A History of Social Justice and Power in the Middle East

From ancient Mesopotamia into the twentieth century, 'the "Circle of Justice"' as a concept has pervaded Middle Eastern political thought and underpinned the exercise of power in the Middle East. The "Circle of Justice" depicts graphically how a government's justice toward the population generates political power, military strength, prosperity, and good administration.

This book traces this set of relationships from its earliest appearance in the political writings of the Sumerians through four millennia of Middle Eastern culture. It explores how people conceptualized and acted upon this powerful insight, how they portrayed it in symbol, painting, and story, and how they transmitted it from one regime to the next. Moving toward the modern day, the author shows how, although the "Circle of Justice" was largely dropped from political discourse, it did not disappear from people's political culture and expectations of government. The book demonstrates the Circle's relevance to the Iranian Revolution and the rise of Islamist movements all over the Middle East, and suggests how the concept remains relevant in an age of capitalism.

A "must read" for students, policymakers, and ordinary citizens, this book will be an important contribution to the areas of Political History, Political Theory, Middle East Studies and Orientalism.

Linda T. Darling has taught Middle Eastern history at the University of Arizona since 1989. Her research has focused on finance administration and political legitimacy in the Middle East. She is the author of *Revenue-Raising and Legitimacy: Tax Collection and Finance Administration in the Ottoman Empire, 1560–1660*. She is a member of the Middle Eastern Studies Association of North America and has published a number of articles in academic journals.

A History of Social Justice and Political Power in the Middle East

The Circle of Justice from Mesopotamia to Globalization

Linda T. Darling

Routledge
Taylor & Francis Group
LONDON AND NEW YORK

First published 2013
by Routledge
2 Park Square, Milton Park, Abingdon, Oxon OX14 4RN

Simultaneously published in the USA and Canada
by Routledge
711 Third Avenue, New York, NY 10017

Routledge is an imprint of the Taylor & Francis Group, an informa business

British Library Cataloguing in Publication Data
A catalogue record for this book is available from the British Library

Library of Congress Cataloging in Publication Data
Darling, Linda T., 1945-
A history of social justice and political power in the Middle East: the Circle of Justice from Mesopotamia to globalization / Linda T. Darling.
Includes bibliographical references and index.
1. Political science–Middle East–Philosophy–History. 2. Middle East–Politics and government. 3. Political culture–Middle East–History. 4. Power (Social sciences)–Middle East–History. 5. Social justice–Middle East–History.
JA84.M53D37 2012
320.95601'1–dc23
2012009743

ISBN 978-0-415-50361-7 (hbk)
ISBN 978-0-415-50362-4 (pbk)
ISBN 978-0-203-09685-7 (ebk)

Typeset in Bembo
by Taylor & Francis Books

MIX
Paper from responsible sources
FSC
www.fsc.org
FSC® C004839

Printed and bound in Great Britain by
TJ International Ltd, Padstow, Cornwall

To my teachers

Contents

Illustrations

Figure

Maps

Preface

Every Middle East crisis for decades has raised the question of Islam and politics. Western politicians' and journalists' reactions to events occurring during the writing of this book – two Gulf Wars, the September 11 destruction of the World Trade Center in New York, US invasions of Afghanistan and Iraq – and public statements by government officials abundantly demonstrate our need for a better understanding of Middle Eastern political culture. Most writers, Western and Middle Eastern, present Islam as the sole indigenous guide to the exercise of political power in the Middle East (other than greed). This preoccupation with Islam has obscured from view other powerful local concepts that contribute to Middle Eastern political expectations, one of the most important of which is the Circle of Justice, a concept that emphasizes the interdependence among rulers, armies, taxes, the taxpaying classes, and the ruler's justice toward them. Specialists often dismiss the Circle of Justice as a literary trope, but this book argues that it was and still is a fundamental concept of Middle Eastern politics, so basic as not to need discussion there, though all but unknown in the West. There are many books on Islam and politics, but they do not fully explain Middle Eastern political thought and behavior because they ignore the relationships encapsulated in the Circle of Justice. This study compiles the history of the Circle (both the saying and the ideas it contains) and examines its role in Middle Eastern political life.

This book is aimed at students and general readers as well as Middle East scholars. It has several goals: to contribute to a narrative of Middle Eastern history centered neither on Islam nor on political structures, to counter stereotypes of Middle Eastern autocracy as universally tyrannical and Middle Easterners as aggressive and dangerous, and to explore a political tradition that is not religious or radical, but that is well known and even taken for granted by Middle Easterners. By offering a single narrative of Middle Eastern history, rather than one broken into ancient, medieval, and modern segments, it highlights cultural continuities and resonances from one era or political regime to another. Tracing the Circle of Justice through Middle Eastern history reveals a basic aspect of Middle Eastern political relationships which is largely ignored today but which is foundational to Middle Eastern political thinking, Islamic or not, in all eras including today.

Thanks go first to the teachers and colleagues at the University of Chicago, who introduced me to the Circle of Justice and gave me the tools to research it, or whose work influenced this study in one way or another: Marshall G. S. Hodgson, R. Stephen Humphreys, Halil İnalcık, John E. Woods, Richard L. Chambers, Robert Dankoff, John R. Perry, JoAnn Scurlock, Cornell H. Fleischer, Wadad al-Qadi, and Lisa Wedeen. I am grateful to the librarians who collected the works studied in this book, especially the staff of the University of Arizona, University of Chicago, and University of Texas libraries, most notably the tireless workers in Interlibrary Loan and Linda Dols, Arizona's ILL chef extraordinaire. I also thank the administrations and staff of Istanbul's Süleymaniye Kütüphanesi and T. C. Başbakanlık Osmanlı Arşivi. I acknowledge my indebtedness to the organizations that have provided funding, time, and space for the research: the American Council of Learned Societies, the American Research Institute in Turkey, the Morris K. Udall Center for Studies in Public Policy, the Institute for Historical Studies at the Department of History, University of Texas, and the University of Arizona's Social and Behavioral Sciences Research Institute and Department of History. I want to thank all those who offered references or suggestions, too many to name. The bibliography relating to the Circle of Justice expanded exponentially during the composition of the book, and I am indebted to those who helped me keep up with it, particularly outside my areas of specialization. Thanks also go to Mahmoud Aziz, who proofread the Arabic, Rebecca Eden, who drew the maps, Marilyn Wheeler, who drew the picture of Ataturk, and the Images Online and Permissions staff at the British Library, who provided the image of Sultan Sanjar. My gratitude goes to the various editors at Routledge Press who worked to eliminate errors and computer glitches. I am especially grateful to those stalwart individuals who read all or part of the manuscript and helped make it shorter, more accurate, and more readable, notably Ziad Abi-Chakra, Serpil Atamaz, Richard Beal, Touraj Daryaee, Ziad Fahmy, Ramon Duarte, Ranin Kazemi, Kate Lang, Amanda Lopez, Beatrice Manz, JoAnn Scurlock, Genoa Shepley, Laura Tabili, Malissa Taylor, Farzin Vejdani, Fariba Zarinebaf, and the students in my course on Religion and State in Islam. The remaining errors and infelicities are, of course, my own. The production process cut the book drastically, and many topics touched on in this book deserve further investigation and longer exposition; I hope that scholars in each area of specialization will take up their study where I have left off.

Abbreviations

AcIr	Acta Iranica
AcOr	Acta Orientalia
AEuras	Archivum Eurasiae Medii Aevi
AHR	American Historical Review
AI	Annales Islamologiques
AJSLL	American Journal of Semitic Languages and Literatures
ANET	Ancient Near Eastern Texts Relating to the Old Testament, ed. James B. Pritchard
AOH	Acta Orientalia Academiae Scientiarum Hungarica
AOtt	Archivum Ottomanicum
ARI 1, 2	Assyrian Royal Inscriptions, Records of the Ancient Near East, 1 and 2, ed. A. K. Grayson
ArsOr	Ars Orientalis
ASQ	Arab Studies Quarterly
AÜDTCFD	Ankara Üniversitesi Dil ve Tarih-Coğrafya Fakültesi Dergisi
AÜSBFD	Ankara Üniversitesi Siyasal Bilgiler Fakültesi Dergisi
BEO	Bulletin d'études orientales
BRIJMES	British Journal of Middle Eastern Studies
BSOAS	Bulletin of the School of Oriental and African Studies
CAH 4	Cambridge Ancient History, 2nd ed., vol. 4: Persia, Greece and the Western Mediterranean, c. 525 to 479 B. C., ed. J. Boardman, D. M. Lewis and M. Ostwald
CAJ	Central Asiatic Journal
CANE	Civilizations of the Ancient Near East, ed. J. M. Sasson
CHI	The Cambridge History of Islam, ed. P. M. Holt, A. K. S. Lambton, and B. Lewis
CHIr	The Cambridge History of Iran, ed. Sir H. Bailey, P. W. Avery, W. B. Fisher, I. Gershevitch and E. Yarshater
CSSAAME	Comparative Studies of South Asia, Africa and the Middle East
CSSH	Comparative Studies in Society and History
EEQ	East European Quarterly
EI2	The Encyclopaedia of Islam (2nd ed., Leiden: E. J. Brill, 1954–2004)
EIr	Encyclopaedia Iranica
HJAS	Harvard Journal of Asiatic Studies
HMEIR	Harvard Middle Eastern and Islamic Review
İA	İslam Ansiklopedisi
IC	Islamic Culture

IJIAS	International Journal of Islamic and Arabic Studies
IJMES	International Journal of Middle East Studies
IJTS	International Journal of Turkish Studies
ILS	Islamic Law and Society
IOS	Israel Oriental Studies
IQ	Islamic Quarterly
Iran	Iran: Journal of the British Institute of Persian Studies
IranS	Iranian Studies
IS	Islamic Studies
İÜİFM	İstanbul Üniversitesi İktisat Fakültesi Mecmuası
JA	Journal asiatique
JAAS	Journal of Asian and African Studies
JAH	Journal of Asian History
JAOS	Journal of the American Oriental Society
JAS	Pakistan Journal of the Asiatic Society of Pakistan
JContempH	Journal of Contemporary History
JCS	Journal of Cuneiform Studies
JEEH	Journal of European Economic History
JEMH	Journal of Early Modern History
JESHO	Journal of the Economic and Social History of the Orient
JIS	Journal of Islamic Studies
JMS	Journal of Mediterranean Studies
JNES	Journal of Near Eastern Studies
JPHS	Journal of the Pakistan Historical Society
JRAS	Journal of the Royal Asiatic Society
JSAI	Jerusalem Studies in Arabic and Islam
JSH	Journal of Social History
JSS	Journal of Semitic Studies
JTS	Journal of Turkish Studies
JWH	Journal of World History
MEEP	Middle East Economic Papers
MEJ	Middle East Journal
MES	Middle Eastern Studies
MHR	Mediterranean Historical Review
MSR	Mamlūk Studies Review
MTM	Milli Tetebbu'lar Mecmuası
MW	The Muslim World
NPT	New Perspectives on Turkey
OA	Osmanlı Araştırmaları
OM	Oriente Moderno
OTAM	Osmanlı Tarihi Araştırma ve Uygyulama Merkezi Dergisi
POF	Prilozi za Orientalnu Filologiju
RA	Revue d'assyriologie/Revue d'assyriologie et d'archéologie orientale
REI	Revue des études islamiques
RHM	Revue d'histoire maghrébine
RIMA 1	Assyrian Rulers of the Third and Second Millennia BC (to 1115 BC), The Royal Inscriptions of Mesopotamia, Assyrian Periods, 1, ed. A. K. Grayson

RIMA 2	Assyrian Rulers of the Early First Millennium BC, I (1114–859 BC), The Royal Inscriptions of Mesopotamia, Assyrian Periods, 2, ed. A. K. Grayson
RIMA 3	Assyrian Rulers of the Early First Millennium BC, II (858–745 BC), Royal Inscriptions of Mesopotamia, Assyrian Periods, 3, ed. A. K. Grayson
RIMB 2	Rulers of Babylonia: From the Second Dynasty of Isin to the End of Assyrian Domination (1157–612 BC), Royal Inscriptions of Mesopotamia, Babylonian Periods, 2, ed. G. Frame
RIME 1	Presargonic Period (2700–2350 BC), The Royal Inscriptions of Mesopotamia, Early Periods, 1, ed. D. R. Frayne
RIME 2	Sargonic and Gutian Periods (2334–2113 BC), Royal Inscriptions of Mesopotamia, Early Periods, 2, ed. D. R. Frayne
RIME 3/2	Ur III Period (2112–2004 BC), Royal Inscriptions of Mesopotamia, Early Periods, 3/2, ed. D. R. Frayne
RIME 4	Old Babylonian Period (2003–1595 BC), Royal Inscriptions of Mesopotamia, Early Periods, 4, ed. D. R. Frayne
RMMM	Revue des Études Méditerranées et du Monde Musulman
RO	Rocznik Orientalistyczny
ROMM	Revue de l'Occident Musulman et de la Méditerranée
SAO	Studia et Acta Orientalia
SI	Studia Islamica
StIr	Studia Iranica
TAD	Tarih Araştırmaları Dergisi
TALID	Türkiye Araştırmaları Literatür Dergisi
TD	Tarih Dergisi
TDAYB	Türk Dili Araştırmaları Yıllığı Belleten
TED	Tarih Enstitüsü Dergisi
THİTM	Türk Hukuk ve İktisat Tarihi Mecmuası
TİD	Tarih İncelemeleri Dergisi
TM	Türkiyat Mecmuası
TOEM	Tarih-i Osmani Encümeni Mecmuası
TSAB	Turkish Studies Association Bulletin
TV	Tarih Vesikaları
WI	Die Welt des Islams
WZKM	Wiener Zeitschrift für die Kunde des Morgenlandes
ZDMG	Zeitschrift der Deutschen Morgenlandischen Gesellschaft

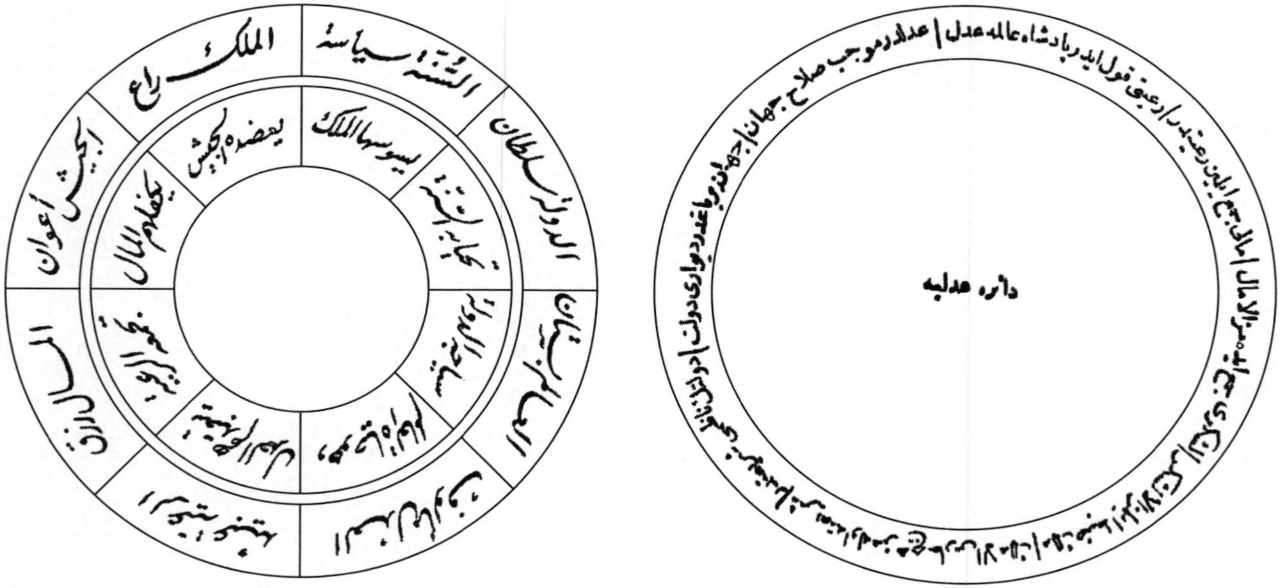

Figure 1 The Circle of Justice: Left circle – Arabic, after ʻAbdurrahman Badawi (ed.), *Fontes Graecae Doctrinarum Politicarum Islamicarum*, 1954. Right circle – Ottoman Turkish, after Kınalızade ʻAli Çelebi, *Ahlāk-i ʻAlāʼī*, 1228/1832–3.

1 Introduction

The Circle of Justice

The Circle of Justice is an ancient Middle Eastern political concept, and this book tells its story. The Circle of Justice is actually a mnemonic, a summarized description, of the interrelationship between Middle Eastern states and their societies. It got its name in the sixteenth century Ottoman Empire, but it had been written in a circle as early as the eleventh century and its circularity had been recognized much earlier; in fact, the earliest written descriptions of this relationship come from the third millennium BCE. Experience has demonstrated vividly how little the West understands Middle Eastern political culture and how poorly adapted Western political science is to that task. In an effort to pay more attention to indigenous political concepts, this book examines a concept of social justice based on interdependence between rulers and ruled, one that underlies their differing degrees of power and obvious conflicts of interest and that holds society together when such conflicts would pull it apart. The book traces the Circle's concept of justice from the earliest manifestation of its elements in ancient Near Eastern texts through the twentieth century, its transmission throughout society and from one regime to the next, the systems and institutions through which it was put into practice, and where we have evidence, the use of those institutions by ordinary people as well as rulers and elites.

What is the Circle of Justice?

The term "Circle of Justice" comes from the sixteenth-century Ottoman writer Kinalizade, whose version of the Circle, actually written in a circle, is in the illustration for this chapter. A saying quoted in many Middle Eastern works on politics expressed this indigenous concept of politics in shorthand form:

> No power without troops,
> No troops without money,
> No money without prosperity,
> No prosperity without justice and good administration.

This little saying encapsulated political relationships visible in the ancient Near Eastern empires of the Babylonians and Assyrians and later those of the Persians and Abbasids, Seljuks and Ottomans. The saying existed in many versions and translations and was quoted or referred to in a variety of literary genres and contexts, but it was more than a set of words. It summarized and idealized a set of interdependent political relationships that originated in the ancient Near Eastern city-states and that is known as the Near

Eastern concept of state.[1] The saying was both a schematic representation of the articulation of the elements of such a state and a recommendation for their optimal functioning.[2] Its full expression, first attested in the tenth century, reads as follows:

> The world is a garden, hedged in by sovereignty
> Sovereignty is lordship, preserved by law
> Law is administration, governed by the king
> The king is a shepherd, supported by the army
> The army are soldiers, fed by money
> Money is revenue, gathered by the people
> The people are servants, subjected by justice
> Justice is happiness, the well-being of the world.

In the Near Eastern concept of state, the ruler, with divine blessing or even divine appointment, protected the realm from external and internal enemies, for which he needed a strong military force. This force had to be supported financially; the money came from taxes, and in an agrarian society revenues could be high only if the cultivators were productive. Productivity was insured by the army's protection of society from invasion, banditry, and civil strife; by the maintenance of the infrastructure of irrigation works, roads, and markets; and by the provision of justice, which included, besides the enforcement of law, the remission or reduction of tax demands in times of disaster and control over the exploitative tendencies of landholders and governmental officials. The Near Eastern concept of state saw the ruler as far above the elites, the ally of the peasants against both elites and outside forces, in contrast to the European concept of kingship in which the king was the leading aristocrat and the nobles his peers. The exaltation of the ruler was one aspect of this concept of state to which Islamic thinkers objected, but its purpose was to grant the ruler unchallenged authority, especially over military and administrative personnel. He also had to be accessible to information and requests from the productive classes of society.

The absence or malfunctioning of any of these elements broke the Circle and threatened state power. If justice were not provided, for example, economic productivity and therefore revenue would decrease, the army would not be paid and would rebel, and the ruler would be unable to exercise power. Cooperation between rulers and ruled was thus the key to political stability.[3] That was not a theory of government but a fact preceding political theorization and one often demonstrated in Middle Eastern history. Philosophers discussed the Circle's concept of justice in terms of "balance" or "equilibrium," but it was less a philosophical concept than a political one. Like patronage systems, this concept of justice involved reciprocal obligations that legitimized claims by inferiors on superiors as well as vice versa.[4] Special institutions developed to deliver this justice: state-supported irrigation systems that ensured fertility and prosperity, laws and revenue surveys that apportioned taxes justly, and courts of petitioning that heard and adjudicated complaints.[5] The continued functioning of these institutions through times of ideological change gave the concept of the Circle greater permanence in Middle Eastern society.

The Near Eastern state contrasts with the governance of the nomadic groups that sometimes gained control of Middle Eastern society. Tribally based, nomadic society tended to be egalitarian and personalistic rather than hierarchical and bureaucratic; the chief was a "first among equals" and the government was wherever he was. The political unit was much more apt to split and divide, and leadership was often contested among the sons of the ruler, all of whom were considered potential heirs to power. Finally, taxation was not an annual collection of the surplus production but an occasional requisition usually for a specific purpose.

This book demonstrates the pervasiveness and importance of the Circle of Justice in the Middle East. While the circular form of the statement is not attested until Islamic times, texts containing the same elements and relationships appeared for millennia before and after the rise of Islam. Expressions in this book like "the ideas of the Circle of Justice" or "the concept of the Circle" refer not only to the circular quotation itself but also to the set of relationships to which it refers. Scholars have often dismissed the Circle of Justice as a purely literary conceit, something known only to writers and readers of mirrors for princes (advice works for current and future kings) or works of *adab* (collections of interesting and useful facts and sayings compiled for elites and courtiers). But the Circle was more than a literary curiosity; it was a description of real political relations in an agrarian empire, an understanding in capsule form of the political and economic interdependence between rulers and ruled that Middle Eastern governments and peoples had already arrived at.

There was a strong degree of consensus across the pre-Islamic and Islamic Middle East with respect to political values and goals, a consensus periodically interrupted, usually by outside invasion, but repeatedly reestablished. Rulers trumpeted these values to legitimize their exercise of power, and people used them to hold their rulers to account – not to thwart or usurp their power, but to induce them to employ it to meet their subjects' needs.[6] This complex of ideas was modified and added to over time; some regimes gave it more importance than others, and when some rulers ignored or discarded it, other segments of society kept the concept alive. We cannot at this late date determine how just any particular ruler or government "really" was, but we can see whether they made public and falsifiable claims of justice and established or maintained institutions and practices to provide justice and prosperity to their people. And while we cannot say how well ordinary people knew the sayings in their literary forms, we can judge whether they understood the ruler's responsibility for justice if they used the institutions he provided and demanded this justice when it was not forthcoming voluntarily. The fact that governments attempted to put the Circle of Justice into practice shows that they recognized the people's demand for justice, and the fact that people acted on it by presenting complaints against government officials indicates that they understood these relationships and considered their acts politically effective. Intellectuals were able to use the Circle for advising and exerting pressure on the ruler precisely because it was not a maxim of deceased pagan rulers out of a dusty old book but one of the ordinary ways most people thought about politics.

Intellectual history studies the origin and development of ideas, and numerous scholars cited in the notes have explicated the Circle of Justice as an idea. This book, as a cultural history, studies the expression, dissemination, and implementation of that idea in society. Because the evidence comes mainly from texts, the literary representation of the Circle holds a prominent place in this analysis, but the purpose of the many quotations and references is not so much to analyze the Circle's conceptual development as to explore its circulation through society and from one society to another. Beyond verbal representations, visible expressions of the concept were a significant form of transmission, and still more significant were its enactments in ritual and in governmental processes, the media that publicized the concept most widely beyond the literate elite. Since we cannot directly evaluate the relative justice of different regimes, the best gauge of the Circle's impact is the extent to which people used the systems of justice provided by the state or developed their own mechanisms for demanding justice from their rulers, even though much less evidence exists for these systems and mechanisms than for the Circle's literary dissemination, especially before the modern period.

Studies of Islamic political thought, perhaps taking their cue from early Arabic writings on politics, tend to focus on the ruler's right to rule and the nature of his power.[7] This book deals with claims to legitimacy that did not depend on the Qur'an and the experience of the early Muslim community.[8] Nevertheless, the Near Eastern concept of justice lay at the basis of Islamic complaints of injustice and remained an important element in Middle Eastern ethics and politics across changes of religion. The principles of the Circle of Justice and the techniques of administration and governance by which they were put into practice, suitably modified to accord with Islamic ideals, became the normal apparatus of most Middle Eastern governments until the modern period. Muslim ideas about kingship and social order, as they developed under sultanic rule, drew on the same sources as the Circle's concept of justice.[9] This book is about the ruler's behavior toward his subjects and the role of the Circle's justice in that aspect of Middle Eastern political culture, particularly the ruler's responsibility to the taxpayers, mostly peasants, whose revenues maintained the state. An equivalent book could be written on justice in rulers' relations with their elites and how those responsibilities were fulfilled, but that is a different project.

Justice has many definitions, but this book includes only the Circle's definition of justice, that is, the maintenance of social balance, the provision of whatever was necessary to maintain taxpayers' productivity and their ability and willingness to support the state. The comparison of the Circle's definition with other concepts of justice is outside the book's scope, as are the Circle's interaction with other ideologies and its international implications. The book's examples do not include all uses of the term justice but only those in which it was used in the sense of the Circle, whether or not the Circle was specifically quoted. Even with respect to the Circle, it is not a full inquiry into all its variations in wording, which often seem to follow no particular pattern, or all the problems presented by its history. Readers should nevertheless be alert to changes in the way the Circle of Justice was expressed or employed over time.

The investigation concentrates on the ruler's relationship to the peasants rather than the elites. It focuses on the core area of the concept's use, the eastern Fertile Crescent and Iran, with extensions to the Ottoman Empire and Morocco. Places and periods where few or no references to the Circle were found are not discussed except in terms of contrast. The book looks back to the first disorganized presentations of the concept in writing, which take us back to the third millennium BCE, and forward to the late twentieth century. It does not argue that the Circle was the only or even the most important understanding of justice at any particular point, but that it was present and influential. Its emphases and omissions reflect the amount and accessibility of surviving evidence and the degree to which different regimes appear to have cited or used the Circle of Justice.

Political ideas similar to the Circle, accompanied by practices for the redress of grievances, can be found outside the Middle East. The Chinese Mandate of Heaven comes immediately to mind, while in Europe similar ideas were connected with Christian concepts of authority, which had a separate route of development through the Roman concept of state. Their examination lies beyond the scope of this book, as does the

Judeo-Christian tradition in the Middle East, which seems largely to have taken different directions. Europe did know the Middle East's Circle of Justice from the eleventh-century advice work *The Secret of Secrets*, popular in Muslim Spain and translated into numerous languages (see Chapter 5). Fourteenth-century French mirrors for princes expressed a surprisingly Middle Eastern idea of justice: "King and justice are brothers," they quoted, and "Justice makes the realm endure."[10] Antoine de Montchrétien in the seventeenth century developed a European version of the Circle appropriate to a commercial society: "It is impossible to make war without men, to amass men without salaries, to furnish their salaries without taxes, or to levy taxes without trade."[11] Western political thought in general, however, could not fathom how the Circle's elements interrelated and found it "paradoxical. Authority was developed in conditions of war, yet war created the demand for finance. Finance required taxation and orderly collection of revenue. This process required, in turn, law and order, which was dependent on disciplined troops. But disciplined troops, which were also the prerequisite to war, also demanded adequate finance. But of course adequate finance was dependent on disciplined troops."[12] In the Middle East the Circle of Justice formed the basis of political relationships, but Europeans ceased to employ it politically, finding that other concepts described their political circumstances more closely.

Some Europeans, however, quoted the Circle historically, and the way they did so helped to establish the modern stereotype concerning it. Gibbon's *Decline and Fall of the Roman Empire* included a version attributed to the Persian ruler Ardashir: "The authority of the prince … must be defended by a military force; that force can only be maintained by taxes; all taxes must, at last, fall upon agriculture; and agriculture can never flourish except under the protection of justice and moderation."[13] The Circle appeared in more modern scholarship in 1815 in the *History of Persia* by Sir John Malcolm, who copied it from an undistinguished contemporary Persian history, though he must have read Gibbon.[14] George Rawlinson cited both these sources in 1876 in *The Seventh Great Oriental Monarchy*, on ancient Persia. The Circle was quoted again in 1913 by Lybyer in his study of the Ottoman government of Suleyman the Magnificent, and in 1935 by Wright in his translation of Defterdar Sarı Mehmed Pasha's advice book. Lewis Thomas cited the latter two sources in his study of Na'ima's use of the Circle, to which most modern citations refer.[15] This route of transmission fostered the belief among scholars that the Circle of Justice was a Persian product, that its use was confined to the literature of advice to kings or mirrors for princes, that it was introduced into Islamic culture by a small and specialized Abbasid scribal class of Persian origin who opposed it to Islamic concepts of political legitimacy derived from Qur'anic precepts and the example of the Prophet Muhammad, and that its function was to justify absolute rule and fiscal exploitation.[16] As this study will show, the scholarly stereotype needs revision on all counts. Tracing back the history of the ideas contained in the Circle of Justice reveals that they were already articulated in the political ideology of the Sumerian city-states around 2500 BCE, that the ancient Persians were strangely slow to realize their interconnectedness, that they affected Islamic culture through many sources other than mirrors for princes, and that they could be and were used to resist as well as to justify absolute rule and fiscal exploitation.

Modern writers on politics, both European and Middle Eastern, usually belittle the effectiveness of the Circle in checking the tyranny of past rulers, preferring the stereotype of unlimited Oriental despotism.[17] Although Middle Eastern rulers typically achieved power through conquest, they needed to win the acquiescence of the ruled to keep down the cost of retaining power. The common people normally tendered their submission in return for protection and justice. The Circle of Justice described a condition of "exploitation," in which the wealth of the subjects supported the military and governing classes.[18] But it was not unmitigated exploitation; in the Near Eastern concept of state, the rulers also had obligations to the ruled, and the Circle could be traversed in both directions. It was a hegemonic idea, disseminated by the ruler to induce consent, but the ruled routinely inverted it to legitimize resistance to aspects of his rule that they found unjust. It implied a moral economy of the Middle Eastern peasant that considered peasants' political and economic support for the ruler to depend on his justice and support for the peasants. Challenges from the people confirmed the legitimacy of the ruler, as they required him to act, but also the legitimacy of the challenge itself, as the ruler responded to his subjects' requests.

Historically, subjects of Middle Eastern states sought their ruler's adherence to the Circle of Justice mainly through petitioning. Studies of everyday forms of peasant resistance such as foot dragging, dissimulation, flight, theft, sabotage, and petty violence generally neglect legitimate forms of protest such as petitioning, seeing the only alternatives to reluctant compliance as violent rebellion or collective defiance, usually too costly for the weak.[19] In the Middle Eastern context, however, petitioning was the main device by which the weak demanded justice from the strong. Its effectiveness was based not on the political power of the weak but on the ideological power of the Circle of Justice. Middle Eastern subjects always had the right to go over the heads of their lords and landholders to petition the king directly, whether about their own needs, against their overlords, or against the king himself or his officials. As we shall see, there is abundant evidence that they did so regularly and often, playing imperial powers off against local authorities, sometimes traveling long distances and spending what may have been inordinate amounts of money to ensure that their voices were heard and their demands met.

Scholars of modern Middle East politics note that even today, political legitimacy depends less on the form of government than on the government's performance in meeting people's needs for protection, economic support, and justice. Some authorities discuss modern Middle Eastern politics in terms of a "social contract" or "ruling bargain" in which people renounce their political rights in exchange for social welfare benefits such as food subsidies, free education and health care, agrarian loan programs, and infrastructure construction.[20] When the state's failure to deliver violates that contract, protest and political violence erupt. The viability of this bargain is surely reinforced by the long history of the Circle of Justice in the region. Although the specific content of the ruling bargain has altered with changing conditions, the interrelations between political actors that it embodies have remained remarkably constant over time. "Even patronage-based authoritarian regimes rely on ruling formulas in their search for legitimacy and accord their ideological principles more than rhetorical attention. When … [this formula] is built around a set of radically populist and redistributive norms, economic crisis becomes a serious ideological issue. The capacity of the regime to fulfill its populist commitments became an important measure of its legitimacy."[21] Rulers complied with popular demands not only out of fear of rebellion but also to be seen as living up to their own announced values. "The moral economy was the obverse of paternalism and the crowd were able to challenge their rulers to fulfill a role which they had assigned themselves."[22] E. P. Thompson's concept of the moral economy is comparable to, for example, the Muslim Brotherhood's vision of Islamic social justice in that both ideas justify compliance with authority as long as authority upholds the values and livelihood of the producing class.[23] The moral economy expresses a collective subsistence ethic: the productive classes are obliged to pay rent and taxes, but elites are "obliged never to demand so much that peasant subsistence is endangered."[24] This moral economy is often tied to the shariah, Islamic law, ignoring the long history of the Near Eastern state. Edmund Burke III, however, states that "it was expressed not only in the language of the 'ulama' [the learned] and works of *fiqh* [jurisprudence], but also in the language of Islamic notions of justice freely available to all, and extra-Islamic forms of legitimation drawn from customary practice."[25] The Circle of Justice, which exchanged taxes and production revenues for good administration and the provision of justice, is the Middle East's historical expression of this ruling bargain.

Most expressions of the Circle of Justice throughout history have come from the state and the elites, and only by reading between the lines and "against the grain" can we infer what ordinary people thought. Yet the continued reintroduction of these ideas by indigenous authors and advisors after their repeated disappearance argues for the strength and pervasiveness of the Circle's concept of rulership among the peoples of the Middle East. That peasants through the ages filed petitions or waged rebellions based on the same sense of justice shows the inviability of assumptions that all such protest was based on religious fanaticism. Although we have little direct evidence from the peasants' perspective, their actions in petitioning for the ruler's intervention, as well as more direct forms of resistance, suggest that they understood the premises of the Circle of Justice well enough to know how to present their demands. The number of instances of such action contradicts the stereotype of the Circle of Justice as merely an elite idea, unknown to illiterate peasants.

The reciprocity and accountability found in the Circle of Justice persist in today's political life but may be unrecognizable when described in the modern political languages of democracy, capitalism, or socialism. The Circle's influence on Middle Eastern political expectations, however, cannot be expected to have disappeared with the institution of modern forms of government in the twentieth century. The popular version of Islamic history today relates the sensationally tyrannical deeds of rulers but edits out the possibility of sultanic justice and ignores the subjects' efforts on behalf of justice and equity. Under its influence, the actual past is discarded as a source of modern political inspiration in favor of an ideal of Islamic government that was never really practiced. This study attempts, among other things, to recover an aspect of the centuries-long struggle for justice in the Middle East. It focuses on the reciprocity and interdependency of state–subject relations in the Circle of Justice in part because of their ongoing centrality to Middle Eastern political thought and their potential usefulness in developing modern political mechanisms that meet the needs of Middle Eastern peoples.

Sources and methods

This book assumes a basic knowledge of Middle Eastern or Islamic history such as can be gained from reading the standard histories that explain, for example, how Islam arose or who the Abbasids were. Retelling the entire narrative of Middle Eastern history in the light of the Circle of Justice would have doubled the length of the manuscript. The book treats the Islamic side of that history very lightly, as a counter to the many narratives that seek to explain everything about the Middle East in terms of religion. No work of this type can be exhaustive; unpublished manuscripts alone prevent that. But this one seeks to be full, to quote different kinds of literature and to reinforce evidence from texts with visual and behavioral evidence. The demands of publishers have condensed the book considerably, but the sometimes abbreviated arguments can be restored through the works referenced in the notes.

Written sources for this study include royal inscriptions and edicts; advice literature and mirrors for princes written mostly by bureaucrats and courtiers; history, poetry, romances, and other works composed for the court and also for more popular audiences; discussions of political economy in philosophical works; and references in the introductions of works written for other purposes. Some of these sources testify to their authors' ideas; others testify to audience appreciation of what others had written; still others record actions and intentions. The dissemination of the Circle can be traced through manuscript copying and literary borrowing; visual sources such as art and architecture; rituals, procedures, and institutions putting the Circle into practice; and popular demands for the Circle's justice, usually in the form of petitions and responses, or evidence of petitioning. Scholars typically discuss political legitimacy on the basis of texts – educated people seek religious or legal forms of legitimation for rulers and their policies – but such arguments bypass the uneducated majority, which looks for reassurances and tangible signs such as remitted taxes and repairs to the infrastructure. A painting of Sultan Sanjar hearing the complaint of an old woman is a reiteration of the Circle of Justice; tax surveys and irrigation repairs are enactments of the Circle of Justice. Copies of earlier works signal later societies' absorption of the ideas they contain; the copying of an old work is almost as significant as the creation of a new one for demonstrating people's adherence to the Circle of Justice, as well as for identifying its routes of transmission. Some of these texts quote the Circle of Justice in its formulaic versions; others contain the ideas of the Circle without quoting it precisely.

Quotations of texts in this book do not employ the reference conventions of every field of study or retain the italics, parentheses, and other devices used to signal linguistic problems in the texts. The arguments do not engage specialist issues but stay as close as possible to the texts themselves. The conclusions do not depend on individual vocabulary items whose translation may be in doubt but on the whole tenor of numerous citations, including many not quoted here. Certain ideas originating in the early pre-Islamic period were still in use in late Islamic times, and the assumption is that they continued as part of the ideology in the intervening period rather than being reinvented later. I do not try to determine how far afield these ideas extended beyond the Middle East, whether they were employed by Israelites, Greeks, Africans, Europeans, or Chinese.

Since this is not a literary study, questions of genre are not central to the analysis. To many literary scholars this is heresy, and it demands explanation. It is commonplace to divide Arabic political writings into the categories of political philosophy, jurisprudence, theology, and belles lettres.[26] Although these are four recognizably different genres of writing, they were not necessarily produced by different men with different styles of thought and different intellectual and moral commitments. The same authors often produced works in more than one of these genres (e.g. al-Ghazali, Razi). In the mind of such a writer, and probably in many readers' minds as well, the watertight divisions assumed by genre categories did not apply. Although the Circle may have made its impact differently in a poem than in a theological work, these differences are less significant to this particular story than the fact of its impact or transmission. I also do not analyze the whole thought of individual authors; the Circle may or may not be the most prominent aspect of their work, although it is the aspect I am interested in. We must all be grateful to earlier specialists in each field who paid attention to political thinking and studied, published, and sometimes translated the relevant works. Many of these works are not known outside small groups of specialists; for that reason, and because even specialists may sometimes find themselves outside their areas of expertise, I reference Western-language translations wherever possible. In the case of citations of the Circle of Justice, I checked the translation against the original text; when I translated or amended a translation, I did so as literally as possible.

Accessing the relevant sources presented certain difficulties that affect the whole field. At the beginning of this project, many medieval sources were available only in manuscript or in inaccessible and crumbling nineteenth-century editions. I therefore gleaned information from (sometimes rather old) secondary sources. In the intervening period, Islamists interested in Islamic texts have published or republished many of the Arabic texts, although numerous Ottoman and Persian texts still languish in manuscript. The problem with modern sources is quite different: the division of the Middle East into over twenty different countries multiplied exponentially the sources of information on political thought and practice, but budgetary and other constraints reduced their acquisition by US libraries. Moreover, the speeches and texts published, collected in libraries, and especially translated, deal almost exclusively with international rather than domestic issues. Only the country experts with the motivation and capability to comb through newspapers, publications, and archives in the countries themselves report on what Middle Eastern leaders say to their own people about their own affairs. Thus, Chapter 10 relies more heavily than earlier chapters on excerpts quoted in secondary sources. That technique is not very satisfactory, but it suggests the richness of the material that could be at our disposal if more resources were devoted to acquiring it. For twenty-first-century sources, the Internet provides a solution.

Because I quote the Circle of Justice across so many centuries, I have been accused of thinking that Middle Eastern thought did not change, of purveying an orientalist view of the "timeless East." I have responded that although the Circle of Justice, like a proverb or a verse of scripture, did not change, what changed was the way people used the concept, who expressed it, and how it governed their actions. But in fact the Circle of Justice did change: the emphases and the relationships among its constituent elements altered and evolved over time, and the quotations indicate some of those changes. The basic idea of the Circle of Justice, however, is one of the bedrock political concepts of the region, and no attempt to discuss Middle Eastern politics can succeed without including the political relations embodied in the Circle.

A few words are in order on the presentation of the material. The names of regimes, places, and most rulers in this book are spelled in the American English fashion. Foreign words found in an unabridged dictionary are not italicized; other foreign words are, but both types are defined in the glossary and at their first appearance in the text. Dates after rulers' names are regnal dates; dates after writers' names are usually death dates, as dates of birth are often unknown. Diacritical marks are omitted in the text, except for the *'ayn* ('), which represents an Arabic consonant not found in Western languages; diacritics are, however, included in the notes. The notes also contain information that may be useful to students and further discussion of disputed points. Transliteration is according to the old *IJMES* style, but with dots under the letters only for Arabic. In the text, the spelling of terms connected with the Ottomans or Turkey uses Turkish rather than Arabic conventions, but simplified for non-specialist readers; j is substituted for c. Variant spellings in quotations are retained. Parentheses found in quotations are original; square brackets mark authorial interpolations. Series titles are included only when they are significant for locating the works. Notes referencing several points or quotations generally cite them in the order in which they occur in the text.

Outline of chapters

The purpose of calling this introduction Chapter 1 is to establish from the beginning what the Circle of Justice is, what the story of this book is about; it cannot be skipped. The actual story of the Circle of Justice begins in antiquity. In Middle East scholarship the Circle is generally traced to pre-Islamic Persian thought, to which most early Muslim commentators attributed it. While pre-Islamic Persia was its immediate source, however, the concept had a much longer history. Elements of it are discernible in the earliest royal inscriptions of Mesopotamia, and it developed extensively before the Persians arrived on the scene. The Persians themselves, even after their conquest of Mesopotamia, were slow to adopt it, finding some of its assumptions alien to their culture and social structure. By the time of the rise of Islam, however, the Circle formed a secure part of Persian political culture and was expressed in writings that survived into Islamic times. Chapters 2 and 3 investigate ancient Mesopotamia's development of the ideas that made up the Circle of Justice and its gradual adoption by the Persians, who added elements from their own culture. These chapters also examine certain institutions by which ancient societies sought to implement these ideas: bureaucratic control of revenue extraction and allocation, governmental provision for the economic infrastructure, and the institution of the ruler's court.

After the rise of Islam, the concepts of the Circle of Justice were associated with issues of the ruler's identity and the nature of the Islamic state. A long controversy in both Islamic and Western scholarship categorizes political writers on the basis of the sources for their ideas of the ideal Muslim state and the selection of its head, whether juristic (Qur'an and *hadith*), philosophical (Plato and Aristotle), or bureaucratic (pre-Islamic Persian writings).[27] What is remarkable, in view of the deep disagreements among these sources, is their high degree of consensus on the question of the ruler's behavior toward the ruled. On that issue the verdicts of these different traditions converged, giving the Circle of Justice a secure place among Islamic political concepts. Chapters 4 and 5 describe that process, together with Muslim society's elaboration of means to enforce the Circle's justice, a development separate from that of Islamic law and the qadi courts.

Invading Turks and Mongols from the steppes brought with them tribal economic and social structures that held no place for a concept of justice based on agrarian relations, although Persian influence on steppe culture had generated some common ideas about rulership. To incorporate conquerors and conquered into a single state, rulers turned to the Persian model of government, the Near Eastern state, and to advisors from the conquered people who bridged the gap between the two cultures. Persian and Islamic concepts of state appeared to them as a continuum rather than an opposition and were increasingly presented as such by the authors of advice literature. The Circle of Justice formed an important part of their advice, a useful mnemonic for understanding how to govern a sedentary society that resonated with nomadic ideas of justice as well. Chapters 6 and 7 discuss the outpouring of advice literature in this period and the gradual rapprochement among Islamic, Persian, and nomadic concepts of justice. By the end of this process, the fourteenth-century historian Ibn Khaldun could write of the Circle of Justice not just as a prescription for good government but as a fundamental description of society and social relations.

After around 1500, the use of gunpowder weapons by large standing armies and the further development of bureaucratic government made possible larger and more stable empires and a more central role for the Circle of Justice, not only in rulers' ideologies but also in governing practices, especially in the Ottoman Empire, as detailed in Chapter 8. With the economic changes of the age of discovery, however, justice for the strong became more difficult to provide, and complaints of its lack formed the main topic in the advice literature of the early seventeenth century. Sultanic injustice to the strong soon produced injustice to the weak. By the eighteenth century, imperial rulers looked to Islam for legitimation, while their subjects gave their loyalty to local provincial leaders, putting the Circle of Justice into the shadow.

Recentralization and modernization in the nineteenth century employed the Circle of Justice as framework and validation. The period's reforms, however, led to the commodification of land and the rise of an agrarian (and after World War I industrial) bourgeoisie, reducing appeals to the Circle of Justice. In the mid-twentieth century the relationships encapsulated in the Circle regained prominence again, but they were expressed in terms of development or socialism, both of which advocated government support for the people's welfare. Although Westerners, in the absence of direct quotation of the Circle, can usually see it behind the modern rhetoric only in the context of its long history in Middle Eastern politics, Middle Easterners to whom this continuity has been proposed say, "Of course!" In socialism the connection of government support with the people's ability to support the state was tacitly understood, while in development ideology it was ostensibly irrelevant. The resistance of Islamist groups to the modern state also contained parallels to the Circle of Justice. The economic downturn beginning in the 1970s made state implementation of the Circle's justice increasingly impossible and shifted political power to the bourgeoisie. At that juncture the people, turning to Islamist groups for support, took up the Circle again as a weapon against the state and quoted it in rebuke of neoliberal economic policies and their unjust effects. Chapters 9 and 10 trace this story of modernization and its discontents.

The chapters of this book, though they deal with different time periods, are not self-contained but build on and refer (overtly or tacitly) to the information in previous chapters. Each chapter begins with an introductory summary and closes with a brief conclusion suggesting its wider implications. Chapter subsections are generally chronological, to facilitate the book's use in courses, but occasional subsections are organized thematically, giving prominence to certain more complex developments. The middle periods of Middle Eastern history are the least well known and are usually skipped over in textbooks, but their importance for the development of governmental practices based on the Circle of Justice warrants a fuller treatment here. Predicting the future of the Circle of Justice is impossible for a historian, but its past records suggest that it is an integral part of Middle Eastern political thinking on the popular as well as the literary level, and that it is unlikely to disappear in the near future.

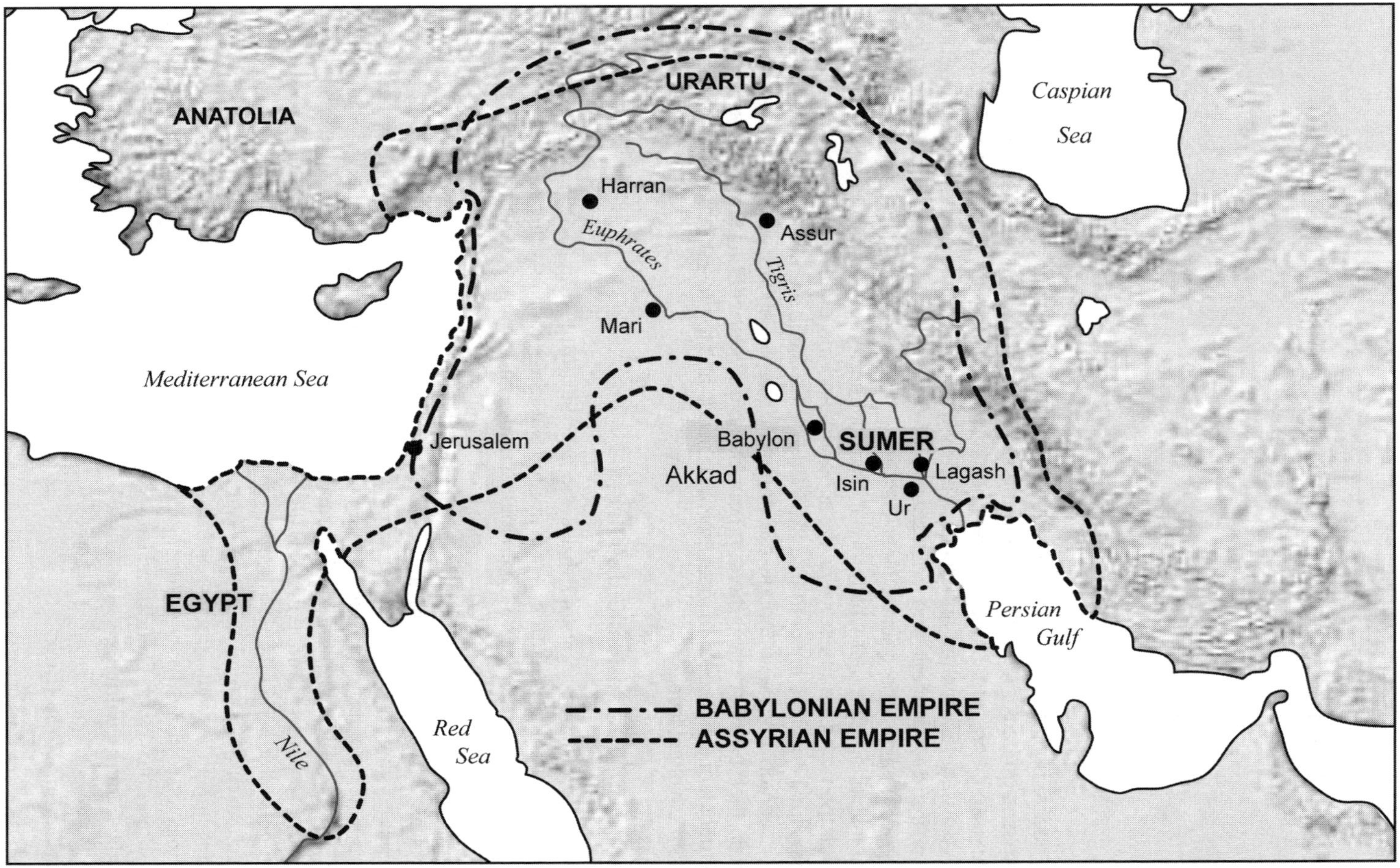

Map 1 The ancient Near East

2 Mesopotamia

"That the strong might not oppress the weak"

The ideas behind the Circle of Justice and the governmental interrelationships it expresses go back much farther than the saying itself. Its main elements came together in the inscriptions of the ancient Mesopotamian empires – the Sumerians, Babylonians, and Assyrians. Excavated and deciphered by modern archaeologists, these inscriptions reveal the development and coalescence of the concepts later encapsulated in the Circle of Justice. The ancient Near Eastern empires also founded administrative and legal institutions through which to put this concept of justice into practice; among the most important were tax surveys, royal courts, and the petition process. Administrative and cultural activities ensured that the ideas of the Circle were known to elites, officials, and common people. Although the common people left no writings of their own to explain their point of view, there is considerable evidence that they used the imperial institutions of justice both to meet their own needs and to protest oppression and injustice up to the highest level.

Sumer and Akkad (2500–1800 BCE)

The elements and relationships that came together in the Circle of Justice can be traced to the oldest political writings surviving today – the royal inscriptions of the Sumerians, who were the first people to have cities, writing, and complex political organization.[1] In their texts, the concepts that later coalesced into the Circle of Justice – divine favor, royal power, military victory, prosperity, and justice – all appeared, and their interrelatedness was clear. Sumer in the third millennium BCE was a loose association of Mesopotamian city-states vying for dominance. Each city-state had its own god, temple, and ruler. The ruler's staff of officials and scribes functioned as political propagandists, proclaiming the rulers' political ideology and achievements in cuneiform inscriptions on clay tablets and cylinders, on palace and temple walls, on stone monuments, and on rock surfaces.[2] Although most people could not read, they probably heard such inscriptions read aloud on ceremonial occasions; even inscriptions buried under temple foundations had copies for reading in public.[3] Poems, hymns, letters, and law collections also conveyed the ideology of royal power and justice. Handed on to the Babylonian and Assyrian dynasties, these ideas were foundational to the moral and political economy of centuries of Middle Eastern civilization.

The elements of the Circle

In ancient Near Eastern inscriptions the elements of the Circle of Justice first appeared separately, but they soon started combining in ways that were later encapsulated in the

Circle. The oldest written records indicate that the Sumerians already had a concept of royal power, its dependence on divine favor, and its role as the source of civilization and social order. The ruler gained power through conquest or inheritance, but ideologically the god, or gods, appointed him to rule as their deputy or viceroy.[4] The first surviving inscriptions (twenty-seventh and twenty-sixth centuries BCE) recorded the rulers' construction of temples and dedication of offerings to the gods.[5] An early example, on a stone mace-head dated about 2550 BCE, stated simply: "Mesilim, king of Kish, temple builder for the god Ningirsu, set up this mace for the god Ningirsu."[6] This inscription shows the ruler working for the god, seeking his favor.

Mesopotamian rulers soon began to leave more complex inscriptions extolling their own accomplishments. The inscriptions of Ur-Nanshe, king of the Sumerian city-state of Lagash in the early twenty-fifth century BCE, developed the theme of building for the god, listing the temples, shrines, and cult statues he had constructed. They also recorded his building of city walls and irrigation canals, which protected people and encouraged agricultural prosperity. His inscriptions described his military victories over other cities, Ur and Gishu, and recorded another action of his: he "had ships of Dilmun [Bahrain] submit timber as tribute from the foreign lands to Lagash," which proclaimed the wide extent of the king's reach.[7] Thus, already around 2500 BCE, royal ideology juxtaposed several elements of the Circle of Justice: divine favor, military strength, and prosperity or productivity.

The element of justice itself appeared in the inscriptions of Ur-Nanshe's grandson Eanatum (*c.*2450 BCE). He was called "the man of just commands" for his measurement of land boundaries. Another of his inscriptions causally linked the god's favor and the king's victory: "As for Eanatum, who is commissioned by the god Ningirsu, because of the strength given by the god Ningirsu, when he rages against the foreign lands, nobody is able to resist him." Making the same point at a later date, a prophecy for one of the kings of Mari warned that the god had brought him to the throne and could also take back what he had given.[8]

If rulers wanted to invoke divine support to legitimize their actions, then those actions must recognizably merit divine approval by protecting or aiding the god or his worshippers. Temple-building obviously fell into that category, but Eanatum did not explain how the destruction of kingdoms benefitted either his subjects or the gods. The idea that divinely-favored conquest brought prosperity to the people was articulated a century later in the inscriptions of Lugalzagesi, king of the city-state of Uruk around 2350 BCE and a conqueror like Eanatum. In this text divine favor and right leadership led to victory, and victory to prosperity and fruitfulness of the land under divinely-ordained leadership.

> When the god Enlil, king of all lands, gave to Lugalzagesi the kingship of the land, directed all the eyes of the land obediently toward him, put all the lands at his feet, and from east to west made them subject to him; then. Enlil permitted him no rival; under him the lands rested contentedly, the people made merry. [And Lugalzagesi prayed,] Under me, may the lands rest contentedly, may the populace become as widespread as the grass, may the nipples of heaven [rain clouds] work properly, and the people experience prosperity. may I always be the leading shepherd.[9]

In modern times these concepts have been explained as sacred kingship, oriental despotism, or the Asiatic mode of production.[10] In all of these explanations, however, the prosperity of the land and people as a sign and a result of successful rule is a significant element. Whatever model we apply today, clearly people of the third millennium BCE were already aware of the interdependence of prosperity and success on one hand and divine favor and right leadership on the other.

The quotation above used the metaphor of the ruler as a shepherd and the populace as sheep feeding in a pasture, suggesting that care and protection of the people were supposed to follow conquest. The defeat of enemies brought peace in the sense of the end of warfare, but it also created a more extensive land where, if the king made people prosperous and content, he would have internal peace – the absence of rebellion and unrest. It was the ruler's task, after he had won foreign wars, to institute the conditions of contentment within his land. In this way the king became more than a chief priest, a work organizer, or a military leader; he became the overseer of society as a whole, responsible for the welfare of its members. A later inscription from the eighteenth century BCE expresses the shepherding responsibility of the ruler most vividly: "The god Marduk gave to me, Samsu-iluna, king of his pleasure, the totality of the lands to shepherd and. to make his nation lie down in pastures and to lead his extensive people in well-being, forever."[11]

Shepherding care and the provision of welfare meant not only satisfying material needs but also granting justice for the ruled. Lugalzagesi's contemporary Urukagina, king of Lagash (*c.*2350 BCE), highlighted this aspect of welfare in his inscriptions. Beyond building temples and digging canals, Urukagina tried to create internal peace by providing justice. At his accession taxes were high and royal officials appropriated from the populace more than their due. The temple organization was subordinated to that of the ruler: "The oxen of the gods ploughed the garlic plot of the ruler, and. the grain of the temple administrators [was] divided up by the work crews of the ruler." Ordinary people became the victims: "Administrators ripped out trees in the orchards of the poor"; workers had to pay to enter the city; even burying a corpse cost high fees to various officials; and "bailiffs held jurisdiction from the boundary of the god Ningirsu to the sea. These were the proprietary rights of former days." But when the god Ningirsu granted kingship to Urukagina, "he restored the customs of former times." He removed government bureaucrats from responsibility over taxation, replacing them with religious personnel, presumably more honest. He also lowered tax rates and cancelled debt servitude. "The administrators no longer plunder the orchards of the poor," and "Urukagina made a binding agreement with the god Ningirsu that he would never subject the orphan or widow to the powerful."[12] The texts describing Urukagina's reforms became classic works of statecraft and were recopied many times in later centuries.[13] Mesopotamian society remembered Urukagina's ideal of providing justice to the weak and powerless long after Urukagina himself was vanquished by Lugalzagesi, who in turn was conquered by Sargon of Akkad (*c.*2330 BCE).

The Akkadian interlude (2334–2154 BCE)

Not everybody in the Middle East employed the Circle's concept of justice. Sargon of Akkad and his successors, who turned the Sumerian assemblage of city-states into a centralized empire, left inscriptions that sounded like those of the Sumerians but contained very different ideas of governance. Although Sargon boasted of feeding his own followers, his inscriptions extolled his conquests as evidence of divine favor and ignored justice and well-being for ordinary people. A typical inscription reads: "Enlil did not let anybody oppose Sargon, the king of the country. Enlil gave him the region from the Upper Sea to the Lower Sea."[14] Sargon's empire lasted nearly two hundred years and stretched from the Mediterranean to the Gulf; his armies made forays to still more distant lands. Tribute and trade brought goods and raw materials to the capital from afar. The fourth king of the line, Naram-Sin, also ascribed his victories to the support of a god: "Mighty Naram-Sin slew Arman and Ibla with the weapon of the god Dagan who aggrandizes his kingdom."[15] These inscriptions glorified the rulers' achievements outside the kingdom but paid little attention to internal conditions.

Naram-Sin of Akkad seems to have been the first ruler to use the title "king of the four quarters," king of everything to the edges of the known world, a claim to universal rule.[16] This title was later adopted by rulers of centralized imperial states, such as the Ur III dynasty, Hammurabi and some of his successors, and many of the Assyrian rulers. Naram-Sin also wrote his name with the sign for divinity, and an inscription stated that "his city wished him to be the god of their city."[17] The meaning of deifying a king is unclear, but he had to be elevated high enough over other kings to dominate them and unify the region. The "Legend of Naram-Sin" expressed later Mesopotamian society's condemnation of such presumption: in the story Naram-Sin goes on campaign in disobedience to the god's warning and is badly defeated. In his depression he mourns, "I am a king who brings no prosperity to his country, a shepherd who brings no prosperity to his people."[18] "Bringing prosperity to the people" may have been Naram-Sin's own understanding of his responsibility, but more likely it was inserted by the later compilers of the legend, since the inscriptions of Sargon and his descendents show little concern for the conditions of their subjects.

The Circle restored

After Sargon's dynasty ended, the pre-Sargonic royal ideology emphasizing prosperity and justice reappeared in the inscriptions of the city of Lagash, ruled by Gudea (2143–2124 BCE). In Gudea's time, as in Urukagina's, claims to care for the people could legitimize a dynasty's rule. He often referred to himself as "shepherd," "faithful shepherd," or "shepherd of his country."[19] In his city, Gudea "barred unnecessary words and he sent crime back to its 'house.' He undid the 'tongue' of the whip and the goad. … No mother would have words with her child, and no child would disobey its mother. No master would hit his slave … and no mistress would slap the face of the slave woman who had misbehaved towards her."[20] This extraordinary condition of justice was not an everyday affair but was part of the preparation for the building of a new temple. To initiate construction in the right way, peace and virtue had to reign in the city. Another part of the preparation was less pleasant: "in those days the ruler imposed a levy on his land, on his realm," a tax of building materials for the new temple (wood, stone, metals, and precious stones, some obtained from distant lands). The dedication of the temple was a time of great justice: "He had caused everything to function as it should in his city … he had debts remitted and he granted pardons … for seven days the slave woman was allowed to be equal to her mistress, the slave was allowed to walk side by side with his master. Days of justice had risen for him, and he set his foot on the neck of evil and complaint."[21] Gudea's activities built on the sense of a causal connection among the righteousness of king and people, the gods' favor, prosperity, and justice affirmed earlier by Urukagina. In addition, these inscriptions show that under ordinary circumstances people sought justice by bringing their complaints to the ruler.

In the following centuries, these two modes of royal legitimation – Sargon's of external victory and Urukagina's of internal care – mingled in the inscriptions of many rulers of city-states in the region. They called themselves both divine, mighty man, conqueror, and also shepherd, righteous husbandman, the shepherd who feeds the flock. This combined claim appears in an inscription of Ur-Nammu (2112–2095 BCE), the founder of the centralized Ur III empire, describing both his power and his justice. As "mighty man" and "king of the lands of Sumer and Akkad," he built the temple of the god Enlil and the canal that fed it; he also made just decisions.[22]

Shulgi (2094–2047 BCE), Ur-Nammu's successor in Ur, also combined these two claims. He dominated the whole of Sumer and beyond, taking Naram-Sin's title, "king of the four quarters." A poem in his honor related how he was born of a goddess to bring prosperity and justice:

> To fill the granaries of the Land with barley,
> To stock the treasuries of the Land with goods,
> To make the foreign lands deliver their yields,
> ...
> To let justice never come to an end,
> To throw evil in the Depths, as if it were a light stone,
> To let no man make his fellow a hireling,
> That Shulgi, after having taken his seat upon the enduring dais,
> The lustrous throne of Sumer's well-built palace,
> The king, Divine Judge, the "seed" of Sumer,
> Shall pronounce the judgment of the Land, that he shall make the decisions for the Land,
> That he shall cause our city, Ur, to lift high its head.[23]

This poem implied that the entire status of the empire depended on the prosperity and justice that the king would provide. Besides conducting ambitious military campaigns, Shulgi reformed the imperial administration, regularized government accounting, standardized weights and measures, and organized an empire-wide messenger service. His justice was supposed to protect the powerless: "So that the strong does not oppress the weak."[24]

Such rhetoric, whether or not it corresponded to reality, embodied society's understanding that the proper use of power was to enact justice and bring prosperity. From an observation, it became a recommendation. At public festivals and in the scribal schools where government bureaucrats were trained, these poems were recited to foster an ideology of centralized rule and universal dependence on the king. Whoever heard them learned that the king was supposed to provide justice and prevent oppression. Official seals from this period portrayed the king seated with a cup, in a god-like position that exhibited his participation in the divine task of rendering justice. His throne represented the authority granted by the gods to make decisions, and the cup of divination in his hand symbolized his insight into the divine will. The seals on which these pictures were carved were the tools by which the ruler delegated part of his authority to subordinate officials. Thus, they stood for the whole centralized administrative system headed by the king through which the Circle's power and justice were exercised.[25]

The Ur III empire collapsed shortly before 2000 BCE, but the kings of subsequent dynasties retained in their titles the claims made by the third-millennium rulers, claims to universality and legitimacy via divine appointment, military victory, prosperity, and shepherding care or justice. That can only have been because the people of their societies continued to see those qualities as establishing someone's right to rule over them. Nur-Adad (1865–1850 BCE), powerful ruler of Ur and Larsa, "mighty man. subduer of the foreign lands," also claimed to be a "shepherd of righteousness" who "removed evil and the cause for any complaint." To him, shepherding meant protecting the weak from the strong: "I destroyed the brigand, the wicked, and the evil-doer in their midst. I made the weak, widow, and orphan content."[26] The kings of Der used similar epithets, while Samsu-iluna of Babylon (1805–1768 BCE) "defeated with weapons. the totality of the land of Sumer and Akkad" and received from the god "a sceptre of justice that makes the land firm."[27]

City-state rulers who made no conquests could apparently claim only the shepherding half of the equation. Rulers whose inscriptions emphasized the king's responsibility to provide for the people included Enlil-bani of Isin (1860–1837 BCE), the "shepherd who makes everything abundant for Nippur," who stressed reduction of taxes and satisfaction of complaints: "I established justice in Nippur. I made righteousness appear. As for sheep I sought out food to eat and fed them with green plants … I established righteousness and justice in Isin … I reduced to one-tenth the grain tax … I made anybody with a complaint a taboo thing. I am a judge who loves righteousness." Similarly, the kings of Larsa provided food and water because they saw themselves as shepherds who cared for their people.[28] These inscriptions contained two main emphases of the Circle of Justice: ensuring safety and security, and providing abundance through construction of irrigation works and elimination of excessive exploitation. A contented populace would not exist without sufficient food and water at reasonable prices. Nor would peace coexist with injustice, oppression, or crime.

Laws, decrees, and judgments (2112–1104 BCE)

Justice and peace were not created only by military force and construction. The legal system was crucial to enacting justice: fighting crime, popular unrest, and oppression by elites. The legal system, so royal inscriptions indicate, was based not on judges but on kings and their decrees. A long process of legal development preceded the famous Code of Hammurabi. Rulers issued decrees on all sorts of problems, specific or general, and by the late third millennium BCE, these decrees were being gathered together into "law-codes." Such texts were not legal codes in the modern sense but compilations of laws "carved in stone," usually with a preamble justifying their issuance. The laws themselves defined various crimes and wrongdoings and listed the penalties to be applied, but our interest lies in the preamble explaining why the compilation was made and what justice meant. The concept of justice in these preambles was clearly that of the Circle with its interdependencies.

Lawcodes of Ur-Nammu and Lipit-Ishtar

The earliest known "lawcode" was the so-called "Code of Ur-Nammu," probably compiled by the founder of the Ur III empire and issued during a general reorganization after his reconquest of Sumerian cities from Anshan to the east.[29] Restoring order involved standardizing weights and measures, planting gardens, and reenacting rituals. Equally important was reestablishing social justice and protection for the weak: "The orphan was not handed over to the rich man, the widow was not handed over to the mighty man. I banished there evil, violence, and any cause for complaint. I established justice in the land."[30] Regulating prices, remitting debts and unpaid taxes, suppressing crime and violence, answering complaints, and protecting the defenseless were all part of the restoration of justice after turmoil. Justice meant more than equality before the law or seeing that everyone got what was coming to him. As the Circle indicated, it meant remedying the imbalance of human society, reining in the powerful and protecting the powerless who could not obtain justice for themselves.

Isin's ruler Lipit-Ishtar (1934–1924 BCE), following Ur-Nammu's example, also promulgated a "code" or compendium of laws whose preamble defined justice as the provision of peace and prosperity. The gods, he said, called "Lipit-Ishtar, the wise shepherd … to the princeship of the land in order to establish justice in the land, to banish complaints, to turn back enmity and rebellion by the force of arms, and to bring well-being to the Sumerians and Akkadians."[31] In the epilogue to his laws, Lipit-Ishtar reiterated that "true justice" meant he had "abolished enmity and rebellion; made weeping, lamentations, outcries … taboo; caused righteousness and truth to exist; brought well-being."[32] These statements included the defeat of enemies, the protection of the weak, and the provision of prosperity in a concept of justice that embraced them all. The whole purpose of kingship in this view was to defend the land against its enemies, to put down rebellion, and to meet the needs of the people, especially when they complained to the king.

Two types of needs, both within a king's power to meet, typically produced complaints from the people: first, oppression by royal officials, and second, natural disasters demanding repair of the infrastructure (canals, buildings) and/or remission of agricultural taxes. If allowed to continue, these problems would cause the loss of well-being and eventual rebellion. Internal unrest equalled foreign conquest in its ability to disrupt the land. To maintain his power, the just ruler dealt with both internal and external difficulties.

The lawcode of Hammurabi

Hammurabi of Babylon (1792–1750 BCE) united Mesopotamia, establishing Babylonia as the leading state in the region and taking the title "king of the four quarters." His "lawcode" was modeled after that of Lipit-Ishtar, and its preamble developed the theme of justice in the Circle's terms: "At that time [the gods] Anum and Enlil named me to promote the welfare of the people, me, Hammurabi, the devout, god-fearing prince, to cause justice to prevail in the land, to destroy the wicked and the evil, that the strong might not oppress the weak. Hammurabi, the Shepherd, called by Enlil am I, the one who makes affluence and plenty abound."[33] In pursuit of this justice, Hammurabi explained, he delimited pastures and watering places for pastoralists, refounded cities for peoples dispersed by invasion and warfare, supplied water in abundance (by digging canals and extending the irrigation system into the conquered areas), and provided security for people and property.

After listing all the laws, he reiterated that justice meant relief for the oppressed: "They prospered under my protection; I have governed them in peace; I have sheltered them in my strength. In order that the strong might not oppress the weak, that justice might be dealt the orphan and the widow … I wrote my precious words on my stela, and in the presence of my statue as king of justice I set it up in order to administer the law of the land, to prescribe the ordinances of the land, to give justice to the oppressed."[34]

The banishing of complaints from the populace had become very important in royal ideology by now, as shown by the code's detailed instructions to complainants: "Let any oppressed man, who has a cause, come into the presence of my statue as the king of justice, and then read my inscribed stela, and give heed to my precious words, and may my stela make the case clear to him; may he understand his cause; may he set his mind at ease!"[35] These provisions were also meant as a model for other rulers: "If such a leader has intelligence and wishes to guide his land aright, he should heed the words which I wrote on my stela, and it shall surely show him the road and the way."[36] Lawcodes, however, were not the only vehicles for providing justice.

Justice decrees

Rulers' claims of justice referred not merely to their general attitude of benevolence or legal rectitude, but to specific acts on behalf of the poor and powerless, most of which had clear economic implications. The kings of this era periodically issued "justice decrees" remitting certain debts, taxes, and tax arrears and cancelling debt-slavery. A justice decree differed from a compendium of laws in that its provisions were not permanent reforms but one-time exemptions that removed the burden of debt accumulated over the years, wiping the slate clean for a fresh beginning. A king might issue a "justice decree" at the beginning of his reign or at a later date, such as after a war or natural disaster.[37] The decree might cover the whole empire or just a particular location. The year of its proclamation or the following year was often named after the issuance of the justice decree: "The year in which so-and-so proclaimed justice."[38]

The written version of one such decree still exists; issued in the reign of the Babylonian king Ammisaduqa (1646–1626 BCE), it lists the debts, tax arrears, and loans that were remitted.[39] Contracts of sales and loans with clauses limiting the effects of justice decrees demonstrate that for two millennia wealthy people genuinely stood to lose money when such decrees were enforced, debts and unpaid taxes were forgiven, land was given back to its original owners, and debt slaves were freed. The greatest loss was in taxes owed to the king, and issuing this type of edict seems to have been one of the deeds that entitled a ruler to call himself a shepherd.[40]

Royal courts of justice

Unlike periodic debt remissions, which happened only occasionally, the provision of justice in response to individual or communal complaints was an ongoing responsibility. Kings had regular days when they sat in judgment to receive appeals from their subjects and to issue edicts on their problems.[41] Cases were also referred from provincial governors or lower courts. A few actual petitions on clay tablets sent by subjects to their kings have been preserved and translated, as well as many royal responses to petitions now lost. These documents show that people took advantage of the possibility of appealing to the ruler to air their grievances, seek judgments against oppressors, and get injustices rectified. The kinds of cases varied widely, and the king was not always in a position to render a just judgment on the spot. His role was often to act as mediator, to stir up his officials to take action, or to repress subordinates who used their power irresponsibly. A few examples of such cases illustrate the variety of complaints and rulers' responses.

One tablet recorded the king's response to a subject's complaint that his land had been seized by a man of higher status; when the government's records were checked, the land did appear to belong to the petitioner, so the ruler ordered the provincial governor that if the seizure had no valid reason, he should restore the land and punish the oppressor. Another tablet concerned a merchant's complaint about a government official who owed him a debt and had not paid anything for three years; the king ordered the governor to make the official pay up. Still another referred to someone's complaint about rent that had originally been submitted to a provincial governor; the governor had forwarded the case to the capital along with his recommendation for a solution, and the extant tablet stated the king's approval of his recommendation. A final example is a case of two brothers making a complaint against their elder brother who had done them an injustice; in the previous two years they had complained several times to the provincial governor with no result and were finally appealing to the king. The tablet in question commanded the provincial governor to submit the case to the capital for judgment.[42]

The complaint process, as these documents show, functioned both as a means of settling disputes and as a way of obtaining redress against the injustices of people of higher status, rich men and officials. It sometimes had little to do with law as such, since it was often concerned with matters outside the jurisdiction of the courts. Bypassing the ordinary legal system, it appealed to the ruler as a judge whose status and power exceeded that of even the most formidable opponent.[43] Beyond the fair settlement of an individual case, justice in these circumstances meant a balancing of the social scales, a leveling of differences in power.

The procedures employed for handling these complaints were similar to those used in the later Persian and Islamic empires. Subjects could complain in person directly to the royal court or indirectly through a provincial official or judge; rulers sat in judgment at regular intervals to hear individuals or read petitions; and they delegated enforcement to provincial officials and their troops. Petitions from distant subjects or officials and royal responses were forwarded over the post system, a royal messenger service carried on swift horses over a road network dotted with post stations. The Babylonian post system was later expanded and maintained by the Assyrians and succeeding dynasties as an essential tool in the distribution of justice from the capital throughout the empire.[44] The use of this mechanism indicates that millennia before the rise of Islam people availed themselves of the ruler's justice, as denoted by the Circle.

Dynasties after Hammurabi's

Despite the international stature of the Babylonian monarchy at this time, the evidence for its political concepts is very thin after about 1600 BCE, but some evidence suggests that the Circle's justice was still highly regarded. Boundary stones from the second dynasty of Isin (1157–1025 BCE) recorded the king's acts in maintaining the irrigation system and providing roads, bridges, and border garrisons as well as royal judgments.[45] The few surviving inscriptions show that Kurigalzu of the Kassite dynasty (1594–1157 BCE) was called a shepherd and a "judge who like Shamash examines the case."[46] Nebuchadnezzar I (1125–1104 BCE), the only king for whom extensive inscriptions survive, called himself the "just king who renders righteous decisions;" he claimed that the Sun-god had "granted him a just sceptre, an eternal throne, and a reign of long duration," and wished "that he might shepherd Sumer and Akkad."[47] Older ideas on royal justice were clearly still current in this later period.

Babylonian ideas of justice did not exist in isolation; similar concepts of royal justice and recommendations on the best method for handling subjects' complaints were current throughout the Middle East in the second millennium BCE. In Syria, Zimri-Lim of Mari (1782–1759 BCE) was told by the local god: "When a petitioner appeals to you, hold court and give them justice. That is the only thing I demand of you." Although the Egyptian concept of justice generally differed from that of Mesopotamia, some Egyptian texts carried similar messages. A ruler of the Old Kingdom (Sheshi, twenty-fourth century BCE) boasted of his justice in his tomb inscription:

> I judged between two so as to content them,
> I rescued the weak from one stronger than he
> As much as was within my power.
> I gave bread to the hungry, clothes to the naked,
> I brought the boatless to land.

An Egyptian text of instruction made justice the mark of the ideal king and warned: "That you may rule the land, govern the shores, increase well being! … I gave to the beggar, I raised the orphan, I gave success to the poor as to the wealthy." A text from about the twentieth century BCE gave advice on how to provide justice: "Do justice, then you endure on earth. Calm the weeper, don't oppress the widow, don't expel a man from his father's property, don't reduce the nobles in their possessions. Beware of punishing wrongfully." A fifteenth-century Egyptian official was told at his installation not to treat petitioners lightly: "Do not pass over a petitioner before you have considered his speech. When a petitioner is about to petition you, don't dismiss what he says as already said. Deny him [only] after you let him hear on what account you have denied him. Lo, it is said: 'A petitioner wants his plea considered rather than have his case adjudged [i.e. he wants a hearing more than a verdict]. Lo, you succeed in this office by doing justice.'"[48] These scattered references can only suggest how the Circle's concept of justice continued to inform the political ideology of the region in this period, but more information exists on the society of Assyria in northern Mesopotamia.

Assyria (2000–539 BCE)

The Assyrians have acquired a terrible reputation, mainly because of the way they were depicted in the Hebrew Bible, but although they were militaristic they exhibited great administrative ability and inclusiveness. The abundant evidence from northern Mesopotamia sheds considerable light not only on the Assyrians' idea of justice, but also on how they put it into practice. Assyrian royal inscriptions expanded the description of the ruler's exploits from a mere mention to an extended annalistic narrative with long descriptions of battles. The narrative emphasized a number of characteristics that were woven into the Circle of Justice, including divine favor, military victory, good administration, and the provision of prosperity, but not justice itself. Justice was an important part of the rulers' governing activity, but at first it did not appear to play any role in their legitimation.

Early Assyrian justice and its role

The Assyrians, who became a territorial power in the last quarter of the second millennium BCE, followed Sumerian models in their form of government and the style of their inscriptions.[49] Their political thought, however, exhibited some differences. The Assyrian concept of kingship was similar to that of Sumer and Akkad in that the ruler was considered the appointee of a god.[50] Assyrians, however, put more stress than Sumerians and Babylonians on the god's position as the real ruler and arbiter of society and the king's subordinate role as high priest and viceroy.[51] The ruler's long inscriptions boasting about his exploits would appear to contradict this humble position, but the gods received credit as first cause of all his success. His legitimacy depended on being the divine favorite, "the king at whose feet the gods … made all rulers and princes bow down."[52] Broadening the borders of the land, capturing booty, incorporating diverse peoples, and imposing tribute, taxes, and the Assyrian "yoke" all proved the greatness of the king, the land, and ultimately the chief god, Ashur.[53] Extending Assyria's boundaries and incorporating foreign peoples into the realm emphasized the potential universality of Assyrian dominion, while booty and tribute symbolized the winner's superiority to the loser.

Like earlier rulers, the kings of Assyria gave the gods their due and the land its prosperity by building temples and walls and digging canals.[54] They also provided justice, as evidenced by an inscription of Lipit-Ishtar's contemporary, the Assyrian Erishum I (1940–1901 BCE), recording his construction of a temple and a gate. The gate held particular importance as the place where justice was served, cases were tried, and complaints were heard; the term "gate" or "door" (and later "Porte," as in "Sublime Porte") came to mean the place of government and, by extension, rule itself. Erishum's gate no longer exists, but its description stated that in the gate were seven judges called "the Seven Judges of the Step Gate" (perhaps statues in niches?); their names were Justice, He-Heard-the-Prayer, Get-Out-Criminal, He-Extolled-Justice, Watch-Over-the-Downtrodden, His-Speech-Is-Upright, and God-Has-Heard.[55] A later inscription indicated that Adad-Narari I (1307–1275 BCE) repaired and restored the Step Gate. Adad-Narari's own inscriptions, however, did not link the provision of justice with military success or prosperity, suggesting that although justice formed a significant part of the ruler's activity, it did not yet have an important place in his ideology of legitimization. Sometime during this period a collection of laws in the tradition of Hammurabi's appeared, but the preamble has been lost; its discussion of justice might have told us more about how the Assyrians regarded that concept.[56] On the other hand, Shalmaneser I (1274–1245 BCE) freely used the epithet of shepherd to describe his rule, showing that in this period care for the people was still a central part of a ruler's task.[57]

Justice and good administration

Even though justice did not contribute to the Assyrian kings' legitimation, good administration became one of their most outstanding royal qualities. Tukulti-Ninurta I (1244–1208 BCE), who brought Babylonia temporarily into the Assyrian Empire, installed Assyrian officials as governors to permit more direct control. He also gave a new emphasis to good administration, calling himself "the one who properly administers peoples and habitations with his just sceptre," or "the prince who accepts their gifts, the shepherd who has charge over them, and the herdsman who properly administers them."[58] While earlier inscriptions had occasionally mentioned palace construction, Tukulti-Ninurta's annals contained a lengthy description of the building of a palace "as a place for the exercise of his rule."[59] He called himself a king "who maintains. populations in good order," and an inscription describing the role of the god in "teaching me just decisions" testified to his active involvement in the provision of justice.[60]

An inscription of Tiglath-Pileser I (1115–1077 BCE), under whom Assyrian power reached from Babylon west toward Phoenicia and north into Anatolia, linked this territorial breadth to royal justice. It stated that the king "named the gates of the palace gates of justice, which give just decisions concerning the rulers of the world, which let in the tribute of sea and mountain countries."[61] Tiglath-Pileser also made several innovations in the format of royal inscriptions, one of which was to include a section describing his activities in reconstructing and repopulating cities and providing for the prosperity of the land. This aspect of the inscriptions helped to balance an earlier emphasis – perhaps overemphasis – on conquest and destruction resulting from the expansion of the military annals. The king announced that he moved people from regions that had been fought over and destroyed, resettling them in newly opened areas or in reconstructed cities; that he allocated fields and planted orchards, and that he rebuilt temples and fortifications, set up garrisons, and established security.[62] He also cultivated a garden containing exotic plants from all the regions he had conquered to symbolize the extent of his control and his ability to make the land prosperous and fertile.[63] He thus demonstrated his good administration and his ability to care for his land and people. This shepherding care went beyond the provision of food and water to the creation of new homes and livelihoods, internal peace, and external security.

Later Assyrian rulers stressed their good administration of the lands and peoples in their charge, as the Circle of Justice linked justice with good administration. The Assyrian idea of good administration included the absorption and assimilation of conquered peoples into the people of Assyria, to be governed by the same standards as the king's own people. For example, after the defeat of the Mushku, Tiglath-Pileser "took the remaining 6,000 of their troops who had fled from my weapons and submitted to me and regarded them as people of my land."[64] An inscription of Tukulti-Ninurta II (890–884 BCE) told a tale of such relocation and re-assimilation after a rebellion; the king relocated the people of the rebellious land to abandoned cities elsewhere and made their ruler take an oath of allegiance to the god Ashur.[65] An inscription of Shalmaneser I had already indicated how far such incorporation could be carried: it related how after subduing "all the land Uruatri … I took a selection of their young men and I chose them to enter my service."[66] Such men were assimilated into the ruling class and could rise to high positions in the government; the most well-known examples are the biblical Joseph and Daniel. Relocation and incorporation, however, were often interpreted as "captivity" by those who experienced them, and the later king Esarhaddon gained political mileage from returning "the captive people of the lands … to their places."[67]

After a period of disintegration, the Assyrians of the ninth century BCE expanded and reconsolidated in what is usually called the Neo-Assyrian Empire. The records left by Ashurnasirpal II (883–859 BCE) contained long tales of his military exploits in which the word "merciless" appeared as a term of approbation.[68] To portray his royal authority, he presided over a development of Assyrian palace art involving the creation of huge narrative wall sculptures depicting him as a successful warrior and hunter and a worshipper of the gods.[69] Along with accounts of destruction and death in his annals, however, came descriptions of this king's reconstruction activities. Like Tiglath-Pileser, he prided himself on his good administration of the kingdom. His inscriptions related that he appointed governors and reorganized the administration of conquered territories, resettled both Assyrians and war refugees in newly conquered or rebuilt towns, irrigated meadows, planted orchards, and provided protection and security to the inhabitants of the land.[70] Ashurnasirpal wanted to be remembered as adding territory to Assyria and people to its population. As he said of himself: "I have subdued and brought under one authority fortified lands, dangerous highlands, and merciless fierce kings from east to west."[71] He clearly wished to be the universal monarch: "shepherd of the four quarters, who has brought all peoples under one authority … whose protection spreads like the rays of the sun over his land and who has governed his people in well-being."[72] The sun was a god, of course, the god of justice, and Ashurnasirpal claimed his support. His successor Shalmaneser III (858–824 BCE), another conqueror and builder, actually claimed to be "the sun (god) of all people," as well as a "faithful shepherd who leads in peace the population of Assyria."[73]

The inscriptions of Tiglath-Pileser III (744–727 BCE) renewed the emphasis on the resettling of conquered peoples, bringing them into the fold and assimilating them to the Assyrians; rather than massacring his opponents, he incorporated them. His inscriptions repeatedly described how after the conquest of an area he ousted the rulers and installed his own officials, put the people on the same footing as the original Assyrians and "considered them as inhabitants of Assyria."[74] Building a city, he settled conquered people in it and "placed upon them the yoke of Ashur as upon the Assyrians."[75] The records of Sargon II (721–705 BCE) made the same point with respect to Samaria, when he relocated its inhabitants and repopulated it with people from other lands he had conquered: "My courtier I placed over them as a governor and duties and tax I imposed upon them as on Assyrians."[76] Both rulers expanded the amount of territory under direct Assyrian rule, increasing the need for organization and assimilation. Sargon's inscriptions also related his efforts to acculturate his new subjects and instruct them in Assyrian ways.[77] Similar policies later appeared in the Ottoman Empire, where they were considered aspects of the good administration that the Circle recommended.

The provision of prosperity

Among the projects of many Neo-Assyrian kings was the creation of prosperity through the foundation of new capital cities and the construction of "brilliant temples and artistic shrines" for the gods and splendid palaces for themselves.[78] Kings initiated construction at the command of the god: "At that time the god Assur, my lord, requested of me a cult centre on the bank opposite my city."[79] Commemorative inscriptions emphasized the fact that no one had previously thought of building on that site, or of renewing it; these inscriptions paid tribute to the intelligence and creativity of the royal minds. The first requirement for the establishment of a city was a source of water, since the inhabitants had to be fed from the fields surrounding the city, and the inscriptions described the digging of canals, rerouting of rivers, and provision of wells. Around Tukulti-Ninurta's city of Kar-Tukulti-Ninurta, he said, "I cut a wide path for a stream which supports life in the land and which provides abundance, and I transformed the plains of my city into irrigated fields."[80] This stream was named the "Canal of Justice;" justice, therefore, included the provision of water. The later ruler Ashurnasirpal rebuilt the ruined city of Kalhu as his capital and settled it with "people whom my hand had conquered." He too dug a canal for it, laid out fields, built temples and a palace, planted a garden with forty-one different kinds of trees, and set up a royal zoo, breeding lions in cages as an exhibition of royal supremacy over nature.[81]

As the empire became more centralized the palace became more important, not only as the ruler's seat, but also as a canvas on which his ideology could be displayed. Sargon II built himself a new capital city, Dur-Sharruken (now Khorsabad), complete with temples, wall, irrigation works, and a palace called "The Palace Without Rival." To exemplify the universality of his rule, he settled his city with people "of foreign tongue and divergent speech," and had the walls of his palace decorated with sculptures of tribute-bearers from the many peoples of the empire. The carvings showed Sargon in all his various roles and included inscriptions that situated the building of his new city within a wider context than those of earlier capitals. Its construction formed part of his larger program for the provision of prosperity, which involved restoring ruined towns, cultivating new fields, and planting orchards in order "to cause the waters of abundance to rise high."[82]

One purpose of this building program was to avert unrest by stimulating economic growth and keeping prices low, so that "the oil of abundance which eases the muscles of men should not be too costly in my land."[83] To quiet dissatisfaction, he compensated those who lost their land to the building program: "In accordance with the name which the great gods have given me [Sargon means 'just king'], to maintain righteousness and justice, to give guidance to the weak, not to injure the feeble, I paid back to their owners the price of the fields and of the town according to the record of the purchase documents, in silver and copper, and to avoid any misgivings I gave to those who did not want to take silver for their lands a field for a field, in a location facing their old field."[84] Nor did Sargon neglect his canal-digging and temple-building elsewhere, "for his life, the welfare of his seed, the destruction of his enemies, the success of the crops of Assyria, the welfare of Assyria." He was rewarded with abundant rains and plentiful crops.[85]

The conquest accounts of Neo-Assyrian rulers paid more attention to the collection of tribute and taxation than did those of earlier kings, who were apparently more interested in recording their prowess as warriors. This new aspect of prosperity and good administration appeared in the inscriptions of Shalmaneser III, which listed in detail the tribute he received from defeated enemies: "Silver, gold, tin, bronze, iron, bronze, red-purple wool, elephant ivory, garments with multicoloured trim, linen garments, oxen, sheep, wine, and ducks."[86] Several rulers' wall sculptures also portrayed deliveries of tribute from foreign peoples as well as "gifts" from Assyrian nobles.[87] Tax and tribute, particularly in kind, required a storehouse, so even before there was money there was a "treasury," filled with treasures – wool, garments, elephant hides, ivory, precious woods, utensils, precious metals, gems, chariots, gear, furniture, and arms. Inscriptions carefully noted the capture of more than one defeated ruler "together with his property, goods, palace treasures."[88] Even more than the taking of booty, the capture of a royal treasury symbolized the subordination of an enemy.

A regular system of taxation implied a higher degree of control and administrative capability than periodic exactions of tribute. Assyrians paid regular taxes; coinage was not introduced until later, but in the eighth century BCE taxes were paid in precious metal measured by weight as well as in goods and labor. In Assyrian ideology, tax and tribute were both the symbol and the medium of submission and belonging. Ceasing to pay was seen as a sign of a change of allegiance and was treated as rebellion: "Mutallum of the land of Kummuhu, a wicked Hittite, who did not fear the name of the gods, a planner of evil, plotter of iniquity, put his trust in Argisti, king of Urartu, an ally who could not save him, and stopped the yearly payment of tribute and tax and withheld his gifts."[89]

The regular payment of taxes, like a proper request for their reduction or remission due to bad harvests, simultaneously recognized the ruler's power and acknowledged his legitimacy. His permanent exemption of a person or place from taxes and dues in kind or in labor was thus both a generous favor and a statement of trust, and maintaining these exemptions became another mark of the just sovereign.[90] The text of privileges for the citizens of Sippar, Nippur, and Babylon prohibited mobilizing the population or imposing forced labor, exacting taxes, fees, fines or bribes, commandeering their animals, or convicting them improperly. Most important was the reason given: "If a king does not heed justice, his people will be thrown into chaos, and his land will be devastated."[91] Shalmaneser V's abrogation of the privileges of the city of Assur was considered to be a valid reason for the god to overthrow his reign and install Sargon as king; Sargon immediately restored the city's exemptions.[92]

People expected justice and good administration in return for their taxes. When they did not get it they rebelled, as shown in a text about the bad administration of a local ruler: "The anger of the great gods was upon him for ruining his land and diminishing his people, and the people were in an uproar, they planned evil. The whole of his land, with one accord, opposed him and deserted him."[93] In contrast, bringing prosperity to the land and increasing its population brought popular approval and legitimation, and made people more willing to pay their taxes.

New aspects of good administration

Controlling extortionate tax collection was the crowning goal of good administration and one of the most important ways that kings could show justice to their subjects. The recording of tax assessments established a firm upper limit to the amount that royal officials could legally collect. Tiglath-Pileser III and his successors greatly strengthened the Assyrian bureaucracy, an improvement that culminated in the seventh-century Harran census, a survey of northern Mesopotamia.[94] The survey registered agricultural lands, buildings, crops, and animals, and it enumerated the residents by family, including their names, occupations, personal status, and tax obligations to the state. Records mentioning the assessment or reassessment of tribute or tax usually give no information on how the amounts were arrived at, but the first translator of the Harran census noted that, even as far back as the third millennium, estates were carefully surveyed, their area computed, their boundaries specified, and the kind of land, type of irrigation, crops cultivated, average yields, and names of cultivators were recorded. Similar information appeared in bills of sale in many periods, and a letter of Hammurabi indicates that land and land use were surveyed and recorded in his time as well.[95]

The tighter administrative control over the provinces established by Tiglath-Pileser III was increased by his successors. Sargon II's inscriptions stressed his appointment of royal officials to govern the conquered lands in place of local elites; one inscription mentioned it eleven times. Another of Sargon's inscriptions enumerated the multiple levels of provincial administration: "the princes of the four regions of the world … the governors of my land, the scribes and superintendents, the nobles, officials, and elders."[96] The administrative organization of the empire had become an achievement to boast about on palace walls. A large tablet, on which Ashurbanipal (668–627 BCE) described his education for the throne, shows how intensively he was trained for rule and administration and how important the scribal arts (divination, arithmetic, the reading of old scripts, and "the intricacies of the art of writing") had become to good government.[97] By the seventh century, the Neo-Assyrian Empire had become much more administratively sophisticated than earlier states, better able to establish direct rule over vast reaches of territory, maintain a road network and post system, coordinate the flow of taxes, goods, and information, and control exploitation by elites, military commanders, and governors.

Sargon's successors continued to employ Sargon's repertoire of claims to legitimacy, but with individual differences in emphasis. Sennacherib (704–681 BCE) described himself as a universal ruler, proud of his might, his conquests, and the extent and diversity of the additions he made to the empire. His "Palace Without Rival" at Nineveh portrayed in its wall reliefs the many origins of the workers and materials contributing to its construction.[98] Esarhaddon (680–669 BCE) wished to be admired for building religious sanctuaries and returning war captives to their homelands. He restored the city of Babylon, which Sennacherib had destroyed, reestablishing its privileges along with those of the city of Assur and exempting its inhabitants from certain taxes.[99] In addition, justice at last re-emerged as a significant legitimizing quality in the rhetoric of the late Assyrian rulers. As far as Sargon was concerned, "Ninmenanna the creator goddess made his sovereignty without peer so that the weak might not be oppressed and to assure justice to the powerless." Sennacherib called himself a lover of justice; Esarhaddon stated that he loved righteousness and hated oppression and falsehood.[100] Ashurbanipal, too, claimed a love of justice that brought prosperity: "Adad sent down his rains for me, Ea opened for me his underground waters ... during my reign there were prosperity and abundance, in my years plenty was heaped up."[101] Sin-shar-ishkun (?–612 BCE) called himself a "just judge, who speaks righteousness and justice."[102] The later Babylonian-Chaldean rulers used the same epithets; for instance, Nebuchadnezzar II (604–562 BCE) and Nabonidus (555–539 BCE) both called themselves lovers of law and justice.[103]

A letter to an unidentified Neo-Assyrian king reveals that people in this later period still understood the promise of justice in the same way as in Lipit-Ishtar's day – as the banishing of complaints and the provision of well-being. The letter urged the ruler to hear patiently the appeals of his subjects: "As for the men who have made appeals to the king, the king my lord should not turn them away; let these men come and appeal, and let the king my lord go into their cases. Any matter which finds favour with the king, let him take into his hands, and any which does not find favour with the king my lord, let him dismiss."[104] Documents of this period recording appeals from subjects to rulers reveal that individuals complained to their kings about the ignoring of tax exemptions, unjust dismissal from office, false accusation, an attempt to evade taxation, a dispute within the family of a city official, a confiscation of sheep, the poverty of a minor bureaucrat, or a ruined harvest. Both officials and ordinary people sent appeals to demand justice in the face of oppression by royal administrators or of circumstances they could not handle themselves. Illiterate people had documents written on their behalf. Kings responded to such complaints with orders to governors and other officials commanding them to look carefully into local affairs, straighten out problems, and not to allow the subjects to be victimized.[105] Other documents record judgments by officials with royal appointments, military commanders, and even gods; it appears that in this period, kings often did not preside over judicial proceedings in person but delegated the task to others. It is impossible to tell if their orders were always obeyed, but the fact that provincial administrators were more often royal officials, rather than vassal kings who had once ruled in their own right, gave rulers better control over their actions.

Conclusion

Assyria in the seventh century BCE had become a multinational empire with a complex system of provincial governance and taxation, an international bureaucracy and army, and extensive systems of long-distance communication and trade. Contrary to its negative image, it was governed by an ideology linking the favor of the gods, royal authority, military victory, productivity, and justice. This concept of state had a long history in the ancient Near East: it had appeared in embryo as early as 2350 BCE in Sumer; its most succinct statement came in Babylonian law collections of the second millennium; and Assyrian rulers put it into practice by means of an effective administration of wide scope. Mesopotamian kings were not simply overbearing despots; as divinely appointed shepherds, they accepted responsibility for providing prosperity and justice for their land and people. To do this they developed an extensive system of public works involving irrigation systems, road networks, temples, and public buildings, and an administrative system involving supervision of trade and prices, regulation of taxation, enactment of rituals, provision of laws and courts, and attention to the needs and complaints of their subjects. These rulers' subjects took the opportunity provided by these systems to seek royal support in adverse circumstances and to enlist the kings in their struggles against oppressive officials. Although obtaining this support was doubtless easier for wealthy and powerful subjects than for poor ones, the poor did have direct access to the ruler, and providing justice to them was an important part of the ideology of rule. The revenues and loyalty generated by public works and the provision of justice supported a program of offensive and defensive military activities aimed at keeping internal discord to a minimum and bringing glory and fame to the rulers and their gods. This ancient Near Eastern concept of state, eventually encapsulated in the Circle of Justice, was adopted by the Persians, who invaded the Fertile Crescent in the late seventh and sixth centuries BCE.

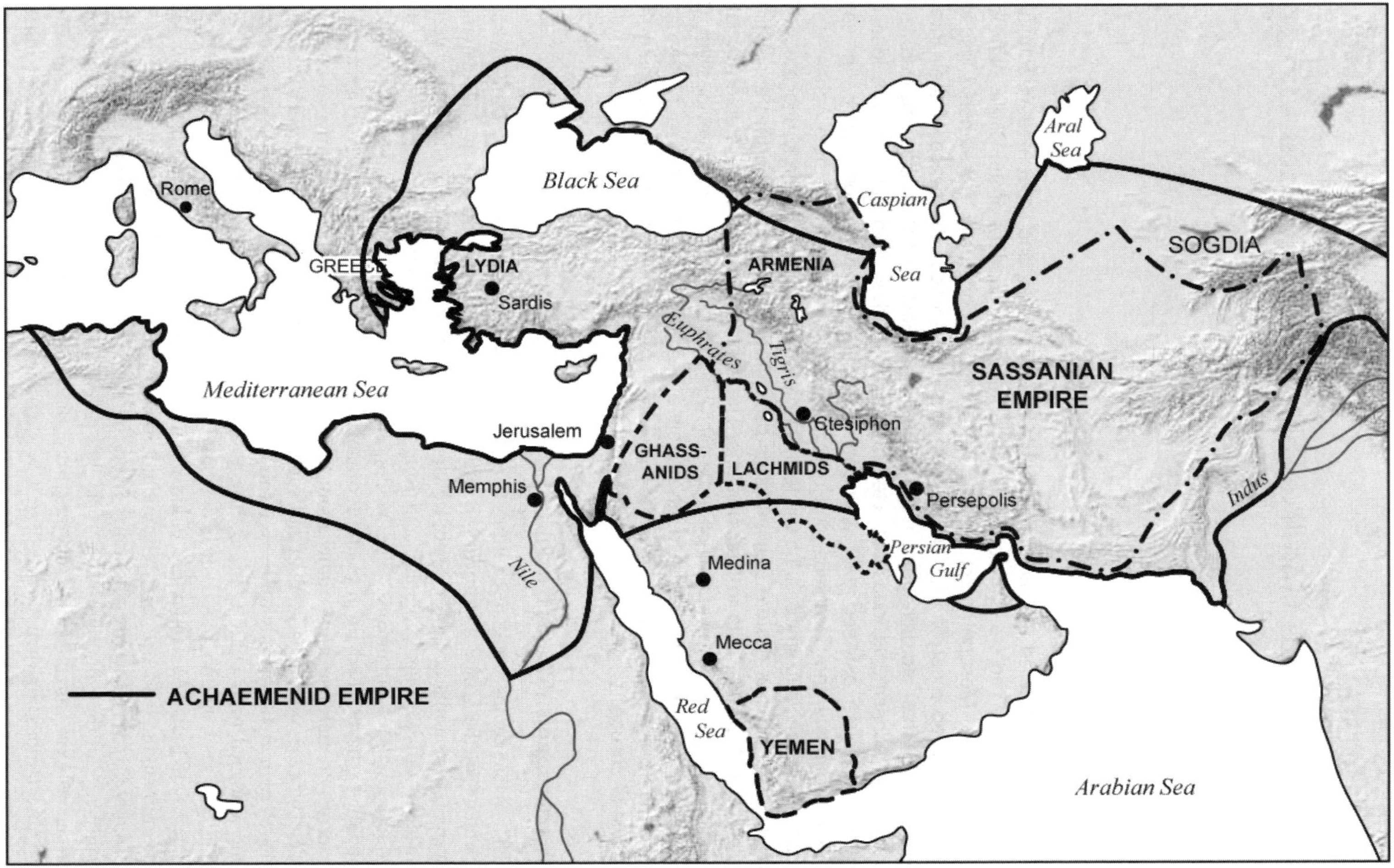

Map 2 Pre-Islamic Persia

3 Persia

"The deeds God likes best are righteousness and justice"

The Arabs considered the Circle of Justice a Persian idea, and most modern scholars follow their line. The pre-Islamic Persians did know the concept of the Circle, but they learned it from Mesopotamian sources, and only very gradually. Achaemenid inscriptions contained most of the Circle's elements, but without the sense of their interdependence that had developed in the ancient Near East. The Seleucids and Parthians preserved Achaemenid ideas but altered them to fit their own cultures. The idea of interdependence between ruler and people apparently revived only under the last Persian dynasty, the Sasanians, and only late in their reign. In collecting Achaemenid texts, the Sasanians stripped the Circle of its Mesopotamian context and relocated it in Parthia. Legends of eastern Persian kings became the primary vehicle for transmitting the concept of the Circle to later Muslims. The impression of just rule created by late Sasanian writings, however, influenced early Muslim historians' view of previous eras of Persian history, and they attributed the Circle of Justice to Persian rulers of all periods. The Persians were also the ones who fully integrated money and the treasury into the Circle of Justice.

Achaemenids (539–311 BCE)

The Achaemenids' rock inscriptions are the oldest Persian writings, and they include elements of the Circle of Justice, though not all its interrelationships. The Achaemenids were a semi-nomadic pastoral people who derived their techniques of imperial governance, record-keeping, monetary and long-distance communications practices from the Medes and Mesopotamians.[1] The Medes, eastern neighbors and conquerors of Assyria, appear to have based their political organization almost completely on Assyrian precedents, though we know little about their ideology, since most of their documents were written on perishable materials such as parchment and papyrus.[2] Around 550 BCE the Persian Achaemenids took over this Assyro-Median empire and its neighbor Elam and absorbed their culture. In 539 the Achaemenids also conquered Babylonia, establishing a new empire that stretched from Egypt and Greece to Central Asia and the borders of India. Alexander the Great reputedly burned the Achaemenids' books, and the remaining evidence on Achaemenid royal ideology and administration is not as extensive as that for Mesopotamia. Most of the Achaemenids' documents have also vanished, but their inscriptions on rock cliffs reveal that their political ideology and social structure were initially quite different from those of Mesopotamia.[3] The Persians later became famous for their justice, but it was a long time before Persian ideas of justice came to resemble Near Eastern concepts of state.

Divine favor, royal authority, and military victory

Achaemenid rulers, like those of the Fertile Crescent, believed they held their kingdom on trust from their chief god, Ahuramazda. An inscription attributed to the early king Ariaramnes put it succinctly: "By the favor of Ahuramazda I am king in this country."[4] Darius I (521–486 BCE) reiterated this belief in divine appointment: "Ahuramazda bestowed the kingdom upon me."[5] In contrast, Cyrus II (539–530 BCE), who conquered the whole region from Central Asia to Egypt, attempted to win the goodwill of his new subjects by having himself crowned in the conquered lands according to local political and religious conventions. Inscriptions in Akkadian modeled on those of Ashurbanipal referred to Cyrus as a worshipper of the Babylonian gods and awarded him the titles of a Babylonian king: "Cyrus, king of the world, great king, powerful king, king of Babylon, king of Sumer and Akkad, king of the four corners of the world."[6] In imitation of Ashurbanipal, Cyrus restored the city of Babylon, built temples, and brought back exiles who had been resettled in distant parts of the empire.

Such concessions to local religions, however, were only for consumption in the conquered areas. At home, Cyrus and the other early Achaemenid rulers described themselves in terms more appropriate to a tribal, stock-raising people. Darius I called himself the ruler of "this kingdom, great, possessed of good horses, possessed of good men."[7] The same terms appeared in inscriptions attributed to his ancestors Ariaramnes and Arsames. Although the latter inscriptions are thought to have been written long after the rulers named in them, this vocabulary suggests that whoever wrote them considered those terms appropriate for Persia's pre-imperial period. Papyrus or parchment copies of the royal inscriptions were made in all the major languages and sent throughout the realm.[8]

Sometime during the reign of Darius I, Persians started seeing their kingship as a universal monarchy like those of Mesopotamia; some of Darius's inscriptions described him very much in Assyrian terms, as "the king of countries having all kinds of men."[9] The Persians are usually credited with the concept of a world empire as a fusion of peoples and cultures. This inclusiveness, however, was already part of Assyrian ideology, although Darius and his successors adopted and intensified it. Darius's palace at Susa, like Sargon's "Palace Without Rival" at Dur-Sharruken and Sennacherib's at Nineveh, was decorated with carvings of subjects from all corners of the empire, and an inscription boasted of all the workers and materials from distant lands that contributed to its construction.[10] The sculptured reliefs of Persepolis, the Achaemenid capital, show people from many lands supporting the ruler's throne or paying him homage. Darius connected the universalization of Persian kingship with the support of the Persian god: "These are the countries which fell to my lot; by the favor of Ahuramazda I was their king," an idea repeated in both the Persian and Akkadian languages in the Persepolis inscription of Xerxes I (485–465 BCE).[11] The Achaemenid kings enacted their sense of universality by rotating their court among several capitals in Mesopotamia and Persia, and their ceremonial entry into each city was organized to mimic the order of the realm. Like the Assyrians, they also brought children of the conquered people to staff the imperial palace at Persepolis, creating a household at the heart of the empire made up of all its peoples.[12]

With regard to military conquest of foreign lands, the Achaemenids' inscriptions stressed, not their victory and dominion, but the less warlike characteristics of breadth of territory and good administration. Describing his conquests, Darius did not emphasize his own might but listed the countries that "came unto me" and "bore tribute to me."

Achaemenid art most often portrayed captive peoples praising the ruler rather than being slaughtered by him, as in Assyrian art.[13] The gods, it was thought, granted victory in recognition of the king's virtue, his espousal of right and truth. The Persians won battles not because they were stronger but because they were honest and righteous, therefore divinely favored. An inscription at Behistun depicting Darius' victory over rebels explained how he gained the god's help: "For this reason Ahuramazda bore aid and the other gods who are, because I was not disloyal, I was no follower of Falsehood, I was no evil-doer, neither I nor my family, but I acted according to righteousness, neither to the powerless nor to the powerful did I do wrong."[14] The accompanying relief did not show Darius' merciless treatment of the defeated rebels as described in the inscription; he had himself depicted as magnanimous in victory. The fact that he repeated these ideas on his tomb at Naqsh-i Rustem indicates their importance in royal ideology.[15]

Like Assyrian rulers, Achaemenid kings suppressed rebellion, but they justified it differently. Darius's inscriptions portray him as re-establishing not peace, but Truth; the rebels lied about their status, pretending to be legitimate rulers, and deceived the people.[16] In Persian belief, Ahuramazda supported the Achaemenid kings because they were truthful, not followers of Falsehood. As in Assyria, however, divine support helped the ruler free society from aggression and oppression. "Provinces were in commotion; one man was smiting the other. The following I brought about by the favour of Ahuramazda, that the one does not smite the other at all, each one is in his place. My law – of that they feel fear, so that the stronger does not smite nor destroy the weak."[17] One purpose for having an all-powerful ruler was that subordinates would "feel fear" and so would remain each in his proper place.

Hierarchy and justice

The Assyrian concept of justice inherited by the Achaemenids involved, as we have seen, the protection of the weak from the strong. The Persians added the idea of protecting the strong from the weak, as an inscription by Darius makes clear: "It is not my desire that the weak man should have wrong done to him by the mighty; nor is that my desire, that the mighty man should have wrong done to him by the weak."[18] This suggests that Persian rulers depended more heavily on "the mighty" than Assyrian rulers, a notion reinforced by the structure of their respective military forces. The Assyrians had had a citizen army; a certain percentage of householders was called up for service, while only the officers and core of the army were career military men. Persian tribesmen, in contrast, formed a separate warrior class of cavalry armed with bows and javelins. Its officers, also Persian, became the courtiers and administrators of the Achaemenid Empire. The warrior class could not be alienated, because it could not be replaced without destroying the empire's identity.[19] Warriors held second place in the class system after priests and were exempt from taxation. Beneath warriors in the class structure were agriculturalists (both cultivators and pastoralists), and beneath them merchants and artisans. This class system was quite rigid; inscriptions reveal that Persian rulers set great store by having everyone and everything "in its proper place."[20] Justice in this system was more akin to order than to equality.

The king at the top of the social pyramid was far above his subjects – literally so in some examples of imperial art, where the king was drawn above the other figures. Persian royal protocol evolved under Darius into a view of the king as not quite divine, yet more than human.[21] He shone with "royal glory," the charismatic token of god-given royalty, and was always portrayed as larger than his followers. The king was the source of law; justice came down from him as from heaven and radiated impersonally upon all. The actions of the king, therefore, established prosperity: "The man who was loyal, him I rewarded well; him who was evil, him I punished well."[22] The king was also the supreme judge, and the administration of justice was indispensable to his legitimacy. In this role, Darius I codified the laws and conducted extensive tax surveys of the land.[23]

Good administration and prosperity

With respect to good administration, the Achaemenids built on earlier imperial practices. Their chancery employed scribes from the conquered peoples as well as Persians, and they issued edicts in all the languages of the empire. These edicts were delivered via the imperial post service and road network, which permitted rapid communication throughout the empire and fostered trade as well as imperial control. Darius I installed a provincial administration run by centrally appointed governors called satraps, whose courts were modeled on that of the ruler.[24]

The Persians' building and rebuilding of cities and their settling of displaced peoples in fertile regions continued earlier imperial practices for providing prosperity to the land. As part of a general restoration by Darius I after the rebellion of Gaumata, for example: "I restored to the people the pastures and the herds, the household slaves and the houses which Gaumata the Magian took away from them. I reestablished the people on its foundation, both Persia and Media and the other provinces. As before, so I brought back what had been taken away."[25] The Achaemenid government invested in irrigation works, completed a canal linking the Nile with the Red Sea, and involved itself in the agriculture and trade of the empire. The Avesta, the Persian scripture, praised agriculture and reclamation of wastelands and made the king, "the Feeder," responsible for the cultivation of the land. When the god was asked where the earth is gladdened He responded: "Wherever grain is most produced … wherever arid land is changed into watered and marshy into dry land."[26] Coins and seals portrayed the king as a hunter and gardener.[27] His gardens housed trees, plants, and animals from all corners of the empire, emphasizing its universality, and subject peoples were symbolically invited to participate in the sumptuousness and variety of the king's table.

Prosperity is usually thought of in terms of money, but money did not yet exist. Royal treasuries had begun to be significant in power relations under the Assyrians, who employed a monetary system using silver by weight. The invention of coinage by the Lydians, and the Achaemenid conquest of Lydia in western Anatolia, brought this new medium of exchange to the Middle East. The use of coinage gave a new impetus to the development of exchange relations, not only in commerce but in governmental activities, facilitating the hiring of mercenary soldiers (especially Greeks) and more effective control of outlying provinces. The treasury became an important part of Achaemenid administration, occupying a huge building complex in Persepolis, with additional treasuries in cities throughout the empire. Its records were written on the spot in Aramaic on papyrus or parchment and were later transferred to clay tablets in Elamite cuneiform.[28] The Achaemenids also collected antiques from around the empire and stored them in their treasury, suggesting that the treasury housed not only their wealth but also their continuity with previous regimes.

The treasury's increased role in administration, however, did not transfer into the symbolic realm. Carved on the grand stairway at Persepolis is a long procession of tribute-payers from all parts of the empire, but this depicts a ceremonial gift-giving, not a tax payment.[29] Regular tax revenues were handled outside the Persepolis treasury in the provincial treasuries of the empire. There is evidence for some kind of cadastral survey to regulate land transfers, tribute, and taxation.[30] Taxes were paid mainly in precious metal, and Darius I instituted a tax reform that stabilized the amount expected from each province in accordance with the average yield of the land as established by the survey. As the empire became monetarized and urbanized, military obligations were also converted into monetary terms. These changes led to the growth of tax farming, the expansion of a class of fiscal middlemen, and the development of a marketing system in which agricultural yields were exchanged for precious metals.[31] Despite its expanded role, however, the treasury does not appear in extant royal inscriptions.

As far as the evidence goes – from the later empire few inscriptions survive – Achaemenid political thought never fully embodied the Circle of Justice as the Assyrians had known it, although it contained the elements of the Circle. In the inscription about Gaumata, those called "the people" were well-to-do landowners, not the poor. Achaemenid inscriptions expressed two distinct political concepts, one of divine favor ensuring military victory, and one of good administration and justice bringing about reconstruction and order. Both occurred in a realm that was broad in extent and diverse in population, but the Achaemenids apparently did not see them as interdependent or integrally related.

Seleucids and Parthians (311 BCE–224 CE)

The conquests of Alexander the Great put an end to the Achaemenids. Despite destroying the Achaemenids' books, Alexander presented himself as a true Persian monarch and became in later times a symbolic carrier of the Circle of Justice. His successors to the rule of Iran, the Greek Seleucids, perpetuated many Achaemenid imperial practices while gradually introducing Greek culture and administration. After two centuries, however, the Parthians invaded from the east and ousted the Seleucids, replacing Greek culture with that of eastern Iran. Eastern Iranian history and legend, with the addition of Alexander's story, became the conduit through which the Circle of Justice passed to their successors.

The Seleucids and the Circle

Direct testimony to the Seleucids' political ideology is lacking, as their records were written on perishable materials rather than clay tablets, but their coins and symbols celebrated their military achievements and strength, depicting them as "dear to the gods."[32] Seleucus himself, the founder of the dynasty, was considered to be Apollo's favorite, and this divine favor led to military victory, which legitimized his kingship. The Greeks deified their kings in order to reinforce loyalty and cohesion among their followers; the king's divine attributes, portrayed symbolically on statues and other objects, raised him above ordinary men.[33] Seleucid rulers continued to be deified for the sake of their Greek subjects, in order to fulfill their expectations and promote loyalty in the distant lands they now inhabited.

The Seleucids also sought – for the sake of their Middle Eastern subjects – to fulfill the Fertile Crescent's reciprocal conception of the king's responsibilities. To heredity and conquest as legitimating factors they added an ethical component of virtue and care for their subjects.[34] Inscriptions in Akkadian show that the Seleucid ruler Antiochus I Soter (280–262 BCE), like the Persian Cyrus, employed Babylonian forms of legitimation. Calling himself "the great king, the mighty king, king of the world, king of Babylon, king of lands," Antiochus prayed for military victory, justice, prosperity, and fertility: "the overthrow of the countries of my enemies, the achievement of my battle-wishes against my enemies, permanent victories, just kingship, a happy reign, years of joy, children in satiety."[35] Seleucid kings portrayed themselves as savior, benefactor, protector, and shepherd of the people, "that the subjects may always enjoy peace and obtain justice promptly in the courts."[36]

Fourth- and third-century Seleucid kings tried to live up to these titles by emphasizing their good administration. They extended patronage to temples and the nobility, preserving the Achaemenid system of obligations between social ranks, but they also improved their governing systems, including the coinage, the taxation system, the bureaucracy, and legal administration. They upgraded communication among their far-flung lands by maintaining the post system, fortifying important trade routes, and strengthening provincial administration, placing fiscal authorities alongside the governors.[37] Seleucid kings repaired religious edifices, surrounding themselves with the arts and styles of bygone empires to symbolize their continuity with past regimes. They founded new cities, established agricultural colonies, and extended irrigation works, cultivating exotic new plants as a sign of prosperity.[38] Various rulers granted protection in the form of tax exemptions in return for political support and, presumably, in cases of natural disaster. Evidence for a new land survey comes from documents allocating tax revenues, which refer to "existing surveys" of villages.[39] A system of royal justice existed, though its procedures and jurisdiction are not known. This scanty evidence suggests that despite the Seleucids' Greek origins, they employed Near Eastern governing practices congruent with the Circle of Justice. In time, however, the empire with its vassal states fragmented into smaller local kingdoms which were conquered by the Romans and Parthians.[40]

The Parthian influence

The Arsacids of Parthians a nomadic people from the northeast who gained control of Persia and Mesopotamia in the second century BCE, continued the decentralization of government begun under the Seleucids and permitted a "feudalization" of the military system. In the east, in Central Asia, the nomadic lifestyle and culture became dominant and bureaucratic governing institutions were allowed to lapse. In the west, however, the Arsacids maintained for some time the imperial government of the Achaemenids and Seleucids, claiming the old royal titles and tracing their genealogy back to those prestigious dynasties.[41] Rock-carved monuments depicted their continued belief in "royal glory" – the divine charisma of the king, symbolized by eagles in flight – which was bestowed by the god and necessary for right rule. The kings were supposedly "inaccessible" and lived in luxury, but they seem to have spent most of their time at the head of armies or hunting parties. Like the just rulers of the past, they built cities, patronized religion, reorganized the administration, and contributed to agricultural prosperity. A considerable expansion of irrigation in the late Parthian period suggests that the population was growing, at least in southern Iran.[42] The ideology behind these activities is obscure because Parthian records are particularly poor; hints of systems of population registration, local justice, and royal audiences survive, but not explanations. We do know that the Parthians acted as middlemen in the Rome–China silk trade, a trade so important that they devoted strenuous efforts to controlling and protecting the stages on the trade routes.[43]

Gradual cultural transformation during the Parthian era eliminated Greek features such as military and administrative techniques, artistic and architectural styles, Greek images and legends on coins, and the unique political arrangements of Greek cities.[44] In their place developed a post-Hellenic mixed culture that was aristocratic in character, well suited to the military commanders, royal bodyguards, and members of noble families who became the important people of the empire as it decentralized.[45] The Arsacids traced their history to the kings of eastern Iran and to an epic tradition of heroic deeds and eternal rivalries among possibly mythical princes of noble families. This epic history, in oral and written forms, became the main literary conduit through which subsequent generations learned the ideology of the Near Eastern state.

The juxtaposition of heroic rulers with bureaucratic justice and good administration was not a comfortable one. In this form, Near Eastern justice was stripped of its institutional supports and personalized, becoming a matter of the wisdom and virtue of individual monarchs rather than an affair of well-regulated administrative systems and official oversight. Outside this epic history, the transmission of the political practices of the past to future generations depended on inherited precepts and institutional survivals, which actually turned out to be quite durable.[46] The absence of written records, however, prevents us from gaining a better look at the Parthians' society and government. In the third century CE they were replaced by the Sasanians.

Sasanians (224–637 CE)

The Sasanians (descendants of Sasan) began as minor rulers from the mountainous western province of Persis (later Fars), where elements of the Achaemenid governmental heritage survived through centuries of change. Wresting control from the Parthians in 224 CE, they inherited a diverse political culture of Near Eastern, Greek, and Persian connections. To this they added (partly by translation, partly by conquest) contemporary practices from India and the Greco-Byzantine world. Ideologically, however, the Sasanians presided over the "restoration" of an imagined Persian past based on eastern Iranian foundations.[47] Sasanian histories portrayed this "restoration" as an immediate result of the establishment of Sasanian rule, but it must in fact have been very gradual, since the decentralized Parthian institutions doubtless provided little help to a dynasty trying to restore a centralized regime. The Sasanians' records of their own early period do not clarify the process: their inscriptions are few, and most of their governmental records are lost.[48]

The Sasanian Circle

The Sasanians' histories treat the first two centuries of their rule in legendary style, painting the kings as epic heroes, and they are reliable only for the later period of the dynasty. These histories portrayed the Sasanian monarchs as just rulers and good administrators; they founded cities, settled war prisoners within their lands, extended irrigation, protected trade, recentralized the empire, developed a bureaucracy, and established the teachings of Zoroaster as the state religion.[49] All these developments were credited to the first Sasanian king, Ardashir I (224–41), although they actually came into full flower only later, in some cases not until the last century of Sasanian rule. A number of Sasanian texts or excerpts survive in later versions from the Islamic period, including histories, religious literature, and wisdom texts full of moral aphorisms and the advice of sages and royal counselors.[50] These texts reveal that Sasanian political ideas resembled the ideas of the Achaemenids more than those of the Parthians to whom they were ascribed, as they were religiously oriented and quite hierarchical.

Like the Greeks and some early Mesopotamian rulers, Sasanian kings considered themselves to be not just divinely appointed but of divine origin, "of the race of the gods," and they portrayed themselves being invested by a god with the insignia of kingship.[51] Royal glory shone from them, symbolized in art by a halo, or a diadem with flowing tails.[52] Divine favor brought victory and wealth, portrayed through hunting scenes where the killing of game symbolized victories over enemy rulers.[53] As under the Parthians, the nobility played a powerful political role and generated much factional strife. Administrative centralization was a gradual process, intensifying late in the Sasanian era. Although Sasanian justice later became legendary, the concept of justice played a minor role in royal ideology except in sources attributed to the reign of Khusrau I Anushirvan (531–79), although it often appeared in the propaganda of rebel movements.[54]

On the other hand, it was a Sasanian source that first introduced money and the treasury into the formula of kingship and sovereignty as the vehicles of prosperity. The *Denkard*, a group of older Persian works compiled by Zoroastrians in the ninth century during the Islamic era, was the earliest version of the Near Eastern concept of state to refer to treasure as an essential element: "The organization of the Sovereignty is based upon these six: King, Religion, forgiveness, ammunition, treasure and army. As evident, when one of these is non-existent, or not co-operating together, the sovereignty is unstable and changeable."[55] The same passage detailed the effect on the other five elements of the absence of each of the six.

> For, when there is no King, the sovereignty is without a name, religion without propagation, ammunition without effect, forgiveness invisible, treasure without sustenance and without protector and the army defeated.
>
> Now when there is no religion, the mandate of the Sovereign is ineffectual, ammunition is used for evil, forgiveness is given to those who deserve a blow, treasure is accumulated by excess and depleted owing to defectiveness, and the army is worthless owing to breach of disciplined command.
>
> When there are no weapons of ammunition, the King is afraid of the non-Iranians, afflicted on account of the heretics, forgiveness is well-inclined to the cavalry hostile to him, treasure without support and army denuded.
>
> When there is no forgiveness, the King has many enemies, religion is scoffed at, ammunition is inefficacious against the enemy, the treasure invisible owing to destruction and the army desirous of separation from the King [or, discontented because of its separation from the King].
>
> When there is no treasure, the King is without property and in want, the weapons of ammunition are broken, forgiveness is for the wicked, the rich are tormented and the army is poor and powerless.
>
> When there is no army, the King is without servants, the religion is without a propagator, ammunition is useless, and forgiveness is without a name and the treasure is without benefit.[56]

This formulation, allegedly taken from the Avesta, exhibited striking continuity with Achaemenid ideas. The stress on religion and righteousness (two components out of six) is familiar, as are the exaltation of the military class and its function (another two) and the king, the centerpiece of sovereignty. As for the last component, treasure, the formula specified that it depended on righteous behavior (forgiveness and religious piety) and that its absence threatened military power (poverty and powerlessness). Notably absent from the *Denkard* passage are the two attributes of prosperity for the land, or support for cultivation, and justice for the weak. The *Denkard*'s was, as the passage itself states, a circle of "Sovereignty and control of the subjects" rather than a circle of justice.[57]

Assyrian and Achaemenid ideologies both indicate the growing importance of treasure as a symbol and a means of power. While extant Achaemenid inscriptions did not mention it, the passage from the *Denkard*, if it truly goes back to the Avesta, suggests that treasure may already have become part of the concept of state. The *Denkard* alleged that its formula was of ancient origin, "expanded from the propitiatory formula of Xšatrevar, Holy Immortal," consisting of "the six Avestan words," one of which was "treasurer, friend of the treasures."[58] The antiquity of the formula cannot be proven, but it is possible that the concept of treasure entered the ideology of kingship in Achaemenid times in a form that survives only in this reference. Still, the passage testifies to the centrality of treasure in Sasanian thought.

The *Denkard* contains another statement on the relationship between kingship and religion that appeared with variations in other Sasanian works: "Kingship is essentially religion and religion kingship according to the teaching of the Good Religion."[59] The relationship of interdependence between religion and kingship was further elaborated in the "Testament of Ardashir," which stated, "Kingdom and religion are twins: religion is the foundation of kingdom and the king is the guardian of religion."[60] Sasanian coins bore the image of the ruler on the face and usually a fire altar on the back, proclaiming to all who used them the ruler's sovereignty and the place of religion in his ideology. The Sasanian kings seem to have taken their role as guardians of religious purity and conformity far more seriously than did earlier dynasties, stressing correct belief over subordination to the god, which was the hallmark of Assyrian rulers. The Sasanian king was not just a devotee of his religion but its definer and protector.

Sasanian society and justice

Justice entered Sasanian political ideology as a component of the ruler's public image. The *Denkard* counted it among the qualities of a good king that he rendered justice in public. The "Testament of Ardashir" proclaimed that there was "no way for the sovereign to be honored but by the justice of his policy."[61] Most Iranian kings went out occasionally on horseback for the purpose of visibly dispensing justice among their subjects. They reportedly commanded that petitioners wear red in order to be easily identified.[62] What the Sasanians meant by justice was similar to what the Babylonians and Assyrians had understood it to be: the protection of the realm and the deliverance of its people from ruin either by oppression or natural disaster. The "Menog i Xrad," a Zoroastrian text that may date back to Sasanian times, defined good government as the provision of prosperity and linked it to the activity of the god: "The creator Ahuramazda produced good government for effecting the protection of the creatures. Good government is that which maintains and directs a province flourishing, the poor untroubled, and the law and customs true, and sets aside improper laws and customs."[63] Like the Assyrian kings, Sasanian monarchs tried to keep "the poor untroubled" by forgiving arrears of taxes at their enthronement.[64]

The *Denkard*'s definition of a bad or unjust king was one who was unable to deal with widespread disaster among his subjects: "If distress appears everywhere, and if he is incapable of putting an end to it by himself, or if he doesn't worry about it or try to find a remedy, then that king, who is weak and can neither overcome the evil nor ameliorate it, is obviously incapable of administering justice in any way, shape, or form; thus other claimants to the throne must challenge him in the name of justice."[65] The king's inability to provide justice disqualified him for rule and made it permissible for his people to overthrow him. This procedure was actually carried out in the case of Khusrau II Parviz (590–628): he was accused of overtaxing the peasantry to support his incessant wars and was deposed by his own son.

Another important aspect of justice was the maintenance of order, but here the Sasanian understanding was very different from the Mesopotamian idea of social order as freedom from rebellion. The *Denkard* represented the social hierarchy as a mirror of the cosmic order of the universe. Order meant a rigidly hierarchical class system, with everyone in his proper place. "Know that the decadence of states begins when one permits the subjects to practice other than their traditional occupations and the activities they know."[66] Scholars often attribute the Sasanians' strong concern for social order to their reaction against the turmoil of the Parthian period, but the "Testament of Ardashir" related it instead to the hierarchy of power: "If the subjects can change their class, then the king can be deposed" (i.e. change his class!).[67] Social class divisions had altered since Achaemenid times: instead of priests, warriors, agriculturalists, and artisans/merchants, the four classes had become warriors, priests, learned men/scribes, and agriculturalists/merchants/artisans/servants. The addition of a new upper class, scribes and the well-educated, pushed those in the middle ranks farther down.[68] Certain behaviors and customs were specified for each social class; a passage in the "Sayings of Ardashir" prescribed the dress and eating behavior of each class. According to this text the class system would be perfected when people accepted their status so completely that they could not dream it was possible to change it.[69] The "Letter of Tansar" decried social climbers, nobles engaging in trade, and humbly born people who became wealthy and important as being contrary to good order and stability.[70]

The top of the social pyramid nevertheless had its own responsibilities: "The king should not do what will cause him to be deposed: greed, anger, frivolity, idleness, envy, fear, tyranny, depravity, inconstancy."[71] The superiority of the king resided uniquely in his capacity to act for the general good of society. Sasanians portrayed this idea mythologically in legends of kings fighting and killing dragons, the bringers of drought.[72] The "Sayings of Ardashir" saw order and justice embodied in the vertical hierarchy that ran from the god to the king to each class of society in turn. As the king had his suite of retainers, lower in rank, so each of them had his suite of lesser men, and so on down to the humblest. The rich were admonished to maintain the network of vertical status relations that was the connective tissue of society.[73]

The justice of Anushirvan

A Sasanian political ideology consistent with Assyrian and Babylonian concepts of justice only becomes visible in the records of the sixth-century monarch Khusrau I Anushirvan (531–79). Sasanian kings wrote, or had someone write, autobiographies or autobiographical epics to be read by later kings as manuals of statecraft.[74] Later generations added the legendary history of earlier times and the story of Alexander the Great. The "Life of Anushirvan," also called the "Book of Deeds," contains a speech in Khusrau's name defining justice.[75] Here for the first time (as far as we know) a Persian ruler proclaimed that receiving the god's favor depended on the provision of justice, and military strength on prosperity and the cultivation of the land:

> I give thanks for all God's benefits since my birth. Gratitude is expressed not only in words but in deeds, and the deeds God likes best are righteousness and justice. I have followed righteousness and justice. I have seen that their fruit is the cultivation of the land, thanks to which men and beasts of burden, birds and wild animals live. When I meditated on this, I found that the warriors are the stipendiaries of the peasants and the peasants are the stipendiaries of the warriors – the warriors exact their salaries from the taxpayers and residents of the countryside, because they defend them and make war on their neighbors. The cultivators ought to pay them their salary entirely, because their crops prosper thanks to the warriors. If the peasants are slow to pay, it weakens them and the enemy grows stronger. When the cultivator is ruined cultivation stops. If the cultivators do not have what they need to live and to cultivate their lands, the warriors will perish. The land can only be cultivated with the surplus remaining in the hands of the peasants.[76]

Warriors and peasants provided for each other, taxes were the link between the two, and the fruit of justice, particularly in revenue matters, was protection and prosperity. The king ruled by the favor of the god, his responsibility was to provide justice, and his rewards were peace and security. This speech seems much closer in spirit to Assyrian and Babylonian concepts of justice than to those of the Achaemenids or earlier Sasanians. This justice is founded not on the hierarchy of the social classes but on their interdependence, an interdependence that included the king himself. Superiority of status should not become an excuse for oppression; rather, "He who tyrannizes the peasants, who wants to destroy our protection which constitutes the buttress and the refuge of the weak, does wrong to us."[77] At about the same time, the pictures on Sasanian metal vessels began to depict an intrinsic relationship between royal glory and prosperity.[78]

Ironically, this heightened awareness of the relationship between prosperity and justice emerged just when the productivity of Mesopotamia, on which the empire depended, was declining. Shifts in the rivers entailed frantic work on the irrigation system, and the arrival of the plague may have killed as much as a third of the working population. Meanwhile, war with Byzantium increased the demand for revenue. A religious revolt led by Mazdak mobilized desperate people with calls for sharing the wealth and eliminating the social hierarchy.[79] Rebellions tied to the worship of Mithra, even closer to the ideas of the Circle of Justice, blamed economic and social disruption on the ruler's injustice, his breaking of the contract between himself and the people.[80] After putting down Mazdak's rebellion and restoring order, Khusrau Anushirvan instituted a series of tax reforms, described in the "Book of Deeds" as the enactment of justice.[81]

Anushirvan's reforms were not confined to remitting taxes as a temporary emergency measure but entailed the reassessment of the entire realm. New tax levels were set by measuring, not the amount of the harvest, but the extent and kind of land (as was already done on crown land) in order to increase and stabilize government revenues, equalize tax rates, and avoid injustices caused by delays in measuring the yield.[82] The reform established a separate revenue administration independent of the provincial governors and commissioned judges to supervise assessment and collection in their districts. Administrators had to remit district accounts to the central government for checking. Anushirvan later invited people to submit complaints about this process to the provincial capitals to be reported to him. When that process did not seem to be proceeding satisfactorily (perhaps no reports were arriving), he instituted a massive inquiry that uncovered corruption and collusion by the governors and the new fiscal hierarchy. He therefore installed a new complaint procedure staffed by scribes, judges, and personnel from the palace. It was only natural, he wrote, for relatives and close retainers of the king to be powerful and sometimes to misuse their power, but it was the duty of the ruler to control their excesses: "Thus I gave them a solid guarantee against the corruption of the functionaries. God has not given our family, servants, and retainers a place near us without demanding from them righteousness and justice."[83]

Khusrau Anushirvan was not the first Sasanian king to be hailed as a good administrator. Ardashir I had initially put the empire together, and later rulers extended irrigation and increased the cultivated land, built new cities and settled them with relocated villagers and prisoners of war, and developed an organization and taxation system for religious minorities. The long reign of Shapur II (309–79) centralized authority, religion, and law under the monarch. But Khusrau Anushirvan's administration found greatest favor among later generations. Besides regularizing the tax system, he improved the bureaucracy, funded irrigation works, sponsored architectural projects, expanded trade, built roads, bridges, and caravanserais, welcomed immigrants, and encouraged literary translation and cultural development.[84] Among these measures, he sheltered Greek philosophers expelled from Christian Byzantium; built a school of medicine staffed by Syrians; employed the great minister Buzurgmihr, who among other things brought chess to Iran; and sponsored the translation of the book *Kalila and Dimna*, a collection of Indian fables on good government much prized by later generations.[85]

No Persian royal archives survive to give us authentic records of how Sasanian people obtained justice from their rulers, but such records must have been kept. The Sasanians had an extensive bureaucracy; the number of bureaus is estimated by the number of different seals used to authenticate documents.[86] Government secretaries were numerous and influential, especially late in the empire's life when a succession of short reigns enhanced the importance of a stable administration. A number of stories about them have been preserved, including one about their violent response to a hapless colleague who dared to find fault with Khusrau Anushirvan's taxation reforms; they beat him to death with their pencases.[87]

The concept of justice and good administration enunciated in Anushirvan's speech was reinforced every New Year's Day, according to later records, by a ceremony in which the king displayed himself to the people. At this ceremony the chief treasurer addressed the king in a speech that reiterated the connections between power, justice, prosperity, and divine favor:

> The application of justice extends the cultivated lands and, thanks to this justice, men are disposed to increase their crops, when they are sure of being delivered from extortion. Then the revenue redoubles; kindness ensures prosperity, while abuses cause misfortune. Where there is treachery, the blessing of God is withdrawn and annihilation befalls; debauchery diminishes the raindrops. Where there is security, divine benediction descends. Where there is no treachery, there is a harvest blessed

> by God. O king, wealth flows from taxation; with wealth one possesses soldiers and the soldiers destroy the enemy, from which results power.[88]

Here justice was equivalent to deliverance from extortion, which led to increased cultivation, revenue growth, and divine blessing; in turn these ensured the strength of the army, military victory, and political power. The "Letter of Tansar" preserved a negative summary of the same set of principles: "When the people have become poor, the royal treasury remains empty, the soldier receives no pay, and the kingdom is lost."[89]

Anushirvan became in subsequent times the model of the just ruler; later generations called him "Anushirvan the Just." Many anecdotes were told about his generosity and provision of justice to poor, elderly, or widowed subjects oppressed by officials or provincial governors. He appointed provincial judges from among the clergy who could see justice done even by the highest authorities. A person who could not obtain justice on the local level could apply directly to the king. Anushirvan reportedly installed a bell outside his palace door that could be rung by anyone seeking justice; that person would immediately be admitted to direct audience with the ruler. He also held two open audiences per year in which he listened to anyone who complained of oppression, starting with those who complained against the king himself. Later commentators described the etiquette for the audiences in detail, perhaps as a model for their own rulers to imitate. They reported that the Sasanians had considered injustice perpetrated by the ruler to be worse than any other sort, because God had confided to him the care of the subjects, to protect them against injustice.[90]

Conclusion

While the formulas of the Sasanians sound very much like Mesopotamian ideas, there were certain differences between Anushirvan's conception of justice and Hammurabi's. The Achaemenid invaders of Mesopotamia had brought with them a concept of political organization appropriate to a society of tribal warriors, and its amalgamation with indigenous ideas and systems did not obscure its strongly hierarchical character. The Parthians reinforced this elitism, and by the time the Sasanians came to power, sharp status differences between aristocrats and common people had become part of the governing ideology. This ideology of distinction tended to work against the idea of interdependence in the Circle of Justice. The Sasanians preserved the Assyrian definition of justice as the protection of the weak from the strong but added to it the need for maintaining the social order and keeping everyone in his place. They also stressed the ethical and doctrinal components of religion over its protective and generative aspects, the requirement of virtue as the way to divine favor and the king's responsibility for defining and protecting true religion. While Achaemenid inscriptions had not connected religion with the provision of prosperity and justice, Sasanian writings – especially those attributed to Anushirvan – did make that connection clear. Finally, the Achaemenids possibly, and the Sasanians definitely, enriched the concept of prosperity by articulating the role played by money and the treasury.

Although Muslim writers ascribed the Near Eastern concept of state and its encapsulation in the Circle of Justice to the Persians in general and the Sasanian Ardashir in particular, we have seen that the idea was common in earlier Mesopotamian thought, that it developed gradually over the centuries through its assimilation into Persian ideology, and that the Sasanians finally enunciated it in full only late in their regime. If the sources reflect Sasanian society at all realistically, all the elements of the Circle of Justice and their interrelationships had become part of Sasanian political culture by the time of Khusrau Anushirvan, during whose reign Muhammad was born. Less than a century from that point, in 637, Arabs from the peninsula captured the Persian capital of Ctesiphon and became the heirs of the Sasanians and their ideology.

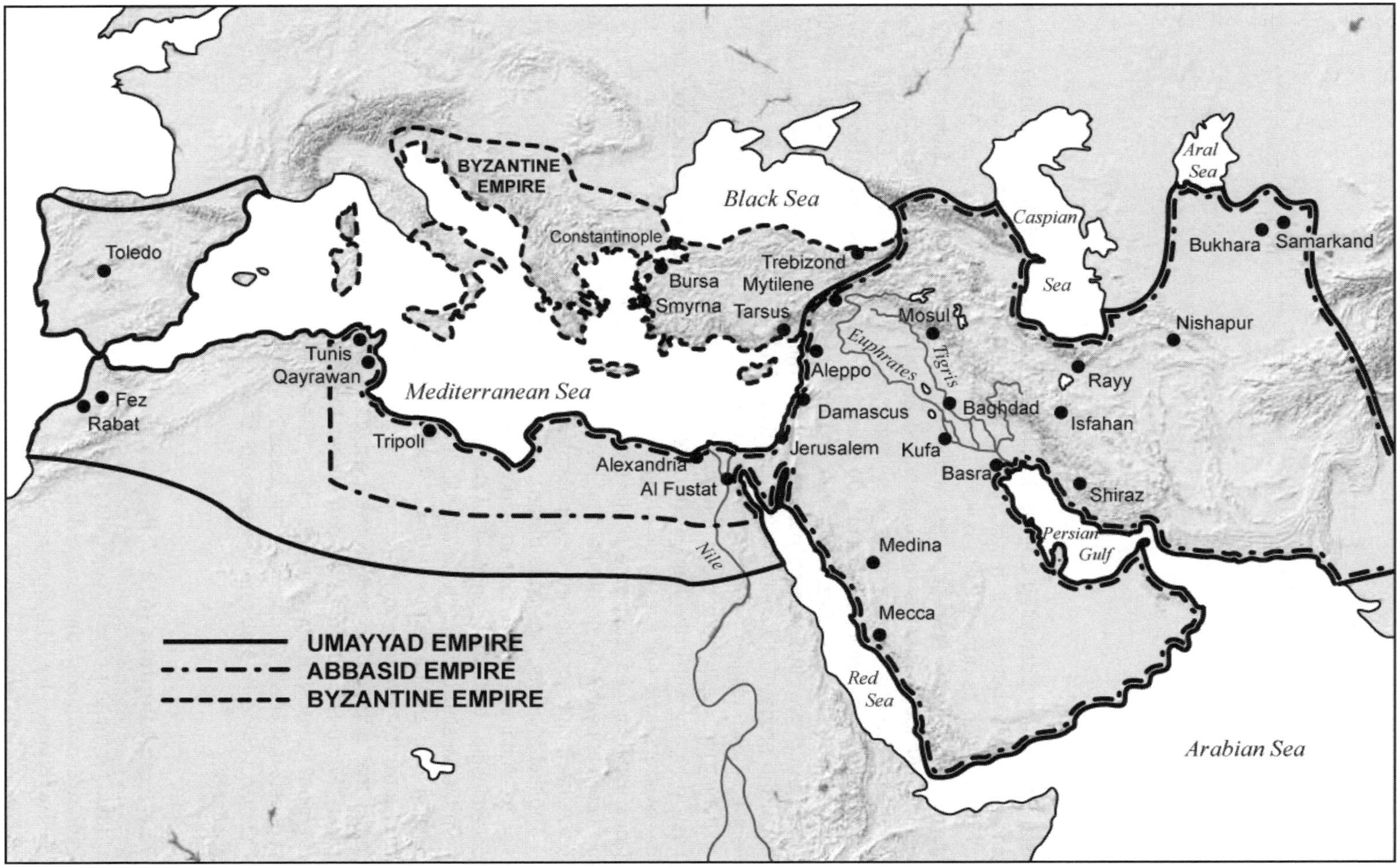

Map 3 The early Islamic empires

4 The Islamic Empire

"No prosperity without justice and good administration"

Islamic theology postulated a sharp break between the era of the revelation of Islam and what came before, but in fact the coming of Islam did not wipe the slate of history clean or oblige its adherents to build a new society from the ground up. The Circle of Justice survived the Arab conquest and re-emerged in the political culture of the conquerors. Although Islam is often described as the religion of the desert Arabs, both peninsular Arabs and the peoples of their empire, especially the Fertile Crescent region, were involved in developing Islamic ideas and practices. Viewed from the Fertile Crescent rather than the Arabian Peninsula, the conquest brought into the region another ruling group from a peripheral pastoral society with a new faith and new customs to begin the process of acculturation once again.[1] Like the Achaemenids, the Muslims kept their own religion after conquering Mesopotamia, but they learned many of their governing concepts from those they conquered. Reconceptualizing the ancient Near Eastern legacy within the framework of Islam, Arabs and non-Arabs together created the civilization we call Islamic or Islamicate (associated with Islam even in its non-religious aspects).[2] As Islamicate political culture developed, kingship within a Circle of Justice reappeared in Arabic political literature, just as it had in Persian writings after the Achaemenids conquered Mesopotamia.[3]

The first Muslims, the Arabs of the peninsula, defined political legitimacy as succession to Muhammad (570–632) as leader of the Muslim community (*umma*), or as a tribal chieftainship. With the conquest of the empire, however, the political unit changed from the Muslim community to the ruler and all his subjects regardless of language or religion. The amalgamation of Greco-Roman, Persian, and Arabic political cultures in an Islamic framework was a productive synthesis, generating new political and social forms that appealed to the diverse peoples of the region. This synthesis is usually called "Perso-Islamic," but that term implies that "Islamic" means "Arabic" and that the "Persian" ingredient was grafted in later; therefore it is called here "Perso-Arabic" to suggest that neither part was necessarily un-Islamic. It was a Muslim Persian historian writing in Arabic in whose work the standard form of the Circle of Justice appeared.

The Arab kingdom (622–750)

Unified for the first time through the preaching of Muhammad, the people of the Arabian Peninsula conquered the southern half of the Roman Empire and the whole of the Persian Empire. By 711 they reunited the Fertile Crescent, brought Arabia into an empire, and spread as far as Spain and India. They also began the process of revising political structures and concepts to accord with Islamic precepts. The relationship between pre-Islamic cultures and the tenets of Islam was a controversial issue. Near Eastern governmental policies were initially assimilated into Islamic law as normative practices (*sunna*) of the early Muslim community. When Muslims redefined the *sunna* to encompass only the practice of the Prophet Muhammad, they saw pre-Islamic concepts of state as conflicting with political precedents derived from Muhammad's reported speech and behavior (*hadith*) that were considered more authentically Islamic.[4] They then ascribed the revival or continuation of ancient Near Eastern political ideas and governmental practices to the conquest of Persia and its imperial system, the emergence of a Persian-style scribal class, and the creation of a Persian-influenced Arabic literature. They considered these influences "foreign to Islam," even though by that time many Muslims were of Persian origin. Paradoxically, however, some elements of the Circle of Justice appeared in early Arabic writings unattributed to Persian precedents and treated as common knowledge. Explicitly Persian political ideas overlaid an existing Arabic conceptual base and were readily adapted to Islamic purposes.

Justice and the early Islamic state

Although the first Muslims did not explicitly invoke the Circle of Justice, the prominence of social justice in the teachings of Islam was doubtless due in part to the long history of justice in Near Eastern politics. The Qur'an itself associated justice with benevolence and commanded care for orphans and the poor: "Hast thou seen him who cries lies to the Doom? That is he who repulses the orphan and urges not the feeding of the needy."[5] In the Qur'an the word "justice" (*'adl*) usually means personal integrity or probity, but a social justice resembling that of the Circle was a key element in Muhammad's message from his earliest days in Mecca.[6] The Muslim community's dispute over the assassination of its third leader (caliph) 'Uthman (644–56) revolved around his responsibility to provide justice and ensure the welfare of the whole society.[7] As the law of Islam, the shariah, developed, equity and public welfare were among its guiding principles.[8] The judge (qadi) produced equity and welfare both in his legal capacity and as an administrator. Legal scholars (ulema) tried to regulate individuals' contributions to the welfare of society by "enjoining the good and forbidding the evil;" through the ordinances of God "the share of the weak was taken back for them from the strong, that of the wronged from the oppressor."[9] These ideas, more than many other quotations on justice, resonate with the Circle of Justice, suggesting that the ancient Near Eastern values they embodied were part of the intellectual furniture of the Muslim community from the first.

To establish sedentary governance and implement the message of Islam on an empire-wide scale, the Muslims developed a monarchical political institution that was first elective and then hereditary. The term for the monarch, caliph (*khalifa*), denoted two different concepts of his authority, delegation by God and succession to the Prophet. This political development was highly controversial; the Muslims divided over caliphal authority and the relationship between its two components.[10] Moreover, they chose the first four caliphs individually, and when the fifth caliph Mu'awiya (661–80) first instituted hereditary succession (creating the Umayyad dynasty, 661–750), they accused him of turning the caliphate into a kingship, arrogating to himself worldly powers inappropriate for the head of a Muslim community. Although sedentary Arabs had long had kingdoms, the Arabs of the desert, defining themselves as "those who had never submitted to a king," rebelled against caliphal rule.[11] They were only reconciled to it by the early caliphs' rejection of royal ceremonies and prerogatives, and they found it ideologically necessary to differentiate the caliphs from ordinary kings both in style and in how they were legitimated. Although most Muslims considered pre-Islamic ideas of divine appointment unbefitting to an Islamic caliph, the ancient practices of royal justice became obligations of all Muslim rulers. A saying directed at the second caliph 'Umar I (634–44) even made justice in taxation the sole characteristic separating caliphs from kings.[12] Through such sayings, Muslims both acknowledged the caliphs' appropriation of royal power and applied to it the limitations developed for pre-Islamic monarchs.

A second model of the caliphate, best represented by Mu'awiya, was that of the Arab tribal chief, a mediator selected by common consent to resolve the community's disputes and to choose its path. Before an Islamic legal system emerged, caliphs rather than judges were primarily responsible for the delivery of justice and public welfare. Early Islamic political thought, however, developing in a nearly stateless society, transferred responsibilities elsewhere granted to the state – including protection of the weak and provision for the needy – not to the caliph but to the community as a whole and to its members as individuals. Islamicate government gradually reintroduced these functions at the state level, but some people continued to see them as illegitimate. The ulema took on the obligation of shunning, limiting, or seeking to control state power.

The experience of the first century of Arab rule was enough to demonstrate that neither the caliphal nor the tribal mode of governance could control and administer a multicontinental and multicultural empire. Under the Umayyads, Muslims employed governmental techniques and political ideas from the surrounding imperial cultures. Although some Muslims rejected Umayyad "kingship" as illegitimate, the Qur'an itself held a more balanced view, condemning the tyrannical god-king Pharaoh, who persecuted the people of God, but approving David, the prophet-king, and saying: "We have appointed thee a viceroy (*khalifa*) in the earth, therefore judge between men justly."[13] Pastoral Arabs readily adopted the shepherding quality of Near Eastern monarchy; early caliphal art indicates that apart from his role as successor to the Prophet, the caliph had a role as the shepherd who provided blessing and justice.[14] Political ideology and institutions soon expanded to accommodate the concept of the caliph as a king or emperor.

Attributing the Near Eastern state to the Persians and maintaining its Persian cultural trappings enabled its proponents to endow it with the aura of success and permanence associated with the Sasanians, while allowing its opponents to stigmatize it as "foreign to Islam."[15] The Muslims' transfer of the capital to Iraq after 750 and their more systematic use of Sasanian royal practices reinforced the centrality of the ancient Near Eastern concept of kingship. Non-Arabs, both Muslim and non-Muslim, played an active role in Islamicate government. Persians worked on the staff of 'Umar I, under whom the first tax surveys were made and other administrative problems addressed in Near Eastern style. Imperial and peninsular Arabs, hellenized Syrians of Damascus, and Coptic and Persian secretaries advised the caliphs and governors and maintained the land records. The Persian Empire's local notables served in the army and as governors, officials, tax collectors, and even religious leaders.[16] From very early on, the contributions of all these groups made Islamicate civilization a blend of Arab and non-Arab elements, although there was a consensus among Muslims that the Arab elements should be cherished and given extra weight.[17]

Umayyad prosperity and justice

The Umayyad dynasty (661–750) held court in Damascus in a manner far removed from that of tribal chieftains and closer to that of the emperors whose lands they had appropriated.[18] They appropriated imperial ideologies as well: Mu'awiya used to have the histories of Arab and Persian kings read to him as models of governance.[19] Although "Persian-style" governance is usually ascribed to the Abbasids (750–945), the Umayyads continued many patterns established by the older empires. They also shared some political ideals with the Byzantines, whose eighth-century Isaurian (Syrian) dynasty connected victory and peace with the provision of social justice and the protection of the weak from the strong. The lawcode issued by the Isaurian emperor Leo III (717–41) echoed earlier Mesopotamian codes, stating that the ruler's task was "to govern in judgement and justice those who are committed by Him [God] to our care, to the end that the bonds of all manner of injustice may be loosened, the oppression of covenants imposed by force may be set at naught, and the assaults of wrongdoers may be repelled, and that thus we may be crowned by His almighty hand with victory over our enemies."[20]

At first the Umayyads imitated Byzantine pomp and display, but in order to differentiate themselves from their major imperial rivals, they soon adopted the styles and customs of the defunct Sasanian Empire. Caliphal palaces in Syria and Baghdad exhibited structures, layouts, and ornamentation already found in Muslim governors' residences in Iraq, the place where Arab, Mesopotamian, and Persian cultures met and blended. Like Mesopotamian and Persian kings, caliphs and their governors also planted gardens to convey their ability to make the world fertile and prosperous, and they collected rare plants and animals from distant regions to illustrate the universality of their rule.[21]

Poetry dedicated to Umayyad caliphs imitated the style and language of pre-Islamic Arabic poetry but expressed ideas of kingship consistent with Mesopotamian and Persian royal ideologies. Although court poets rarely cited Persian precedents and never Mesopotamian ones, they were clearly reworking older political ideologies both to praise the ruler and to express his power and obligations. They called the Umayyad caliphs "pillars of religion," reminiscent of the Sasanian kings' role as protectors of the faith, or "the shepherd of God on earth," with the Muslim community as the flock for which they were responsible.[22] The caliphs' task was to guard and keep the people: Mu'awiya was spoken of as a refuge where protection could be found. 'Abd al-Malik (685-705), like a Babylonian or Assyrian king, was hailed as one "whom God has made victorious. the vicegerent of God, from him we expect rain." His successors al-Walid I (705–15) and Sulayman (715–17) were also expected to control fertility by bringing rain. A poem by the caliph al-Walid II (743–44) put his own accession in a similar light: "The shrewd and evilbringing one is dead; the rain is already falling."[23] Such works ascribed to the Umayyads the Circle's qualities of divine support, military victory, protective care, justice, and the prosperity of the land.

The later Umayyads themselves shared the poets' view that the caliph was obligated to enact the Circle's values. Al-Yazid III (744), to justify his seizure of the throne, claimed that he would not allow the mighty to oppress the weak, nor overtax the peasantry and force them to flee, nor squander the treasury on women, palaces or irrigation works, but would treat his distant subjects the same as those nearby and would pay stipends promptly. His just rule would build up the treasury to protect the empire. A proclamation probably composed for Marwan II (744–50) used the same concept of justice but stated it negatively, proclaiming that rebellion led to injustice and injustice to poverty and decay.[24] By the end of the Umayyad period, despite disclaimers of any resemblance between the two types of leadership, Muslims found the kingly obligation of providing justice solidly entrenched in the rhetoric and function of the caliphate.

The provincial governors of Iraq, unburdened by succession to Muhammad but entrusted with similar military, fiscal, and religious responsibilities, also bore characteristics of the region's pre-Islamic rulers. According to Ziyad, governor of Iraq under Mu'awiya, they were empowered by God's authority, given victory by God, and commissioned to spend the revenues of the conquered lands on protection and justice.[25] A poem praised Ziyad as a provider of prosperity:

> Victorious by God's command, helping
> when the flock goes astray, you do not oppress.
> Plentiful milk streams through your hands
> of what they wanted from the world for themselves.
> You apportion equally, and neither rich
> nor poor complains to you about injustice.[26]

Here the image of the shepherd, still the primary metaphor for the just ruler, was embellished with details appropriate to a pastoral setting.

Opponents of the Umayyads deployed the Circle's concept of justice to criticize the caliphs and their deeds, emphasizing the need for justice in practice. Extremist rebels awaited justice from a *mahdi*, a messianic figure, whose justice resembled that of the Circle: he would "fill the world with justice and equity as it is now filled with tyranny and oppression," for in his time "the heavens would not withhold rain; the earth would give bountiful crops and surrender her precious metals."[27] The developing Shi'i movement anticipated a messiah from the family of the Prophet who, as "protector of the weak," would "distribute equally among the people and. establish justice among his subjects."[28] The figure of 'Ali, the fourth caliph and first Shi'i Imam (leader), emerged as the spokesman for the struggle against oppression and was endowed with attributes of Near Eastern kingship. He was chosen by God, a shepherd of his sheep, without whom worship and prayers were not accepted; he was the pillar of the earth, the father of orphans, the judge, the interpreter of God's commands; he was the light toward which people walk, a rain cloud of blessings and kindness and a clear spring that flows at God's command, the owner of all the land and fresh waters and the treasures of the earth.[29] The Khariji rebels stressed the practical side of the Circle of Justice over the apocalyptic, forbidding their followers to pay taxes to the Umayyad caliph because he could not provide protection and exhorting them, "Do not allow these tyrants to oppress the weak."[30]

The Umayyads and good administration

Beyond an ideology and symbolism of kingship recalling pre-Islamic empires, the Umayyads employed many past administrative practices, adapting them to suit the changed geographical and economic situation and the new religious ethos. Simply by going on using them, they ensured that pre-Islamic mechanisms for checking injustice, such as land surveys, bureaucratic control of taxation, and the ruler's accessibility to petitioners, were incorporated into Islamicate governance. People then identified these practices as Islamic, the normal practices of the Muslim community. Although pre-Islamic ideologies earned the condemnation of purists, these governing mechanisms won general acceptance.[31]

Papyrus finance records reveal that Egypt's Muslim administrators prepared registers of population and landholdings, assessed taxes according to the registers, and issued receipts for taxes paid. A late seventh-century document in Greek referred to a land survey performed in Palestine, and Iraq was surveyed in the early eighth century.[32] Another document instructed tax officials not to take more than the amount assessed. A letter to a provincial governor from the year 710 explained the link between justice and prosperity: "Restrain your functionaries and restrain yourself from oppressing the country people, because the land will not support injustice and injustice will not last; and if the country people are exposed to oppression and loss by those who are charged with their welfare, it will be their ruin."[33] Ordinary people demanded that the caliph and his officials accept responsibility for providing justice; surviving documents contain appeals from the populace to the central authorities against oppression by tax collectors and other problems. The people of a region sometimes mobilized as a group to make representations and complaints, as is shown by a letter from late seventh-century Palestine recruiting a delegation from several cities to protest a tax assessment.[34] An Umayyad governor of Egypt advised his subordinate to listen carefully to such appeals: "Devote yourself to the people of your administrative district, hearing what they say and giving just judgment to each, not shutting yourself off but allowing them free access to you."[35] Clearly, the demand for "justice and good administration" was central to the shaping of Islamicate governance.

People appealing to rulers expected to be taken seriously, and by the second Islamic century there is evidence that some caliphs genuinely tried to act on their ideologies of justice. People told stories of Hisham's (723–45) scrupulous administration; they said his tax register was the most "beneficial both to the common people and to the government."[36] A caliph's letter to the judge Abu Musa, attributed to 'Umar I but probably written in the late Umayyad period, shows how pre-Islamic judicial practices were integrated into an Islamic context. It contained instructions on court procedure reinforced by references to the Qur'an and the example of the early Muslim community, but it also offered advice echoing ancient texts from Egypt and Iran: "So neither the man of high station will expect you to be partial, nor will the humble despair of justice from you," and "Avoid fatigue and the display of weariness or annoyance at the litigants in the courts of justice."[37]

The new Muslim administrators' need for detailed information on prior governing institutions inspired translations of older political and administrative literature. The earliest known translations date from the reign of Hisham, when interest in imperial precedents was high.[38] The man who headed the Umayyad scribal staff in those years, Abu al-'Ala' Salim, translated several pre-Islamic works of political thought, including the apocryphal "Letters of Aristotle to Alexander," supposedly containing Aristotle's advice on governing conquered territories.[39] Besides this work's debt to Greek political ideology, it included recommendations based on Near Eastern precedents, notably that the ruler should hold an audience daily to hear appeals for justice and should see that the legal system redressed the grievances of the people.[40] It also contained an admonition related to the Circle of Justice that put the peasants before the soldiers: "Know that the support of the villages is the cities, the support of the cities is the fortresses, the support of the fortresses is the soldiers, the support of the soldiers is provisions and arms, and these will not exist without justice."[41]

Salim's successor 'Abd al-Hamid (d.750), Marwan II's chief scribe, won fame both for his elegant epistolary style in Arabic and for his "Epistle to the Secretaries," the first in a long line of Arabic handbooks for scribes that reproduced the values of the Persian scribal corps, adapted for Muslims.[42] The secretarial class of the Islamic era was more limited in scope than the Sasanian learned class; the Islamic social system's grouping of philosophers, doctors, and other intellectuals with the religio-legal scholars as ulema left the scribes and bureaucrats in a class by themselves. When the Fertile Crescent was conquered by outside invaders, these scribes, like their predecessors, took responsibility for maintaining imperial administration and instructing the rulers.

Only one generation after the conquest of Iraq, Mu'awiya's revenue official, Ibn Durraj, rediscovered and employed the records of the Sasanian crown lands; he also reinstituted Sasanian ceremonies, such as mass payment of taxes on New Year's Day (Nawruz, the first day of spring). For generations afterward, a Persian fiscal secretary, Zadhanfarrukh (d.701) and his descendants maintained tax records for the eastern half of the empire.[43] Zadhanfarrukh's protégé and successor was the Persian convert Salih ibn 'Abd al-Rahman (d.717), who translated the tax records of Iraq from Persian to Arabic in 697 during the caliphate of 'Abd al-Malik. Here, too, Iraq set the example and the rest of the empire followed suit. Salih trained the next generation of secretaries, possibly including Ibn al-Muqaffa' (d.757), who served during the first decade of Abbasid rule.[44] This amazing continuity transmitted scribal lore across changes of regime and allowed the scribes to retain and build on older governing practices. By about 750, therefore, the Arab rulers of the Middle East possessed an ideology of governmental justice to the poor and weak employed by officials and their supporters, and also by their opponents and critics, and a mature administrative mechanism equal to those of prior empires that could implement the justice of the Circle.

Abbasid political culture (750–945)

The Abbasids, the second dynasty of caliphs, rebelled against the Umayyads in 750 from a base of support in eastern Iran. Their takeover intensified the existing interest in Persian political and administrative systems. The Abbasids brought into the government an increasing number of Muslims of Persian background, of whom the most prominent were the Barmakids; these men did not introduce but reinforced Near Eastern styles of governance.[45] The "Persianization" of the Abbasid caliphate was not just a reversion to the bad old past, as the regime's critics claimed. Already under the Umayyads, Muslims had begun to create a new cultural and political synthesis that assimilated Persian and Greek political concepts and institutions together with ideas and practices derived from the Arab heritage.[46] The remolding of these ideas under the inspiration of an Islamic view of life gave the major political institutions of Islamicate civilization – law, bureaucratic administration, monarchical rule – their classical form. And Abbasid literature produced the first extant version of the four-line Circle of Justice.

Imperial ideology and justice

The Abbasid caliphs defined the duties of government as defense of the frontiers, internal security, and the provision of justice; the last of these was especially important in legitimating their takeover from the Umayyads, whom they labeled corrupt.[47] The caliph al-Ma'mun (813–33) courted popular support by judging cases in person at the great mosque; he defined the caliph as a deputy of God, divinely chosen, entrusted with authority over creation, and responsible for justice on earth.[48] Abbasid poets portrayed caliphal justice in metaphors alluding to Sasanian kings, palaces, and governing practices. The Abbasids also improved the administrative mechanisms of justice, centralizing revenue collection, resurveying parts of the empire, and regularizing the taxation of Muslims, many of whom by now were practicing agriculture in the conquered lands. The tenth-century official al-Khwarazmi, in his essay on secretaryship, described Abbasid land and tax registers, which were scrupulously kept in detailed and summarized forms.[49]

These administrative developments began as early as the reign of the second Abbasid caliph al-Mansur (754–75), although outwardly he retained the style of an Arab tribal chief as a rebuke to the "kingship" of the Umayyads. The later caliphs continued such practices and added the external trappings of the Sasanian kings – their elaborate dress, royal banquets, and lavish entertainments.[50] On the ceremonial stage, the caliphs reenacted the Sasanian emperors' role as pinnacle of the social pyramid, protector of the realm, religious arbiter, divine representative, and shadow of God on earth. "Shadow of God on Earth," the caliphal title that the piety-minded saw as most presumptuous, was current in Assyrian and Sasanian as well as Abbasid times; it referred to the quality of protection afforded by the shade in the Near Eastern climate, which the ruler was supposed to provide.[51]

Court poetry expressed this ideology, endowing the Abbasid caliphs with the attributes of earlier kings: virtue, the divine light, victory, and the ability to renew the world.

> Through you the expanses of the land have become fertile.
> How can the world be barren when you are its protector?[52]

These qualities extended to the caliph's agents: one of the Abbasid viziers, Muhammad al-Zayyat, was compared to the abundant rain that nourished the sterile ground.[53] The caliph was not only the rain but the sun:

> Harun came and all was bright.
> Again the sun shoots forth his rays.[54]

The Abbasid caliphs themselves adopted the concept of the Circle of Justice in political testaments left for their heirs. The historian al-Tabari recorded that the caliph al-Mansur told his son, "The country will not last without justice, the prosperity of the Sultan and obedience to him will not last without money." Al-Tabari's version of al-Mansur's testament noted the dependence of caliphal power on a full treasury supplied by taxation and devoted to the salaries of the army and the needs of the frontiers. It called justice "the most effective means of preventing unrest" but ignored its role in the creation of power and revenue.[55] The caliph al-Ma'mun instructed his successor that justice toward the people benefitted the ruler as well: "Do not neglect the affairs of the subjects; keep your subjects and the common people perpetually in mind! For the maintenance of royal power comes only through them and through your continual concern for the Muslims and their welfare. Take from the powerful subjects and give to the weak ones. Do not impose any intolerable burden upon them, and ensure that justice is meted out between all individuals with fairness."[56] The Abbasids, by modeling aspects of their caliphate on the model of Sasanian kingship, clearly sought to evoke in their subjects the reverence and loyalty seemingly commanded by those monarchs. Caliphal supporters, in contrast, used Persian metaphors of kingship prescriptively, urging the caliphs to dispense the justice and prosperity that Sasanian subjects reputedly enjoyed.

Opponents of Abbasid rule stressed similar ideologies of justice. The Qarmatian movement, an Islamic parallel to the pre-Islamic Mazdakites, emphasized social equality and the just distribution of wealth.[57] The various Shi'i movements opposed the Abbasids through both violent rebellion and ideological separation. Resistance to oppression and the search for justice became foundational elements in Shi'i theology, justified by the Qur'anic command to "enjoin the good and forbid the evil" and symbolized in key events such as the massacre of Husayn by the Umayyads, Abu Dharr's chiding of 'Uthman on behalf of the oppressed, and the Abbasids' execution of their revolutionary propagandist Abu Muslim. Since they did not usually control the state, the justice they advocated lay more in the private religious realm. Many such movements announced the coming of a *mahdi*, a messianic figure, who would replace for the oppressive Abbasids with a regime indubitably just. Feeling that social justice, the justice of the Circle, had failed, they sought to replace it with an apocalyptic justice beyond the reach of royal power.

The influence of Persian literature

The translation of Persian literary and political works into Arabic further stimulated Muslim society's assimilation of Near Eastern ideals, ideals understood as Persian because they were articulated in speeches by Persian kings. The courtier Ibn al-Muqaffa' translated a number of such works, some of which were discussed in the previous chapter: the "Sayings of Ardashir," from an anthology of rules and customs of the Sasanian royal court; the *Book of the Crown*, where the Circle of Justice appeared in the speeches of Anushirvan; *Kalila and Dimna*, a collection of political fables advocating maintenance of the inherited social hierarchy; and the "Letter of Tansar" and "Testament of Ardashir," replete with political advice.[58] Other translations he made included the *Book of Kings*, containing the history of the Persian kings as understood by the Sasanians, and *The Great Book of Etiquette (Adab),* a book of advice for kings and courtiers, which explained principles of good government and courtly behavior attributed to the Ancients.[59] He also wrote original works in Arabic, mainly political thought and advice, including the *Essay on Royal Companions*, which proposed a plan for a Persian-style Islamic monarchy without mentioning Persian precedents.[60]

Following Ibn al-Muqaffa', Persian culture began to affect non-Persians through the medium of Arabic literature. His Arabic prose style aroused great admiration, and his books immediately became classics for scribal training. He started a fashion for translating and compiling political and historical literature. Other authors translated parts of the *Book of Kings* not included in his version and re-translated some sections.[61] The ninth century also saw a wave of translations from Greek and Syriac into Arabic; the first work translated from Greek was Plato's *Republic*, with its division of society into rulers, soldiers, and the productive classes.[62] These translations, compiling selections interesting to a Muslim audience and omitting un-Islamic elements, reflect a new valuation by Arabic speakers of the worth of the non-Arab intellectual and political cultures as well as a new appreciation by non-Arabs of the Arabic language.

This reevaluation of non-Arab cultures also affected the work of Muslim religious scholars writing on public law, who began to express the Circle's concept of justice. Yahya ibn Adam's collection of *hadith* on taxation, which attributed some of its sayings to the fourth caliph 'Ali, recommended leniency in taxation, adjustment of taxes to the taxpayer's capacity to pay, and collection only of the surplus, not necessities such as seed grain, the peasant's cow, or the shirt off his back.[63] A strong influence from Near Eastern political thought and practice also colored the *Book of Taxation*, a legal work written by the jurist Abu Yusuf (d.798) for the caliph Harun al-Rashid (786–809). This was one of several works produced under Abbasid auspices to bring the taxation system into harmony with Islamic values and support it with Islamic authorities.[64] According to Abu Yusuf, his book was "designed to avert oppression from his subjects and to benefit their interests."[65] His attribution of most of his advice to Muslim sources has sometimes been interpreted as a deliberate refutation of "the prevailing cult of the Sasanian tradition," but that assessment is overstated. He did not reject advice that he could not support by quotations from Muslim authorities; he merely presented it as his own idea, even if it had Sasanian origins.[66]

Abu Yusuf associated the dispensation of justice with accuracy and fairness in taxation. He discussed the ruler as shepherd over the flocks of God, the light or illumination given to rulers by God, the responsibility of rulers for their people's prosperity and its result, a greater yield from the land tax, and the provision of welfare through preventing oppression and injustice. The Circle of Justice clearly lay behind these ideas, even though they were not explicitly attributed to the Persians. In comparison, the Fatimid Qadi al-Nu'man expressed a concern for justice outside the Near Eastern state tradition, using images of tribal enmity and battle between champions.[67] Abu Yusuf's vision of justice was urban rather than tribal: the construction of a building on a firm foundation, "a paved road, well-established practice and accepted legal sources."[68] The results of such justice would be "taxes in abundance" and the loyalty of the subjects, as well as divine approval, long life, and heavenly bliss. Abu Yusuf presented the Near Eastern state as the normal form of an imperial state, Islamic or otherwise, not as a foreign idea. That he could support it by verses from the Qur'an and references to Islamic concepts, rather than by Persian statecraft and precedents, indicates the extent to which the idea was an intrinsic part of Islamic political thought rather than an import from outside.

A mirror for princes composed by a provincial governor in 821 expressed the concepts of the Circle of Justice in a Persian genre but in the Arabic language. This work took the form of a letter of advice from the semi-autonomous governor of Khurasan, Tahir Dhu al-Yaminain, to his son, also a governor. Tahir described the governor in terms similar to those used by Anushirvan and Lugalzagesi:

> a watchman, and a shepherd; the people in your realm are only called "your flock" because you are their shepherd and their overseer; you take from them that which they hand over to you from their surplus income and subsistence means, and you expend it on things which will ensure their continued material well-being and spiritual welfare and which will alleviate their burdens. The land under your rule will burgeon with fertility, the yield from the land tax will increase, and your income in kind will be proportionately expanded. By this means you will be able to strengthen the bonds linking your army to you, and you will bring contentment to your people through the personal largess which you will be able to lavish upon them.[69]

Because of the ruler's protective care, the people produced a surplus paid as taxes, which the ruler used to foster the productivity of the land, the welfare of the people, and the loyalty of the military forces. This epistle was distributed as a manual of government by the Abbasid caliph al-Ma'mun, conveying the ideals of the Circle of Justice to every administrator in the empire.

Ulema in this period tended to see government service as corrupting, to be undertaken unwillingly and only to preserve Muslim society from worse evils.[70] Ordinary people, however, expected to be governed by the Circle of Justice, within which their role was to pay fair taxes and complain of injustices. The population of Rayy in Iran, to convince their military commander that he should remain in their region and protect them, reportedly told him to "impose on us as taxes on our private property whatever you think we can bear."[71] When the Abbasid caliph visited Damascus in 857, the populace appeared before him to protest the injustice of the officials, their embezzlement of tax revenues, and their oppression of the weak; the caliph ordered an investigation, since in an earlier incident the officials' refusal to listen to peasant petitioners had sparked a revolt. Even more revealing was the rebellion in 811 of Abu al-'Umaytir, a messianic rebel who expelled the governor of Damascus and proclaimed himself caliph, appointing officials and adjudicating disputes. Surviving histories called his judgments unjust, which may be true or may be official slander.[72] The assumption that he would sit in judgment, however, indicates that people considered this an indispensable duty of the ruler, and the fact that unjust judgments could be food for slander implies that rulers' judgments ordinarily had to satisfy a popular sense of justice.

The anonymous *Book of the Crown* indicates how strongly the customs and patterns of Near Eastern kingship dominated the caliphal court. The book introduced Sasanian justice in connection with the royal obligation to hold open court on festival days, especially Nawruz and Mihrgan. This good custom of all Sasanian kings had been abandoned by Yazdagird, "the guilty, the sinner," who by ceasing to administer justice overturned the world and oppressed the people. He decreed that the flock could not claim justice from the shepherd, the people had no right to complain to the kings, the humble were in no way equal to the powerful. This unnatural attitude brought down the judgment of heaven, and Yazdagird was miraculously killed by a kick from a magical white horse.[73] No stronger sermon could be preached on the kingly duty of justice.

This definition of justice as hearing the claims of the people, drawn from the chapter on the king's duties, contrasts with a definition of justice as "the king giving to each his proper status and to each class its due" that can be drawn from a chapter on the king's companions.[74] The *Book of the Crown* employed the four-layered Sasanian class system of warriors and princes, clergy and ascetics, scribes and scientists, and farmers and artisans. The contradiction between justice toward courtiers and the powerful and justice toward the common people was one of the realities of daily life in a monarchical system. Political literature mandated that containing the resulting tensions was the king's job, an essential one if the society were not to dissolve in civil war. The Circle of Justice made it clear that ultimately the ruler's ability to grant justice to the powerful, in the form of ranks and rewards, depended on his justice toward the humble in the form of protection from exploitation and redress of grievances. As a political concept, it established intrinsic connections between conquerors and conquered, Muslims and non-Muslims, rich and poor. Kingship within the Circle of Justice was kingship for all, not just for a segment of society. That may have been why, despite resistance from those wanting to reenact the early Muslim community's experience of government by religious authorities, the ancient Near Eastern state and its understanding of justice remained a foundational concept in Middle Eastern politics.

Abbasid historians and the Circle of Justice (*c*.850–950)

In the histories of the Abbasid period the Circle of Justice began to be used in a new way, and its first appearance in its standardized form came in the work of the historian Ibn Qutayba. Expressions of the Near Eastern concept of state in the literature of the early Islamic era were prescriptive, recommendations for governmental success. Tahir's widely-circulated mirror for princes, court literature and poetry addressed to the caliphs, and translations of Persian works made by courtiers and secretaries could all be characterized as efforts to control rulers' behavior. In that sense, the stereotype of the Circle of Justice as belonging to practical rather than theoretical politics reflects its role in the first two centuries. After the middle of the ninth century, however, the Circle's concept of justice began to be used descriptively and it gained a wider audience. The introduction of paper around the year 800 facilitated book production and encouraged the writing of diverse literary genres. Collections of maxims and anecdotes made for entertainment and instruction (the literature of *adab*) introduced the Circle of Justice outside the Persian context and developed its standard formula of expression. The idea also appeared in works of philosophy. In addition, justice became central to the descriptions of kings in historical literature, which was undergoing a transformation at just this time.

Pre-Islamic cultures in Arabic histories

Histories written in the ninth century incorporated the pre-Islamic past as a vital part of the story of the foundation of Islam. Early Islamic historical writing had dealt primarily with the Arab and Muslim past, including the life and sayings of Muhammad, narratives of the conquests, information on the Muslim community, and stories of the pre-Islamic Arabs. The non-Arab pasts were understood as having ended with the coming of Islam, to which only portions of the Arab past were at all relevant.[75] Gradually, however, the stories of prophets before Muhammad and the histories of other nations were included in the Islamic narrative.[76] The new "universal histories" narrated the history of the world beginning with creation, continued through the histories of the various peoples of the earth (including the Arabs, the Jews, the Greeks, the Persians, even sometimes the Indians and Chinese) and culminated with the history of the Muslim community. These histories treated not only the Arabs' pre-Islamic past, but the pre-Islamic pasts of all the Muslim peoples, as prefatory to the coming of the revelation. All of those pasts, together with that revelation, became the common heritage of all the Muslims. The ninth-century author al-Jahiz (d.868), for example, saw Islam as heir to all the world civilizations, claiming the best ideas and accomplishments of the past.[77] This realization permitted aspects of the non-Arab pasts, including parts of Persian political culture like the Circle of Justice, to be carried legitimately into the Islamic present. Near Eastern customs and ideas could now be recommended to rulers not as the dubious counsels of infidels, but as the wisdom of the centuries on the management of empires.[78]

Ninth-century historians implemented this transformation both methodologically and substantively. Al-Dinawari (d.898) drew on Greek learning and science as well as Arabic philology and the Islamic sciences, and his history of the world centered on Iran ("a walled garden") rather than the Arabian Peninsula.[79] The universal history of al-Ya'qubi (d.897) saw time as beginning with the people of Israel and the rulers of ancient Mesopotamia, moving on to the Greeks and Romans, Indians and Persians, the Turks, Chinese, Egyptians, and Africans, and finally the pre-Islamic Arabs, before reaching fulfillment in the Muslim community.[80] Ibn Qutayba (828–89), although he was an orthodox theologian and judge and a proponent of Arabic culture, by no means despised the non-Arabic literatures. Besides the Persian works translated by Ibn al-Muqaffa' and others, his sources included Greek or pseudo-Greek literature and translations of the Old and New Testaments as well as the Qur'an and the history of the Arabs. His history incorporated the Parthian-Sasanian historical narrative in its recital of the Persian rulers and their achievements, from the legendary kings of old to the later and more historical monarchs.[81]

Ibn Qutayba and the four-line Circle of Justice

Ibn Qutayba was the earliest writer we know of to quote the shorter formula for the Circle of Justice, though not in his history but in a book called *Fountains of Information*. This was a work of *adab*, a literary genre compiling information necessary for someone to function as a knowledgeable and cultivated member of a particular social class or profession, especially the caliphal court.[82] A chapter entitled "Authority," a collection of quotable quotes and anecdotes on good government, contained the four-part version of the Circle of Justice:

> There can be no government without men,
> No men without money,
> No money without prosperity,
> And no prosperity without justice and good government.[83]

The chapter also contained two versions of the Persian saying, "Government and religion are brothers," one of which was cited without attribution and another, more extensive, attributed to Ardashir I.[84]

In this chapter, Ibn Qutayba freely mingled recommendations from Persian and Greek sources, such as the "Testament of Ardashir," the "Sayings of Ardashir," and the apocryphal letters of Aristotle to Alexander, with material drawn from the history of the Muslim community, Arabic poetry, and quotations from the *hadith*, the sayings of the Prophet. He explained that outside the strictly religious realm, good could be found in many places: "This book, although not dealing with Qur'an or Sunna, the religious law or the knowledge of what is lawful and what is forbidden, yet leads on to the heights of things and shows the way to noble character; it restrains from baseness, turns away from ugly things, incites to right conduct and fair management, to mild administration and to rendering the land prosperous."[85] Ibn Qutayba chided those Muslims who, in absorbing the learning of the non-Muslims, abandoned that of the Muslim community; his goal was to bring the two together.[86] He saw his Persian and Greek material as supplementing the Qur'an and Islamic precedents to provide guidance for Muslims in the political arena.

The quotations in Ibn Qutayba's chapter on authority came from a wide variety of sources, but they reiterated a common set of ideas on the just use of authority. To the Prophet he attributed the saying, "God has his guards; his guards in the sky are the angels, his guards on earth those that are in charge of the *diwan* [treasury]"; while Ziyad, the governor of Iraq under Mu'awiya, was supposed to have said, "Act kindly towards the farmers, you will remain fat as long as they are fat."[87] Citations from *hadith*, Arab history, Sasanian or Greek culture illustrated aspects of the Circle of Justice, by now the standard definition of good government. As a supporter of Arab superiority, Ibn Qutayba was not likely to have represented Persian ideas as an important current of political thought unless they were fully assimilated into Islamic culture.

Ibn Qutayba did not claim that his rendition of the Circle of Justice was his own invention but presented it as a citation from an earlier authority. Unfortunately, the words with which he introduced the quotation, "it has been said," indicated a composite account from unidentified sources.[88] A variety of possible sources, now lost, circulated through the Muslim world at that time. Some attributed the quotation to Ardashir or Anushirvan; others, like the source used by Ibn 'Abd Rabbih of Andalusia (d.940) in his *adab* collection *The Incomparable Necklace*, ascribed it to the early Arab general and governor of Egypt 'Amr ibn al-'As.[89] It was clearly a common idea to which many were eager to lay claim.

Uses of the four-line Circle

Although the precise origin of the Muslims' version of the Circle of Justice cannot now be traced, we can follow its uses in later hands. The idea appeared about this time in the work of certain philosophers with an interest in politics, such as Abu Zayd al-Balkhi (850–934), whose essay on politics employed an analysis based on Aristotelian theories of causation, couched in the terminology of the Muslim jurists, but defined politics as "a craft that allows the cultivation of a country and the protection of the human beings in it to take shape," a definition that set the goals of politics in accordance with the Circle of Justice.[90] Qudama ibn Ja'far (873?–948?), a representative of secretarial circles with an interest in philosophy, argued in the foreword to his taxation manual that the rules of statecraft and secretarial practice associated with the Circle of Justice and the Near Eastern state were not opposed to Islamic law but were part of it: "Whereas the right to govern has no foundation if not based on divine religious authorization, it is clear that the rules of al-Kitabah [the secretarial art] must be a branch of the religious law [shariah]."[91] In a chapter on politics he cited both Aristotle and Ardashir, including the latter's dictum, "Religion and kingship are brothers," but he also offered a new version of this aphorism that could only have arisen in an Islamic context: "Kingship cannot exist without religion and law, and religion cannot exist without kingship and taxation."[92]

Even as conservative a historian as al-Tabari (d.923), who drew most of his information from the transmitters of *hadith*, followed the practice of the universal historians and began his narrative with the histories of the pre-Islamic peoples. He valued the continuity and clarity of the Persian narrative, and although he edited out its epic and magical elements, he retained its descriptions of the justice and injustice of kings.[93] His version of the oration of the fabled king Manuchihr expressed a concept of kingship based on mutual interdependence: "For the king has a claim on his subjects, and his subjects have a claim on him; whereas their obligation to the ruler is that they obey him, give him good counsel, and fight his enemy, the king's obligation to them is to provide them with their sustenance in its proper times, for they cannot rely on anything else, and that is their commerce. The king's obligation to his subjects is that he take care of them, treat them kindly, and not impose on them what they cannot do."[94] Al-Tabari's endorsement of the Persian historical narrative allowed it, and the values it carried, to become a standard element in Muslim universal histories down to the modern period.

Al-Mas'udi (d.956), in his history *Fields of Gold and Mines of Gems*, presented the Circle of Justice not as a snippet of history, ethics, or linguistics but as a governing tool.[95] Al-Mas'udi's writings exhibited the synthesis of Arab, Greek, and Persian traditions that constituted Islamicate culture in its mature form. To gather information he traveled widely throughout the Muslim world and read the works of Ibn Qutayba and his contemporaries, the Persian translations of Ibn al-Muqaffa', the ancient tales of the peoples he wrote about, and works by contemporary Muslim and Christian authors. Al-Mas'udi's work also showed the influence of the currents of Greek learning that were sweeping the Islamic intellectual world in the ninth and tenth centuries.[96]

In the chapters on the Persians in his *Fields of Gold*, al-Mas'udi demonstrated how the kings had used the Circle of Justice, carefully explaining "the foundations of monarchical authority and how useful it is to people to have kings and to be governed."[97] Like the historians of the previous century, he based his account of the Persian kings on the Sasanian epic-historical narrative. He began at the creation of the world with the legendary Gayomart, first king of the Persians, who prayed "to follow the good path toward justice which makes order and harmony reign in the world."[98] For Ardashir I, the founder of the Sasanian dynasty, justice was essential to kingship: "A king must be overflowing with justice. Justice is the source of all good; it is a citadel raised for the defense of the state against destruction and ruin; the suppression of justice is the first sign of the decline of a country. When the banners of tyranny wave over a people, the eagles of justice must combat them and put them to flight."[99]

Al-Mas'udi portrayed Bahram II as a reformer who conformed to the Circle of Justice: he returned confiscated land to its rightful owners, compiled registers, and restored ancient customs (of taxation, presumably) and the vitality of agriculture. The land and people became prosperous, the taxes filled the treasury, and the army renewed its strength, defeating enemies and protecting the frontiers. This state of justice supposedly occurred because Bahram followed the advice of his courtiers, offered as the moral of a cautionary tale about Bahram himself. In this tale the king passed by a ruined village where two owls were hooting. On asking what they were saying, he learned that the two owls were to be married, and that the female owl had demanded as a wedding present twenty ruined villages like this one so that she could hoot in them. The male owl responded that if the king continued in his unjust ways, he would easily be able to give her a thousand ruined villages. The lesson Bahram's advisors drew from this story paraphrased the Circle of Justice: "The strength of a realm rests on the law and obedience to God and the execution of His will. The law cannot be upheld except by the king, and the king owes his power to men, but what upholds men is money, which only comes from the flourishing state of agriculture; now prosperity does not exist without justice."[100] In the sayings of Anushirvan another statement of the Circle of Justice appeared, this version, like Bahram's, having seven terms that detailed how justice should be carried out: "The kingdom rests on the army, the army on the finances, the finances on the land tax, taxes on agriculture, agriculture on justice, justice on the [reform] of agents, and this on the rectitude of ministers."[101]

Al-Mas'udi's understanding of society has been analyzed as reflecting Greek philosophical and scientific thought. Al-Farabi (d.950), the great proponent of Greek political philosophy, was al-Mas'udi's contemporary and had a powerful influence.[102] But to limit the list of al-Mas'udi's influences to the Greek understates his debt to ancient Near Eastern concepts of state. For al-Mas'udi, justice held the highest position in the ethical hierarchy and was "the mainstay of the social order"; kingship was the institution that carried it out. The idea of justice implied, as for the Persians, a strict social hierarchy graduated in rank, along with protection for the rights of all, the strong and the weak. The ruler's justice generated prosperity for the land, envisaged as the Assyrians had seen it in the construction of cities, fair taxation, and constant care for agriculture and maintenance of canals, roads, and frontier posts. Lack of justice and decay of the bond between kingship and religion allowed contenders for power to arise and the kingdom to decline.[103]

While the events of late Sasanian history abundantly illustrated this last point, al-Mas'udi also applied it to his own day, when the Abbasid Empire was disintegrating. The extant text of his history was written in 943 and revised in 947, when the caliphs were becoming increasingly unable to fulfill their responsibilities, not just from personal corruption, but because of the institutional weakness of their office and a spiraling economic and social crisis.[104] Al-Mas'udi's stories from Sasanian history may have served as inspirational reading for the officials on whom the burden of governance increasingly devolved. Perhaps the growing ineffectiveness of caliphal politics in ordering the realm made the Near Eastern state tradition appear more useful.

Conclusion

The Near Eastern concept of state was one of the key strands in Islamicate political development. Decentering Islam in the history of this development allows us to set aside the negative valuation that many Islamic scholars, concerned for retaining the godliness of Prophetic guidance and caliphal rule, placed on imperial forms and ideologies. Muslim rulers and administrators seeking to govern the immense region they had conquered found useful tools in the governmental systems already developed in the region. Associates of the caliphs – secretaries, governors, and court poets – recommended these systems and their accompanying ideology, and because of their centrality to vital aspects of government such as taxation, caliphal authority, and redress of grievances, most of the empire's people supported them strongly. The Circle of Justice, as a statement of the relationships among the elements of the ideology, was bound to become an often-repeated maxim of governance.

By the time the Abbasid caliphs lost control of their empire in the mid-tenth century, concepts and practices of the Near Eastern state were deeply embedded in Islamic government. The caliphs were considered as divinely selected for their roles and responsible for the order and justice of Muslim society. They were aided by a complex administration, part of whose task was to maintain the army and the empire's infrastructure without unfair taxation and to protect the common people from exploitation by the great. Although the rulers themselves were generally hidden from the people, they maintained routes of access through which people could appeal for justice. These caliphal roles and responsibilities were enshrined, not in Islamic law (which developed more or less independently of the state) or religious doctrine (which often developed in opposition to political and social trends), but in Arabic literature: poetry, history, essays, and works of advice, which developed mainly at the caliphal court. The standardized Arabic form in which the Circle would be repeated throughout the history of Islamic civilization made its first appearance in the *adab* and advice works. Yet, apart from the words in which it was expressed, the Circle of Justice was not merely a literary device known to essayists. Its underlying concept, the interdependence between ruler and people, already had a long history in the Middle East and fueled popular demands for good administration and redress of grievances. In 945 the caliphs lost power to a family of Persian warlords, but there was no need for the new rulers to import "Persian-style" political ideas into Islamic politics; they were already firmly established there.

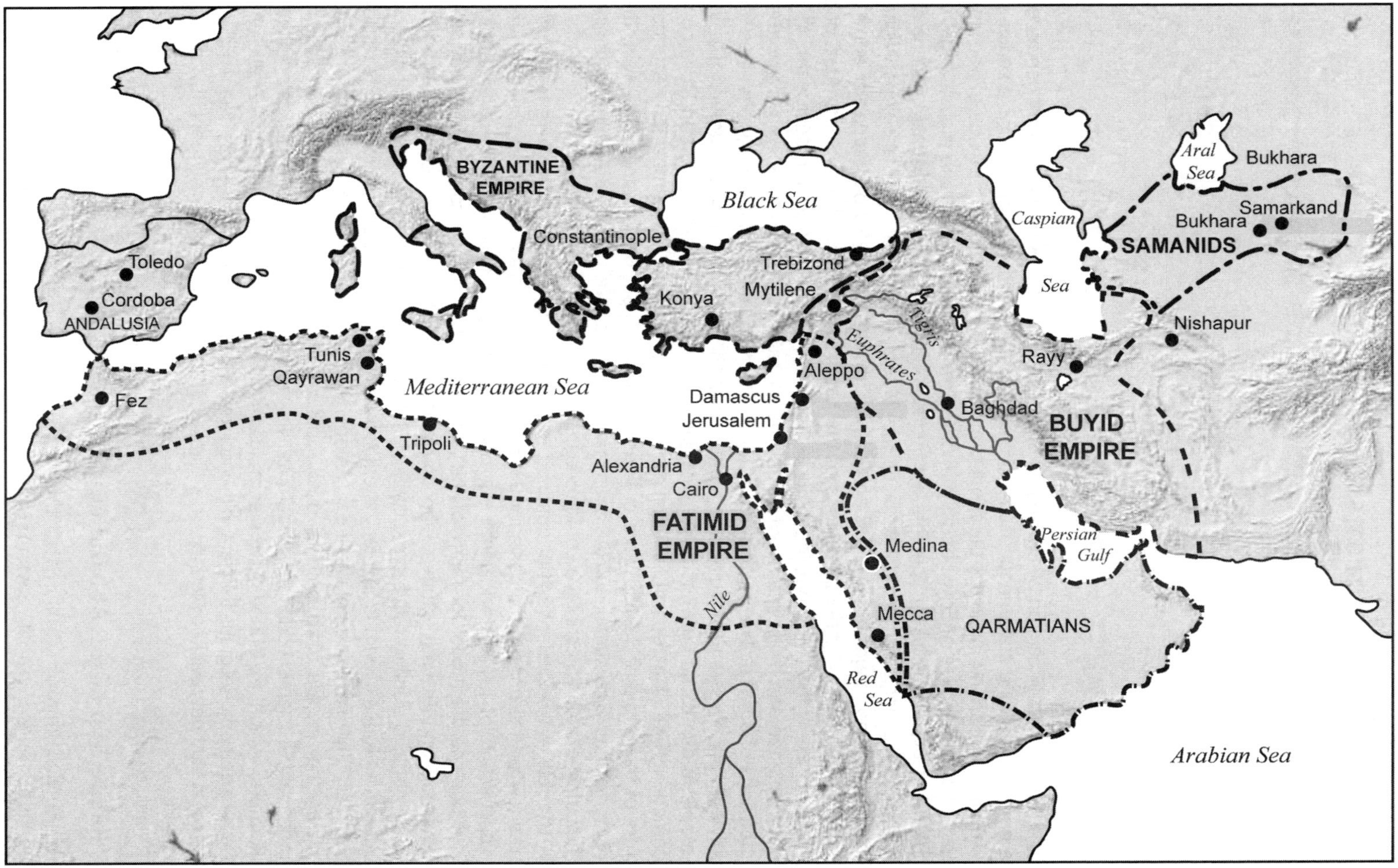

Map 4 The Buyid and Fatimid empires

5 Politics in transition

"Curb the strong from riding on the weak"

The political turmoil caused by the ending of the Muslim caliph's political power generated a number of strong statements of the Circle of Justice. In the tenth century, a series of warlords, rivals, and invaders, the most powerful of whom were the Buyids of Iraq and Iran and the Fatimids of Egypt and Syria, broke the Abbasid Empire into pieces. Most of the rulers of the empire's fragments continued to acknowledge the Abbasid caliphs as dispensers of legitimacy and heads of the Muslim community in a religious sense, though they no longer governed it politically. These rulers developed separate administrative structures in different regions of the Middle East, Central and South Asia, and North Africa where they employed local languages and political arrangements. The fragmentation and multiplication of governments, rather than turning society away from the Circle of Justice as a political ideology, instead provided enlarged opportunities for advisors and writers to develop the themes of justice and good administration and for people to demand it from the authorities, who now might be less distant and less concerned with other modes of legitimation. In this setting two of the most powerful carriers of the Circle of Justice were created, Firdausi's epic on the kings of Persia, the *Book of Kings* (*Shahnama*), and the anonymous *Secret of Secrets* (*Sirr al-Asrar*), containing the oldest extant representation of this idea actually written in a circle.

The role of the Circle was not confined to literary ornamentation or advice to kings. It also formed the conceptual basis for the ongoing activities of tax reassessment and the dispensation of justice. Additionally, it became part of a new political understanding that became the model for many of the Abbasid Empire's successor states. Provincial governors and Shi'i adventurers, who dominated parts of the former Abbasid realm, imitated Abbasid administrative organization. They introduced governance by non-caliphal authorities together with (and later instead of) the caliphs, and non-shariah courts run by political authorities to complement shariah courts with Islamically trained judges; evidence shows that people used both to obtain justice. The Circle of Justice became more prominent in Islamic concepts of state as well as in Arabic literature, especially political literature, which expanded to cover much of the territory pioneered by Greek and Persian authors. Religious thinkers, although they continued to condemn pre-Islamic ideas of royal authority, acknowledged the Circle of Justice as a core element in caliphal ideology.[1]

The breakup of the Abbasid empire (*c*.850–999)

As Abbasid control weakened in the ninth century, Muslim society felt a need for powerful and impartial government to defend against aggression, maintain social harmony, and provide justice to the people, but the Abbasids themselves could not supply it.[2] After 833, the caliphs became dependent on their bodyguard of Turkish slave soldiers, imported to replace their untrustworthy Arab and Persian troops. Over the next hundred years, the Turkish forces became disruptive and over-powerful, masterminding the succession to the caliphate, seizing provincial governorships, and controlling provincial finances. From 936 on, the Abbasids acknowledged their loss of control over the capital by appointing a commander-in-chief with sovereign authority.[3] In this period of caliphal weakness, the empire depended on its high officials, especially the viziers, the heads of the administration, to one of whom a version of the Circle of Justice was attributed: "The prosperity of exploitation and the augmentation of the revenue rest on the maintenance of agriculture, which cannot be obtained but by justice."[4]

In the provinces the Abbasids lost control gradually, in several stages, starting when for stability's sake they awarded hereditary governorships – including control over both military and financial affairs – to the Tahirids and others in the early ninth century.[5] Later in the century the caliphs were forced to recognize as their "governors" men who seized or already held power in a region, such as the Persian Saffarids and Samanids. The fiction of "governorship" became still thinner in the tenth century with the independent rule of the Buyids and Ghaznavids. The Umayyads of Spain even claimed the title of caliph for themselves, as did the Shi'i Fatimids of Egypt. Like the Umayyads' governors, these governors and local rulers acquired the attributes of kingship. Except for the Fatimids and the Umayyads of Spain, none of them claimed to be successors of the Prophet, but they were still required to provide the Circle's attributes of victory, prosperity, and justice. Only sending taxes to the Abbasid caliph separated "loyal" governors from independent rulers, who retained the revenues to support their own military forces.

The Circle in New Persian culture

The multiplication of courts around the various governing families, often Persian by descent or acculturation, expanded patronage of Persianate literary and political culture.[6] The Saffarids, who seized power in eastern Iran, compelled court poets to address them in Persian and allegedly wanted to revive Sasanian rule. The Tahirid governors of Khurasan, loyal to the caliphs but proud of their elite Persian descent, employed their fluent Arabic to convey Persian political ideas and were applauded for being "concerned for the restoration of agriculture and the preservation of the peasants from undue exploitation."[7] The Samanids, who succeeded the Tahirids in Khurasan, linked their genealogy to that of the Sasanian kings and patronized Persianate culture. At their court in Bukhara, the growth of a New Persian language using Arabic script and vocabulary ignited a literary and linguistic renaissance in Persian.

The Samanids sponsored a number of works in New Persian containing the concept of the Circle of Justice; the greatest was Firdausi's *Book of Kings* (discussed below). The Samanid vizier and scholar Bal'ami (d.974) translated the history of al-Tabari into Persian and added to it from other sources, including the Sasanian *Book of Kings*, which must be the source for a speech of Anushirvan's not reported by al-Tabari listing the elements of the Circle: "As the Almighty has been more beneficent to me than to my ancestors, and has enlarged my country, it is necessary that I should exceed them in justice. I have looked into the affairs of men, and I see a king must be helpless without a treasury. I cannot protect my country without an army nor can an army be maintained without means, and those means must be derived from the people."[8]

Bal'ami also put the Circle of Justice into the mouth of Purandukht, daughter of the deposed Khusrau II Parviz, who ruled in her own right for over a year late in the Sasanian era: "This kingdom cannot be governed by valor nor by wealth, but by the power of God. The sovereign cannot exercise power except by justice and good administration. The army cannot triumph over the enemy unless it is paid, and one cannot keep an army except by justice, equity, and discipline."[9] Khusrau Parviz was accused of demanding tax arrears twenty and thirty years old, while Purandukht cancelled arrears and erased the registers. Khusrau Parviz in self-justification pointed out the two pavilions of justice he had erected, where he went one morning every month to hear petitions.

Local histories also flourished under the Samanids. Most are now lost, but one that survived, Narshakhi's history of Bukhara, listed in its opening chapter the city's most illustrious Islamic scholars and judges, praising their justice. The second chapter was also an encomium on justice, but the central figure was the ruler of the city at the Arab conquest, a woman called simply Khatun ("Lady"), serving as regent for her young son. The chapter compared her administration of justice with that of the great Sasanian monarchs: "She had the custom every day of coming out of the gate of the fortress of Bukhara on a horse and halting at the gate. She issued orders and prohibitions, and gave a robe of honor to whomsoever she wished and punishment to whom she wished."[10] Samarqand, the second city of the realm, also became a center of literary production, not for the court but for ordinary people. There the *hadith* expert Ibn Hibban compiled a collection of noteworthy sayings that included a Circle of Justice centered on the vizier rather than the monarch:

> A king's kingdom does not last unless the officials obey him, and officials do not obey without a vizier, and it does not happen unless the vizier is devoted and loyal, and that is not found in the vizier without integrity and good judgment, and that formidable foundation does not come about without money, and money is not found without the cultivation [or thriving] of the people, and the people do not cultivate [or thrive] except by the performance of justice, so it is as if the stability of the kingdom is not possible without the requirement of justice, and the disappearance of the one is not possible without the disappearance of the other.[11]

Another *hadith* scholar, al-Khwarizmi (933/4–994/5), quoted Ibn Qutayba's four-line version of the Circle in a speech of Moses to Pharaoh. Since Moses was considered Pharaoh's vizier before he fled Egypt, al-Khwarizmi's quotation, like Ibn Hibban's, may reflect an increase in the political importance of viziers under the Samanids. The anonymous *Proper Behavior for Sultans and Viziers* stressed the function of both sultans and viziers as shepherds and their responsibility for the people confided to their care; their greatest duty was to be just, and justice was the root of the order of the world. As the landed aristocracy did not "show a desire to read an Arabic book," Narshakhi's history was translated into New Persian, as was the political allegory *Kalila and Dimna*, the latter illustrated by Chinese artists.[12] The Samanids employed the Persian language not to set themselves apart from other Muslims but to convey to their Persian-speaking subjects the Islamic worldview, history, and political ideas, and to locate the Persians within the realm of Islamicate culture. Their works preserved the concepts and procedures of the Near Eastern state through changes of language, religion, and government and disseminated them to new audiences.[13]

The Shahnama *of Firdausi*

The greatest exponent of Islamicate Persian literature in the Samanid realm was Firdausi, whose *Shahnama* retold in the New Persian language the old Persian historical myths, suitably edited for a Persian-speaking but Muslim audience.[14] Firdausi finished his poem for the Ghaznavid ruler Mahmud I (999-1030), but he wrote most of it under the Samanids, and its emphasis on how a ruler should govern rather than how he should be chosen reflected the shift in power from the caliph to local warlords.[15] The *Shahnama* revolved around the legendary kings and heroes of ancient eastern Iran and stories of victory, valor, and virtue. Among the ancient kings, only Kai Khusrau gave the land prosperity by his justice, making it a fertile garden.[16] The story of Alexander the Great did introduce as his advisor the figure of Aristotle the philosopher, to whom later generations attributed the eight-line Circle of Justice.

In Firdausi's portrayal of the historical Sasanian monarchs, justice appeared in most of their enthronement speeches. Ardashir, of course, was an exemplar of justice; his accession speech proclaimed, "In this world my treasure is justice and the whole universe has been revived through my efforts," while his last words contained the saying, "Religion and royalty are brothers."[17] His attention to the provision of justice was described in loving detail: his administration of justice in public, his charge to provincial governors to use justice, his remission of taxes in times of drought or enemy destruction, and his employment of tax revenues on public works. The wickedness of Yazdagird I appeared in that "he answered no petitions," but his successor proved his fitness to rule (and his similarity to Mesopotamian kings) by cancelling arrears of taxes and burning the registers. Firdausi celebrated Anushirvan's justice to the hilt – his remission of taxes, resurveying of the land, reform of the bureaucracy, and attention to petitions from his subjects. So marvelous was his justice that he seemed an apocalyptic savior:

> He filled with justice all the face of earth,
> And cultivated all the barren lands;
> Both great and small slept safely on the waste,
> And sheep and wolf came to one trough.[18]

Firdausi saw the espousal of justice as a mark of true royalty, and justice brought about prosperity. Rightly spent, the resulting treasure paid for useful works and numerous troops, ensuring their loyalty and defense of the realm. This was the same Circle of Justice the Assyrians had known, now colorfully embellished with legendary battles, miraculous tales, and the jewel-encrusted crowns of Persian kings.

If Firdausi's great achievement was, as scholars say, to make the Near Eastern state tradition a permanent part of Islamicate Persian culture, then the achievement of men like Abu Yusuf, Ibn Qutayba, and al-Mas'udi was to secure its place in Islamicate culture as a whole, despite its association with controversial concepts of kingship. Even an exemplary qadi could now be praised in the language of the Circle of Justice when he "established good laws with impartiality and justice, so that the strong could not tyrannize the weak."[19] The significant point was not the use of the Persian language, the preservation of antique texts, or the establishment of Persianate monarchies, but the deployment in an Islamic context of Near Eastern ideas of legitimacy and justice associated with Persian history.

On the other hand, three centuries after the Arab conquest and the establishment of the caliphate, Persian-style kingship still had enormous legitimacy among the populace, especially in the east. Provincial governors and rebel leaders employed thrones and crowns and other pre-Islamic symbols of sovereignty to win popular support.[20] Some went much farther than the Samanids toward the restoration of a Persian monarchy: a *hadith* attributed to the Prophet foretold the reign of a non-Arab from Khurasan, while astrologers predicted the overthrow of the Arab caliphate by a Persian dynasty – a "king from the east," or a "man of Isfahan."[21] The titles "king" (*malik*) and "king of kings" (*shahanshah*) came back into favor, though the title most characteristic of non-caliphal rulers was "authority" (*sultan*). The Ziyarids in northern Iran claimed royal Sasanian descent and the Samanids aristocratic Persian roots, whereas the Buyids' lack of royal lineage hurt their relations with their followers.[22] The Ziyarid ruler Mardavij (d.935) attempted to create a real Persian monarchy: after conquering large parts of the Iranian plateau, he introduced Persian court ceremony, celebrated Zoroastrian holidays, and persecuted Islam. He employed all the symbolism of crowns and thrones and royal exaltation, and he wanted to restore the ruined Hall of Khusrau (*Iwan Kisra*) in Baghdad to serve as his seat.[23]

Al-Mas'udi, writing in 956, related that some Persians hoped and believed that power would return to them and their empire would be re-established.[24] What actually took place, however, was not a restoration of Persian rule, but a new appreciation of monarchy in Islamicate society. New types of rule sprang up beside the caliphate and ultimately supplanted it; new peoples conquered Muslim society and were themselves conquered by it; new political concepts and ideas of justice were amalgamated with the old.

Buyids and Fatimids (945–1171)

The era of the Buyid and Fatimid regimes witnessed major changes in both structures of government and ideas of authority. The Abbasid caliphs remained in place after 945, but they surrendered political power to new rulers with other religious or secular claims to leadership. The Muslim world divided into rival political bodies whose competitive wars replaced the now unmanageable wars of expansion. The fracturing of the Abbasid polity might have meant the marginalization or disappearance of the Circle of Justice, as it had after the Akkadian, Achaemenid, and Arab invasions. Instead, the Abbasids' successor states employed elements of the Circle of Justice in their own political ideologies. The rise in importance of local administration also made the search for justice easier by reducing the distance between rulers and people. It was in this context that the longer statement of the Circle of Justice appeared.

The Buyids and the Persian past

The Buyids, who conquered most of Iran and took Baghdad in 945, began as generals of the Samanids and the Ziyarid Mardavij but did not follow the latter in rejecting Islam. They came from Daylam, an autonomous region of northern Iran where Persian culture was still strong.[25] Most of the region had gradually accepted Islam in one of its Shi'i forms, but Persian titles and personal names continued in use and Persian was the official as well as the spoken language. Once in power, the Buyids devised a genealogy going back to the Sasanians, employed Persian ceremonies, and portrayed themselves as Persian monarchs on coins and medals with inscriptions in pre-Islamic Persian script.[26] Although they stopped short of eliminating the Abbasid caliphs, they decreased the power and dignity of the caliphal office, limiting access to him by controlling his audiences, his correspondence, and his funding. In their multiple capitals, they instituted Shi'i ceremonies and extended toleration to heretical Muslims and to non-Muslims, employing them in government positions. They took over the position of commander-in-chief (*amir*, their favorite title) and added to it the titles of king (*malik*) and emperor (*shahanshah*). Compelling the caliph to delegate his temporal power to them, they made the position of commander permanent and hereditary within their family. They presided over an increasingly hierarchical society; their military chiefs developed into a landholding nobility, and even ordinary soldiers won tax exemptions and hereditary proprietorships of the lands that provided their salaries, reuniting military and fiscal authority and making it difficult for the state to control abuses or to ensure that irrigation systems were maintained.[27]

Like the Umayyad governors, the Buyid *amirs* adopted the royal and caliphal qualities of shield, shepherd, and shadow of God on earth.[28] 'Adud al-Dawla (944–83) compared himself to Alexander the Great and to the Persian kings, and on his coins he called himself "The Just *Amir*."[29] He embodied his claims in royal inscriptions carved on Darius's palace at Persepolis; palatial and urban construction; irrigation canals, dams, and ports; bridges, roads, and post stations; religious edifices; and support for culture and education. His fellow *amir* Mu'izz al-Dawla (945–67) worked with his own hands on irrigation repairs, as the rulers of antiquity used to do, in order to advertise his commitment to the welfare of the people.[30] The Buyids' Persian vizier Ibn 'Abbad (d.995) quoted the Circle of Justice and recommended that every king should engrave it on his pectoral jewel as a reminder.[31]

Despite their Persian descent, the Buyids in Baghdad presided over an Arabic-speaking court where a literary and cultural florescence took place. The court's cultural diversity introduced new sources for political ideas that rapidly entered Arabic political literature. If one hallmark of this Buyid renaissance was the expression of Persian-style governing ideas in Arabic texts, another was the continued translation into Arabic of Greek and Syriac philosphical and literary works, including Greek materials on Alexander the Great. Political philosophy linked Greek philosophical approaches with ideas of Persian origin found in mirrors for princes. Under Buyid auspices, the Zoroastrian leadership in Baghdad recompiled the *Denkard* and other texts. A mystical group in Basra called the Brethren of Purity (*Ikhwan al-Safa'*) also produced a compilation of texts, the *Epistles*, which reinterpreted the Greek sciences according to the group's esoteric theology. They argued that the community could not have stability without both religious and political leadership, for "Kingship and religion are twin brothers."[32]

The Fatimids and the Muslim mission

The Fatimids of Egypt (969–1171) also proclaimed themselves to their Sunni and non-Muslim subjects as just rulers despite their divergent religious orientation. The Isma'ili Shi'i movement, to which the Fatimids belonged, encompassed a powerful sense of social justice and an expectation of a charismatic ruler to enact it. The precise nature of the ruler's charisma was a secret imparted only to Isma'ili initiates, but his reforming role was part of the movement's official propaganda. The Isma'ili *Book of Debates* established "the need of the people for someone to govern them. restrain the wrongdoer, and render justice to the wronged."[33] As Shi'is, the Fatimids saw the political system as a microcosm of the cosmic order with God at the pinnacle; the prerequisite for a just political order was the right man in the headship.

In public festivals and processions, the Fatimid caliphs drew on the common people's ideology of the caliph as the font of justice to whom petitions were addressed, bestower of prosperity and sponsor of the infrastructure, victorious warrior, and religious arbiter.[34] In partial fulfillment of these roles, the Fatimids stressed their ability to supply grain and bread to the people of Cairo and to control the grain merchants.[35] They made a land survey in 1121 to stabilize tax demands and eliminate corruption by officials and tax collectors. They also paid for the construction and repair of irrigation works, provided public safety, granted land to petitioners, and presided over the courts of justice in person.[36]

A compendium of Isma'ili law written by the Fatimid Qadi al-Nu'man included a political testament that addressed the ruler as a source of justice, warning him to listen to God, who "hearkens to the prayer of every oppressed one. for the discontent of the common people outweighs the contentment of the retinue." The testament, stressing the interdependence of all social groups and the contribution of that interdependence to society's prosperity, recommended that rulers maintain the populace in good order: "Take care of those who pay the *kharaj* [tax] and consider everything that will keep them in good estate, for upon their welfare rests that of others. They and none other are the mainstay of the state, and the people are dependent on them. Therefore you should care for the cultivation of their land and the favorable state of their livelihood more than for the easy collection of their *kharaj*." In the first century of their rule, the Fatimids could take credit for a rise in Egyptian prosperity, according to Persian poet and pilgrim Nasir-i Khusrau, who visited Cairo in the 1040s and found people "so secure under the sultan's reign that no one fears his agents, and they rely on him neither to inflict injustice nor to have designs on anyone's property."[37]

The turn in this period toward royal symbols and behavior did not generally indicate a turn away from Islam. The assumption by the Fatimid caliph al-Hakim (996–1021) of the messianic role of god-king and the attempt by Mardavij to restore the Persian *shahanshah* were exceptional cases.[38] More often, the Fatimid and Buyid rulers did not intend to replace Islamic rule as such, but to replace its main instrument, the caliphate, because it had proven incapable of holding the Islamic Empire together or of exemplifying the ideals of just rule held by most segments of society. This failure could not be attributed merely to weak or unjust caliphs; it was a structural problem. Although the caliphate had become the source of authority for religious institutions as well as for governance, the concept of the caliph as successor to the Prophet was too far removed from the needs of a government whose institutions rested on the ideology of Near Eastern kingship and the reality of military power and thus demanded different qualities in their head.[39]

Justice under divided authority

It is easy to see the contrast of the political roles of caliph and king in the dual headship institutionalized by the Buyids, who retained the caliphs as spiritual heads and bestowers of legitimacy and added themselves as military and political executors. Even before 945, however, the Abbasid caliphs were aware of the distinction between those two roles and their different demands; in fact, the employment of Turkish troops would have required the caliphs to appeal also to tribal modes of legitimation, and the loss of the Turks' loyalty may well be related to their failure to do so.[40] The division of authority between two individuals in most of the Muslim world after 945 permitted the caliphs to represent the ultimate sovereignty of God while non-caliphs governed the Islamic realms as *amirs*, commanders or uncrowned kings.

The new arrangement produced a theoretical reconfiguration of political responsibilities. The tenth-century philosopher al-'Amiri saw two indispensable political necessities: "true prophecy" and "real royal authority," both gifts from God. He paraphrased a Persian saying often attributed to Ardashir to state that "the relationship of religion to royal authority is like that of the foundation to the building erected upon it."[41] He wished both of these political necessities to be met by the caliph, but his theoretical separation of the two roles tended to legitimize their actual separation. The philosopher al-Farabi was apparently quite ready to separate religious from secular leadership if the necessary qualities could not be found in a single person. Al-Farabi's philosophy treated religion as a symbolic representation of the truth; for the caliphate to hold only symbolic power, then, would not be inappropriate.[42] Whoever held royal authority carried the ancient responsibility for justice.

Shi'i sources published during the Buyid period denigrated or ignored the Abbasid caliphs' provision of justice. An eleventh-century Shi'i *hadith* collection included a quotation from the eighth Imam 'Ali al-Rida chiding the caliphs for injustice that echoed sentiments expressed to Anushirvan and the Umayyads: "When rulers lie and issue unrightful decrees, rain is imprisoned in the sky. When kings act with injustice, their dynasty will be thrown down."[43] *The Highway of Eloquence*, a collection of sermons, letters, and sayings attributed to the caliph 'Ali, included a letter from 'Ali to his governor of Egypt, al-Malik al-Ashtar, another version of the text of the Fatimid Qadi al-Nu'man's political testament. This letter described the Muslim community as the embodiment, under God, of the Circle of Justice, composed of interdependent categories of people: soldiers protected the people but needed sustenance through taxes; soldiers and tax collectors needed judges and administrators who attended to the people's welfare; none of them could do without traders and craftsmen; the destitute needed help from the whole community; and the community prospered through each group's receiving its due.[44] This version of the text stressed the element of the community, lacking in the Fatimid version, and so increased the interdependence displayed by the passage. Interestingly, this version's instructions on holding regular court sessions sound very much like the advice given to ancient Egyptian rulers: "Assign part of your time to petitioners, and give them your full attention. Accord them the opportunity of a public audience."[45]

Other works of the time laid the responsibility for justice explicitly on the *amirs*, transplanting older formulations into the new political context. A book of advice written by an anonymous finance scribe for his new Buyid rulers recommended that "the king must keep the realm by his soldiers, keep his soldiers by money, which is received from the collectors of land tax, paid by the peasants in the cultivated regions; the latter can be kept only by justice."[46] In the vizier al-Abi's collection of literary gems, the simple four-part Circle accompanied a more elaborate version attributed to the Sasanian ruler Shapur and addressed to the Buyids: "Know that the preservation of your realm depends on the flow of the *kharadj* [tax], and the flow of the *kharadj* depends on agriculture, and the way to the greatest success in this sphere is to care for the well-being of its people through justice and aid."[47] The reformulation of the Circle in contemporary contexts speaks to its use not just as a literary ornament but as a practical recommendation for people in ruling positions.

The eight-line Circle: The Secret of Secrets

The most complete statement of the Circle of Justice in this period has been traced to a lost work, "The Book of Policy on the Management of Government." This work, supposedly compiled for Alexander the Great by Aristotle, resembled the *Epistles* of the Brethren of Purity in adding concepts of cosmology to political advice from Greek and Persian sources. It apparently formed the foundation of a later and more comprehensive work that still exists in several versions. This later compendium, entitled *The Secret of Secrets*, combined advice to kings with information on an encyclopedic variety of subjects, such as politics, history, science, philosophy, medicine, alchemy, and magic.[48] Translated first in medieval Iberia and then in the Crusader state of Tripoli, *The Secret of Secrets* gained great popularity in the West through its claim to contain the wisdom of Aristotle. It was translated into Latin, Spanish, Old French, Middle High German, English, Russian, and Hebrew, and was utilized by the mystical Andalusian theologian Ibn al-'Arabi and edited by the English scientist Roger Bacon.[49] It purported to be a translation from Greek made about 150 years earlier by a secretary of the caliph al-Ma'mun, Yuhanna ibn al-Batrik (d.815), and perhaps parts of it were.[50] The book as we know it, however, was apparently compiled from a variety of sources between 950 and 980; surviving copies date to the mid-eleventh century. Much of the "Greek" and "Hindu" wisdom it contained was actually derived from works of Persian history and advice circulating in the ninth and tenth centuries, and it also owed a great deal to the Alexander romances and other pseudo-Greek material as well as to Arabic sources. One version proclaimed that the ruler could dominate the bodies of his subjects either by justice or by force, but only by justice could he capture their hearts, and it quoted the Arabic proverb, "Act favorably toward the peasants; you will be fat as long as they are."[51]

Among its other secrets, *The Secret of Secrets* contained an eight-part statement of the Circle of Justice extending and elaborating the four-line version cited by Ibn Qutayba and Ibn 'Abd Rabbih and the seven-part version of al-Mas'udi. Its eight sentences constituted the first version of the Circle of Justice to bring it full circle and join the end to the beginning; "each sentence was connected to the ones before and after it, and the last to the first." In some recensions the sentences were actually written in a circle or octagon, a figure that *The Secret of Secrets* itself called "the essence of this book … it is with justice that the earth is populated, kingdoms are established … and rulers become immune from all sorts of evils."[52] The book placed the eight sentences at the close of a long discourse on justice full of Persian proverbs, claiming that Aristotle had invented them for Alexander. Early versions of the text gave six different variations of the sentences, one of which was attributed to 'Ali ibn Abi Talib. In an interesting reversal, the version attributed to 'Ali based justice on "law, which is the life of the state," while the version attributed to Anushirvan by al-Mas'udi made justice depend on "the reform of agents" and "the rectitude of ministers" (i.e. on the personal qualities of leaders). Here the major variations in wording are incorporated into a single rendition:

> The world is a garden/foundation, hedged in by sovereignty/dynasty/dominion/state
> Sovereignty is lordship, preserved/sheltered/veiled by law/custom
> Law is administration/guidance/an open road, governing/governed by the king/imam
> The king is a shepherd/crown/arm, supported by/mustering the army
> The army are soldiers/helpers/dragons, fed by money/property/wealth
> Money is revenue/food/livelihood, gathered by the people/the many
> The people are servants, subjected/enfolded/enthralled by justice
> Justice is happiness/harmony, the establishment/prosperity/well-being/repair of the world.[53]

The eight sentences expanded on the four-line form of the Circle of Justice by stating its propositions positively rather than negatively, by defining the elements in terms of images, and by adding three elements: the world, the state, and the law. Al-Mas'udi's seven-part version had already emphasized the element of law and had introduced the realm or kingdom as the context for justice, but the eight sentences expanded the context to the whole world. These three elements provided the context in which justice was to be carried out: a world-state, or a world of states, governed by law. On this foundation and within these boundaries the king was to perform his functions, feed his armies, raise his taxes, and satisfy his people. The word used for law, *sunna*, meant custom or precedent, referring to the divinely guided behavior of the Prophet Muhammad and his community rather than to a specific code of laws. The "hedged garden" of the world was a pasture, and the word for people, *ra'iyya*, was derived from "flock." In one corner of this garden hungry dragons (bringers of drought and devastation) howled to be fed, and the people had to produce food for the dragon army as well as for themselves. Justice, administered by the shepherd-king, kept the dragons in their corner and allowed the garden and all its inhabitants to prosper. The garden was thus the rural or pastoral counterpart of the Platonic city as the locus of politics.[54] This portrait of the realm as a garden made fertile by justice coincided in time with the similar portrait painted by Firdausi, and it soon became a stock image in Islamic art and poetry. Rulers even planted flourishing gardens as symbols of their just rule and traveled to them in rotation, like the sun.[55]

Uses of the eight-line Circle

The existence of several different versions of the eight sentences in *The Secret of Secrets* suggests a multiplicity of earlier sources no longer extant. As with the four-line version, the origins of this longer version are obscure but its uses can be traced. The eight sentences were anthologized by numerous writers, collectors of fine sayings as well as compilers of advice to kings. They became popular first in Spain, spreading eastward over time.[56] Ibn Juljul of Andalusia quoted them in Cordoba around 980 in a biography of Aristotle for his book *The Generations of Physicians and Sages*, according to which Aristotle before his death had these eight sentences written around an eight-sided dome.[57] Another Cordoban, the qadi Ibn 'Abd al-Barr, identified them as a Persian saying attributed to Aristotle and included them along with the four-line version in an *adab* collection he compiled in the eleventh century. The early twelfth-century author al-Muradi of Qayrawan also quoted them in his book of advice on the conduct of rulership written for the Almoravid rulers of North Africa.[58] They appeared around 1050 among the sayings of Aristotle in an *adab* anthology from Cairo, the *Choice Wise Sayings and Fine Statements* of al-Mubashshir ibn Fatik, who used the version replacing the "king" with the "imam."[59] Eastern writings apparently did not include the eight sentences until some centuries later, although they often quoted the four-line version.

The Buyid philosopher and historian Miskawayh (932–1030), without quoting the Circle of Justice, developed a concept of justice that harmonized with it.[60] Miskawayh assimilated Persian, Greek, Indian, Arabic, and Islamic political concepts; he knew the wisdom literature of pre-Islamic times and preserved the sayings of Anushirvan and the testament of Aristotle.[61] He saw justice in Greek philosophical terms as an equilibrium, a balance among potentially opposing forces, but this concept had a number of consequences that interlocked with the Circle.[62] Contributing to the prosperity of the state formed "the essence of 'political justice'." The idea of equilibrium was equally powerful on the social level: social stability rested on a balance of interests among people unequal in power, and doing justice meant maintaining that balance.[63] It was the duty of the government to oversee social justice, providing protection, education, and care for productive activities. Like Miskawayh, many authors of the period valued justice above the identity or even the personal faith of the ruler, quoting the saying, "The realm will endure with unbelief but not with injustice."[64]

A history of the Iranian city of Qumm written in 988 gives evidence that Buyid society envisioned the concept of justice as a preservation of the social balance of power, not only in the theoretical and literary context but in the realm of ordinary practice. Its author, Hasan Qummi, listed eight revenue surveys of Qumm made between 804 and 914, some of them in response to petitions by the inhabitants.[65] He noted that officials took care to record measurements accurately and to secure the agreement of cultivators and landlords to the amounts assessed, because they believed that strict adherence to the assessments constituted justice in taxation. Peasants and landowners typically employed the concept of justice to avoid payment or to obtain lower assessments by pleading poverty and demanding relief from oppression. On lands not subject to regular assessment, in contrast, peasants had no recourse against landlords' revenue demands. As exploitative as the state might be, its ideology of justice and the regular intervention of its surveyors and officials gave peasants leverage against their landlords' exactions or officials' overcollection. In the Buyid period, however, the state administration was not large enough or sophisticated enough to perform surveys throughout its territory often enough to allow peasants to bring that leverage into play.[66]

Caliphs, power, and justice (945–1055)

While philosophers discoursed on balance and ulema proclaimed the primacy of religion, the actual division of power between caliph and *amir* tended to subordinate the religious to the secular.[67] The early Buyid *amirs* held the Abbasid caliphs in their grip, deposing some, seizing their treasury, providing small and irregular stipends, assuming their prerogatives, and giving them orders they could not refuse. But the later Buyids were weaker rulers, often absent from Baghdad, and the caliphs began to be able to exercise some limited authority.[68] They received support from the Sunni Ghaznavids, who established themselves in Afghanistan and in 1029 attacked the Buyids in Iran. Although the Ghaznavids were subsequently less successful, the rising Oghuz Turks took up the caliph's cause. With their backing, the caliphs obtained somewhat bigger and more regular stipends with which they could recruit a larger and more talented staff, wrest greater symbolic submission from the Buyids (who needed caliphal support in their internecine struggles and against the Fatimids), and exert firmer control over religious taxation and the appointment of religious and judicial personnel. The emerging balance legitimated in practice the division of responsibility between the heirs of "true prophecy" and "royal authority" that the philosophers had earlier theorized.

Members of the caliphal court of al-Qa'im (1031–75) wrote several works in the late Buyid period discussing the roles and responsibilities of caliphs, *amirs*, and other officials in the new order.[69] Among these were *The Ordinances of Government* by al-Mawardi (974–1058) and the *Rules of the Caliphal Court* by Hilal al-Sabi' (969–1056), both written before 1055. These works contributed to a reformulation of the position and responsibilities of the caliphate within an Islamic state. They both continued to sanction a division of power between caliph and *amir*, though they wished to alter its terms. Together they reveal how thoroughly the Circle of Justice and Near Eastern kingship had been assimilated into Islamic political thought.

Al-Mawardi and the caliph's responsibilities

Al-Mawardi, a teacher, qadi, and representative of the caliph to the later Buyid *amirs*, presented an analysis of government in terms of Islamic law in his book, *The Ordinances of Government.*[70] He wrote this book at the point when the caliphs, having lost almost all their power to the Buyids, were beginning to take it back again, "that he [the caliph] may know the views of the jurists as to those ordinances which define his rights, that he may exact them in full."[71] Al-Mawardi couched his analysis of the caliphate, succession to office, delegation of responsibility, and the conduct of war, pilgrimage, and prayer in terms of Islamic history and legal tradition. In his view, the caliph united succession to the Prophet with kingship or royal authority, ruling in accordance with Islamic law and public welfare and supplementing Islamic law with government regulation where it was incomplete, since religion and state were twins. An *amir* or commander-in-chief, though holding full authority in state affairs, must be subordinate to the caliph and must maintain the religion and law of Islam.[72]

When al-Mawardi enumerated the caliph's duties, however, the ideas of the Circle of Justice came to the fore. The execution of justice was high on the list of duties, along with defense of the frontiers, provision of security, appointment of capable officials, collection of taxes and their proper disbursement, and good administration.[73] Al-Mawardi directed the caliph to adhere to official registers in setting the salaries of officials and the levels of peasant taxation, enjoining him to "curb the strong from riding on the weak, and encourage the weak to take his due in face of the strong."[74] Although these duties are usually discussed within a framework of early Islamic precedent, their dependence on the Near Eastern idea of kingship virtually leaps from the page. The Near Eastern concept of state had become so well assimilated in Islamic thought by this time that al-Mawardi, like Abu Yusuf, unquestioningly accepted its values and priorities as constituting good government. He mentioned Persian precedents only in connection with specific practical matters, such as the taxation of the former Sasanian crown lands, irrigation works and reclamation of waste land, coinage, and the practice of justice in the ruler's court (*mazalim*).[75] If indeed al-Mawardi employed in this work only Islamic legal sources, as is said, then the ideals of the Circle of Justice were deeply embedded in the corpus of Islamic law.[76]

Beyond his studies of the Qur'an and Islamic institutions, al-Mawardi's advice works reveal his familiarity with the elements of that genre, including the Circle of Justice and its centrality to Islamic politics. Numerous manuals of ethics and behavior either written by him or attributed to him – two for kings, two for viziers, one long one for judges, and two for the common people – quoted ideas on justice from Greek and Persian kings and philosophers as well as Islamic sources.[77] *The Royal Gift on Political Etiquette* included the Circle itself, along with stories about kings like David and Anushirvan. *Rules for the Vizierate* quoted Plato in introducing its central theme, the concept of justice.[78] Through these works, addressed to all segments of society, al-Mawardi sought to recreate a godly political life in the Muslim realm.

Courts of Justice: Mazalim *justice beyond Islamic law*

One of the greatest accolades al-Mawardi could bestow upon a ruler was that he attended to justice through the *mazalim* court. The term *mazalim* meant acts of injustice, and this court institutionalized the ruler's duty to right wrongs of oppression – especially those committed by his own officials – and to redress the grievances of the people.[79] It was the place where the taxpayers of the Circle could seek the Circle's justice. *Mazalim* justice was not part of the regular legal system but a public service; the *mazalim* courts operated beside and outside the jurisdiction of Islamic law, accepted cases not covered by the shariah, and dispensed with shariah rules of procedure. At times this could lead to a real tug of war between the two judicial systems, a conflict whose outcome clearly indicated the balance of power between civil government and the religious establishment.[80] More often, the two courts divided responsibility between them.

The types of cases people brought to the *mazalim* court included crimes against the state or by the state, crimes for which Islamic law had no ruling, and cases decided in shariah courts whose verdicts the qadis could not enforce. Among these were acts of injustice or tyranny perpetrated by the ruler or his governors; injustice in the levying of taxes or the behavior of bureaucratic officials; claims for pay on the part of troops or for property taken by force, either by an official or by a private person; and demands for enforcement of laws and decisions that had been ignored. Certain types of cases could be heard by governors or other responsible officials; others were reserved for the ruler himself. Most cases dealt with taxation or official injustice, and the Abbasids had a special treasury for money recovered from officials found guilty of oppression.[81] The ruler's hearing cases in person was a mark of a just sovereign, and the hearing of *mazalim* was taken as a sign of legitimacy. Alexander the Great is supposed to have declared that any day on which no one came to obtain justice could not be counted as a day of his reign.[82]

In the ancient Near East, rulers had usually heard *mazalim* cases in person at regular intervals, and we have seen the responses of Hammurabi and other rulers to these cases. According to al-Mawardi, while the Prophet may have decided such cases occasionally, the Umayyad ʻAbd al-Malik was the first Muslim ruler to establish a regular day for *mazalim* court; the ceremonies opening court sessions included the recitation of poetry about justice. Muʻawiya received petitions and complaints of injustice both informally in the mosque and formally in the palace. The Abbasids established a government bureau to collect (and later hear) petitions, and Abbasid caliphs, viziers, governors, and qadis held *mazalim* court with increasing frequency. Harun al-Rashid had to be urged to hold court once a month, or at least once a year, and Caliph al-Hadi (785–6) incurred criticism "for not receiving petitions and hearing complaints (*mazalim*) for three whole days," but most tenth-century rulers regularly sat in *mazalim* once or twice a week. The caliphal palace in Baghdad's city center, where court was held, symbolized the caliph's accessibility as well as his authority, and when the caliphs moved their residence to Samarra they probably received petitions at the palace gate. The Samanids had a special official, the *amir-i dad*, to supervise the *mazalim* court. Qudama ibn Jaʻfar's *Book of Taxation and the Scribal Art* had an entire section on *mazalim* court procedure, the behavior of the judge and court scribes, and the storage and retrieval of petitions and information.[83]

Some areas admitted *mazalim* as part of Islamic law; where the Maliki legal school prevailed, a qadi court under a separate *mazalim* judge tried cases outside the regular legal system. The first evidence of such a court comes from North Africa in the year 851. In Muslim Spain, *mazalim* judges dealt with complaints against officials and cases which could not be satisfactorily resolved under the shariah. In Sicily the *mazalim* court remained in operation even after the Norman conquest, presided over by Roger II (1095–1154), "where the oppressed could take their complaints and seek justice, even against his own son." In areas outside caliphal jurisdiction, the duty of dispensing *mazalim* justice fell on *amirs* and sultans, who sometimes delegated it to a vizier or qadi. At least once, a woman was appointed to hear *mazalim* cases, and some Muslim scholars felt there to be no intrinsic gender bar.[84]

The Buyids usually delegated the *mazalim* courts to subordinates, but the Fatimids exalted *mazalim* justice, as their caliph was the source of legal interpretation, "the infallible oracle in all matters, temporal and spiritual."[85] The exercise of *mazalim* by the caliphs or their officials was highly esteemed.[86] The Fatimid political testament recorded by Qadi al-Nu'man called the judicial office "the balance of God's justice which He has established on earth to vindicate the offended against the offender, to defend the weak against the strong"; it urged rulers to hear the grievances of the people and lighten their tax burden in times of distress and recommended that judges not be impatient, "get angry with the contenders, or be exasperated at the halting speech of stammerers."[87] Ibn al-Sayrafi, author of a Fatimid treatise on bureaucracy, saw the people's petitions as improving the state's reputation by bringing injustices to the attention of the ruler, initiating investigations, and promoting the good behavior of officials.[88] All sorts of people used the *mazalim* court: Muslims and non-Muslims, city dwellers and country folk, rich and poor sent petitions or brought their cases to the court in Cairo and obtained responses to their pleas.

Considerable information exists about Fatimid *mazalim* procedures because, in addition to detailed descriptions in secretarial manuals, a number of petitions and rulers' responses have survived. The Fatimids probably invented the petition format used in later times; Abbasid and earlier petitions took the form of a simple letter. People presented petitions at court either orally or in writing, or they handed their written petitions to the caliph when he processed through the city. When court was in session, the caliph or his official either made a decision on the spot or requested the governor or qadi to investigate the case. A "secretary of the thin pen" recorded the decision on the back or in the margin of the petition, and the "secretary of the thick pen" put it into proper formal wording. The secretaries also made a permanent record in the chancery and, if necessary, composed a decree regarding the problem, returning the annotated petition to the petitioner as evidence of the court's decision. Petitions from this period concerned cases of murder and theft, loans and debts, forced labor, conflicts over offices, construction of a synagogue, repair of churches, land seizure, Bedouin raids and harm to pilgrims, renewal of privileges for the monastery of St. Catherine in the Sinai, onerous new taxes, and sectarian strife.[89]

Although the rules and practices of the *mazalim* court closely followed the Sasanian example, the concept was so popular that everyone wanted to claim it. Muslim authors like al-Mawardi ascribed the *mazalim* court to early Arab customs as part of the role of the tribal chieftain and of the Prophet in his governing capacity, regarding Persian precedents as merely analogous. The "Letters of Aristotle to Alexander," by contrast, appealed to Greek values in recommending the establishment of such a court.[90]

Justice in the royal court: al-Sabi'

Quite different from al-Mawardi's work was another important treatise on the caliphal prerogative, *The Rules of the Caliphal Court* by Hilal al-Sabi'.[91] Like al-Mawardi, Hilal recorded the ordinances surrounding the caliphate as a foundation for the renewal of Abbasid prestige; his book described caliphal court ceremony and etiquette. Hilal al-Sabi' was not a qadi but a caliphal secretary, and the ordinances he recorded were not those of Islamic or caliphal law but those of court protocol and the scribal art. He described the rules for attendance at court; the proprieties of dress and ceremony; and the correct form for writing letters. Many of the ordinances of the Abbasid court, although attributed to Muslim caliphs and courtiers, were derived from ancient practices; he saw justice as one of the pillars of the caliph's court. In his opening praises of the caliph al-Qa'im, al-Sabi' acknowledged that God, whose deeds were "based on justice and truth and in full accord with wisdom and the public interest," had chosen al-Qa'im as his vicegerent. The family of the Prophet, to which al-Qa'im belonged, guarded religion and preserved order, protected the people and defended the needy. The Buyid *amirs* meanwhile were described as obedient to God and conquerors of "enemy lands difficult to conquer;" they "built mosques, dug rivers and sought the welfare of all the provinces." These terms, so similar to those with which the Assyrian and Sasanian kings were described, incorporated Islamic juristic concepts into a framework based on Near Eastern political thought. An imperial ruler guarded and guided by God would care for his people as the Circle recommended: "He would encompass the East and the West with justice, as he has filled them with abundant favor; and he shall pervade them with beautiful works as he has extended his beneficence over them."[92]

The literature of the period disseminated the Circle of Justice beyond the court to the wider society, where it became part of the heritage of the literate in all walks of life and a theme in popular oral literature as well. The four-line version even appeared in the *Thousand and One Nights* in a story about Anushirvan that resembled the tale of Bahram and the owls relayed by al-Mas'udi. This version depicted Anushirvan as wanting to restore ruined villages but being unable to find any in his realm, having been instructed by his ministers, "Religion (is) by kingship and kingship by the army and the army by revenue and revenue by the prosperity of the country and the prosperity of the country by justice to the people."[93] This story, like other contexts in which the Circle of Justice was quoted, would be repeated frequently in the literature of the Islamic world in times to come.

Conclusion

Although the concepts of the Circle of Justice had originated with the historic Near Eastern state, by the eleventh century they were so well integrated into Islamic political thinking that they could appear even in court literature without being justified by stories about Persian rulership. Many jurists accepted them as the ordinary description of good government, not needing to be attributed to pre-Islamic sources but fully in harmony with Qur'anic pronouncements and Islamic precedents. Philosophers saw them as the results of the application of a justice conceived in Greek terms as a balance of opposing forces. The formulations of men of religion like Abu Yusuf and al-Mawardi contradict Gibb's opinion that the ideals of Near Eastern kingship formed an indigestible "kernel of derangement" in Islamic political thought.[94]

The Circle of Justice itself was enunciated in its four-part form in a variety of settings, embroidered with pastoral or imperial imagery, and ascribed to different speakers, both Persian and Arab. Its more elaborate eight-part form was usually credited to the Greek heritage, a source of valuable ideas and information on numerous scientific and political topics. Through these means Muslims appropriated and Islamicized the Near Eastern state tradition in its Persian incarnation, merging it with Greek political ideas and those derived from the political experience of the Muslim community to create a new concept of universal kingship. This new kind of rule accorded with Qur'anic values but at the same time had the capacity to control an empire.[95]

The Near Eastern concept of state, which had developed over many centuries through repeated conquests and changes in the ruling group, embodied the demands made by agrarian citied society on imperial rulers and vice versa, and shaped the structures and activities through which those demands could be met. These structures now included caliphal and non-caliphal imperial governments and rulers' *mazalim* courts, together with the legitimation for cooperation between religious and non-religious authorities. Attempting to return to the governing style of the early community would have required the Muslims to divest themselves of their empire and go back to a tribal organization. Instead they regarded their empire as evidence of God's choice of the Muslims for governance and embraced Near Eastern political ideas, modifying them to their own purposes and imbuing them with their own ethos. Many of the ordinances of the Abbasid court, although attributed to Muslim caliphs and courtiers, derived from ancient practices. Such ordinances, as Hilal al-Sabi' stated, constituted not only proper behavior toward a powerful monarch but also "a path to the appreciation of the glory that Allah has given to the Hashemite cause and to the prestige of the Abbasid caliphate." An imperial ruler guarded and guided by God would not merely achieve success and renown for himself or his dynasty but would care for his people as the Circle recommended. "He would encompass the East and the West with justice, as he has filled them with abundant favor; and he shall pervade them with beautiful works as he has extended his beneficence over them."[96]

Beyond the literary arena, the institutionalization of administrative mechanisms for providing justice enabled the productive classes of society to press their interpretation of justice and their demands for redress. Peasants and townspeople used petitions and *mazalim* courts to request reassessment of taxes and punishment of corrupt and tyrannous officials; they understood quite well the procedures by which the Circle of Justice could be invoked. The *Thousand and One Nights* reflected this understanding in numerous stories telling how the petitions of common people, especially the poorest and most helpless of them, called unjust princes to rectitude.[97] Although the Turkish and Mongol invaders of the next two centuries brought both the Abbasid and the Fatimid caliphates to an end, they themselves developed a concept of state that incorporated Turco-Mongol values into the Perso-Arabic synthesis that had already been created, a synthesis that upheld the shariah and was in harmony with the Circle of Justice.

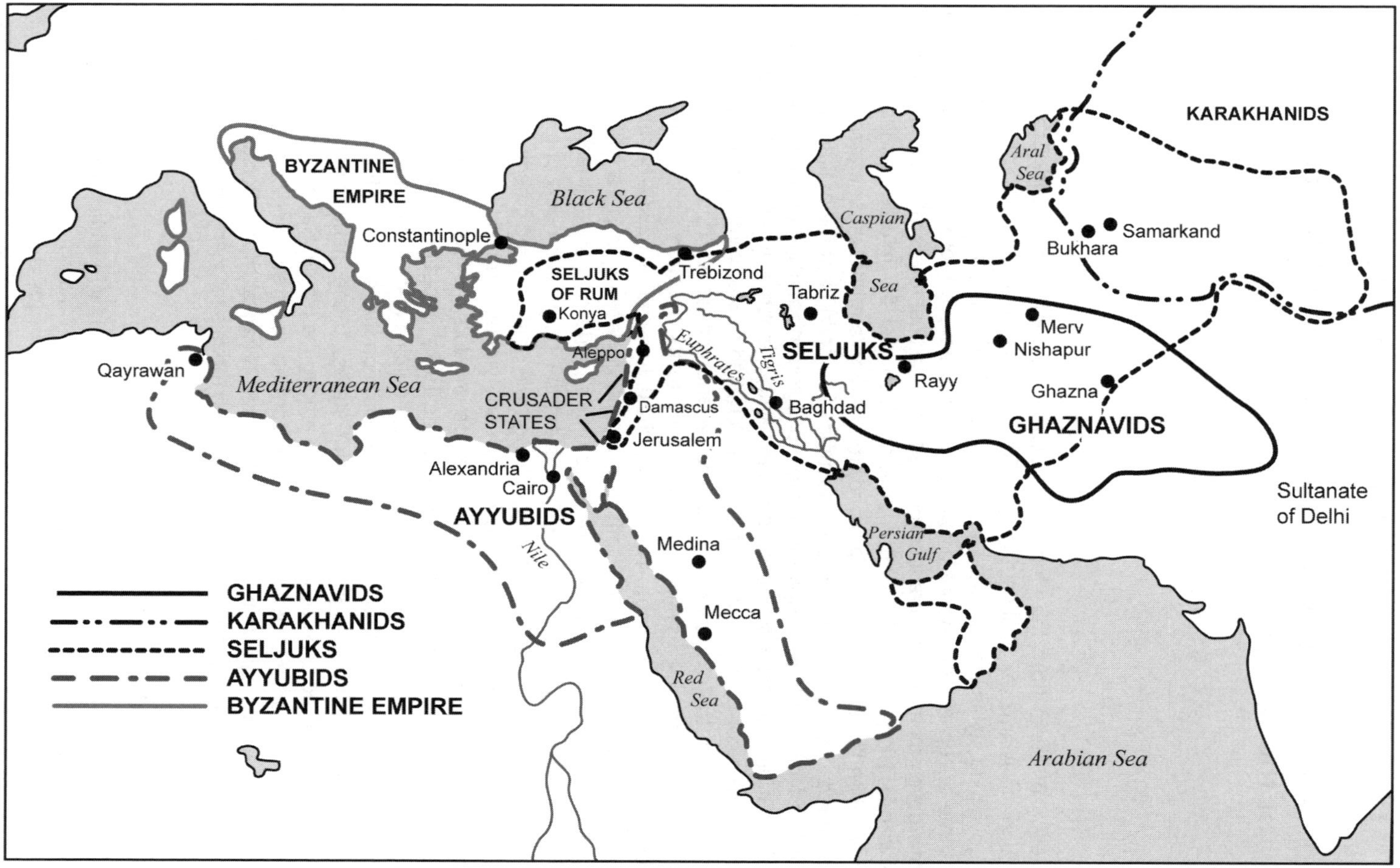
KARAKHANIDS
BYZANTINE
EMPIRE
Black Sea
Caspian
Sea
Aral
Sea
Samarkand
Bukhara
Constantinople
Trebizond
SELJUKS
OF RUM
Konya
Tabriz
Merv
Nishapur
Aleppo
Euphrates
Tigris
SELJUKS
Rayy
Qayrawan
Mediterranean Sea
Ghazna
CRUSADER
STATES
Damascus
Baghdad
GHAZNAVIDS
Jerusalem
Alexandria
Cairo
Sultanate
of Delhi
AYYUBIDS
Persian
Gulf
Nile
Medina
Mecca
Red
Sea
Arabian Sea
GHAZNAVIDS
KARAKHANIDS
SELJUKS
AYYUBIDS
BYZANTINE EMPIRE

Map 5 Turkish empires through the Seljuks

6 The Turks and Islamic civilization

"The most penetrating of arrows is the prayer of the oppressed"

The entry of Turks from the steppes of Central Asia into the Middle East gave new directions to Islamicate political thought. The process of acculturating them to sedentary governing styles brought the Circle of Justice to the fore in political culture and life. For some observers, the Abbasid caliphate would always represent the high point of Islamic government, but others incorporated new political forms into their definitions of Islamic rule. History textbooks often omit or gloss over the middle periods of Islamic history, when the once-unified Islamic realm split into a multitude of states with fluctuating boundaries, governed in different fashions for varying lengths of time, and often at war with each other. New peoples invaded the region, introducing their own cultures and politics but also destroying documents and killing members of the old regimes whose job it was to record events for posterity. They created new governing institutions whose differences from the old were seen as decline and corruption. It is fatally easy just to skip over these troubled times and go directly to the modern period, where politics again takes on a familiar shape. Yet it was in these tumultuous middle centuries that the Circle of Justice proved its worth both as a governing ideology and as a way to introduce outsiders from nomad societies to the structures of sedentary government.

Modern stereotypes do not generally present the Turks as models of justice, and at first medieval Muslims, too, saw the governing style of the nomadic peoples as clashing with the Perso-Arabic synthesis they had already worked out. Yet similarities between ideas of social organization and justice that the invaders brought from the steppes and aspects of the Near Eastern state facilitated the Turks' adoption of Near Eastern forms and concepts of governance. The Seljuk Turkish sultans and their officials succeeded in creating institutions of justice and good administration that outlasted the regime itself to become standard practices in its successor states. These institutions and the ideas behind them achieved wide acceptance, even among the ulema. Seljuk authors produced great literary and artistic vehicles of that integrated understanding, including the two most well-known statements of the Circle of Justice, Nizam al-Mulk's *Book of Government* and al-Ghazali's *Counsel for Kings*, which became models for many later regimes.

Early Turkish empires (522–1186)

The Turks originated in southern Siberia and gained their livelihood through pastoral nomadism, raiding, and trade.[1] Mobility and superb archery gave them a military advantage that, when they were unified, could outweigh the superior numbers and weaponry of the sedentary empires on their borders. They were unified only rarely, however, as their tribal structure and the division of territory among the ruler's sons caused their politics to alternate between fragile confederations, easily dissolved, and brief periods of strong charismatic rule. Through interaction with the Persians and Chinese, the Turks developed an imperial ideology of their own, adapted to a nomadic culture and shamanic religion but sharing several features with the concept of the Circle of Justice. During the short-lived Kok Turk Empire of the early eighth century they recorded this ideology in the Orkhon inscriptions, carved in runes on a group of royal tombstones along the Orkhon River in Siberia.

Justice and Turkish tribalism

The Orkhon inscriptions advised the Turks to unite under a single supreme tribal ruler, the *khagan*, who belonged to the charismatic ruling family, controlled the sacred homeland, and was successful as a conqueror. The Turkish *khagan*, like his Mesopotamian, Persian, and Chinese counterparts, received divine appointment to his position. In the Orkhon inscriptions Bilge Khagan (d.734) declared that "since Heaven was gracious, and since I was granted with fortune, I succeeded to the throne."[2] All members of the Turkish ruling family inherited the charisma of rulership, and their "presence assured the good fortune of heaven."[3] The Turks characterized the *khagan*'s dominion in terms reminiscent of the Assyrian inscriptions, despite vast differences in their society and culture: he ruled "all the peoples in the four quarters of the world," extending "eastwards to the sunrise, southwards to the mountains, westwards as far as the sunset, and northwards to the midnight."[4]

Military victory maintained their independence, but it was also the route to prosperity. Prosperity in this pastoral society did not depend on the fertility of the earth or the abundance of water through rain or irrigation. It resulted from numbers and organization, which determined the amount of grazing land the society could control and the size of its flocks and herds. The Orkhon inscriptions repeatedly brought together organization, victory, and the nourishment of the people as responsibilities of Turkish rulers, and cited organization as the primary achievement of successful leaders.[5]

After uniting the tribes, establishing the law was the *khagan*'s most important function. The ruler's law, the law of his own tribe, became the law for all under his control. Rulers' revival of laws and customs brought victory, increase in numbers, and control of territories and grazing grounds: "In accordance with the state rules, my uncle succeeded to the throne … he organized and nourished the Turkish people anew." The goal of this effort was prosperity for the people; as Bilge Khagan boasted, "I did not become ruler over a wealthy and prosperous people at all; on the contrary, I became ruler over a poor and miserable people who were foodless in the inside and clothless on the outside. I furnished the naked people with clothes and I made the poor people rich and the few people numerous. I made them superior to the peoples who have great states and esteemed rulers."[6] This ideology contained elements of the Circle of Justice, although nomadic politics lacked the bureaucracy and legal institutions of the Middle Eastern empires.

In the mid-eighth century, however, the Turkish empire fragmented again, and over the ninth and tenth centuries the Tahirid and Samanid governors conquered southern Central Asia for the Abbasids. The frontier Turks converted to Islam in the tenth century. Like the Abbasids, the Samanids employed Turkish war captives and slaves as pages, palace guards, and soldiers, an old Assyrian practice, and since they were treated well and had access to power they assimilated rapidly. Turkish slave soldiers were the most important body of troops in the Samanid army, and they soon became officers and political actors.[7] As the Samanid grip weakened in the late tenth century, some Turkish generals and governors made their power hereditary and created new polities in the Middle East.

The Ghaznavids and ruler's justice

The most successful of the Samanids' Turkish generals were the Ghaznavids in Afghanistan (999–1186), where Sebuktegin and his son Mahmud (999–1030) created an independent sultanate with its capital at Ghazna. Their humble origins as steppe warriors and Samanid slaves, said the historian Bayhaqi (995?–1077?), made God's choice of the Ghaznavids as sovereigns especially poignant.[8] A universal history written by the courtier Tha'alibi around 1020, *The Splendors of the Lives of the Kings*, compared the Ghaznavids to Alexander the Great, who came out of relative obscurity to conquer the known world. This history, like the contemporary *Shahnama* and the slightly earlier *Secret of Secrets*, compared Iran to a royal garden inhabited by subjects, protected by troops, and maintained by the treasury. Tha'alibi's depiction of the pre-Islamic Persian kings, though it drew on many of the same sources as Firdausi's, was less a celebration of their magnificence than a demand for royal virtue, the pairing of kingship and religion. The four-line Circle of Justice of Ardashir, the first Sasanian monarch, was his first quotation and represented also a call for justice from the Ghaznavids.[9]

The Ghaznavids were familiar with the Circle of Justice, but they seemed to have some difficulty putting it into practice. Sebuktegin patterned his rule on the Perso-Arabic administration of the Abbasids and Samanids, employing Samanid officials and maintaining Abbasid court practices and ideologies. A treatise of counsel he left for his son Mahmud alluded to the Circle of Justice in a definition of good rulership resembling that of the Samanid historian Bal'ami: "The first thing you should do is to keep the private and public treasuries in a prosperous condition; for a kingdom can only be retained by wealth. If you do not possess money, gold, or wealth, nobody [i.e. no troops] will obey you. Wealth cannot be acquired except by good government and wise statesmanship, and good government cannot be achieved except through justice and righteousness." In Sebuktegin's opinion, the most important aspect of justice was legality in taxation and strict control of extortionate revenue collectors. Sebuktegin counselled Mahmud on the proper use of power: "You should encourage needy persons to approach you, and avenge the oppressed on their oppressors."[10]

Sebuktegin became known as "The Just Amir," and stories were told of his justice and forbearance. Mahmud, as an ideal king, held a daily *mazalim* court to administer justice and redress grievances; his vizier also held court every day.[11] The Ghaznavids sought legitimacy through construction, building bridges, mosques, and irrigation channels; an arch resembling the Hall of Khusrau and a monumental inscription in the rhythm of the *Shahnama* suggested the Circle of Justice more directly.[12] They also imitated the Samanids' Sunni orthodoxy, waging war against the Shi'i Buyids and the pagans of India. Shortly after Mahmud's death, the historian 'Utbi (d.1036 or 1040) wrote a panegyric history of his and Sebuktegin's reigns, haloing them with a coruscation of Persian-style royal imagery and praising their justice.[13] Their successors tried to appear as dispensers of justice by following their example, holding regular court and occasionally remitting taxes.

At bottom, however, most Ghaznavid sultans seemed more interested in wealth than in justice; while painting themselves as just rulers, they oppressed their subjects beyond endurance. Under the onerous taxation that funded the conquests, the common people played an increasingly passive role as "sheep" whose part was not to engage in political activity but merely to pay. In fact, Sultan Mahmud rebuked the people of Balkh for resisting Karakhanid attacks and blamed them for the city's destruction, while he praised Nishapur for paying its taxes to whichever military group gained victory.[14] Sultan Ibrahim was depicted as being oblivious to a famine in his capital under his very window until the city was nearly depopulated, saying "Why did you not inform us?" and fearing that rival kings would slander him, not for indifference but for the "great shame" of being too poor to feed his subjects. People transferred the tale of the owls hooting in the ruined village from the Sasanians to the Ghaznavids. Poetry for these rulers warned them to balance conquest with prosperity. Controlling unjust officials was part of the ruler's justice, but the histories were filled with stories of rapacious officials and their executions. The tension between ideal and reality became a major concern for historians. Bayhaqi made references to Alexander the Great and Ardashir, but only to draw a new and ironic parallel with the Ghaznavids. Their conquests and their justice were great, he said, but they are gone; Sebuktegin also made conquests and exercised justice, and may the Ghaznavids last forever …[15] The Ghaznavids seem to have adopted the outward forms of Perso-Arabic governance without the substance.[16]

Justice and good administration distinguished divinely assisted rulers from tyrants and usurpers. But a new social ideal arose, combining the military victory of the ancient kings with the call to Islam of the recent past: the ideal of the *ghazi*, the warrior for the faith. The nomadic Turkish influx may have propelled this shift toward heroic values; despite their conversion and adoption of Perso-Arabic culture the Ghaznavids still spoke Turkish, clung to steppe values, and sponsored Turkish immigration from Central Asia.[17] *Ghazi* warriors formed a significant component of the Samanid army, and when the fall of the Samanids and the conversion of the steppe Turks ended "holy war" in Transoxiana, *ghazi* fighters rushed westward to the Byzantine frontier or southward to join Ghaznavid raids on idol-worshippers in India.[18] By this time, Central Asia had developed an Islamicate culture with numerous ties to the Middle East.

The Karakhanids and royal glory

The Near Eastern idea of justice expressed in eleventh-century Ghaznavid literature reached the Turks of the steppe under the Karakhanid dynasty (999–1165). At the eastern Karakhanid capital of Kashghar (western China) in 1069–70, the court chamberlain Yusuf Khass Hajib composed a long Turkish work of political advice entitled *Wisdom of Royal Glory*, detailing the qualities necessary for a strong, stable kingdom. Yusuf's accomplishment was to make Perso-Arabic statecraft compatible with both Islam and the Turkish concept of kingship. His discussion of justice and his portrait of an ideal ruler, however, came straight from the Circle of Justice: "Troops are needed to maintain the state, and wealth is needed to pay the troops; a prosperous people is needed to attain this wealth, and for the people to be prosperous, you must maintain justice. If any one of these is lacking, all four are left behind, and when this occurs, princely rule disintegrates."[19] The ideal king was justice personified; his justice increased his territory and brought prosperity to the realm. His courtyard was the seat of justice, and he ruled through good administration: "The ruler takes control of his realm by the sword, and keeps it under control by the pen." He was expected to answer petitions, and Yusuf identified the chamberlain as the key official in the petition process: "Whether the indigent or widows or orphans present him with petitions, he [the chamberlain] must listen to one and all and present them to the prince … it is he who controls access of the petitioners."[20]

Yusuf paired Near Eastern and Islamic ideas of royal justice with Turkish concepts of organization and law that would generate prosperity and order: "The king straightened his heart from that time forth, and constantly laid down good law for his subjects. The people lived contented, the thin grew fat, his friends flourished, and his enemies grew weak."[21] The Karakhanids' amalgamation of Turkish and Near Eastern concepts of state seems to have been more thorough than that of the Ghaznavids, who adopted the Perso-Arabic tradition wholesale but failed to live up to it. As the book's translator pointed out, however, whatever influence *Wisdom of Royal Glory* had in Central Asia, it was not read by Turkish rulers in the Middle East.[22]

Seljuks and their advisors (1038–1318)

In the Middle East, Turkish rulers turned for advice to works in the New Persian language written by Persian scribes and the ulema, subjects of the Seljuks. The Seljuks (the family of Seljuk) led a group of islamicized Turks from the Oghuz tribal confederation into Ghaznavid Khurasan in the 1030s, moving on to conquer Iran, Iraq, Syria, and Anatolia. Local Persian elites became Seljuk advisors, exploiting their literary skills and knowledge of governance and culture. Their books of advice, quoting the Circle of Justice in various ways, became literary classics read all over the Muslim world from then on. The Seljuks were also more successful than earlier Turkish dynasties in developing institutions to enact the Circle's justice.

Invasion of the Seljuks

The Seljuk sultans, on conquering the Middle East, rapidly added Islamicate legitimation to that of the steppe. Coming from around the Caspian Sea, they were apparently familiar with urban institutions and Near Eastern ideology; they were members of the tribal elite, not the ignorant savages that contemporary and later historians painted them, and not all their followers were nomads.[23] When they took the Khurasanian capital of Nishapur in 1038, they immediately organized a state in the Near Eastern manner, appointing officials and adopting Islamic symbols of sovereignty. They were counseled to "render justice, and listen to those who have suffered tyranny," and indeed Tughril Beg (1040–63) was called "The Just Ruler" and presided over a *mazalim* court at Nishapur.[24] At the city of Merv he "sat in the seat of command and destroyed tyranny and injustice," and the letter he wrote to the caliph announcing his conquests reported that "justice had been established in Khurasan."[25]

After conquering most of Iran, the Seljuks reached Baghdad in 1055 and dispossessed the fragmented Buyids, stepping directly into the Buyid role as sultans, although they allowed the Abbasid caliphs a greater role.[26] They legitimated their conquest by restoring stability, providing justice, and supporting Sunni Islam and Persianate literary culture. Besides displacing their Shi'i predecessors and defeating the Fatimids, they opposed the Isma'ilis, who were trying to eliminate the Sunni leadership; an Isma'ili assassin killed the vizier Nizam al-Mulk by posing as a supplicant, taking advantage of his concern for petitioners.[27] The sultans replaced their Turkish tribal forces with a standing army of free and slave soldiers that provided an alternative power base to the ungovernable tribesmen.

It also gave rise to a "military patronage state," one in which power and its benefits flowed downward from the sultans and their personal troops through their patronage of weaker social groups.[28] Government servants, military and civilian, were remunerated by the continuation of a Buyid governing device, the *iqta*, a conditional grant of financial and administrative rights over land in return for service.[29]

The Seljuk sultans, aware that their strength now rested on the agrarian economy of the Middle East, channeled their tribal forces toward pasturelands in the Caucasus and Byzantine Anatolia, where they engaged in *ghaza*. Conquering Anatolia and Syria, the tribesmen added Fatimid and Byzantine practices to those of the Fertile Crescent and Iran to create new models of Islamic governance more cosmopolitan in culture and with a stronger nomadic element than in the central Middle East.[30] This cosmopolitanism could be seen in the walls of Konya, the Seljuk capital, which were decorated with reused inscriptions, reliefs, and ancient Greco-Roman statues taken from the Byzantines "with the sword of Khusrau" by Turkish sultans named after Persian heroes from the *Shahnama* and bearing the title of "Roman Caesar."[31] The Seljuks made Persian the literary language of Anatolia, and Persian histories and secretarial manuals transmitted Near Eastern concepts of administration and justice.[32]

Although the Seljuks adopted the languages and customs of the lands they conquered, they also, like the Ghaznavids, retained elements of tribal culture, such as the *tughra* or mark of sovereignty in the form of a bow and arrow on royal documents, the feasting of their followers at the royal table as a symbol of their ability to provide for their people, and most importantly the notion of the charismatic legitimacy of the entire ruling family, which led to repeated divisions of the realm among the dynasty's heirs; in later years the Seljuk realm split into separate sultanates. The battles for sovereignty rarely involved the general population, but they preoccupied the military class and heightened its dominance over government and society. Despite this in-fighting by the ruling class, Seljuk rule was a time of material growth and cultural florescence. Leading religious scholars wrote histories, mainly in the hope, as Ibn al-Athir put it, that "when the kings read in the history books about the biographies of just rulers and how they were highly esteemed by their subjects, they would try to follow their examples."[33] A Seljuk-period history of the province of Fars, the Sasanian homeland, quoted the four-line Circle of Justice in Arabic as the legacy of the Persian kings, bestowed on the Muslims through the marriage of Yazdagird's daughter with Muhammad's great-grandson.[34] With such an illustrious genealogy, the Circle had to be acknowledged as legitimately Islamic.

Another important vehicle for political ideas was imaginative literature. Since love was based on interdependence, romances became places where political virtues like justice were discussed. The essential relationship between the just ruler and his able vizier formed the theme of several sections of the five-part collection by Nizami (d.1203) called the *Quintet* (*Khamsa*), especially the epic of Alexander the Great and his quest for the Fountain of Life under the guidance of the capable but mysterious Khizr. Nizami also elaborated on justice in the other parts of the *Quintet*; in *The Seven Beauties*, for example, the king, as shepherd of his flock, brought to justice an unjust vizier who left the treasury empty, the troops unequipped, and the petitioners imprisoned. The *Quintet* also contained a critique of royal ethics, *The Treasury of Mysteries*, where the ruler's justice formed the point of several anecdotes, including stories of the tyrannical king and the truthful man, Sultan Sanjar and the old woman wrongly accused, and Anushirvan and his vizier, a retelling of al-Mas'udi's story of Bahram and the owls in which the birds turned Anushirvan to justice by enumerating how many ruined villages would result from his injustice.[35] "There's no tax on ruined villages," said a proverb recommending tax remissions in times of disaster that Nizami quoted in another anecdote.[36]

To acculturate their rulers to agrarian society, secretaries and officials turned out works of advice literature and mirrors for princes, seeking to harness Turkish military might to the task of constructing a politically centralized, religiously united, and administratively sophisticated Muslim polity – or, short of that, to secure the Turks' adherence to the amalgam of Islamic and Near Eastern practices and values that Muslim society had already produced.[37] The Seljuk sultans' adoption of sedentary culture and court protocol rapidly broke down the early cultural dichotomy between conquerors and subjects. Turkish political thought had analogies to the Perso-Arabic synthesis; agrarian administrative procedures and social structures differed greatly from tribal customs, but the steppe concepts of the ruler's divine appointment, charismatic leadership, and care for his people were similar to Near Eastern ideas.[38] Three Seljuk advice works are famous for their quotation of the Circle of Justice.

The Book of Ka'us

The first of these works of advice, the *Book of Ka'us*, or *Qabusnama*, was written in 1082 by Kai Ka'us (or Qabus), a descendant of the Ziyarid prince Mardavij who became a Seljuk vassal and governor of Tabaristan, south of the Caspian Sea. He depicted kingship in the Perso-Arabic style, quoting the sayings of Anushirvan and borrowing illustrations from Islamic history. Like Yusuf Khass Hajib he framed his advice within a story, a story of his son's need to practice a profession other than kingship. Within this frame story, he described ideal (or at least typical) behavior for different classes of court personnel as well as for people in various walks of life: trade, agriculture, the learned professions, and the religious sciences. On kingship he had only a brief chapter near the end of the book, since "it is a rarely acquired profession and not everyone attains to it." Much of his "advice" was actually a humorous exposé of the tricks and foibles of each craft and profession; his first precept on the conduct of kingship, for example, was to "keep eye and hand away from other Muslims' women-folk."[39] His intended audience for the book was clearly not just his own son but also people in other walks of life.

To aspiring kings Kai Ka'us recommended: "Be circumspect. never consent to injustice, and scrutinize every deed and word." Justice was inseparable from rulership, and Kai Ka'us, alluding to the Circle of Justice, advised the king to protect the taxpayers' livelihood: "In the same way that the people's submissiveness is secured by the soldiery, so the maintenance of the soldiery is made possible by the people. And it is through the people that the country is made prosperous, for the revenues are earned by the people, who remain settled and prosperous if given what is rightfully theirs. Therefore let there be no place in your heart for extortion." He addressed the vizier in more traditional terms: "Good government is secured by armed troops, armed troops are maintained with gold, gold is acquired through cultivation and cultivation is sustained through payment of what is due to the peasantry by just dealing and fairness."[40] Kai Ka'us recommended that a king should be ever truthful, secluded from public gaze, advised by a wise old vizier and well informed by spies, harsh with robbers and the disobedient but like a shepherd over his own people, generous with gifts and rewards, and diligent to keep everyone in his proper place and employment. Simultaneously practical and inspirational, the *Book of Ka'us* became widely popular and was translated into Turkish several times, carrying the Near Eastern concept of justice to new circles of readers.

The Book of Government, *or* Rules for Kings

The most well-known Persian advice work was the *Book of Government*, a mirror for princes attributed to the vizier Nizam al-Mulk (d.1092), who wrote it in response to a demand from Sultan Malikshah (1073–92). This work, which became a standard source for writers on good government and political justice, reflected a vision of kingship blending the concepts of the Circle of Justice with Islamic theories of governance in ways that might appeal to a steppe ruler.[41] The idea of God's granting kingship to a human being specially chosen and endowed belonged to Turkish belief as well as to Near Eastern theory, but it was the Muslim standard of righteousness, the "divine laws" and the "commands of The Truth," to which the king would answer on the day of resurrection. The *Book of Government* tied the Near Eastern and steppe concept of the provision of justice and prosperity to the Islamic concept of obedience to God: "It is for kings to observe His pleasure (His name be glorified) and the pleasure of The Truth is in the charity which is done to His creatures and in the justice which is spread among them." The image of the king as shepherd was also one with which a ruler of tribal origin could identify: "Caliphs and kings have always guarded the sheep from the wolves … [and] kept their officials in check."[42]

The author advised that the sultan was the shadow of God as much as the caliph, and that the subjects should "duly pass their time in the shadow of his justice." Unlike the caliph, he was not the sun, but he was "a taper from which many lamps have been lighted." No less than the caliph, the sultan must "be acquainted with the divine precepts and prohibitions and put them into practice," because "kingship and religion are like two brothers."[43] The just ruler chose his subordinates carefully, maintained the social order, restrained the inevitable aggression of his more powerful subjects, and worked toward prosperity through advancing civilization, "such as constructing underground channels, digging main canals, building bridges across great waters, rehabilitating villages and farms, raising fortifications, building new towns, and erecting lofty buildings and magnificent dwellings; he will have inns built on the highways and schools for those who seek knowledge."[44]

The first specific royal duty that the author listed was for the sultan to hold court twice a week for the redress of wrongs (*mazalim*), to hear subjects' complaints with his own ears and to accept written petitions. A chapter on judges, illustrated by the story of Yazdagird and the miraculous horse, explained the Sasanian practice of receiving petitions at Nawruz and the procedures for hearing cases against the king himself. The author expected the king's judgments to follow the shariah, and if he was ignorant of Islamic law he should appoint knowledgeable qadis as deputies. He must monitor viziers, tax collectors, and potential oppressors, going out personally in disguise to catch transgressors unaware, and must appoint spies and informers to investigate officials' injustices. The author summed up the Circle of Justice in his description of the good vizier: "When the vazir is of good character and sound judgment, the kingdom is prosperous, the army and peasantry are contented, peaceful, and well supplied, and the king is free from anxiety."[45]

Just as al-Mawardi's *Ordinances* had assimilated the Circle of Justice into a juristic analysis of the caliphate for a caliph trying to regain political power, so the *Book of Government* assimilated the Islamic shariah into a bureaucratic analysis of the Near Eastern state for a sultan trying to exercise political virtue.[46] Might did not make right; no matter how the ruler was chosen, the standard of rightness was set by Islamic law and its representatives, and the sultan's enforcement of justice produced prosperity and legitimacy, as the Circle of Justice described. On the basis of this integration of political ideas, religious scholars, who had previously scorned government service as corrupting, now began writing advice literature for rulers and assuming an active role in government.

The Book of Counsel for Kings

The first and most famous of these ulema advisors was al-Ghazali (1058-1111), to whom another great mirror for princes is attributed: *The Book of Counsel for Kings*, written for the Seljuk sultan.[47] There is some disagreement about which sultan, because the book's two parts have such different emphases that some scholars think they were written by different people.[48] However, al-Ghazali authored several books on politics and ethics, each within a different literary tradition and employing a different vocabulary and set of ideas; it is possible that he wrote two mirrors for different princes that were later combined into a single book. The fact that most readers of the *Counsel for Kings*, past and present, have regarded its two parts as a single whole shows how successfully ideas and practices with different starting points and motive forces were integrated into a unified political conception.

The second part of the *Counsel for Kings*, whose Arabic translation dedicated it to Sultan Muhammad ibn Malikshah (1104–18), described kingship in the style of the *Book of Government*, combining pre-Islamic and Islamic sources into a portrait of the ideal ruler. This part of the *Counsel for Kings* linked kingship with prophethood at the top of the human hierarchy: "To guide his slaves to Him, He sent prophets; and to preserve them from one another, He sent kings." Kingship depended on religion ("because monarchy and religion are like brothers"), but even more on justice, "for the Prophet stated that 'sovereignty endures even when there is unbelief, but will not endure when there is injustice'." The author understood the phrase "the Sultan is God's Shadow on earth" to mean "he is high-ranking and the Lord's delegate over His creatures," referring to status and power rather than shade or protection, but he quoted Anushirvan's definition of the most admired king, "the one of whom the enemies are most afraid, by whom the highways are kept most safe, and in the shadow of whose justice the subjects are best protected."[49]

The Circle's justice differentiated the civilized ruler from the leader of a warrior band, as had been seen many times before.

> The kings … whom we have mentioned all showed concern for justice; they developed the world and kept the troops under control through strict discipline. Remains of their buildings and works are still visible in the world, and every city is named after one or another king. They founded villages, excavated irrigation tunnels and brought out all the waters that were being wasted to give life to the land. The efforts of these kings to develop the world were made because they knew that the greater the prosperity, the longer would be their rule and the more numerous would be their subjects. They also knew that the sages had spoken rightly when they said: The religion depends on the monarchy, the monarchy on the army, the army on supplies, supplies on prosperity, and prosperity on justice.[50]

In the midst of change, continuity with past ruling practices was vitally necessary to preserve justice, and the ruins of older cities brought that continuity vividly to the eye. To attain the fame of the ancient kings, the ruler must adopt their behavior, including the Circle of Justice as quoted above. This section legitimated Muslim imitation of pre-Islamic rulers by recounting the just caliph al-Ma'mun's discovery of the tomb of Anushirvan and his endorsement of Anushirvan's advice.[51]

The first part of the *Counsel for Kings* was of a very different character. This part was probably composed for the young Sultan Sanjar (1118–57), remembered for his justice. It enumerated the roots and branches of the tree of faith and the springs that watered it; that is, the principles of the Muslim creed and the behaviors it entailed, including the ruler's adherence to the pillars of Islam and his justice toward his subjects. The concept of kingship was quite different from that in the second part of the book; the first part did not say that the sultan was appointed by God or superior to other men. After listing the ten "roots" or principles of Islam, the author turned to the ten "branches" or principles of justice, supporting each with Islamic sayings and anecdotes from Islamic rather than Persian history. He ignored the fruits of justice in this world to concentrate on its results in the next; the past was irrelevant except as a source of lessons. The just sultan was the first person to be sheltered by God on the day of resurrection and the unjust ruler the first to suffer hellfire, for the holders of authority were shepherds of God's sheep. The concept of sultanic justice in this section included the righteousness of the ruler, his supervision of his officials, and his care for the subjects, but not the connection of justice to irrigation and development, prosperity and civilization, or military victory. The motive for adhering to these ideals was not benevolence or worldly success but the transitoriness of life and the certainty of judgment: "The ruler should not disregard the attendance of petitioners at his court … for redressing the grievances of the Muslims is more meritorious than any work of supererogation."[52]

Al-Ghazali wrote a number of other books employing different traditions of political thought and different styles of writing. In works on the caliphate, he used al-Mawardi's description of caliphal duties in terms of the Circle of Justice.[53] His book on Sufism and the search for happiness, *The Scales of Action*, spoke of justice in philosophical terms as the harmonious order of the faculties and employed political justice, the ancient hierarchies of the state, as an analogy for the justice of the soul: "When a praiseworthy hierarchy is established between the king, his army and his subjects, a hierarchy manifested by the fact that the king is farseeing and dominant, the army is strong and obedient, and the people are docile and submissive, it is said that justice is established in that country."[54] The different classes of people had their proper places in society and their proper contributions to make toward its purpose, the realization of God's law. Kings provided order and harmony: "For this reason, it is said that 'Religion and temporal authority are twins'."[55] Besides demonstrating personal virtue, the sultans contributed by presiding over an administration that could put this advice into effect.

Justice and Seljuk administration

Works on the Seljuks – medieval and modern – sometimes read as if the ideals of the advice writers were descriptions of how the Seljuk government actually operated. There is, however, little hard evidence on the extent to which these ideals were carried out, although later eras remembered the Seljuks as just rulers. Government revenues increased over the Seljuk period, but this growth cannot be directly linked to state policies toward agriculture and the peasants, as no contemporary petitions or government documents exist.[56] Copies of some documents do survive in manuals compiled for secretaries, such as Juvayni's *The Writer's Threshold* and Baghdadi's *Introduction to the Art of Letter-Writing*.[57] Royal orders, usually those granting offices and *iqta*s, cited the Circle's concept of justice, which meant that it was not confined to intellectuals but was disseminated to all in official positions, as in this appointment order for a provincial governor: "The foundation of kingship and the basis of rulership consists in making the world prosperous; and the world becomes prosperous only through justice and equity; and the justice and equity of a ruler are attainable only through efficient governors of good conduct and officials of praiseworthy beliefs and laudable ways of life, and only so does prosperity reach the people of the world."[58] All who read the order, or heard it announced, learned this definition of justice. The order could then be used by superiors or inferiors to hold the official to account and make claims against him.

Governors and local officials were considered extensions of the ruler, who was accountable for their misbehavior or oppression. A governor's appointment order explained, "His actions … are tantamount to a decree and order from ourselves," and it commanded him to maintain order, collect taxes, and redress grievances.[59] Governors, military officers, and *iqta* holders were ordered to exercise *mazalim* justice within their jurisdictions as delegates of the ruler. Civilian officials called district heads oversaw the people's welfare; an appointment order for one district head warned him "not to allow … officials to oppress the people or the people to oppress one another" nor to "place the burden of the strong on the weak." Another such order widened access to justice by commanding the appointment of deputies in every city "so that the affairs of the subjects may be conducted with justice."[60] By delegating justice to their officials, the sultans sought to extend royal justice beyond their own courts to the remote corners of their realm.

Just taxation was the key to a peaceable relationship between rulers and people, and Seljuk documentary procedures aimed at making the revenue process run smoothly and predictably. Secretarial manuals describe the compilation of census and property registers that decided land rights and set just taxation levels.[61] Strict adherence to official registers was regarded as the foundation of just administration; an appointment document for an irrigation official ordered him to adhere to the records, to see that each person received his share of water, and to ensure that the strong did not oppress the weak.[62] Since overtaxation would ruin the countryside and reduce the ruler's revenue, tax remissions were often granted in cases of special distress or natural disaster.

A letter attributed to Nizam al-Mulk recommended care for irrigation, rivers, and springs so that all would receive their water rights; it said that since agriculture depended on scarce water supplies, to allow anyone to exercise tyranny over water would cause blessing and abundance to depart from the world. Accordingly, rulers and elites financed dams, canals, and irrigation works. Agricultural manuals affirmed that a flourishing agriculture was the foundation of prosperity, and in most of the Middle East agriculture depended on maintaining irrigation works and organizing water use and thus on the political will of the rich and powerful. The demand for stability created by this dependency was recognized at the highest levels; an appointment document from Sultan Sanjar proclaimed: "The stability of the empire and the ordering of the affairs of the kingdom are among the fruits of the spreading of justice and the dispensation of compassion."[63]

Enforcing Seljuk justice

The enforcement of justice depended, as in any society, on personal relationships and on the extent to which subordinates shared the ruler's ideology or feared his discipline.

Complaints from those experiencing injustice notified higher authorities of where that discipline should be brought to bear. Edicts in secretarial handbooks reveal that people regularly complained about harassment by raiders, crop failures, over-taxation, and oppression by royal officials, all expressed as problems that the ruler was bound to correct.[64] Although obtaining an audience was not easy or cheap, subjects had the right to present their grievances directly to the throne. To advertise that right, Sultan Malikshah sent heralds around, put up notice boards, and had preachers "proclaim from the pulpits that he would personally hear and investigate every complaint of injustice."[65] The partition of the empire and proliferation of smaller governments in the later Seljuk period probably improved peasants' access to redress of grievances, as it made rulers' courts less distant and less exalted. Connections to highly placed officials eased petitioners' access to rulers, and patronage ties between military and producing classes became an important political mechanism. If petitioning failed, peasants could use more direct means of protest, such as concealment of revenue, flight from the land, or even rebellion. Because such acts would reduce prosperity and lower the revenue, rulers had an interest in preventing them by commanding their officials to improve conditions and act justly.

The Seljuk legal system gave a prominent place to the administration of justice; the steppe tradition of rulers' law and organization reinforced the Perso-Arabic stress on royal justice to make the *mazalim* court a potent symbol of sovereignty. Seljuk sultans sat in *mazalim* in person and conferred decision-making powers on subordinates. Qadis and viziers also consulted with the *mazalim* court and sometimes presided over it in the sultan's name. Governors and military officers, besides holding their own courts, also enforced the judgments of the shariah courts, fulfilling their responsibility to preserve order, punish criminals, and keep the roads safe.[66]

Reconciling Islamic and royal justice continued to be difficult because of the great differences between the shariah, steppe customs, and Near Eastern views on the agrarian economy, taxation, the role of the military, and the use of public funds. Still, the ulema in this period were less likely than before to remain aloof from or opposed to the ruler. Many even became his deputies in administering the kingdom, working as judges, ambassadors, viziers, and governors. Provincial qadis functioned both as spokesmen for the people and as local administrators for the state.[67] Expansion of the pious endowment (*waqf*) system improved financial support for religious personnel, allowing them to participate in government on a more independent footing. This multiplication of officials, ulema, and enforcement mechanisms improved the delivery of justice, and the Seljuks earned a better reputation for just rule than their initial portrayal suggests.

An integrated legacy (*c.*1100–1308)

The division of Seljuk territory among the sultan's heirs multiplied the number of courts whose princes supported intellectual production, and writers around the Seljuk realm expanded on the synthesis of kingly and Islamic values. Religious scholars as well as scribes authored advice works that integrated Islamic and Near Eastern political concepts. This was their opportunity to infuse the Perso-Arabic political synthesis with Islamic norms and values, giving the term "Posio-Islamic" some real meaning, and quite a few took advantage of it, becoming almost as likely as scribes to quote from Sasanian sources or refer to the Circle of Justice.[68] Al-Nasafi of Bukhara (d.1142), author of an Islamic creed, and the Sufi poet 'Attar (d. around 1200) both alluded to it.[69] The mirror for princes by the Spanish qadi al-Turtushi of Tortosa (1059–1126?), *The Flambeau of Kings*, quoted the four-line Circle and maintained that a just ruler was better than abundant rain and a tyrannical ruler worse than a fierce lion. "O King," he wrote, "be more glad at what remains in your subjects' hands than at what you take from them."[70] Even non-Muslim writers like the Egyptian Christian historian Jirjis al-Makin (1205–73) "likened the world unto a garden, the wall of which is king-craft," and quoted the entire eight-line Circle.[71] Expressed in varied ways by authors from Spain to Central Asia, the Near Eastern concept of justice became part of universal Islamicate culture and the responsibility of caliphs and sultans alike.

Later Seljuk authors

Authors in some parts of the Seljuk realm (e.g. Syria, Iran, Anatolia) referred to the Circle of Justice with greater regularity than their contemporaries. Syrian authors, involved in fighting the Crusaders, cited the Circle in books discussing *ghaza*. In mid-twelfth century Aleppo, an anonymous religious scholar composed *The Sea of Precious Virtues* in Persian for the *ghazi* sultan Nur al-Din Zangi (1146–74), who had built a "House of Justice" in Damascus.[72] This author quoted the Circle of Justice in a form supposedly inscribed on Anushirvan's table: "No one can rule without subjects; subjects are won only by wealth; wealth is obtained only by prosperity; and prosperity can be achieved only by justice."[73] The author considered most kinds of royal income illegal according to Islamic law, including tithes and customs dues as well as bribes and confiscated funds, but he nevertheless found them necessary, for "the spirit and the life of kingship lie in three things, the army, the treasury, and prosperity; and these three can only be achieved through justice."[74] Most of this author's versions of the Circle of Justice omitted the role of the military and seem to have visualized creating prosperity and justice by peaceful or even mystical means. The military's duty, however, was to wage holy war against the infidel, as Nur al-Din did against the Crusaders. In this regard, the author defined justice as a struggle on the path of God, for the first time integrating *ghaza* with the Near Eastern concept of state.[75]

In the Syrian environment of *The Sea of Precious Virtues*, the "wandering ascetic," envoy and spy al-Harawi (d.1215) quoted the eight-part Circle in his mirror for princes, *Harawi's Memorandum on the Ruses of War*. This book discussed the military and political qualities necessary for *ghaza*, advised that all was maintained by justice and lost by oppression.[76] Such works indicate that in the twelfth century a new synthesis of political thought percolated through at least the educated population. This synthesis included al-Ghazali's awareness of the eternal consequences of royal injustice but was more strongly influenced by Nizam al-Mulk's dynamic conception of the king's need to provide justice, follow the shariah, and consult with religious scholars to solve current problems. For these Syrian writers, the need for rulers to maintain local support while engaged in war for Islam seems to have made the justice of the Circle especially relevant.

Iranian authors of this period referenced the Circle's justice in works of history. The recommendation of justice animated the *Book of the Seljuks* by Zahir al-Din (d.1186?) of Nishapur in eastern Iran, where Seljuk rule crumbled at an early date. Zahir al-Din evaluated the sultans according to their Islamic piety and adherence to the Circle's justice; in his view, the later Seljuks' failure to provide justice and care for their flock led to the dynasty's fall.[77] The historian Ravandi (d. after 1207), who lived through Tughril's death in 1194 and the splintering of the kingdom, dedicated his history, *The Comfort of Hearts*, to the Seljuks of Anatolia. Ravandi explicitly connected justice, prosperity, taxation, military strength, and sovereignty; because of the virtuous behavior of its kings:

> the land grew prosperous and its provinces populous ... then the army was better equipped and the kings more comfortable and wealthy.
>
> A king who robs the people of their wealth
> Weakens the wall and makes the roof to fall.[78]

Meanwhile, in turbulent eastern Iran, Afdal al-Din Kirmani (d. after 1189) wrote a history of political turmoil idealizing the justice and absolute power of earlier strong rulers. Good administration meant maintaining all classes of people in their proper place and appointing righteous judges and pious governors. Kirmani ascribed to Alexander the Great the idea that the agricultural development of an area and the wealth of its peasants reflected the justice of the ruler.[79] These Iranian historians referred to the justice of the Circle in the face of ethical and political decline, less as a recommendation they hoped rulers would follow than as an explanation for the regime's decay.

While the eastern Seljuk realms disintegrated and disappeared, the remaining Seljuk territory in Anatolia developed into a unitary state with a growing population of Turkish and Persian refugees fleeing the disorder of the Seljuk breakup and the Mongol invasions to the east.[80] In this context, the secretary Yahya ibn Sa'ad composed a mirror for princes called *Gardens of Virtues*, stating that the exemplary sultan was chosen by God to expand both justice and the faith. As the "sun" of his people, he should think constantly of their welfare and be accessible to all. In a metaphor resonating with nomadic life, he compared the realm to a tent whose poles, stakes, and cords maintained a stable balance and justice supplied the solidity. A chapter on injustice emphasized the ruler's need to make himself available to petitioners, as "the most penetrating of arrows is the prayer of the oppressed."[81]

The Sufi thinker Najm al-Din Razi (or Daye, d. 1256), another Iranian refugee, wrote a book on the mystical journey, *The Path of God's Bondsmen from Origin to Return*, proposing that true kingship included prophethood rather than simply being paired with it, so the ruler was required to exercise justice in person. Justice meant obedience to God and "maintaining equilibrium among his subjects, so that the strong do not oppress the weak, nor the wealthy impose burdens on the poor." In a pastoral analogy, "If the flock contains both horned rams and ewes without horns, the ram will wish to oppress the ewe and transgress against it; this evil too the shepherd must prevent."[82] Another advice book by an Iranian emigré, *The Subtleties of Wisdom*, reminded the ineffectual late Seljuk rulers that injustice led the population to flee and the revenue to drop. If the king provided justice and ordered affairs rightly, plants and animals would become fertile, people would experience security and low prices, and he would acquire merit in the hereafter.[83] These authors presented the Circle's justice as incumbent on a truly Islamic ruler and a necessary element of a flourishing kingdom.

The successful integration of Near Eastern and Islamic concepts of justice and good administration helped transform the image of the Turks from superb fighters to masters of governance. In adopting Perso-Islamic norms, however, the Seljuks left those of the nomads behind, and they were unable to assimilate Turkic concepts of law and organization into their governing ideology. Abandoning tribal concepts of rule may have worked to their advantage in urbanized Iraq and Iran, but on the frontiers, where the nomadic element was greater, it detracted from their legitimacy. In 1153 the Turkish tribes of Khurasan in the northeast rebelled against Sultan Sanjar, captured him, and held him for two years, perhaps in an effort to reacculturate him to tribal values. On the Anatolian frontier in the west, nomadic tribes led an unsuccessful revolt against the central government, together with Sufis preaching an ideology of justice and denouncing royal oppression.[84] The tribal warriors' disaffection fatally weakened Seljuk resistance to the Mongol invasion of Anatolia in 1243. Assimilating Perso-Islamic norms and methods kept the Seljuks from taking full advantage of steppe traditions of unity and legitimacy. It enabled them to govern an agrarian society in accordance with its customs and values but did not provide sufficient cohesion to a ruling group operating under the Turkic concept of divided rule. The legal and organizational tools for maintaining a strong and unified state of broad geographical scope and an effective central administration were not yet available to the Seljuks or their successors.

Seljuk successors

During the twelfth century the Seljuks were snuffed out one by one and were replaced in central Iraq by the Abbasid caliphs and elsewhere by their own officials or vassals. Besides the Seljuks of Anatolia (1071–1308) and the Sultans of Delhi in India (1206–1526), the most important of the new rulers were the Khwarazmshahs (1150–1220), descendants of Sanjar's cup-bearer on the throne of Khwarazm (south of the Aral Sea), and the Ayyubids (1171–1250), descendants of a Zangid officer, ruling Egypt and Syria. These sultans had "few if any of the attributes of sacral kingship,"[85] but they bolstered the dubious legitimacy of conquest with adherence to Seljuk governing practices, which still enjoyed great prestige. Reports of the provision of justice under their rule portray it as more intermittent and less reliable than under the Seljuks.

Saladin (Salah al-Din ibn Ayyub, 1171–93), who grew up among Seljuk officials, replaced the faltering Fatimids in Egypt. His biography by the religious scholar Ibn Shaddad described Saladin as a just governor, and in that role he performed a revenue survey, remitted non-Qur'anic taxes (restored by later sultans),[86] and regularly held *mazalim* court:

> Every Monday and Thursday he sat in public to administer justice, and on these occasions jurisconsults, kadis, and men learned in the law were present. Every one who had a grievance was admitted – great and small, aged women and feeble men. He sat thus, not only when he was in the city, but even when he was travelling; and he always received with his own hand the petitions that were presented to him, and did his utmost to put an end to every form of oppression that was reported. Every day, either during the daytime or in the night, he spent an hour with his secretary, and wrote on each petition, in the terms which God suggested to him, an answer to its prayer.[87]

In this receptive atmosphere, new literature on justice began to emerge. A work on the virtues of leadership written for Saladin by the Syrian al-Shayzari, *The Straight Path Regarding the Politics of Kings*, presented three versions of the Circle: the standard four-line form attributed to 'Amr ibn al-'As, the Muslim conqueror of Egypt; the eight-line version attributed to Anushirvan; and a new version putting the Circle into a practical context for a soldier king fighting against the Crusaders: "The things that protect kings and their borders are five: water, mountains, deserts, castles and men; the best are men, then castles; castles are strengthened by men, and men are strengthened by wealth; the best wealth is food, and the collection of food and its acquision are realized by justice."[88]

Although other Ayyubid rulers do not seem to have shared Saladin's concern for justice, the institutional mechanisms for delivering justice developed under the Fatimids continued to operate under the Ayyubids. People presented petitions in "Houses of Justice" in Aleppo and Cairo, which were built in imitation of the one constructed by Nur al-Din Zangi in Damascus. Rulers handled petitions privately as well, considering cases with the aid of a panel of qadis and transmitting their decrees not by mere secretaries but by high court officials and religious scholars, as under the Seljuks.[89] Documents were registered before being issued, and governors, deputies, headmen and holders of *iqta*s enforced the sultan's orders. The few decrees still extant show that Ayyubid administrators emphasized the need "to protect the subjects whose affairs were entrusted to us by God."[90]

In Iran and Transoxiana, the Khwarazmshahs developed a reputation for injustice and were considered tyrannical and ruthless conquerors, as they competed to fill the vacuum left by Seljuk disintegration.[91] There the theologian and philosopher Fakhr al-Din Razi (d.1209) wrote a *Compendium of Sciences*, stressing the need for justice and order.[92] Living in a time of violence, Razi regarded any ruler who could maintain order and keep peace as the Shadow of God and the representative of the Prophet.[93] The Khwarazmshahs may have had a military court that functioned as a *mazalim* court, but no records of their administration of justice have survived. They did, however, have an official responsible for developing the country. His diploma of appointment was based on the Circle of Justice, a concept that its writer seems to have had some difficulty explaining:

> The most important principle and the strongest pillar of kingship ... is the cultivation, development, tilling, and husbandry of the province, because the affairs of the government of the world are made strong by cultivation and [agricultural] development, and the state of the kingdom depends upon husbandry: 'There is no kingdom without men, no men without money and no money without [agricultural] development.' If negligence and slackness are shown over cultivation ... there will be a deficit ... and if ... there are straitened circumstances and the incoming sums decrease, the defraying of expenses becomes impossible and the wages necessary for the retinue of the ruler are not paid, and this causes a conflict of views ... and thoughts of dispersal and a desire for ascendancy are formed in their hearts, and if steps are not taken by him to remedy that ... kingship vanishes and the basis of the kingdom is destroyed.[94]

This confused babble suggests that the simple Circle was not widespread in Khwarazm, although it expressed a vital truth. The printed edition of Razi's compendium of sciences contains the eight-sided Circle of Justice, but it is absent from early manuscripts and was probably added by a later copyist.[95] Its assumptions of stability, legality, and reciprocal support seem alien to the troubled regime of the Khwarazmshahs. In hindsight, later historians remembered them as just rulers, but their rule in Iran and Transoxiana was based solely on violence. They could not win the loyalty of those they conquered, and in the face of the Mongol hordes they found themselves unsupported. They fled through Afghanistan to India and then through Iran to the Caspian Sea. The Mongols, in relentless pursuit, annihilated cities and towns in their path that offered any resistance, killing the inhabitants, demolishing the buildings, and ruining agricultural fields and irrigation works; some areas never recovered.[96]

Sheltered from Mongol devastation, Shiraz under the Turkish Salghurid dynasty became a center for Persian cultural production. Here flourished the poet Sa'di (d.1292), whose work *The Garden* portrayed the prince to whom it was dedicated as another Anushirvan, renowned for justice, who spread his protecting shade above the world and provided a "wall" like Alexander's against the Mongols. Although it did not quote the Circle of Justice directly, its first chapter contained all of its terms:

> Keep watch upon the poor and needy, for by virtue of the people the emperor holds his crown … The militia that is not content with the prince will not keep watch on the borders of the realm … When the merchants heard the news that there was tyranny in that clumsy one's domain, they cut from thence all purchase and vending; cultivation stopped; the populace was consumed! … The treasury is not for me alone: the vaults are kept full for the sake of the army … For your own sake, care for the yeoman, for the happy labourer does more work! … A tree, your subjects are: husband them, and fruit you'll eat to the heart's content … The mind's distress of one seeking justice will cast out the emperor from his realm.[97]

Good advice if it were followed, but the "wall" of Shiraz was made not of stone but of gold (i.e. tribute payments) and was therefore easily penetrated. In the end the province was conquered by subordinates of the Mongols and became part of their empire.

Conclusion

Throughout the region dominated by these Turkish Muslim dynasties, the concepts and ideals of the Circle of Justice became commonplaces of political thought and were expressed in advice literature, history, poetry, philosophy, letters, and imperial orders. Although some critics still considered them outside the range of political ideas sanctioned by the Prophet Muhammad, for most they formed an inseparable part of Islamic political thought. Nur al-Din Zangi made the House of Justice in Damascus a component of his Islamic counter to the Crusades;[98] he clearly considered this method of dispensing justice part of Islamic practice. Writers across the region deployed the Circle of Justice to legitimate rulers, to evaluate them, to flatter and to criticize them. Rulers varied, of course, in the extent to which they lived up to the ideal, but they generally saw the advantage of maintaining the *mazalim* institutions where their subjects could seek justice and bring complaints. They also seem to have retained Seljuk policies regarding taxation and care for the infrastructure, except when the government's weakness or small size made it impossible to check the depredations of invaders, punish distant officials, or renew the revenue surveys.

Despite the great cultural similarities among the post-Seljuk polities and their common Sunni orientation, however, no motive for unification was strong enough to override the rivalries between multiple claimants to the sultanate. While such disunity may have had few immediate consequences at the local level – and, as we have seen, some of those consequences may have been positive – it left the region easy prey to Mongol invaders by making it impossible for any one ruler to harness its full military potential. On the other hand, the integration of shariah and *ghaza* with the Near Eastern concept of state linked Islamic opposition to the pagan invaders with defense of the state and may have strengthened political loyalties.

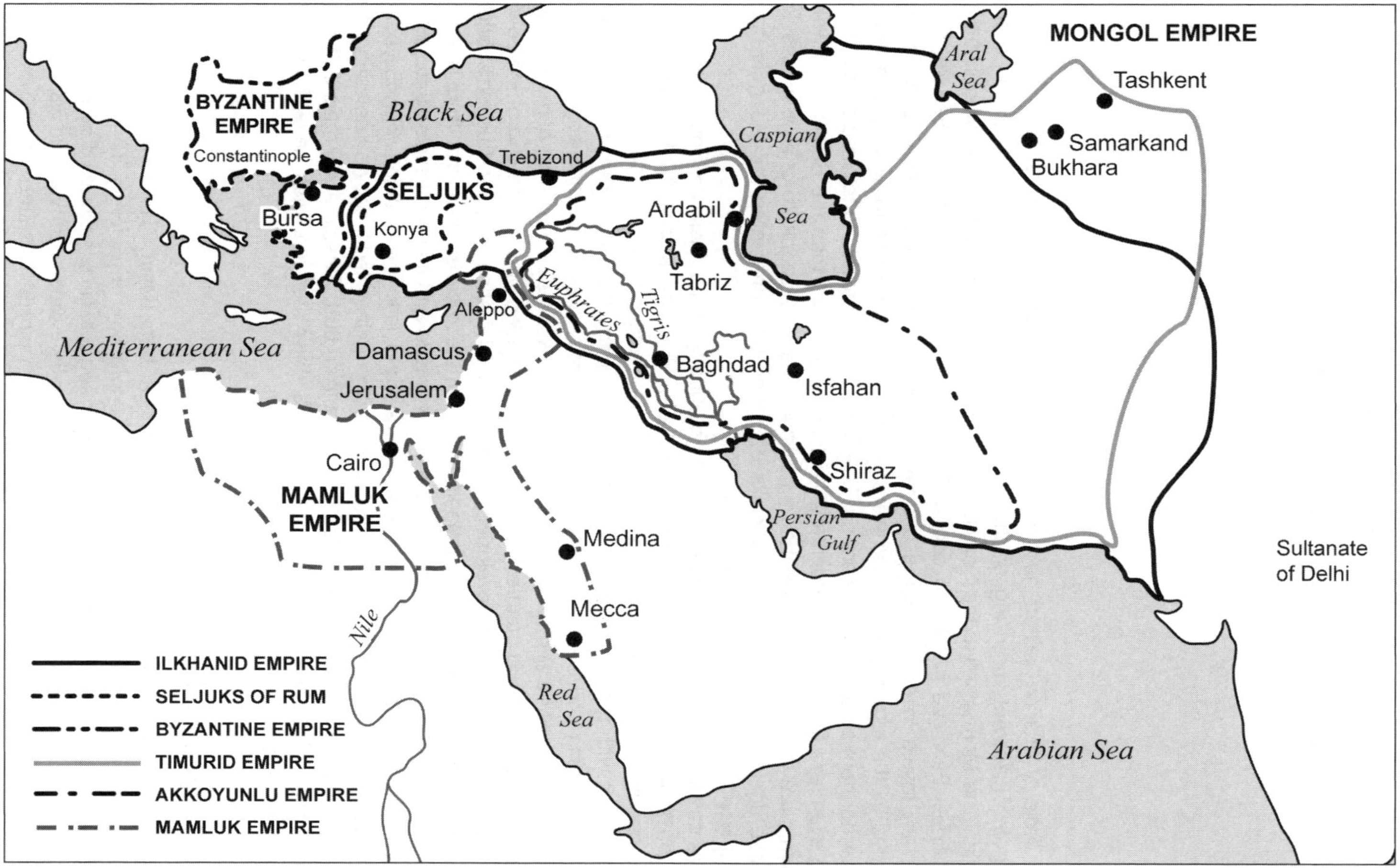

Map 6 The Mongols and their successors

7 Mongols and Mamluks

"Fierce toward offenders, and in judgements just"

The Circle of Justice gained new and persuasive cultural representations under the Mongols. This is not surprising, as their acculturation was more difficult than that of the Seljuks. The Mongols, like the Seljuks, were Central Asian tribal nomads who invaded the Middle East and ruled it in cooperation with local elites. Unlike the Seljuks, they were not losers in some steppe quarrel but winners who had already defeated or coopted all the region's tribes and were well on their way to conquering China. From the far northern steppes, they were not Muslims on their arrival in the Middle East; they were even less familiar with sedentary life and government than the Seljuks and were known more for destructiveness than for justice. The only people to offer a successful defense against them were the Mamluks of Egypt, who prevented the Mongols from taking North Africa and the Syrian coast.

Any consideration of the Mongols has to compensate for their ferocious reputation and for the fact that later generations blamed all their miseries on them. For in the end, the Mongols also adopted Islam and with it the Perso-Islamic model of governance, enhancing it with their own steppe concept of the divine mandate, administrative practices from China and Central Asia, and a new devotion to organization and law. Their numbers and prestige allowed them to retain these aspects of their own heritage while beginning a political and cultural integration that extended beyond the end of their own rule. Like the Seljuks, they developed mechanisms of justice and good administration that outlasted their regime and helped to legitimate their successors. And like the Seljuks, they and their successors created new artistic and literary vehicles that transmitted the Circle of Justice to wider audiences and later generations. The Egyptian Mamluks, Turkish and Circassian slave soldiers who gained legitimacy by defeating the Mongols and the Crusaders, inherited the Circle from both Turkish and Arabic cultures. Despite their difficulties in fulfilling its demands, their literature also gave it broader distribution in both languages.

The Mongols of the steppe (1206–1260)

The Mongols came from Siberia beyond the Orkhon River. Their partly legendary tribal chronicle, *The Secret History of the Mongols*, told how their leader Temujin (1206–27) climbed to power from the depths of poverty and weakness.[1] Deserted by his tribe in childhood after the murder of his father, he heroically escaped captivity and assassination to gather a following based not on tribal ties but on personal loyalties. By 1206 all the steppe peoples acknowledged his rule and gave him the title of Genghis Khan (in Mongol *Chinggis Qan*, "Oceanic Ruler").[2]

Mongol ideology and law

Mongol ideology contained several parallels to the Turks' Orkhon inscriptions and the Circle of Justice. Genghis Khan's astounding military success and the wide extent of his rule gave his followers reason to believe in his divine appointment. He himself began to believe in the guidance of Heaven at a young age; an early victory gave him a sense of being

> Appointed by mighty Heaven,
> Invited by Mother Earth.[3]

This concept of divine appointment to world dominion continued the ideology of the Turks' Orkhon inscriptions, but Genghis Khan was the most successful steppe ruler in putting that rhetoric into action.[4] His repeated victories expanded his people's prosperity and the frontiers of his dominion.[5] After his death, his followers continued to believe that God's will was to unite all the kingdoms of the earth under Mongol leadership:

> In Heaven there is God, the One, Eternal, Immortal, Most High,
> On Earth Genghis Khan is the only and supreme Lord.[6]

These lines appeared in edicts addressed to European monarchs and the pope inviting them to become Mongol vassals or be destroyed. Not to choose vassalage was to rebel against Heaven and deserve annihilation, as the Khwarazmshah Muhammad discovered when in 1218 he defied the Mongols and killed their envoys.[7]

As in the Orkhon inscriptions, organization was the route to prosperity on the steppe. Genghis Khan organized the tribesmen under his command, using a decimal system of tens, hundreds, thousands, and ten thousands that cut across family and tribal lines to become a new focus of loyalty centered on himself and his family. He divided allies and captives among his fighting leaders and his sons, and distributed rewards, pasturelands, and areas for conquest. He recruited his elite personal guard from all the tribes and included "hostages" of vassal rulers, usually sons, brought up in close contact with the supreme ruler, as in Assyrian practice.[8]

As his responsibilities increased, Genghis Khan issued decrees and ordinances (*yasas*) regarding military decisions and appointments, punishments and rewards, and financial matters. References in the *Secret History* to these decrees increased in number over time, as his continued military success gave his words new authority. His successor Ogedei (1229–41) renewed the decrees of his father: "How aforetime were they wont to act by the edict of my father the Qahan? Let them now act in the same manner."[9] The *Secret History* portrayed Ogedei's entire reign not as a series of events, but as a series of laws embodying and extending the regime of Genghis Khan: "First of all he made a *yasa* that such ordinances and commands as had previously been issued by Chingiz-Khan should be maintained, and secured, and protected against the evils of change, and alteration, and confusion."[10]

By the mid-thirteenth century these decrees were compiled into an authoritative legal document (*yasa*), and each Mongol ruler possessed a copy. Consequently, scholars thought that the *yasa* of Genghis Khan had been a lawcode promulgated by that ruler and now lost.[11] Like the *khagans* of the Orkhon inscriptions, however, Genghis Khan on his accession to power applied his tribe's customary law to his whole following, adding his own practices, orders, and advice. His prestige caused his successors to revere and renew his ways, assimilating their decision-making to that of their great progenitor. Thus the *yasa* of Genghis Khan, the foundational law of all subsequent Mongol states, was not something looked back to but something continually created by its adherents.[12] The Mongols' reverence for the *yasa* was well known; familiarity with the *yasa* became a qualification for rule and an issue in the choice of Genghis Khan's successors.[13] Its prestige eased the way for a wider acceptance of ruler's law outside the shariah but roused a prejudice against it in virulently anti-Mongol quarters. Some Muslims saw the *yasa* as rivaling the shariah, and reconciling the two forms of law was a long process.

Mongol conquest of the Middle East

After uniting the steppe tribes, Genghis Khan's aim, like that of previous tribal confederations, was to capture China's legendary wealth. His Middle East campaign of 1219–21 was not originally a conquest but a punitive expedition against the Khwarazmshah for killing Mongol envoys and massacring merchants.[14] Capture of the Khwarazmian cities of Bukhara, Samarqand, Balkh, and Nishapur was followed by punishment: massacres, plunder, and conversion of agricultural land to pasture. This was not mere barbarism or ignorance of the customs of agrarian society. The extreme contrast between the Mongols' destructiveness in Transoxiana and Khurasan and their tolerance and moderation in eastern Turkestan indicates that their atrocities in Khwarazm and Iran were politically motivated.[15]

After Genghis Khan's death in 1227, the Mongols pushed the conquest of the Middle East forward in stages. Seljuk Anatolia became a vassal in 1243, and the Fertile Crescent fell in 1256–58 when the fourth *khagan* Mongke (1251–9) sent an army there under his brother Hulegu. After defeating the Isma'ilis in northern Iran, Hulegu captured Baghdad, killing the caliph and all his family except a distant cousin who escaped to Cairo and established a "shadow" caliphate, not acknowledged by all Muslims. Hulegu's invasion brought to the Middle East a full 20 percent of steppe Mongols and Turks with their families and herds, estimated at 850,000 people, 3–5 million horses, and 17 million sheep.[16] This was a major migration many times larger than that of the Seljuks. As conqueror and semi-autonomous ruler of the former Seljuk lands, Hulegu (1256–82) held the title of *Ilkhan* (provincial khan), and his dynasty is known as the Ilkhanids.

The sudden vast increase of nomads in the Middle East's population and military forces made nomadic ideologies and forms of organization more central to Mongol legitimacy than they had been to the Seljuks. The Mongols did not initially adopt the culture of the sedentary civilizations they conquered, and the percolation of the Circle of Justice into Mongol ideology was a long, slow process. In fact, the story circulated that after the conquest of North China they had planned to destroy the agrarian and urban base and turn the region into pastureland and were only dissuaded when their Chinese advisor convinced them they could obtain more wealth from the sedentary people by taxing them than by killing them.[17] They did institute a policy of counting the conquered peoples for taxation and military recruitment, adding to the regular tax on crops the irregular levies of nomadic taxation and collecting them, it was said, not once or twice but, like Khusrau Parviz, twenty or thirty times a year.[18]

A lament by the poet Pur-i Baha illustrated the taxpayers' despair over the Mongol levies *qalan* and *qopchur* and the resulting population flight, which broke the Circle of Justice:

> The whole world has become scattered and homeless
> Because of the immense *qalan* and endless *qopchur*.
> The census, that in thirty years was taken once,
> Now every two or three days launches some new *qopchur*.[19]

Between the destruction of conquest, death and emigration, and Mongol military levies, the population of some parts of Iran fell drastically. The impact on wealthy Khurasan was the most severe, and that province was home to the historians whose works shaped later views of the conquest. In their opinion, only if the Mongol rulers could be persuaded to adopt the norms of Near Eastern governance (or, better yet, the religion of Islam) would security and prosperity return to the region. The clash between Near Eastern norms and those of nomadic rule generated factionalism in the ruling cadre as Mongol leaders from opposition groups, intent on extracting the maximum of wealth and resentful of administrative centralization, undercut Ogedei's efforts to regularize taxation and restore prosperity.[20] Not until Mongke's accession did Mongol rule begin to reflect the values of the Circle of Justice.

Mongol regime and Near Eastern state (1258–1335)

By the time the Mongols conquered Baghdad in 1258, some members of the ruling family were anxious to recruit administrators trained in the Perso-Islamic tradition. Mongke consulted local experts to learn "how the people's lot might be alleviated … and the lands restored to prosperity," declaring that he was "concerned for the welfare of the subjects, not [only] for the proliferation of treasury revenues." Like the Assyrians, Mongke brought conquered people into the ranks of the ruler's household and awarded them high offices. Among the most outstanding was the former Khwarazmian official Mahmud Yalavach (d.1254), who reduced occasional taxation in Transoxiana to once a year and eliminated compulsory military service; as a result "those scattered and dispersed in nooks and crannies were by the magnet of his justice and clemency attracted back to their former homes."[21] His policy succeeded so well that by 1260 Transoxiana approached its former level of prosperity.[22] He was then promoted to the province of North China, where his reforms proved so effective that Mongke adopted them as a model for the whole empire.

Mongke's reform replaced the irregular levies of nomad taxation with an annual tax based on a population census and collected by the ruler's own personnel. In an empire-wide survey in 1252, teams of central and local administrators in each province counted households, revenue sources, and military-age men. Repeated censuses reduced oppression by regularizing taxation, systematically distributing the revenues among the Mongol elite.[23] Other steps Mongke took to organize the empire also echoed ancient Near Eastern practices, such as the resettlement and repopulation of lands devastated by war, or the reform of the post service, the essential linking device of this far-flung empire. More than just a messenger service, the post system was the conduit for the flow of tribute and taxes, petitions and royal judgments, government and military supplies, and royal and private trade across the empire.

Tusi and other Near Eastern advisors

The creation of a Mongol version of the Near Eastern state indicates the rulers' growing awareness of their dependence on agrarian revenue from the conquered people as well as nomadic resources, and thus on agrarian ideologies. As a token of this awareness, Mongke commissioned Hulegu, when he reached the Middle East, to seek out the Isma'ili philosopher and astronomer Nasir al-Din Tusi (1207–74), author of a famous Persian ethical/political work, *The Nasirean Ethics*. After defeating the Isma'ilis in 1256, Hulegu made Tusi his advisor and consulted him about a warning he had received that if he attacked the caliph in Baghdad the sun would not rise, rain would not fall, plants would cease to grow, there would be hurricanes and earthquakes, horses and men would suffer pestilence, and the Mongol *khagan* would die.[24] Tusi advised Hulegu to ignore this ancient Near Eastern superstition, which was based on the same interrelationships as the Circle of Justice. Tusi's own works, however, cited the Circle together with Islamic, philosophical, and nomadic concepts of governance, blending them into a single set of ideas.

The introduction Tusi wrote for a new set of astronomical tables acknowledged the divine origin of the Mongols' power and celebrated their institution of good laws that "adorned the world with justice and equity" and "kept the people in tranquillity and peace."[25] His *Nasirean Ethics*, rewritten for the Ilkhanids, analyzed justice as a philosophical "midpoint" or mean, requiring for its attainment the "correspondence" of the different classes of society, the men of the Pen, Sword, Negotiation, and Husbandry. This philosophical definition took for granted a definition derived from the Circle that became an analogy for the just behavior of Everyman, the recipient of God's gifts: "Why should he [Everyman] not be virtuous as the just ruler? As an effect of *his* governance, roads and realms are tranquil and well-maintained; his justice is apparent and renowned in distant parts and local territories; he lets no second pass in waste or negligence, in his defence of women and the protection of the kingdom's integrity, in preventing men from oppressing one another, and in facilitating the means to Man's best interest in this world and the next."[26]

As administrator of pious foundations, Tusi wrote a short work on taxation in response to the ruler's demand to know "the ways and regulations of the ancient kings in those provinces, which regulations maintained the world in a flourishing state, and the army and the subjects in contentment and good order." To maximize revenue over the long term, the Ilkhanids had to maintain the taxation levels and exemptions established by the census and recorded in the provincial registers. Strict observation of the finance regulations would prevent rebellion and generate tranquillity and prosperity, values which his treatise on ethics had associated with justice; this justice would give the ruler a good name and a surplus in the treasury.[27] Here he brought the discussion of justice full circle again to state that the wealth of the kingdom depended on the just treatment of those who produced it.

Writers of the period used various means to convey the concepts of the Circle. The anonymous bureaucrat who wrote *The Royal History* around 1281 described justice as dependent on the ruler's fiscal and administrative measures, his guiding hand, and his oversight of his officials. To another anonymous author writing after 1258, justice involved supporting agriculture, "an alchemy that changes earth into gold," and preventing officials' injustices. A contemporary encyclopedia of philosophy, *The Pearly Crown*, explained in a section on political philosophy that "when the king practices justice, equity, and good government, and is occupied with improving the condition of his subjects, his reign brings peace, verdure, low prices, abundant harvests of plants and animals, and an increasing population." The Syrian Christian Bar Hebraeus characterized the Ilkhanids' Anatolian vassal as "fierce toward offenders, and in judgements just."[28] The Mongols thus acquired the Circle of Justice as part of the heritage of Islamicate civilization which they had just conquered and were soon to join.

The Juvayni brothers

The Ilkhans, like the Seljuks, recruited Persian and Arab officials who worked to acculturate their new rulers, as the scribes of old had done.[29] These bureaucrats played no small part in the region's recovery from the devastation of conquest.[30] The highest-ranking of them were the Juvayni brothers, from a family whose service in the scribal corps went back to early Abbasid times. Shams al-Din Juvayni (d.1284), the Ilkhanids' finance minister, won praise for his just reorganization of Anatolia's finances after its revolt in 1277–8.[31] His brother 'Ala al-Din 'Ata Malik Juvayni (d.1283) served as governor of Iraq and wrote a history of the Mongols.[32]

In this history, written for Hulegu, Juvayni faced the problem of reconciling conquest by non-Muslims with Islamic notions of God's hand in history. He justified Mongol rule as destined by God, since Genghis Khan was an even better conqueror than Alexander the Great.[33] The Mongols' destructiveness was God's chastisement, but through them God also destroyed enemies of the Muslims, like the Isma'ilis. Juvayni portrayed the Mongols as just rulers, revitalizers of the world. Mongke, like the pre-Islamic monarchs and Umayyad caliphs, resembled "the sun in the zenith of his power," and his justice compared favorably with that of Anushirvan. At his enthronement "the surface of the face of the earth was again decked out and adorned because of his all-embracing justice, and the affairs of mankind in general and the concerns of the Moslems in particular took on a new freshness and brilliance;" God "place[d] the crown of kingship and the diadem of sovereignty upon his head, so that by his justice and equity the desolate world may bloom again."[34]

The most salient aspect of Mongol justice for Juvayni was Genghis Khan's law, the *yasa*. As a Muslim, Juvayni could not grant the *yasa* the near-sanctity which the Mongols accorded it, but he did allow that it "established such usages as were praiseworthy from the point of view of reason," many of which conformed to the shariah, and provided "that no man should injure another nor the strong impose upon the weak." Juvayni found the *yasa* similar to the shariah on many points but drew attention to its differences: annihilation of those who refused to submit, equality of religions, avoidance of ceremony, and the military as an armed peasantry. Also impossible for Muslims were Mongol *yasa*s about killing animals and prohibiting washing in running water. Juvayni understood the Mongol *yasa* in terms of the Middle Eastern legal tradition of ruler's law. Justice was defined by "the book and the balance," the revelation of the Qur'an and the awareness of final judgment, but it was to be enacted by the Mongol khan, whose "august shadow extends over all mankind."[35]

We have no written record of the Ilkhans' own position during this period, but their patronage and continued employment of Muslim administrators suggest general approval of their ideas on governance. The architectural constructions they sponsored, such as the observatory they built for Tusi at Maragha, visibly indicated their willingness to adopt portions of the Near Eastern heritage as their own.[36] Hulegu's successor Abaqa (1265–82) erected a magnificent palace whose location and decoration evoked the Circle of Justice many times over. The palace, called "Solomon's Throne," was built over a Zoroastrian fire temple in Azerbaijan thought to have been the coronation site of the Sasanian kings. This palace was decorated with imagery of Sasanian royal palaces from the *Shahnama* and was linked by an inscription with Mahmud of Ghazna, whose justice had also become the stuff of legend. Built around a spring-fed lake and embellished with appropriate inscriptions, the palace also recalled Alexander's quest for the Fountain of Life.[37] This quest in turn was a well-known metaphor for the mystical quest for God, and here a link was formed with the Islamic heritage and its use of the universal heroic past as an image for the universality of faith. In non-verbal form this palace proclaimed the Mongols' incorporation of Near Eastern governing ideology.

Abaqa's successor Ahmad Teguder (1282–4) actually converted to Islam, but the ruling family and the Mongol chieftains could not accept his new allegiance and quickly deposed him.[38] Their rejection of Islam and of sedentary life strengthened dissident Mongol factions and made the rulers' reform efforts ineffective. It took increased conversion to Islam over the next two decades, and Ilkhanid independence from the Mongol Empire after Kubilai Khan's death in China (1291), to create wider acceptance of Ghazan's conversion. Ghazan Khan (1295–1304) and his successors were all Muslims, considered themselves Middle Eastern rulers, and adopted Perso-Islamic governing mechanisms.[39] The scribes' tradition of service to steppe rulers within an Islamic framework had once again borne fruit.

Rashid al-Din

In place of Juvayni's organic metaphors of blossoming spring, Ghazan Khan's vizier Rashid al-Din (d.1318) described Ghazan's justice in terms of accurate paperwork, firm control of subordinates, and equitable, balanced treatment of petitioners and officials. This change of diction registered how far the Ilkhanids had come in two generations toward fulfilling the demands of Perso-Islamic kingship. Rashid al-Din, like Juvayni, wrote a history that situated the Mongols within Islamic and world history. He compared Ghazan Khan to Solomon and Anushirvan, reporting that he decreed "justice and equity, and there was to be no oppression of the weak by the strong."[40] He attributed to Ghazan a speech describing kingship in the style of Anushirvan, in which the divine mandate to rule formed an occasion for thanksgiving and generated a corresponding responsibility toward the subjects: "I am not unaware that the giving of thanks by a hundred-thousand tongues is incumbent and necessary for the fact that, through His grace and bounty, He has brought into the compass of submission to me all of the peoples of the Iranian lands who are, as so many charge, entrusted to me by the Majesty of the God-head. wherefore, rather than that they should be oppressed, it is better that His servants should be relieved of any molestation from me and, instead, be glad of, and avid for, my rule."[41]

Rashid al-Din, thoroughly versed in Perso-Islamic ideals of governance, believed that raising the revenue and diminishing revolt required the restoration of agriculture and the proper treatment of the common people. Letters attributed to him contained a version of the four-line Circle of Justice, drawn in circular form and written in Persian and Arabic.[42] He set a personal example of just administration on the extensive lands he owned or controlled, building canals and irrigation works and founding or repopulating villages and towns as well as the "Rashidian quarter" in the capital, Tabriz. He was also one of the prime movers in the reform of coinage and the expansion of international trade. In fact, Rashid al-Din is thought to be the man who was behind the reforms of Ghazan Khan.[43]

The reforms of Ghazan Khan (1295–1303)

Ghazan Khan instituted a number of reforms designed to restore order and prosperity to the empire after a period of runaway exploitation and embezzlement under his immediate predecessors. "He established a new cadaster and he stipulated the procedures that were to be followed in all fiscal and financial operations. By these means, the affairs of the provinces were restored to order."[44] Ghazan's new laws mandated good administration and routes to prosperity suitable for a sedentarizing society, and they employed a variety of metaphors for justice and allusions to aspects of the Circle.[45]

Prosperity, agriculture, finances, and the military

In order to "maintain the world in a flourishing state," Ghazan Khan ordered a new census registering areas never before surveyed. This order prescribed justice in taxation, commanding that tax levels be set by finance secretaries from the central government rather than local landlords, allowing people to appeal against their assessments, forbidding collection of more than the surveyed amounts, regulating the compilation and central storage of accurate registers, publicizing tax assessments and allowable provincial expenditures, standardizing the forms of documents, and cursing anyone who destroyed tax records. Similar orders banned interest-taking to stop extortionate loans, granted tax remissions for cultivating wastelands, appointed agricultural agents in the provinces, and provided draft animals and seed to peasants. Some of these nuances were of Chinese origin; the rest were standard Middle Eastern practices of good administration.[46] Another edict revived the *iqta* system to support the army, which by this time was abandoning nomadic pastoralism and "had the desire for estates and for the practice of agriculture."[47] Other edicts mandated improvements in such areas as the post system, revenue assignments, the judicial system, treasury inventories, public drinking, begging by camel-drivers, and highway robbery.[48]

Ghazan's reform edicts deployed Near Eastern and Islamic concepts of justice to legitimize their provisions. For example, an edict on property deeds began with quotations from the Qur'an and *hadith*, but continued: "We exert all our care to secure the wellbeing of our people, and desire that the shadow of our justice may be generally spread everywhere, so that the powerful may not be able to oppress the feeble, that right may not be undone by wrong."[49] The edict restoring the *iqta* system required recipients of *iqta*s to pledge "to make justice pervasive and uprightness widespread." A metaphor in a taxation edict echoed ancient Near Eastern ideology: "It is necessary that the emperor's justice should reach everyone in every place, like the light of the sun." The announcement of an agricultural reform reiterated the elements of the Circle: "When fallow lands are made to flourish, grain will be cheap; and when expeditions are mounted for obligatory actions on the borders, provisions will be readily available. Money will also flow into the treasury and increase. Lords and property owners will gain a new prestige and confidence, the peasants will enjoy peace of mind and ease, and we will have a heavenly reward and enjoy a good name."[50]

Rashid al-Din's history asserted that the "justice and fair administration" of Ghazan's reign could be proven by "comparing the registers of the revenue bases and revenue expenditures belonging to the rulers of the past, all of which have been deposited in the register archive, with the similar registers belonging to this present reign."[51] These registers no longer exist, and their loss has allowed modern critics to speculate that Mongol policies reduced overall prosperity by up to 90 percent. Even if that was the case, it appears to have been temporary. By the late Mongol period, areas not devastated by conquest, such as Mesopotamia and southern Iran, were probably at least as prosperous as in the disturbed middle Abbasid period. This assumption implies a 200 percent inflation in the value of silver over the intervening 450 years, and it yields overall revenue totals not much lower than at earlier periods, despite deeper declines in some provinces.[52] Agriculture and irrigation in Khurasan had recovered by the fourteenth century, and the new capital region of Azerbaijan produced five times as much as before. Anatolia's revenues increased by a factor of twenty-five; such a huge increase cannot have resulted merely from higher taxation but must be due to real economic growth.[53] Central budget figures, however, are not the best indicators of the empire's prosperity, since they measure the condition of the central treasury rather than the economy as a whole. A drastic decrease in revenue collected from Khuzistan, for example, probably resulted not from the province's ruin but from the grant of much of its land to the tax-exempt Rashid al-Din. Contemporaries felt, contrary to modern stereotypes, that Ghazan and his officials had considerably restored irrigation works and revived agricultural production: "Previously they destroyed things to the extent that they now make improvements."[54]

Yasa, *Shariah, and* Mazalim

Despite Ghazan's loyalty to the Mongol *yasa*, his new legislation was a far cry from the *yasa* of Genghis Khan. Ghazan's edict on the *iqta* system, for example, began with praises of the *yasa*, but the military organization it mandated bore little resemblance to Genghis Khan's decimal system. Yet so great had the prestige of the *yasa* become, so large a role did it play in legitimating the ruler, that it could not be abandoned after conversion to Islam. When the Central Asian Mongol khan Tarmashirin tried to do so, "his subjects opposed this most vehemently."[55] Consequently, when the Ilkhanid rulers became Muslims, they retained the *yasa* and assimilated it to the Perso-Islamic institution of ruler's decrees and the *mazalim* court.

Mongol courts already resembled the Muslim ruler's court in certain respects. Their main purposes were to maintain peace and order and to judge misbehaving officials and rebels. While still on the steppes, the Mongols also had a "complaint box" hung on a pole with string, and "if a man had a complaint or had suffered an injustice, he would write his grievance in a petition, seal it, and place it in this box. When Friday came, the king would. discover the injustices suffered by people."[56] In these situations Mongol justice functioned much like the *mazalim* court, so the transfer of ideology from one to the other must not have been too difficult. The judicial reform of Ghazan Khan established a dual court system: Islamic courts under officially appointed qadis, and the *mazalim* court, which added Mongol judges to the Muslim qadis and met in a mosque; its decisions were supposed to harmonize *yasa* and shariah.[57] These courts did not leave any records, but presumably the kinds of complaints people presented there were much the same as in earlier centuries. Problems in the delivery of justice in this period have been subsumed under the general violence and dislocation of the conquests, but overall population decrease, due to conquest and later the Black Death, may have made land and employment widely available, reducing ordinary crime and lawsuits.[58]

This legal compromise was paralleled in art. The emergence of Persian miniature painting has been traced to a magnificent royal copy of the *Shahnama* produced in the fourteenth century. The *Shahnama*, linking pre-Islamic, Islamic, and steppe cultures in a masterpiece of rulership, romance, and heroism, became a powerful cultural icon for the Mongols. The miniatures of the "Great Mongol *Shahnama*" illustrated themes of justice and legitimacy, symbolized by Alexander the Great and Ardashir. Alexander, as a foreign world-conqueror who became a legitimate Iranian monarch, was the Mongols' model, and the parallel was highlighted by paintings of Alexander resembling Ghazan and his successors. The *Shahnama*, besides being copied in book form, decorated Ilkhanid royal palaces in the form of quotations on tile friezes and images on metalwork and ceramics, constantly reminding palace residents of the ancient governing ideals of the civilization into which they had been integrated.[59]

Ghazan's untimely death interrupted his reforming efforts, but reforms continued under his successors Oljeitu (1304–14) and Abu Sa'id (1314–35) thanks to their viziers Rashid al-Din and his son Giyath al-Din (d.1336). By the end of the Ilkhanid regime, Ghiyath al-Din's economic and taxation measures had significantly increased population and wealth. A discourse on royal ethics written for Oljeitu explained: "Money can only satisfy a few people … but through the spread of justice which contains within itself all the benefits of religion and of the state, and which in no way fails to satisfy the needs of life and property, there shines forth suddenly in bridal splendor the rule of the world, in a phrase: Through justice heaven and earth exist."[60]

The author of this discourse, the historian Vassaf, had the opportunity to enact the Circle's justice when he obtained a revenue contract for a territory that needed restoration. He related that he relieved the condition of the peasants, gave them seed, and brought peasants from neighboring districts to augment the labor force; within a month the land was populated and under cultivation and the revenue rose. The next year, however, the district was awarded to someone who did not understand the principles of justice in agriculture, and because of renewed exploitation the yield decreased again. This incident reinforces the conclusion that a shortage of trained and experienced officials contributed to the Mongols' purported injustice. The rulers went so far as to recruit the people as watchdogs, carving the government's tax demands – and their limits – into the walls of buildings and towns. An inscription of 1330 in the citadel of Ankara specified the taxes to be collected and cursed anyone who demanded more.[61]

By this time the Ilkhanids employed mainly sedentary methods of administration, although their political goals remained closer to the nomadic model: maintaining or increasing the territory and peoples under their rule and organizing and providing for their subjects. The later khans repaired the ravages of conquest and restored the trust that most Muslims had denied to a government of pagans. They also struggled to accommodate their less acculturated followers and wrestled with the economic and social effects of massive nomadic migration into the Middle East. After seventy-seven years of Mongol rule, the Perso-Islamic culture and administrative practices adopted early by the rulers were still being assimilated by those more recently converted or sedentarized. Reconciling Mongol and Near Eastern concepts of justice and good government preoccupied the Ilkhanids' successors in the Middle East for over a century.

Post-Mongol polities (1335–1506)

In 1335 the Mongol sultan Abu Sa'id died without heirs and was succeeded by an assortment of contenders for power.[62] As in the late Seljuk period, however, the decentralization of politics did not imply a break in political culture. Already Oljeitu had been called the Emperor of Islam, the Mightiest Sultan, and the Most Noble *Khagan*, uniting in himself the three main political currents of his age – Islamic, Perso-Arabic, and Turco-Mongol. This ideological cross-fertilization was also visible in law. The *yasa* was no longer an active lawcode, but it remained a watchword for the dynasty; rulers only distantly related to Genghis Khan made claims to legitimacy based on it. The prestige attached to the *yasa* expanded to cover dynastic law as a whole and enabled it to take a place beside custom as an auxiliary to the shariah. The shariah itself, it was claimed, sanctioned ruler-made law that did not contravene the law of God, and this claim recurred in stock phrases of edicts, such as "according to the law of justice [the shariah] and the *yasa*."[63] The two types of law began to work together, diluting the earlier sense that the religious law presented a challenge and a rebuke to that of the state. The Mongols' successor states, many ruled by Turkish dynasties, inherited this dual system of justice, but they also inherited a pattern of competition among heirs to the sultanate and among powerful tribal forces that interfered with putting that justice into practice.

Poets of imperial disintegration

The level of turmoil caused by the Mongol breakup made the enforcement of justice difficult, but political fragmentation spread arts and literatures embodying the Circle of Justice to wider audiences. Outside the royal courts, commercial workshops developed where calligraphers penned less lavish versions of the *Shahnama* and Nizami's romances for wealthy nobles and merchants, and artists sold pictures of romantic lovers and kings granting justice.[64] Competing rulers patronized living artists whose works instilled justice and good administration. The court poet Ibn-i Yamin (d.1368), for example, asserted that justice remained a legitimating quality even for rulers who could never match the great conquests of the Ilkhans:

> If the praise of the King of the World is, like the fame of his justice,
> Spread abroad throughout the earth, the praise-producing talent is mine![65]

The satirist 'Ubayd Zakani (d.1371), in contrast, inculcated the idea of justice by commenting on its absence among the great men of state. His book, *The Ethics of the Aristocracy*, purported to explain to the humble how the mighty redefined the laws of virtue. In the past, "kings, emirs, and noblemen always tried to be just and look after their subjects and soldiers as the means for attaining good repute," but now they regarded justice as weakness and injustice as strength, and only injustice and tyranny made the kingdom run smoothly:

> One who practices justice (God forbid) and refrains from beating, killing, and fining his subjects, and who does not get drunk and make an uproar and quarrel with them, will not be feared by anyone. As long as the kings of Iran, such as Zahhak the Arab and Yazdigird the Sinner. practiced injustice, their kingdoms prospered and flourished. But when the time of Khosrow Anushirvan arrived, he followed the

counsel of feeble-minded ministers and chose the way of justice. Before long the pinnacles of his palace fell to the ground. Since the poor Abu Sa'id was obsessed with the idea of justice and distinguished himself with this quality, before long the days of his monarchy were numbered, and the House of Hulagu and his endeavors disappeared.[66]

Zakani mocked those who seemed to think that the practice of justice was out of date and ridiculed their idea of government by force. Just as he appeared to admire the villains of Firdausi's *Shahnama* and pity the heroes, so he saw the disorder and competition of a time of turmoil apparently overturning all moral values. The virtue of justice, however, had not really changed, although it now went unrewarded. His satire charted the worth of the ostensibly discarded values of the past. These works suggest that the disintegration of centralized rule after the death of Abu Sa'id did not mean the end of the Mongol achievement. As princes, generals, and governors squabbled for power and political disintegration began to affect economic prosperity, rulers of the successor states continued to employ elements of Ilkhanid administration. Even the tyrannous warlord Malik Ashraf Chobani tried to improve his image by having a bell and "chain of justice" hung outside his door which could be rung by those seeking redress.[67]

Secretarial handbooks and the Jalayirids

Ongoing service by scribes from old bureaucratic families represented a structural continuity underlying all the period's wars, changes of dynasty, and factional struggles. Historical chronicles and biographical dictionaries omitted the writers and government scribes who were the agents of this continuity.[68] Instead, scribal manuals recorded how Ilkhanid prodecures continued in use beyond the end of the dynasty. Three finance manuals are still in existence, the surviving copies of which come from Anatolia, indicating that the Mongol administrative system laid the foundation for governance in the emerging Turkish principalities.[69] The Jalayirids (1340–1410), who ruled eastern Anatolia, western Iran, and the former Mongol capital of Tabriz, played the largest role in maintaining Ilkhanid practices and the Circle's governance, and they inherited the Ilkhanids' bureaucracy, where the finance manuals were copied and preserved. These manuals explained and illustrated the procedures for proper tax assessment and accounting and detailed how the registers should be kept and the money spent to avoid injustices.

The historian Khwandamir characterized the Jalayirid ruler Shaykh Uvays (1356–74) as "a padishah of perfect equity who showed great concern for his subjects and exercised justice and clemency." Even his rival Timur praised his justice.[70] A book by the secretary Nakhjavani written during his reign, called *Rules for Scribes on the Assignment of Ranks*, represented another type of scribal manual, a collection of model appointment documents that Nakhjavani, who had served in the late Ilkhanid bureaucracy, assembled "to set out the canons of government and care for the subjects." The book gave Shaykh Uvays the titles of "resurrector of the traditions of the Changiz-khanid state" and "unfurler of the banners of the Sacred Law," testifying to the ongoing rapprochement between *yasa* and shariah. Its documents spelled out the duties and functions of government officials; the vizier's duties were "to make the country prosperous and populous," to appoint competent officials, to levy appropriate taxes, and to sit in *mazalim* once a week. Documents also instructed the tax collector "to supervise the operations of his province, which consist of expenditure and reception of income … rendering the district fruitful and increasing its production … to entice those who are absent to return to their accustomed homeland through his clemency and put them to work in building up and cultivating the district."[71] Thus, the Circle of Justice provided the blueprint for Jalayirid rulers' attempts to overcome the baleful effects on the land of tribal and dynastic contention. These attempts proved unsuccessful, and the Jalayirid dynasty and its contemporaries fell to a powerful new conqueror, Timur (1370–1405).

Justice and injustice under the Timurids

Timur (Tamer lane), from the Chagatai Mongol khanate in Central Asia, attacked the Middle East to suppress upstart dynasties in Mongol territory. His dynasty ruled Iran and Central Asia until 1506; despite its sometimes savage behavior, its culture came to dominate the Middle East and South Asia and conveyed the eight-part Circle of Justice to the great empires of the early modern period. Despite ruling a Mongol province, Timur was not descended from Genghis Khan, so he sought legitimacy in other terms, some related to the Circle of Justice. After he plundered those he conquered to finance his magnificent constructions, he repaired the damaged cities and irrigation works and fostered economic life, both agrarian and commercial. He conducted investigations of oppression, and it was reported that a wealthy widow could travel in perfect safety across the whole empire unaccompanied by armed guards.[72] Later in life he sponsored extensive cultural production, but in his time the Circle's concept of justice was articulated only in a book of disputed authenticity, the *Political and Military Institutes of Tamerlane*, which stated that "by justice and equity I gained the affections of the people of God … for the ruin of the subject causes a diminution of the imperial treasures and a diminution of the imperial treasures effects the dispersion of the troops and the dispersion of the troops produces the extinction of the imperial power."[73]

The subjects' deep need for justice in daily life has been inferred from the brutality of Timur's conquests and the battles among his successors, but it was also represented in Timurid art. Miniature painting developed a new repertory of gestures and color schemes to portray "disappointed suitors, suppliants, beggars, and other unfortunates," and scenes of a petitioner before the sultan were frequently painted. The Timurids revered Alexander the Great as the Mongols' model conqueror, and a Timurid *Shahnama*, which was painted about 1400, illustrated the Alexander story almost as lavishly as the Great Mongol *Shahnama*. Miniatures of rulers enacting justice also decorated the many new copies of Nizami's Alexander epic and *The Treasury of Mysteries*, as well as of the complete *Quintet*, parts of which had been neglected since Seljuk times. The late Timurid poets Jami and Nava'i retold the Alexander legend, and several poets composed their own Quintets. Jami's had a section on "The Chain of Gold," referring to the chain of the bell that could be rung by petitioners. Repeated illustration of the stories of Alexander, Anushirvan and the ruined village, and Sultan Sanjar and the old woman secured a place at the heart of Persian miniature painting for the Circle's concept of justice.[74]

At his death, Timur's heirs and local princes divided his territories in Iran and Central Asia. Justice formed one criterion on which they were evaluated, but many apparently fell short in performance. Timur's immediate successor Shahrukh (1405–47) gave rise to conflicting reports: Armenian manuscript writers in 1421 called him a "benevolent and just king," but in 1430 he became "the wicked Shahrukh who plundered our Armenian land." Administrative development occurred during his reign, new secretarial and accounting manuals were composed, and the letters of Rashid al-Din containing the four-line Circle of Justice were compiled. According to Khwandamir, "while he was in power no officeholder was able to indulge in tyranny," and an assassin got close enough to stab him by pretending to offer a petition.[75] His biographer Dawlatshah, however, raised doubts of Shahrukh's justice; although he spoke of "a king who passes his days in justice and equity," he avoided saying directly that Shahrukh was that king.[76]

The Timurids, like the Sasanians, fully embraced the Circle of Justice only toward the end of their regime. Prince Baysunghur patronized Persianate culture and presided over the *mazalim* court; meanwhile, Ulugh Beg (1447–9) stood by the *yasa* and tradition of Genghis Khan. Abu Sa'id (1451–69) followed Islamic law but left room for the *yasa*; he favored agriculture and was considered "a good shepherd to his flock" who reputedly did not sleep during the day lest a petitioner come seeking justice. His namesake, the prince Shaykh-Abusa'id, was just the opposite: he multiplied the taxes by ten, because of which "women, heads and feet bared, their hair blowing in the wind, ran to the divan and begged helplessly for justice."[77] Only the last Timurid, Sultan-Husayn Bayqara (1470–1506), was consistently described – and described himself – in terms of the Circle of Justice.

In his "Apologia," Sultan-Husayn boasted that during his time the poor had not felt the aggression of the mighty, the roads were free of robbers and lined with caravanserais, religion was supported and the arts flourished. It was reported that "the poor and peasants of Khurasan live in welfare and ease under the shadow of his protection," and that he expanded irrigation works and supported agriculture. His policies had intermittent success in "restoring justice, in improving the conditions of the populace, and in building up the land," but in the end they failed because of political opposition from nobles whose power and revenue he tried to curtail, and their failure contributed to the breakup of the Timurid empire.[78]

The ideology behind these policies, however, became a Timurid legacy to later societies. The historian Mir Khwand (d.1498) quoted the Circle among the sayings of Ardashir.[79] An agricultural manual from the end of the Timurid period emphasized the interdependence of agriculture and political stability, maintaining that "effort in agriculture" was one of the principles of salvation and relating that Anushirvan had tried to make sure there was not a single uncultivated place in his realm, since a flourishing agriculture made possible by Sasanian-like justice and the shariah would increase the tax yield.[80] A manual of ethics written by Husayn Va'iz Kashifi known as *The Muhsinian Ethics* translated Tusi's concept of social "correspondence:" "Without the protection of justice, the powerful in society would destroy the weak, and if the weak are destroyed, the powerful will not retain their place, because the people are linked by their means of subsistence, and only justice permits the organization of human society." In his definition, "Justice is this, that they should give redress to the oppressed." The result would be "the endurance of the kingdom and its happiness, a full treasury and the flourishing condition of villages and cities," for "the subsistence of mankind is connected with their mutual dependence." Husayn Va'iz paraphrased the Circle of Justice in different ways and quoted half of it, in Arabic, at the end of the manual.[81] The full eight-line Circle of Justice entered the Timurid legacy through its illustration in an illuminated manuscript of the *Counsels of Alexander*.[82]

The Akkoyunlu struggle for justice

The Timurids' decline in the east brought artists and their manuscripts westward to new power centers that continued their artistic and governmental practices and perpetuated their ideology of justice. Two Turkic tribal confederations, the Karakoyunlu (1389–1469) and Akkoyunlu (1378–1501), gained control of eastern Anatolia and western Iran as the Jalayirids decayed. Surviving manuscripts do not describe the Karakoyunlu as interested in justice, but they did ally themselves with the last of the Jalayirids and adopted Ilkhanid political forms and Timurid refugee artists.[83] The Akkoyunlu began as raiders and *ghazis* under the Timurids, conquered the Karakoyunlu, and legitimized their rule by pairing an islamicized Turkish tribal ideology with Near Eastern administrative practices. A letter of advice attributed to the Akkoyunlu sultan Kara Osman (1403–35) called on the justice of Anushirvan, but in its concept of the Circle the ruler depended on the nomads of the warband as well as the peasants: "Without warriors and land and peasants, kingship is impossible."[84] Akkoyunlu rulers united Perso-Islamic and Turkish claims to legitimacy, calling themselves simultaneously "shadow of God, heir to the glories of Oghuz Khan and the achievements of Anushirvan." Despite a strong commitment to nomadism, they developed a bureaucracy, issued lawcodes on commerce and taxation, and in 1491 re-surveyed the revenue.[85] It was through the Akkoyunlu author Davani that the eight-line Circle of Justice passed to the Ottomans.

Jalal al-Din Davani (d.1503) dedicated *The Jalalian Ethics*, a translation and islamicization of Tusi's *Nasirean Ethics*, to the Akkoyunlu Sultan Uzun Hasan (1457–78):

> So awesome is the justice of his sway,
> The wolf does guide a lambkin gone astray.[86]

Dispensing justice followed both ancient Persian and Islamic precedents: "The kings of Persia used to have an appointed time for giving public audience to all classes of men. His Holiness the refuge of prophethood [Muhammad] had declared to the effect that a person, who is entrusted with any authority over the Muslim. and who closes his door to the needy and the offended, God Almighty shall close the door of His mercy to him."[87] To enact this justice, Uzun Hasan made himself accessible to petitioners: "When Uzun Hasan had finished the morning prayer, the 'drum of justice' would be sounded to indicate the convening of the court of appeals. There he would appear in person."[88] Davani closed his work with the advice of Aristotle to Alexander and the eight-part Circle of Justice. This Persian Circle conveyed a somewhat different sense from the Arabic one in *The Secret of Secrets* and *The Counsels of Alexander* because of slight differences in wording and in the meaning of words common to Arabic and Persian.

> The world is a garden irrigated by good fortune (or, the dynasty)
> Good fortune is a sultan whose chamberlain is the law
> Shariah is governance protected by the kingdom
> The kingdom is a city brought into being by the army
> The army is supported by money
> Money is collected from the people
> The people are servants subjected by justice
> Justice is the pivot of the welfare of the world.[89]

In this version of the Circle, kings ruled over a bounded world, not a pasture but an irrigated garden in an urban, even a palatial, setting (with no room for the dragons of the earlier version). Law was codified in the shariah and sovereignty was personified in the king, for whom the term "shepherd" no longer seemed appropriate. Justice here was even more central (the "pivot"), but its definition appeared less clear as pastoral imagery gave way to the hierarchy and pragmatism of the "city."[90] This reworking of the Circle of Justice seems to clash with nomadic ideology, but it may reflect the sedentarization and islamicization of the Mongols' successor states. It also embodied a strong hierarchical tendency reinforced by the system of landholding. The Akkoyunlu used the severe post-Mongol *iqta* system that gave landholders nearly sovereign rights over land and people. During his reign, Uzun Hasan balanced the divisiveness of these powerful landholders with a strengthened imperial administration, for which he probably had the Ilkhanid finance manuals recopied. He also instituted new taxes, perhaps to replace revenues alienated to the landholders.[91]

A description of the just society by Fazlullah ibn Ruzbihan, the greatest political thinker of the age, retained the Circle's sense of interdependence among people, revenue, army, and ruler but reached a harsher conclusion: "The support and allowances of the people of Islam are from the proceeds of the land tax, because the livelihood of the inhabitants of the regions of Islam comes from agriculture, the good order and preservation of which depends upon the army; and the stability of the army depends upon its wages and its wages come from the land tax. Therefore, if the sultan shows negligence in the collection of the land tax or abandons it, disorder will occur."[92] Fazlullah tried to bring Uzun Hasan's reforms into line with orthodox Islamic law, stressing the Islamic legality of agricultural taxes and the illegitimacy of administrative dues and trade levies, some of Mongol origin. Powerful landholders resisted such changes, and the epic struggles over this issue divided and weakened the empire.

The conflict over reform generated a discourse on justice that pervaded the histories of the period.[93] Fazlullah argued that the Akkoyunlu Sultan Ya'qub (1478–90) was the restorer of the age, since he cancelled illegal taxes, compensated peasants for crops destroyed by his soldiers, and enforced Islamic law.[94] Davani, who favored revenue grants for the ulema, called Ya'qub's tax-cutting agenda "tyranny and oppression" and refused to engage in government service until this injustice was rectified. Authors portrayed Sultan Ahmad (1497) either as the introducer of the rules of justice or as a prince of exceptional villainy. He was determined to base his regime on revenues legalized by Islamic law and to abolish tribal law even if he had to fight all the tribal leaders to do so, but the historian Idris Bitlisi considered that the injustice and violence of his warfare lost the Akkoyunlu their mandate to rule.[95] As significant as the destructive warfare and competition for revenue among these leaders was their ideological conflict over what constituted justice, particularly in taxation and revenue allocation. In the region dominated by these tribal polities, the process of integrating Turco-Mongol and Perso-Islamic norms into a single whole was a precarious one. No more than the Ilkhanids and Timurids could the Akkoyunlu settle the issue within the short lifetime of their dynasty. Nevertheless, they sought to balance the demands of nomadic warlords against different conceptions of the needs of the subjects, and their struggles for leadership constituted an argument about the definition of justice and good rulership.

Mamluks and Ibn Khaldun (1250–1517)

The only Middle Eastern regime to stand against the Mongols was the Mamluks. The Mamluk rulers of Egypt and Syria, like the Seljuks and Mongols, traced their origins to the steppe, but they came to the Middle East not as tribes or hordes but as individuals, separated from steppe culture and converted to Islam at an early age. They were originally slaves (*mamluks*), purchased as adolescents and intensively trained as elite troops. Manumitted at graduation, they retained close ties to their former masters, advancing with them through the ranks. The sultan's *mamluks* could even aspire to rule: in 1250 the slave generals overthrew their enfeebled Ayyubid masters and took the throne, initiating the Mamluk Sultanate. Legitimated by unexpected victories over the Mongols and the Crusaders under Louis IX, they passed the throne to sons or fellow *mamluks* by combat or intrigue for two-and-a-half centuries.

Despite the Mamluks' slave origin, Mamluk society was class-based and strongly hierarchical, distinguishing sharply between Mamluks and civilians. The Mamluk sultans obtained legitimation from the shadow caliph, but they also claimed to be chosen by God and independent of the caliph's will. The qadi Ibn Jama'a (d.1333) and many of his contemporaries, like the advice writers of Seljuk Anatolia, transferred to the sultan the functions that al-Mawardi had allocated to the caliph: protecting religion, providing justice, collecting taxes, and maintaining order.[96] A similar solution appeared in the works of Ibn Taimiya (d.1328); although he recommended a public policy based completely on the Qur'an and *hadith* (a *siyasa shar'iyya*), he too awarded to the sultan the authority to administer justice, wage holy war, lead prayers, and relieve the oppressed, and on that account designated him as God's Shadow on Earth, quoting the proverb, "The world can endure with justice and unbelief, but it can not endure with injustice and Islam."[97]

The Circle of Justice in Mamluk culture

Ibn Jama'a saw no discontinuity between the precepts of the Qur'an and Near Eastern concepts of state, writing in his political advice book that "justice is the cause of the increase of blessings and of the growth of prosperity, but that injustice and tyranny are the reason for the destruction of empires."[98] He even quoted the Circle of Justice, though in a garbled form: "The kingdom is a building supported by the army. The army are soldiers assembled by money. Money is sustenance obtained from prosperity, and prosperity is an accomplishment brought about by justice. And the wise men say that the world is a garden whose walls are the state. The state is authority supported by the soldiers. The soldiers are an army assembled by money. Money is sustenance gathered by the subjects. The subjects are servants raised up by justice."[99]

The offhand way in which Ibn Jama'a relayed this passage suggests that he knew his readers were familiar with it. They could have encountered it in a biography of Aristotle in the collection of medical biographies by the thirteenth-century Egyptian author Ibn Abi Usaybi'a (d.1270) called *Sources of Information on the Generations of Physicians*. This book listed among the sayings of Aristotle the eight sentences which he desired to be written at his death on the sides of his costly tomb. The eight sentences, carefully numbered, were marked on an eight-sided diagram (of the tomb?).[100] In a book on ethics, al-Watwat (d.1318) paraphrased the last line, clearly expecting his readers to recognize the quotation:

> For justice is the support of the world and the faith,
> And the cause of the health of all creation.[101]

Mamluk authors and encyclopedists, whose books could be read in private and public libraries throughout the city, cited the Circle of Justice as part of the intellectual heritage of the past.[102] The administrator al-Nuwayri (d.1331), in his encyclopedic reference work of *adab* and history, attributed it to 'Amr ibn al-'As, and al-Ibshihi (d.1446), in his anthology of "wise maxims," gave it five terms and traced it to Anushirvan.[103] The eight-line version appeared in *The Principal Influences on the Progression of Dynasties* by al-'Abbasi (d.1310), introduced by the note that Alexander had between his hands an eight-sided wheel or ball of gold which Aristotle had invented, on each side of which was written a political sentence on which he should act. This version seems to be the first to islamicize the concept by inserting the term "shariah" in place of *siyasa*, policy, making the Circle consistent with Ibn Taymiya's political ideal. Ibn al-Azraq (d.1491) also quoted the eight-line version (without "shariah") in his *Marvellous Lines on the Nature of Authority*, an analytical advice work based on Ibn Khaldun.[104]

The Circle of Justice provided Mamluk subjects with criteria for legitimating and praising the ruler: a fifteenth-century writer praised the sultan for protecting helpless subjects against robbery and brigandage and maintaining order in the cities. Mamluk rulers also adopted it as a standard of behavior: Sultan Baybars (1260–77), during the grain crisis of 1264, took responsibility for feeding the poor for three months, and Sultan Kitbugha (1295–97) did the same in 1295. Memoranda by Sultan Qalawun (1310–41) prioritized adherence to the shariah and provision of justice. He knew that "justice results in the cultivation of the land and financial profits which are the essential element, or basis, of the armies," so he ordered his deputy to "collect proper petitions from all the people to discuss them in order to preserve that golden age" because "the strong must not use their power to dominate the weak."[105]

Mazalim, *Mamluk style*

Predictably, a prominent element in Mamluk administration was *mazalim*, lauded by the finance official al-Qalqashandi (d.1418) in his secretarial manual *Daybreak for the Blind* as "rendering justice to the victim of a wrong against the one who committed it, delivering the right from the wrong, succoring the weak against the strong, assuring the observation of the rules of justice throughout the realm." The Mamluk sultans maintained Fatimid and Ayyubid institutions of justice, but during times of political upheaval the *mazalim* court was not convened. Reopened when the crisis came under control, it symbolized the stability and order provided by a powerful sultan, hearing cases against qadis, the great men of the realm, and even the sultan himself. The *mazalim* court, however, changed over time from an imitation of Ayyubid judicial practice to a ceremonial occasion renewing the ruler's legitimacy, while royal judicial activity was transferred to other locations.[106]

Cases were first heard in the Ayyubids' House of Justice in one of the schools of Cairo. In 1262, to reinforce the independence of the Mamluk regime, Sultan Baybars built a new House of Justice near the Citadel. Al-Nasir Muhammad (1294–97, 1299–1309) constructed a second House of Justice inside the Citadel in 1315; its open sides suggested the sultan's accessibility. In 1387 Sultan Barquq (1382–89, 1390–99) started hearing *mazalim* cases in the Royal Stables below the Citadel, surrounded by the chief qadis, government officials, and military officers. This was not an insult; in Turkish practice, stables and posthouses were places of political sanctuary.[107] The House of Justice inside the Citadel became the place where the sultan "held court" ceremonially. Special sittings of the *mazalim* court acclaimed the enthronement of new sultans. The hearing of petitions became a symbol legitimating the ruler's power and may have lost some of its effectiveness as a means of complaining against governmental oppression.[108]

If the petition process became ineffectual, however, the Egyptian populace could resort to mass demonstrations. Because the rulers looked askance at popular political participation, they had to maintain a certain level of responsiveness to petitions as a safety valve. When the authorities became too oppressive, people took their demands for justice to the streets. An upsurge of crime, urban rioting, or Bedouin incursions indicated a lapse in the ruler's ability to govern: "Every grain crisis thus became a … political struggle." In 1412 the sultan punished grocers who closed their shops in the wake of currency alterations, since the people's inability to buy bread could be interpreted as the ruler's inability to feed his flock; his "sheer fury" recalls the Ghaznavid Sultan Ibrahim's "great shame" at his incapacity to provide for his subjects.[109]

To maintain public order, Mamluk sultans dispensed free grain to the poor during times of shortage and tried to control elite violence.[110] Sultan al-Ghuri (1501–16), to enhance his image as the fountain of justice, demolished the House of Justice and built a bigger, more magnificent one. An advice book written for him addressed the intricacies of judging *mazalim* cases. He also restored the Nilometer, posing as bestower of the people's well-being by praying for the annual Nile flood. His predecessor Qaytbay (1468–96) similarly used his judicial role in *mazalim* to emphasize his solidarity with his subjects, intervening personally in cases of official dereliction and announcing his return to health after a riding accident by presiding over the *mazalim* court.[111]

According to the historian Ibn Iyas (d. 1522), however, royal injustice contributed to the Mamluks' fall in 1517. Sultan al-Ghuri's preparations for war with the Ottomans included oppressive levies on peasant villages and extortion of money from women who sacrificed their dowries to pay. In the very first battle the Sultan was killed and his body lost, never to be buried in the magnificent tomb for which he had squeezed so much money from the people. He was commemorated in a verse describing the disastrous effects of injustice:

> Look with wonder at al-Ashraf al-Ghuri,
> Who, after his tyranny had reached its height in Cairo,
> Lost his kingdom in an hour,
> Lost this world and the world to come.

His successor Tuman Bay (1517), commissioned to "abolish the tyrannical innovations of al-Ghuri," tore down the stone *mastaba*, the seat or throne that al-Ghuri had erected, and replaced it with a simple wooden dais:

> The Dais of Justice has come back,
> The "Mastabah" of Injustice has been pulled down;
> Tuman Bai has become amongst the people
> As one who causes the wolf to live with the sheep in peace.
> Oh! what a King he is! his justice has become notorious
> Amongst Arabs, and people of other countries.

He also punished advisors who recommended oppressive measures, even to raise money for an army bonus, and tried to enforce Islamic law. His justice came too late, though; in the last battle his troops fled, leaving him to defeat. The Ottomans legitimized their conquest of Egypt specifically by replacing Mamluk justice with their own.[112]

The Circle in Mamluk administration

Like the Seljuk and Mongol armies, the Mamluk troops were supported mainly by *iqtas*, and it was through the *iqta* administration that the rural population felt the ruler's justice or injustice most directly. "Good administration" meant the proper allocation of *iqtas* and the fair assessment and collection of taxes, obtained by regular surveys of land and agricultural production. Ordinarily government agents set taxation levels on the basis of the height of the Nile flood and refined the assessment by surveying the actual area planted to crops. "This," said al-Nuwayri in his secretarial handbook, "is justice and equity, and whoever departs from it has erred and done wrong." A handbook by the late Ayyubid finance official al-Nabulusi had decreed "failure to make a survey of all private and public property annually, by faithful and recognized assessors, together with honest and intelligent soldiers who are heedful, scribes who are expert in surveying, and two or three of the most faithful accountants, who fear for their honor" to be "amazing negligence."[113] Under the Mamluks, however, *iqta* recipients participated in making the surveys and keeping the records, which left ample room for abuses like those in the Akkoyunlu *iqta* system.

According to al-Maqrizi, another type of survey, estimating the average yield from each plot, was supposed to be done every thirty years but had been neglected for a long time.[114] A third kind of survey, allocating the *iqtas* among their holders, was made only twice, in 1298 and 1315. These surveys centralized landholding in the hands of the elite: the first took *iqtas* from ordinary soldiers and redistributed them to Mamluk officers, while the second put more *iqtas* under the sultan's direct control. Despite this centralization, later Mamluk sultans could not maintain the irrigation works or force *iqta* holders to do so, and demands for heightened revenue were not matched by improvements in production. People responded to increasingly oppressive tax collection not with open rebellion but with foot-dragging and evasion, using petitioning as a last resort.[115] They could present petitions directly to the sultan, but according to al-Qalqashandi, most petitions went through administrative channels. At least eight other secretarial manuals appeared during the Mamluk period, and they show that Mamluk petition forms and practices resembled those of the Fatimids. Topics of complaint in the few surviving documents include interference with a poor man's palm trees, Bedouin raids on St. Catherine's monastery in the Sinai, and an *iqta* holder's taking revenue he was not entitled to.[116]

The Mamluks generally minimized Turkish elements in their culture, but like the Karakhanids they gave the chamberlain a prominent role in facilitating the petition process and in judging disputes outside the shariah. As judge of the army, the chamberlain became the repository of Turkish customary law and the Mongol *yasa*. Descriptions of the Ilkhanids' legal alterations after their conversion made a pun on the words *yasa* and *siyasa* (ruler's policy, state regulation), and al-Maqrizi, who was vehemently opposed to assimilation between Mongol and Muslim practices, cited this play on words as "proof" that *siyasa* was derived from the non-Islamic *yasa*. He then used that derivation to denigrate ruler's law, the chamberlain's role in it, and Mamluk governance in general.[117]

In the last Mamluk century the chamberlain's jurisdiction spread from the army to the civilian population, and he began judging shariah cases as well as those covered by ruler's law. His office expanded to include numerous assistants, all Mamluks. Some gained good reputations as *mazalim* judges, like Sudun, who "invariably supported the weak against the strong," and Taghri Birdi, who "never heard a petition sent [to him] without struggling to do justice, as he saw it." These stories contrast sharply with tales of oppression and arbitrariness by Mamluk soldiers, who commonly violated laws and oppressed civilians because they could only be tried in the *mazalim* court. People reluctantly put up with their injustices because of their military ability and defense of Islam.[118]

The Circle of Justice received some emphasis in Mamluk cultural media. Tiles, carpets, and book illustrations in eastern styles created by artists trained in the Timurid tradition became vehicles for or reminders of Near Eastern concepts of justice. Karakoyunlu painters in Cairo in 1468 illustrated a Turkish version of the Alexander legend by the Anatolian poet Ahmedi. In 1511, the royal manuscript workshop issued a *Shahnama* in Turkish with 62 illustrations. Some were copied from older manuscripts, but many were original paintings depicting the Mamluk court in Timurid style, a gesture suggesting appreciation of the Timurids' political ideals along with their dress and literature.[119]

Arabic political literature was not neglected; *Kalila and Dimna* was highly popular, and during the fourteenth century the *Thousand and One Nights* took its more-or-less final form, including the story of Anushirvan and the ruined villages. Advice works written for Sultan al-Ghuri referred to the justice of Alexander the Great and the Persian kings. In the nearby court of Tunis, the qadi Ibn Radwan al-Andalusi (d.1381) wrote *Brilliant Blazes on Practical Politics*, using the four-line Circle of Justice to show that justice, not military force, was the real foundation of society. The contemporary Moroccan sultan Abu Hammu II (1323–89) also wrote a book of politics called *The Mediator of Behavior for the Policy of Kings*, where he quoted the four-line Circle to support the idea that "the kingdom is a building and justice is its foundation."[120]

Ibn Khaldun and his Introduction to History

Perhaps the most outstanding cultural product of this period was the history of Ibn Khaldun (1332–1406), with its well-known *Introduction to History* (*Muqaddimah*) containing one of the most famous citations of the Circle of Justice. Ibn Khaldun served as a *mazalim* judge, qadi, and royal advisor in both Morocco and Egypt, watching Mamluk and North African dynasties rise and fall and meditating on the nature of human society.[121] He saw royal authority as having a life-cycle of initial success, adoption of civilization and justice by the conquerors, increasing luxury and exploitation, and final debilitation and ruin, leading to conquest by a new and energetic power. He is often cited as the main transmitter of the Circle of Justice, but unlike its other transmitters he considered it no mere literary gem nor even a piece of good advice to a ruler. To him it epitomized the real nature of human association and formed the key to the science of civilization which he felt he had been led by God to understand and set forth. At the beginning of his *Introduction* he quoted the Circle in three versions: the tale of Bahram and the owls as relayed by al-Mas'udi, the four-line saying of Anushirvan, and the eight sentences of Aristotle. He credited the author of *The Secret of Secrets* with the circular arrangement of the eight sentences but expressed his disapproval of all previous writers for not supporting this crucial statement with arguments or pursuing its historical implications, as he intended to do.[122]

According to Ibn Khaldun, struggle for power did not in itself delegitimate kingship, but a king's power could be dissipated by injustice. The ruler and his army lived on the wealth of the conquered cities, returning the people's taxes in the form of gifts and public works. They would be successful as long as they remained just, but as the level of luxury among the rulers increased so did the level of exploitation, and injustice soon produced division and "the ruin of civilization." So strongly did Ibn Khaldun insist on this point that in discussing the injurious effects of injustice on society he retold the entire story of Bahram and the owls, ending with the vizier's advice from the Circle of Justice:

> "O King, the might of royal authority materializes only through the religious law, obedience toward God, and compliance with His commands and prohibitions. The religious law persists only through royal authority. Mighty royal authority is achieved only through men. Men persist only with the help of property. The only way to property is through cultivation. The only way to cultivation is through justice. Justice is a balance set up among mankind. The Lord set it up and appointed an overseer of it, and that is the ruler." The lesson this story teaches is that injustice ruins civilization. The ruin of civilization has as its consequence the complete destruction of the dynasty.[123]

In his history, Ibn Khaldun managed to do something previously only achieved by the philosophers: he set the Circle of Justice within an analysis of human existence. In this context, justice formed an essential element in the working of society rather than an optional added virtue or attribute of the rulers, desirable but not intrinsic to the system, as both jurists and advice writers had described it. Earlier analyses of justice in society by philosophers had described justice as a mean or equilibrium; among philosophical works, only Davani's specifically cited the Circle, and even for him it was an afterthought. Ibn Khaldun, however, based his social analysis on the full Circle of Justice as relayed by the advice writers. Moreover, the society in which he saw the Circle at work was not a visionary utopia but actual human history with all its flaws and injustices. His insight into society's workings was unique for his time, but perhaps it was facilitated by an increasing ability of Middle Eastern regimes to institutionalize the Near Eastern concept of justice in its islamicized form.

Conclusion

Ibn Khaldun's cyclical concept of royal authority seemed to deny the possibility of progress or development from one conquest regime to another. In the Middle Eastern context, however, successive regimes built upon the experiences of their predecessors both ideologically and administratively. This was made possible by a governmental class of great continuity that preserved the procedures and literatures of the past and improved on them over generations.[124] In Egypt and the Fertile Crescent, the scribal class retained all the power and influence, if not the independence, of bygone eras, leaving monuments in the form of histories and manuals as impressive as the mosques and palaces of the rulers, and possibly more useful. Paradoxically, the Mongol conquest, although destructive, contributed to this process by the Mongols' dependence on their Persian administrators, as well as by their addition of Chinese administrators and technicians to the mix and their encouragement of a cross-fertilization of ideas and methods.

Building on Seljuk and Ayyubid precedents, Turco-Mongol steppe practices and Chinese bureaucratic methods, Mongol and Mamluk administrators found solutions for problems in Middle Eastern governance that would make possible the great stable empires of the early modern period. The boost given by the veneration of Genghis

Khan's bloodline to the ideology of the divine selection of an entire dynasty not related to the Prophet legitimated rule by other Muslim dynasties of non-Arab extraction. The Mongol census with its Chinese admixture made a highly sophisticated foundation for agrarian organization in the new empires, and the prestige awarded by the *yasa* to rulers' law in general facilitated the provision of royal justice and raised the status of *mazalim*, allowing rulers to regulate more closely matters outside (and even inside) the provenance of the shariah. The subsequent dynasties of the early modern period improved upon Mongol and post-Mongol procedures and ideas to create a new kind of state in the Middle East whose longevity and good organization Ibn Khaldun himself could not have predicted.

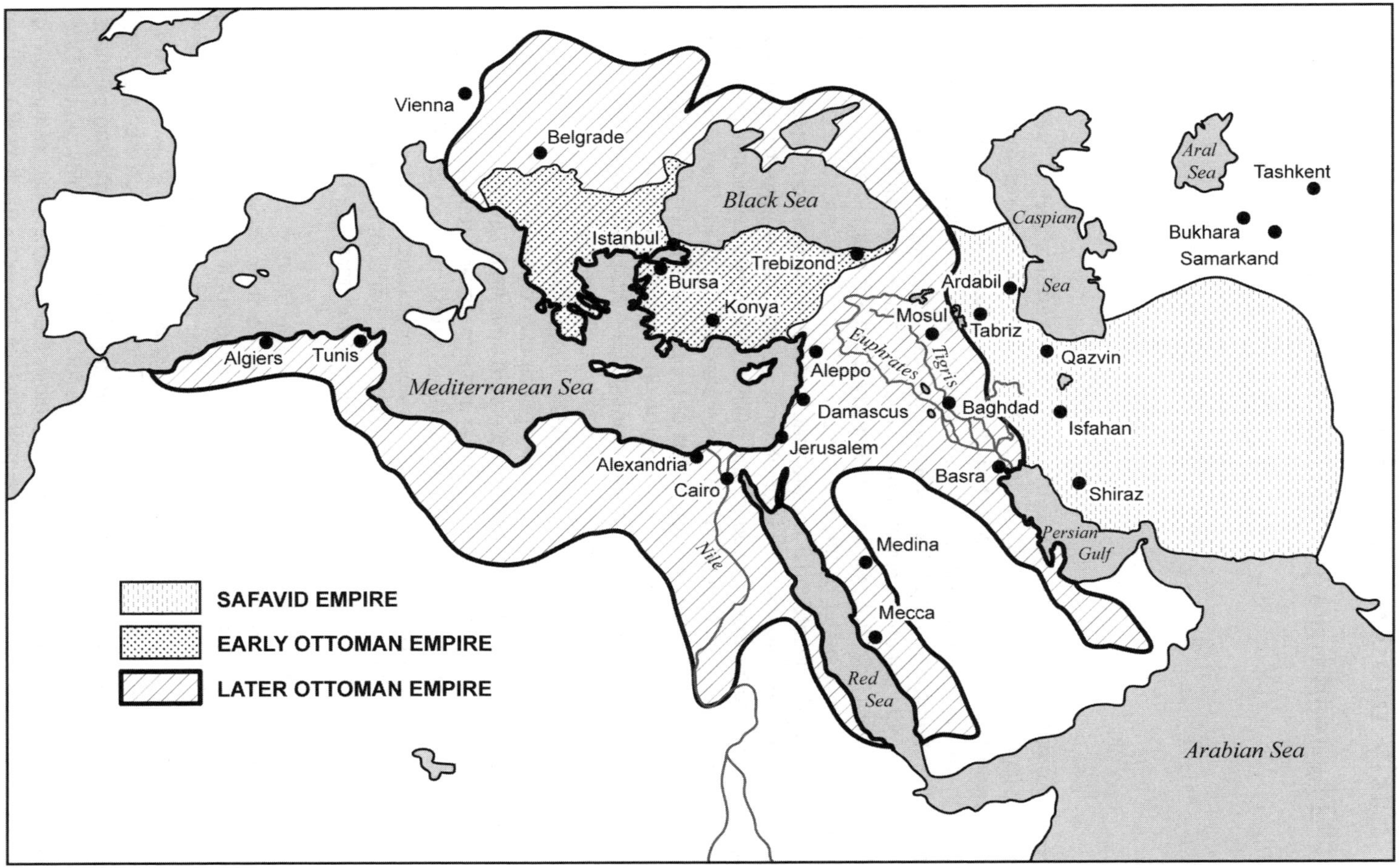

Map 7 The Ottoman and Safavid empires

8 Early modern empires

"The world is a garden, its wall is the state"

By the early modern period, the Circle of Justice was a secure part of the Islamicate political heritage, essential to political relations in the new empires arising in that period.[1] These empires all had Turco-Mongol origins, but they overcame nomadic instability to create "Well-Protected Domains," larger and more stable territories that endured for centuries rather than the decades of earlier regimes, with more consistent boundaries and more effective central control. The tug of war between the central state and its warrior nobility did not pull these states apart but left them intact, stronger and more independent, in a better position to put the recommendations of the advice writers into practice. The institutional transformations of the period from 1500 to 1800 created large urbanized states with sophisticated administrative systems, centralized revenue collection, gunpowder weapons, and political ideologies in which the reciprocal obligations of the Circle of Justice formed a core element. For them, the Circle was not problematic in any way; it was an integral part of their political thought and behavior.

The first of these new empires to appear in the Middle East was the Ottoman Empire in the central Middle East and the Balkans (1299–1923), followed by the Safavid Empire in Iran (1501–1722).[2] The early Ottoman principality emerged on the west coast of Asia Minor, one of the dozen or so small principalities into which Anatolia split when the Mongol Empire broke up. The Ottoman principality eventually incorporated the others, expanded into the Balkans, and conquered all the Arab lands except Morocco and Oman. In its first two centuries of conquest and expansion it resembled the rapidly changing sultanates of the post-Mongol period, but it was able to contain the centrifugal force of the warrior elite to become a stable bureaucratic empire in the early modern period. The Safavids, whose empire included parts of the Akkoyunlu and Timurid realms, formed as a bureaucratic state in an Iran torn apart by the elites of those empires.

For the Ottomans, the Circle of Justice was not a mere literary curiosity but a foundational element in the empire's ideology and a key to their transformation; for the Safavids it was an important part of the Persian heritage but it played a more marginal role in their political life, reflected in their more marginal treatment here. At the end of the sixteenth century, the image of Ottoman justice grew tarnished by official corruption, economic difficulties, and institutional change. The Circle of Justice then appeared in the new advice works written to critique Ottoman policies and recommend solutions. These works are usually considered a primary site for the Circle's deployment in Ottoman literature, but strangely, it played less of a role in them than in political literature of earlier and later centuries. Moreover, the problems of the early modern era did not respond to the solutions presented by the seventeenth-century advice writers.

Geopolitical and technological changes demanded the development of new systems and institutions, and justice eventually became less central to Ottoman concerns than military power or financial solvency, though the demand for justice did not disappear.

The era of expansion (1299–1520)

The Ottoman and Safavid Empires were expansive states in the early modern age of expansion. Unlike so many conquerors in Middle Eastern history, these dynasties did not adopt the Near Eastern state as outsiders but were acquainted with it from the start. In both the Seljuk and Ilkhanid cases, Persian administrators had imposed the Circle of Justice on tribal ruling elites, but in the early modern empires the initiative was ascribed to the rulers themselves. The Ottomans initially created a conquest state with institutions geared for rapid expansion, but their reputation for justice accompanied or even preceded their early conquests.[3] By the fifteenth century the Circle of Justice was repeated extensively in Ottoman literature, and the provision of justice was institutionalized in Ottoman administration.

Justice in early Ottoman culture

Fifteenth-century Ottoman chronicles romanticized the founder Osman (1280–1324) and his forebears as simple tribal nomads who migrated from Khurasan to the border between the Seljuk and Byzantine empires, away from sedentary civilization. Khurasan, however, was not the pagan steppe but the heartland of eastern Islam, where nomadic life had long been pursued amid imperial governance and Perso-Islamic civilization. The Ottomans, who lacked dynastic or religious claims to legitimacy, stressed justice as establishing their right to rule and reduced taxes to retain popular loyalty. Towns surrendered and peasants moved from other regions to Ottoman-controlled areas to partake of their justice.[4] The first extant Ottoman historical narrative, Ahmedi's *Tale of Alexander* (1410), superimposed justice over divine approval and military victory, praising the Ottomans as "people of justice … who first to last were both Muslims and just rulers."[5] The ideal just regime described in Seljuk and Ilkhanid sources became for the Ottomans a real political goal.

The literary history of Anatolia demonstrates that from the start the Anatolian principalities had access to Perso-Islamic governmental models in which the Circle of Justice played a significant role. The works composed in western Anatolia in or just after the last quarter of the thirteenth century include a collection of model documents called *A Garden for Scribes* (1279); Ibn Bibi's history of the Seljuks (1282); *The Scales* (or *Pavilion*) *of Justice* (1284), an advice book; Aksarayi's chronicle (1323), which quoted Nizam al-Mulk and Nizami, cited the proverb "there's no tax on ruined villages," and quoted part of the Circle; and several scribal manuals produced between 1280 and 1310 for an Ilkhanid governor on the western frontier, one of which contained two sample letters of complaint.[6] Documentary evidence is lacking for the reign of Osman, but his successor Orhan (1324–62) appointed officials and produced documents in Seljuk and Ilkhanid styles.[7]

The disappearance of Seljuk and Ilkhanid cultural patronage in Anatolia after 1335 opened space for a more popular political vision; tales of the frontier mystic Sarı Saltuk, for example, showed him preaching justice and equity, good treatment of the weak, and control of the powerful men of state from outside the royal court.[8] Toward mid-century, however, a translation movement produced Turkish versions of Arabic and Persian classics conveying the Circle of Justice, such as *Kalila and Dimna*, the *Book of*

Ka'us, selections from Nizami, and the *History* of al-Tabari.[9] Najm al-Din Razi's *The Path of God's Bondsmen* was also popular; several of the existing copies date from the mid-fourteenth century.[10] New literature for sultans appearing after the end of the century combined folk and classical influences.

Ottoman organizational development largely followed Seljuk and Ilkhanid precedents in the bureaucracy, centralized army, and mechanisms of justice. But where the Mongols employed sedentary governing techniques to serve nomadic goals, the Ottomans embedded nomadic elements, such as the feasting of followers at the ruler's table or the right of all his sons to vie for rulership, within a typical Near Eastern imperial administration. The Ottomans also adopted the ancient Assyrian practice of bringing up the children of defeated enemies in the ruler's palace to become his closest servants, bodyguards, and officials, creating a household that mirrored the diversity of the empire; Greeks, Serbians, Bosnians, Albanians, and later Georgians and Circassians became the sultan's pages, officers, and high officials. The collection of these children (*devshirme*) also supplied the elite military slaves of the standing forces, the janissary infantry, artillery, and palace cavalry.[11] The Ottomans, like the Seljuks and Mongols, replaced their tribal forces with heavy cavalry and infantry with siege machinery and cannon. To support the non-nomadic horsemen they developed a version of the *iqta* system called *timar*, which centralized land and revenue grants and increased bureaucratic and sultanic oversight to prevent injustice.

Timar-holders, like *iqta* recipients, collected peasants' taxes in lieu of salary, but they were less like feudal lords and more like government officials: they were organized into provinces and districts under centrally appointed commander/governors and rotated regularly to prevent construction of a local power base.[12] The *timar* system started in western Anatolia, and Bayezid I (1389–1402) extended it to the newly conquered territories on the frontiers.[13] Unlike the free-wheeling and exploitative post-Mongol *iqta*, the Ottoman *timar* system preserved governmental control over land use and peasant taxation; few *timars* were free of "the pens and the feet" of the ruler's agents. This improved ability to safeguard peasants' interests, along with lower taxes and religious toleration, enhanced the Ottomans' legitimacy.

Taxes were determined by a land survey, justified in terms of social interdependence; an edict authorized surveys "in order that the populace of the province (who are the source of the continued prosperity of the state and the cause of its good order) would be sheltered from oppression and attain a prosperous condition."[14] Like the Harran census, survey registers listed the sources of revenue, the names of taxpayers and their crops, and the residents and revenue-producing activities of the towns. Despite episodes of peasant mockery or even murder of surveyors, the surveys brought central and local administrators together with *timar*-holders and peasants to negotiate mutually acceptable tax totals.[15] The *timar* system made powerful military commanders dependent on the state, provided agrarian oversight and rural policing, and created a public record of tax assessments, enabling peasants and townsmen to appeal against violations. Since all peasants regardless of religion could petition the sultan directly, they had a powerful ally against oppression by the military-administrative class.

Civil war and cultural reassessment

If the Ottomans employed Ilkhanid and Byzantine administrative techniques and assimilated Timurid cultural trends, ideologically they resembled the Seljuk advice writers, who integrated Islamic and Near Eastern ideas of legitimacy in a way that can truly be called Perso-Islamic.[16] Ottoman writers portrayed their rulers as true Muslims and their conquests as *ghaza* but judged their rule preferable to the Byzantines' because of their justice, seen in God's selection of them and in their shepherding care of the flock. This ideological mixture was visible in the oldest narrative of Ottoman history still extant, the last part of Ahmedi's *Tale of Alexander*. This epic appeared in the aftermath of the Ottomans' catastrophic defeat by Timur in 1402 and the subsequent war for the throne among the sons of Bayezid I. The story was based on Nizami's *Tale of Alexander*, which along with its parent work, the *Shahnama*, became popular throughout the Middle East around that time.[17]

Ahmedi's work included a panegyric to the Ottoman sultans, their justice and their *ghaza*; "the business of all of them was to fight with the unbelievers," while the Mongols "openly oppressed the people, they oppressed the people by means of the law, without bloodying their hands, oppression by law and taxation."[18] The juxtaposition of this theme with the stories of Alexander and the pre-Islamic kings immediately recalls similar combinations of Islamic and Near Eastern themes in the mirrors for princes of Kai Ka'us and Najm al-Din Razi, or the tile-lined palace of Ahmad Teguder. Like them, it was as much a prescription for rectitude as a description of the sultans' deeds, contrasting their early piety and justice with later failures.[19] By attaching his critique of the Mongols to the tale of Alexander and the history of sultans famous for justice, Ahmedi implied that he was not opposed to imperial governance as such but to its unjust application.

The work's paramount illustration of the theme of just versus unjust rule was Ahmedi's patron, Bayezid I. Bayezid's *timar* registers and tax surveys made him the first Ottoman ruler who could claim legitimacy through good administration. "There was not any place in all of Rum which was not developed with his justice." Later sources blamed Bayezid's officials and their Byzantine backgrounds for "Christian" corruptions such as wine-drinking and for "Byzantine" imperial practices of elaborate court protocol and *timar* taxation.[20] Ahmedi attributed Bayezid's defeat by Timur to the Ottoman forces' rejection of his corruption and injustice. The war for the throne after Timur's departure brought Mehmed I (1413–21) to the throne as restorer of the empire. He and his successors prudently based their legitimacy on their military achievements and bowed to Timurid political pressure and cultural superiority.[21]

At the same time, fifteenth-century Ottoman sultans preserved Bayezid I's administrative advances. Even while the civil war was still in progress Mehmed I had one of the Ilkhanid finance manuals recopied.[22] When he re-established control over former Ottoman territory he enforced the *timar* system and land registration, making surveys and keeping registers.[23] The sultans established provincial regulations called *kanun* that eliminated abusive or un-Islamic taxes and specified the rights of *timar*-holders and peasants. Both groups defined justice as obedience to *kanun*: for peasants, *kanun* justice signified limits on taxation, and for *timar* holders it meant gaining *timar*s properly as rewards for loyalty and valor.[24]

Scribal and advice literature situated these developments within the ideology of Perso-Islamic governance. The Ottomans and other Anatolian principalities were familiar with classical political thought and administrative practice and by the early fifteenth century were contributing to both. The Turkish work *Treasure of the Great* (1400), based on *The Path of God's Bondsmen*, recommended that rulers should be just to both soldiers and common people, since kingship and justice were twins. An original work of ethics in the style of Tusi, *The Treasure of Happiness*, was dedicated to Mehmed I, and the first illuminated version of Ahmedi's *Tale of Alexander* also appeared during his reign.[25]

At this time, too, Amasi wrote his *Mirror for Princes*, a work of philosophical ethics in the style of Tusi with sections on ethics, economics, and politics. Within an extended medical metaphor of the ills of society and himself as a doctor providing remedies to restore it to health, he quoted the Circle of Justice in a story about Anushirvan the Just borrowed from al-Ghazali. In this story, Anushirvan one day announced that he was ill and ordered that the kingdom be searched for an old tile which could be pulverized to make a medication. No old tiles could be found, and Anushirvan rejoiced, because his real purpose had been to discover the condition of his kingdom, which the new tiles showed was flourishing. The intelligent agreed that this proved the maxim that religion is founded on kingship, and kingship on the army, and the army on money, and money on the prosperity of the country, and the prosperity of the country on justice among the believers.[26]

Murad II (1421–51), whose *ghazi* credentials were extolled in a *Book of Ghaza*, supported further contributions to the literature of justice and good administration. The administrative literature included the first original secretarial handbooks in Turkish, authored by Ahmed Da'i and Hafiz Husam.[27] Murad sponsored new translations of the standard advice works and composed his own book of advice for his son Mehmed to teach him to govern with justice and compassion. Other new advice works included Ahmed Da'i's Turkish version of the *Testament of Anushirvan the Just* and his poem telling how all the ends of the earth sought out the justice of the Ottoman sultans.[28] Early fifteenth-century Ottoman ideology and organization paired the expansion of the empire with its just governance and good administration.

Mehmed the Conqueror and ruler's law

The Ottoman conquest of Constantinople in 1453 fulfilled Islamic society's oldest dream, the capture of the elusive "Red Apple," the unattainable prize, the capital of Christendom.[29] This victory transformed the Ottoman state from a successful border kingdom to a world-class empire and reinforced the sense that divine favor produced military victory. Mehmed II, the Conqueror (1451–81), like Alexander and Timur, was "eager to conquer the whole world, and to rule greater empires than any of those who came before him." Like the Sasanian kings and the caliph Mu'awiya, he had the histories of earlier kings read to him nightly. His vizier, Sinan Pasha (d.1486), wrote him an ethics book, *The Book of Instruction*, that was steeped in the Perso-Islamic heritage, although it did not quote the Circle of Justice directly. The sultan's justice, he said,

> is a right hand to his prosperity and a helper to his glory, an assistant to his felicity, a support for his nobility, a watchman of his property, an exalter of his kingdom. It bestows his presence on his flock and his gratitude on his gifts; it attracts those who beg for alms and brings about rewards for the worthy. One hour of it is worth a thousand years of obedience, and one measure of it brings religion alive. All people of intelligence agree with this, that for rulers there is no army stronger than justice, and for the people of the world there is no bread more wholesome than security. There is nothing like justice to preserve the sultanate and nothing like security to give the kingdom repose.[30]

Mehmed conquered the legendary empires of east and west, retaking once-Byzantine lands in Europe and defeating Uzun Hasan, the Akkoyunlu heir to Mongol supremacy, in 1473. Greek musicians played at Mehmed's court and Italian artists painted his portrait, while Greek authors compared him to Alexander the Great, described his construction of fortifications, a palace, and a walled city (like Assyrian kings), and praised his might, his intelligence, and his justice.[31] He sent gifts to illustrious Persian authors to try to lure them to his court, among them the Timurid poets Jami and Nava'i and the Akkoyunlu author Davani. Davani's *Jalalian Ethics* transmitted the eight-fold Circle of Justice to the Ottomans, while the translation of Nizami's *Quintet* into Turkish enriched the concept with the airs of romance. Paintings of kings dispensing justice in *Shahnama* and *Quintet* manuscripts furnished visual icons for the same idea.[32]

Mehmed's policies aimed at creating a reign of justice both symbolically and practically. Topkapi Palace, which he had built for himself at the heart of Istanbul, symbolized his place at the heart of the empire overlooking the two lands and the two seas, as well as his provision of justice. The gate, or Porte, was the site of imperial administration and the place where taxes were paid. The second courtyard housed the council hall, where viziers and court secretaries met four times weekly to hear petitions and transact government business; the hall's open sides represented the accessibility of Ottoman justice. Above it rose the Tower of Justice, from which the sultan could – metaphorically, at least – spy out injustice in the land. His throne room was called the Chamber of Petitions; there his officials offered their own petitions and their answers to those presented in the council hall for his decision and approval.[33] Outside the palace, too, the sultans imitated ancient forms for the dispensation of justice. Whenever they rode abroad, on campaign, to the hunt, or merely in town, members of their entourage accepted petitions from people lining the roads. These petitions were not mere window-dressing; even provincial governors were dismissed or executed because of complaints of oppression. Through ritual and administrative behavior, the sultan and his officials demonstrated not only the social hierarchies on which their rule rested but also the justice that legitimized it.[34]

Mehmed's enactment of justice took concrete form in the codification of law. As the successor to both the Mongol khan and the Byzantine emperor, Mehmed II was in a position to issue a "lawcode" (*kanunname*), a compilation of edicts and ruler's law. Three compilations of laws, concerning crime, the *timar* system, and the organization of officials, are attributed to his initiative.[35] The laws balanced the interests of different social groups and checked abuses; a note stated that their purpose was "to protect the common people against the oppression of the authorities." Although the aim was to increase revenue, tax extraction was limited to maintain the subjects' prosperity and good administration.[36]

Ruler's law played a greater role in Ottoman governance than in any Muslim regime since the Ilkhanids. Thanks to the precedent of Genghis Khan's *yasa*, the legal structure rested not simply on the will of a powerful leader but on the prestige and divine sanction of the whole ruling dynasty. The *yasa* was a pagan law, and the reform edicts of Ghazan Khan were never codified or merged with the legal heritage of the past, but Ottoman ruler's law was issued by a Muslim sultan and was intended from the start to coexist with Islamic law. While the Ilkhanids operated separate court systems for shariah and non-shariah cases, and the Mamluks allowed non-shariah judges to judge shariah cases, the Ottomans administered both Islamic and dynastic law in the shariah courts and enforced both by the provincial governors and their men. Ottoman shariah courts also performed *mazalim* functions, hearing petitions and forwarding cases to the ruler's court.[37] This unified legal administration led to a desire to harmonize dynastic law with Islamic law, which was accomplished in the reign of Suleyman the Magnificent (1520–66) – or, as he was known to the Ottomans, Suleyman the Lawgiver – bringing about a reconciliation that Muslim society had been working toward for centuries. The danger now was that further modifications might be seen as corrupting the system rather than improving it.

Mehmed also provided tangible signs of justice. His replacement of warring states with a single political and economic unit increased security; the roads were safe, and towns moved from inaccessible hilltops to the rich valleys beside rivers and roads. He restored cultivation in abandoned areas, settling captives in villages around Istanbul. He regulated prices in the market and manipulated trade relations and customs taxes to put more wealth into the hands of his subjects. He and his chief officials founded charitable institutions in the city's neighborhoods, including public kitchens where the needy were fed, and his biographer noted that the supply of bread was of primary concern to him.[38]

Justice was central enough to fifteenth-century Ottoman behavior to be noticed by foreigners such as the Burgundian envoy Bertrandon de la Brocquière, who reported on Murad II's generosity, his care for his people, and his "great and remarkable examples of justice, which procures him perfect obedience at home and abroad."[39] Constantine Mihailovich, a Serbian captive in the Ottoman army, also remarked in his memoirs on Ottoman institutions of justice: "No one who does an injustice to the poor is long tolerated by the emperor, for he will take [his position] from him and give it to another. And it is the emperor's special precaution that every year he sends four lords from his court to the four corners of his land in order to inspect and observe whether somewhere some injustice is being done to the poor people by their masters."[40] And an Egyptian physician, Shams al-Din, described the early sultans' administration of justice, before Topkapi's council hall was built: "Early in the morning the Ottoman ruler would sit on a wide, raised sofa. The people stood some distance away, in a place whence they could see the sultan, and anyone who had suffered wrong would come to him and state his complaint."[41]

Fifteenth-century sultans used the concepts of the Circle of Justice to justify their administrative centralization, creating social order and protecting the poor. Elites claimed lands and positions of power as their just rewards for service to the ruler. Peasants and townsmen demanded fair taxation and social order in the name of justice. Rebels fought against sultanic oppression and official corruption. The proper functioning of the Circle was a goal that concerned groups throughout Ottoman society.

War, cultural exchange, and the Safavids (1501–1722)

In the years around 1500, while the Ottoman Empire grew territorially and institutionally, Safavid Iran (1501–1722) emerged from a union of the Akkoyunlu dynasty with a Shi'i Sufi order north of Tabriz, the Safavi order.[42] Over the sixteenth century, the Safavid Empire expanded and centralized, developing a gunpowder army on the Ottoman model, expanding its commerce, and developing religion's role in its ideology.[43] The Ottomans under Bayezid II (1481–1512) expanded their navy and gained control of the eastern Mediterranean. Bayezid's successor Selim I (1512–20) defeated the Safavids (1514) and Mamluks (1516–17), acquiring most of the Arab lands and western Iran.

Athough they fought the Safavids, however, the Ottomans continued to appreciate and employ Persian cultural products.

Bayezid II and Persian culture

Bayezid II came to the throne with a promise to reverse Mehmed II's divisive taxation policies, since Mehmed's amassing of new resources for military expansion had aroused strong opposition. Besides taking uncultivated or unawarded land to bestow as *timars* on ordinary soldiers or his slave troops, he confiscated lands from private owners and pious foundations and re-awarded them as *timars* to make their holders provide military service.[44] Although this policy expanded the ruler's opportunity to provide justice to taxpaying peasants, it was seen as injustice to the powerful, particularly the prominent Turkish warrior families and Sufi foundations enriched by lands from the early conquests. The elites reacted by bringing Mehmed's son Bayezid to the throne and forcing him to return confiscated lands, eliminate military demands on religious foundations and private property owners, and raise money by levying extraordinary taxes on the common people.[45]

Bayezid legitimated himself by turning away from European culture and conquest, providing a more thoroughly Islamic culture and a more prominent role in governmental affairs for the ulema and their concerns. He patronized eastern-style painters and calligraphers for classical Persian political works, and new ones such as a mirror for princes by the Timurid poet Jami. Under his patronage Ahmed Rizvan retold the *Tale of Alexander*, and the first new Ottoman *Quintets* appeared.[46] Bayezid promulgated his own lawcode in 1501 and issued most of the earliest surviving provincial codes.[47] He also sponsored histories in Turkish representing him as a just ruler and the Ottomans as worthy successors to the Seljuks and Abbasids.

The historian Tursun Beg enunciated a political ideology based on the Circle of Justice in the introduction to his *History of the Conqueror*, delineating the foundations of empire and translating the old proverb, "A kingdom will not endure without justice." His section on political philosophy, based on Tusi's *Nasirean Ethics*, explained that justice meant maintaining social order and preventing conflict and rapacity. The just ruler should be generous to the military but not increase the tax burden of the subjects. He must implement both sultanic and Islamic law, ensuring prosperity in this world and felicity in the next. Since God had granted rule to Bayezid, he should be obeyed as the "Shadow of God on Earth" who had "drawn the sword of right and justice from its sheath and caused oppression and falsehood to submit to him."[48] The anonymous *Tale of Bayezid* painted his reign in the colors of justice:

> The surface of the earth turned so prosperous from the sown fields
> that the sky became the skirt of the ones who gathered the crop.
> In such a way the affairs of the world were put right,
> the earth and the epoch came to be filled with righteousness.
> The pay of the soldiers was multiplied tenfold by the grace of the ruler.[49]

The provision of justice, under the Mongols and their successors often a matter of attempting to put rambunctious warriors in their place, among the Ottomans was more concerned with maintaining a flourishing agriculture and distributing the surplus.

Toward the end of Bayezid's centralizing reign, powerful subjects, tribes, and heterodox groups that were losing their independence revived the accusations of administrative injustice that Ahmedi's epic had raised earlier. Bayezid's son Korkud, in a 1508 treatise, condemned Ottoman government in much the same way that Ilkhanid and even Umayyad and Abbasid government had been criticized before: its claim to justice was false and its *ghaza* was illegal because it had strayed too far from the ideals of Islamic law and the image of the early Muslim community.[50] This sense of the state's injustice, which was fomented by Safavi religious propaganda, generated a massive rebellion that was put down by Bayezid's son Selim, who seized the throne in 1512.

Selim I and the early Safavids

The rebellion in Anatolia, followed by further Safavid military and ideological challenges, spurred the empire's eastern conquests and adoption of religious orthodoxy. Sultan Selim I (1512–20) became the defender of Sunni Islam against Safavid Shi'ism and mystical heterodoxy, and after his conquest of the Arab lands, the protector of the Holy Places and the annual pilgrimage. He also claimed the title "The Just" (although today he is remembered as "The Grim") and made a conscious effort to present Ottoman dominion as a reign of justice. He revised Bayezid's lawcode, conducted new surveys of the lands he conquered, renewed the surveys of the empire's heartlands, and read petitions every night.[51] The Arabic preamble to a 1519 land code for one of the Syrian provinces proclaimed that justice was "bonded in the character of the Ottoman sultans" and underlaid their tax policies.[52]

Selim's justice was celebrated by Idris Bitlisi (d.1520), an Akkoyunlu official who fled from defeat to the victorious Selim I and "the dynasty of justice and generosity." Bitlisi's *Imperial Code* was not a lawcode but an advice work warning that justice, on which the world's continuation depended, meant keeping everyone in his proper place. As the "Shadow of God," the sultan had to reward state servants appropriately and treat the people compassionately; both *timar*-holders and peasants had to be free to petition the sultan with their needs. He must organize and provide for the army, since "the sultanate cannot exist without an army, the army cannot exist without the sultan, the sultan cannot exist without the subjects, and the subjects cannot exist without wealth." Financial weakness divided the army, and military disorder and factionalism led to the kingdom's disintegration.[53] Strong imperial control and firm taxation were thus manifestations of justice.

Selim temporarily occupied Safavid Tabriz in 1514 and brought back to the Ottoman court over a hundred artists and calligraphers, some of whom the Safavids had relocated from the Timurid capital of Herat when they captured it in 1506. The son of Sultan-Husayn Bayqara also fled to Istanbul in 1515 with his followers. Books, albums, and illustrated manuscripts came west with them; admiration for Timurid culture made these objects great prizes of war, and they raised the prominence of Perso-Islamic political thought.[54] Ongoing warfare and ideological competition with the Safavids, however, tarnished the Persians' image, while the conquest and incorporation of the Arab lands in 1516–17 strengthened Ottoman ties to the Arabic cultural heritage. The conquest of Cairo brought the contents of Egyptian libraries to Istanbul, including the works of Ibn Khaldun along with many older manuscripts.[55]

Although both Safavid and Ottoman literature contained the Circle of Justice, the Circle was less central to Safavid ideology. The Safavids founded their empire on the messianic ideology of Shi'i Islam and a justice symbolized by the Imam 'Ali, and the Circle of Justice had to fit in around the edges of the dominant religious culture. The first shah, Isma'il (1501–24), traced his lineage to the founder of the Safavi Sufi order and the daughter of the Akkoyunlu sultan, the Shi'i martyr Husayn and the daughter of the last Sasanian ruler, adding to his Sufi spiritual leadership, Shi'i imamate, and local kingship the legitimating force of descent from the Prophet, "royal glory," and military invincibility.[56] In 1501, on defeating the Akkoyunlu, Isma'il declared Shi'ism the religion of the Iranian (now Safavid) Empire and began to conquer the rest of Iran. When he marched into Anatolia, however, the Ottomans retaliated with cannon, and Isma'il's disastrous loss to Sultan Selim at the 1514 battle of Chaldiran ended his claims of invincibility. Accentuating instead his monarchical role as the Safavid shah, Isma'il adopted Perso-Islamic political forms but downplayed the idea of the Circle; Shi'i theology supported the shah's exercise of the absolute authority of the Imam but had no place for his interdependence with the common people.

The Shi'i ulema were divided about whether kingship was inherently unjust in the absence of the true Imam or whether people should be "ruled by a king who will rule with justice and follow the practice and tradition of the Imam," since "if there is no just and judicious king to administer and rule this world, the affairs will end in chaos and disintegration."[57] As in times past, the ulema confronted rulers on behalf of the common people, but their advocacy of justice for the poor and oppressed weakened as they gained control of land revenues and joined the ranks of officials. In the end, the Safavids were legitimized by success; they kept the throne, beat off attackers, and enriched the country, fostering internal security and developing trade with Europe. Safavid shahs of the seventeenth century acted as political monarchs, similar in practice to the Sunni sultans, and they developed a bureaucratic administration, a slave army, and centrally controlled land grants.[58]

New artistic renditions of the Circle of Justice proliferated in sixteenth-century Persia. The Akkoyunlu libraries, workshops, and treasury – and their personnel – fell into Safavid hands at the conquest of Tabriz in 1501, and the Timurid workshops and artists in 1506 with the conquest of Herat. These artists, relocated to Iran, produced new copies of the *Shahnama* and Nizami's *Quintet* for successive Safavid rulers, legitimating them as true Persian monarchs. Their masterpiece was a magnificently illustrated version of the *Shahnama*, one of the finest Islamic manuscripts ever created, with 258 miniatures, several depicting kings dispensing justice to the poor and weak.[59] This manuscript accredited Isma'il's son Shah Tahmasp (1524–76), who had little of Isma'il's charisma but aspired to provide order, security, and justice. Once his legitimacy was established, however, he gave the manuscript as an accession gift to the young Ottoman sultan Selim II (1566–76) and withdrew his patronage from secular arts. Court painters went to work for provincial governors or in commercial studios selling copies of the *Shahnama* and *Quintet* to wealthy patrons. Although a *Shahnama* continued to be illustrated for each reigning shah, after the mid-seventeenth century the economy declined, tastes changed, and these texts went out of fashion.[60] Safavid architecture showed a similar pattern. Safavid rulers lived not in fortresses but in garden pavilions, earthly paradises, that symbolized Near Eastern concepts of state in a way even the illiterate could "read." The palace of Isfahan represented the prosperity and life that rulers gave to the kingdom through a lavish use of water and plants. Its "forty-pillared hall" imitated the royal hall of Sasanian Persepolis, and in front of the palace gate the council of justice met. New palace and mosque construction, however, also diminished in the seventeenth century.[61]

The Circle among the Safavids

The Circle of Justice appeared rarely in Safavid literature, which was preoccupied with religious and romantic themes. Popular storytellers recited the *Shahnama* and *Tale of Alexander* in streets and coffeehouses, but literature discussing justice did not generally quote the Circle. The great works of philosophical ethics by Miskawayh, Tusi, Kashifi, and Davani, some of which contained the Circle, were read and occasionally imitated.[62] A mirror for princes written for Shah Tahmasp defined justice in philosophical terms as "spiritual balance and equipoise." The Circle also appeared in older Persian literature copied in Safavid times and in imitations of the *Shahnama* starring the early Safavid shahs. In the later seventeenth and eighteenth centuries, however, quotations of the Circle were few, while Shi'i religious literature was abundant. Only a manual of Safavid administration written in 1725 portrayed the Safavids as attached to the Circle of Justice. This manual, *A Memorial for Kings*, instructed the grand vizier to remit taxes in time of need: "If for some creditable reasons a diminution appears in the Divan revenue and, in the Grand Vazir's presence, the tax-payers report the facts and show that they merit attention and endorsement, then in order to solicit the blessings of the subjects and to secure their tranquility and the prosperity of the realm, the collection of the former sum is considered an injustice, and the acknowledgement of deficit a reasonable procedure, and a [document] of alleviation is issued."[63]

Although the Circle of Justice played little part in Safavid legitimacy claims, which admitted only rule by the Shi'i Imams, the shahs sitting in judgment formed the highest court. Thousands presented their grievances at the palace or stopped the shah as he rode along the road. The grand vizier also had an important role in dealing with petitions, sometimes responding to two hundred in a morning. Provincial and urban officials dispensed justice and enforced customary and criminal law – which, unlike Ottoman law, was never written down. As later shahs weakened, the ulema resumed protecting the people from oppression, and late in the seventeenth century the cleric Majlisi (d.1700) wrote an essay, based on Muhammad's words to Abu Dharr and numerous *hadith*s, stressing the ruler's duty to act justly toward the people.[64]

In Safavid ideology, the duty of protecting peasants fell more heavily on landlords than on rulers. Royal documents granting land and revenues tried to restrain landlords from exploiting their labor force by commanding them to follow the Circle of Justice; administrators were well aware that "there's no tax on ruined villages."[65] A document awarding to a Safavid dignitary the revenue from land "which he has brought into a flourishing condition" warned government officials to "keep their feet and pens away" and not to demand extraordinary taxes. Another document called on dispersed peasants "to return to their places and homes with every good expectation" and decreed that nobody should impede them or demand extra taxes, while the governor should recover and restore "the money wrongfully taken from them."[66]

Late in the seventeenth century, internal order disappeared and revenue was funneled to the army instead of the irrigation system. Agricultural production declined as a result, causing uprisings throughout the eighteenth century.[67] In 1722, invading Afghan tribesmen conquered the Safavids' capital, destroyed their archives, and initiated decades of instability and militarism. The Afshar chief Nadir Shah (1736–47) cynically employed the mechanisms of the Circle of Justice to raise revenue for his conquest of Iran and military exploits in India. His most forceful efforts to extract taxes from the impoverished peasants, however, only brought in one-third of the revenue that the last Safavid shah could collect. Death and migration reduced the population so far that old women kept shop and farmers returned to nomadism. Nadir Shah was urged to adhere to the Circle of Justice, but in vain; finally an arrow was shot through his window bearing the message, "If you are a king, cherish and protect your people."[68]

Karim Khan Zand (1750–79) seized the throne in the mid-eighteenth century and adopted the title "Representative of the People," promising at last a struggle against oppression. The carvings on the Marble Throne, one of the few surviving remnants of his destroyed palace, depicted his authority as "champion of justice and order against the powers of darkness."[69] Although this was a messianic notion of justice, it contained elements of the Circle. Karim Khan was portrayed as the archetypal good king who tried to ensure that officials collected no more than was due. He provided justice in person, setting apart a specific time every day to sit in *mazalim*.

> He was one day on the point of retiring from his judgment-seat, harassed and fatigued with a long attendance, when a man rushed forward in apparent distraction, calling out in a loud voice for justice. 'Who are you?' said Kurreem [Karim]. – 'I am a merchant,' replied the man, 'and have been robbed and plundered by some thieves of all I possess.' – 'What were you about,' said the prince, 'when you were robbed?' – 'I was asleep,' answered the man. – 'And why did you sleep?' exclaimed Kurreem in a peevish and impatient tone. – 'Because,' said the undaunted Persian, 'I made a mistake, and thought you were awake.'[70]

Karim Khan's successors were not of his caliber, and again in the late eighteenth century turmoil convulsed the country, allowing the Qajar tribe to seize the throne.

The Safavids and their successors, though symbolic carriers of the Circle of Justice, proved unable to put it into practice over the long term. In the seventeenth and eighteenth centuries, subordinate groups and tribes strengthened their position against the central government, and popular loyalties seem to have shifted to them. The empire may have become less important and the Circle of Justice less convincing for structuring imperial interrelationships as the economy began to alter and provincial groups gained power. A similar pattern is observable in the Ottoman Empire; after a long period of imperial consolidation and institutional centralization, power and loyalty shifted to the provinces in the eighteenth century.

The "Golden Age" of Suleyman the Magnificent (1520–1566)

The sixteenth to eighteenth centuries saw expansion for Western Europe and contraction on the part of China; Europeans not only colonized the New World but participated in the trade of Asia.[71] The Ottomans and Safavids also expanded, the Ottomans advancing north of the Danube River and the Black Sea and south into Africa and the Indian Ocean. They interacted roughly as equals with the powers to their east and west, and their organization and wealth staggered Western visitors. Agricultural productivity peaked because of a century of generous rainfall, supporting a population growth ranging from 40 to 278 percent, depending on location.[72] Migration to the cities swelled the ranks of artisans and students and fostered crafts and arts. An expanding treasury funded larger and more successful military forces.

In the mid-sixteenth century the Ottoman Empire became a Great Power coexisting with other states, dominant but not world-conquering. Although the Ottomans made further territorial conquests, their main efforts centered on building rather than conquering, ruling and improving the realm rather than enlarging it, regularizing the administration and investing in economic and cultural life.[73] The greatest rewards and highest offices went to administrators rather than warriors; royal heirs were no longer assigned to lead armies or govern provinces. Military expenditures increasingly funded protection and policing rather than expansion. Justice and good administration became the hallmarks of imperial rhetoric and the promises of Sultan Suleyman to his subjects.

People found the Ottoman rhetoric of justice credible because the sixteenth century was an era of unprecedented wealth and prosperity. Vast resources were devoted to cultural production and the flourishing of the arts and sciences. The sultans could afford to be generous, not only to court artists, but to taxpayers seeking remissions and to soldiers and administrators seeking jobs. Social unrest, which in Mehmed II's day had arisen from vassals being subordinated and warriors being brought under central control, now came from soldiers seeking permanent positions in the army and students wanting administrative and clerical employment – people not resisting the state but seeking incorporation into it.[74] The sense that the state had reached its ultimate form and condition gave rise to the feeling that change should be resisted as a decline from perfection.

Suleyman's reign of justice

The consolidation of the Ottoman Empire made law and justice yet more "pivotal" in imperial ideology than during the time of rapid conquest, when victory was its own validation. Suleyman became the personification of the Ottoman just ruler, the one who executed law and exercised power on behalf of the poor and weak. He deliberately highlighted his divine selection for his role and fostered the image of his greatness.

Suleyman sought to make sultanic justice the crowning glory of the Ottoman regime. "Every virtue flows from justice," he wrote in a letter to a commander. He inaugurated his reign with deeds of symbolic justice, dismissing or executing officials guilty of oppression and abuse of power, in order to appear as the messianic ruler who would fill the world with justice as it had been filled with injustice.[75] His contemporaries acclaimed him as embodying all the qualities of the perfect ruler: more just than Anushirvan, wise like Solomon, "Darius returned, the king, Suleyman the blessed, of equity and justness' realm that royal rider." He received petitions when he rode out to prayer or to the hunt, and pictures were painted of him posed on horseback like Sultan Sanjar, listening to the complaint of an old woman.[76]

The literature and art of Suleyman's reign connected him with the just heroes of the past. The *Shahnama*'s Turkish translations were frequently copied and lavishly illustrated in his honor. The link between the Ottoman dynasty and the *Shahname* became proverbial; foreign monarchs often sent ornate copies as gifts to Ottoman sultans.[77] The histories of Suleyman's conquests, also called *Shahname* or *Suleymanname* replaced the portrayal of sultanic exploits as *ghaza* with one that bestowed on them the *Shahname*'s prestige and universality.[78] In Eyyubi's *Deeds of Sultan Suleyman*, the sultans' justice unrolled like a carpet over the world. The illustrations in Arifi's *Suleymanname* portrayed the sultan hunting and sitting in judgment, making conquests and executing rebels, deeds that were "the visible expression of justice."[79] In other genres, Ansari's *The Present of Time* was an advice work prescribing the rules of just government, one of the first Ottoman works to emphasize the treasury's role. Around 1540, 'Ala' al-Din 'Ali Çelebi adapted *The Emperor's Tale*, renamed in Suleyman's honor, from Husayn Va'iz Kashifi's ornate version of *Kalila and Dimna*. Kashifi's *Muhsinian Ethics* was also translated, and poets translated parts of the *Quintet* or wrote *Quintets* of their own.[80]

All these works alluded to the Circle of Justice as a characteristic of Suleyman's reign, but one quoted it in its full eight-line form. 'Ali Kinalizade (d.1572) composed *The 'Alian Ethics* in 1565, modeling it on Tusi and Davani.[81] Key to prosperity and social order was the ruler's active oversight of the conditions of the subjects; he must provide for the needs of his officials and free the common people from oppression, for which he needed to hear their petitions. In the section on politics, Kinalizade quoted the Circle of Justice and gave it its name. His version was not an exact translation of either Davani's Circle or Ibn Khaldun's, but Kinalizade's own interpretation. Once again minor alterations and the translation of terms into a new language gave the Circle a different thrust in its new setting.

> The world is a garden, its wall is the state
> The Arranger of the state is the shariah
> There can be no guard for the shariah except the sovereign
> The sovereign cannot govern without the army
> He cannot assemble the army without wealth
> Those who gather the wealth are the subjects
> Justice enslaves the subjects to the banner of the sultan
> It is justice that is the cause of the goodness of the world.[82]

This version eliminated almost all the picturesque metaphors of the earlier renditions; there are no dragons here, no irrigation works, no shepherds feeding their hungry sheep. The only remaining vestige of poetry is the image in the first line of the world as a walled garden. This was a potent image for the Ottomans; lyrics of the period pictured the world as the garden of paradise, or the Empire as a protected garden in the wilderness of the world. In the real world, too, the sultan's palace at the heart of the Empire sat at the heart of a walled garden. The remaining lines were similarly realistic and presented not a fantastic portrait of an ideal state but the interlocking of existing Ottoman institutions. Indeed, to Kinalizade, the religious, administrative, and social perfection that the empire had actually reached by the end of Suleyman's reign was worthy of comparison with Plato's utopian vision of the Virtuous City.[83] This focus on the real suggests that people in Suleyman's time considered "the goodness of the world" not just a poetic metaphor but an attainable goal. It is against this backdrop of heightened expectations that every flaw in the state assumed apocalyptic proportions, that every problem became a sign of decline.

Even Suleyman's reign had problems, and to address them he issued justice decrees.[84] These were not tax remissions like Assyrian justice decrees, but edicts forbidding specific forms of oppression, such as tax inequities, problems in the *timar* system, or steep judicial fees. Like earlier monarchs, the Ottoman sultans issued these decrees on their enthronement, in response to petitions, or after an inspection of the provinces. They sent copies to all major cities with orders to read them aloud in marketplaces and other locations where people gathered and to record them in judges' registers for future reference. Writers in distant provinces praised the Ottoman sultans for adhering to the shariah, establishing order, and treating their subjects with justice.[85]

Suleyman the lawgiver

The exploit that gave Suleyman his Turkish nickname was not conquest or magnificence but the promulgation of law. Suleyman "the Lawgiver" reaped the benefit of the long development of Ottoman law under his ancestors. He had new revenue surveys made for every province to standardize local laws on taxation and landholding. The preamble to the provincial laws of Egypt for 1524–5 proclaimed that since "the sultan was God's Shadow on Earth and every oppressed person takes refuge with him," these laws made sultanic justice and the noble shariah the foundations of the Ottoman regime.[86] Suleyman also promulgated a general lawcode revising Selim's and Bayezid's, stating in its preamble that its purpose was to combat oppression and regulate taxation: "My late, blessed father and grandfather – may Almighty God glorify their resting-places – considered and saw that oppressors tyrannized over the oppressed and violated the [God-given] limits, and the condition of the peasants became distressing, and because of that they issued the Ottoman Lawcode. And I too order that provincial governors and district governors and troop leaders and town captains and cavalrymen should levy their taxes and fees from the peasants in accordance with this Ottoman Lawcode, and if they practice any more oppression they deserve my painful reprimand."[87]

The truly innovative aspect of Suleyman's law was its reconciliation of Islamic law and ruler's law, shariah and *kanun*, achieved by the empire's highest religious official, Abu Su'ud. This reconciliation went in both directions: Ottoman land law and criminal law incorporated shariah provisions and categories, while issues undecided in Islamic law were decided by the sultan.[88] The harmonization of law was so successful that many later commentators saw no incompatibility between *kanun* and shariah, comparing Ottoman law to Ibn Taymiyya's concept of shariah-guided politics (*siyasa shar'iyya*).[89] Copies of the new lawcode were distributed to every court in the empire and were read aloud in public. Results appeared immediately: legal experts quoted *kanun* as well as shariah in their opinions, judges investigated cases "according to shariah and *kanun*," and court records show that they issued verdicts according to these codes. This legal reconciliation became the hallmark of Suleyman's reign, and officialdom expanded to implement the law throughout the empire and to create the good administration of the advice writers.[90]

The main purpose of *kanun* was to regulate the *timar* system, the basic system of landholding and military-bureaucratic compensation. Although grand vizier Lutfi Pasha reiterated the old standard that surveys should be made every thirty years, during the sixteenth century they were made more frequently, sometimes only five or ten years apart. The tax and *timar* registers and the laws governing them became symbols of Ottoman imperial dominion and means of implementing justice, so much so that when in the seventeenth century the *timar* system lost its centrality because of the military transformation from *timar*-holding cavalry to salaried infantry with guns, some thought it meant the decline of the empire itself.[91]

Other *kanuns* regulated the status and functions of officials. The empire's early expansion created new positions in the military-bureaucratic establishment and made advancement and even entry into the ruling elite possible for almost anyone, including peasants, nomads, non-Muslims, slaves, and foreigners. Selim's conquest of the Arab lands and Suleyman's acquisitions further expanded military and bureaucratic positions, and the construction of mosques, schools, and courts created employment for the ulema. Contrary to Persian-style advice recommending strict maintenance of the social order, the Ottoman Empire actually functioned through the recruitment and upward mobility of "outsiders." Objections to the change of class were overridden, in the case of the *timar* system by a sultanic edict dated 1531. Already before mid-century, however, the empire's expansion slowed, population expanded, elite employment became harder to find, and advice writers began to insist that *timars* not be awarded to peasants, even for valor. The ranks of the ruling class began to close, and crossing the line between the ruled and the rulers came to be seen as "resulting in harm to the world order and ... the cause of injustice and treachery."[92] After mid-century, unrest increased as the acceptance of social mobility seen in previous generations diminished in favor of a more rigid social ranking.

A distinguishing mark of the elite was proper behavior, and new and translated books of ethics and manners (*adab*) gained popularity. As the sultan spent more time in the capital issuing laws than on the battlefield making conquests, ethical advice and ethical checks on sultanic power became more central to Ottoman governance, and the literature of advice often quoted the Circle of Justice as a key to royal behavior.[93] One example was Mustafa Jelalzade's *adab* work, *Gifts of God on the Degrees of Ethics*, or, *The Sultan's Companion*.[94] Jelalzade translated the four-line Circle into Turkish and summarized the eight-part Circle in a unique version attributed to the caliph 'Ali:

> The ruler resembles a shepherd who with an army becomes strong
> The army is helpers who by money are fed
> Money is bounty by the people collected
> The people are a prosperous district by justice enslaved
> Justice is the foundation that the peoples of the world rest upon.[95]

Suleyman's magnificent sultanate improved the empire's organization from a collection of separate provincial bureaucracies to a unified administration organized by function, permitting the highest degree of centralized control yet achieved in a multinational empire outside China.[96] Economic growth, population increase, territorial expansion, and cultural florescence appeared to extend indefinitely. Such progress was not, however, unidirectional or conflict-free; deep divisions persisted in the religious, political, and social spheres. The choking off of opportunity after mid-century caused dissatisfaction within the military and religious cadres and rebellion among unemployed religious students. Restlessness among the common people also increased as the population grew and the average size of landholdings shrank; thousands left the villages to become urban artisans or take up arms as retainers of provincial magnates and governors.[97] Both flight and petitioning formed alternatives to the more dangerous path of rebellion, but peasant flight was thought to signal rural injustice and officials were ordered to investigate.[98]

Now that the claim to enact justice could plausibly be made, people found fault with others' definition and implementation of justice. Critics during Suleyman's reign pointed to moral flaws in those around the ruler: his wife, his sons, his grand viziers, or the powerful. The goal of the ethical works of Jelalzade and Kinalizade was to improve elite behavior. The same goal animated Lutfi Pasha, another of Suleyman's grand viziers and author of the *Book of Asaph*, who stated that the road to good administration ran through the morals and conduct of the leading officials.[99] Lutfi Pasha stressed proper management of the army, treasury, and people: "The Sultanate stands on its treasury. The treasury stands by good management. By injustice it falls."[100] Despite the era's celebration of Suleyman's justice, Lutfi Pasha still felt it necessary to employ the Circle of Justice as a warning.

Justice in the courts

A key official in the delivery of "good management" and elimination of oppression was the judge. The Ottoman qadi was not only the representative of Islamic law on the local level but also the guarantor of the *timar* system, the local administrator for sultanic *kanuns* on taxation and crime, and "a source of redress against the Ottoman officials."[101] With no enforcement mechanism of their own, judges had to check the behavior of powerful officials and their troops, and their frequent failures generated numerous petitions. Complaints about corruption in the qadis' ranks extend back to the first Ottoman century, showing what a sensitive position they held in administration and imperial legitimacy. Accusations most often concerned abuse of their role as tax and fee collectors and collusion with oppressive governors, bandits, or rebels.[102]

In the expansive conditions of the sixteenth century, with new territories added to the empire and population increases turning villages into towns, the number of judgeships grew rapidly, giving more people access to legal services.[103] In contrast to earlier times, thousands of documents from this period survive, providing a detailed look at the process of justice. Qadis heard people's complaints and supervised local officials. Problems they could not solve they forwarded to the imperial council, and they served as pipelines for petitions to the ruler. There was no separate *mazalim* court; the shariah court exercised *mazalim* functions, as did provincial governors' courts.[104]

The imperial council and bureaucracy served as a higher court, deciding cases forwarded by from the provinces, and as a *mazalim* court for cases brought directly before them. These cases generally concerned problems the state was supposed to rectify, such as complaints about government operations, taxation, and oppression, or issues of Islamic and customary law that could not be reconciled or enforced in the shariah courts. To reflect the council's central role, Suleyman reconstructed the council hall and treasury in the late 1520s; the rebuilt Chamber of Petitions was said to be stupefyingly rich, with a gilded globe hanging from the ceiling to represent the universality of its justice.[105]

As in earlier regimes, petitions were read in council, directed to appropriate government bureaus for study, annotated in the margins with relevant information, inscribed with the decision of the sultan or grand vizier, and given to scribes who drafted and calligraphed the response. Responses took the form of orders to officials to take appropriate action, while the annotated petitions were returned to petitioners as evidence that the matter was attended to. The administration kept large registers recording its responses, and provincial governors and military commanders also kept complaint registers. These detailed records of complaints indicate the importance the Ottomans assigned to the hearing of subjects' requests even as the process itself became more bureaucratized.[106]

All subjects of the sultan – men, women, Muslims, non-Muslims, rich, poor – had the right to petition the ruler directly, and thousands upon thousands of petition records survive to show that they exercised that right regularly. People from all walks of life brought their petitions to the sultan's court and presented them, orally or in writing, to the assembled viziers and chief scribes. Governmental and military personnel, judges, townspeople, villagers, and nomads also sent petitions to the capital through the post system.[107] Women, including Christians and peasants, often petitioned the sultan, and some journeyed from distant provinces to attend the sultan's court in person and receive justice from the ruler.[108] Those who could not travel to the sultan's palace presented petitions in the shariah court and had them forwarded to the capital, or they got judges to write petitions for them.

Responses to complaints affirmed the government's desire to control oppression and see its orders enforced. "Those who demand justice should be consulted," said one imperial edict, "and. those scoundrels [about whom they complained] must be caught and be judged." Make sure, said a taxation order, that the official "collects the taxes according to the register … and anything taken contrary to the law and the register must be returned." Written records and laws were the final authority: "When my noble order arrives it must be acted on … and you must not cause harm to anyone by demanding more [money] contrary to the shariah and *kanun*."[109] Imperial orders emphasized legality, justice, and adherence to edicts and registers. The development and growth of the central administration and its control over taxation in the provinces made the central government increasingly not the last resort of provincial petitioners but the first, especially in cases of official misconduct or tax violations. The hearing of petitions became not just the personal act of rulers who wished to be seen as just, but the perennial administrative function of a bureaucratic state that enacted justice on a daily basis in its tax bureaus and official departments, as well as in the courts.

An increase of complaints after the mid-sixteenth century, often taken to indicate an increase in corruption and the empire's decline, instead reveals increased literacy, recordkeeping, bureaucratization, centralization of taxation, provincial involvement with the capital, scope of the sultanic court's judicial activity, and/or expectations of favorable response.[110] Officials understood that the refusal to pay taxes was a protest against oppression.[111] Ottoman peasants usually protested revenue demands and official or illegal exactions through "everyday forms of resistance" rather than the risky violence of rebellion and official reprisal. Their tactics ranged from simple disobedience or poaching to petitions and court cases, and ultimately to boycotts and strikes, such as closing shops to protest price regulation, leaving the land to avoid heavy taxes or oppression, and abandoning work in the mines because of unchecked banditry. As discussed earlier, the idea that the empire was in decline was a recurring one having little to do with any actual decline. But a growth in complaints after the death of Suleyman did make political commentators newley aware of problems that they interpreted in terms of the decline of empires.

The post-classical era (1566–1789)

The period after Suleyman has been considered the Ottomans' age of decline, but mounting evidence argues against that simple assessment. The decline stereotype blamed Ottoman military losses and geopolitical weakness in later centuries on governmental corruption and social fragmentation in the late sixteenth; the Ottomans supposedly declined externally because they had first declined internally.[112] While they experienced a sixteenth-century "time of troubles," however, those troubles were not the permanent effects of Ottoman decay and corruption but the symptoms of historical trends affecting Europe and the Far East as well, trends labeled by historians the "little ice age," the "price revolution," the "military revolution," and the "seventeenth-century crisis." The description of this period also suffers from a sort of optical illusion in the source material, the effect of moving from an era praised by all to an era criticized by all. If the praises of

Suleyman's justice obscure the problems of his reign, the complaints of the seventeenth century overshadow that era's achievements. The Ottomans' economy expanded, their culture developed, and their strength won respect until the mid-eighteenth century. The decline of the Ottomans' geopolitical position took place after that and was due not to the "corruption" of the Ottoman system but to the great acceleration of change in Western Europe in the eighteenth and nineteenth centuries.[113]

The Ottoman "time of troubles"

Although the growing number of complaints in the late sixteenth century did not signal the stereotyped "decline of the Ottoman Empire," the apocalyptic expectation of Suleyman's reign surely made people in the following era regard their own times as anticlimactic. Official rhetoric changed from providing justice to remedying injustice, suggesting that justice had come to be perceived as the norm.[114] Imperial administrative expansion facilitated access to the ruler for protection against local officials, turning the spotlight from the mere ability to complain toward the causes for complaint. This change also reflects the ebbing of that wave of favorable weather and agrarian prosperity that had crested in the middle of the century, and the inception of a period of climate change, when population growth outstripped production and individual economic conditions worsened. People whose prosperity was declining were more likely to complain and seek immediate redress, even if the government was not at fault. As economic hardship intensified conflicts between producers and revenue collectors, both peasants and officials invoked the ideology of justice against economic oppression and the loss of land.[115]

Urban artisans also turned to imperial justice to protect their place in the production system against elite profiteers and external pressures upsetting the market. The expansion of demand intensified commercial competition; commerce became lucrative enough to attract competitors from the military classes, and the monetization of the economy accelerated. Global economic events also impinged on the Ottoman economy: the price revolution that had accompanied Europe's importation of silver from the New World reached the Ottoman Empire in the 1570s and 1580s, causing coinage debasement and counterfeiting, rampant inflation, and economic distress, especially among government employees, paid in debased coin.[116]

The military revolution of the period was an even greater factor in Ottoman budgetary deficits than the price revolution. The advent of hand-held gunpowder weapons, and the replacement of *timar*-holding cavalry forces by infantry recruited from peasants and paid in cash, escalated military expenditures and radically altered the social structure of the Ottoman army. Land revenues were transferred from the *timar* system to support gun-bearing infantry in the sultan's troops and governors' retinues.[117] The expense of supplying them increased the cost of warfare for both the treasury and the peasants. The other expenses of two long wars – one against Iran (1578–1590) and one against Austria (1593–1606) – ballooned with inflation, as did official salaries. Decreased security in the countryside, due to the *timar*-holders' absence on campaign, left an open field for marauding troops and bandits; governors bolstered their local forces, and the sultans allowed peasants to arm themselves against attacks on their villages. These simultaneous changes generated a "time of troubles," when the disappearance of prosperity, changes overturning *kanun* in the military and tax systems and in elite career patterns, and a rise in banditry by the surplus population of armed young men multiplied the occasions for complaint and heightened the moral demands critics made on the state.[118]

During these difficult times, the sultanate fell into the hands of a series of less capable descendants of Osman. Some were still children at the time of their accession, some were mentally handicapped or otherwise incompetent, and some were merely less attentive to duty than their forebears. As sultans retired from the military and public aspects of rule, palace servants and dynastic women emerged as political figures.[119] Advice literature (*nasihat*) also took on a new importance as the sultans appeared more in need of advice.[120] Its authors, largely current or former bureaucrats, contrasted their era with the imagined perfection of an earlier day – the reign of Mehmed II or Suleyman – to fit Ottoman history into a paradigm of decline recapitulated the story of the Garden of Eden or the empires of antiquity. Unlike past advice works, concerned to create a just and effective state, these works were concerned with remedying the specific problems generated by late sixteenth- to early seventeenth-century conditions. The advice works are generally associated with the Circle of Justice, but although the Circle's structure undergirded the social relations they discussed, they specifically invoked the Circle only when discussing peasants, and peasants occupied very little space in these works. Their quotations of the Circle actually functioned to reinforce the traditional social hierarchy; the assumption was that if the elite were treated properly, the common people's problems would disappear.

The Circle of Justice in the advice literature

The first of these political writers after Suleyman's death was Mustafa 'Ali (d.1600), who traced the empire's problems to the infiltration of the elite by men from other social classes. As he noted in his 1581 advice manual, *Counsel for Sultans*, "Justice means putting things in the places where they belong"; that is, sultans should "grant high offices to those who qualify, so that the prominent and conspicuous persons excel over the low-bred persons."[121] Beyond sour grapes over his own inability to attain high rank, he considered the appointment of officials from other social groups to impair the delivery of justice. His analysis did not encompass the economic forces driving social mobility; he simply felt that since there was "No sovereign without men, no men without money," the transfer of men out of the taxpaying class jeopardized the empire's strength, presumably because they paid no more taxes.[122] The omission of "justice and good administration" from his quotation confirmed that his main concern was not peasant welfare.

'Ali concluded in *The Essence of History* that the fall of dynasties resulted from injustice; this could mean heightened taxation (injustice to the weak), but primarily it meant the disruption of promotion patterns (injustice to the strong).[123] He recognized that sultans needed troops, troops needed artisans and suppliers, and all needed the peasants, but he was not interested in the peasants' problems. He focused instead on the troops and their support, decrying the promotion of corrupt or incompetent officials who accepted bribes and allowed state land to pass into private hands. The troops were angry over not receiving proper rewards for their service, and their discontent threatened the empire's solidarity. 'Ali favored a return to the standards of Mehmed II's time, but the empire's circumstances made that impossible; the two long wars decimated the *timar* cavalry and demanded the recruitment of soldiers from the peasantry, palace servants, and the retinues of men of state, and bureaucrats from outside the palace elite.[124]

The Bosnian judge Hasan Kafi Akhisari (d.1616), wrote *Philosophical Principles Concerning the Order of the World* during the war with Austria to bring the Circle of Justice to bear on the military situation. He quoted the standard four-line form of the Circle as a tool for exercising sovereignty: justice created prosperity, generated loyalty, and made the dynasty endure.[125] No more than 'Ali did he identify the population growth and monetary inflation that produced fiscal injustice, but he did discuss recent European innovations in gunpowder weaponry and the poor performance of the *timar*-holding cavalry.[126] He recommended peace with Austria so the Ottoman Empire could set its house in order; a powerful sultan, enacting justice to the strong, would be able to remedy the empire's deficiencies. Akhisari's advice was not taken; war continued until 1606, necessitating continued recruitment of gunbearing infantry from the peasantry. When not on campaign, these men remained outside the social hierarchy; no longer peasants, they became bandits and were condemned as "Jelalis," rebels. Their violence, and that of the government in putting them down, created insecurity and injustice in the Ottoman countryside for several decades.[127]

Between the Austrian war and the reign of Osman II (1618–22), when the Circle of Justice was next quoted, the economy continued to worsen. The *timar*-holding cavalrymen had lost their political power along with their military effectiveness. The janissaries and palace corps were now the sole elite troops in the capital and were sent as security forces to provincial cities, where they became involved in the local economy.[128] The Circle of Justice appeared in an anonymous critique written to explain the janissaries' lackluster performance in the Polish campaign of 1621. This critique, *The Excellent Book*, proposed that the janissaries were unfit for combat partly because of their lack of pay, caused by the treasury's emptiness. Three things were necessary for the sultanate to endure: peasants, treasury, and army; the peasants supplied the treasury and the treasury supplied the army. Good administration and justice had characterized the conquering Ottoman state, but now the janissaries had become disordered and the peasants of Anatolia scattered and impoverished, and both had become Jelalis. This was the first analysis, however brief, of the peasants' situation. The book concluded that restoring justice demanded a grand vizier who could enforce order and a sultan who adhered to Islam and the *kanun*.[129]

The official Kochi Bey quoted the Circle of Justice in a slightly more extended analysis of the peasants' condition. His *Treatise*, written in 1630 for the young sultan Murad IV (1624–40) as he came of age, also saw the peasants' main problem as meeting the need for revenue to pay the inflated military salaries. Although the economy was improving, he felt that the demand for more taxes threatened the ruin of the world, since "the world will endure with unbelief but it will not endure with injustice." He used the Circle of Justice to enumerate ideals of government that were not being met: "In short, the exalted sultan's might and power come through the army, and the soldiers survive by means of the treasury, and the treasury's gain is through the peasants, and the peasants endure through justice. Now because the world is ruined and the peasants dispersed and the treasury empty, the men of the sword are in this condition."[130] Restoring peasant agriculture and just taxation, the supports of the Circle, would preserve the empire. This was the same analysis as that of *The Excellent Book*, but neither author said how this restoration could be accomplished.

Kochi Bey wrote a second treatise for Sultan Ibrahim (1640–8) when he took the throne after Murad IV's death. This treatise explained the Ottoman government in very simple terms for Ibrahim's diminished capacity. It did not quote the Circle of Justice but was clearly based on it, as it named the peasants "the treasure of the Padishahs" who must be "protected against injustice and oppression" because "as long as they enjoy prosperity and are not oppressed the treasury is full." It also instructed the sultan how to handle petitions that were presented to him, what to say to the petitioner, and how to command the grand vizier to handle the matters raised in the petitions.[131] Ibrahim, however, was incapable of ruling or of controlling the great men (and women) of state; after grand vizier Kemankesh Kara Mustafa Pasha, who had balanced the budget, was replaced in 1644, the empire fell into insolvency and factionalism.

By 1653, the empire's dire fiscal situation impelled retired finance official Katib Chelebi (d.1657) to write his advice work, *Norms of Activity for the Reform of Defectivity*. Uniquely, he started by discussing peasant conditions, quoting a forceful version of the Circle of Justice: "There can be no royal authority without men, no men without the sword, no sword without money, no money without the peasants, and no peasants without justice."[132] What he took from it, however, was not the urgency of justice but the state's need for troops, money, and peasants, the topics of the work's three main chapters. Katib Chelebi knew that "the world is not destroyed by unbelief but by injustice."[133] If the peasants' taxes, collected in advance for the past two years, were reduced and collected by honest men, their ability to pay would recover. Since the corrupt elites would never agree to this, the only solution was for a "man of the sword" to control extortion by force. In another work, Katib Chelebi admitted he did not think that would happen,[134] but he was wrong; in 1656, Koprulu Mehmed Pasha (1656–61) became grand vizier with a mandate to control the situation by whatever means was necessary.

The late seventeenth-century Koprulu era

Koprulu Mehmed, as a "man of the sword," restored the balance of society by killing or exiling ten thousand of the elite and defeating a massive Jelali uprising under Abaza Hasan. By this victory Koprulu gained control of political factionalism and military expenditure. He remained in office for only five years, but his relatives succeeded him for the next half-century and filled government offices with their supporters. Katib Chelebi's advice work had acknowledged that social balance could be restored only by the application of force, and the result would not be justice but order. Nobody ever praised Koprulu's justice, but the absence of complaints about tax collectors' extortions in the complaint register of 1675 suggests that he and his successor did something to curb illegal taxation.[135]

In the Koprulu period the Circle of Justice was not often quoted. The full eight-line Circle appeared only in distant Morocco in a letter of remonstrance that the Sufi sheikh al-Yusi (d.1691) wrote to the Moroccan sultan.[136] Ottoman political literature of the later seventeenth century abandoned the form and language of the advice work for the more stringent diction of the lawcode. In the 1670s two political writers wrote "lawcodes" to control the numbers and salaries of government personnel; these were the *Kanunname* of Eyyubi Efendi, largely a ceremonial code, and the *Explanatory Plan for the Laws of the House of Osman* by Hezarfen Huseyin (d.1678?).[137] These authors set forth a new elite status quo that would balance the budget and prepare the empire for renewed conquests, but they did not discuss justice for peasants and townsmen. Actual lawcodes also emerged in this period; in the 1670s the official Tevki'i Abdurrahman Pasha compiled both a new general *kanunname* and a ceremonial code regulating the ranks and responsibilities of palace and administrative personnel.[138]

As in Iran, justice for the peasants was increasingly left to local officials and notables (*ayan*), who controlled land and taxation in the provinces. The new lawcode mandated that provincial and district governors should hear complaints.[139] Qadis and courts in various locations also continued to deal with local petitions. Petitions presented to the sultan from people in villages and small towns also grew in number, many of which complained about the new officials' administration.[140]

Another group contributing petitions in this period was urban guild members, who petitioned about taxes, guild regulations, pricing and supplies, internal disputes, and guild leadership. Guildsmen also petitioned to institute new practices or abolish old ones; when the price of wheat bread was fixed by law, for example, the bakers' guild petitioned for the right to bake white bread, which was less subject to price controls.[141] People saw rising bread prices and shrinking supply as violations of justice; in Aleppo bread riots broke out in 1771, 1797, 1804, and 1819, and the same problem generated violence in Cairo in the late seventeenth century, almost always because of hoarding of grain by the wealthy. The state took seriously its responsibility for urban justice and assiduously maintained the mechanisms for grain supply, pricing, and market and bakery supervision through which to "feed the flock." In provincial cities this responsibility fell on the judge rather than the governor, and problems in its execution sometimes led to charges of qadi corruption.[142]

Historians in this period harped on Ibn Khaldun's analysis of the decline of empires, but unlike Ibn Khaldun, they insisted that decay could be reversed by justice. The history of Munejjimbashi (d.1702), *Chronicle Pages on the Events of the Ages*, which he called a piece of advice (*nasiha*), maintained that the Ottoman state, unlike its predecessors, was founded on justice, and that its law had improved the subjects' condition over that of Mongol times. Because the Ottomans removed oppression, the conquered peoples preferred their rule. A long section contrasting Suleyman with his successors praised the justice of his reign. Although after him the Ottomans had entered Ibn Khaldun's stage of luxury and debilitation, the high degree of justice in the previous era should enable them with effort to return to it.[143]

Naima (d.1716), more pessimistic, wrote his history, *The Garden of Husayn, Being the Choicest of News of East and West*, as a history of the "time of troubles," beginning it in the year 1000 (1591–2). He reintroduced the Circle of Justice into political discourse in his book's first preface, presented as an advice work to grand vizier Amjazade Huseyin Koprulu (1699–1702).[144] Combining the metaphors of the body's humors and the stages of the life-cycle, he described the state as suffering from internal disequilibrium, which had brought the elite to the stage of laxness and lethargy, to be followed by disintegration unless some remedy could be applied. He offered Kinalizade's eight-part Circle of Justice as a path to this remedy, stating: "The kingdom and state exist by means of soldiers and men, they are found by money, and money is gathered by the subjects and the subjects are (ordered) by justice. The weakness and lassitude that threaten the entire state are always caused by the disorder of these four pillars."[145] Had he finished his history, Naima would doubtless have analyzed how the Ottomans should manage their condition, and even in the part he wrote he proposed numerous improvements. To restore social equilibrium, he recommended balancing the budget, paying government employees on time and in full, bringing the military to full strength and eliminating absentees, enforcing justice in the provinces, and facing the future positively.[146] Greater observation of these recommendations in the early eighteenth century pacified the elite. Accusations of justice came instead from the artisan class, which became politically active during this period.

Rebellion and the Circle in the eighteenth century

In the eighteenth century, a series of popular rebellions manifested demands for justice from the urban populace, especially in the capital. The 1687 rebellion that unseated Mehmed IV, the 1703 rebellion that toppled Mustafa II (1695–1703), and the 1730 rebellion of Patrona Halil that deposed Ahmed III (1703–30) all combined protests by janissaries, urban workers and artisans, and ulema with a rhetoric of injustice that delegitimated sultans and their advisors. In 1687 high taxes, food shortages, and starvation resulting from the War of the Holy League caused unpaid janissaries to rebel in conjunction with common people and the notables and ulema of Istanbul. The 1703 rebellion responded to oppression by Feyzullah Efendi, the chief religious official, who seized control of the administration and milked it for himself and his faction. Protests by janissaries whose pay Feyzullah had confiscated, overtaxed artisans and merchants of Istanbul, and religious students denied employment by Feyzullah's faction resulted in Mustafa II's deposition and Feyzullah's execution.[147] Caught up in these changes was the imperial treasurer, Sari Mehmed, for whom the Circle of Justice was a warning against just such events.

Sari Mehmed's 1703 advice work, *The Book of Counsel for Viziers and Governors*, recommended that the sultan, in gratitude for being granted imperial rule, should watch over his flock like a shepherd and supply protection, order, and prosperity to the governed: "There is no state save with men and no men save with wealth."[148] This book, less original than Naima's, covered the standard topics – viziers and other office holders, janissaries and *timar*-holders, and the condition of the peasants. His admonitions to viziers, the primary enforcers of justice, culminated in a paraphrase of the eight-line Circle of Justice:

> A country endures not unless there be men.
> But for men of substance wealth is needed.
> Wealth is produced by the subject people.
> It comes from the culture of vineyard and garden.
> Unless there be justice the subjects are restless.
> Without justice the tent becomes not a lasting home.
> Justice is the basis of the order of the world.[149]

Sari Mehmed urged provincial governors to protect the peasants, referring to Sultan Suleyman's remark that peasants were the real benefactors of mankind because they fed all the rest.[150] He recommended making a survey every thirty years to record *timar*-holders' and peasants' conditions, and the Ottomans did make several such surveys in succeeding years (they later returned to recruiting paid troops).[151] The peasants, concluded Sari Mehmed, should not be made *timar*-holders nor alienated by tyranny, lest they stop paying taxes and the prosperity of the realm be destroyed.[152] This concern for the peasants recalls earlier works of the sixteenth century and before rather than those of the more recent past, which may indicate that the pressure on the elites had decreased somewhat.

Although the next sultan, Ahmed III, tried to control both external enemies and internal disruption, the third of Istanbul's justice-seeking rebellions in this period, the Patrona Halil revolt of 1730, ended his reign and with it the Tulip Era. The Tulip Era (1718–30), masterminded by Damad Ibrahim Pasha, Ahmed III's grand vizier, was a period of opening, usually seen as Westernization. Military techniques and elite entertainment did become more Westernized in this period, but the Ottomans also borrowed from Persian culture, notably in the arts.[153] The new taxation mechanism of life term tax farming (*malikane*) diverted provincial wealth to Istanbul and into the hands of powerful official elites, who alone were allowed to purchase these lucrative tax collection contracts. Their new wealth altered consumption patterns, while architectural and artistic patronage by the palace elite renovated the face of the city.[154] Intellectual life also flourished; many works were translated, including part of Ibn Khaldun's *Introduction to History* by Pirizade, which then influenced several later writers. In contrast, the first Ottoman printer, Ibrahim Muteferrika, composed and published an advice work that did not quote the Circle of Justice.[155]

Change in lifestyle was not confined to the elite; the elaborate and ephemeral palaces of the rich confronted coffeehouses and taverns that served as intellectual and cultural centers for the humble.[156] The urban lower classes and provincial migrants found the city's luxurious lifestyle barred to them; they underwent unemployment and poverty, while military weakness and a Venetian blockade of Istanbul led to high food prices and starvation. In one of the new urban coffeehouses the Albanian migrant Patrona Halil, a janissary, former marine, and old-clothes dealer, and his artisan companions (grocer, pickle vendor, coffee seller, wood seller, and janissary houndsman) hatched and directed the rebellion of 1730.[157] The rebels, claiming to enact justice on behalf of the whole city, governed Istanbul for several weeks, maintaining order, protecting shopkeepers, and punishing looters. They secured the sultan's deposition and the grand vizier's execution, but the new sultan, Mahmud I (1730–54), defeated and executed them. A speech of advice for Mahmud (possibly fictional) recommended that he wield his power in line with the Circle of Justice, supply the markets and ensure low prices, keep the treasury filled to support the troops, and listen to the complaints of soldiers and the common people.[158]

The revolt in the capital sparked other protests in the provinces; people demonstrated in the streets, closed their shops, enlisted high-status men as spokesmen for their demands, and sometimes descended to violence. Through these protests the conservative ulema, allies of the artisans and janissaries, developed an anti-state discourse condemning Westernizing influences as un-Islamic. This discourse made orthodox Islam the only valid basis of Ottoman legitimacy and put advocates of the Circle of Justice on the defensive.[159] The idea that remedying injustice demanded officials' piety and isolation from non-Muslim culture was more divisive than the Circle of Justice and less successful in generating policies for the empire's whole population. Thus began a tension that contributed greatly to the empire's dissolution.

The Circle of Justice and people's protests

The entry of the masses into Istanbul's politics injected a new political significance into popular procedures for seeking justice. Bread riots started up again at mid-century; Damascus's bread riots noticeably concided with moments of political crisis.[160] Eighteenth-century conditions again brought forward the Circle's justice as legitimation and critique. The people of Syria continued to define good government as "harmony in the streets, justice in the marketplace, and fair taxation," and the Bosnians as "order and stability." The head of al-Azhar seminary in Egypt, al-Damanhuri (d.1778), quoted the four-line Circle of Justice in a traditional-style *adab* work for the sultan, while in Tunisia, all the historians praised the justice of their local ruler Husayn Bey (1705–40) and quoted the story of the owls in the ruined village about his nephew and heir.[161]

Eighteenth-century tax reforms improved the empire's fiscal position, and the absence of foreign war in mid-century freed up funds for provincial security. The Ottomans, however, did not reshape their legal and economic systems to encourage long-term investment in growth, so their new wealth proved unsustainable. Central officials' monopolization of life term tax farms increased absentee landlordism in the countryside. After about 1760 the peasants' economic condition worsened greatly at the hands of provincial elites. The Ottoman Empire definitively became part of the capitalist world economy dominated by the West, and actual conditions in the countryside began to match the decline mythology. Renewed war against Russia and Austria concluded in 1774 with permanent territorial losses and a depleted treasury and was followed in 1787–92 by another war with Russia that sent the treasury into bankruptcy. These wars revealed that the janissaries had become nearly militarily useless and that provisioning the troops, formerly one of the Ottomans' strengths, had become a real problem.[162] In 1793, immediately after the second war, the state tightened its control of the grain supply by establishing the Grain Administration, a central bureau overseeing all aspects of bread production, from grain transport to baking to marketing. High government officials and even the sultan involved themselves personally in bread policy negotiations, balancing the need to supply the military against the amount of bread available to the public, which symbolized the ruler's justice.[163]

After the first of the Russian wars, new advice works started appearing as part of a debate on modernizing the empire. One that quoted the Circle of Justice was Nehifi Mehmed Efendi's *The Road that Brings to the Policy of Kings*, an Ottoman translation of a twelfth-century *adab* work written for Saladin by al-Shayzari.[164] Nehifi translated this work in 1775 because of its relevance to contemporary conditions; when it was first written, invasion and disorder had filled the Muslim lands. Both Saladin and Sultan Selim I, into whose hands the book had later come, had valued it, and Naima had wanted to translate it.[165] It contained the treasured thoughts of the ages on governance, including quotations on justice from Ardashir, Anushirvan, Plato, and Aristotle, as well as the eight-line Circle of Justice (with explanations of its terms) attributed to Buzurgmihr, Anushirvan's vizier, who inscribed it on a dome.[166] In the second half of the eighteenth century the Russian wars depleted the treasury and made the Ottomans less able to provide justice, as did Ottoman incorporation into the world economy after 1750 and the 1789 revolution in France, the Ottomans' main trading partner.

Public responses in 1787 to the second war with Russia show that people found new ways to wield the shared understanding of the Circle of Justice to challenge the state. This war was the first time that broadside sheets – posted on walls or distributed in mosques – were used to convey Ottoman public opinion. One of these broadsides recommended to the sultan a time-honored Near Eastern practice: "You should immediately venture out in public in disguise and mingle with your subjects to get a sense of the public mood and initiate negotiations for peace. Recall the standards from the battlefield and bring the troops home – or, by God, you will later regret it."[167] They were right: this war allowed Russia to dominate the Black Sea, discredited the military, bankrupted the treasury, and initiated a period of chaotic unrest in the Balkans.

Peasant conditions worsened further in the last decade of the century as war financing generated new taxes, imposed either by the central administration or by governors and local authorities. Military recruitment and provisioning, apportionment of communal tax burdens, and, often enough, local justice enforcement were entrusted to local agents and provincial notables and judges.[168] Most of these men were not government officials, and the state could not discipline them or force them to disburse tax revenues to their proper recipients.[169] The same was true of landholders, comprising local notables (*ayan*), wealthy tax farmers, and even bandits who had gained control of land; the state had little control over their actions and they felt little responsibility to provide good administration. Corrupt or impoverished governors took advantage of wartime tax increases to add new taxes of their own, causing the jurist Ibn Abidin of Damascus to complain, "Most of the extraordinary taxes imposed on villages these days are not for the purpose of preservation of either property or people, but are mere oppression and aggression."[170] The government's lack of control was obvious to the population; people in Bosnia in the last decades of the century stopped bringing their disputes to the centrally appointed governor, finding the local qadi a better recourse for justice.[171] The state supported local notables who could reliably keep order and provide revenue, but their increasing independence and the strengthening of their financial base made possible the growing autonomy of the provinces and their break from the empire in the nineteenth and early twentieth centuries.

In the post-classical era the Ottoman Empire struggled against adverse conditions, and the Circle of Justice became, not a blueprint for state development, but a rebuke to state inadequacies. The difficulties of the period generated a stream of advice works in which the Circle appeared, almost always to critique injustice to the peasants which harmed their ability to pay taxes. Although the Circle could not explain the economic and technological changes responsible for the peasants' problems, it was able to identify precisely where the problems lay and the threats they posed to peasant prosperity and sultanic legitimacy. After the hiatus of the Koprulu period, when the need for advice appears to have diminished, the Circle of Justice was cited again in the eighteenth century, this time not only by advice-writing officials but also by rebellious peasants and artisans, for whom it encapsulated their expectations of the state. By the end of the eighteenth century, however, the state could no longer meet those expectations.

Conclusion

The Ottomans apparently intended from the start to govern in accordance with the Circle of Justice. Early Ottoman political institutions and ethics had the Circle at their heart. By the reign of Suleyman they thought they had attained just governance, or that it was within their grasp. The severe disappointment of the following decades, when economic downturn and social unrest put justice out of reach, contributed to the sense of decline so apparent in the advice literature. The Koprulu era downplayed justice in favor of order, but in the eighteenth century demands for justice began to come from urban workers, a newly powerful social group. Meeting their demands depended on the absence of war and budgetary deficit, becoming impossible in the late eighteenth century. Meanwhile, the Safavids enjoyed the literature of justice but made less effort to put it into practice.

By the late eighteenth century, provincial leaders exercised political power, but their primary interests lay in their provinces and localities. Although their identities and loyalties usually belonged to the empire, they were impatient of supervision and could not be prevented from exploiting the lands and peasants under their control.[172] Their financial investment was directed in political rather than productive directions. They competed with each other as well as with the central government, causing such disorder that their suppression began to seem an act of justice. In the nineteenth century, resistance to their oppression gradually turned into nationalist rebellion.[173]

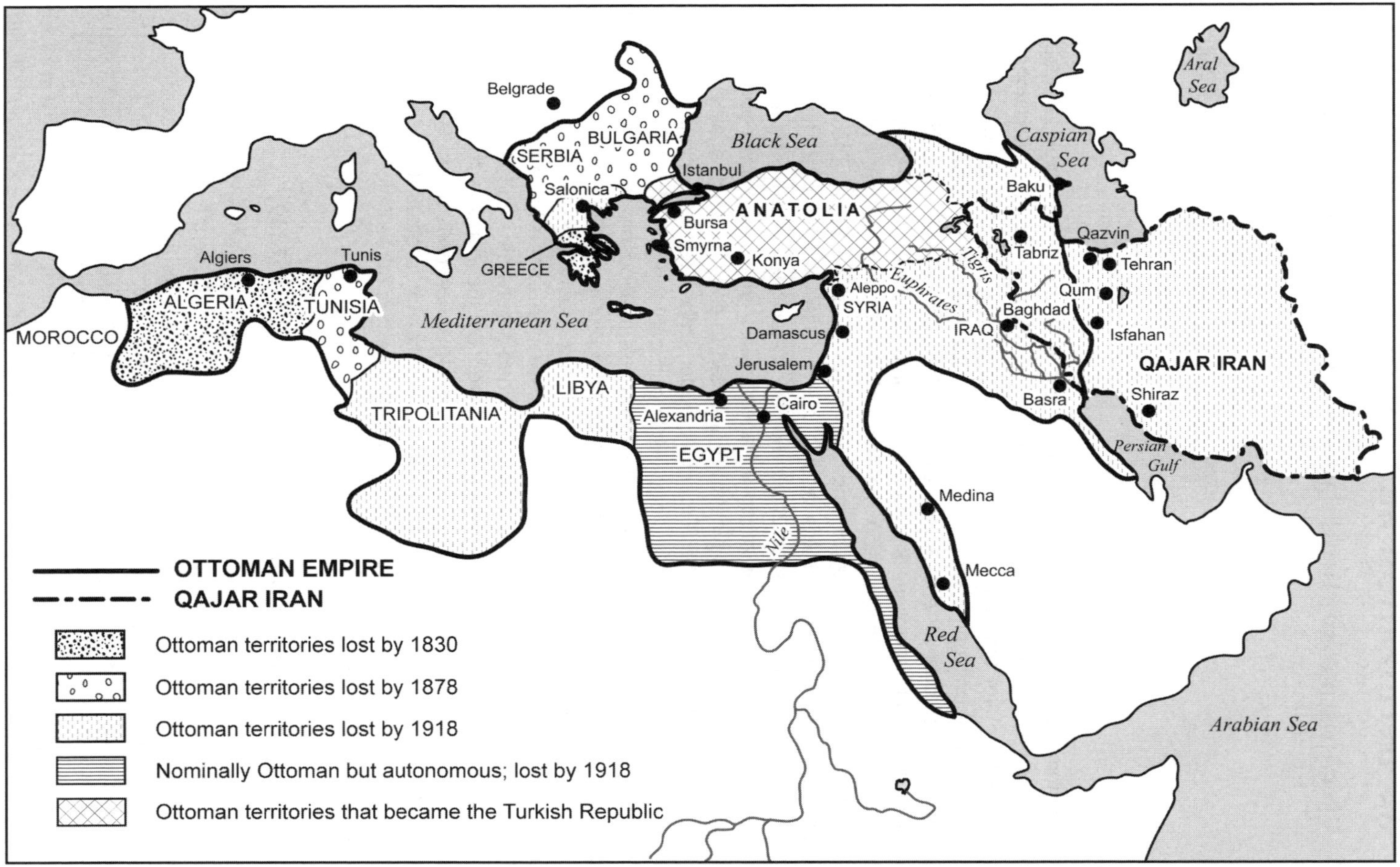

Map 8 The Ottoman and Qajar empires in the nineteenth century

9 Modernization and revolution

"No justice without law applied equally to all"

Middle Eastern modernizers of the nineteenth century found in the Circle of Justice a model for reform, a stimulus to change, and a justification for the alterations they wished to make.[1] Not until the advent of capitalism late in the century did the Circle cease to represent political relations in the Middle East. Modernization altered political organization to conform at least superficially to Western models – first constitutional monarchies and later republics. An older scholarship described these changes as the importation of foreign practices and the "reform" of ailing institutions, motivated by Napoleon's 1798 invasion of Egypt and the "impact" of the West. These changes, however, also had indigenous roots and in many cases helped rulers to fulfill the requirements of the Circle of Justice under the new conditions of the period. New forms of technological and social organization enhanced rulers' ability to protect and provide for their people, while new political institutions aimed to secure justice against the unilateral power of sultans and shahs. Technical modernization altered administrative and social organization as well as technology, while political modernization meant not only new political institutions but new concepts of people's relationship to the state. Late in the century, the spread of capitalist relations and the Westernization of political culture caused the Circle to disappear from the worldview and vocabulary of most elites; it then became a synonym for constitutionalism and a weapon in the hands of those who challenged top-down modernization. It also remained a defensive tool for the peasants and lower classes, whose security was threatened by the period's transformations. Rulers and states paid more attention to administrative, economic, and technological modernization than to political participation, especially of non-elites. Popular and elite efforts to broaden participation were alike unavailing, leading to revolution in the Ottoman Empire and Iran after the end of the century.

Justice and the beginnings of modernization (1789–1839)

The Circle of Justice represented the political departure point for modernization efforts across the Middle East.[2] Its demand that the ruler protect his people from foreign conquest and domestic exploitation justified many of the changes made over the next two centuries. Centralization and economic growth were the primary issues. Provincial notables in the late eighteenth-century Ottoman Empire, by managing tax collection and military procurement, had amassed enough economic and political power to aspire to replace central government elites as a check on the sultan. In Iran, too, tribal warlords controlled military forces and economic resources sufficient to challenge the central state. The initial purpose of modernization in both empires was to enhance the ruler's power over these elites in order to dampen both their tendency to exploit the people and their ability to control the ruler himself. External pressure came from the expansion of the world economy, Western imperialism, and the combined imposition and allure of Western culture.

Amassing the resources to undertake the necessary measures provided another stimulus for change, because central government finances were increasingly problematic. Ottoman revenues grew in the eighteenth century, but not enough to subsidize major wars, and provincial notables sent less revenue to the central treasury. Iran's rulers could scarcely control or tax their own followers and allies, much less provincial magnates. During the nineteenth century, rulers across the Middle East struggled to recentralize their administrations and improve revenue collection and the health of the treasury. At first they legitimated these changes with the Circle's arguments about military strength and prosperity; later in the century they employed Western rhetorics of modernization and progress.

Imperial power and the Circle of Justice

The Ottoman sultan Selim III (1789–1807) proposed to strengthen his military force by creating an expensive "New Model Army" with modern weapons and training, supported by a centralized institutional and financial structure separate from the existing system. His justification echoed the political ideology of the Circle: improving the army was necessary to protect the realm, but it could not succeed without sufficient revenue, and revenue would not grow without justice and prosperity among the subjects.[3] Despite this conservative gloss, the reforms' centralization and tax demands threatened the independence and wealth of officials, janissaries, and provincial notables. These groups joined and deposed Selim in 1807, claiming that central government corruption caused provincial injustice.[4] Other notables marched on Istanbul in support of sultan and empire, enthroned Mahmud II (1808–39), and signed a "Document of Agreement," applying the Circle of Justice to reform somewhat differently. These notables agreed to submit full and accurate tax payments, build up the army, deliver justice within their own territories, and guarantee each other's "protection of the flock and the poor" as long as the sultan recognized their local autonomy and assessed taxes justly and fairly.[5]

This event, so early in the modernization process, exposed the key power struggle dominating the nineteenth and twentieth centuries, the struggle of rulers to strengthen the state to compete in a world of nation-states, and therefore to increase its wealth and power of intervention, against landowners and notables resisting the loss of their autonomy, their local position and wealth, and their function as intermediaries between state and subjects. Burdened by dysfunctional provincial governments, ordinary people supported state centralization, but they also bore the greatest costs. Despite some political and economic gains, over the century their ancient protections eroded and the gap between them and the rich widened due to privatization of landholding and the Middle East's incorporation into the world economic system. The justice of the Circle became harder to obtain, although the need for it remained or even increased.

Mahmud II, unable to achieve military victory against Greeks or Russians and fearing further opposition from notables, cautiously avoided major changes. Instead he eradicated roadblocks to change, eliminating conservative *timar* holders and janissaries, whose recent behavior had tarnished their reputation for upholding justice, although such policies caused him to be seen as attacking Ottoman society and abandoning justice.[6] Many smaller changes that Mahmud introduced were extensions of existing practices, justifiable by the Circle of Justice. For example, he renewed the centralizing practice of population and revenue surveys, making a census of the empire's interior provinces in 1831.[7] He also reestablished the post system to permit closer supervision of provincial officials.[8] In 1838 he founded the Supreme Council of Judicial Enactments to produce reform legislation for the empire; it also took on the function of a *mazalim* court, adjudicating violations and hearing appeals.[9] These measures were consistent with the Circle of Justice but fostered Mahmud's modernization goals.

Modernization elsewhere in the Middle East also grew from a foundation in the Circle of Justice. In Iran, Aqa Mohammed Shah (1785–97) brought to power the Qajar dynasty (under which Iran's modernization later began), restored centralized power, and reestablished the Circle as a governing idea. Descended from followers of the Safavids, the Qajars instituted new "traditions" imitating what they knew of Safavid practices, particularly the dispensation of justice.[10] Aqa Mohammed, brought up at the court of Karim Khan Zand, consciously took on the role of a Near Eastern king: he was "rigid in the administration of justice" and heard petitioners daily.[11]

Building on that foundation, the second Qajar king, Fath 'Ali Shah (1797–1834), revived a political vocabulary related to the Circle of Justice, taking the royal titles of *Shahanshah* (King of Kings), Asylum of the Universe, Arbitrator of His People, Guardian of the Flock, Protector of the Unfortunate, and Shadow of God on Earth. His coronation exemplified the Circle's values: "He promised the people justice and benevolence and remitted to the landowners of the provinces of the empire tax-arrears."[12] Fath 'Ali surrounded himself with images of justice, sponsoring wall paintings in restored Safavid palaces and adding rock reliefs to those of the Achaemenids and Sasanians. His Marble Throne was modeled on pictures of the throne of Solomon and decorated with carvings of the king as champion of justice and order.[13] He dispensed justice through a central court that won the common people's approval, but it threatened officials' autonomy and was soon abolished.[14]

A literary renaissance at court produced texts containing the Circle of Justice and a large literature advising the Qajar rulers on ethics and princely conduct in the style of the classical mirrors for princes. The chief court poet composed a lavishly illustrated *Shahanshahnama* that celebrated the Qajar dynasty in the manner of the *Shahnama*. A tract entitled *A Gift for Kings* quoted the four-line Circle of Justice attributed to Ardashir.[15] A treatise by Muhammad Marvazi, citing *The Highway of Eloquence*, presented the caliph 'Ali as the archetypal just ruler who demanded that the government "take into account the interests of the common people more than those of the elite" and "keep an eye on the cultivation of the land more than on the cultivation of revenue," because revenue "cannot be had without cultivation, and whoever asks for revenue without cultivation ruins the land and brings death to the people."[16]

Rulers of this period used the Circle of Justice in different ways. The Qajars made historical references to it to support the restoration of traditional rule in Iran, while the Ottomans employed it to justify modernization. Other rulers and governors across the Middle East also wielded aspects of the Circle, often to legitimize themselves in the face of foreign invasion.

Western encroachment and the Circle of Justice

Napoleon's 1798 invasion of Egypt opened the Arabs' modernization period, which also used the Circle of Justice as a guide. The historian al-Jabarti (d.1825) argued in the introduction to his history that the ideal ruler "holds office for the welfare of the people and the improvement of the country. He is under obligation to settle people's quarrels and to put an end to strife."[17] Egypt in the late eighteenth century, however, was a land without justice, judging by the inadequacy of the Nile flood, famine and the high price of food, and the fact that people traveled great distances to the capital to complain of oppression by governors. Decay and crime also signaled injustice: business came to a standstill, the marketplace was filled with dust, thugs and pickpockets controlled the streets, bandits made the roads unsafe, and violence and murder flared up in the countryside.[18]

A restoration of order and justice was clearly needed. Unlikely as it sounds, Napoleon adopted the Circle's language, proclaiming to the Egyptian public that the French invaders would "restore the people's rights from those who had oppressed them" and prevent "the strong from oppressing the weak." This effort to gain acceptance failed because the French could not implement reforms due to the turmoil of conquest. The people of Cairo in turn invoked the Circle in their defense, petitioning against French assaults, extraordinary taxation, and other injustices and supporting the 1805 coup of Muhammad 'Ali (1805–48) based on his early image as a just ruler.[19] He was reputed to sit in judgment for eight to ten hours daily and to state that it was government's first duty to secure the well-being of the people, who must not be prevented from petitioning officials or even the pasha himself.[20]

The Egyptians were not alone in employing the Circle of Justice against an invader; North Africans also used the Circle to define a legitimate ruler as opposed to a usurper. A pledge of allegiance to a new Moroccan sultan asserted that God had made the sultan the protector of people's lives, goods, and honor, the one who would restrain the arms of the oppressors, in whose spacious shadow the strong and the weak would find shelter.[21] When the French invaded Algeria in 1830, some Algerians, feeling themselves unprotected by the rulers of Algiers and the Ottoman Empire, switched their allegiance to the sultan of Morocco because he could provide justice: "if he rules them with justice, mercy, equity and correctness. then he is the lieutenant of God on Earth, and God's shadow on his servants."[22] The leader of Algerian tribal resistance against French colonization, 'Abd al-Qadir (d.1883), invoked Islamic principles and called his struggle a *jihad*, but his 1832 accession speech showed that his Islamic principles included the Circle's concept of justice: "I accept this position as emir, although with reluctance, hoping it will be a vehicle for Muslims, for preventing strife and dissension among them, for assuring the safety of the roads, for terminating activities which are contrary to the pure Shari'a, for protecting the country from the enemy, and for establishing law and justice for the powerful and for the feeble alike."[23]

The nineteenth-century Tunisian historian and bureaucrat Bin Diyaf (d.1874) quoted the Circle of Justice and summarized the history of justice in Tunisia in the history book he wrote for the modernizing ruler Ahmad Bey (1837–55). Bin Diyaf described Husayn ibn 'Ali (1705–40), the founder of the dynasty, as "righting injustices" and "providing security in return for taxes."[24] Hammuda Pasha (1782-1814), he said, controlled his governors, exploited his land to give the profits to the poor, reduced taxes in bad years, and defended people's petitions before the tribunal. These rulers exercised justice in *mazalim* courts; the beys of Tunis received complaints every morning from 8 to 12 (9 to 12 in winter); the *dey* of Algiers heard complaints 6–7 hours a day, four days a week; and although the Moroccan sultan heard complaints only once a week, subjects could hand him a petition at any time.[25] Such policies were considered to increase wealth and population, foster construction and industry, and enhance the country's prestige and the people's satisfaction.

In the early nineteenth century, rulers across the Middle East and North Africa utilized symbols and enacted measures drawing on the legitimizing power of the Circle of Justice. Modernizing or not, facing foreign invaders or their own elites, they found aspects of the Circle useful in preserving and improving their states. The common people, too, made justice one of their primary demands. Already in 1838 they combined this demand with references to their rights as the sultan's subjects: "We know it to be the will of the sultan that we should enjoy our rights; we have suffered much, too much from your oppressions, and as subjects of the Sultan we demand justice."[26] When Ottoman modernization moved into high gear and Iranian modernization stepped up in the 1840s and 1850s, references to the Circle might be expected to have decreased, but they did not; the Circle of Justice supported modernization as well as tradition.

Institutional modernization and the *Tanzimat* (1839–1876)

Middle Eastern modernization was propelled by an awareness that implementing society's ideals in the face of enhanced Western power demanded new measures. As effective as it was in creating loyalty, the exercise of justice alone could not defend people against the expanding power of the West. Rulers also needed to centralize administration and develop their economies in order to modernize their military forces.[27] These changes were couched in terms of the provision of justice.

Historians often depict Middle Eastern modernization as imposed by the West, and the West did set the pace both technologically and ideologically, but the Middle East also came to modernization through its own observations. The Ottoman ambassador to Vienna in 1837, Sadik Rifat, analyzed European states using Near Eastern political concepts: "The sovereigns of the world were only vouchsafed the grace of God in order to protect and safeguard the welfare and prosperity of countries."[28] Enumerating the four traditional ranks of society, he suggested that increasing the prosperity of the lowest rank, the farmers and workers, would give them a greater stake in society. Justice was the starting point for achieving national prosperity: "It is impossible for a country not grounded on this foundation and [acting] contrary to law and reason and equity and justice to be settled and enduring."[29] Despite their traditional sound, in a modern economy these ideas were quietly revolutionary, since enlarging and strengthening the state no longer meant simply increasing the size of its territory and the number of tax-paying subjects who supported it. Growth depended on increasing the percentage of revenue that the subjects could deliver in taxes and thus on improving their productivity. The ambassador's memo described the innovations in agriculture, trade, transportation, education, and taxation that would make the greater productivity possible. Modern conditions, in other words, induced Middle Easterners to reconsider how justice might be brought about in society and what roles the state and elites should take to implement it.

Prosperity and justice in the Ottoman Tanzimat

The Ottoman modernization program known as the *Tanzimat* drew heavily on the Circle of Justice for its legitimation. The political and administrative changes introduced in 1839 by Sultan Abdulmejid I (1839–61) gave their name to the whole period up to

1876. The real movers of the *Tanzimat* program, Mustafa Reshid Pasha (d.1858) and his proteges 'Ali (d.1871) and Fuad (d.1869), were bureaucrats committed to Westernization. 'Ali Pasha, although he quoted the Circle of Justice to subordinates, thought of politics in Western terms; his political testament, a summary of his own political views, contained nothing resembling the Circle.[30] The sultans, however, leaned more heavily than the bureaucrats on traditional legitimization for innovative change. The sultan's edict initiating the *Tanzimat*, the 1839 "Noble Rescript of the Rose Garden," justified its modernization of conscription and taxation with the Circle's formula for state centralization, the interconnection between justice, popular prosperity, good administration, military power, and the strength of the state: "A state certainly needs armies and other necessary services in order to preserve its lands; and this is done with money, and money is obtained from the taxes of the subjects. [therefore] henceforth each of the empire's people should be assessed a tax in proportion to his wealth and possessions, and it should be impossible for anything more to be exacted from him."[31]

While the *Tanzimat* edict incorporated new governing ideas derived from the West, it introduced these new ideas very carefully, retaining the terminology and much of the content of Islamic and Near Eastern ideas of justice and good government. Their specific applications may have owed much to Western political ideas and Western pressure, but the rescript designated them all as "Islamic laws" *(kavanin-i Şeriye)*.[32] Subsequent edicts by Sultan Abdulmejid conveyed the idea that a new era of justice and equity had commenced: "The basic purpose of the *Tanzimat* was the application of the foundations of justice … and the guaranteeing of the good order of land and people." On a commemorative medallion the sultan proclaimed "Equal justice for all" and "Protecting the weak."[33]

The Circle of Justice had more than a rhetorical effect on these new measures; it also affected how they were promulgated and enacted. The rescript was read aloud in public squares, appealing to popular practices of justice.[34] This appeal stimulated an immediate response; people's complaints and petitions shortly began to arrive at the Supreme Council of Judicial Enactments. Provincial councils were instituted to ensure compliance with *Tanzimat* legislation, control extortionate officials, and respond to people's complaints. The petition process itself was modernized: the sultan still received petitions when he went out to the mosque, but a new government bureau, the Bureau of Petitions of the Stirrup, recorded the requests and the sultan's responses week by week.[35] The *Tanzimat* produced institutional change through regulatory councils and response to petitions as well as through legal modernization based on Western lawcodes. Edicts of 1840 and 1841 verify their effectiveness; governors and tax officials collecting illegal revenue were dismissed or even imprisoned.[36]

The *Tanzimat* state also resumed making regular revenue surveys and censuses; these surveys contributed to modernizing the empire while fulfilling the demands of the Circle of Justice. They identified new sources of wealth, but they also helped protect the realm by regulating military conscription and other state obligations, and they reduced oppression by rectifying taxation inequities and permitting greater central control of local officials. The explanatory document for the 1831 census stressed the need "to secure comfort and repose for all the poor subjects and the destitute of the provinces in our justice dispensing realm."[37] The sultan appealed to his subjects in terms of the Circle of Justice, citing concern for "the security and prosperity of my subjects from all classes," in order "to protect every single person from being oppressed and wronged."[38]

Although the changes introduced by the Rose Garden rescript were legitimated by traditional formulas, they did not reinforce traditional social patterns. The *Tanzimat* bureaucrats intended tax reforms to shift more of the fiscal burden to urban wealth. They attempted unsuccessfully to abolish tax farming and succeeded in centralizing provincial government and state-*ayan* relations.[39] They aimed to exert direct state control over the empire's subjects as individuals rather than dealing with groups through privileged local notables.

Besides new modes of communication, direct control demanded a centralized modern bureaucracy, which grew into the most powerful element in the state.[40] Bureaucrats on state councils wrote new laws, administered taxation and budgets, controlled the army and navy, and governed the provinces. Membership on these councils also empowered new social groups such as wealthy provincial families, the urban middle class, and non-Muslims, reducing the influence of the old elites. The Circle of Justice served as both justification and critique of these changes. They were advertised as good administration, but people whose interests were harmed by them saw them as the overturning of the social order, an intensification of oppression, and a violation of the state's role as protector of its subjects.[41]

The second major *Tanzimat* edict, the "Imperial Rescript of 1856," reasserted the state's role of protecting its subjects, simultaneously promising judicial reform, commercial and agricultural improvement, and equality for all the empire's subjects, particularly non-Muslims. The fruits of modernization were unevenly distributed, however; the middle and upper classes profited more than the lower classes, and urban conditions improved faster than rural ones. Despite better security, productivity in some regions apparently declined, and where it expanded it fed the European industrial economy more than the Ottoman.[42] As a result, many people identified modernization with injustice, especially when they discovered *Tanzimat* officials milking the system. Conflicts of interest between those who gained from the changes and those who lost created new social tensions, and the frequent delivery of tax demands before state services or equality produced new economic difficulties and injustices.[43]

In order for the Circle of Justice to justify a modernization that benefitted new social groups and created greater equality, the ideological emphasis had to shift from preservation of the social order to the prosperity resulting from good administration. Thus the sultan, in the Rose Garden decree, protested that "ever since the day of our enthronement, the thought of the public welfare, of the improvement of the provinces and regions, and of relief to the people and the poor has not ceased to engage [our mind]."[44] In the Imperial Rescript of 1856 he declared his support for popular welfare: "Thanks to the Almighty, [my] unceasing efforts have already been productive of numerous useful results. From day to day the happiness of the nation and the wealth of my dominions go on augmenting."[45] The year 1856, however, capped a half-century of inflation worse than anything since the price revolution of the late sixteenth century, as well as two decades of destruction of Ottoman manufacturing. People began to rebel on the grounds of injustice in the reform process, although they disagreed about where that injustice lay. A revolt in Vidin (modern Bulgaria) in 1850 was set off by those whose privileged status was threatened by the changes; one in Kisrawan (modern Lebanon) in 1858 was fueled by peasants who demanded more and faster change.[46]

Provincial competition to deliver justice

Claims to increase prosperity and justice dovetailed neatly with the new ideology of modernization, and rulers and governors all over the Middle East were making such claims at this time. The different regions of the Ottoman Empire maintained strong local identities, and modernized provincial government and new relations with the West encouraged local leaders to aspire to greater autonomy. They began to compete with the sultan as reformers and modernizers, and echoes of the Circle of Justice appear in their actions.

Muhammad 'Ali in Egypt was one governor who understood how to present modernizing change in traditional dress. A number of his measures fulfilled the demands of the Circle of Justice, although their purpose was to centralize revenue and land in his own hands. Instituting a census and eliminating local tax farmers decreased oppression by provincial magnates while it strengthened the governor's treasury.[47] Muhammad 'Ali made land surveys and censuses in tandem with the Ottoman government; arguing in 1845 that censuses were among the causes of progress in civilization, a modernized version of good administration.[48] Once the surveys were completed and taxes assessed, he encouraged peasants to bring complaints against tax farmers who transgressed the registers. Traveling throughout the country to inspect his officials, he accepted petitions personally from villagers and townsmen, seeking to make himself the sole source of justice and recourse against oppression in Egypt, as the Ottoman sultan was for the empire as a whole.

To control state officials, Muhammad 'Ali issued a performance manual commanding them to follow proper procedures and refrain from injustice.[49] He created a network of inspectors to check on local administrators, and he read their reports carefully; he also expanded the irrigation system, reducing officials' exploitation. Modernization of the judicial system contributed to centralization as well as justice by curbing the power of provincial governors.[50] The Cairo Council of Egyptian Judicial Rulings made rulings and reviewed petitions against officials.[51] Like the Istanbul councils, the Cairo Council adopted the role of *mazalim* court: it belonged to the administration and was staffed by officials rather than ulema, and it received petitions and decided cases according to the ruler's decrees rather than Islamic law. It also served as a court of appeal from lower echelons of the administration, functioning alongside the shariah courts and the new police stations. These institutions simultaneously enhanced the delivery of justice and fostered dependence on the state and its officials.[52]

The Circle of Justice was not just a tool for the ruler, however; the concept also supported peasant resistance to heavier taxation for irrigation and agricultural improvements. Resistance took shape in petitions as well as uprisings, social banditry, migration, pilfering, or sabotage. Peasants also manipulated the new state services to meet their needs, petitioning the police as well as the ruler.[53] Rather than abandoning the quest for justice, they pursued it through modern as well as traditional institutions.

The Egyptian social commentator Rifa'a al-Tahtawi (d.1873), Muhammad 'Ali's representative in France, saw Middle Eastern ideals of justice as congruent with French ideas of liberty and modernization, their aims the security of the regime and the upbuilding of the country. He started a description of French government by quoting the Circle of Justice, observing that even without divine revelation the French understood justice in similar terms: "[French] intellect has decided that justice and equity are the causes for the civilization of kingdoms, [and] the well-being of subjects. There is no strength without the support of men, whereas there are no men without money, no money without civilization, and no civilization without justice."[54] He measured the French constitutional charter of 1814 against the Circle's concept of justice, noting that the French observed justice as equality before the law: "What they hold dear and call liberty is what we call equity and justice, for to rule according to liberty means to establish equality through judgments and laws, so that the ruler cannot wrong anybody."[55] He saw this concept of justice as universal; a prominent theme of his book was the just European ruler's role as shepherd of his people, and he noted that "in a well-ordered country, the subjects are not found without a shepherd."[56]

Muhammad 'Ali, however, was more of a merchant than a shepherd, using state monopolies and export controls to build up his treasury. Still, under his rule security was at its height, the land was better watered and yields increased, taxes rose no faster than inflation, and rebellions actually decreased. Despite his despotic methods, therefore, he could plausibly claim precedence as "the refuge of the poor and the sanctuary of the weak."[57]

Other governors in Lebanon and Syria also competed with the Ottoman sultans for credit as the source of justice and benevolence, sometimes generating tension between the provincial and imperial levels. Syria's provincial governors began to make new censuses early in the nineteenth century; the records of an 1817 land census still survive. Here too, people saw census-taking as a mark of justice: when the governor Dawud Pasha surveyed property and readjusted taxes, they praised his keen sense of justice and zealousness in building up the country.[58] In the 1840s, Amir Bashir II of Mount Lebanon (1788–1840), like Muhammad 'Ali and Ahmad Bey, made himself the source of power and justice for his province. He centralized the administration, subordinating local notables to himself, and exercised his own justice throughout his territory. Over one of the doorways in his new palace of Bayt al-Din, built on the model of Topkapi Palace in Istanbul, he put the saying, "One hour of justice is worth three thousand hours of prayer." Because he could not suppress rebellion, however, he was dismissed from office and his program collapsed.[59]

A few years later, the successful deputy governor Bashir Ahmad (1854–8) was characterized by his historian in the language of justice: "His regime was devoted to justice, and he set about restoring rights which had been trampled and abandoned. He restrained the strong from harming the weak by his bravery and great courage."[60] His harsh policy toward landowners, however, generated factional rivalries that contributed to the Lebanese civil war of 1858-60. Most of the rebels' statements during the civil war incorporated traditional demands for justice, such as tax collection in accordance with the registers, the repayment of illegal taxes, and the appointment of just officials. More radical peasant groups insisted on the social and political equality promised by the Ottoman *Tanzimat*. Tanyus Shahin, the leader of one such group, dramatized his equality with the notables by hosting travelers and sitting in judgment on wrongdoers, validating the new social hierarchy through traditional acts of hospitality and justice. Officials and peasants both knew how to wield the symbols of the Circle of Justice to their own advantage.[61]

Modernization of provincial governance employed techniques that have been represented as new but that actually expanded on existing means of enforcing a justice based on the Circle. Sending inspectors to provincial trouble-spots was a classic technique for disciplining local officials and restoring order and solvency.[62] After 1839 the state often sent such inspectors to hot spots, such as Lebanon and Bulgaria, to discover the sources of local dissatisfaction. Encouraging provincial inhabitants to send delegations and petitions to the capital to inform the central government when justice had broken down in the province was another time-honored practice. Petitioners, however, began to request political readjustments in the province and the modernization of local facilities. They extended the concept of provisionary justice from agrarian and pastoral issues to urban problems, reflecting the new political importance of urban, commercial society. Provincial councils established by the *Tanzimat* acted as dispensers of *mazalim* justice, as the governor and his subordinates had formerly done, but the councils, made up of local representatives, bargained with the center over provincial requests as governors had not done before.[63] The efforts of provincial governors, councils, and even rebels to be regarded as bringers of a justice congruent with that of the Circle indicate how significant that kind of justice still was to the empire's population. In some areas, the Circle of Justice even acquired a role as a vehicle of anticolonial resistance.

Modernization with justice as resistance to the West

In North Africa, modernization became a form of resistance to European imperialism. After the French conquest of Algeria in 1830, messianic figures or *mahdi*s arose to deliver the Muslims from the infidel, promising an apocalyptic or prophetic justice.[64] Dynastic rulers such as Tunisia's Ahmad Bey, in contrast, espoused modernization rather than revolt as a strategy for resistance and found the Circle of Justice and the redress of grievances a more solid basis for legitimacy. A Hanafi jurist wrote a commentary for Ahmad Bey on the Circle of Justice, which the Bey seems to have taken as his governmental philosophy. His chronicler, Bin Diyaf, also quoted the Circle but recast the interdependence between the ruler and his subjects in the modern terms of social contract and consent of the people; loss of consent made the ruler illegitimate.[65] Political commentators warned that military victory and protection demanded a modern army capable of fighting in formation, and that military success was conditional on the ruler's "following the path of justice," which included "succouring the oppressed, staying the hand of the oppressor, keeping the strong from the weak, and caring for the poor and needy." Taking this advice, Ahmad Bey expanded the delivery of justice; besides the regular Islamic courts, he employed two officials who heard complaints daily, one for the Turkish military and ruling class and the other for the Arab subjects. Other officials adjudicated crimes occurring at night, cases involving foreigners, or minor crimes among the military. To strengthen his government against a French takeover, Ahmad Bey also labored to build up its administrative, fiscal, and military capacity. He regulated the tithe by measuring the harvest rather than the fields, and to enlarge and centralize his administration he imported European methods, grafting modern councils and tribunals onto the existing bureaucracy.[66]

The financial strain generated by even this minimal modernization roused disaffection and unrest, also expressed as adherence to the Circle of Justice. Some tribesmen sent a petition to Ahmad Bey relaying their complaint about heavy taxation and their intent to avoid it by leaving the country. They stressed that their departure was not a rebellion against authority but a protest against injustice, stating paradoxically, "We want you to know now that escape in front of power is a form of obedience."[67] Reform legislation in 1857 and a constitution in 1861 failed to solve the problem but eliminated indigenous means of handling discontent, escalating peasant unrest to province-wide rebellion in 1864. The rebels demanded the closure of Ahmad Bey's new tribunals due to their slowness in delivering justice, the reduction of taxes that had suddenly been doubled, and the repeal of the 1861 constitution with its prohibition on slavery.[68] The prohibition of slavery presumably struck at the protestors' fragile economic security; in fact, their list of demands reads like a critique of the negative impact of Tunisia's modernization on the local economic arrangements and sense of justice. The rebels specified that taxes be paid when the crops were ripe and that the ruler personally sit in judgment in the customary way and restore the shariah courts; these complaints reveal that their taxes were collected in advance of income and that the new tribunals were perceived as unjust. Another key demand was the elimination of European "protection," since the Ottoman sultan was the proper refuge against unjust local officials and outside attacks.[69] The rebellion's failure, due largely to European intervention, provoked massive retaliations and economic disruption, facilitating the French takeover of Tunisia. In Algeria, too, colonial dependency deepened due to the failure of rebellions to end local involvement with the international market.[70] North Africa simultaneously fell under colonial control and lost the institutions that provided a sense of just rule.

Iran's Qajar rulers also adopted modernization after successive military defeats by Russia in 1813, 1818, and 1828. Crown prince Abbas Mirza employed European military advisors and sent students abroad for training in modern methods. Financing such measures demanded new taxes, more efficient collection, tighter accounting, greater control over the bureaucracy, and a more regular system of conscription. Iran at this time had no centralized irrigation and no large bureaucracy, and thus no means for achieving these goals. Iranians, moreover, resisted Western-style modernization because of mortification at their loss to Russia in 1828 and the staggering war reparations. Largely still governed by the norms of the Circle of Justice, they petitioned or rebelled against the new taxes, threatening disorder or abandonment of cultivation. In their view the shah's job was to protect the kingdom, preserve order, and bring prosperity; the shah's inability to fulfill these responsibilities inflated their resistance.[71]

The Iranian ulema had an oppositional role as supporters of justice. They were "an alternative source of information and protest, and even a rival source of authority to the Shah's representatives. The people have a right to appeal to them in all ordinary cases, where there appears an outrage against law and justice."[72] In contrast to government officials, who extracted taxes and labor, the ulema were sources of help and advice. They called for balance in society and, in the face of repression and autocracy, reminded people to look for messianic justice.

As foreign powers intervened more frequently during the reign of Muhammad Shah (1834–48), petitions appeared from bazaar merchants complaining of Western commercial competition. Religious movements and revolts also called for the Circle's justice, perhaps in reaction to dislocations caused by foreign competition and investment. The *Babi* messianic movement, for example, which spread from merchants to the peasant class, protested the disruption of social and economic conditions by European imperialism and preached redistribution of income and provision for orphans, widows, and the poor.[73] The Baha'i movement stressed the state's duty to care for the poor, establishing a "house of justice" in Tehran in 1878.[74] Both the state and non-state groups justified modernizing measures in the Circle's terms as protection and justice for the people, as the provision of wealth for the treasury and the ruler's defense of the realm, as good administration. The Circle of Justice also supported protests both against current conditions and against the often oppressive changes brought by modernization.

The quest for political modernization (1848–1876)

After the middle of the nineteenth century, it became apparent that modernization intensified a structural opposition between two aspects of the Circle – the state's need for revenue and the demand that it protect the revenue producers – that had not been as severe in agrarian society.[75] This contradiction generated a debate throughout the Middle East pitting administrative reform, centralization, and technical modernization against autonomy, traditional privilege, and political participation. These concerns gained a new salience as the high costs of institutional and technical modernization evoked calls for political liberalization and a more popular political voice. Advocates of political modernization introduced Western political concepts and institutions, but they also found the Circle of Justice a useful resource for demanding the institution of reciprocal checks and balances. The long rule of the Qajar shah Nasir al-Din embodied this shift in emphasis from technological to political change as well as the Circle's role in political debates.

Political modernization and justice in Iran

Nasir al-Din Shah (1848–96), the longest-reigning of the Qajars, bore several titles linking him to the Circle of Justice: world conqueror of Alexandrian magnitude, possessor of Khusrau's splendor and Timur's vehemence, fortuitous sultan, shadow of God, king of the Well-Protected Domains of Iran.[76] The shah in his documents repeatedly declared that his main functions were to establish justice and provide for his people. Receiving petitions and chastening governors legitimized his rule and renewed the people's loyalty. The Circle of Justice provided an accurate description of the structure of his dominion. Because credit was unavailable, a full treasury was an essential support for royal power. The army and the subjects were the other two pillars of the realm: "The children of the rule are the trained army and the reliable subjects. Everybody who oppresses these two classes of people has to risk punishment by the king."[77]

Influenced by his prime minister Amir Kabir, Nasir al-Din began his rule as a technological reformer. Amir Kabir initiated technical modernization like that of the *Tanzimat*, but like the Ottoman bureaucrats he was uninterested in political liberalization. Nasir al-Din also centralized and modernized the dispensation of justice by subordinating provincial and bureaucratic courts to a new Ministry of Justice. Centralization, however, did not necessarily mean effectiveness; a number of his new ministries quickly disappeared or had to be refounded years later. The Ministry of Justice was reestablished several times; a plan for a House of Justice was also abortive. Most of the ulema opposed such centralization, in part because it would strengthen the state's control and in part because improving communications would open the country to Europeans and their way of life, which the ulema found threatening to Muslims.[78]

Technical and institutional modernization also suffered from lack of funds and opposition from Britain and Russia; few public works were constructed and agriculture was not greatly improved. Two councils did form to amend the tax system and to take censuses of the major cities; better communications and the installation of telegraph lines helped the government exercise direct control over provincial governors. Such piecemeal reforms seem to have been fairly effective and increased the likelihood of justice, but systemic modernization was blocked by the personal interests of powerful men of state as well as by fluctuations in Nasir al-Din's determination to push his changes through barriers of entrenched custom and stubborn opposition.[79]

Throughout these shifts in technological modernization, Nasir al-Din maintained an interest in the delivery of justice; his genuine concern for the *mazalim* process is verified by his own notes. Mu'ayyir al-Mamalik, brought up at his court, praised its openness to petitioners: "Members of the lower classes were easily able to obtain an audience and present their complaints orally. In short there was a possibility of escape from tyranny and oppression for the people; they knew there was someone who would give them redress."[80] Nasir al-Din instituted a variety of systems for hearing complaints, first promulgating a new official calendar: "Saturday, special and public audiences. Sunday, sessions of the court of complaints and inquiries into the petitions submitted by the chief magistrate's court." Petitioners mostly appeared in person to present their complaints. Post-riders brought petitions from distant locations in a special bag, scribes summarized the written petitions, and the shah read the summaries and wrote his decisions in the margins. This system soon seems to have disappeared.[81]

Undiscouraged, Nasir al-Din Shah tried several other experiments for receiving and handling petitions. In the 1860s and 1870s, it was the "Chest of Justice:" locked boxes installed in the major towns into which, for a few years, oppressed persons could deposit petitions that were periodically sent to the capital. Government ministers answered them, writing their responses in the margins. "Not even a feeble old woman will be oppressed in the whole of Persia," declared the royal rescript, "and should she be subjected to ill-treatment, on the case being represented to His Majesty a full stop without delay will be put on that oppression and tyranny."[82] Later in the century the shah established the Council for the Investigation of Grievances, which was heavily patronized. Records still exist of several thousand petitions sent to this council in the 1880s by peasants, artisans, and workers. Almost half complained about governors or other officials, and another one-fourth about powerful individuals such as landowners and moneylenders. The petitioners, whatever their social status, claimed that they were poor and that if their needs were not met they would have to leave their land. In most cases the complaint was referred to the appropriate official or the religious court, and occasionally an official was dismissed for injustice.[83] When followed, these varied procedures seemed capable of producing a degree of justice; petitioners using them clearly expected their petitions to have a positive effect. They enhanced the shah's legitimacy by showing him as attentive to his subjects' needs, but since they depended on his and his officials' personal involvement, they stopped working whenever official interest flagged.

The unreliability of royal justice roused a demand for the rule of law. Customary law was unwritten, royal law was uncodified, and Islamic law was not accessible to laymen, so court decisions appeared arbitrary and unsystematic. Presenting legal codification as the key to modernization, the royal official Mirza Yusuf in 1870 wrote a book called *One Word*; the word was law (*kanun*), codified, approved by government and people, and published in the common tongue. Mirza Yusuf saw lawcodes as the source of European progress; law was the instrument of justice and justice was the foundation of prosperity. His book became a handbook for several secret societies founded around the turn of the century to push for political liberalization and a constitution.[84] An effort was made in 1898 to codify Iranian law, and translations of the French Code Napoleon and the Ottoman and Indian lawcodes were started but never completed. A Western-style codification of Iranian law did not take place, but royal law did expand its jurisdiction.[85] This cry for law, and the key role that the demand for government to be regulated by law played in Iran's Constitutional Revolution, reveal an absence of regulatory law that contrasts vividly with the Ottomans' centuries-old stress on *kanun* and rulers' law.

As Nasir al-Din aged, he appeared to become more conservative, more arbitrary, less interested in reform. Perhaps, like the Ottoman sultan Abdulhamid II, he had always desired centralization more than political change; although centralization looked like modernization because of the introduction of modern technology, it did not provide political rights. As Nasir al-Din withdrew, other state officials actively began to demand and implement change.[86] Prime Minister Mirza Husayn (d.1881) attempted to modernize the bureaucracy, creating separate departments, including a court of appeals to receive petitions. His decrees justified these innovations in terms of the Circle of Justice, the restoration of ancient practices, and the principles of Islamic law but linked those traditional notions with examples presented by wealthy, powerful nations in the modern world. The royal translator Malkum Khan (d.1908), influenced by developments in Europe and the Ottoman Empire, advocated constitutionalism and the rule of law to strengthen the state and furnish justice and good administration.[87]

People outside the government also pressed for change. Already in 1862 Malkum Khan's father Yaqub Khan issued a pamphlet critiquing the shah's policies in terms of the Circle: "The prosperity of a country depends upon agriculture and commerce, and for a long time past there has been no protection for the cattle of the cultivator nor for the capital of the merchant … the protection of a realm and the maintenance of its credit are dependent on the soldiery and the civil officers; and these are reduced to … utter distress."[88] Yaqub's pamphlet warned the shah to relieve his people's afflictions before they took more serious measures, comparing a regime without a constitution to a land without water, both unfruitful. The writer Mirza Aqa Khan Kirmani, on the other hand, saw pre-Islamic Persian culture and religion as a good guide for modern political life, since the ancient Persians had purportedly lived under law and justice.[89]

The interest in constitutionalism was not just a Westernizing fad. Technical modernization by itself proved deficient because it introduced new conditions that were detrimental to the largest population groups: peasants, artisans, most merchants, and women. Any modernization that opened the economy to Western commerce rapidly raised prices, put local artisans out of work, transferred profits from indigenous into Western hands, and increased the level of violence in society. Without opportunities for judicial recourse and political input, ordinary people lost even the minor rights and low level of comfort they previously enjoyed. Expanding trade with the West increased commercial agriculture and large-scale landholding and introduced modern private property ownership, in which landlords acquired proprietary rights while peasants lost their traditional usufruct rights and fell into debt, usually becoming landless sharecroppers. Landowners gained local administrative and judicial powers as well, and village headmen became their agents rather than the villagers'. Peasants lost access to outside authorities and turned from petitioning to pilferage and foot-dragging as modes of resistance.[90]

If the peasants were depoliticized, the urban lower classes were becoming politicized. After mid-century, urban bread riots merged with overtly political opposition to government policies. During Iran's 1856 war with England, people ignored a call for *jihad* because of economic oppression.[91] In February of 1861 serious bread riots broke out that directly threatened the shah. Returning from hunting, he was surrounded by five or six thousand unveiled women with mud on their heads as a sign of misfortune, crying for bread. The throng of unveiled women in the street signaled, as it had for the Timurid Shaykh-Abusa'id, disorder and lack of prosperity, the breaking of the Circle. Although the shah executed the mayor for manipulating food supplies, famine and grain hoarding by officials continued. Another famine struck during the years 1869–72, owing in part to landlords' shift from food crops to opium, a more lucrative crop on the world market. This famine provoked the statesman Majd al-Mulk to write a tract criticizing the government's failure to provide justice and protect the peasants, whom he called the mainstay of the state.[92]

The shah's inability to shelter his people from Western economic imperialism meant that the state was not fulfilling its responsibilities of protection and justice. Seeing this, some ulema chose to intervene in politics, turning for a solution to Western political thought: if the shah failed to provide protection and security, the people could remove him and choose another ruler. Acting on the same understanding, Mirza Reza Kirmani assassinated Nasir al-Din Shah in 1896, approaching him by pretending to offer a petition. His explanation for his deed resonated with the Circle of Justice: "A king to whom, after he has reigned for fifty years, affairs can be misrepresented in this fashion, and who does not investigate them; a tree whereof the fruits, after all these years, are such as the [officials of state], and such low-born rogues and scoundrels, who are the plagues of the lives of the Muslim community; such a tree, I say, bearing such fruits, ought to be cut down, that it may bear such fruits no longer. Are not these poor folk, and this handful of Persian people a trust from God?"[93]

This image of justice as a tree also appeared in an article in a weekly journal. "Divine Plato," the author asserted, "has said that the world is a garden whose tree is the state." The men of state had to cooperate to cultivate their political garden, which was blighted by despotism. Contemporary drawings and political cartoons often depicted justice and injustice as trees. One such drawing showed loyal subjects uprooting the tree of tyranny; another showed justice-loving people breaking the branches of the tree of despotism. A third portrayed a tree of justice being given water, while on the other side someone threatened to cut it down.[94] These images of danger to the garden contrasted dramatically with older images of walled gardens as places of security and prosperity and reflected Iran's precarious geopolitical position. The state's failure to nourish the tree of justice led to revolution after the turn of the century; Iran led the way, but the Ottoman Empire followed close behind.

The Circle of Justice in Ottoman political modernization

In the last third of the nineteenth century, a combined appeal to the Circle of Justice and the ideology of modernization became widespread. Ottoman officials made the same connection as Iran's prime minister Mirza Husayn between the discourse of justice and the discourses of modernization and Western politics. Fuad Pasha, as governor of Syria from 1860 to 1861, described the 1860 massacre of Christians in Damascus both as unjust and oppressive and as "contrary to the principle of civilization current in the world." The Lebanese political thinker Fransis al-Marrash noted that overseeing education, commerce, and industry as well as agriculture and general prosperity formed the modern version of the government's "care for the general welfare."[95] As common people became politically active in provincial capitals and port cities, the language of complaint broadened to include not only demands for tax remission and the hearing of petitions but requests for modernization and rights for individuals and groups, terms that appealed to wider audiences.[96] Modernization was supposed to bring justice; when it did not, resistance to it took up the cry for justice, laying the foundation for the introduction of modern concepts of social justice at the end of the century. The Ottoman Empire, as a non-industrial state, could not protect itself militarily and modernize its infrastructure while keeping official salaries high enough to prevent corruption and tax and conscription levels low enough to prevent rebellion. Protest, migration, and revolt intensified, and the empire could neither repress them completely nor meet the demands they articulated.[97]

The injustices resulting from heedless application of modernizing regulations caused a new generation to reject the *Tanzimat*'s bureaucratic centralization and imitative Westernization. These new thinkers, the Young Ottomans, found in the Circle of Justice a perfect critique of the dark side of modernization: its rigid centralization, onerous fiscal exactions, elimination of traditional tax exemptions, promotion patterns that overturned social hierarchies, and suppression of provincial autonomy. They did not wish to undo prior economic and technological advances but to temper bureaucratic autocracy through individual political participation and a more central role for Islam, and to bring modernization to people outside the reach of Western thought. They therefore installed a constitution and a parliament, the modern Western protections against royal oppression; in 1876 these institutions transformed the sultanate briefly into a constitutional monarchy. For the Young Ottomans, as for the critics of Nasir al-Din Shah, the answer to injustice lay in the rule of law, Islamic and constitutional, for which the Circle was a kind of shorthand.[98]

The printing of books on the Bulaq Press in Cairo (1821) and the Imperial Press in Istanbul (1832), as well as private presses, brought the political debate to a wider audience. Besides translations of European political works by Enlightenment critics, these presses published older Middle Eastern political literature, much of which quoted the Circle of Justice.[99] The *'Alian Ethics* of Kinalizade, first printed in 1833 on the Bulaq press, was reprinted several times. The Bulaq press also printed Ibn Khaldun's *Introduction to History*, and the historian Jevdet finished Pirizade's Turkish translation and published it in Istanbul. In a search for historic precedents for new political rights, Kochi Bey's *Treatise* was printed twice before 1870, and al-Akhisari's *Philosophical Principles* and Nehifi's translation of al-Shayzari's *The Straight Path* were each printed three times.[100]

New advice literature, some referencing the Circle, also appeared in this period. Mehmed Said Efendi's *Hamidian Ethics*, written for Sultan Abdulhamid II (1876–1909), drew on Aristotle and the *Ethics* of Davani and Kinalizade, although it did not quote the Circle of Justice. Mehmed Nusret Pasha inserted the Circle into the introduction to his translation of Ibn Abi al-Rabi's ninth-century *The King's Comportment in the Country's Management*. In 1887, the judge Ahmed Lutfi Bey published *The Mirror of Justice* on the Ottoman just order. This literature supported the Young Ottomans' movement for political liberalization by advocating controls, at least ethical controls, on the arbitrary power of the ruler.[101] It responded to people's need for direction and kept the Circle of Justice alive as a political idea.

The Young Ottomans, far from contrasting European political ideas with the Middle Eastern Circle of Justice, saw them as coinciding and used the Circle's language to refer to ideas gleaned from Western texts. Writing in the 1860s and 1870s, they gave the definition of justice a political meaning new in the Middle East – the constitutional protection of individual rights. For Namik Kemal (d.1888), the most famous writer of the time, justice stood for the state's respect for the political rights and wishes of the citizens as expressed by their representatives. He was the only author to refer directly to the philosophical sources of the Circle of Justice: Tusi, Kashifi, Davani, and Kinalizade. From the last of these he learned the term "Circle of Justice," which he used in an 1868 newspaper article to refer to constitutionalism: "For the government to stay within that Circle of Justice, there are two basic measures, of which the first is to announce to the world that it has the purpose of freeing the basic organizations of the administration … The second is the plan for a council which … is to take from the hands of the men of the government [the bureaucrats] the power of laying down the law."[102]

Some Young Ottoman thinkers followed his lead. Shinasi wrote in an ode to *Tanzimat* minister Mustafa Reshid Pasha: "Your justice is a lantern to guard us from the blast of oppression. Your law is an act of manumission for men." The law he revered was constitutional law, which like the Circle of Justice "informs the Sultan of his limits." The exiled Egyptian prince Mustafa Fazil saw justice as protection of the fundamental rights of the citizens by a representative body. Where these rights were not protected, the citizens would be impoverished and unable to pay their taxes; when the revenue decreased, tyranny would increase, for "an official insufficiently paid is an official who extorts the population." Ali Suavi viewed the *mazalim* court as a precursor of representative government; it fulfilled the sultan's duty to protect his subjects from the tyranny of the bureaucracy and made him aware of the need for popular representation.[103]

Other Young Ottomans continued to discuss justice more in economic than in legal terms, as the Circle itself did. Kamil Pasha, a high government official, identified the role of the modern capitalist in the provision of justice: "A man of state amasses power by the service of men of property and by the production of wealth through the fruits of their efforts, and by means of that power he executes justice."[104] The Syrian author Shibli Shumayyil devised a version of the Circle of Justice that incorporated modern economic concepts: "There can be no justice without freedom; no learning without justice; when knowledge is absent, there is no strength because strength is contingent on wealth, and the instruments of wealth (agriculture, commerce and industry) are dependent for success on education."[105] He quoted Aristotle's eight-part Circle but decried its hierarchical basis, advocating a new and scientific basis in which the parts of society would be equal as the cells in the body were equal. The Egyptian Husayn al-Marsafi emphasized a social and economic justice echoing both the Circle and European socialism: "Justice consists in each one doing his work perfectly, work useful to others, and for which others pay what it is worth. If someone does not do his work and yet takes its value, or does it incompletely and takes its full value, he is unjust. If he does his work and is not paid its value, he is treated unjustly."[106]

The modernist thinker Jamal al-Din al-Afghani defined the enlightened government as one that would fulfill the demands of the Circle of Justice, "discern the welfare of the people, the measures for producing prosperity in the country, the means for preventing internal corruption and the ways of averting external catastrophes. These things will only come to pass by levying equitable taxes." In another work, al-Afghani retold the story of Abu Dharr, who warned the Umayyads to be just and not to arouse their subjects' anger by seizing their wealth to spend on luxury and corruption.[107] Mahmud Nedim, more conservative, wrote in *The Mirror of State* that it was justice, not equality, that made government work. Whereas the Egyptian reformer Muhammad 'Abduh cited Ibn Khaldun as the source of the idea that unity and political supremacy were mutually interdependent, Mustafa Kamil ascribed the saying, "Religion and nationalism are inseparable twins," to Bismarck. He called the people "Egypt's backbone," and chided, "Do you not see that the great men are great only because the people carry them on their heads and obey their orders?" – a circle of injustice that would appear later as a statement of resistance.[108]

One North African statesman and author espoused both economic and political justice, the two sides of the Young Ottoman position. The Tunisian Khayr al-Din al-Tunisi (chief minister 1873–7) struggled to institute modernization because increased government efficiency would help resist Western encroachment and provide for people's needs. He reorganized taxes and encouraged economic growth, citing the Circle of Justice to legitimate these changes, and he installed a complaint box to ensure that protests were heard. In his book, *The Surest Path to Acquaintance with the Conditions of the Nations*, Khayr al-Din justified his approach by the idea that God made prosperity result from justice.[109] He discussed the virtues of European governments in the context of the Circle of Justice, attributed to Aristotle:

> The basic requirement is good government from which is born that security, hope and proficiency in work to be seen in the European kingdoms. Europe has attained these ends and progress in the sciences and industries through *tanzimat* based on political justice. It is God's custom in His world that justice, good management and an administrative system duly complied with be the causes of an increase in wealth, peoples and property. And one of the wise maxims of Aristotle pictures
>
> > the world as a garden whose fence is the state.
> > The state is the legitimate authority through which the *umma* is given life.
> > The *sunna* is the policy followed by the king.
> > The king is the organizer who is supported by the army.
> > The army is the bodyguard paid by the treasury.
> > The treasury is the wealth accumulated by the subjects.
> > The subjects are slaves protected by justice.
> > Justice is custom, which serves as the foundation of the world.[110]

The linking of progress and order to unity and social justice was compatible not only with the Circle of Justice and the needs of the state but with some European modernizing philosophies. Important elements of this agenda were the encouragement of production through science, the establishment of a regular budget, and equality of taxation. Tunisia's provincial government, however, could not enforce equal taxation because its treasury was subordinate to that of Istanbul and had to remit its surpluses to the imperial capital rather than finance local enforcement.[111] Khayr al-Din worked to increase provincial government's contribution to economic growth and local reforms, evaluating his success by the traditional yardstick, popular prosperity and safety of the roads: "In this period one saw women traveling by themselves from one village to another in areas where one scarcely used to risk going except in a numerous and well-armed company. Even the Arab nomads … finding security and honest gain, renounced their raids."[112] The degree of modernization he was able to achieve in his four-year term of office was nevertheless insufficient to fend off French colonization of Tunisia in 1881.

Midhat Pasha (d.1884) was the most active of the Young Ottomans; as governor of several Ottoman provinces, he had a box for receipt of petitions in front of his mansion and would open the box and investigate the complaints in person. Sent to pacify Bulgaria, Midhat invited the notables to present their complaints, and in response he constructed 2,000 miles of roads and over 1,400 bridges, allowing people to market their crops without fear of brigandage. As governor of Iraq, he raised the economic level of peasants and tribesmen by granting them ownership of the land they cultivated, lowering taxes, draining marshland, and improving the navigability of the Tigris and Euphrates. In Syria he planned another road system to help develop local resources and tried to centralize provincial administration, but this alienated local notables. He also tried to assure the quick and fair administration of justice but was prevented by imperial orders prohibiting governors' intervention in judicial affairs.[113]

Midhat's policies got him into great trouble. His educational reforms in Bulgaria backfired because they mixed Muslim and Christian students. In Iraq, his land reform alienated tribesmen by demanding the registration of land ownership, raising fears of military conscription and heavier taxation. By the time Midhat became governor of Syria, Abdulhamid II was on the throne, and although the sultan wanted modernization, he also insisted on firm central control. Because Midhat's policies introduced too much provincial autonomy, he had him arrested. At his trial Midhat defended his policy of provincial enrichment by comparing it to the Western ideal of state activity as indirect; European governments did not build factories but guaranteed the safety of private investments.[114] The sultan, however, rejected his liberal concept of the state.

By 1876, the centralization initiated by Mahmud II had strengthened the sultanate enough that Abdulhamid II could subordinate the councils and parliament and govern through his ministries and staff. His modernization policies included bureaucratic reorganization, finance reform, and foreign debt reduction, with the resulting funds devoted to road and railroad construction, post and telegraph service, and agricultural and commercial development. Ottoman administration penetrated more deeply into the provinces, suppressing local autonomy and introducing new reforms and services. Population censuses provided data for military recruitment, and the educational system expanded greatly. Modernization of the judicial system introduced French-style court procedures and a codified version of Islamic civil law, together with Western-influenced commercial and international codes.[115] Despite all the technical modernization, however, this did not become an era of justice, not only because of Abdulhamid's autocracy, but also because economic expansion was limited and industrial development prevented by agreements with European powers that kept the Ottoman Empire a peripheral state in the world economy, and by the bankruptcy of the Ottoman treasury and the establishment of European budgetary control in 1881 through the Ottoman Public Debt Administration. The cities gained some modern infrastructure, but without industrial development they teemed with the unemployed and impoverished. Politically, no liberalizing changes occurred, and urban workers still sought state help through petitions that pressed the values of the Circle of Justice.[116]

The growing tension laid the groundwork for revolution in both the Ottoman Empire and Iran in the early twentieth century. Technical modernization improved the means of communication, bringing more people into direct contact with the state and giving them ways of critiquing its measures. The failure to broaden political participation, however, meant that when petitions could not correct their problems, people had no recourse but revolt.

Injustice and revolution (1876–1911)

In 1876 modernization was not very far advanced, but in the last quarter of the nineteenth century it made rapid progress. The financial and political costs of this progress grew burdensome, and the autocratic way these costs were recovered violated popular ideals of justice. The effects of modernization bore increasingly heavily on the unmodernized segments of society. Protests from peasants, provincial notables, and even government officials culminated in the Iranian Constitutional Revolution of 1906 and the Young Turk Revolution of 1908. These developments are usually discussed in modern

Western political terms, but through the changes in political language it is possible to see where the concept of justice referenced by the Circle continued to influence people's political actions and desires, as well as where it did not.

The social basis of revolution

Attempts to correct the state's political problems foundered on the rock of social change. The Young Ottomans, with Midhat Pasha as one of the prime movers, proposed to institute a constitution to limit the sultan's autocratic power. The Constitution of 1876, however, failed to achieve their goals. The Young Ottomans drafted a highly liberal constitution, but the political compromises leading to its enactment completely altered it. As finally promulgated, the Constitution dropped all reference to the Circle of Justice and all Islamic language; rhetorically it resembled Western constitutions. Its actual provisions, however, created not a constitutional monarchy balanced by a parliament, nor even a sultanate in interdependence with elite and popular forces, but a monarchy with complete sovereignty through the caliphate and absolute control over ministers, legislation, and parliament, which became only a consultative body. It also established Islam as the state religion and source of sovereignty, acknowledged both state law and Islamic law, and used both sets of laws to limit popular rights and freedoms rather than enlarge them. Although the autocratic Abdulhamid II dismissed parliament in 1877 and refused to reopen it, he could still claim to be governing according to the Constitution.[117]

The shift of the 1876 Constitution away from the Circle of Justice reflected not only changes in political thought and power relations, but also social transformations among the elite. Nineteenth-century economic and legal changes greatly altered Middle Eastern social structures. Control of land was no longer an administrative responsibility in which the ruler's appointees collected taxes in an area and oversaw security and prosperity on behalf of the state. Land became a commodity whose value lay in its ability to produce for the market. In conjunction with the growth of agrarian capitalism and monetarization of the economy, the Ottoman and Egyptian Land Laws of 1858 encouraged personal proprietorship of land and gave landholders security of title. The effects of these laws far exceeded their actual provisions and differed in different parts of the Middle East; in some areas peasants managed to keep the land they farmed, but in many places it ended up in landowners' hands.[118] The commercialization of landholding created a new upper class in the Middle East, large landowners (and later businessmen) producing for the world market, whose position depended not on state appointment but on wealth, and urban merchants, intermediaries in this agricultural commerce.[119] Since their role was not governmental, the members of this newly powerful bourgeoisie felt no need to adhere to the Circle of Justice, which prescribed how a state should maintain its power and prosperity. Their function was not to protect the peasants but to profit from them.

In the 1830s farmers' and workers' conditions throughout the Middle East compared favorably with those in England, but by the 1870s they were far more desperate.[120] The decline coincided with a multi-year drought, the worldwide economic depression of the 1870s, and tax increases to subsidize reform and modernization. Widespread rebellion in the Balkans and Syria protested the contradictions raised by the 1858 Land Law and the changes in property-holding.[121] Consular reports from Damascus began to be filled with "the theme of justice as a commercial commodity which was bought and sold like any other commodity" in the markets.[122] Inability to protect the peasants from loss of land and indebtedness delegitimated the state and drove peasants to emigrate, to protest in terms of the Circle of Justice, to adopt new forms of protest such as rent strikes, or to support revolutionaries like Colonel Ahmad 'Urabi of Egypt.[123]

Around this time, references to the Circle of Justice decreased in Middle Eastern political discourse, to be replaced by political language borrowed from the West. The Circle of Justice had recommended justice both in the judicial sense and as the provision of infrastructural supports that would enable peasants, artisans, and merchants to produce a surplus for the treasury. In the late nineteenth century, the language of bureaucratic efficiency and order was commonly employed to discuss the enactment of judicial justice, while the rhetoric of progress and civilization, which stressed the importance of science, development, and increase of wealth, expressed in modern terms the fostering of prosperity. By 1919, even the sermons of modernist ulema were couched in such terms: "It is by independence that men will be able to expend their efforts in the pursuit of their interests which are also the interests of their nation. Among these are the improvement of communications, the construction of railroads, and the fostering of commerce, agriculture, and all other forms of economic activity. This is the independence of which the prophet approved, the independence advocated by Islam."[124]

Protesting against injustice

The disappearance of the Circle's vocabulary reflected the adoption of a new political language and set of concepts appropriate to a propertied middle class. It did not, however, mean that the idea of interdependence between the state and its people disappeared, particularly on the popular level. Statements by common people and their advocates at the turn of the century still emphasized this interdependence. The Egyptian reformer Muhammad 'Abduh (d.1905) described the ideal society as one in which "the government does not own, but manages public property and acts as the trustee of the people to ensure its interests." Peasants and townsmen continued to petition their rulers to provide the means of life and to cease oppression; in 1904 sixty-eight villagers in Egypt sent a petition to the King of England to complain of oppression, appealing to the king's "glorious sense of justice." New forms of protest also emerged, often employing the vocabulary of European radicalism, but embodying demands for justice in the sense conveyed by the Circle and appealing to existing frameworks of complaint.[125]

Protests against the economic difficulties of the 1870s exhibited this transition. History books focus on the Balkan wars, in which popular protests escalated into rebellion under pressure from Austrian and Russian agents, but Egypt also faced high food prices and a flood of petitions from guild workers as well as a great increase in brigandage. In Syria drought and poor harvests generated rising bread prices and protests by women. Famine in Iran provoked such unrest, including violent demonstrations by women, that the provincial governor of Fars opened almshouses in urban areas. Anatolia also experienced famine; however, there, too, elite intervention stopped popular protest short of social upheaval.[126]

The military crisis leading to Egypt's 'Urabi revolt in 1881–2 began with petitions from army officers complaining about budget reductions. The petition campaign escalated from complaints about specific grievances to requests for a "just consultative government," a chamber of deputies, to regulate Egyptian society and economy on the basis of justice and freedom. European investments and government indebtedness siphoned off a considerable percentage of Egypt's wealth, creating unrest in the countryside. A solution to peasant deprivation was offered by one village headman: eliminate private property, restore the old landholding system, and put the sugar factory and viceregal lands into the people's possession. This sort of proto-socialism, besides demanding a return to familiar social interdependencies, had millenarian overtones that were fueled by prophecies of the abolition of injustice upon the approach of a comet and the turn of the century (1882 was the year 1300 in the Muslim calendar).[127]

As the village headman's recommendation indicates, the spread of commercial agriculture sharpened the contradiction between the government's need for support from the propertied classes and its responsibility for the welfare of the peasants. Lack of state protection and justice generated popular protests against the breakdown of the Circle's interdependencies. The journal *Le Tunisien* warned in 1907, after the passage of Tunisia's land law, that the creation of private property in land was detrimental to peasants. A few wealthy peasants benefitted, but many more poor peasants lost their security or livelihood. Hundreds of Palestinian villagers and Bedouin petitioned the Ottoman government over policy changes, land ownership, tax increases, dispossession, and abuse of power. Leaving the land signaled a lapse in the ruler's protection and justice; in Syria and Lebanon, a million peasants unable to get reductions in tax and conscription levels or increases in services abandoned cultivation and migrated en masse to Europe, Africa, and the Americas. Resistance to increased taxation in Libya manifested itself as wholesale destruction of olive groves. In Algeria, tribesmen resisted French occupation, monetary exactions, and the rearrangement of tribal lands by refusing to give up traditional farming methods and by supporting brigands and bandits. Anatolian villagers murdered tax collectors and blocked grain transfers from the villages. Groups of Egyptian peasant leaders, sometimes quite numerous, complained on behalf of peasants from entire regions, and the first successful agricultural strike occurred in 1882.[128]

Urban resistance also began to intensify in Egypt around 1880; riots in the cities lasted longer and became more severe, since there were no resources to meet popular demands. Non-Muslim groups in Iran were infected with messianism, and within Islam reformist religious ideas, which had molded resistance to Western colonial encroachments in India and Africa around the purification of Islam and a return to Islamic rule as in the Prophet's day, began to be heard closer to the imperial centers. These ideas often echoed the Circle of Justice; the Syrian reformist al-Kawakibi (d.1902), for example, opposed Ottoman rule on the grounds of deficiencies in both the Ottomans' Arabness and their Islam that caused the Ottomans to neglect the practice of justice and allow the strong to kill the weak. He proposed a combination of Islam and socialism to counter the appropriation of wealth from the poor by the rich.[129] By the end of the century, these popular protests coalesced into movements for political reform.

The Young Turk and Iranian Constitutional Revolutions

After 1876, Sultan Abdulhamid II worked to keep the Ottoman Empire together and put down revolts by strengthening the central government through technical modernization, against growing resistance from the population. He badly needed to raise more men and money, but his harsh methods made people unwilling to contribute. Heightened European intervention in the economy also alienated elites and caused popular disturbances that took new forms. A variety of political opposition groups, collectively called the Young Turks, combined in the Committee of Union and Progress, forming underground groups in Ottoman cities and in the military. Their rebellion was spurred by tax revolts by peasants suffering from bad harvests, riots by urban artisans feeling the economic pressures of Westernization, and protests by soldiers and bureaucrats whose salaries went unpaid. When Abdulhamid sent out spies to locate the ringleaders, Committee members in the army began a guerrilla resistance. To undercut their main demand, Abdulhamid recalled the parliament, effectively putting the Constitution back into practice. Young Turks were immediately elected to political offices and dominated the government.[130] This Young Turk Revolution of 1908 took place only two years after the Constitutional Revolution of 1906 in Iran and repeated many of its themes.

Iran in the last days of Nasir al-Din and Muzaffar al-Din Shah (1896–1907) exhibited signs of royal injustice: neglect of irrigation systems produced desertification, the treasury went empty while men of state grew rich, and Iranian territory and resources were prey to British and Russian exploitation. Iranian society, already economically stressed by increasing tax demands and incorporation into the world capitalist economy, massively protested the sale of the country's resources to Europeans. The commercial middle class, bureaucracy, and intelligentsia began to work together against Qajar policies. In the great tobacco boycott of 1891–92, the whole country including the shah's harem stopped smoking for months to protest the sale of a tobacco monopoly to a British company, the Imperial Tobacco Corporation. The 1901 sale of oil rights to D'Arcy, a British entrepreneur, did not arouse such alarm, but the lease of the customs dues to the Belgian M. Naus generated new protests that ignited the Constitutional Revolution of 1906.

During the tobacco boycott, the ulema emerged as leaders of the opposition – or were pushed into leadership; the legal opinion (*fatwa*) authorizing the boycott, we now know, was authored not by the head of the ulema but by a group of merchants. The ulema opposed the state's ventures because the ruler failed to protect the people from outside incursions or provide justice and the means of subsistence, a discourse based on the Circle of Justice as part of Islamic doctrine. The merchants attracted the lower classes to their cause by supporting their demands for cheap bread as food prices rose throughout 1905.[131]

Protesters held a strike against the Belgian customs regime in April 1905, taking sanctuary with the ulema in the 'Abd al-Azim shrine. They were joined by radicals who proposed a revolutionary program echoing the Circle of Justice at many points; it demanded a land survey, military and taxation reforms, replacement of foreign customs officials, regulations for provincial governors, a written legal code, and a House of Justice "to attend to the subjects' petitions and grievances and to treat them with justice and equity."[132] The establishment of a House of Justice as an alternative source of redress to the ruler was a tactic familiar from the 1870s, often tried but not yet successful. The shah promised compliance but did not fulfill these requests. A second protest in December 1905 followed the same pattern and renewed the demand for a House of Justice, as defined by Sayyid Muhammad Tabataba'i, the chief ulema protester: "We want justice, we want a *majles* in which the shah and the beggar are equal before the law." After six weeks of protest and argument, the shah did issue an edict for a House of Justice but did not specify its composition or meeting time, so it could not convene.[133]

Tensions rose during the first half of 1906, and in June Tabataba'i preached a sermon quoting the Circle of Justice but warning that it had broken down; petitions to the shah were being blocked and the shah was dangerously unaware of the injustices committed by his officials. Should he be killed for speaking "in the path of justice," he said, "my blood will water the tree of justice." That prophecy was fulfilled by proxy in July, when the shooting of a religious student at a rally ignited massive protests that this time proved effective. The demonstrators took refuge in the British Embassy grounds and were joined in a huge strike by 14,000 others, mainly urban workers, who demanded a written constitution and an elected national parliament.[134]

Although the shah was not deposed, elections were held and in October a parliament convened; several members were former "Representatives of the People" or their relatives. The parliament drafted a constitution that enshrined the qualities of "law, system, and equality," the modern keys to justice in Iran. As a newspaper article put it, the power of the state depended on the prosperity of the subjects; the prosperity of the subjects depended on justice; and there was no justice without law applied equally to all.[135] The Western concept of justice as equality before the law was thus drafted into the service of the Near Eastern concept, provision of prosperity as the source of strength.

The new governing mechanisms and laws aroused hope, and people inundated Parliament with petitions; petitions from rural villagers also multiplied in the columns of newspapers. Their authors clearly considered that whoever held power was responsible for redressing grievances. Deluged with requests, Parliament constituted a Commission of Grievances to receive petitions and became preoccupied with basic demands, postponing structural changes that would reduce inquality.[136] Councils were set up all over Iran to improve local government, collect taxes, institute reforms, and address complaints; their social-democratic agenda had much in common with the Circle of Justice. As Parliament took over the ruler's responsibility to respond to petitions, these councils substituted for the ulema in representing popular grievances and meeting local needs. The populace had a lot to complain about: revolutionary promises to reduce food prices, lower taxes, and end corruption were not being kept. In ordinary people's eyes, liberal democracy and legal reform were no substitute for the provision of bread and the elimination of oppression. The contradiction between reform and provision broke into the open in June 1907 in Tabriz, where radicals were the strongest group. Their demands for independence from colonialism, freedom of the press, an eight-hour workday, and collective bargaining gained them the adherence of many in the upper and middle classes and the modern working class, but they lost the support of the discontented poor, the most numerous group, whose need was for the most basic levels of food and housing. An extended clash ended in their defeat by opponents of reform.[137]

Conservatives gained power in the Iranian capital as well, reversing the liberal direction of the revolution's early days. Since the new laws transferred the shah's power to Parliament, he refused to ratify them; most ulema also opposed codifying the law, as it would diminish their authority. Parliament's actual accomplishments proved far less impressive than its revolutionary promises, and a reaction against it began to gain ground. Most delegates elected after 1907 came from the merchant and landowning classes; backed by palace officials, they undercut the radicals' reforms. Land reform, for example, ended up benefitting the treasury but not the peasants: elites returned land grants to the government, but the government did not distribute them to peasants or reduce the tax burden. The creation of private property in land allowed the emergence of a new class of landlords who held their titles independent of the state and its oversight.[138]

Because the liberal parliament had not instituted legal measures to help the less fortunate, the poor and disenfranchised turned to the conservatives, whose legitimation came from Islam. These petitioners, mainly women and urban groups, once again rioted for bread, this time against the liberal parliament rather than the shah. They were joined by some of the revolutionary ulema, now disillusioned by the secular nature of Parliament's laws. The revolution's extension of suffrage to all adult males also brought into the electorate rural elites and peasants who elected a very conservative group of representatives in 1909. These conservatives ensured that the radical proposals of the original revolutionaries were not enacted, that the social hierarchy was not overturned, that women did not gain political rights, and that landowners increased their power in the countryside.[139] Reformers, deprived of support from both elites and common people, were forced to turn to military strongmen such as Reza Khan, who made himself Reza Shah in 1924, and to give up political liberalization for the sake of modernization. The same was true, with variations, in the Ottoman Empire and its successor states in the Middle East. The modern search for justice in the twentieth century had to contend with modern forms of conservatism and inequality.

Conclusion

During the nineteenth century, Middle Eastern political discourse adopted and adapted the terminology of the West but used it to describe the relationships encapsulated in the Circle of Justice. The ruler as the source of prosperity, the people's need for military protection and administrative rectitude, the state's demand for the productive surplus and its enlargement, and the cry for justice from officials and people alike did not vanish because the language of politics changed. Technological and institutional modernization, however, altered (sometimes unrecognizably) the mechanisms for producing and identifying a surplus, defining and providing military protection and administrative rectitude, and delivering justice. Agricultural transformation, modern military weaponry and organization, new forms of taxation and census-taking, and new governmental bureaus for the administration of justice replaced the face-to-face contact and personal responsibility of earlier times with more impersonal forms of interaction. Political modernization had the ambitious goal of changing the fundamental relationship between ruler and subjects by shifting sovereignty to the people, so it should have had a more detrimental effect on the employment of the Circle of Justice. Instead, it was the political modernizers who found the Circle most useful as a precedent for checking the ruler's unbridled exercise of power and restoring social balance.

The shift to capitalist economic relations during the last quarter of the century meant that the Circle of Justice no longer expressed the actual relationship among peasants, landholders, and the state, although it remained a widespread ideal, especially among those disadvantaged by the growth of capitalism. A number of mirrors for princes were republished in the early years of the twentieth century, and new ones also appeared. Rulers' preoccupation with climatic disaster and famine, Western economic encroachment, and the suppression of the resulting protests interfered with the institutionalization of political checks and balances. Many of those protests were shaped by the Circle of Justice and its call for balance among the different social groups. The suppression of protest proved to be counterproductive; it stimulated revolutions that sought to reestablish justice by instituting new political forms to govern the Middle East.

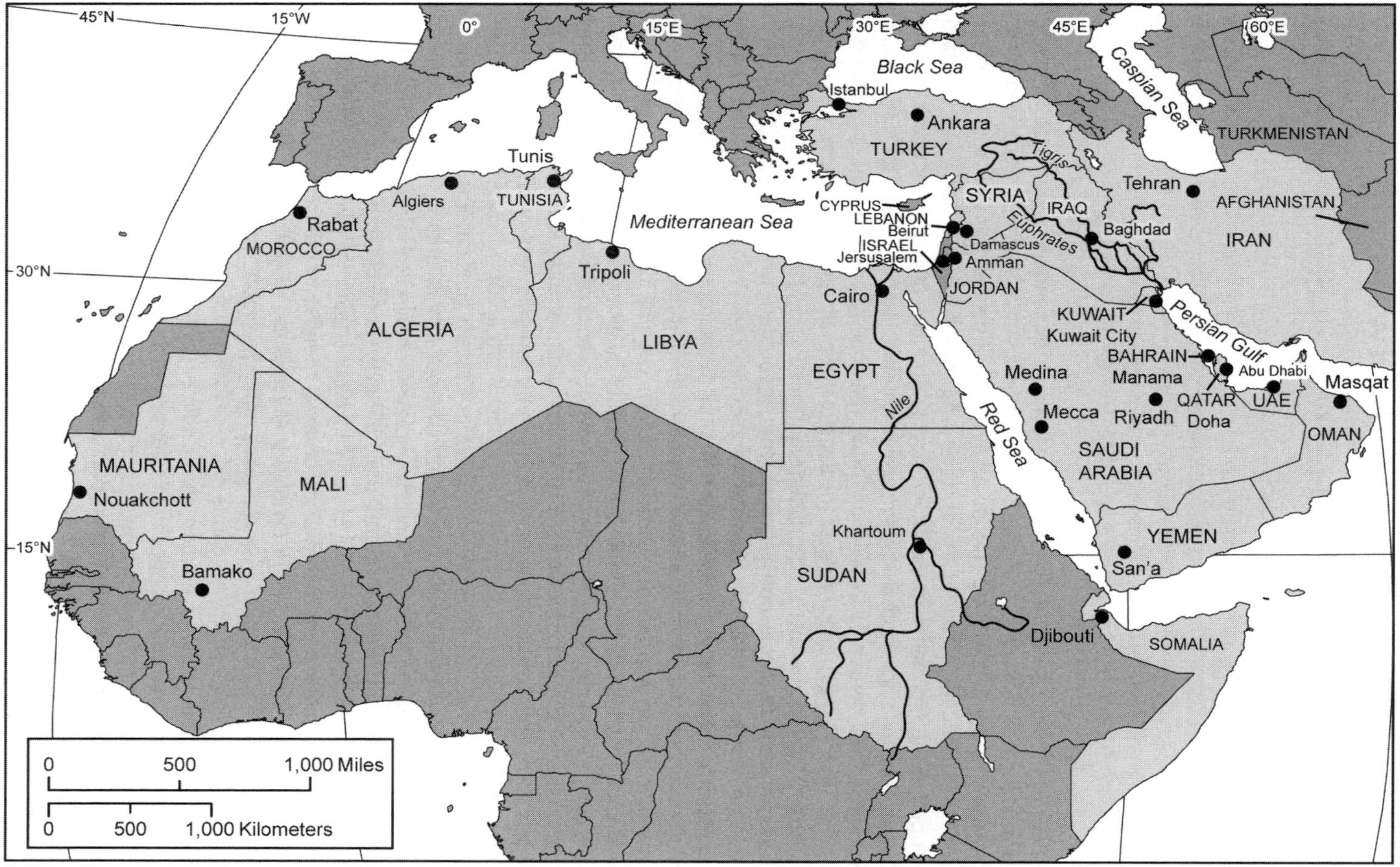

Map 9 The modern Middle East

10 The Middle East in the twentieth century

"The regime will endure with unbelief, but not with injustice"

The twentieth century saw Middle Easterners gain independence from historic empires and European colonial powers and establish national states with modern governments.[1] In these states the Circle of Justice as a saying disappeared from political rhetoric, no longer quoted except by historians and the shah of Iran. In the bourgeois states that developed in the first half of the century, however, critics of the government continued to stress the need for justice and the government's responsibility to the producing classes. By mid-century it was clear that national rulers – kings, presidents, or dictators – were again being forced to reenact the political relationships embodied in the Circle. Numerous experts report state activities and leaders' pronouncements, as well as people's requests and protests, that resonated with, although they did not quote, the Circle of Justice. Despite employing the modern languages of constitutionalism, democracy, and socialism, the rulers addressed people who persistently demanded adherence to the culture's established standard of justice. This concept of justice survived or resurfaced in Middle Eastern political culture not merely because of peasant conservatism but because the Circle of Justice still described some aspects of people's relationship with the state. The new concepts of nationhood and citizenship did not replace, but were added to, older concepts of interdependency and justice between rulers and people. While the Circle's influence cannot in most cases be proven, its ubiquity and persistence through the centuries argue for a fundamental role for the understandings it describes in modern Middle Eastern political thinking. The Circle's heritage does not explain these ideologies fully, but it highlights a recurrent aspect of Middle Eastern politics that was long downplayed or even missing from Western and modern analyses, the expectation that the state is responsible to provide the means of protection, prosperity, and social justice or to compensate for their lack. Having been part of people's thinking and behavior for so long, the idea of the Circle of Justice could not be eliminated from the culture simply by eliminating the saying.

In the modern monarchies and republics that developed after World War I, condemnations of violations by indigenous elites or foreign rulers and demands for just rule from national governments echoed the Circle's definition of justice.[2] Some rulers consciously drew on it to legitimize their rule; others incorporated it into their policies in response to demands from their subjects. Kings tended more than presidents to retain institutions connected with the Circle, particularly the receipt of petitions. Other rulers installed policies and institutions that drew on the interdependence of the Circle but expressed it in the new vocabularies of development and socialism. As the promises of these Western panaceas failed to materialize, the ideas of the Circle also became tools for a popular critique of government, especially but not only within Islamic discourse.

The justice these critiques demanded was sometimes called "social justice" and ascribed to secular politics, and sometimes "Islamic" and traced back to the Qur'an, but in both cases it resembled that of the Circle in its demand that the state support the producing class on which it depended for taxes and goods. Despite this similarity, the socialist and Islamic demands for justice were often at odds with each other, and those who used Islamic terms frequently rejected any connection to more secular ideologies. Yet the structure of demands made by Islamic as well as secular critics bore the unmistakable shape of the Circle of Justice.

In both secular and religious ideologies, the ruler – or the state – was supposed to protect and care for the subjects or citizens, not fleece or oppress them. The ruler or state also had to provide an infrastructure allowing people to work freely and to contribute their labor and revenue to the state and (now) society. In the modern era, this infrastructure included electricity and running water, housing, health care, affordable bread or food, education, jobs, and a good work environment, in addition to roads, bridges, markets, courts, a fair tax system, and military protection from attack and oppression. While specific provisions were based on modern needs and influenced by socialist and democratic ideologies, this demand for support was consistent with the framework of the Circle of Justice and, like the Circle, provided a test of the government's legitimacy and effectiveness. Modernization also generated new versions of the Circle itself that incorporated modern political and economic concepts into a recognizable framework of interdependency. As regimes and their policies changed over the course of the century, people employed these new versions, as they had in the past, to chide those who ruled them for failing to provide and protect.

The "bourgeois patronage state" (1908–1952)

In the early twentieth century, new states developed across the Middle East under Western influence. These new states may be termed "bourgeois patronage states," on the model of the military patronage states of the past. In a bourgeois patronage state, power and its benefits flowed downward from a bourgeois ruling class to its clients, whose access to power lay through patronage links to landowners, wealthy merchants, and industrialists.[3] Western imperialists imported their own political and economic ideas and structures (as outside invaders had done before), including a powerful capitalism that supported an elite of landowners and businessmen, indigenous and foreign, and an ideology of nationalism and economic advancement rather than political responsibility and social justice.[4] Unlike the elites of the military patronage states, the modern bourgeoisie did not function as the state's agents. Although they benefitted from state wealth, they took no responsibility for the state's duties, in particular that of providing justice. Whether these states were European colonies, mandate states (indigenous Western-style states under European "protection"), or independent monarchies or republics, their leaders were preoccupied with other problems and forgot or ignored the close connection between military protection, the treasury's health, the people's ability to provide resources, and the state's provision of justice.

Bourgeois patronage states and the demand for justice

The establishment of the Republic of Turkey out of the break-up of the Ottoman Empire after World War I created a bourgeois patronage state where measures fulfilling a justice like that of the Circle could not be enacted. Ziya Gökalp, the ideologue of the modern Turkish state, defined justice as "the freedom of the individual from any sort of attack."[5] This definition rejected oppression by elites or outsiders but ignored both the state's responsibility for the individual and the individual's responsibility to the state. Popular logic, in contrast, envisioned justice as shepherding care ensured by the constitution; an old Turkish peasant complained about the constitution, "But we thought that everything could be rectified; taxes would be collected justly and peacefully; murderers and thieves in the village would be reformed; our children who go to military service would not be kept hungry and naked for years, but would be discharged in time; officials would not do things as they pleased and everything would be changed. But so far nothing has happened."[6]

The speeches of Ataturk (1924–45), founder of the Turkish Republic, employed the Circle-of-Justice view of the peasant, presumably because it resonated with his audience: "The real Lord of Turkey is the peasant who is the real producer."[7] In practice, however, the new government developed the commercial and industrial middle class and supported large landowners because they had the resources to support the state. Large landowners and big businessmen received privileges and opportunities from the state and dispensed patronage to those at lower social levels.[8] To enact economic and social change, therefore, Ataturk developed statism, a policy that made the bureaucracy the agent of development and redistribution of wealth, the ruler's role in the Circle of Justice. This ideological turn was legitimized by reference to the Orkhon inscriptions, making Atatürk the heir to Bilge Kaghan.[9] Statism, however, also struggled against bourgeois opposition; for example, the government passed a land reform law in 1945, but landlord pressure made it ineffectual.[10]

Multiparty politics beginning in 1950 brought into power the landholding elites, who won peasant votes by supporting rural development and popular religion. The mechanization of agriculture, however, eliminated landlords' dependence on peasant farmers and reduced the peasants' bargaining power and their ablity to obtain justice. Thousands left the land, starting the explosive urban growth that became such a severe problem later in the century. While national struggles and the formation of political parties encouraged alliances between the middle and lower classes, economic and cultural competition set them against each other.[11] Once peasants lost their economic centrality as the main supporters of the treasury, their demands for justice became ineffective. That cry was taken up by the urban lower classes.

Like Turkey, other new states in the interwar period gave bourgeois elites control over patronage and enacted their values. In Syria under the French mandate, large landowners possessed 85 percent of agrarian land and received credit, irrigation projects, and land from the mandate government; in turn they controlled and patronized the peasants.[12] The Egyptian government, still partly under British control, relegated social services to private and religious organizations until World War II; even then, the social service efforts of King Farouk (1936–52) were not enough to win him popular legitimacy.[13] In independent Iran a statist political configuration also emerged; its reforms benefitted the state and elites more than the popular classes. Reza Shah (1924–1941) gained peasant support because of his crackdown on bandits and tribal raiders, but his policies were repressive. He made the village headmen legally the landlords' representatives rather than the peasants', and he favored landowners, merchants, industrialists, and the military. He brought the country the technical modernization it had not achieved in the nineteenth century, but the peasants' standard of living did not noticeably improve.[14]

If rulers and elites in the first half of the twentieth century neglected or discarded the Circle of Justice, ordinary people did not. Middle Eastern populations in the interwar period, in the face of their states' minimal social concern, mobilized through petitioning, collective action, and violent resistance to put pressure on their governments to enact justice. Between 1915 and 1921, northwestern Iran's provincial notables and democratic reformers rose up against the centralizing state, demanding land redistribution and tax reductions for the producers. Egypt in 1919 faced a peasant uprising against the reimposition of the colonial economy as well as an urban revolt sparked by the British arrest of nationalist leaders. Peasants in parts of the Nile Delta destroyed the infrastructure of cotton growing and export; others inundated the cotton fields and planted rice, which they could eat. Still others attacked the houses of elites, crying, "We want bread!"[15] In interwar Morocco, mountain tribes employed traditional protest mechanisms, such as refusing to pay taxes and abandoning the land, to make modern demands on French colonizers for schools, markets, and employment. Demonstrations in Damascus and petitions to the short-lived Arab government in 1919 tried to awaken the government's responsibility to its citizens. Repeated petitions to the French mandate governments of Syria and Lebanon demanded political reform as well as education, health care, industrial growth, and worker protection.[16] Egypt's rural notables and peasants mounted petition campaigns to demand reductions in land rents but failed, raising rural poverty to over 50 percent by 1950.

As the bourgeois patronage states matured, their public spending increased, but social services were not available to all in need, either through the Circle's justice or the justice of rights as in a modern welfare state. Rather, state services became the coin in which bourgeois patronage governments dispensed political favors. In the late 1920s Syrian social and workers' groups began to obtain roads, schools, clinics, and electricity, but the French mandate government dispensed the largest benefits to the groups that posed the greatest threat, not those that had the greatest need. When the French did increase social spending in the 1930s, it was only to fend off demands for self-government. In Iran, the 1930s were also a period of development spending on roads, railways, factories, and schools, but the goal was to strengthen the state. New governments often argued that they should postpone social spending until the national state was secure, and only marginalized political groups on the ideological left spoke up for the needs of the poor and marginalized population. Secularist and Muslim reformist modernizers then competed to become the principal spokesmen for the demands of the needy and to gain the legitimacy granted to those who provided justice.[17]

Ideologies: Justice against the state

Intellectuals were slow to articulate the contest between the bourgeois patronage states and popular demands. The great controversial statements of the 1920s, such as 'Ali 'Abd al-Raziq's claim that the caliphate was a secular institution and there was no "Islamic government," and Taha Husayn's claim that pre-Islamic Arabic poetry in its current form was a creation of the Islamic period, concerned the validity of the standard Islamic narrative of origins and its value for national identity construction.[18] When critiques of the bourgeois state emerged, however, their rhetoric echoed the Circle of Justice. Without using the Circle's terminology, they emphasized the state's responsibility for its people's welfare.

Members of the Muslim Brotherhood, a reformist group founded in 1928, were among the first to respond. Muhammad al-Ghazzali and Sayyid Qutb analyzed Islamic history to show how rulers, representing the rich capitalists, had always allowed maldistribution of land and wealth and foreign economic exploitation, while the poor paid high taxes and lived in intolerable conditions. Al-Ghazzali, in his 1951 book *Our Beginning in Wisdom*, argued that Islam was an instrument for eliminating the state's injustice. Charity, though one of the five pillars of Islam, was not meant to satisfy all the needs of the poor, only their emergencies. Meeting their ongoing needs was the function of the state, which should help them provide for themselves, especially by expanding jobs for the growing non-agrarian population: "Providing work for all is the responsibility of the government."[19] Sayyid Qutb's *Social Justice in Islam* (1949) condemned governments and elites for doing so little about the condition of the poor and praised Abu Dharr, the Companion of the Prophet, for his opposition to excessive accumulation of wealth. Although he defined justice as integrity and godliness, a religious definition that owed nothing to the social interdependence of the Circle, Qutb emphasized social interdependence in his demand that the government establish "mutual social responsibility," by which he meant state enforcement of the responsibility of the rich to provide for workers and those unable to work, as well as of the workers' responsibility to contribute labor and taxes. Maududi's Islamic critique of Western influence rejected Darwinism because it made a virtue – or a right – out of the oppression of the weak by the strong, and capitalism because it took from the rich all responsibility for the plight of the poor and needy.[20]

Secular condemnations of governmental injustice brandished similar terms. Taha Husayn published seven books between 1945 and 1950 condemning governments that "strove to please the prosperous" rather than the "wretched, who burned with a yearning for justice."[21] The Egyptian Khalid M. Khalid, in his 1950 work *From Here We Start*, rejected a religious state but demanded social justice, stating categorically, "The government that does not provide food for its people is not even a government."[22] He too acclaimed Abu Dharr for criticizing the hard-heartedness of early Muslim rulers and distributing his property to the needy. The socialist or social democratic tinge of these ideologies reflected not only Western influence but the continuing power of the Circle of Justice and Islamic notions of equity in popular thought.

The governmental response to both Islamists and secularists was suppression. Consequently, religious and secular critics joined the anti-imperialist struggles erupting all over the Middle East in the hope that independent national governments would address the grievances of workers and the poor. At the end of World War II the colonial powers divested themselves of their Middle Eastern mandates. Their denial to the new states of financial aid, military support, and ideological understanding aroused the resentment of many Middle Easterners, and in the Cold War conditions of the 1950s, resentment of the West was expressed in alliances with the Soviet bloc and entailed at least a rhetorical adoption of some form of socialism. The 1950s and 1960s saw violent changes of government in the region, and many governments in that period – both monarchies and republics – adopted ideologies of socialism, social welfare, and social justice.

The modern kings and *mazalim* (1924–*c.*1975)

The kings of the twentieth-century Middle East were more likely than elected leaders to retain the rhetoric of the Circle of Justice. The reasons range from their premodern roots in sultanates or tribal sheikhdoms to their relative independence from Western political ideologies, their largely tribal populations, and their preservation of older institutions of governance. As the Circle had legitimated tribal sheikhs and premodern sultans, it continued to legitimate kings as modern dispensers of justice who reenacted more or less convincingly the old myth of the just sultan.[23] In a modernized, even Westernized, form the institutions of justice became a key element in these kingdoms' bureaucracies. Whenever kings failed to deliver on their promises, the Circle of Justice became a tool of the opposition.

Modern Arab monarchies and royal justice

Modern Arab kings found justice in response to petitions, the justice of *mazalim* courts, a useful vehicle for their relations with the ruled. The rulers of Kuwait, chiefs of the dominant tribal group, accepted appeals from their people at regular gatherings held for that purpose. Petitioning in Yemen ranged from oral complaint in the street or mosque to written documentation presented in offices, in a complaint box, or through the mail.[24] King ʻAbd al-Aziz ibn Saʻud (1902–53), who established the Saudi state in 1924, based its legal system on a modernized Ottoman law linking shariah and ruler's law; he also set up complaint boxes and received petitions in person.[25] In 1955 the Saudi kings institutionalized *mazalim* in a Board of Grievances (*Diwan al-Mazalim*), which handled complaints against the state.[26] From the early 1950s Saudi workers began striking to demand greater rights; in exchange for their political quiescence, the kings, in a sort of social contract, poured the country's oil revenues into development projects such as paved roads, electricity and water, telephone systems, housing, education, health care, welfare, and social security. Around the same time, the Yemeni constitution declared that "social justice is the basis of taxation and public expenditure."[27] Other Middle Eastern kings struck the same bargain with their subjects.

King Abdullah (1923–51) of Transjordan (Jordan after independence), who grew up in tribal Arabia, won over Jordan's tribes by enacting the role of a chief among them in constant personal visits, providing for their needs and settling disputes, as the Circle mandated. His grandson King Hussein (1952–99) carried on the practice: "I love these visits. Tribesmen sometimes present petitions when they hear I am visiting them, and most are so simple I can deal with them on the spot."[28] Despite his Western education, King Hussein gained the loyalty of the tribes by indigenous practices of dispensing patronage, judging disputes, and accepting petitions; he also received petitions from the urban poor. To hear middle-class opinions he went out disguised as a taxi driver and questioned passengers on their problems. Like the Saudi kings, he withheld political rights, stating that his people were unready.[29]

Royal authority legitimized Morocco's regular judicial system, but the king retained personal *mazalim* functions. Hassan II (1961–99) encouraged individuals or delegations to bring their complaints directly to the king, as they formerly did in the "Feast of Students," an annual carnevalesque reversal centered on the granting of petitions. A student, invested with the royal parasol, would act as sultan for three weeks and grant petitions; at the end of the period he petitioned for whatever he wanted.[30] Prosperity was an obligation of Morocco's ruler; the king's blessing or *baraka* was thought to bring rain, abundant crops, healthy children, and national prosperity, while its absence brought troubles, drought, famine, and the failure of fruit to ripen. "Injustice brings ruin and justice brings prosperity," wrote the scholar al-Kattani (d.1927). The state was supposed to meet the needs of all its subjects, in modern times through development rather than miracles.[31]

Hassan II invoked the values of the Circle of Justice to support economic development, flood relief, and workers' rights. He employed the unemployed on big, visible development projects: reclaiming land, building roads, dikes, and canals, drilling for water, planting forests, or building houses, schools, irrigation works, dams and power stations, turning the first spade himself in imitation of the brick-carrying kings of ancient Mesopotamia.[32] He represented the monarchy as the supreme dispenser of justice in Morocco, but it was also the supreme dispenser of patronage. Independence and development increased the patronage at the king's disposal, and with this economic leverage he addressed the needs of the elite and gained their cooperation. He did not reform landholding but distributed state lands as private property to managerial companies, while many peasants remained landless.[33] He attempted to blunt criticism and project the image of a just ruler by solving technical problems of economic development and food production: "While they [Algerians] extract oil, I build dams."[34]

To justify his policies, Hassan redefined democracy in terms of the Circle of Justice: "Democracy does not consist only in a collection of political organizations and representative institutions. Real democracy is rather that which guarantees to individuals and groups effective protection against illness and ignorance."[35] Although Hassan said many times that he was constructing a social and economic democracy, he certainly did not construct a political democracy. Tensions multiplied between his promises of prosperity for all and the limited distribution of wealth and land, between his promises of justice for all and his harsh suppression of political opposition, and between his announced role as defender of the faith and his use of the army to assert royal authority and punish dissent. These tensions gained force from the contradiction between the king's behavior and popular expectations raised by an ideology so dependent on the Circle of Justice.

The Circle of Justice in Iranian national ideology

In Iran the Circle of Justice served both as authorization for the ruler's policies and as a banner of the opposition. More than other monarchs, the twentieth-century shahs of Iran had a special relationship to Near Eastern ideology: because of its attribution to Persian origins, the Circle became an integral part of Persian national mythology, though not of the modern monarchy itself. When Reza Shah came to power, he adopted the pre-Islamic Persian term Pahlavi as the name of his dynasty and used aspects of ancient Persian history in the ideology of the new national state. He revived the old Persian calendar, sponsored an urban architecture modeled on the ruins of ancient Persia uncovered by archaeologists, and like earlier shahs put forward the *Shahnama* as a model for Iranian politics, having it cheaply published and making schoolchildren memorize it. The interdependence of the Circle of Justice, however, did not guide Reza Shah's policies; he favored a new social hierarchy like those of the mandate states, controlled by the bourgeoisie, large landowners, and military officers. Although he had the *Testament of Ardashir* translated into modern Persian, he did not govern according to its advice.[36]

His successor Muhammad Reza Shah (1941–79), the only modern ruler to quote the Circle of Justice, nevertheless worked as hard as his father to suppress political dissent and popular calls for justice. He wanted to create a modern society and economy, but like Abdulhamid he wanted it completely controlled by himself and the state. His quotation of the Circle emphasized the hierarchical rigidity of its Iranian interpretation and its ability to lend divine sanction to his rule. The quotation occurred near the beginning of his first book, *Mission for My Country* (1961): "According to Ardeshir I, the first Sasanian ruler, 'There can be no power without an army, no army without money, no money without agriculture, and no agriculture without justice'."[37] This quotation, he said, showed how Iran could benefit the rest of the world, presumably by modeling a successful autocracy leavened by justice.

In his 1967 book *The White Revolution* Muhammad Reza Shah explained and justified his development program, consisting of six points, the most crucial of which was land reform. The program incorporated the idea (shared with Morocco's Hassan II) that "political democracy has no meaning unless it is complemented by economic democracy." The shah also established village "Houses of Equity" for resolving disputes, citing the precedent of Sasanian kings who gave justice in person and quoting the proverb attributed to the Prophet: "An irreligious state can survive, an unjust one never." *The White Revolution* proposed a new sort of Circle, based on modern concepts of social justice: "Today, political rights which are divorced from social rights, and legal justice that does not include social justice, and political democracy without economic democracy, are devoid of real meaning."[38] The Iranian state, however, was a "rentier state," dependent not on people's taxes but on oil revenues; the shah kept his throne not by popular support but by his security forces.[39] The state was brought closer to the people, intervening in their lives in new and more intrusive ways, but the people were not brought closer to the state; in fact, they were discouraged from political participation by state terrorism.

"The Shah and his technocrats abhorred being the rulers of peasants and donkeys," observed an anthropologist.[40] Despite the rhetoric of justice surrounding the land reform program and the socialist tendencies of some of the officials in charge, the shah did not grant equality to the lower classes or raise agricultural productivity. He broke the political power of the landowning class; moved investment from land into industry, creating an industrial bourgeoisie; capitalized agriculture and its bases, such as land, water, fertilizer, and labor; removed the buffer of the landlords between the state and the mass of its subjects, in the process impoverishing millions of middle-class people who lost all the savings they had invested in land; and deprived peasants without cultivation rights of agricultural jobs and moved them into the cities, where they became consumers and cheap labor for industrial and commercial enterprises.[41]

The land reform's attack on the bourgeois patronage state roused a massive response. Landlords from whom land had been taken, ulema opposing the loss of revenue from foundation lands and their exclusion from decisions with religious implications, and liberals afraid of "creeping despotism" staged a riot in Tehran in June 1963 which was bloodily suppressed. Khomeini's speech at this riot and his subsequent arrest first made him a public figure. Socioeconomic modernization was not matched by an equivalent political modernization or an extension of political participation to the newly urbanized and educated populations created by land reform. Rather than reinforcing the interdependence of state and society, as the shah's rhetoric promised, Iran's policies emphasized their antagonism and set their interests in conflict. Peasants in the countryside grew independent, critical, even defiant; in urban areas the politically active population expanded.[42]

The expectations of prosperity and justice formerly articulated in the Circle of Justice were now expressed largely in the political language of the West. Contradictions between those expectations and actual state policies produced a sense of betrayal and lent urgency to popular protests. In emphasizing the Circle's hierarchical side, the ruler's responsibility to create order and prosperity for his obedient subjects, the shah seems to have forgotten that the Circle could be traversed in both directions. The failure of his justice became for his subjects a signal of his illegitimacy, his lack of divine approval, potential military defeat, and ultimately the loss of prosperity, order, and justice in society. The Circle's claims, repeatedly stressed in the shah's propaganda, turned into a weapon against his regime.

Arab socialism, the "just welfare state" (1952–*c.*1975)

Most Arab countries gained independence in mid-century and, in reaction against the bourgeois patronage states they emerged from, adopted republican governments and socialist ideologies, some for rhetorical purposes and some genuine. Their development strategies paralleled those of the monarchies, with a stress on industrialization supplemented by the provision of rural and urban social justice in the form of irrigation works, producer and consumer cooperatives, health care, education, loans, and subsidies. Socialist republics employed a very different vocabulary from the Circle of Justice, but like the Circle their priorities included the state's provision of justice for the productive classes and their obligation to support the state in return. Building their political position on the critiques of opposition writers gave these states a powerful tool for legitimation. Already in 1949, for example, Egypt's new Civil Code, explicitly rejecting the liberal individualism of early legal reform efforts, stated that it "stands behind the weak to protect him" and "implements social justice."[43]

Socialist thinkers saw the state as the ally of peasants and workers and expected it to fulfill and expand the sultan's role of protecting them from exploitation by landowners and capitalists.[44] They revised the myth of the just sultan into the myth of the just welfare state, a myth, declared the scholar who identified it, that was "known and accepted literally as a political goal … in much of the Middle East."[45] Socialist republics recreated in modern dress the political relationships of the pre-colonial past. Under the colonial and bourgeois governments of the early twentieth century, people had had no recourse to the state for protection from local authorities. They favored socialism because socialist governments announced their support for the peasants and the poor and their protection from oppression on the local scene.[46] Socialist government, in other words, reassumed the pre-colonial state's task of enforcing the Circle of Justice.

In contrast to the personal justice dispensed by monarchs, socialist justice was to be delivered by means of structural changes in economy and society. The strong state tradition in the Middle East meant that even under a modern government, people would find a state-directed politics and economy familiar. Socialism's popularity rested not only on its opposition to the capitalism of the imperial powers and indigenous bourgeoisie, but also on popular belief in the state's responsibility to create a just and moral social order. Its goal, that "the citizens … will be enabled to live in the shadow of a just social order," fitted directly into Near Eastern political ideology.[47] Socialism contained no compensatory justice for the powerful bourgeois elites who lost their dominant position in the political scene; in the socialist definition, "democracy means the establishment of social justice and equity for the oppressed class as against the oppressive class."[48]

Egypt's Arab socialism

The major exponent of socialism was Gamal Abdel Nasser, Egypt's president from 1956 to 1970 and a leader of the 1952 revolution. Social change in Egypt began with a land reform that dispossessed large landowners and distributed land to peasants. Its economic effects were moderate, but its political effects were revolutionary.[49] The reform broke the political power of the large landowning class and reduced or rechanneled its wealth. It lessened rural poverty and hunger and allowed farm children to stop working and go to school. Justified by the need to give peasants the means of making a living and escaping the exploitation of the rich, the land reform echoed the demands of the Circle of Justice.[50]

Some of the consequences of land reform, however, eroded people's sense of the state's justice. While land redistribution favored smallholders, the accompanying mechanization, loan policies, and resource cooperatives benefitted the more substantial farmers who held local power. Enlarging the irrigated area created new farmland for distribution, increased the food supply, and diminished rural poverty, but land reform did not improve agricultural productivity or eliminate landlessness.[51] It increased rural unemployment; landless peasants lost jobs on the disappearing large estates. Migration to the cities rose rapidly, and better public health and food production fostered population growth. The cities mushroomed and urban poverty redoubled.[52] The "just welfare state" came into being to subsidize food and fuel for the urban poor and to provide birth control, health care, education, and employment.

Egypt's National Charter of 1961 proclaimed: "Socialism has become both a means and an end, namely sufficiency and justice."[53] Sufficiency meant growth in national prosperity, and justice demanded its fair distribution. The National Charter explained the relationship between justice, prosperity, and military victory in terms remarkably close to the Circle of Justice: "The new society, which is now being built on the basis of sufficiency and justice, needs the armed forces as a shield to defend the reconstruction of Egyptian society against external dangers. A strong army is a necessity, but the needs of defense should never have precedence over the needs of development – because without economic and social development no army can withstand the strain of long campaigns."[54] In premodern conditions these goals were thought to depend on a strong social hierarchy, but under modern conditions they demanded a more egalitarian society. Arab socialism maintained that a degree of economic equality was a prerequisite for democracy in order to prevent domination by an economically powerful minority.

Nasser's speeches made justice the path to liberty and democracy as well: "When we say that we want political liberty we mean that there should be economic and social justice."[55] Political democracy could only function on the basis of social democracy. Like Morocco's King Hassan II and the shah of Iran, Nasser proclaimed: "The freedom to earn a living is a necessary guarantee to the freedom to vote."[56] The concept of the Circle thus formed the foundation for newer concepts of political justice depending on popular participation.

The state's development reforms and social services raised production and introduced greater equality of distribution; in 1970 Egypt's per capita income increased 3 percent faster than population; employment and working conditions improved markedly.[57] Many people had better education, better health care, more social security, and more equality; but there were always many who did not. By the end of Nasser's presidency, his vision of social justice and the great strides taken toward that goal were overshadowed by a sense of the state's injustice stemming from the large number of people for whom food subsidies and social services were still inadequate, diversion of resources away from social programs to the military, corruption in government, denial of political participation to newly educated and modernized groups, and violent suppression of criticism and dissent. Newly mobilized groups called for justice from outside the political system, adding to the cry for food and services new demands for democracy and freedom and for ethics in government. The government's inadequacy in the face of these demands for justice was a major factor in its loss of legitimacy.[58]

Nasser insisted that realizing his long-term goal of establishing democracy was impossible in the short term because only the elites and the army were ready to exercise political power. Mobilization of the poor and peasants would be unsuccessful without a long period of education and politicization, and for that reason peasants were under-represented in the political system. The middle class, however, required a much shorter preparatory period than Nasser had anticipated, and by the end of his regime even peasants were using the political concepts of Arab socialism and the modern state's mechanisms of justice – the police, the party, and civil authorities – to address their problems. In the late 1960s, when an oppressive landowner deprived of his property murdered a rabble-rousing socialist peasant leader in the "Kamshish affair," both peasants and landowners marshalled the rhetoric of social justice to support their positions.[59]

Nasser's "Arab socialism" was not dissimilar to the Muslim Brotherhood's "Islamic socialism," especially when Nasser began to counter accusations of communism by linking his ideology to popular culture and Islam, referring to the justice of 'Umar and Abu Dharr.[60] Other policies of the Egyptian state contradicted its Islamic claims, and international events also stood in the way of Arab socialism's success. By the time of Nasser's death in 1970, the legitimacy of states based on non-Islamic models and the relationship between social justice and religion were in question.

Islamic socialism, the Muslim Brotherhood, and the Baath

After centuries when Islam's sanctioning of social justice seemed unproblematic, the introduction of "godless" socialism raised new issues of religion and state. Egypt's Muslim Brothers criticized both secular socialist ideology and the state's faulty implementation of social goals; they supported state welfare policies but sought to derive them from the teachings of Islam, including the ideas of the Circle of Justice, rather than secular political thought. The Brotherhood acted on its vision, sometimes more successfully than the state, founding mosques and schools throughout the country; bringing health care, clinics, and sanitation to villages; distributing food and clothing; and providing welfare and social services to poor families, the aged, the homeless, and orphans.[61]

The Brotherhood's vision of an Islamic social justice spread beyond Egypt to Muslims elsewhere. The Syrian Muslim Brother Mustafa al-Siba'i, in his 1959 book *The Socialism of Islam*, argued that socialism was in accord with Islam: "The task of prophets and reformers in various ages has been to preach that we should be fair to the unfortunate, to show mercy to the poor, and to sweep away injustice." Islamic socialism resembled Arab socialism but refused to use its vocabulary. In place of "social justice," Islamic socialism used Sayyid Qutb's term, "mutual social responsibility:" the rich were responsible for the care of the lower classes, who were responsible for production and taxation. The state's role was to manage these relations, controlling wealth, providing gainful employment and economic assistance, organizing production and collecting taxes.[62] When in the 1970s the state turned away from socialism, Islamic socialism became the main oppositional ideology. This move injected a sectarian element into what had been a nationalist and populist movement for social justice.

The relationship between Islam and socialism evolved differently in different countries. Libya's 1969 revolution under Muammar al-Qaddafi, for example, was modeled on

Egypt's under Nasser; Qaddafi's socialism, however, did not conciliate Islam but incorporated it. His "Third Universal Theory" made Islam an intrinsic part of Libyan socialism and set up that combination as a rival to capitalism and communism for the world to imitate.[63] "The Islamic Religion," declared Qaddafi, "is a socialist creed." As a Libyan popular song expressed it:

> The universal theory has seen the light,
> Bringing to Mankind peace and delight,
> The tree, oh, of justice, people's rule and socialism,
> Completely different from laissez-faire and capitalism,
> Based on religion and nationalism.[64]

The Libyan Constitutional Declaration of December 1969 embraced social justice in Article 6: "The State aims at realizing socialism through social justice that prevents all forms of exploitation and through sufficiency in production and just distribution of national wealth."[65] In 1969 Qaddafi launched a "Green Revolution" to raise agricultural productivity in the Fezzan valley, proclaiming: "The Jefara Plain, the great Jebel al-Akhdar ... the Fezzan valleys are witnessing the great agricultural revolution that will enable the Libyan people to earn their living, to eat freely ... the food that was normally imported from overseas ... this is freedom, this is independence and this is revolution."[66] This is the Circle of Justice again, in modern terms.

In contrast to Libya's "Third Universal Theory," the socialism of Syria and Iraq was nonsectarian. The Baath (Resurrection) Party, founded in 1947 by the Muslim Salahuddin Bitar and the Christian Michel Aflaq, called for the creation of a "just economic order" that would guarantee a more universal social justice: "All humanity is mutually responsible for its common welfare, and collectively responsible for its protection and civilization." Aflaq consciously broke with the bourgeois patronage state to demand a social justice based on structural changes rather than elite favors, declaring: "The problem of rising prices can only be solved by the application of socialist principles ... by nationalizing the foreign companies and freeing the people from their exploitation of such basic needs as water, electricity and transport, and by distributing land to the small farmers." The Baath Party Programme of 1965, like Egypt's National Charter, declared that "a rise in the standard of living must keep pace with justice in distribution and with an accompanying diminution in the differences between classes as well as in the exploitation of one man by another."[67]

Syria's national state retained the structures of the French mandate, and it had almost always been a loosely governed province of some larger empire rather than a centralized state. Syrians had no tradition of implementing the Circle of Justice through the state, only through leading men, who dispensed favors through personal patronage rather than state power.[68] They therefore had more difficulty than the Egyptians in developing a state that would act as a dispenser of justice. Bourgeois patronage politics dominated the state from the mandate period until Syria's union with Egypt as the United Arab Republic (UAR, 1958–1961), which introduced Egypt's state socialism to Syria. It survived the death of the UAR; the Baath Constitution of 1964 called for redistribution of property, education, health and employment services, workers' rights, and retirement benefits. The Baath Cabinet used the stress on social justice to justify state-controlled reforms: "Economic freedom, freedom [from] capitalist imperialism, overcoming scientific, social and economic underdevelopment, the eradication of class differences and the provision of culture, hygienic conditions, food and clothing for the people – all these objectives cannot be realized within a framework of social relations based on the exploitation of one man by another and one class by another. In choosing socialism, we chose the only answer to this challenge."[69] The process of introducing these reforms created a strong central apparatus able to contain social conflict – or any popular political action outside the state.[70]

The Baath political apparatus brought to power army officers from rural areas, where strong leaders mediated quarrels and gave protection to the weak. The military presence in the state, it was hoped, would prevent a takeover by either the old bourgeoisie or the new radicals. Syria's land policy set tighter limits on the size of landholdings; roughly 25 percent of farming families received land; compared to Egypt, agricultural investment and production increased significantly, reducing rural discontent.[71] The opposite was true, however, of the Baath Party's business and industrial reforms. In contrast to Egypt, where the nationalization of businesses struck at foreign colonizers, in Syria it struck at indigenous urban merchants, almost 50 percent of the population, cutting off their political participation and leaving the urban middle class at odds with the state.

After the Arabs' 1967 defeat by Israel, the Baath Party wanted to stop social development and build up the economy to prepare for future war. In 1970 the military wing took over the party; the officers, though sympathetic to rural justice concerns, were more concerned about military expansion. It was this military wing that brought Hafiz al-Asad to power in 1970.[72] With a vastly strengthened state, and the party as the only channel of patronage, it became impossible to press for social justice or popular representation. Even Michel Aflaq became *persona non grata* in the new Baath state and moved to Iraq, where a Baath government had also been installed.

Iraq, the Baath, and the Near Eastern past

In Iraq, where the Circle of Justice was conceived, social justice concerns were central to state policy for only a brief period in the twentieth century. The British-backed monarchy was not considered serious about social justice; it did not expropriate the big landowners on the grounds that Iraq's terrain was perfect for large-scale machine agriculture, and in 1951 it spent only one-third of its development budget.[73] Turning Iraq toward social justice took a series of national uprisings, each one spurred by a sharp rise in inflation as well as by international circumstances. A revolution in 1958, including a central government coup and a peasant uprising, installed a republican government that expanded social services and imposed a land reform. President Qassem (1958–63) emphasized the interdependence between rich and poor, writing: "Sons of the people, I am Abdel Karim Qassem and stronger and more resolute for the sake of the poor," and concurrently, "I also protect the rich," because "rich and poor support one another."[74] In 1963 the republic was replaced by a Baath-led socialist government and in 1968 by a single-party socialist system that collectivized agriculture, lowering production and galvanizing urban migration.[75]

Iraq's socialist leaders legitimized their program by relating it to historic concepts of governance in the region. Iraqi Prime Minister Bazzaz (1965–6) traced socialism to the Arab heritage: "The socialism which is good for Iraq is the one that emanates from the Arab nature of the Iraqi people."[76] Baath Party official Tariq Aziz linked socialism with a key aspect of ancient Near Eastern political thought: "The Baʻth Party revolution … won great victories. Then it began to falter. The fundamental, but not the only reason for this, was that it was unable to 'put things in their right place'."[77] President Aref (1963–6) related social justice to older images of the fertility of the land: "Our fertile land and plentiful water supply require the peasant to take care of this good earth which brings forth its blessings. Citizens, Your revolutionary Government is bent upon its policy of development, reform and social justice."[78]

Such references to ancient Mesopotamian ideas drew on the context of the Circle of Justice, although they did not quote it directly. The first Revolution Day celebration in 1959 included floats portraying ancient Mesopotamia; one representing the stele engraved with Hammurabi's laws was entitled "Justice is the Foundation of Government." The Iraqi National Assembly house was named the Hammurabi Building "to establish a strong link between ancient and modern Iraqi law-givers."[79] The use of ancient names and titles, archaeological reconstructions, and celebrations of ancient festivals tied Iraqi national identity to a respected governmental past. Modern rulers identified themselves with the ancient kings; a drawing entitled "From Nebuchadnezzar to Saddam Husayn, Babylon Is Rising Again," showed Saddam Hussein carrying a brick to rebuild the wall of Nebuchadnezzar's palace.[80] It should not be surprising if such associations raised expectations that modern rulers, no matter how autocratic, would revive ancient norms of justice.

When Saddam Hussein came to power in Iraq in 1970, it was clear that, propaganda aside, neither land reform nor agrarian collectivization nor oil investments had been able to increase productivity very much. The proportion of the population in agriculture fell from 50 to 30 percent; rural migration to the cities grew, necessitating a wider distribution of development's benefits. Increased oil revenues brought electricity and new roads to the villages, and industry, transportation and communication systems, and housing to the cities. Food consumption increased and more people took advantage of free health care and education; illiteracy dropped, and women gained new social and occupational roles. Prosperity, literacy, and economic opportunity did not lead to enhanced political mobilization, however, but to greater political oppression. Uniting society to combat foreign opposition meant the suppression of internal divisions, and the Iran–Iraq War ended prosperity in the 1980s.[81]

In view of his background as an assassin and state torturer, Saddam had to make special efforts to present himself as a just ruler. He identified himself with the ancient Near Eastern kings who had made Mesopotamia great, using the slogan, "Yesterday Nebuchadnezzar, today Saddam Hussein." A source close to the Hussein family remembered: "Again and again in his speeches, Saddam told us that Iraq was the modern-day successor of Nebuchadnezzar's fabled kingdom." Iraqi art often depicted Mesopotamian themes, as in a painting of Hammurabi's stele surrounded by factories and oil rigs. The Babylon Festival of 1988 included an international symposium on Hammurabi's code. For other such festivals Saddam rebuilt parts of Babylon, the ancient city of Nebuchadnezzar, stamping the bricks with his own name like that ancient ruler, while postage stamps portrayed him reconstructing the city of Basra after the Iran–Iraq War.[82]

Though ferocious toward opposition, Saddam wanted people to see their prosperity as a direct result of his personal intervention and patronage. Like past kings, he toured the countrysides and urban neighborhoods accepting petitions and speaking to schoolboys, shepherds, monks, and housewives, until assassination attempts ended such visits. He intervened in cases of bureaucratic oppression, chiding state officials for not eliminating obstacles to people's paying their taxes or utility bills, accessing their bank accounts, or obtaining building permits. He repeatedly stated, "We want the citizens to feel that they are living in a country where justice reigns, not connections." He had a direct telephone line for hearing complaints and received letters from Iraqi citizens; he also held weekly meetings at the Presidential Palace to which hundreds of Iraqis brought their problems and complaints. An ongoing television program called "Discussion of the Month" allowed people to phone in questions to officials.[83]

The Islamic heritage in Iraq also resonated with themes of justice. Historic individuals and groups who challenged injustice and tyranny and sought to help the poor, such as Husayn the martyr and Abu Dharr or the egalitarian Kharijis and Qarmatians, became household words. Movements bringing social justice to the downtrodden cited precedents from Islamic history of those who called the state to account. The idea that rulers and people were interdependent was still alive in religious as well as secular contexts.

Throughout the Middle East between about 1950 and 1975, in the socialist republics and in some of the monarchies as well, ideas of social justice resembling the ancient Near Eastern concept of the Circle of Justice entered modern national ideologies. These ideas emphasized the state's responsibility to protect the population and to provide for their needs: land, irrigation water, sufficient food at affordable prices, jobs, social services, and the infrastructure that enabled them in their turn to be productive and to contribute to the state's functions of national prosperity and defense. Through these provisions, the numbers and health of the population increased, they gained literacy and skills, their countries' infrastructure and industry developed, and their agricultural output soared. In the process, they created authoritarian governments, monarchical or republican, that disempowered aristocratic and bourgeois elites and suppressed dissent, sometimes violently.

These new governments have been labeled "authoritarian populist" for their attempts to meet popular demands for economic and social benefits while not granting political rights.[84] The military origins of most of the republican leaders encouraged them to dispense with democratic or consultative institutions and to create hierarchical bureaucratic states and command economies. They diverted funds from industrialization and social services to military preparedness and increasingly repressed political dissent and agitation for democratic reforms. The new states, like the old, attempted to prevent the concentration of economic or political power and restricted the role of civil society associations to addressing individual grievances. This position became unacceptable toward the end of the century with the growing politicization of the populace and the increasing authoritarianism of the states themselves. On the credit side, they did carry out their provisionary responsibilities, often to an acceptable degree, and aroused perennial hope that they could do so even better in the future. This hope was doomed to disappointment, because a global economic downturn made these states' economic and social goals unattainable and created new exploitative relations between the Middle East and the West that changed the direction of development.

Globalization and the Circle of Justice (*c.*1975–2000)

Unlike the Turks and Mongols, Western imperialists did not stay long enough in the Middle East to adopt the governing ideals of the people they ruled. The Western-style governments they left in their wake inherited this role, including the task of adapting Western state forms to Middle Eastern political values.[85] This adjustment became visible during the second half of the twentieth century but was not complete by the century's end. Changing priorities during the last quarter of the twentieth century generated a rhetorical shift reducing the discussion of justice to a minimum. Echoes of the Circle of Justice reverberated more in actual conditions and people's responses to them than in the statements of leaders. These conditions revealed that the region faced a crisis of justice unmatched by anything earlier in the century.

The "ruling bargain" and its violation

Most analyses of the Middle East in the modern period read as if the Middle Eastern states were failures; they are almost invariably written to explain "what went wrong."[86] But that approach fails to explain, because much of the modern history of the Middle East was a success story. The governments of the 1950s and 1960s achieved both their initial political goals of independence and statehood and their initial economic goals, the elimination of the agrarian bourgeoisie and the rapid creation of a basic industrial sector. In the next two decades, "the historical social contract in the region generated 'unprecedented levels of economic growth and social development'."[87] By around 1970, annual economic growth even in the non-oil-producing countries ranged from 4 to 8 percent, and in the oil-producing countries it was much higher, up to 21 percent, while population growth was under 4 percent per year. Egypt's gross domestic product doubled between 1961 and 1970 and again between 1975 and 1985. Per capita income and standards of living rose throughout that period by over 2 percent per year and in several countries by about 7 percent. Between 1952 and 1980 food production outstripped population growth; until 1980 total agricultural production (including food) increased by 2.7 percent per year and population by only 2.1 percent, decreasing rural poverty by almost 20 percent. Average life expectancy increased by 15 years; infant mortality declined over 50 percent; the birthrate dropped by around 25 percent; the percentage of the population with access to clean water, electricity, and sanitation climbed to 80–90 percent; and literacy rates rose from 20 percent to over 80 percent.[88] In the two decades from 1950 to 1970, social justice reached millions of people and their lives improved radically. These governments and their policies were not failures, although coherent statistics on this astounding progress and any real appreciation of this achievement are hard to find.

Such advances, however, fell short of fulfilling the aspirations of many in the Middle East. It was not possible in two decades for the new states to build national economies that could meet their development needs, keep pace with their rapidly growing populations, and match the exploding economies of the postwar West. Moreover, these advances had multiple costs. The initial cost for such rapid progress was political: in order to push populist measures past the opposition of the wealthy bourgeoisie that held political power in the first half of the century, Middle Eastern governments had to abandon democracy and become highly authoritarian. They feared that if the rich had democratic rights they would immediately dominate the government again, due to their wealth and political capability, and would reverse the social progress already made. These states made a "ruling bargain" with their citizens, a sort of social contract, to forgo political participation in exchange for rapid social progress.[89] This contract, though often despotic, was not totally one-sided, and it embodied some of the interdependence of the Circle of Justice. Another cost was economic: routing resources away from industrial development to meet social needs threatened the long-term success of economic development as a whole. Massive debt, resulting from price increases and from the attempt to do everything at once, and coinciding with a worldwide rise in interest rates set off by the United States, left the Middle Eastern states prey to creditors from the West.

Around 1975 Middle Eastern states found their ruling bargains impossible to keep, not because authoritarian politics generated an inefficient economy or because authoritarian rule exhausted its legitimacy or its compulsive capacity, as has been claimed, but for several other reasons beyond their control. First of all, conflict in the region, especially the Arab-Israeli conflict, demanded an enormous investment in military forces and armaments, siphoning off revenue mainly to Western arms manufacturers.[90]

Second, the global financial crisis and the oil embargo of 1973 caused a fall in the US dollar and a 300 percent increase in the price of oil. As oil production and the industrial and service sectors of the economy grew, the predominance of agriculture and peasants in the political equation fell. The oil-rich countries became "rentier" states, dependent on income rather than taxes, which released them from the need to address people's demands to secure their revenue. Simultaneously the oil-poor countries grew unable to satisfy their publics as galloping inflation priced food, goods, and services above what their remaining resources could cover. Changes in consumption patterns, especially the increased consumption of meat by the better-off, increased agricultural shortages and food imports, particularly of grain. Land reform, although it reduced individual poverty, did not expand agrarian production enough to cover the gap, and a shift in global food production patterns around 1980 necessitated the importation of food from developed countries and intensified the search for hard currency.[91]

Middle Eastern countries going into debt and trying to borrow from the International Monetary Fund (IMF) and the World Bank were denied loans unless they eliminated food subsidies and social services from their budgets, reversed their land reform policies, devoted their revenues to debt repayment or to development opportunities that fed back into US and European companies, and opened their economies to Western investment; this was called "economic restructuring" or "structural adjustment."[92] In a process eerily reminiscent of the Ottoman and Egyptian debt crises of the 1870s, creditors demanded economic changes that favored their own investments and those of the Middle Eastern bourgeoisie rather than the mass of the population. The return of the bourgeois-dominated state diverted government spending from domestic to export industries. The economic growth rate fell to under 1 percent and the standard of living fell markedly.[93] This downturn was related in part to cyclical economic changes, but its unjust handling aroused new calls for justice.

Third, the social and educational policies of the previous two decades had created new politically active classes: a large middle and working class ready for political participation but denied it due to the authoritarian structure of their governments, a landowning peasantry exploited to benefit the economy's modern sector that was beginning to find its own political voice, and an enormous group of migrants from the countryside to the fast-growing cities for whom industrial employment was not expanding and whose social services were shrinking due to economic restructuring.[94] Readjustment policies opened political participation not to them but to potential economic investors (i.e. wealthy elites; this was labeled "democratization") and replaced direct aid to the poor with the chance of limited social mobility. The new political elites were concerned with security and state solvency rather than with social justice or provision for the people. In terms of the Circle of Justice, the Circle was breaking down, and the violence of popular responses – the "food riots" of the late 1970s and 1980s – suggests how central the Circle's justice still was to people's political understanding. Attempts by governments in Syria and Egypt to hedge on the IMF's demands and retain some populist measures indicate rulers' awareness that structural adjustment risked loss of legitimacy, since it upset people's ingrained beliefs about the duty of the state. Widespread protests against the 1991 Gulf War expressed popular grievances against the political and economic dominance of the new oil elites and against US support for the restructured status quo, while Saddam Hussein emerged as an unlikely spokesman for the powerless and marginalized.[95]

Finally, education and urbanization mobilized formerly quiescent population groups. The process of demanding state aid helped create a politically active public. People disappointed with the state's performance lacked secular opposition groups due to governmental repression of leftists, so they turned to the Islamist opposition, which advocated social justice at home and freedom from oppression and cultural domination internationally. For people uprooted from rural villages and thrown into a rapidly changing urban environment with insufficient support, Islamic groups represented a source of strong social bonds that could recreate the sense of community and mutuality that the village once provided. Islamist political parties promised responsible, uncorrupt government that would enact the values of the common people and speak with their voice.[96]

Although the concepts represented by the Circle of Justice remained central to the political equation, people did not quote the Circle itself. Most urban dwellers and some rural people reaching adulthood in the 1970s had been exposed all their lives to Western-style education. Popularized Western political concepts reached ordinary people as well as the educated, and political science replaced *adab* literature and mirrors for princes. Calling on the Circle of Justice was no longer as effective a strategy as it once had been. Even more noticeable was the effect of Islamist discourse on political rhetoric. Popularized in the aftermath of the 1967 Six-Day War with Israel, Islamist discourse blamed the Arabs' difficulties on socialism's corruption of Islam.[97] In this discourse, purifying Islamic thought and practice would bring divine favor and military strength, while adhering to Islamic private property and charity laws would revive the economy and fill the treasury. Islamist discourse employed not the Circle of Justice, nor the language of Western political science, but the terms of religious revival. It was only in the process of challenging the state and meeting people's needs that Islamic groups rediscovered the Circle of Justice. In their hands the Circle again became the possession of critics of the state.

Social justice from the state to the Islamists

When Middle Eastern states turned away from socialism, the call for social justice sounded outside the state. Egypt, the ideological leader in the socialist period, also led the retreat from socialism, the transition to capitalism, and the reworking of the ideology of justice into a tool of resistance. President Anwar Sadat (1970–81) encouraged the development of private industry and opened the economy to foreign investment in a program called *infitah* ("opening"). He returned to large landowners the lands confiscated from them in the reforms of prior decades, gave newly reclaimed land to special interests (engineers, war heroes) rather than peasants, dismantled rent controls and peasants' legal security, and redressed the grievances of the rich.[98] The income gap between rich and poor grew wider. As one critic said, "Sadat's early days led people to believe they would be heard, and the government would be responsible. However the new open-door economic policies, *infitah*, soon showed that the rich could be heard louder."[99]

Infitah failed in its initial efforts to improve the economy; the first six years have been called an utter disaster. Its long-term effects were more economically productive, but at the price of social equity. The policy left the government deep in debt, dependent on international banking firms, and prey to a conflict of interests between rich and poor.[100] The IMF and World Bank insisted as a condition on any further loans that the Egyptian government eliminate its subsidies on food and essential items. In January 1977, the overnight elimination of subsidies on sugar, tea, and bottled gas raised the cost of living 15 percent for the poor and unleashed three days of rioting more violent than anything since the 1952 Revolution. As one local commentator observed, "Bread riots ... are meant to 'prick the rulers' conscience' and 'send them messages' that something is amiss in their rule." In the aftermath of the riots, the government restored the subsidies and rewrote the social contract, making the subsidies "the symbol of the regime's understanding with the poor" and the key to state legitimacy.[101]

Criticism of the state came from both secular and Islamic groups, and the outlawed Muslim Brotherhood began to reappear. Newly educated but dissatisfied people developed their own understanding of Islam based on reading the Qur'an and other early sources for themselves, discarding centuries of Islamic exegesis in a search for sure and simple rules for navigating the modern age. After radicals assassinated Sadat, the new president Hosni Mubarak (1981–2011) initially refrained from attacking food subsidies; he spoke about social justice and maintained a safety net of price supports to protect the poorest levels of the urban population. Once he was secure in office, he developed a restructuring plan of his own that decreased subsidies gradually, lowered wages and benefits, and eliminated guaranteed employment. External debt decreased markedly, but the cost of food more than doubled, forcing ordinary people and the poor to eat less. Despite a rhetoric of care for the poor, Egypt's structural adjustment plan paid little attention to the urban lower class, small rural landholders, and the landless. People adversely affected, at least one-fourth of the country's population, complained of harm to their productive ability, increased demands on women's unpaid labor, and the detrimental effects of cuts in food, health care, and education on their children.[102]

Other countries where economic restructuring was installed had similar experiences. In Morocco two-thirds of the population had moved to the cities within a couple of decades, in Iran over half; in every country urban migration was substantial. Industrial expansion and job creation could not keep pace, and unemployment rates ranged from 20 to 46 percent. The unemployed or underemployed population depended for survival on state subsidies of staple foods and basic necessities. These subsidies were reduced or eliminated in response to World Bank/IMF demands and prices rose by 40 to 100 percent overnight, while real wages dropped from 10 to 50 percent.[103] Massive riots broke out wherever these draconian subsidy cuts were made, expressing not only people's material want, but their sense of justice denied. Two huge food riots in Morocco and one in Tunisia in the early 1980s resulted in hundreds of people killed and thousands arrested.[104] In Jordan in 1996, the king forcibly put down demonstrators and cut subsidies still further. The next election produced an Islamist victory in the Jordanian parliament, since the Muslim Brothers, the best organized opposition group, promised relief for the poor, unemployed, and undereducated.[105]

Some countries, like Algeria, Syria, and Iraq, did not deal with Western banks but mounted their own structural adjustment programs, but the results were similar. Young people in Algiers initiated three days of violence in October 1988 that devastated the main shopping street, attacking symbols of wealth and state properties. The rich filled their swimming pools, they complained, while the poor suffered water shortages. When protesters gathered to listen to a preacher, security forces fired on the crowd, killing forty. The country's "ruling bargain" had suppressed popular political participation for the sake of rapid progress and urban social welfare, but the economic downturn combined with state corruption and violent repression undermined that bargain. The government answered calls for welfare services with a pledge to "democratize" the political process, which gave new elites a voice in the political process but provided no help or access to the poor.[106] The Tunisian government in the 1980s also exchanged social welfare for economic liberalism; protesters responded not in the language of rights but in the language of social justice, supported by Islamic values.[107]

Syria under President Hafiz al-Asad (1970–99) likewise pulled back from the socialist policies of the 1960s. Syrian socialism had attacked the interests of large landowners and big businessmen, but Asad's emphasis on large-scale industrial development and commercial agriculture revived their fortunes. The agricultural surplus went not to improve living standards but to build up the military. Syria's Muslim Brotherhood blamed the state and elites for the growing gap between rich and poor and called for social justice through Islamically lawful policies. The Brotherhood advocated an Islamic political system harking back to what has been called "the myth of the just Caliphate," which grafted the "myth of the just welfare state" onto the story of the Muslim community. "The primary duty of the state is to protect its citizens against the following: autocracy; bondage; unjust laws; emergency legislation; wrong police practices; economic exploitation; political suppression; administrative pressure; party, class, and sectarian domination; and any other form of injustice in the society."[108]

In view of the state's abdication of its duty, the Muslim Brothers began again to organize the opposition. Army raids on suspected Brotherhood hideouts in the town of Hama roused tradespeople, merchants, and small manufacturers in a huge revolt, crushed only by a massacre of over 10,000.[109] After the revolt, Syria continued its voluntary *infitah* program, opening the economy to capitalism and emphasizing exports, and channeling the benefits of growth to the elites. Combined with a population growth rate among the world's highest, the lack of economic improvement for the majority generated a critique of the state that could be expressed only indirectly for fear of reprisal. A political cartoon from the late 1980s, for example, portrayed a circle of injustice: a peasant bent to water the roots of the tree of justice, while on his back stood a rich man eating the fruit from the tree. People considered that the state had broken its "ruling bargain" trading economic advancement for political liberty, and they wanted back their half of the bargain, their political compliance. By the 1990s, complaints about individual problems or low-level political issues, which had been published in newspapers for some time, gave way to calls for democracy.[110]

In Iraq, the large growth in oil revenues after 1973 made possible significant investment in private agriculture and industry and a growth in social services. The Iran–Iraq War of the 1980s and the subsequent Gulf War and economic sanctions intensified Iraq's retreat from socialism.[111] In 1988, as Iraq–Iran peace talks faltered, Saddam Hussein introduced a new "ruling bargain" promising freedom of speech, constitutional reform and multiparty government in exchange for support. What he delivered was freedom to complain, the expansion of *mazalim* in modern forms. Newspaper complaint pages appeared, headed with Saddam's statement: "Write what you like without fear," and filled with letters on administrative problems and police abuse.[112]

The West African country of Mali enacted *mazalim* justice on television. In 1991 the president initiated the "Forum for Democratic Consultation," where any citizen with a complaint against the government could address the prime minister and cabinet on national television, with local and international representatives as watchdogs to ensure action. Complaints ranged from the lack of elementary schools to bad conditions in the prisons, from salary complaints by airport workers to rights for the elderly. The government, required to respond, passed laws banning unjust practices and providing clean water and electricity. The expectations of justice generated by this practice had broader results; after experiencing the injustices of economic restructuring, the people of Mali sued the World Bank and filmed the trial for international distribution. Similarly, Egyptian cabinet members visiting government projects were televised responding to complaints from the population. The shah of Iran, in order to show that he was "rooting out corruption," televised the proceedings of the Imperial Commission for Efficient Resource Application, which investigated development projects.[113] Rulers and viewers still valued the interrelationships of the Circle of Justice, even when it was not explicitly invoked.

Socialist policies throughout the Middle East, flawed as they were, had brought about significant improvements in education, health care, and food supply, but the greatest benefit of structural adjustment was improvement in the balance of payments. While people in a truly Islamic society were supposed to take care of the poor primarily out of their own wealth, the Near Eastern state was supposed to ensure justice. The scope of poverty in a modernizing society had magnified the state's role. Now, in the face of the government's withdrawal from social welfare services, populist Islamic groups surged forward to rescue the peasantry and urban masses.[114] While their arguments and proposals differed from one another, a common thread was their appeal to concepts of interdependency that drew their strength from the centrality of the Circle of Justice in Middle Eastern political culture.

Islamist protests and the Circle of Justice

Parallel to the state's retreat from socialism, a popular ideology of Islamist welfare sprang up. In the last quarter of the twentieth century Islamist groups took up the cry for social justice, calling the state to account and creating their own social service organizations to meet needs that the state no longer would or could meet. The Islamists' rapid response to an Algerian earthquake in 1989 exposed the government's incompetence in the social sphere and won popular support for Islamist political parties. Social justice also formed one of the three pillars of the Islamic economy envisaged by Iraq's chief clerical critic of the state, Muhammad Baqir al-Sadr (d.1980), the other two being a mixed economy and limitations on economic liberty.[115]

Lebanon, a bourgeois patronage state since its foundation in 1943, was gripped by civil war in the mid-1970s; since it was unable to provide even basic services, justice and social services fell into the hands of confessional militias. The Lebanese Forces, a mostly Maronite militia, gained support by engaging in public services that the government had stopped providing, such as crime control, public utilities, social welfare, health care, and education. Similarly, the Shi'i militia Hezbollah built a social welfare infrastructure for the disempowered Shi'i community, including jobs, schools, clinics, hospitals, research institutes, and orphanages. The Shi'i cleric Musa al-Sadr (disappeared 1978) developed a discourse featuring Lebanese Shi'is as "the wretched of the earth," the "disinherited" or "deprived," and implying that this disinheritance justified revolt against the state. The reestablishment of national government in the 1980s occasioned speeches promising that the state would resume its responsibility to protect the people and provide social justice.[116] Whatever the hopes of those who made the war, however, those who made the peace reimposed the old social hierarchy.

As the Egyptian government of the 1970s withdrew support for subsistence agriculture and urban welfare, mosque preachers in various parts of Egypt began to scold the state for not providing social justice. Shaykh Uthman of Minya criticized the withdrawal of food and health care subsidies: "Today we hear much about matters of security, but what does the citizen want? The ordinary person, the man on the street, he wants to be assured of a good piece of bread first of all, and to be assured of security so he can live in peace."[117] The Muslim Brothers began again to emphasize the concept of socio-economic justice as the foundation for an Islamic state that would be productive yet not exploitative. Major Islamist organizations rejected violence as a tactic, turning instead to the "winning of hearts" and the gaining of votes and profits through political participation and the construction of hospitals, clinics, daycare centers, and schools. The success of Islamist groups has been attributed to their representation of the religious worldview of the recently mobilized masses, but it was also due to their espousal of popular concepts of justice and good administration.[118]

An important demonstration of Islamist social justice took place in October 1992, when a major earthquake hit Cairo. Professional unions, dominated by Islamist delegates, leaped into action. The doctors' syndicate set up tents for slum dwellers whose houses were demolished, treated the ill and injured, and distributed food and medicine, while the engineers' syndicate sent inspectors to examine the stability of housing. The media highlighted the effectiveness of the Islamic relief operations and the state's inactivity. The state, reacting against the bad publicity, sent troops to raze the tents and halt the housing inspections and banned private organizations from offering disaster relief. The earthquake and its aftermath dramatically revealed both the regime's inability or unwillingness to provide goods and services to the needy and its fear of competition from Islamic organizations.[119]

The growth of North African Islamism was also a response to economic injustice and repression of dissent by states claiming to act in the name of Islam and the people. Two works appeared in 1974 that resonated with the Circle of Justice while articulating an Islamist ideology of resistance. Abdellatif al-Soltani's book, *Socialism is the Descendant of Mazdakism*, critiqued state socialism in terms derived from early Islamic critiques of Iran's "libertine" and "communist" Mazdakism, presenting Islam as a doctrine of social justice containing the solution to all socioeconomic problems. In the same year, Abdessalam Yassine published *Islam or the Deluge*, an open letter to the king of Morocco emphasizing the reciprocal obligations of ruler and ruled and warning him that by continuing his inegalitarian policies and unjust methods he was sealing his own doom.[120]

The Islamist critique took different forms in different political circumstances; in monarchist Morocco it expressed itself in social movements, the largest of which was Yassine's Movement of Justice and Benevolence. In Tunisia the Islamic Tendency Movement (MTI) mobilized young rural migrants who had gained an education in the cities but whose social mobility was blocked by the economic crisis. The movement's spokesman, Rachid Ghannouchi, enunciated its solidarity with the oppressed and their advocates: "One of Islam's fundamental objectives is to establish justice in the world. The value of justice is the greatest value in Islam, and Just is one of the attributes of God. How could we then have embroiled ourselves in opposing those, even if they were Marxists, who struggled for securing the interests of the poor and the oppressed?"[121] In Algeria, the Islamists instead formed political parties, one of which, the Islamic Salvation

Front (FIS), was elected to local offices in 1990. The FIS and other Islamist groups built support by providing social services such as soup kitchens, free clothing, housing, emergency aid, medical care, mosque-building, and intervention with the bureaucracy. A striking instance of their effectiveness was their response to the 1989 earthquake; the Islamists brought in emergency medical care even before state officials arrived on the scene. The army-run state retained control by establishing martial law and declaring the national election of FIS candidates in 1992 null and void, an act that transformed a political competition into a violent struggle.[122]

A concept of government that turned the provision of justice from food and social services to cultural and spiritual development appeared in the preamble to the Turkish constitution of 1982.[123] Turkey's Islamist Welfare (*Refah*) Party, trumpeting the absence of social justice, won municipal elections in Istanbul and many other cities by landslide votes in 1994. The Welfare Party revived the discourse of social justice and connected it to the Islamic heritage. As one politician commented: "In a country like Turkey that widely experiences such injustice, poverty, and inequality, people, the folk, the population seek a way out, because they're tired of being pressured in the mangle of life. Not being able to bring home bread, remaining unemployed, not being able to educate their children ... [or] to take advantage of health facilities – they want to be saved from all this."[124] Nejmettin Erbakan, the party's ideologue, linked social justice to the Islamic heritage in *The Just Economic Order*, which analyzed injustice as stemming from the diversion of the "fruits of modernization" to the rich and to foreign powers. Erbakan's "just order" combined capitalism and socialism without their flaws: banning interest would reduce elite profiteering and exploitation of the poor and would increase profit-sharing investment. Besides regulating production, the state should provide justice, water, roads, health, education, transport, communications, and security. The younger leaders of the party stressed civic responsibility, urban social problems, and human rights.[125]

At election time, the Welfare Party appealed directly to the people by distributing food, clothing, and fuel to the needy. Women went door-to-door in poorer neighborhoods, offering the party's welfare, health, and educational services. The Welfare Party in one Istanbul municipality put out a water cooler on the sidewalk and gave free drinking water to passers-by, recalling the public fountains of Ottoman times. Istanbul's Welfare mayor Tayyip Erdoğan provided justice in the form of public services: beefed-up trash collection removing "hills of garbage" and repairs to the city's water supply. More importantly, he banned city employees from taking bribes and advertised their freedom from corruption. These practices were so successful that secularists began imitating them.[126]

Mayors of municipalities also held regular meetings where people could bring their complaints and problems, appealing to the ideology of *mazalim* justice. One such mayor hoped that the meetings would encourage popular participation in government, asking, "Could a higher image of justice be conceived?"[127] When the state broke the "ruling bargain" by providing inadequate assistance after a 1999 earthquake that devastated the Istanbul region and by failing to protect national economic interests, people began to vote for Islamist parties at the national level, putting them in power after the turn of the century.[128] At the same time, a more secular leftist radicalism rose among Turkey's non-Sunni population. People from all walks of life, from workmen to university professors, organized visits to Ataturk's tomb in Ankara, often carrying written petitions or writing their complaints into the visitors' book, and turning Ataturk into a symbol of justice. And indeed, one classic photograph showed him, in a modern parallel to Sultan Sanjar, leaning out the window of a train to accept a petition. More recently, visitors to the shrine of Hajji Bektash have observed Bektashi worshippers praying before the statue of Ataturk that stands outside the shrine.[129]

In Saudi Arabia, where oil revenues supported the elites in style, the discontented protested injustice and exclusion from the political process by seizing the Grand Mosque of Mecca in 1979 and proclaiming a former theology student as the *mahdi*, the restorer of justice. After suppressing the rebels the king replaced provincial governors with Saudi princes, who controlled more funding for social projects and who held daily public *majlis*, petition-receiving sessions, to handle grievances. Citing Islam as their inspiration, they reestablished the social hierarchy that kept "individuals and classes in their place."[130] These measures neither (*nasiha*) satisfied popular demands for political participation nor provided socioeconomic equality. In the early 1990s, therefore, drawing on the tradition of advice literature and on the religious duty to critique the ruler, Saudis began writing letters of advice to the king, some of which were published.[131] The king promulgated a new constitution in 1992 that made the state responsible for social services as well as defense. It reiterated the importance of the royal courts open to all citizens, where anyone with a complaint could receive justice. The constitution called the relationship between ruler and subjects a "social contract" and likened it to a shepherd and his sheep. However, the contradiction between the state's claim to protect its people and the stationing of US troops in Saudi Arabia in the 1990s undercut the credibility of this rhetoric.[132] Throughout the Middle East, people's loss of confidence in their states' ability to protect them from encroachment or to provide justice caused disaffection, rioting, and attempts to change the government, legally or illegally.

The call for justice and the Islamic Revolution

The most dramatic governmental overthrow took place in Iran in 1979. Iran's Islamic Revolution was not the triumph of justice over oppression that its participants hoped for, but a conflict between masses of the poor and needy seeking social and economic justice together with groups fighting on their behalf, and a new set of authorities who paid lip service to their cries for justice but were more concerned for their own interests. The new authorities did not uphold the Circle of Justice or the "ruling bargain;" the quality of life declined under their rule, but they granted no political rights in its stead.[133]

In Iran, as in Saudi Arabia, the oil boom of the 1970s brought unprecedented wealth but skewed its distribution; while business and political figures became fabulously rich, others were impoverished or could no longer afford ordinary goods and services. Economic growth increased by 17 to 42 percent, but inflation skyrocketed from zero to 24 to 200 percent and over half the population lived in poverty. Rapid population growth made the shah's modernization goals impossible to attain; soon Iran was importing over 70 percent of its food. Peasant farmers, forced into debt, left the villages in droves, migrating to the cities and becoming a pool of cheap labor. The state could neither employ the urban migrants nor provide enough services for them.[134] Islamist groups, well-organized and quick to seize the opportunity, filled the gap, providing welfare services, channels of association, and basic religious education in the cities. After a 1978 earthquake they jumped in with emergency relief before government agencies could get organized.[135]

Against the growing discontent, the shah appealed to the ideology of the Circle of Justice, the benevolent monarch as the source of prosperity and justice, confirming that this ideology was still a powerful political force among varied social groups. His programs, however, often failed to deliver the promised justice because of poor planning or political favoritism. People whose education had included stories of justice from the *Shahnama* began to complain of injustice in society, while people appealing to Western values complained of the absence of democracy. Secular writers such as Jalal Al-e Ahmad criticized the shah's heedless Westernization as inauthentic.[136] Religious critics like 'Ali Shari'ati compared the shah to the tyrannical Umayyad dynasty that had murdered Husayn, the grandson of the prophet Muhammad. In Shari'ati's view, Husayn's death was not just a tragic act of sacrifice but part of a larger struggle against oppressive and unjust regimes that trampled on the rights of the lowly and killed the poor, a struggle that contemporary Iranians were also involved in. He popularized the figure of Abu Dharr (Abu Zarr in Iran), whose biography he had translated from Arabic, as "the first Muslim socialist" and the spokesman for "the Islam of the people, of the exploited, and of the poor."[137]

The idea of fighting for an Islamic social justice won people away from the Marxist and secular leftist parties, which in any case were being suppressed.[138] People blamed both the economic problems and increased repression on the shah, his advisors, and the United States, which supported him. Leftist leaders saw Ayatollah Khomeini, recently exiled from Iraq to Paris, as a perfect revolutionary figurehead because of his long opposition to the shah and his potential to unite religious and secular opposition, so they invited him to head the movement.[139] Khomeini had been in active opposition since 1963, when he protested against votes for women and non-Muslims and rejected the White Revolution as a phony program insufficient to the size of the need. Exiled to Iraq, he (like earlier Islamists) developed a concept of justice as against the state, one that would replace state oppression with divine justice, transformed into governance by ulema knowledgeable in Islamic law. He still referred frequently, however, to social justice, drawing on the historic "mirrors for princes" literature and the ideas attributed to 'Ali in *The Highway of Eloquence* as well as more recent writers like Sayyid Qutb, newly translated into Persian.[140]

The revolution, spurred initially by students and professionals, drew participants from all levels of society and was accomplished less by military contention than by huge strikes in oil fields, factories, and government offices that threatened the budget and massive demonstrations that impelled the shah to leave the country. After the shah's departure, the revolutionaries immediately installed a republic and went to work on a constitution decrying oppression and promising economic and social justice. During the first years many social justice measures were passed and the income gap between rich and poor began to narrow, only to increase again later. The Islamic Republic had an elected parliament (*majles*), a president, and a Council of Guardians made up of top-level ulema to vet the laws passed by parliament. Unlike before, ulema ran for office and were elected to executive and legislative posts.[141] A struggle for power ensued among the secular and religious factions that had brought about the revolution.

The period of uncertainty ended with Khomeini in complete charge and his rivals dead, imprisoned, or exiled. The new government's violent suppression of dissent did much to taint the Republic's (and Khomeini's) aura of justice. Most revolutionaries had not fought for ulema rule but for a just and ethical society embodied in Islamic terms, or even in Marxist or socialist terms. The Islamic Republic suppressed the image of the pre-Islamic past in favor of the Islamic heritage, but those educated under the shah found their expectations of a just society stated in the Circle of Justice, and references to pre-Islamic concepts became a form of resistance.[142] The Islamic Republic did have a social program, executed by the Reconstruction Crusade (*Jahad-e Sazandegi*). This organization, with five times the funding of the White Revolution and the enthusiasm of crowds of young people concerned for social justice, provided roads, water, and electricity, development operations, agricultural and veterinary services, housing, health care, literacy and educational activities, and support services for the war with Iraq. Its results far surpassed those of the shah's White Revolution; according to official publications, 4,761 villages were connected to electricity in less than two years, as opposed to 4,547 in two decades under the shah, and 7,482 kilometers of roads were built, as opposed to 4,308 under the shah.[143]

War with Iraq (1981–8) interrupted the state's development plans, absorbing the country's money and manpower and causing extensive damage. Per capita agricultural production fell below its 1976 level. Legalist ulema, who had opposed the shah's land reform on the grounds of Islam's support for private property, now opposed Khomeini's; after being revised several times, the land reform legislation failed to pass, and a repressive labor law was enacted.[144] Many social justice measures passed in the early years of the Republic were later reversed on the grounds that they contravened Islamic law. Islamic law, developed in a precapitalist society, did not produce social justice under modern conditions, and the powerful Council of Guardians opted for Islamic law over social justice. The real eradication of poverty, moreover, would have threatened the clergy's power of patronage.[145] Khomeini admitted to Banisadr, the second president, that he did not feel bound by the egalitarian promises he had made before the revolution. His new speeches played down social justice values: "Did you give the blood of your children for asphalted roads?" Religious or secular groups that tried to fight these decisions were mercilessly crushed.[146]

By the 1990s, a decade of war and economic mismanagement forced the state to seek help from the property-owning bourgeoisie and professionals, most of whom had not previously supported the regime. Times had changed, and the economic and political climate was one of rampant capitalism, private property rights, and a growing gulf between rich and poor. After Khomeini's death in 1989, Iran underwent structural adjustment on the IMF and World Bank model in order to pump up the economy, attract investment, and create jobs for the 20 percent of the population that was unemployed. As in other countries, however, loans and restructuring came with conditions that disadvantaged the group that had brought about the revolution, the dispossessed and needy and their advocates, who lost influence as the economy moved away from social welfare toward a capitalist system.[147]

Despite its Islamic and republican ideology, the shape of the new government was remarkably similar to the old: direction from the top, a heavy emphasis on ideological correctness and censorship, a rather standard development policy based on oil revenues, and dependence on the middle classes and technocrats. Like the shah, who disdained to rule peasants and donkeys, the Islamic Republic's Minister of Agriculture confessed, "We thought the farmers were nobodies. We wanted to impose everything on them." Complaints against the Islamic Republic sounded distressingly similar to the complaints against the shah: arbitrary arrest, torture, and execution; corruption in government; failure to fulfill social welfare promises; failure to control inflation and unemployment or to reduce dependence on the West. The Islamic government permitted greater popular participation in politics and initially gave more emphasis to social welfare, but it also put much greater stress on social conformity and on coercion through torture and execution.

This condition gave rise to a new political form of the Circle of Justice linking justice with freedom: "Without justice, there can be no durable order and without liberty there can be no justice."[148]

In a climate of war, governmental oppression, and worsening economic conditions, people continued to articulate their own concepts of justice. Slogans shouted in the streets after the revolution sent messages based on the demand for provision, such as, "Give us uninterrupted electricity or give us back the traitorous Shah!" The popular idea of Islamic government, as stated by peasants to academic interviewers, was that it "should provide for the well-being of its subjects;" that is, that it should govern in accordance with the Circle of Justice. Peasants interpreted the shah's land reform as a work of justice, the elimination of oppression, stating: "It was the Shah, not the mullahs, who took off the yoke of the landlords' oppression from our shoulders."[149]

The reiteration of these ideas invoked ancient associations among divine authority, victory, prosperity, and justice. The newspaper *Salam* highlighted the relationship between divine approval and social justice when it questioned whether post-revolutionary Iranian society was truly Islamic since the poor were still suffering. National victory, not of armies but of soccer teams, drew young men and women into the streets for celebratory parades that were simultaneously demonstrations against state oppression. Letters to the newspapers publicly aired their writers' ideas about the justice of the regime. At least one reader, quoting the old proverb attributed to the Prophet, "The realm can survive with unbelief but not with injustice," questioned whether in view of its nepotism, discrimination, price hikes, shortages, and widening of the socioeconomic gap the Islamic Republic could be considered a just government.[150]

The case of Ahmad Batebi demonstrated even more clearly that at the end of the twentieth century the ideas of the Circle of Justice still governed political relations in popular consciousness. A film student, Batebi went to cover a demonstration in which a friend was participating. Finding that his friend had been shot dead by the Revolutionary Guard, he held in the air his bloody T-shirt and was photographed by a foreign journalist. The state arrested him on the grounds that he, rather than its own policies, had embarrassed the regime.[151] Imprisoned and tortured, initially given the death penalty, he managed to write an open letter to the head of the judiciary describing the circumstances of his imprisonment, detailing his tortures and those of other victims of the judicial system, and criticizing Iran's system of so-called justice. This gruesome letter, which was published in the press and subsequently on the Internet, began with a quotation from *The Highway of Eloquence* about the elimination of oppression and culminated, despite Batebi's modern education, by quoting the same time-honored proverb, "A dominion can live on without faith in God but never with injustice."[152]

Conclusion

Taking back the state from the bourgeois classes that held it at the beginning of the century, Middle Eastern peoples and their leaders in the mid-twentieth century sought to institute a social justice that fulfilled the demands of the Circle, or at least to make motions toward that goal. Throughout the modernization of political forms, interdependence between state and society was an essential element of Middle Eastern political culture, ingrained in the population and recognized by kings and presidents. Politics based on this interdependence succeeded in bringing health care, literacy, and the basis of prosperity to the populations of socialist republics and monarchies alike. When funding this growth became impossible and Middle Eastern states turned to Western funding agencies for help, they were required to give up their social justice policies and turn away from the ideology of the Circle. The Circle of Justice then became a tool of the opposition, particularly the Islamist opposition. Ironically, in Iran, the one place where the opposition successfully captured the state, it found itself duplicating the trajectory of the socialist states, abandoning the rhetoric and policies of social justice to its critics and opponents. These opponents echoed the Circle of Justice in their struggle to delegitimate what they considered an unjust government.

Conclusion

The Middle East was long ruled in an autocratic style disparaged as oriental despotism, divine kingship, or patriarchal monarchy. Autocracy in this region nevertheless contained a tradition of responsiveness to the people and their needs that has not been sufficiently appreciated either by foreign critics or its own heirs, both of whom have had reasons to see it in a negative light. The Circle of Justice is one of the oldest political ideas in the Middle East, appearing in some of the earliest written inscriptions in the region and retaining its currency until the modern era. It animated much of the governmental and judicial activity of Middle Eastern regimes, tempering their autocracy and giving people a channel for protesting abuses. Moreover, conquerors invading from outside repeatedly found it necessary to adopt the ideas of the Circle in order to govern their Middle Eastern conquests. The concept appeared and reappeared in political literature and art across the region for over four thousand years and was translated into practice through royal institutions of government and through the petitioning activity of Middle Eastern peoples. Only in the modern period has it been seen by some as superfluous, "traditional," even "fictional."[1] For most of those four millennia, it served as a legitimating idea for the people in power, as a guide to good political relations, and as a spur to the subjects of empires to bring their complaints to the ruler or his representative, even if those complaints lay against the ruler himself.

On numerous occasions, the idea of the Circle of Justice disappeared from political discourse – times like the Akkadian invasion of Sumer, or the Mongol destruction of Baghdad, or the expansion of private property in land. In those periods, the Circle always resurfaced as an ideology holding together the conflicting interests of disparate classes and groups in Middle Eastern society and permitting the people to challenge their rulers and elites nonviolently. Although peasants and townsmen could not exercise direct political power for most of that time, the ideology of the Circle continually reminded the powerful (and they needed reminding) that if the weak did not receive the justice they sought, the powerful would not be able to collect the revenue they sought.

Political and economic systems changed during the twentieth century, but the demand for justice remained, if not always in official rhetoric, at least among the populace, and it underlay many of their efforts of resistance. In response, modern governments in the Middle East, both monarchies and republics, socialist and otherwise, gave the Circle's justice at least lip service and often more, attempting to meet popular demands for social justice and to provide their populations with what they needed to create prosperity. If leaders had to become more autocratic to do so, the majority of their populations were willing to forego their political rights on condition of obtaining greater social benefits and economic equality. Toward the end of the twentieth century, as rising costs and the demands of capitalist finance made the Circle's goals increasingly unattainable, the Circle of Justice became less prevalent as a model for government but intensified its function as a critique of governmental behavior. When Islamist groups presented themselves as the carriers of a justice opposed to state policies, many people supported them as much or more for their promise of justice, interpreted in the light of the Circle, as for their Islam, or saw them as part and parcel of the same message.

By the last decade of the twentieth century the excesses of the radical Islamist movement had driven away much of its mass following. The experience of Iran in particular, where Kholmeini's repressive and bloody regime disappointed people's hopes for justice after the fall of the Shah, discredited the Islamist solution. The rule of the Taliban in Afghanistan and the September 11, 2001, attack by al-Qaida terrorists on the US World Trade Center kept Islamism in the news, but not as a movement for justice. In those years, the advent of right-wing regimes around the world and the proliferation of state terrorism made social and political justice seem increasingly remote. Yet ordinary people's repeated returns to the Circle of Justice through quotation or action suggest that it still expressed an essential element of political culture in the region and that any attempt to devise a successful political ideology for Middle Eastern peoples must include the Circle's reciprocal demands on state and society.

At the end of the twentieth century the new political mantra became "democracy," the panacea that would ensure that ordinary people's values and needs were represented in state decision-making and that would be compatible with an urban and capitalist society. Reciprocal justice is not a core value of democratization; installing genuine Western-style democracy in the Middle East might result in abandoning the Circle. The Circle's justice, however, remained alive as an aspiration in the Middle East. The "Arab Spring" democracy movement of 2011, according to Egyptian commentators, was a form of "active expression against different forms of abuse" that aimed "to reach a new social contract," one that included both a "liberation from domestic tyranny" and a refusal to "die in lines for bread, water or medical care."[2] The justice of the Circle could thus contribute not only to a reassessment of the region's past but to the construction of healthier approaches to an indigenous modern government in the future. The idea that government and people are interdependent in certain important ways runs as a thread through historic pre-Islamic and Islamic governments. It is observable in the earliest Middle Eastern regimes for which we have records, and it forms part of the most central ruling ideologies of the region. It repeatedly emerged after being suppressed by invasions from outside, and it was key to the invaders' continued exercise of power in the region, despite changes in ideology, religion, or form of government. The demand for reciprocal justice embodied in the Circle remains part of Middle Eastern political culture, and a democracy assimilated to Middle Eastern political values will find a way to incorporate it.

Glossary

Adab Breeding, training; collections of interesting and useful facts and sayings compiled for elites and courtiers.
Agrarian Related to agriculture or agricultural society.
Amir Military commander, sometimes with governing powers.
Amirate Governorship.
Apocalyptic Related to the end of the world and the coming of the messiah.
Ayan Local notables (ulema, landholders, big merchants, and military-administrative leaders).
Baraka Divine blessing transmitted by a ruler or saint; holiness.
Cadaster (adj. cadastral) Land register used in apportioning taxes; land survey to create such a register.
Caliph (*khalifa*, adj. caliphal) Successor of Muhammad as head of the Muslim community; deputy of God for its administration.
Caliphate Office of caliph.
Caravanserai Fortified stopping place on caravan route.
Chancery Scribal office under the grand vizier.
Cuneiform Writing composed of wedge-shaped characters used in the ancient Middle East.
Devshirme Ottomans' collection of non-Muslim youths for janissary corps and administration.
Duty Tax, especially customs tax.
Epistolary Relating to a letter or letters.
Fiscal Relating to taxation and public revenue.
Ghaza Holy war, raiding; struggle on the path of God.
Ghazi Raider on behalf of Islam.
Hadith Report of the words and deeds of Muhammad, to be followed by Muslims.
Imam Leader of prayer; leader of the Muslims.
Intentional religious community One that people join by choice, not by birth.
Iqta Lands/land revenues assigned to functionaries, usually soldiers, in lieu of salary.
Islamicate Belonging to the society of which Islam is the primary religion, but not necessarily religious in character.
Janissary Ottoman slave soldier.
Jelali (T. *Celali*) Bandit, rebel.
Kanun Ottoman ruler's law.
Kanunname Ottoman lawcode.
Khagan/khaqan Khan of khans; Turco-Mongol emperor.
Kharaj Tax on land owned by non-Muslims at the conquest.

Khariji Branch of Islam based on all Muslims' right to leadership.
Mahdi The Muslim messianic figure; for Shi'is, the Twelfth Imam.
Malik King, prince.
Malikane Life-term tax farm.
Mamluk Slave, owned person.
Mastaba Stone bench, platform.
Mazalim Court for the redress of wrongs, usually a royal court.
Millennium (pl. millennia) A thousand years.
Mirror for princes Political advice work depicting the ideal prince or king.
Moral economy The ethical management of economic life.
Muhtasib Market inspector, responsible for public order and justice.
Nama (T. *name*) Piece of writing, book.
Nasiha (pl. *nasihat*) Advice, literature of advice, esp. political advice.
Papyrus Writing material made from the papyrus plant.
Padishah Emperor.
Panegyric Poem of praise for a ruler.
Pastoral Related to animal raising, usually nomadic in the Middle East.
Persianate Influenced by Persian culture, but not necessarily made or done by Persians.
Polity Politically organized unit.
Popular Of or belonging to the people.
Qadi Islamic judge.
Qur'an Scripture of the Muslims.
Ra'iyya (T. *reaya*) The people, the flock.
Rune One of or resembling the letters of the ancient Germanic alphabet.
Satrap Ancient Persian governor.
Scribe Secretary, official.
Sedentary Not nomadic.
Shahanshah Shah of shahs; king of kings in Persian.
Shahnama/Shahname *Book of Kings*, epic poem of ancient Iranian history.
Shariah Islamic law; the path of God.
Shi'i Branch of Islam based on struggle for 'Ali's right to the caliphate.
Shu'ubiyya Controversy over the value of the non-Arab heritage.
Siyasa Regulation, ruler's law, policy.
Siyasa shar'iyya Public policy based on Islamic law.
Steppe Grassland, relatively flat.
Sufi Islamic mystic.
Sultan Authority; secular ruler.
Sunna Custom, esp. Muhammad's example.
Sunni Branch of Islam based on submission to actual caliphs.
Tax farming Private contracting of tax collection.
Testament Legacy of wisdom and advice.
Timar Ottoman system of assigning land revenues to soldiers and officials in lieu of salary.
Topçular Cannoneers.
Tore Turkish ruler's law.
Ulema (A. *'ulama'*) Men skilled in Islamic learning, especially law; Islamic religious elite.
'Urf (T. *örf*) Custom, customary laws, legalized by the ruler.
Yasa Mongol ruler's law.
Zoroaster Reformer of pre-Islamic Persian religion.

Notes

1 Introduction

1 The terms "Near East" and "Middle East" come out of Europe's old colonial relationships; in modern usage, Near East refers most often to the ancient Fertile Crescent plus Egypt and Iran, while Middle East is used for the Muslim world between Egypt, or even Morocco, and Iran or Afghanistan. These terms are not satisfactory, but at this time there is no better alternative; the term MENA (Middle East and North Africa) has not yet gained wide acceptance.

2 See H. İnalcık, "The Origin and Definition of the Circle of Justice (Dâire-i Adâlet)," in M. Demirci (ed.) *Selçuklu'dan Osmanlı'ya bilim, kültür ve sanat: Prof. Dr. Mikâil Bayram'a armağan*, Konya: Kömen, 2009. A good analysis of the state in an agrarian empire is R. Thapar, "The State as Empire," in H. J. M. Claessen and P. Skalnik (eds) *The Study of the State*, The Hague: Mouton, 1981, 409–26. I use the term "state" for both premodern and modern states, as shorthand for a much more complex phenomenon (or "claim"): D. Sayer, "Everyday Forms of State Formation: some dissident remarks on 'hegemony'," in G. M. Joseph and D. Nugent (eds) *Everyday Forms of State Formation: revolution and the negotiation of rule in modern Mexico*, Durham, NC: Duke University Press, 1994, 371.

3 "The effectiveness of any premodern regime depended at least as much on the subject's acceptance as on the monarch's power of coercion;" J. Miller (ed.) *Absolutism in Seventeenth-Century Europe*, Basingstoke, UK: Macmillan Education, 1990, 13.

4 The ideology of patronage: S. Silverman, "Patronage as Myth," in E. Gellner and J. Waterbury (eds) *Patrons and Clients in Mediterranean Societies*, London: Duckworth, 1977, 7–19.

5 L. T. Darling, *Revenue-Raising and Legitimacy: tax collection and finance administration in the Ottoman Empire, 1560–1660*, Leiden: Brill, 1996, 283–99, examines the Circle of Justice as a legitimating device in the context of Ottoman fiscal administration.

6 There is a tendency to deny that an autocratic ruler could exercise justice or benevolence at any time; this is perhaps too severe. Karateke points out that normative ideologies of legitimacy had to be supported by convincing behavior, although he ignores the Circle of Justice as a norm; H. T. Karateke, "Legitimizing the Ottoman Sultanate: a framework for historical analysis," in H. T. Karateke and M. Reinkowski (eds) *Legitimizing the Order: the Ottoman rhetoric of state power*, Leiden: Brill, 2005, 35.

7 See E. I. J. Rosenthal, *Political Thought in Medieval Islam: an introductory outline*, Cambridge: Cambridge University Press, 1962, repr. Westport, CT: Greenwood, 1985; W. M. Watt, *Islamic Political Thought*, Edinburgh: Edinburgh University Press, 1968; A. K. S. Lambton, *State and Government in Medieval Islam, an introduction to the study of Islamic political theory: the jurists*, Oxford: Oxford University Press, 1981; S. A. Arjomand, *The Shadow of God and the Hidden Imam: religion, political order, and societal change in Shi'ite Iran from the beginning to 1890*, Chicago, IL: University of Chicago Press, 1984; A. Black, *The History of Islamic Political Thought: from the Prophet to the present*, Edinburgh: Edinburgh University Press, 2001, or P. Crone, *God's Rule: six centuries of medieval Islamic political thought*, New York: Columbia University Press, 2004.

8 The Islamic/Qur'ānic concept of justice: M. Hadi Hussain and A.-H. Kamali, *The Nature of the Islamic State*, Karachi: National Book Foundation, 1977; L. Rosen, "Islamic Concepts of Justice," in M. King (ed.) *God's Law versus State Law: the construction of an Islamic identity in Western Europe*, London: Grey Seal, 1995, 62–72; M. Ayoub, "The Islamic Concept of Justice," in N. H. Barazangi,

M. R. Zaman, and O. Afzal (eds) *Islamic Identity and the Struggle for Justice*, Gainesville: University Press of Florida, 1996, 19–26; L. Rosen, *The Justice of Islam: comparative perspectives on Islamic law and society*, Oxford: Oxford University Press, 2000; K. Ahmad and A. Hassan, "Distributive Justice: the Islamic perspective," *Intellectual Discourse* 8, 2000: 159–72; M. H. Kamali, *Freedom, Equality and Justice in Islam*, Cambridge: Islamic Texts Society, 2002.

9 A. al-Azmeh, *Muslim Kingship: power and the sacred in Muslim, Christian, and Pagan polities*, London: IB Tauris, 1997; L. Marlow, *Hierarchy and Egalitarianism in Islamic Thought*, Cambridge: Cambridge University Press, 1997. Lambton hypothesizes that this legitimating concept arose after 1258, when pagan rulers governed much of the Middle East; A. K. S. Lambton, "Introduction," in K. Ferdinand and M. Mozaffari (eds) *Islam: state and society*, London: Curzon, 1988, 4. The disappearance of rule justified by Islamic arguments for caliphal legitimacy, however, merely revealed the persistence of a discourse legitimizing the ruler by his behavior that had been muffled by Islamic political discourse based on the history of the Muslim community.

10 J. Krynen, *Idéal du prince et pouvoir royale en France à la fin du moyen age (1380–1440)*, Paris: A. et J. Picard, 1981, 184–96; quotations on 184 and 185.

11 A. de Montchrétien, *Traicté de l'œconomie politique*, Paris: Librairie Plon, 1889, 142.

12 A. Vincent, *Theories of the State*, Oxford: Blackwell, 1987, 49.

13 D'Herbelot, *Bibliotheque Orientale*, s.v. "Ardashir" quoted in E. Gibbon, *The History of the Decline and Fall of the Roman Empire*, new ed., London: Lackington, Harding, Hughes, Mavor, and Jones, 1820, 1:341.

14 J. Malcolm, *The History of Persia, from the most early period to the present time*, London: J. Murray and Longman, 1815, 1: 9, citing 'Alī Reẓa al-Sharīf Shahavārī, *Zīnat al-tavārīkh* (*c.*1803), an unpublished work, two manuscripts of which are in the British Museum: C. A. Storey, *Persian Literature: a bio-bibliographical survey*, vol. 1: *Qur'anic Literature, History and Biography*, Part 1, London: Luzac, 1927–39, 134.

15 G. Rawlinson, *The Seventh Great Oriental Monarchy*, London: Longmans, Green, 1876, repr. Tehran: Imperial Organization for Social Services, 1976, 61 and n. 3; A. H. Lybyer, *The Government of the Ottoman Empire in the Time of Suleiman the Magnificent*, Cambridge: Harvard University Press, 1913, 20, quoting Rawlinson as well as Yūsuf Khāṣṣ Ḥājib, *Uigurische Sprachmonumente und das Kudatku bilik*, ed. and trans. Á. Vámbéry, Innsbruck: Wagner Universitäts-Buchdruckerei, 1870, 118; Sarı Mehmed Pasha, the Defterdār, *Ottoman Statecraft: the book of counsel for vezirs and governors*, trans. W. L. Wright, Jr., Princeton, NJ: Princeton University Press, 1935; repr. Westport, CT: Greenwood Press, 1971, 119; L. V. Thomas, *A Study of Naima*, ed. N. Itzkowitz, New York: New York University Press, 1972, 123, n. 21.

16 Watt (*Islamic Political Thought*, 80) was one of the few scholars to recognize that the "Persian" element in Islamic political thought actually went back to Sumer and Akkad, though he did not draw the conclusion of its importance outside the literary genre of "mirrors for princes."

17 See H. Enayat, *Modern Islamic Political Thought*, Austin: University of Texas Press, 1982, 14; L. Valensi, *The Birth of the Despot: Venice and the Sublime Porte*, Ithaca, NY: Cornell University Press, 1993.

18 E. B. Mitchell, "Institution and Destitution: patronage tales of old Stamboul," PhD diss., University of California, Los Angeles, 1993, 102–7.

19 J. C. Scott, *The Moral Economy of the Peasant: rebellion and subsistence in Southeast Asia*, New Haven, CT: Yale University Press, 1976; S. N. Eisenstadt, *The Political Systems of Empires*, London, New York: Free Press of Glencoe, 1963; E. Atilla Aytekin, "Neither 'Monarchism' nor 'Weapons of the Weak': peasant protest in the late ottoman empire," in *Perspectives on Ottoman Studies*, ed. Ekrem Čaušević, Nenad Moačanin and Vjeran Kursar, Berlin: Lit Verlag Dr. W. Hopf, 2010, 105–19.

20 D. Brumberg, "Survival Strategies vs. Democratic Bargains: the politics of economic reform in contemporary Egypt," in H. J. Barkey (ed.) *The Politics of Economic Reform in the Middle East*, New York: St. Martin's, 1992, 73–104.

21 S. Heydemann, "The Political Logic of Economic Rationality: selective stabilization in Syria," in Barkey, *Politics of Economic Reform*, 16; a similar but less explicit statement is R. A. Hinnebusch, *Authoritarian Power and State Formation in Ba'thist Syria: army, party, and peasant*, Boulder, CO: Westview, 1990, 322–3.

22 A. Charlesworth and A. J. Randall, "Comment: Morals, Markets and the English Crowd in 1766," *Past & Present* 114, 1987: 212.

23 J. Beinin, "Islam, Marxism, and the Subra al-Khayma Textile Workers: Muslim Brothers and Communists in the Egyptian trade union movement," in E. Burke III and I. M. Lapidus (eds)

Islam, Politics, and Social Movements, Berkeley: University of California Press, 1988, 218. See E. P. Thompson, *The Making of the English Working Class*, New York: Vintage Books, 1966, 67–73; E. P. Thompson, *Customs in Common: studies in traditional popular culture*, New York: The New Press, 1993, 271, 293, 300, 338. The concept of justice lies behind much modern Islamic thinking about the economy; T. Kuran, "On the Notion of Economic Justice in Contemporary Islamic Thought," *IJMES* 21, 1989: 171–91. How Islam formulates the moral economy in a modern capitalist society: C. Tripp, *Islam and the Moral Economy: the challenge of capitalism*, Cambridge: Cambridge University Press, 2006.

24 N. J. Brown, *Peasant Politics in Modern Egypt: the struggle against the state*, New Haven, CT: Yale University Press, 1990, 17.

25 E. Burke III, "Understanding Arab Protest Movements," *Maghreb Review* 11.1, 1986: 27–32; repr. in *ASQ* 8, 1986: 335, 343.

26 C. E. Butterworth, "State and Authority in Arabic Political Thought," in G. Salamé (ed.) *The Foundations of the Arab State*, London: Croom Helm, 1987, 93; Lambton, *State and Government*.

27 Lambton (*State and Government*) made the point that juristic theory formed only one strand of Islamic political thought, and her study clearly reveals its dependence on the ideas of philosophers and statesmen.

2 Mesopotamia

1 On the Sumerians see S. N. Kramer, *The Sumerians: their history, culture, and character*, Chicago, IL: University of Chicago Press, 1963; G. Roux, *Ancient Iraq*, London: George Allen & Unwin, 1964; 2nd ed. Harmondsworth, UK: Penguin, 1980; and A. L. Oppenheim, *Ancient Mesopotamia: portrait of a dead civilization*, rev. ed. completed by E. Reiner, Chicago, IL: University of Chicago Press, 1977. On Mesopotamia as a whole, J. M. Sasson (ed.) *Civilizations of the Ancient Near East*, 4 vols, New York: Scribner/Simon & Schuster Macmillan, 1995 (hereafter *CANE*).

2 A. L. Oppenheim, "A Note on the Scribes in Mesopotamia," *Studies in Honor of Benno Landsberger on His Seventy-Fifth Birthday*, Oriental Institute Assyriological Studies, 16, Chicago, IL: University of Chicago Press, 1965, 253-6; P. Michalowski, "Charisma and Control: on continuity and change in early Mesopotamian bureaucratic systems," in M. Gibson and R. D. Biggs (eds) *The Organization of Power: aspects of bureaucracy in the ancient Near East*, Chicago, IL: Oriental Institute, 1987, 63; H. Tadmor, "Propaganda, Literature, Historiography: cracking the code of the Assyrian royal inscriptions," in S. Parpola and R. M. Whiting (eds) *Assyria 1995: proceedings of the 10th anniversary symposium of the Neo-Assyrian text corpus project*, Helsinki: The Neo-Assyrian Text Corpus Project, 1997, 325–38.

3 B. N. Porter, *Images, Power, and Politics: figurative aspects of Esarhaddon's Babylonian policy*, Philadelphia, PA: American Philosophical Society, 1993, 105–15.

4 Oppenheim, *Ancient Mesopotamia*, 98; S. Smith, "The Practice of Kingship in Early Semitic Kingdoms," in S. H. Hooke (ed.) *Myth, Ritual, and Kingship: essays on the theory and practice of kingship in the ancient Near East and in Israel*, Oxford: Clarendon, 1958, 25–7. A broader view of royal ideology: *CANE* 1: 395–411.

5 The ruler's titles were "governor" or "great man:" M.-J. Seux, *Épithetes royales akkadiennes et sumériennes*, Paris: Letouzey et Ané, 1967, 399 (*ensí*), 421–2 (*lugal*); also 110–16 (*iššiaku*). Some scholars see him as the foreman of the temple labor force: T. Fish, "Some Aspects of Kingship in the Sumerian City and Kingdom of Ur," *Bulletin of the John Rylands Library*, 34, 1951: 37–43.

6 D. R. Frayne, *Presargonic Period (2700–2350 BCE)*, Royal Inscriptions of Mesopotamia, Early Periods, 1, Toronto: University of Toronto Press, 2008 (hereafter RIME 1), 70. Pre-Sargonic dates are from J. S. Cooper, *Presargonic Inscriptions*, Sumerian and Akkadian Royal Inscriptions, 1, New Haven, CT: American Oriental Society, 1986, thought to be accurate to within 65 years.

7 RIME 1: 104; the most complete inscription: RIME 1: 91–3.

8 Cited in B. Lafont, "Le roi de Mari et les prophètes du dieu Adad," *RA* 78, 1984: 10–11; the king was Zimri-Lim. Quotations in RIME 1: 131, 153.

9 RIME 1, 436–7. Similar ideas occur in the Bible: Psalm 72, a psalm of Solomon. On the Biblical concept of justice: E. Nardoni, *Rise Up, O Judge: a study of justice in the Biblical world*, Peabody, MA: Hendrickson, 2004.

10 A. M. Hocart, *Kings and Councillors: an essay in the comparative anatomy of human society*, ed. R. Needham, Chicago, IL: University of Chicago Press, 1970; K. A. Wittfogel, *Oriental Despotism:*

a comparative study of total power, New Haven, CT: Yale University Press, 1957; L. Krader, *The Asiatic Mode of Production: sources, development and critique in the writings of Karl Marx*, Assen: Van Gorcum, 1975.

11 D. R. Frayne, *Old Babylonian Period (2003–1595 BC)*, Royal Inscriptions of Mesopotamia, Early Periods, 4, Toronto: University of Toronto Press, 1990 (hereafter RIME 4), 381. Examples of the continuous use of the title of shepherd from the third millennium through the sixth century: Seux, *Épithetes*, 243–50; Sumerian examples, ibid., 441–2.

12 RIME 1: 259–65. Some authorities read Urukagina's name as Uru'inimgina. Further references in F. C. Fensham, "Widow, Orphan, and the Poor in Ancient Near Eastern Legal and Wisdom Literature," *JNES* 21, 1962: 129-39; Z. Yang, "King of Justice," *Aula Orientalia* 9, 1991: 245–6.

13 B. Hruška, "Die Reformtexte Urukaginas: der verspätete Versuch einer Konsolidierung des stadtstaates von Lagas," in P. Garelli (ed.) *Le palais et la royauté (archéologie et civilisation)*, Rencontre assyriologique internationale, 19th, Paris, 1971, Paris: Paul Geuthner, 1974, 153.

14 Inscription on a statue's pedestal: J. B. Pritchard, *Ancient Near Eastern Texts Relating to the Old Testament*, 2nd ed., Princeton, NJ: Princeton University Press, 1955 (hereafter *ANET*), 267; D. R. Frayne, *Sargonic and Gutian Periods (2334–2113 BCE)*, Royal Inscriptions of Mesopotamia, Early Periods, 2, Toronto: University of Toronto Press, 1993 (hereafter RIME 2), 11, 14, 29, 31; *CANE*, 2: 833.

15 I. J. Gelb and B. Kienast, *Die Altakkadischen Königsinschriften des dritten Jahrtausends vor Chr.*, Freiburger Altorientalische Studien, 7, Stuttgart: F. Steiner, 1990, 89; *ANET*, 286.

16 Seux, *Épithetes*, 305& nn214 and 215; M. T. Larsen, "The Tradition of Empire in Mesopotamia," in *Power and Propaganda: a symposium on ancient empires*, ed. M. T. Larsen, Mesopotamia: Copenhagen Studies in Assyriology, 7, Copenhagen: Akademisk Forlag, 1979, 90.

17 Gelb and Kienast, *Altakkadischen Königsinschriften*, 42–4 (seals of governmental bureaucrats); *CANE* 2: 834; also W. Farber, "Die Vergöttlichung Narām-Sîns," *Orientalia* 52, 1983: 67–72. I. J. Winter, "Legitimation of Authority through Image and Legend: seals belonging to officials in the administrative bureaucracy of the Ur III state," in Gibson and Biggs, *The Organization of Power*, 70, 87–8.

18 O. R. Gurney, "The Sultantepe Tablets (continued): IV. The Cuthaean legend of Naram-Sin," *Anatolian Studies* 5, 1955: 103.

19 Seux, *Épithetes*, 442–5. Inscriptions of Lagash: H. Steible, *Die Neusumerischen Bau- und Weihinschriften*, 2 vols, Freiburger Altorientalische Studien, 9, Stuttgart: Franz Steiner, 1991; D. O. Edzard, *Gudea and His Dynasty*, Royal Inscriptions of Mesopotamia, Early Periods, 3/1, Toronto: University of Toronto Press, 1997 (hereafter RIME 3/1). Post-Sargonic dating follows Oppenheim, *Ancient Mesopotamia*, and Seux, *Épithetes*.

20 RIME 3/1: 77; also Warad-Sin, who, during the rebuilding of the wall of Ur, "removed any cause for complaint from my land;" RIME 4: 240, 243.

21 RIME 3/1: 78–9; 98. A hymn to the goddess Nanshe associated Gudea's building of "a proper house" with the goddess's provision of fertility and justice: T. Jacobsen, *The Harps That Once…: Sumerian poetry in translation,* New Haven, CT: Yale University Press, 1987, 127–8.

22 D. R. Frayne, *Ur III Period (2112–2004 BC)*, Royal Inscriptions of Mesopotamia, Early Periods, 3/2, Toronto: University of Toronto Press, 1997, 64 (hereafter RIME 3/2).

23 Unattributed quotation, *CANE* 2: 851; see also S. N. Kramer, "Kingship in Sumer and Akkad: the ideal king," in Garelli, *Le palais et la royauté*, 165. Poems repeatedly referred to Shulgi as a shepherd.

24 *CANE* 2: 853; J. Klein, *Three Šulgi Hymns: Sumerian royal hymns glorifying King Šulgi of Ur*, Ramat-Gan, Israel: Bar-Ilan University Press, 1981, 145. Shulgi's reforms: *CANE* 1: 402, 2: 844.

25 Michalowski, "Charisma," 66; I. J. Winter, "The King and the Cup: iconography of the royal presentation scene on Ur III seals," in M. Kelly Buccellati (ed.) *Insight through Images: studies in honor of Edith Porada*, Bibliotheca Mesopotamica, 21, Malibu, CA: Undena, 1986, 259–64.

26 RIME 4: 142, 144, 148.

27 RIME 4: 376, 378, 676; Seux, *Épithetes*, 66, 89, 98; B. Andre-Salvini and M. Salvini, "Ein König von Dér," *Altorientalische Forschungen*, 24, 1997: 39. See Hammurabi: RIME 4: 336, 338, 351.

28 RIME 4: 78–85, 242, 293; quotations on 89–90.

29 Ur-Nammu's "code" may have been promulgated by his reforming successor Shulgi; S. N. Kramer, "The Ur-Nammu Code: who was its author?" *Orientalia* n.s. 52, 1983: 453–6; P. Steinkeller, "The Administrative and Economic Organization of the Ur III State: the core and the periphery," in Gibson and Biggs, *The Organization of Power*, 20–1; P. Michalowski and C. B. F. Walker, "A New Sumerian 'Law Code'," in H. Behrens, D. Loding, and M. T. Roth (eds) *Dumm-e$_2$-dub-ba-a:*

Studies in Honor of Ake W. Sjöberg, Philadelphia, PA: Samuel Noah Kramer Fund, 1989, 383–96; RIME 3/2: 44–5; J. V. Canby, *The "Ur-Nammu" Stela*, Philadelphia: University of Pennsylvania Museum of Archaeology and Anthropology, 2001, 50–1. On Mesopotamian justice generally, *CANE* 1: 469–84.

30 RIME 3/2: 49; F. Yıldız, "A Tablet of Codex Ur-Nammu from Sippar," *Orientalia* n.s. 50, 1981: 95; M. T. Roth, *Law Collections from Mesopotamia and Asia Minor*, 2nd ed., Atlanta, GA: Scholars Press, 1997, 15–21.

31 *ANET*, 159; also E. Sollberger and J.-R. Kupper, *Inscriptions royales sumériennes et akkadiennes*, Littératures anciennes du proche-orient, Paris: Éditions du Cerf, 1971, 175–7. Lipit-Ishtar's titles: RIME 4: 48, 49, 54, 56, 60.

32 *ANET*, 161.

33 Ibid., 164. His name should perhaps be spelled Hammurapi: *CANE* 2: 902.

34 *ANET*, 177–8; A. Westenholz, "How Do We Understand Ancient History, and why study it at all?" *Kaskal: rivista di storia, ambiente e culture del Vicino Oriente antico* 1, 2004: 185.

35 *ANET*, 178.

36 Quoted in *CANE* 2: 908.

37 R. D. Biggs, J. A. Brinkman, M. Civil, W. Farber, I. J. Gelb, A. L. Oppenheim, E. Reiner, M. T. Roth, and M. W. Stolper (eds) *The Assyrian Dictionary*, Chicago, IL: Oriental Institute, 1956–2010 (hereafter *CAD*), s.v. "*anduraru*", "*misharu*". On these concepts and associated procedures, J. A. Scurlock, "'Freedom' and 'Justice': the Neo-Assyrian response to socio-economic crises (934–612 B.C.)," paper presented to the Association of Ancient Historians, Madison, WI, 5–7 May 1983. Inscriptions of Entemena of Lagash (*c.*2400 BCE) show the cancellation of obligations: Cooper, *Presargonic Inscriptions*, 58, La 5.4.

38 J. J. Finkelstein, "Some New *Misharum* Material and Its Implications," *Studies in Honor of Benno Landsberger on His Seventy-Fifth Birthday*, Oriental Institute Assyriological Studies, 16, Chicago, IL: University of Chicago Press, 1965, 243–6.

39 F. R. Kraus, *Ein Edikt des Königs Ammi-Saduqa von Babylon*, Studia et Documenta ad Iura Orientis Antiqui Pertinentia, 5, Leiden: Brill, 1958; J. J. Finkelstein, "The Edict of Ammisaduqa, a New Text," *RA* 63, 1969: 45–64.

40 Finkelstein, "*Misharum* Material," 236; J. P. J. Olivier, "Restitution as Economic Redress: the fine print of the Old Babylonian *mēšarum*-edict of Ammiṣaduqa," *Zeitschrift für Altbabylonische und Biblische Rechtsgeschichte* 3, 1997, 13; F. van Koppen, "The Geography of the Slave Trade and Northern Mesopotamia in the Late Old Babylonian Period," in H. Hunger and R. Pruzsinszky (eds) *Mesopotamian Dark Age Revisited*, Vienna: Österreischischen Akademie der Wissenschaften, 2004, 11; Scurlock, "'Freedom'," 8; J. J. Finkelstein, "Ammisaduqa's Edict and the Babylonian 'Law Codes'," *JCS* 15, 1961: 101n15.

41 In fourth-century BCE India, kings were expected to attend court daily to "look into the affairs of the citizens and the country people:" G. Wojtilla, "The Royal Diary in Ancient India and Its Criticism," in *Speculum Regis*, ed. I. Tar and G. Wojtilla, Acta Antiqua et Archaeologica, 26, Szeged, Hungary: Universitas de Atilla Jószef, 1994, 8. Royal power was considered necessary for social order, the prerequisite for economic sufficiency, the basis of all higher aspirations: Aziz al-Azmeh, *Muslim Kingship: power and the sacred in Muslim, Christian, and Pagan polities*, London: IB Tauris, 1997, 59–61.

42 R. Frankena, *Briefe aus dem British Museum (LIH und CT2–33)*, Altbabylonische Briefe im Umschrift und Übersetzung, 2, Leiden: Brill, 1966, 5 (no. 6), 15 (no. 24), 17 (no. 28), 45 (no. 74); see also cases collected in W. F. Leemans, "King Ḫammurapi as Judge," in J. A. Ankum, R. Feenstra and W. F. Leemans (eds) *Symbolae Iuridicae et Historicae Martino David Dedicatae*, Leiden: Brill, 1968, 2:107–29; and W. H. van Soldt, *Letters in the British Museum, Part 2*, Altbabylonische Briefe im Umschrift und Übersetzung, 13, Leiden: Brill, 1994, 5 (no. 4), 13 (no. 10), 15 (nos. 12 and 13), 23 (no. 21), 27 (no. 27), 39 (no. 43).

43 Frivolous complaints were discouraged, as in the example of a family appealing to Samsu-iluna: "Since they were not unjustly treated and since they approached the king without a cause, the judges imposed punishment on them;" G. Voet and K. van Lerberghe, "A Long Lasting Life," in Behrens *et al.*, *Dumm-e_2-dub-ba-a*, 528.

44 On the post system, part of the ruler's information network, in this and later periods, F. Dvornik, *Origins of Intelligence Services: the ancient Near East, Persia, Greece, Rome, Byzantium, the Arab Muslim empires, the Mongol Empire, China, Muscovy*, New Brunswick, NJ: Rutgers University Press, 1974; A. J. Silverstein, *Postal Systems in the Pre-Modern Islamic World*, Cambridge: Cambridge University Press, 2007.

45 J. A. Brinkman, "Provincial Administration in Babylonia under the Second Dynasty of Isin," *JESHO* 6, 1953: 239–41.
46 J. A. Brinkman, "The Monarchy in the Time of the Kassite Dynasty," in Garelli, *Le palais et la royauté*, 395-8. W. Sommerfeld, "Die Kurigalzu-Text MAH 15922," *Archiv für Orientforschung* 32, 1985: 3–22; A. Boissier, "Document cassite," *RA* 29, 1932: 93–104. Shepherd: Seux, *Épithetes*, 217; judge: Seux, *Épithetes*, 66; Boissier, 100.
47 G. Frame, *Rulers of Babylonia: from the second dynasty of Isin to the end of Assyrian domination (1157–612 BC)*, Royal Inscriptions of Mesopotamia, Babylonian Periods, 2, Toronto: University of Toronto Press, 1995 (hereafter RIMB 2), 34, 32; W. J. Hinke, *A New Boundary Stone of Nebuchadrezzar I from Nippur, with a concordance of proper names and a glossary of the kudurru inscriptions thus far published*, The Babylonian Expedition of the University of Pennsylvania, Series D: Researches and Treatises, 4, Philadelphia: University of Pennsylvania, 1907, 145.
48 M. Lichtheim, *Ancient Egyptian Literature: a book of readings*, Berkeley: University of California Press, 1973–80, 1: 17, 100, 135; 2: 23. Zimri-Lim's instructions: Lafont, "Le roi de Mari," 11. Egyptian concepts of justice: Nardoni, *Rise Up*, 21–41. The Egyptian god Amon-Re was worshipped as "Lord of the Silent, who comes at the voice of the poor. who gives bread to him who has none. father of the orphan, husband of the widow."; quoted in E. Peters, *Lord of the Silent*, New York: HarperCollins, 2001.
49 Illustrated overview of Assyrian history: J. E. Curtis and J. E. Reade (eds) *Art and Empire: treasures from Assyria in the British Museum*, London: British Museum Press, 1995.
50 Ibid., 112-14; M. T. Larsen, "The City and Its King: on the Old Assyrian notion of Kingship," in Garelli, *Le palais et la royauté*, 287–8.
51 A. K. Grayson, *Assyrian Royal Inscriptions*, Records of the Ancient Near East, 1 and 2, Wiesbaden: Harrassowitz, 1972-6 (hereafter ARI), 1: 5; Seux, *Épithetes*, 112; S. W. Holloway, *Aššur is King! Aššur is King! religion in the exercise of power in the Neo-Assyrian Empire*, Leiden: Brill, 2002, 183.
52 Inscription of Adad-Narari I (1307–1275), in ARI 1: 58; A. K. Grayson, *Assyrian Rulers of the Third and Second Millennia BD (to 1115 BCE)*, Royal Inscriptions of Mesopotamia, Assyrian Periods, 1, Toronto: University of Toronto Press, 1987 (hereafter RIMA 1), 131. Sennacherib (704–681): "Favorite of the great gods am I. Aššur, father of the gods, has looked upon me, among all princes, with his sure favor, and above all those who dwell in palaces, has made powerful my weapons;" D. D. Luckenbill, *Ancient Records of Assyria and Babylonia*, Chicago, IL: University of Chicago Press, 1926–7, 2: 147.
53 Larsen, "Tradition of Empire," 90; the term "yoke" was used by the Assyrians themselves to refer to their domination.
54 Inscriptions of Aššur-uballit I (1363–1328) and Arik-din-ili (1317–1306): RIMA 1: 112, 121.
55 RIMA 1: 20–1; ARI 1: 12–13
56 Translation of the laws without the preamble: Roth, *Law Collections*, 155–92.
57 RIMA 1: 182, 183, 192.
58 RIMA 1: 240, 237. The Assyrian emphasis on administration and provision may be attributable to Assyria's mercantile background; *CANE* 1: 406–7.
59 RIMA 1: 242. On Tukulti-Ninurta's administration, RIMA 1: 244–5; A. T. Olmstead, *History of Assyria*, Chicago, IL: University of Chicago Press, 1923, 53, 606. The number of governors expanded greatly under later Assyrian rulers.
60 Justice: RIMA 1: 234; Seux, *Épithetes*, 90. Order: Seux, *Épithetes*, 176. The idea that the king was the source of order was expressed in reverse by inscriptions calling non-Assyrians "those in confusion;" P. Machinist, "Assyrians on Assyria in the First Millennium B.C.," in K. Raaflaub and E. Müller-Luckner (eds) *Anfänge politischen Denkens in der Antike: Die nahöstlichen Kulturen und die Griechen*, Munich: R. Oldenbourg, 1993, 85.
61 *CAD*, vol. M/2, s.v. "*misharu*," 117; see RIMA 2: 7–8.
62 A. K. Grayson, *Assyrian Rulers of the Early First Millennium BCE, I (1114–859 BCE)*, Royal Inscriptions of Mesopotamia, Assyrian Periods, 2, Toronto: University of Toronto Press, 1991 (hereafter RIMA 2), 26–9.
63 M. Novak, "The Artificial Paradise: programme and ideology of royal gardens," in S. Parpola and R. M. Whiting (eds) *Sex and Gender in the Ancient Near East*, Helsinki: Neo-Assyrian Text Corpus Project, 2002: 2: 445.
64 RIMA 2: 14.

65 RIMA 2: 172. On the Assyrian ideology and process of relocation and resettlement, J. A. Scurlock, "Assyrian 'Colonization'," paper presented to the Association of Ancient Historians, Lubbock, TX, 1–3 May 1986, which describes the care with which the settlers were treated; they were listed by name and provided with food and clothing.
66 RIMA 1: 183. The practice of filling the royal service with officials from the defeated peoples who had been educated in the palace was followed by later Assyrian and Achaemenid rulers; it also formed the basis of the Ottoman *devşirme*.
67 Luckenbill, *Ancient Records* 2: 225.
68 Examples in RIMA 2: 194, 225, 239, 276.
69 Curtis and Reade, *Art and Empire*, 42–59. As these authors complained, "The barbarous and callous character of the Assyrians has often been stressed" (32), but inscriptions and reliefs portraying the brutal punishment of enemies and rebels were intended as warnings in an era when direct control of a diverse population was logistically impossible.
70 RIMA 2: 242–3, 252, 261, 289–91; Novak, "Artificial Paradise," 446. Sargon II (721–705), who titled himself "guardian of justice" (Luckenbill, *Ancient Records*, 2:83), followed the same procedures (ibid., 2: 62–3). On similar resettlement practices in an even earlier age, D. Charpin, "Immigrés, refugiés et déportés en Babylonie sous Hammu-rabi et ses successeurs," in D. Charpin and F. Joannès (eds) *La circulations des biens, des personnes et des idées dans le Proche-orient ancien*, Paris: Éditions Recherche sur les Civilisations, 1992, 207–18.
71 RIMA 2: 221–2, 224–5; quotation on 281.
72 RIMA 2: 308. This text, called the Standard Inscription of Nineveh, was engraved numerous times on Ashurnasirpal's constructions in that city.
73 A. K. Grayson, *Assyrian Rulers of the Early First Millennium BCE, II (858–745 BCE)*, Royal Inscriptions of Mesopotamia, Assyrian Periods, 3, Toronto: University of Toronto Press, 1996 (hereafter RIMA 3), 7. A hymn to Shamash, the sun-god, praised his justice: "The *Šamaš* Hymn," in W. G. Lambert (ed.) *Babylonian Wisdom Literature*, Oxford: Clarendon, 1960, 133.
74 H. Tadmor, *The Inscriptions of Tiglath-Pileser III, King of Assyria*, Jerusalem: Israel Academy of Sciences and Humanities, 1994, 45, 47, 49, 59, 63, 67–9. The Ottoman sultan Mehmed the Conqueror followed the same procedure after his conquest of Constantinople in 1453.
75 Tadmor, *Inscriptions*, 43.
76 Quoted in H. Tadmor, "The Campaigns of Sargon II of Assur: a chronological-historical study," *JCS* 12, 1958: 34.
77 Machinist, "Assyrians," 96; Scurlock, "Assyrian 'Colonization'."
78 Sargon at Dur-Sharruken (formerly Dur-Sharrukīn): Luckenbill, *Ancient Records*, 2: 37.
79 Tukulti-Ninurta I: RIMA 1: 270.
80 RIMA 1: 273, 276. On royal intelligence: M. W. Helms, *Craft and the Kingly Ideal: art, trade and power*, Austin: University of Texas Press, 1993.
81 *ARI* 2: 172–6; Novak, "Artificial," 446.
82 I. J. Winter, "'Seat of Kingship'/'A Wonder to Behold': the palace as construct in the ancient Near East," *ArsOr* 23, 1993, 36; Luckenbill, *Ancient Records*, 2: 44; quotations from Curtis and Reade, *Art and Empire*, 64, and Luckenbill, *Ancient Records*, 2: 62.
83 Luckenbill, *Ancient Records*, 2: 63.
84 Cylinder Inscription of Sargon, trans. H. Tadmor, "Sennacherib, King of Justice," in C. Cohen, A. Hurvitz, and S. M. Paul (eds) *The Moshe Weinfeld Jubilee Volume*, Winona Lake, IN: Eisenbrauns, 2004, 386; Tadmor points out that this obvious self-aggrandizement was supported by a deed granting new land tax-free to evicted people. Sargon also proclaimed himself opposed to oppression, as did Esarhaddon and Ashurbanipal; Seux, *Épithetes*, 107.
85 Luckenbill, *Ancient Records*, 2: 62–3, 113.
86 RIMA 3: 10–11; other examples, 14–25, 31, 37–8, 47. Some of this material apparently constituted offerings in support of the worship of Aššur, provision of which was a mark of incorporation into his land: J. N. Postgate, "The Land of Assur and the Yoke of Assur," *World Archaeology* 23, 1992: 252. Lavish descriptions of Egyptian royal treasures: W. L. Moran (ed. and trans.) *The Amarna Letters*, Baltimore, MD: Johns Hopkins, 1992: 9–37.
87 H. Gopnik, "Death and Taxes in the Neo-Assyrian Reliefs," in S. E. Orel (ed.) *Death and Taxes in the Ancient Near East*, Lewiston: Edwin Mellen, 1992, 63–4.
88 This idea occurs seven times in Sargon's Display Inscription: Luckenbill, *Ancient Records*, 2: 29–34; list of treasures: ibid., 23.

89 Luckenbill, *Ancient Records*, 2: 32; Postgate, "Land of Assur," 254; also Luckenbill, *Ancient Records*, 2: 13, where a revolt was signaled when a rebellious king "plotted in his heart to withhold his tribute."

90 Luckenbill, *Ancient Records*, 2: 55, 71; Tadmor, "Sennacherib," 387. Exemptions were usually granted to cities that were seats of gods and were more frequent in conquered territories than in the Assyrian heartland, where loyalty was taken for granted (R. Beal, personal communication). For these exemptions and their implications, Holloway, *Aššur*, 293–302.

91 "Advice to a Prince," trans. Lambert, *Babylonian Wisdom Literature*, 110–15; cf. V. A. Hurowitz, "Advice to a Prince: a message from Ea," *State Archives of Assyria Bulletin* 12, 1998: 49. The text's political context: H. Tadmor, "Monarchy and the Elite in Assyria and Babylonia: the question of royal accountability," in S. N. Eisenstadt (ed.) *The Origins and Diversity of Axial Age Civilizations*, Albany: State University of New York Press, 1986, 203–24.

92 H. W. F. Saggs, "Historical Texts and Fragments of Sargon II of Assyria," *Iraq* 37, 1975: 13–17.

93 Luckenbill, *Ancient Records*, 2: 109.

94 C. H. W. Johns, *An Assyrian Doomsday Book: or, liber censualis of the district round Harran, in the seventh century* BCE, Assyriologische Bibliothek, 17, Leipzig: J. C. Hinrichs, 1901; republished by F. M. Fales, *Censimenti e catasti di epoca neo-assira*, Studia Economici e Tecnologici, 2, Rome: Centro per le Antichità e la Storia dell'Arte del Vicino Oriente, 1973.

95 Johns, *Assyrian Domesday Book*, v. 3. On land records, called *kudurru* documents or "boundary stones," L. W. King, *Babylonian Boundary-Stones and Memorial-Tablets in the British Museum*, London: Trustees of the British Museum, 1912. On the land-tenure system that employed these boundary stones, *CANE* 2: 920–25.

96 Luckenbill, *Ancient Records*, 2: 5–25, quotation on 50–1.

97 Ibid., 2: 292, 379.

98 J. M. Russell, *Sennacherib's Palace without Rival at Nineveh*, Chicago, IL: University of Chicago Press, 1991; Luckenbill, *Ancient Records*, 2: 160–79. Sargon's palace at Dur-Sharruken, constructed during Sennacherib's formative years, greatly influenced his own project (Luckenbill, *Ancient Records*, 2: 37–9, 48–55), but Sennacherib vastly outdid his predecessor in provision of gardens and orchards, some for ordinary citizens, watered by massive irrigation projects: T. Jacobsen and S. Lloyd, *Sennacherib's Aqueduct at Jerwan*, Oriental Institute Publications, 24, Chicago, IL: University of Chicago Press, 1935; Luckenbill, *Ancient Records*, 2: 160–98.

99 Luckenbill, *Ancient Records*, 2: 203–4, 225–7, 247, 253, 272, 282. On the Assyrian ruler Esarhaddon's rebuilding of Babylonian temples as a claim for the legitimacy of his kingship over Babylonia, Porter, *Images*.

100 Sargon: Seux, *Épithetes*, 368; he was also "guardian of justice" (Luckenbill, *Ancient Records*, 2:83). Sennacherib: Seux, *Épithetes*, 202, 236, 237; Luckenbill, *Ancient Records*, 2: 115, 128, 186, 190; Tadmor, "Sennacherib." Esarhaddon: Seux, *Épithetes*, 107; Luckenbill, *Ancient Records*, 2: 208, 248, 263.

101 *CANE* 1: 408–9; also Seux, *Épithetes*, 237; RIMB 2: 226. The same king appointed his brother to the kingship of Babylon "in order that the strong might not harm the weak"; RIMB 2: 200–1, 204, 206, 207, 209.

102 Luckenbill, *Ancient Records*, 2: 414.

103 Seux, *Épithetes*, 132, 237; P.-A. Beaulieu, *The Reign of Nabonidus, King of Babylon (556–539* BCE*)*, Yale Near East Researches, 10, New Haven, CT: Yale University Press, 1989, 4, 29. Titles of Marduk-apli-iddina II (721–710): Seux, *Épithetes*, passim.

104 Letter, trans. J. N. Postgate, "'Princeps Iudex' in Assyria," *RA* 74, 1980: 180–2.

105 J. N. Postgate, "Royal Exercise of Justice under the Assyrian Empire," in Garelli, *Le palais et la royauté*, 419&n10; A. L. Oppenheim, *Letters from Mesopotamia: official, business, and private letters on clay tablets from two millennia*, Chicago, IL: University of Chicago Press, 1967, 152, 179–80, 192–3; S. Parpola, *The Correspondence of Sargon II, Part I: letters from Assyria and the West*, State Archives of Assyria, 1, Helsinki: Helsinki University Press, 1987, 95 (no. 188), 150 (no. 190), 185 (no. 237); see also the other volumes in the State Archives of Assyria series.

3 Persia

1 On Persian history see H. Bailey, P. W. Avery, W. B. Fisher, I. Gershevitch and E. Yarshater (eds) *The Cambridge History of Iran*, 7 vols, Cambridge: Cambridge University Press, 1968–91 (hereafter *CHIr*); M. A. Dandamayev and V. G. Lukonin, *The Cultural and Social Institutions of Ancient Iran*, trans. P. L. Kohl and D. J. Dadson, Cambridge: Cambridge University Press, 1989.

2 R. N. Frye, *The Heritage of Persia*, London: Weidenfeld & Nicolson, 1962, 102–3; Jack M. Sasson (ed.) *Civilizations of the Ancient Near East*, 4 vols, New York: Scribner/Simon & Schuster Macmillan, 1995 (hereafter *CANE*) 2: 1002.

3 On Achaemenid history: P. Briant, *Histoire de L'empire perse de Cyrus à Alexandre*, Paris: Fayard, 1996. Elamite documents exist but do not yet add to our understanding of Achaemenid concepts of justice. Elamite copies of royal inscriptions: F. W. König, *Die elamischen Königsinschriften*, Archiv für Orientforschung, Beiheft 16, Graz: Archiv für Orientforschung, 1965; Elamite economic documents: R. T. Hallock, *Persepolis Fortification Tablets*, Oriental Institute Publications, 92, Chicago, IL: University of Chicago Press, 1969; G. G. Cameron, *Persepolis Treasury Tablets*, Oriental Institute Publications, 65, Chicago, IL: University of Chicago Press, 1948; *CHIr*, 2: 588–609; Elamite history: D. T. Potts, *The Archaeology of Elam: formation and transformation of an ancient Iranian site*, Cambridge: Cambridge University Press, 1999.

4 Ariamnes at Hamadan, in R. G. Kent, *Old Persian: grammar, texts, lexicon*, 2nd ed., New Haven, CT: American Oriental Society, 1953, 116. This text may have been written in the fourth century BCE; J. M. Cook, *The Persian Empire*, New York: Schocken, 1983, 8.

5 Darius at Behistun, in Kent, *Old Persian*, 119; cf. R. Schmitt, *The Bisitun Inscriptions of Darius the Great: Old Persian Text*, Corpus Inscriptionum Iranicarum, pt. 1, vol. 1, London: School of Oriental and African Studies, 1991, 49. Although the Zoroastrian reform of Iranian religion was not fully accepted in Achaemenid Persia, Ahuramazda was the most important god, the only one mentioned in most inscriptions. H. Sancisi-Weerdenburg, "Political Concepts in Old-Persian Royal Inscriptions," in K. Raaflaub and E. Müller-Luckner (eds) *Anfänge politischen Denkens in der Antike: Die nahöstlichen Kulturen und die Griechen*, Munich: R. Oldenbourg, 1993, 157.

6 W. Eilers, "Le texte cunéiforme du Cylindre de Cyrus," *Commémoration Cyrus, Hommage universel: actes du congrès de Shiraz 1971*, AcIr ser. 1, vols 1–3, Leiden: Brill, 1974, 2:33; J. B. Pritchard (ed.) *Ancient Near Eastern Texts Relating to the Old Testament*, 2nd ed., Princeton, NJ: Princeton University Press, 1955 (hereafter *ANET*), 315–16; M.-J. Seux, *Épithetes royales akkadiennes et sumériennes*, Literature ancien de la proche orient, Paris: Letouzey et Ané, 1967, 218; A. Kuhrt, "Usurpation, Conquest and Ceremonial: from Babylon to Persia," in D. Cannadine and S. Price (eds) *Rituals of Royalty: power and ceremonial in traditional societies*, Cambridge: Cambridge University Press, 1987, 50. Cyrus's successor Cambyses II (530–522) followed his example: J. Boardman *et al.* (eds) *Cambridge Ancient History*, 2nd ed., vol. 4: *Persia, Greece and the Western Mediterranean, c.525 to 479 B.C.*, Cambridge: Cambridge University Press, 1988 (hereafter *CAH* 4), 40. Cambyses also legitimized his rule over Egypt by taking the king's role in Egyptian religious rituals; A. Kuhrt, *The Ancient Near East, c.3000–330 BCE*, London: Routledge, 1994, 2: 663–4.

7 Darius at Persepolis F, in Kent, *Old Persian*, 143–4; cf. ibid., 116, 136. The training of Achaemenid kings was not scribal and intellectual as it sometimes was in Mesopotamia but almost exclusively concerned with weapons and horses; Cook, *Persian Empire*, 134; cf. Darius at Naqsh-i Rustam B, in Kent, *Old Persian*, 140. On Mesopotamian royal training see, in addition to Ashurbanipal's comments in Ch. 2, Esarhaddon's literacy and education, CANE 2: 951. Shulgi had earlier boasted of his studies in the scribal art ("Of the nobility, nobody was able to write a tablet like me;" ibid., 2: 853).

8 J. Wiesehöfer, *Ancient Persia: from 550 BCE to 650 AD*, trans. A. Azodi, London: IB Tauris, 1996, 18–19. These inscriptions have largely been ignored and the Achaemenids characterized by their Babylonian inscriptions.

9 Darius at Naqš-i-Rustem A and Susa E and F, in Kent, *Old Persian*, 138, 142, 144. Darius, however, was still "a Persian, son of a Persian, an Aryan, having Aryan lineage." On the development of imperial ideology under Darius I, C. Herrenschmidt, "Désignation de l'empire et concepts politiques de Darius Ier d'après ses inscriptions en vieux-perse," 5, 1976: 33–65; M. C. Root, *The King and Kingship in Achaemenid Art: essays on the creation of an iconography of empire*, AcIr 19, ser. 3, vol. 9, Leiden: Brill, 1979. Achaemenid royal art apparently descended directly from Assyrian; Sancisi-Weerdenburg, "Political Concepts," 154–5.

10 Darius at Susa F, in Kent, *Old Persian*, 144; cf. 119, 142, 145. Similar decorations adorned Cyrus's constructions at Pasargadae; *CAH* 4: 46. The Persepolis palace and Naqsh-i Rustam contain inscriptions by Darius listing the countries he ruled; Kent, *Old Persian*, 136, 138. Egyptian precedents for these lists: Root, *King*, 138–44, 160.

11 Darius at Behistun, in Schmitt, *Bisitun*, 49; cf. Kent, *Old Persian*, 119. Xerxes I at Persepolis, in Kent, *Old Persian*, 151; Akkadian version of the latter inscription in *ANET*, 316–17.

12 Briant, *Histoire*, 201–3; M. Dandamayev, "Achaemenid Babylonia," in I. M. Diakonoff (ed.) *Ancient Mesopotamia, Socio-Economic History: a collection of studies by Soviet scholars*, USSR Academy of Sciences, Institute of the Peoples of Asia, Moscow: "Nauka" Publishing House, 1969, 309.

13 Darius at Behistun, in Kent, *Old Persian*, 119; statues described in Root, *King*, 144–7, 192–4.

14 Darius at Behistun IV, in Schmitt, *Bisitun*, 71; cf. Kent, *Old Persian*, 132.

15 Schmitt, *Bisitun*, 140.

16 Darius at Behistun, in Schmitt, *Bisitun*, 51, 67–9; 78–80; cf. Kent, *Old Persian*, 119, 123, 131. The same idea in Sasanian times: H. Humback and P. O. Skjaervø, *The Sassanian Inscription of Paikuli*, Wiesbaden: Ludwig Reichert, 1983, vol. 3, pt 1, 29, 46, 55; Touraj Daryaee, "The Use of Religio-Political Propaganda on the Coinage of Xusrō II," *American Journal of Numismatics* 9, 1997: 46.

17 Darius at Susa E, in Kent, *Old Persian*, 142.

18 Darius at Naqsh-i Rustam B, in Kent, *Old Persian*, 110; *CANE* 1: 522.

19 F. Regourd, "Le rôle de l'élite perse dans la formation de l'armée et de l'état achéménides," *Commémoration Cyrus, Hommage universel: actes du congrès de Shiraz 1971*, AcIr ser. 1, Leiden: Brill, 1974, 103. Several of Darius I's monuments emphasize his dependence on the military support of his nobility; Root, *King*, 76, 282. All Persian children, including the future king, were trained as riders, archers, and javelin throwers; Dandamaev and Lukonin, *Cultural*, 223; Frye, *Heritage*, 104. The imperial forces also had contingents of other origins, many of whom were footsoldiers, and tribal forces were gradually replaced by professionals; R. N. Frye, "Pre-Islamic and Early Islamic Cultures in Central Asia," in R. L. Canfield (ed.) *Turko-Persia in Historical Perspective*, Cambridge: Cambridge University Press, 1991, 40.

20 Darius at Behistun, in Schmitt, *Bisitun*, 53; cf. Kent, *Old Persian*, 120; and Susa E, in Kent, *Old Persian*, 142. The four classes: A. E. Christensen, *L'Empire des Sassanides: le peuple, l'état, la cour*, Copenhagen: B. Lunos, 1907, 19. The concept of justice as maintenance of the social order is separate from (although interconnected with) that of justice as interdependent provision and is analyzed in many of the general studies listed here.

21 Frye, *Heritage*, 95–6; *CAH* 4: 81–82; Root, *King*, 131, 296. On the idea of divine kingship in Iran and Mesopotamian influence on Iranian ideas of kingship, G. Widengren, "The Sacral Kingship of Iran," in *The Sacral Kingship*, Studies in the History of Religions, 4 (Supplements to *Numen*), Leiden: Brill, 1959, 242–57; H. P. L'Orange, "Expressions of Cosmic Kingship in the Ancient World," in ibid., 481–92; H. P. L'Orange, *Studies on the Iconography of Cosmic Kingship in the Ancient World*, Cambridge, MA: Harvard University Press, 1953; and G. Gnoli, "Note su xšāyaθiya-e xšaça," in *Ex Orbe Religionum: studia Geo Widengren oblata*, Leiden: Brill, 1972, 2: 88–97.

22 Darius at Behistun, in Kent, *Old Persian*, 119; Schmitt, *Bisitun*, 50. Royal iconography portrayed the king as calm and passionless, dwelling in an ideal realm; Root, *King*, 310.

23 C. Huart, *Ancient Persia and Iranian Civilization*, trans. M. R. Dobie, New York: A. A. Knopf, 1927, 78. On legal codes and tax surveys, Frye, *Heritage*, 105, 113–14; Cook, *Persian Empire*, 71; R. N. Frye, *The History of Ancient Iran*, Munich: C. H. Beck, 1984, 117.

24 Dandamaev and Lukonin, *Cultural*, 107–10; A. E. Christensen, *L'Iran sous les Sassanides*, 2nd ed., Osnabrück: O. Zeller, 1971, 136–40.

25 Darius at Behistun, in Kent, *Old Persian*, 120; Schmitt, *Bisitun*, 53.

26 *Vendidad*, quoted in A. K. S. Lambton, *Landlord and Peasant in Persia*, rev. ed. London: Oxford University Press, 1969; repr. London: IB Tauris, 1991, xviii–xix.

27 Briant, *Histoire*, 213–15, 226, 246.

28 Dandamaev and Lukonin, *Cultural*, 206–7; *CAH* 4: 83; G. G. Cameron, "Persepolis Treasury Tablets Old and New," *JNES* 17, 1958:168–72; D. N. Wilber, *Persepolis: the archaeology of Parsa, seat of the Persian kings*, rev. ed., Princeton, NJ: Darwin, 1989, 16. These tablets list payments to workers and reimbursements for official purchases.

29 Root, *King*, 227, 282–4.

30 Wilber, *Persepolis*, 64; N. Cahill, "The Treasury at Persepolis," *American Journal of Archaeology* 89, 1985: 373; Briant, *Histoire*, 424–6.

31 See G. Cardescia, (ed. and trans.), *Les archives des Murasû, une famille d'hommes d'affaires babyloniens à l'époque perse (455–403 av. J.-C.)*, Paris: Imprimerie nationale, 1951.

32 S. Sherwin-White and A. Kuhrt, *From Samarkhand to Sardis: a new approach to the Seleucid Empire*, Berkeley: University of California Press, 1993, 23.

33 R. R. R. Smith, *Hellenistic Royal Portraits*, Oxford: Clarendon, 1988, 38–50. Deification also reflected a conception of the king's role as source of law and savior of the state; E. R. Goodenough, "The Political Philosophy of Hellenistic Kingship," *Yale Classical Studies* 1, 1928: 66–7.

34 Smith, *Hellenistic*, 49. Smith wishes to attribute this care for the subjects to the values of the Greek polis, but his own discussion of the Nemrut Dağ sculptures of Commagene reveals at least one Seleucid ruler appropriating Fertile Crescent and Iranian royal themes; ibid., 102–4, 121. The Ptolemies of Egypt also promoted their own divinity and their role as "protectors of the people against the administration"; a number of subjects' petitions show "the concept of the king as the direct source of benefit and justice to the populace;" A. E. Samuel, "The Ptolemies and the Ideology of Kingship," in P. Green (ed.) *Hellenistic History and Culture*, Berkeley: University of California Press, 1993, 190–2. An older Greek attitude from Thucydides: "The strong do what they have the power to do and the weak accept what they have to accept," quoted in R. A. Billows, *Kings and Colonists: aspects of Macedonian imperialism*, Leiden: Brill, 1995, 24. On the integration of Egyptian and Persian ideas into Hellenistic concepts of kingship, Goodenough, "Political Philosophy," 78–9.

35 Cylinder of Antiochus I, trans. A. Kuhrt and S. Sherwin-White, "Aspects of Seleucid Royal Ideology: the cylinder of Antiochus I from Borsippa," *Journal of Hellenic Studies* 111, 1991: 77; *ANET*, 317.

36 Quotation F. W. Walbank, "Monarchies and Monarchic Ideas," in *CAH* 7, pt. 1, *The Hellenistic World*, Cambridge: Cambridge University Press, 1984, 82–3, from appeals by Egyptian peasants to Ptolemaic kings for aid against the bureaucracy. By this time the Greeks themselves had turned from democracy to the "unity and order" provided by a single strong and virtuous ruler; ibid., 55–7. Still, Hellenistic philosophers continued to externalize justice as adherence to law (divine or natural or embodied in the true king), in contrast to the Mesopotamian view of justice as the fruit of human interdependence; Goodenough, "Political Philosophy," 65.

37 S. Sherwin-White, "Seleucid Babylonia: a case study for the installation and development of Greek rule," in A. Kuhrt and S. Sherwin-White (eds) *Hellenism in the East: the interaction of Greek and non-Greek civilizations from Syria to Central Asia after Alexander*, London: Duckworth, 1987, 9, 15; J.-F. Salles, "The Arab-Persian Gulf under the Seleucids," in ibid., 88; Sherwin-White and Kuhrt, *From Samarkhand*, 12. JoAnn Scurlock (personal communication) identifies these commercial "fortifications" as caravanserais.

38 R. J. van der Spek, "The Babylonian City," in Kuhrt and Sherwin-White, *Hellenism*, 57–8; Sherwin-White and Kuhrt, *From Samarkhand*, 20, 27, 127, 143–4; G. G. Aperghis, *The Seleukid Royal Economy: the finances and financial administration of the Seleukid Empire*, Cambridge: Cambridge University Press, 2004, 31, 297, 299–300.

39 Briant, *Rois, tributs*, 16, 105; Sherwin-White and Kuhrt, *From Samarkhand*, 47–50, 74, 133, 150, 194.

40 G. Downey, "The Seleucids: the theory of monarchy," in *The Greek Political Experience: studies in honor of William Kelly Prentice*, repr. ed., New York: Russell and Russell, 1969, 162–72; Frye, "Pre-Islamic," 46.

41 J. Harmatta, "Parthia and Elymais in the 2nd Century B.C.," *Acta Antiqua Academiae Scientiarum Hungaricae* 29, 1981: 203–5; M. A. R. Colledge, *The Parthians*, New York: Praeger, 1967, 33; Frye, *Heritage*, 191–2; Frye, "Pre-Islamic," 47.

42 Frye, *Ancient Iran*, 216–17; Colledge, *Parthians*, 87; R. J. Wenke, "Imperial Investments and Agricultural Developments in Parthian and Sassanian Khuzestan: 150 B.C. to A.D. 640," PhD diss., University of Michigan, 1975, 273.

43 On Parthian trade routes: Isidore of Charax, *Parthian Stations, by Isidore of Charax: an account of the overland trade route between the Levant and India in the first century B.C.*, ed. and trans. W. H. Schoff, Philadelphia, PA: Commercial Museum, 1914; repr. Chicago, IL: Ares, 1976.

44 Colledge, *Parthians*, 51, 59, 67, 175; Colledge, *Parthian Art*, London: Paul Elek, 1977, 14. R. Ghirshman, *Iran: Parthians and Sasanians*, trans. S. Gilbert and J. Emmans, [London]: Thames & Hudson, 1962.

45 Frye, *Ancient Iran*, 219, 283; J. Wolski, *L'Empire des Arsacides*, *AcIr* 32, ser. 3, *Textes et Mémoires*, 18, Louvain: Peeters, 1993, 99–108.

46 Babylonians, Jews, and Greeks in Mesopotamia preserved more complete information on Near Eastern rule; E. Yarshater, "Were the Sasanians Heirs to the Achaemenids?" in *La Persia nel Medioevo*, Accademia Nazionale dei Lincei, Quaderno No. 160, Rome: Accademia Nazionale dei

Lincei, 1971, 524. Also Frye, *Heritage*, 197; A. Kuhrt, "Berossus' *Babyloniaka* and Seleucid Rule in Babylonia," in Kuhrt and Sherwin-White, *Hellenism*, 45. On transmission of artistic forms, Wiesehöfer, *Ancient Persia*, 127.

47 The Sasanians are usually described as ignorant of the Achaemenid past, but they may have chosen to adopt new ideological directions; R. N. Frye, *The Golden Age of Persia: the Arabs in the East*, London: Weidenfeld & Nicolson, 1975, 1; Yarshater, "Were the Sasanians?"; G. Gnoli, *The Idea of Iran: an essay on its origin*, Rome: Istituto Italiano per il Medio ed Estremo Oriente, 1989, 124–5; T. Daryaee, "National History or Keyanid History? the nature of Sasanid Zoroastrian historiography," *IranS* 28, 1995: 129–41; M. Roaf, "Persepolitan Echoes in Sasanian Architecture: did the Sasanians attempt to re-create the Achaemenid Empire?" in V. S. Curtis *et al.* (eds) *The Art and Archaeology of Ancient Persia: new light on the Parthian and Sasanian Empires*, London: IB Tauris, 1998, 5.

48 Sasanian inscriptions: M. Back, *Die Sassanidischen Staatsinschriften: Studien zur Orthographie und Phonologie des Mittelpersischen*, AcIr 18, ser. 3, vol. 8, Leiden: Brill, 1978, 279–498.

49 Some of these cities, irrigation works, and fortifications have been located through archaeology, and the Sasanian period was one of general economic expansion; R. M. Adams, "Agriculture and Urban Life in Early Southwestern Iran," *Science* n.s. 136, no. 3511, 13 April 1962: 116–19; P. Christensen, *The Decline of Iranshahr: irrigation and environments in the history of the Middle East, 500 B.C. to A.D. 1500*, trans. S. Sampson, Odense, Denmark: University of Copenhagen Museum Tusculanum Press, 1993, 29.

50 These texts were reworked and preserved by Zoroastrians under Islamic rule or translated into Arabic by Persian Muslims. Their authenticity has been questioned; A. E. Christensen was criticized for using information from Arabic-Islamic sources for the pre-Islamic Sasanians. S. Shaked, however, believes that most Sasanian throne speeches and testaments recorded in Arabic are direct translations of Pahlavi writings; *EIr*, s.v. "Andarz." Many Sasanian monuments survived into the tenth century; the castle of Shīz in Iran was a center for Sasanian history and culture housing manuscripts in Pahlavi. Arabic writers often cited Zoroastrian clergy as information sources, and some Pahlavi texts were included in a tenth-century Islamic bibliography; K. Inostranzev, *Iranian Influence on Moslem Literature*, trans. G. K. Nariman, Bombay: D. B. Taraporevala Sons, 1918, 10, 19–21, 25, 38.

51 Ghirshman, *Iran*, 119; *CHIr*, 3, pt. 2: 694; Wiesehöfer, *Ancient Persia*, 155, 165–7. Falcons as symbols of royal glory and legitimacy: Daryaee, "Religio-Political Propaganda," 44–9.

52 Royal glory was considered to emanate from the god or gods; A. Soudavar, *The Aura of Kings: legitimacy and divine sanction in Iranian kingship*, Costa Mesa, CA: Mazda, 2003. For its representation on Sasanian coinage, Daryaee, "Religio-Political Propaganda," 46–9. Crowns and diadems may also have been symbols of it; P. O. Harper and P. Meyers, *Silver Vessels of the Sasanian Period*, vol. 1: *Royal Imagery*, New York: Metropolitan Museum of Art, 1981, 98, 114; O. Grabar, *Sasanian Silver: late antique and early mediaeval arts of luxury from Iran*, Ann Arbor: University of Michigan Museum of Art, 1967, 69; Smith, *Hellenistic*, 34–8, 42. The royal glory of Mesopotamian kings was not represented in their art.

53 Frye, *Ancient Iran*, 300; Harper and Meyers, *Silver*, 139. Assyrian reliefs and Islamic court art also depict the hunting theme for similar purposes.

54 P. Pourshariati, *Decline and Fall of the Sasanian Empire: the Sasanian-Parthian confederacy and the Arab conquest of Iran*, London: IB Tauris, 2008, 381, 400, 458.

55 *Denkard,* Book III, Chapter 134, trans. M. F. Kanga, "Kingship and Religion in Iran," *Commémoration Cyrus, Hommage universel: actes du congrès de Shiraz 1971*, AcIr 1–3, ser. 1, vols 1–3, Leiden: Brill, 1974, 3: 224. As A. E. Christensen pointed out (*L'Iran*, 261), the *Denkard* embodies the viewpoint of the Zoroastrian clergy after the fall of the Persian Empire. It is not always possible to tell whether its elements are authentically ancient or whether they are later versions or redactions or even later compositions.

56 *Denkard*, Book III, Chapter 134, trans. Kanga, "Kingship," 224–5, amended according to J. de Ménasce (trans.) *Le troisième livre du Dēnkart*, Paris: C. Klincksieck, 1973, 138–9.

57 *Denkard,* Book III, Chapter 134, trans. Kanga, "Kingship," 224. This circle had not only practical but cosmic implications, since the framework of society supported the king in the struggle of Good against Evil; *CHIr*, 4: 557.

58 *Denkard,* Book III, Chapter 134, trans. Kanga, "Kingship," 224. Sasanian scholars now spell this name as *Šahrēwar* (T. Daryaee, personal communication). The Sasanian treasury: Dandamaev and Lukonin, *Cultural*, 206–9; Sasanian finance bureaucracy, Christensen, *L'Iran,* 122–6.

59 *Denkard,* Book III, Chapter 58, trans. P. Gignoux, "Church-State Relations in the Sasanian Period," in *Monarchies and Socio-Religious Traditions in the Ancient Near East*, ed. T. Mikasa, Wiesbaden: Harrassowitz, 1984, 73. Shaked reads the text to say that religion and kingship are "fellow-countrymen," citing a ninth-century Zoroastrian text which calls them "kinsmen"; S. Shaked, "From Iran to Islam: notes on some themes in transmission," *JSAI* 4, 1984: 38–9. Other texts call them "brothers," "sisters," or "twins," possibly the original reading. In the Sasanian period this formula seems to have been a call for the king to control the religion; in the Islamic period it was a recommendation that the religion control the king.

60 "'Ahd Ardashīr," trans. M. Grignaschi, "Quelques spécimens de la littérature sassanide conservés dans les bibliothèques d'Istanbul," *JA* 254, 1966: 70; also R. C. Zaehner, *The Dawn and Twilight of Zoroastrianism*, New York: G. P. Putnam's Sons, 1961, 296–7. The "Testament of Ardashīr" was published and edited by I. Abbas, *'Ahd Ardashīr* (Beirut: Dar Sader, 1967). It is not certain when or by whom the text was written; it was attributed to the early Sasanians by Shaked ("From Iran to Islam: notes," 55n22), to the reign of Khusrau I (531–579) by M. Boyce ("Middle Persian Literature," in B. Spuler and I. Gershevitch (eds) *Handbuch der Orientalistik,* sect. 1, vol. 4, pt 2, fasc. 1, [Leiden: Brill, 1968], 60–1), and to Yazdegird III (633–651), son of Ardashir III (628–630), by Grignaschi; "Quelques spécimens," 2–3. The testament was preserved in Firdausi's *Shāhnāma*, Mas'ūdī's *Murūj al-Dhahab*, and Miskawayh's *Kitāb Tajārib al-'Umam*, and Grignaschi discovered a copy now in a manuscript in Istanbul's Süleymaniye Library (MS K.1608, in "Quelques spécimens," text, 46–67; trans., 68–90); that manuscript also includes other Sasanian works in Arabic translation.

61 "'Ahd Ardashīr," trans. Grignaschi, "Quelques spécimens," 72.

62 Christensen, *L'Empire*, 80, citing B. Sanjana, R. E. Kohiyar, and D. Darab (eds and trans.) *The Dinkard*, Bombay: Duftur Ashkara, 1874–1928, 3: 180ff.; Christensen, *L'Iran*, 261–2, 301.

63 "Dînâ-î Maîrôg-î Khirad," in E. W. West (ed. and trans.) *Pahlavi Texts*, pt 3, Sacred Books of the East, 24, Oxford: Clarendon, 1885, 43; a newer Persian translation: A. Tafazzolī, *Mēnō-ye Xerad*, Tehran, Tus, 1364/1985.

64 Christensen, *L'Iran*, 124.

65 Sanjana (ed.) *Dinkard*, 2: 115; trans. Christensen, *L'Empire*, 80.

66 "'Ahd Ardashīr," trans. Grignaschi, "Quelques spécimens," 73. On the rigidity of the class system, Christensen, *L'Iran*, 316–21; J. K. Choksy, "Sacral Kingship in Sasanian Iran," *Bulletin of the Asia Institute*, n.s. 2, 1988: 37–8. The main criterion for nobility and office-holding was lineage; the members of the topmost ranks were all known and could be listed in a rock inscription; Wiesehöfer, *Ancient Persia*, 171. This social rigidity was also advocated by Plato: E. I. J. Rosenthal, *Averroes' Commentary on Plato's Republic*, Cambridge: Cambridge University Press, 1969, 115, 160.

67 " 'Ahd Ardashīr," trans. Grignaschi, "Quelques spécimens," 74.

68 The literate class contained not just scribes and bureaucrats but accountants, doctors, poets, and astrologers; Christensen, *L'Iran*, 98. Merchants ranked higher in the class system of commercial Sogdia, between aristocrats and workers; Frye, *Golden Age*, 99.

69 "Ayin-i Ardashir," trans. Grignaschi, "Quelques spécimens," 114–15. Christensen (*L'Iran*, 316–22) suggested that resistance against the inflexible class system was a motivation for the Mazdakite movement, and the *Denkard* recorded that the hierarchical system was reinforced after the Mazdakite movement failed; D. M. Madan (ed.) *The Complete Text of the Pahlavi Dinkard*, Bombay: Society for the Promotion of Researches into the Zoroastrian Religion, 1911, 412–15; trans. Zaehner, *Dawn*, 176.

70 According to its translator, the "Letter of Tansar" was first written in the time of Ardashir I, adapted in the time of Anushirvan, translated into Arabic with comments by the Umayyad scribe Ibn al-Muqaffa', and reworked and translated into modern Persian by Ibn Isfandiyar. The final version, the only one extant, contains these statements; M. Boyce (trans.) *The Letter of Tansar*, Literary and Historical Texts from Iran, 1, Rome: Istituto Italiano per il Medio ed Estremo Oriente, 1968, 39, 44.

71 " 'Ahd Ardashīr," trans. Grignaschi, "Quelques spécimens," 77.

72 Choksy, "Sacral Kingship," 38; see also C. Watkins, *How to Kill a Dragon: aspects of Indo-European poetics*, New York: Oxford University Press, 1995. See *Denkard,* Book III, ch. 46, trans. de Ménasce, *Troisième livre du Denkart*, 57–8, trans. from French by J. E. Woods.

73 "Ayin-i Ardashīr," trans. Grignaschi, "Quelques spécimens," 119.

74 Grignaschi, "Quelques spécimens," 7–8; Boyce, "Middle Persian," 59–60; this practice performed the same function as the Sumerian and Assyrian kings' wall inscriptions. Anushirvan is also reported

to have collected stories of the ancient Iranian kings in the *Khudaynamag* or *Book of Kings*; J. Rypka, *History of Iranian Literature*, Dordrecht, Netherlands: D. Reidel, 1968, 55.

75 "Kārnāmag-i Anūshirvān," as contained in Miskawayh's *Tajārib al Umam* (trans. Grignaschi, "Quelques spécimens," 16–45). Miskawayh also mentions a Life of Ardashīr ("Kārnāmag-i Ardashīr") partly preserved in a Pahlavi text and in quotations by Arabic historians.

76 "Kārnāmag-i Anūshirvān," trans. Grignaschi, "Quelques spécimens," 25–6.

77 Ibid., 23.

78 B. I. Marshak, "The Decoration of Some Late Sasanian Silver Vessels and Its Subject-Matter," in Curtis, Hillenbrand, and Rogers, *Art*, London: IB Tauris, 1998, 85.

79 Christensen, *Decline*, 38, 73–4, 81–3, 248; P. Crone, "Kavād's Heresy and Mazdak's Revolt," *Iran* 29, 1991: 21–42. Revenue demands rose even higher under the later ruler Khusrau II Parviz, but he was deposed for excessive tyranny; R. M. Adams, *Land behind Baghdad: a history of settlement on the Diyala plains*, Chicago, IL: University of Chicago Press, 1965, 71.

80 Pourshariati, *Decline*, 342–92, esp. 351–7; 457.

81 "Kārnāmag-i Anūshirvān," trans. Grignaschi, "Quelques spécimens," 17–18, 20–3. These reforms were begun by Khusrau's father Kavād I (488–531). Kavād also appointed officials known as "protectors of the poor," advocates (mages functioning as judges) for those living in virtuous poverty; J. de Ménasce, "Le protecteur des pauvres dans l'Iran sassanide," in *Mélanges d'orientalisme offerts à Henri Massé*, Tehran: Imprimerie de l'Université, 1963, 282–7. On these officials and their antecedents, A. Perikhanian (trans.) *The Book of a Thousand Judgements (a Sasanian law-book)*, trans. from Russian by N. Garsoian, Costa Mesa, CA: Mazda, 1997, 214, 354; S. Shaked, "Some Legal and Administrative Terms of the Sasanian Period," *Monumentum H. S. Nyberg*, AcIr 4–7, ser. 2, vols 1–4, Leiden: Brill, 1975, 2: 213–15.

82 Christensen, *Decline*, 38; Z. Rubin, "The Reforms of Khusro Anūshirwān," in A. Cameron (ed.) *The Byzantine and Early Islamic Near East, III: states, resources and armies*, Princeton, NJ: Darwin, 1995, 227–97; Frye, *Heritage*, 218; Frye, *Ancient Iran*, 324–6. Whereas Frye characterized this reform as the inception of a service nobility in the aftermath of the egalitarian Mazdakite movement, Pourshariati sees it as injustice to the strong and a cause of the Sasanians' fall; Pourshariati, *Decline*, 85–94, 456. The Sasanian tax system also included personal taxes, extraordinary levies, and "gifts." The three upper classes (priests, nobles and soldiers, and bureaucrats) were exempt from taxation, but not from gifts; Christensen, *L'Iran*, 367.

83 "Kārnāmag-i Anūshirvān," trans. Grignaschi, "Quelques spécimens," 22.

84 Sasanian and Achaemenid achievements in the provision of bridges, roads, and the post system: A. Mez, *The Renaissance of Islam*, trans. S. Khuda Bakhsh and D. S. Margoliouth, London: Luzac, 1937, repr. New York: AMS Press, 1975, 494–5, 501–2.

85 Rypka, *History*, 55–6; I. G. N. Keith-Falconer (trans.), *Kalilah and Dimnah, or, The Fables of Bidpai*, Cambridge: Cambridge University Press, 1885; repr. Amsterdam: Philo Press, 1970. Arguments for the identity of Buzurgmihr with Burzöë, the translator of the book, are presented by A. E. Christensen, "La légende du sage Buzurjmihr," *AcOr* 8, 1930: 81–128; against it is Shaked, "From Iran to Islam: notes," 51n8.

86 Later Arabic sources related that Anushirvan's seal for tax matters was engraved with the word "justice," and that the same word appeared on a seal of the mythical Persian king Jamshid which was used on complaints against iniquity; S. Shaked, "From Iran to Islam: on some symbols of royalty," *JSAI* 7, 1986: 86.

87 Christensen, *L'Iran*, 381; see Frye, *Golden Age*, 17.

88 "Kitāb al-Tāj," trans. Grignaschi, "Quelques spécimens," 129–30. Grignaschi proposed (ibid., 4–5) that this portion of the manuscript he translated was a copy of the lost *Book of the Crown* (*Kitāb al-Tāj*) by Ibn al-Muqaffā' and was compiled from information received from elderly Persian informants.

89 Boyce, trans., *Letter*, 49.

90 Christensen, *L'Iran*, 300-3; 374–9; M. G. Morony, *Iraq after the Muslim Conquest*, Princeton, NJ: Princeton University Press, 1984, 85. Islamic reports on Sasanian judicial processes are confirmed by surviving Sasanian records of procedures applied to Christian martyrs (Frye, *Ancient Iran*, 314). For the clergy's role in administration, S. Shaked, "Administrative Functions of Priests in the Sasanian Period," in G. Gnoli and A. Panaino (eds) *Proceedings of the First European Conference of Iranian Studies*, pt 1, *Old and Middle Iranian Studies*, Rome: Istituto Italiano per il Medio ed Estremo Oriente, 1990, 261–73. Chinese antecedents of Anushirvan's bell: E. A. Kracke, Jr., "Early Visions of Justice for the Humble in East and West," *JAOS* 16, 1976: 492–8.

4 The Islamic empire

1 A detailed survey of Islamic history is M. G. S. Hodgson, *The Venture of Islam: conscience and history in a world civilization*, 3 vols, Chicago, IL: University of Chicago Press, 1974. Reference: H. A. R. Gibb, J. H. Kramers, E. Lévi-Provonçal, J. Schacht, B. Lewis, and C. Pellat (eds) *The Encyclopaedia of Islam*, 2nd ed., Leiden: Brill, 1954–2004 (hereafter *EI2*).

2 The term "Islamicate" refers to a civilization in which Islam does not determine everything, but where cultural elements even in non-religious spheres are associated with the dominant religion; Hodgson, *Venture*, 1: 57–60. On Islamicate society: M. G. Morony, *Iraq after the Muslim Conquest*, Princeton, NJ: Princeton University Press, 1984, 507–26; I. M. Lapidus, "The Arab Conquests and the Formation of Islamic Society," in G. H. A. Juynboll (ed.) *Studies on the First Century of Islamic Society*, Carbondale: Southern Illinois University Press, 1982, 49–72.

3 This process gave Islamic civilization a universal appeal it might not otherwise have had. "Had Islam continued to be ruled from the secluded oases of central Arabia or from a poor and inaccessible region like the central Maghrib, it might have preserved a certain religious purity, but it would never have become the lasting cultural force it did become"; O. Grabar, *The Formation of Islamic Art*, New Haven, CT: New Haven, CT: Yale University Press, 1973, 35. That this argument must be made is a measure of the theoretical completeness of Arab-Islamic cultural hegemony.

4 *EI2*, s.v. "Ḳānūn, iii – Financial and Public Administration"; see E. I. J. Rosenthal, *Political Thought in Medieval Islam: an introductory outline*, Cambridge: Cambridge University Press, 1962, repr. Westport, CT: Greenwood, 1985, 22. *Ḥadīth* and other evidence confirms Wellhausen's argument that the Arab conquest and the Islamic faith were two separate projects for about the first hundred years; S. Bashear, *Arabs and Others in Early Islam*, Princeton, NJ: Darwin, 1997, 116, 118; F. M. Donner, "From Believers to Muslims: confessional self-identity in the early Islamic community," *Al-Abḥāth* 50–1, 2002–3: 9–53.

5 Qur'ān 107: 1–3, English version A. J. Arberry, *The Koran Interpreted*, New York: Macmillan, 1955, 2: 351. Caring for widows and orphans and the weak was similarly lauded in the Bible (e.g. James 1: 27) and became one aspect of the Christian definition of justice; W. S. Monroe, "*Via Iustitiae*: the Biblical sources of justice in Gregory of Tours," in K. Mitchell and I. N. Wood (eds) *The World of Gregory of Tours*, Leiden: Brill, 2002, 105.

6 "As for the orphan, do not oppress him, and as for the beggar, scold him not"; Qur'ān 93: 10–11, Arberry, *Koran*, 2: 342. The idea of justice as a mean or balance (*qist*), present in both Greek and Persian thought, was also influential in the Islamic concept of justice. The Qur'ān, however, usually advocated justice in the sense of bearing witness without bias (Qur'ān, 4: 135, 5: 8), and in the sphere of Islamic law and the courts, justice (*'adāla*, defined as uprightness or probity) tended to be regarded more as a quality of the individual participants than as a quality of the outcome, whereas the word injustice (*ẓulm*) carried the Circle's definition of justice; F. J. Ziadeh, "Integrity (*'Adālah*) in Classical Islamic Law," in N. Heer (ed.) *Islamic Law and Jurisprudence*, Seattle: University of Washington Press, 1990, 73–93; M. Ayoub, "The Islamic Concept of Justice," in N. H. Barazangi, M. R. Zaman, and O. Afzal (eds) *Islamic Identity and the Struggle for Justice*, Gainesville: University Press of Florida, 1996, 19; L. Rosen, *The Justice of Islam: comparative perspectives on Islamic law and society*, Oxford: Oxford University Press, 2000, 155. In later years the usage changed, and *'adl* or *'adāla* (*adâlet*) carried the common meaning of justice, though always with the added nuance of integrity.

7 This dispute generated the split between Sunni and Shi'i Muslims; Abū Ja'far Muḥammad b. Jarīr al-Ṭabarī, *The History of al-Ṭabarī*, vol. 15: *The Crisis of the Early Caliphate*, trans. R. S. Humphreys, Albany: State University of New York Press, 1988, 221–3.

8 EI2, s.v. "*maslaḥa*," "*istiḥsān* and *istiṣlāḥ*"; see also I. A. Bagby, "The Issue of *Maslaḥah* in Classical Islamic Legal Theory," *IJIAS* 2, 1985: 1–11. *'Urf*, customary law, was also seen as safeguarding communal welfare.

9 M. A. Cook, *Commanding Right and Forbidding Wrong in Islamic Thought*, Cambridge: Cambridge University Press, 2000. Quotation from 'Ubayd Allāh b. al-Ḥasan al-'Anbarī (d.784/5), trans. M. Q. Zaman, *Religion and Politics under the Early 'Abbāsids: the emergence of the proto-Sunnī elite*, Leiden: Brill, 1997, 86. This is clearly the same as the ancient Near Eastern concept of justice; in contrast to Gerber and others who see "Iranian" ideas as an influence from "outside" Islam, I see at least this important element as already "inside." Cf. H. Gerber, *Islamic Law and Culture, 1600–1840*, Leiden: Brill, 1999, 50.

10 A. K. S. Lambton, *State and Government in Medieval Islam, an introduction to the study of Islamic political theory: the jurists*, Oxford: Oxford University Press, 1981, 1–42. On the title *khalīfat Allāh* see I. Goldziher, "Du sens propre des expressions Ombre de Dieu, Khalife de Dieu, pour designer les chefs d'Islam," *Revue de l'histoire des religions* 35, 1897: 335–8; P. Crone and M. Hinds, *God's Caliph: religious authority in the first centuries of Islam*, Cambridge: Cambridge University Press, 1986, 37; A. al-Azmeh, *Muslim Kingship: power and the sacred in Muslim, Christian, and Pagan polities*, London: IB Tauris, 1997, 74–6. Some early commentators thought the caliph's function on earth was "to cultivate"; W. al-Qāḍī, "The Term 'Khalifa' in Early Exegetical Literature," *WI* 28, 1988: 407.

11 Arabic had a special word for this concept, *laqāḥ*; M. Ullmann, *Wörterbuch der klassischen arabischen Sprache*, Wiesbaden: Harrassowitz, 1978–, 2: 1075–6, s.v. *laqāḥ*. At the rise of Islam, state formation was spreading into areas that had previously been stateless and tribally organized, and the incorporation of the Arabs was about to occur in any case; F. M. Donner, *The Early Islamic Conquests*, Princeton, NJ: Princeton University Press, 1981, 39–43; I. M. Lapidus, "Tribes and State Formation in Islamic History," in P. S. Khoury and J. Kostiner (eds) *Tribes and State Formation in the Middle East*, Berkeley: University of California Press, 1990, 26. Davis shows in the case of modern Libya how statelessness and anti-state attitudes flow logically from tribal politics; J. Davis, *Libyan Politics: an account of the Zuwaya and their government*, London: IB Tauris, 1987. The rejection of monarchy is not unique to Islam but is shared with Hebrew and Greek thought; J. Dakhlia, *Le Divan des rois: le politique et le religieux dans l'Islam*, Paris: Aubier, 1998, 83.

12 al-Ṭabarī, "Tā'rīkh," trans. B. Lewis, "Monarchy in the Middle East," in J. Kostiner (ed.) *Middle East Monarchies: the challenge of modernity*, Boulder, CO: Lynne Reinner, 2000, 17.

13 Qur'ān 38: 25–6; Arberry, *Koran*, 1: 160.

14 al-Ṭabarī, *History*, 15: 6; O. Grabar, *Sasanian Silver: late antique and early mediaeval arts of luxury from Iran*, Ann Arbor: University of Michigan Museum of Art, 1967, 20–1. Other political and intellectual interpretations of Islamic communal leadership were simultaneously being made, by the Khārijīs, for example.

15 It has been suggested that for that reason monarchy was not embraced with sufficient thoroughness to create a workable Islamic politics; P. Crone, *Slaves on Horses: the evolution of the Islamic polity*, Cambridge: Cambridge University Press, 1980. However, religious thought in Islam, based, as Hodgson showed, on populist and anti-aristocratic principles, tended to write off all government as a priori unjust; F. Rosenthal, "Political Justice and the Just Ruler," in J. L. Kraemer and I. Alon (eds) *Religion and Government in the World of Islam*, *IOS* 10, 1983: 96.

16 M. G. Morony, "Conquerors and Conquered: Iran," in Juynboll, *Studies*, 74–5; I. Goldziher, "'Arab and 'Ajam," in S. M. Stern (ed.) *Muslim Studies*, trans. C. R. Barber and S. M. Stern, London: G. Allen & Unwin, 1889–90, 1: 109–10.

17 B. Spuler, "Iran: the persistent heritage," in G. E. von Grunebaum (ed.) *Unity and Variety in Muslim Civilization*, Chicago, IL: University of Chicago Press, 1955, 171. Early Muslims struggled to keep the Arabs from imitating non-Arab ways; Bashear, *Arabs*, 33–6.

18 O. Grabar, "Notes sur les cérémonies umayyades," in M. Rosen-Ayalon (ed.) *Studies in Memory of Gaston Wiet*, Jerusalem: Institute of Asian and African Studies, Hebrew University of Jerusalem, 1977, 53–7; Grabar, *Formation*, 148–9.

19 A. A. Faruqhi, *Early Muslim Historiography: a study of early transmitters of Arab history from the rise of Islam up to the end of the Umayyad period, 612–750 A.D.*, Delhi: Idarah-i Adabiyat-i Dehli, 1979, 187.

20 "Ecloga of Leo the Isaurian," trans. E. Barker, *Social and Political Thought in Byzantium: from Justinian I to the last Palaeologus*, Oxford: Clarendon, 1957, 85; H. Ahrweiler, *L'idéologie politique de l'Empire byzantin*, Paris: Presses universitaires de France, 1975, 25–6. Byzantine emperors of other origins did not describe justice in the Circle's terms.

21 D. Sourdel, "Questions de cérémonial abbaside," *REI* 28, 1960: 123–32; O. Grabar, "Al-Mushatta, Baghdād, and Wāsiṭ," in J. Kritzek and R. B. Winder (eds) *The World of Islam: studies in honor of P. K. Hitti*, London: Macmillan, 1959, 99–108; Sourdel, "Notes," 52; Sourdel, *Formation*, 58, 153; Morony, *Iraq*, 10, 74–9. More broadly, M. Azarnoush, "From Persepolis to al-Fustat: continuation of Achaemenid architectural concepts," in B. G. Fragner C. Fragner, G. Gnoli, R. Haag-Higuchi, M. Maggi, and P. Orsatti (eds) *Proceedings of the Second European Conference of Iranian Studies*, Rome: Istituto Italiano per il Medio ed Estremo Oriente, 1995, 47–52. Gardens: A. M. Watson, "Botanical Gardens in the Early Islamic World," in E. Robbins and S. Sandahl (eds) *Corolla Torontonensis:*

studies in honour of Ronald Morton Smith, Toronto: TSAR and The Centre for Korean Studies, 1994, 105–11. On Iraq's economy in this period: Christensen, *Decline*, 85–92.

22 Quotations from H. Ringgren, "Some Religious Aspects of the Caliphate," in *The Sacral Kingship*, Studies in the History of Religions, 4 (Supplements to *Numen*), Leiden: Brill, 1959, 737–48; W. Thomson, "The Character of Early Semitic Sects," in S. Löwinger and J. Somogyi (eds) *Ignace Goldziher Memorial Volume*, Budapest: Globus, 1948; Jerusalem: Rubin Mass, 1958, 1: 91–2. A *ḥadīth* reported that 'Umar I called Mu'āwiya "the Khusrau of the Arabs"; Bashear, *Arabs*, 18.

23 Goldziher, "Ombre de Dieu," 335; quotation from Akhṭāl, trans. H. Lammens, "Le chantre des Omiades: notes biographiques et littéraires sur le poète arabe Aḫtal," *JA*, ser. 9, vol. 4, 1894: 163–4; Crone and Hinds, *God's Caliph*, 9; quotation from Al-Walīd II, trans. Ringgren, "Religious Aspects," 740. Crone (*God's Rule*, 41–2) attributes the use of these images to messianism, ignoring their relationship to the Near Eastern concept of state.

24 Yazīd III's accession speech, trans. Crone and Hinds, *God's Caliph*, 68; G. R. Hawting, *The First Dynasty of Islam: the Umayyad caliphate*, AD *661–750*, London: Croom Helm, 1986, 95. Proclamation by 'Abd al-Ḥamīd, trans. W. al-Qāḍī, "The Religious Foundation of Late Umayyad Ideology and Practice," in *Saber Religioso y Poder Político en el Islam*, Madrid: Agencia Española de Cooperación Internacional, 1994, 267.

25 Abū Ja'far Muḥammad b. Jarīr al-Ṭabarī, *The History of al-Ṭabarī*, vol. 18, *Between Civil Wars: The Caliphate of Mu'āwiyah*, trans. M. G. Morony, Albany: State University of New York Press, 1987, 80–1.

26 al-Ṭabarī, *History*, 18: 84. On pastoral imagery in early Arabic poetry see J. Stetkevych, *The Zephyrs of Najd: the poetics of nostalgia in the classical Arabic nasib*, Chicago, IL: University of Chicago Press, 1993.

27 Unattributed quotation, trans. B. Lewis, "On the Revolutions in Early Islam," *SI* 32, 1970: 225; see I. Friedlander, "The Heterodoxies of the Shi'ites in the Presentation of Ibn Hazm," *JAOS* 28, 1907: 43–4. This concept reappears in later works like the twelfth-century Sufi Muhyī al-Dīn b. al-'Arabī's *Les illuminations de La Mecque = The Meccan Illuminations: textes choisis = selected texts*, trans. M. Chodkiewicz, Paris: Sindbad, 1988, 121; other texts: J. A. Williams (ed.) *Themes of Islamic Civilization*, Berkeley: University of California Press, 1971, 66–7, 194–6, 206–7, 219.

28 Attributed to the fifth Imām Muḥammad al-Bāqir: A. A. Sachedina, *Islamic Messianism: the idea of Mahdi in Twelver Shi'ism*, Albany: State University of New York Press, 1981, 39. Other *ḥadīth*s about the *mahdī*: Ibn Khaldūn, *The Muqaddimah: an introduction to history*, trans. F. Rosenthal, New York: Pantheon, 1958, 2: 170, 168, 181.

29 "The Characteristics of the Imama," from *Kitāb al-Hujja*, in *al-'Usūl min al-Kāfi* by Muḥammad b. Yā'qub al-Kulaynī (d.940), trans. Sachedina, *Islamic Messianism*, 188–92. On the figure of 'Alī, see M. Dorraj, *From Zarathustra to Khomeini: populism and dissent in Iran*, Boulder, CO: Lynne Reinner, 1990, 44–66.

30 Exhortation of Ḥamza, *Tārīkh-i Sistān*, ed. M. T. Bahār, Tehran: Zavvār, 1935, 169, trans. J. S. Meisami, *Persian Historiography: to the end of the twelfth century*, Edinburgh: Edinburgh University Press, 1999, 114–15.

31 P. L. Heck, *The Construction of Knowledge in Islamic Civilization: Qudāma b. Ja'far and his* Kitāb al-kharāj wa-ṣinā'at al-kitāba, Leiden: Brill, 2002, 147. G. Frantz-Murphy, "A Comparison of the Arabic and Earlier Egyptian Contract Formularies, Part II: terminology in the Arabic warranty and the idiom of clearing/cleaning," *JNES* 44, 1985: 99–114; W. B. Hallaq, "Model *Shurūṭ* Works and the Dialectic of Doctrine and Practice," *ILS* 2, 1995: 113&n14. Umayyad contributions to the prosperity of the land: O. Grabar, "Umayyad 'Palace' and the 'Abbasid 'Revolution'," *SI* 18, 1963: 5–18; Umayyad irrigation works: E. Ashtor, *A Social and Economic History of the Near East in the Middle Ages*, Berkeley: University of California Press, 1976, 46–8.

32 Documents in A. Grohmann, *Arabic Papyri in the Egyptian Library*, Cairo: Egyptian Library Press, 1938, 3: 186, 191 (surveyors' reports), 195–203 (land survey); H. I. Bell, "Translations of the Greek Aphrodito Papyri in the British Museum," *Der Islam* 2, 1911: 272–3; 3 (1912): 133–40, 369–73; 4 (1913): 87–96; C. J. Kraemer, Jr., *Excavations at Nessana*, vol. 3, *Non-Literary Papyri*, Princeton, NJ: Princeton University Press, 1958, 170; F. M. Donner, "The Formation of the Islamic State," *JAOS* 106, 1980: 287, 292.

33 Letter, trans. R. G. Khoury, *Chrestomathie de papyrologie arabe: documents relatifs à la vie privée, sociale et administrative dans les premiers siècles islamiques, préparée par Adolf Grohmann*, Leiden: Brill, 1993, 157, 159–60. Similar injunctions appear in documents in Grohmann, *Arabic Papyri*, 3: 14; Bell,

"Translations," 276, 281; N. Abbott, *The Ḳurrah Papyri from Aphrodito in the Oriental Institute*, Studies in Ancient Oriental Civilizations, 15, Chicago, IL: University of Chicago Press, 1938, 65–6.

34 Documents in Grohmann, *Arabic Papyri*, 3: 70, 111; U. Rebstock, "Observations on the Diwan al-Kharaj and the Assessment of Taxes in Umayyad Syria," in M. A. Bakhit and R. Schick (eds) *The History of Bilad al-Sham During the Umayyad Period (Fourth International Conference, 1987)*, Amman: Bilad al-Sham History Committee, 1989, 238; G. Khan, *Arabic Papyri: selected material from the Khalili Collection*, Oxford: Nour Foundation and Oxford University Press, 1992, 138; Kraemer, *Excavations at Nessana*, 212–13. Donner, "Formation," 285, 287, 288–9, 292, 293.

35 Document in Bell, "Translations," 2, 1911, 281–82. Calling on the ruler as a source of justice was one way to control the behavior of officials; Heck, *Construction*, 167, 171–2.

36 Abū Ja'far Muḥammad b. Jarīr al-Ṭabarī, *The History of al-Ṭabarī*, vol. 26, *The Waning of the Umayyad Caliphate*, trans. C. Hillenbrand, Albany: State University of New York Press, 1989, 75.

37 Letter, trans. D. S. Margoliouth, "Omar's Instructions to the Kadi," *JRAS*, 1910: 311–12; see R. B. Serjeant, "The Caliph 'Umar's Letters to Abū Mūsā al-Ash'arī and Mu'āwiya," *JSS* 29, 1984: 65–79. See Chs 2 and 3 for parallel texts.

38 H. A. R. Gibb, "The Evolution of Government in Early Islam," *SI* 4, 1955: 1–17. Works purporting to be translated directly from earlier texts were often actually recombinations of other materials: al-Azmeh, *Muslim Kingship*, 84–9.

39 M. Grignaschi, "Les 'Rasā'il 'Āristāṭālīsa 'ilā-l-Iskandar' de Sālim Abū-l-'Alā' et l'activité culturelle à l'époque omayyade," *BEO* 19, 1965–6: 7–83; Grignaschi, "Le roman épistolaire classique conservé dans la version arabe de Sālim Abū-l-'Alā'," *Le Muséon* 80, 1967: 211–64; S. M. Stern, *Aristotle on the World State*, Columbia, SC: University of South Carolina Press, 1968, 2&n2. Admonitions to justice: J. Bielawski, trans., *Lettre d'Aristote à Alexandre sur la politique envers les cités*, Wroclaw: Polskiej Akademii Nauk, 1970. The romance of Alexander had already been translated into Armenian and Pahlavi and from the latter into Syriac; T. Hägg, "The Oriental Reception of Greek Novels: a survey with some preliminary considerations," *Symbolae Osloenses* 61, 1986: 104, 123n23.

40 Grignaschi, "Rasā'il 'Āristāṭālīsa," 9–12; M. Grignaschi, "Un roman épistolaire gréco-arabe: la correspondence entre Aristote et Alexandre," in M. Bridges and J. C. Bürgel (eds) *The Problematics of Power: Eastern and Western representations of Alexander the Great*, Bern: P. Lang, 1996, 109n1.

41 Abū al-'Alā' Sālim, "Letters of Aristotle to Alexander," trans. M. Grignaschi, "La 'Siyâsatu-l-Âmmiyya' et l'influence iranienne sur la pensée politique islamique," *Monumentum H. S. Nyberg*, AcIr 6, ser. 2, Leiden: Brill, 1975, 3: 191; the Arabic reads: "A'lam 'an qawām al-qurra' bi'l-mudun wa-qawām al-mudun bi'l-ḥusūn wa-qawām al-ḥusūn bi'l-rijāl wa-qawām al-rijāl bi'l-zād wa'l-salāḥ wa-lan tajad dhālik illā bi'l-'adl." The concept of justice here is reciprocal, going well beyond the parallel passage adduced by Grignaschi from the *Kitāb al-Tāj*, which was a power circle like that of the *Denkard*, also starting with peasants: "From kharaj flows wealth, by wealth exist armies, by armies the enemy is suppressed and power is [conferred]"; trans. "Quelques spécimens," 104.

42 Abd al-Ḥamīd, "Risāla ilá al-Kuttāb," in M. Kurd Ali (ed.) *Rasā'il al-Bulaghā'*, Cairo: Dār al-Kutub al-'Arabiyya al-Kubrá, 1913, 172–6; I. Abbas (ed.) *'Abd al-Ḥamīd bin Yaḥyá al-Kātib wa-mā tabaqqā min rasā'ilihī wa-rasā'il Sālim Abi al-'Alā'*, Amman: Dār al-Shurūq, 1988, 281–7; T. Khalidi, *Arabic Historical Thought in the Classical Period*, Cambridge: Cambridge University Press, 1994, 87–96. Secretaries and their literary works: Muḥammad b. Isḥāq b. al-Nadīm, *The Fihrist of al-Nadīm: a tenth-century survey of Muslim culture*, ed. and trans. B. Dodge, New York: Columbia University Press, 1970, 1: 256–306.

43 The early Muslim government's Persian scribal functionaries and their translation of administrative documents and literary works from Persian to Arabic: M. Sprengling, "From Persian to Arabic," *American Journal of Semitic Languages and Literatures* 56, 1939: 175–224, 325–36; 57, 1940: 302–5. The many cases of hereditary service in government formed a natural route of transmission for administrative practice and ideology; Morony, *Iraq*, 97, 171, 176, 179, 210. Rulers employed non-Arab scribal families because their dependence made them trustworthy; J. Lassner, *The Shaping of 'Abbāsid Rule*, Princeton, NJ: Princeton University Press, 1980, 98–106.

44 J. D. Latham, "The Beginnings of Arabic Prose Literature: the epistolary genre," in A. F. L. Beeston, T. M. Johnstone, R. B. Serjeant and G. R. Smith (eds) *Arabic Literature to the End of the Umayyad Period*, The Cambridge History of Arabic Literature, 1, Cambridge: Cambridge University Press, 1983, 163.

45 EI2, s.v. "Barāmika"; L. Bouvat, *Les Barmécides d'après les historiens arabes et perses*, Paris: Ernest Leroux, 1912; D. W. Biddle, "The Development of the Bureaucracy of the Islamic Empire during the Late Umayyad and Early Abbasid Period," PhD diss., University of Texas, 1972, 68–72.

46 Spuler, "Iran: the persistent heritage," 172–4; D. Gutas, *Greek Thought, Arabic Culture: the Graeco-Arabic translation movement in Baghdad and early 'Abbāsid society (2nd–4th/8th–10th centuries)*, London: Routledge, 1998, 29.
47 Abū al-Ḥasan 'Alī b. al-Ḥusayn al-Mas'ūdī, *The Meadows of Gold: the Abbasids*, trans. and ed. P. Lunde and C. Stone, London: Kegan Paul International, 1989, 25.
48 Crone and Hinds, *God's Caliph*, 135; E. L. Daniel, *The Political and Social History of Khurasan under Abbasid Rule, 747–820*, Minneapolis, MN: Bibliotheca Islamica, 1979, 178; A. Arazi and 'A. El'ad, "'L'épître à l'armée': al-Ma'mūn et la seconde da'wa," *SI* 66, 1988: 45–6.
49 J. S. Meisami, "Places in the Past: the poetics/politics of nostalgia," *Edebiyat* 8, 1998: 76. Khwārazmī, cited in A. Mez, *The Renaissance of Islam*, trans. S. Khuda Bakhsh and D. S. Margoliouth, London: Luzac, 1936, repr. 1957, 109; H. Kennedy, "The Barmakid Revolution in Islamic Government," in *History and Literature in Iran: Persian and Islamic studies in honour of P. W. Avery*, ed. C. Melville, London: British Academic Press of IB Tauris, 1990, 1998, 93.
50 Al-Manṣūr's administrative developments: Abū Ja'far Muḥammad b. Jarīr al-Ṭabarī, *The History of al-Ṭabarī: The Early 'Abbāsī Empire*, trans. J. A. Williams, Albany: State University of New York Press, 1989, 2: 7, 38; on his simple lifestyle, ibid., 2: 37, 41 (simple clothing), 2: 21 (austere bedroom), 2: 29 (no wine at table). On later caliphs, Sourdel, "Questions," 136–46.
51 Goldziher, "Ombre de Dieu," 333–5; Ringgren, "Religious Aspects," 745–6.
52 Al-Buḥturī, for the caliph al-Mutawakkil (847–861), trans. S. Sperl, "Islamic Kingship and Arabic Panegyric Poetry in the Early 9th Century," *Journal of Arabic Literature* 8, 1977: 24.
53 By Abū Tammām (d.858), trans. O. Petit and W. Voisin, *La poésie arabe classique: études textuelles*, Paris: Publisud, avec le Centre Nationale des Lettres, 1989, 67. Abū Tammām's combination of Islamic and pre-Islamic symbols of legitimacy: S. P. Stetkevych, *Abū Tammām and the Poetics of the 'Abbāsid Age*, Leiden: Brill, 1991, 115–30.
54 Isḥāq al-Mawsilī, for the caliph Hārūn al-Rashīd (786–809), trans. J. D. Carlyle, in W. A. Clouston (ed.), *Arabian Poetry for English Readers*, Glasgow: n.p., 1881, 110; Isḥāq al-Mawsilī was the principal musician at the court of Baghdad. Hārūn as a source of rain: Crone and Hinds, *God's Caliph*, 82–152.
55 Al-Manṣūr, in Abū Ja'far Muḥammad b. Jarīr al-Ṭabarī, *The History of al-Ṭabarī*, vol. 29, *Al-Manṣūr and al-Mahdī*, trans. H. Kennedy, Albany: State University of New York Press, 1990, 106, 150; A. K. S. Lambton, "Islamic Political Thought," in J. Schacht and C. E. Bosworth (eds) *The Legacy of Islam*, 2nd ed., Oxford: Oxford University Press, 1979, c1974, 417.
56 Al-Ma'mūn, in al-Ṭabarī, *History*, 32: 227–8.
57 M. H. Khan, "Mediaeval Muslim Political Theories of Rebellion against the State," *IC* 18, 1944: 43. The Qarmatian movement went so far as to espouse community of goods: S. M. Stern, "Ismā'īlīs and Qarmatians," in *Studies in Early Ismā'īlism*, Jerusalem: Magnes Press, 1983, 289–98. Also under the name Qarmatian was a movement in Bahrain that attempted to enforce prosperity and equal economic opportunity: Hodgson, *Venture*, 1: 491.
58 See Ch. 3; F. Gabrieli, "L'opera di Ibn al-Muqaffa'," *Rivista degli studi orientali* 13, 1931–2: 197–247; G. Richter, *Studien zur Geschichte der älteren arabischen Fürstenspiegel*, Leipzig: J. C. Hinrichs, 1932; J. D. Latham, "Ibn al-Muqaffa' and Early 'Abbasid Prose," in J. Ashtiany, T. M. Johnstone, J. D. Latham, R. B. Serjeant and G. R. Smith (eds) *Abbasid Belles-Lettres*, The Cambridge History of Arabic Literature, 2, Cambridge: Cambridge University Press, 1990, 48–77; EI2, s.v. "Ibn al-Muqaffā'". Of his works we possess only portions, none of which indisputably belongs in its current form to Ibn al-Muqaffā' himself.
59 Abdallāh b. al-Muqaffā', *Adab al-kabīr*, in Kurd Ali, *Rasā'il al-Bulaghā'*, 55–114; J. Tardy, "Traduction d'*Al-adab al-kabīr* d'Ibn al-Muqaffa'," *AI* 27, 1993: 181–223.
60 Abdallāh b. al-Muqaffā', *Risāla fi al-saḥāba*, in Kurd Ali, *Rasā'il al-Bulaghā'*, 120–31; see Abdallāh b. al-Muqaffā', *"Conseilleur" du Calife (Kitāb al-Saḥāba)*, ed. and trans. C. Pellat, Paris: G.-P. Maisonneuve et Larose, 1976. Ibn al-Muqaffā''s sources: M. Zakeri, "'Alī ibn 'Ubaida ar-Raihānī: a forgotten belletrist (*adīb*) and Pahlavi translator," *Oriens* 34, 1994: 92–7, 101.
61 C. Pellat, "Une charge contre les secrétaires d'état attribuée à Ǧāḥiẓ," *Hespéris* 43, 1956: 35; translation in C. Pellat, *The Life and Works of Jāḥiẓ: translations of selected texts*, trans. D. M. Hawke, Berkeley: University of California Press, 1969, 274. Most of these works survive only in quotations by later authors or citations in the tenth-century bibliography of Ibn al-Nadīm, *Fihrist*, 1: 259–60.
62 Lambton, *State*, 44.

63 M. J. Kister, "The Social and Political Implications of Three Traditions in the *Kitab al-kharādj* of Yahya b. Adam," *JESHO* 3, 1960: 326–34; C. Kallek, "Yaḥyā ibn Ādam's *Kitāb al-kharādj*: religious guidelines for public finance," *JESHO* 44, 2001: 111, 119.

64 Daniel, *Political*, 196; Khalidi, *Arabic Historical Thought*, 45–47.

65 Abū Yūsuf, *Kitāb al-kharāj*, ed. and trans. A. Ben Shemesh, *Taxation in Islam*, vol. 3, *Abū Yūsuf's Kitāb al-kharāj*, Leiden: Brill, 1969, 35–9; also B. Lewis, *Islam: from the Prophet Muhammad to the capture of Constantinople*, New York: Harper & Row, Harper Torchbooks, 1974, 1: 152–5. Taxation was the most important field in which pre-Islamic regulation, enforced by the will of the ruler, became accepted in Islamic law; *EI2*, s.v. "Ḳānūn." Abū Yūsuf reports that the early caliphs distinguished between the taxation of urban and rural people on the grounds that "the rural folk must provide for armies … because they are producers"; cited in C. F. Robinson, *Empire and Elites after the Muslim Conquest: the transformation of northern Mesopotamia*, Cambridge: Cambridge University Press, 2000, 3.

66 Quotation from Gibb, "Evolution of Government," 45, but see Abū Yūsuf, *Kitāb al-kharāj*, 105–7 (tax farming), 118–19 (dead land), and 122–3 (islands in the Tigris and Euphrates rivers).

67 G. Salinger, "A Muslim Mirror for Princes," *MW* 46, 1956: 28.

68 Abū Yūsuf, *Kitāb al-kharāj*, 36.

69 Ṭāhir Dhū al-Yamīnain, trans. C. E. Bosworth, "An Early Arabic Mirror for Princes: Ṭāhir Dhū'l-Yamīnain's epistle to his son 'Abdallāh (206/821)," *JNES* 29, 1970: 37–8; see Abū Ja'far Muḥammad b. Jarīr al-Ṭabarī, *The History of al-Ṭabarī*, vol. 32, *The Reunification of the 'Abbasid Caliphate*, trans. C. E. Bosworth, Albany: State University of New York Press, 1987, 110–28. Ṭāhir's dynasty of governors: C. E. Bosworth, "The Tahirids and Arabic Culture," *JSS* 14, 1969: 45–79.

70 Mez, *Renaissance*, 218; W. Madelung, "A Treatise of the Sharīf al-Murtaḍā on the Legality of Working for the Government (*mas'ala fī'l-'amal ma'a'l-sulṭān*)," *BSOAS* 43, 1980: 18–31.

71 Abū Ja'far Muḥammad b. Jarīr al-Ṭabarī, *The History of al-Ṭabarī*, vol. 34, *The Revolt of the Zanj*, trans. D. Waines, Albany: State University of New York Press, 1992, 26; quoted in M. S. Gordon, *The Breaking of a Thousand Swords: a history of the Turkish military of Samarra (A.H. 200–275/815–889 C.E.)*, Albany: State University of New York Press, 2001, 123.

72 P. M. Cobb, *White Banners: contention in 'Abbāsid Syria, 750–880*, Albany: State University of New York Press, 2001, 53–62, 113, 189n21; also 116–18.

73 C. Pellat, trans., *Le livre de la couronne, attribué à Ǧaḥiẓ*, Paris: Société d'Édition "Les Belles Lettres," 1954, 179–82; on this book's origins see L. Marlow, *Hierarchy and Egalitarianism in Islamic Thought*, Cambridge: Cambridge University Press, 1997, 66n1.

74 Lambton, "Islamic Political Thought," 410&n2. These and other translated texts as they relate to the issue of social hierarchy: Marlow, *Hierarchy*, 66–90.

75 H. A. R. Gibb, "Tā'rīkh," in S. J. Shaw and W. K. Polk (eds) *Studies on the Civilization of Islam*, Boston, MA: Beacon Press, 1962, 108–37; A. A. Duri, *The Rise of Historical Writing among the Arabs*, ed. and trans. L. I. Conrad, Princeton, NJ: Princeton University Press, 1983, 64–71; F. Rosenthal, *A History of Muslim Historiography*, 2nd rev. ed., Leiden: Brill, 1968: 90–1. Further on early Arabic historiography: F. M. Donner, *Narratives of Islamic Origins: the beginnings of Islamic historical writing*, Princeton, NJ: Darwin, 1998; A. Noth and L. I. Conrad, *The Early Arabic Historical Tradition: a source-critical study*, trans. M. Bonner, Princeton, NJ: Darwin, 1994.

76 Gibb, "Tā'rīkh," 116–18; Duri, *Rise*, 156-9; Rosenthal, *History*, 133–6; C. Cahen, "History and Historians," in M. J. L. Young, J. D. Latham, and R. B. Serjeant (eds) *Religion, Learning and Science in the Abbasid Period*, The Cambridge History of Arabic Literature, 3, Cambridge: Cambridge University Press, 1990, 189–95.

77 Khalidi, *Arabic Historical Thought*, 104. Haytham b. 'Adī even tried to relate the Turks to the Arabs as descendants of Abraham; Bashear, *Arabs*, 71. Grabar, speaking of Iran, called this process "the islamization of the collective memory of the Iranian past" (*Formation*, 38), whereas Gibb imputed the inclusion of all these histories to the desire of knowledge for its own sake; "Tā'rīkh," 118.

78 Gibb described this process negatively when he wrote of Islamic jurists who, "seeking to justify the historical process, were forced to attempt to integrate the concept of 'universal empire' with Islam"; "Evolution," 45.

79 *EI2*, s.v. "al-Dīnawarī"; Abū Ḥanīfa al-Dīnawarī, *Kitāb al-akhbār al-ṭiwāl*, ed. V. Guirgass, Leiden: Brill, 1888, 114. Another example of this universalism: E. G. Browne, "Some Account of the Arabic Work Entitled 'Nihāyetu'l-irab fi akhbāri'l-furs wa'l-'Arab,' particularly of that part which treats of the Persian kings," *JRAS* 1900: 195–259; M. Grignaschi, "La Nihāyatu-l-'arab fī aḫbāri-l-Furs wa-l-'Arab," *BEO* 22, 1969: 15–67; 26, 1973: 83–184. Walled gardens:

E. B. Moynihan, *Paradise as a Garden: in Persia and Mughal India*, New York: George Braziller, 1979, 1.

80 Aḥmad b. Abī Ya'qūb Ya'qūbī, *Tā'rīkh Aḥmad ibn Abī Ya'qūb*, ed. M. T. Houtsma as *Ibn Wādhih qui dicitur al-Ja'qubī, Historiae*, 2 vols, Leiden: Brill, 1883; *EI2*, s.v. "al-Yaḳūbī."

81 Abdallāh b. Muslim ibn Qutayba, *al-Ma'ārif: Ibn Coteiba's Handbuch der Geschichte*, ed. F. Wüstenfeld, Göttingen: Vandenhoeck and Ruprecht, 1850; Duri, *Rise*, 159; G. Lecomte, *Ibn Qutayba (mort en 276/889): l'homme, son oeuvre, ses idées*, Damascus: Institut français de Damas, 1965, 428–30.

82 *Adab* literature has been called "the normative codification of the culture" (Lecomte, *Ibn Qutayba*, 422). *EI2*, s.v. "*adab*"; S. A. Bonebakker, "*Adab* and the Concept of Belles-Lettres," in Ashtiany, *Abbasid Belles-Lettres*, 16–30. Later *adab* works often contained chapters on justice and injustice; Rosenthal, "Political Justice," 100.

83 'Abdallāh b. Muslim b. Qutayba, *Kitāb 'uyūn al-akhbār*, Cairo: Dār al-Kutub al-Miṣriyya, 1925–30, 1:9; trans. Lewis, *Islam*, 1: 185; Ibn Qutayba, *Kitāb 'uyūn al-akhbār*, trans. J. Horovitz, "Ibn Quteiba's 'Uyun al-Akhbar," *IC* 4, 1930: 193. The Arabic text reads: "Kāna yuqālū: lā sulṭān illā bi-rijāl, wa-lā rijāl illā bi-māl, wa-lā māl illā bi-'imāra, wa-lā 'imāra illā bi-'adl wa-husn siyāsa."

84 Ibn Qutayba, *'Uyūn*, trans. Horovitz, 188, 197. This saying sometimes appeared in Arabic with the word "sisters" or "twins" in place of "brothers."

85 Ibn Qutayba, *'Uyūn*, trans. Horovitz, 173; I. M. Husaini, *The Life and Works of Ibn Qutayba*, Beirut: American Press, 1950, 31.

86 G. Lecomte, "L'Introduction du *Kitāb adab al-kātib* d'Ibn Qutayba," in *Mélanges Louis Massignon*, Damascus: Institut français de Damas, 1956–7, 3: 53–5, 60.

87 Ibn Qutayba, *'Uyūn*, trans. Horovitz, 186, 193. According to Madā'inī, the Umayyad caliphs appointed themselves as guards of the *dīwān*, "which exempted them from the obligation of going out on raids"; al-Ṭabarī, *History*, 26: 74; cited in M. Bonner, *Aristocratic Violence and Holy War: studies in the jihad and the Arab-Byzantine frontier*, New Haven, CT: American Oriental Society, 1996, 100. Multiple attribution as a literary technique: al-Azmeh, *Muslim Kingship*, 90–2; J. Sadan, "A 'Closed-Circuit' Saying on Practical Justice," *JSAI* 10, 1987: 332–4. Sadan lists a number of citations for the Circle of Justice; others appear under "other sayings of Ardashir" in Abbas, ed., *'Ahd Ardashīr*, 98n16.

88 In Arabic, *kāna yuqālū*; Ibn Qutayba's contemporary, the historian Balādhurī (d.892), employed "they have said" (*qālū*) in the same way; T. Khalidi, *Islamic Historiography: the histories of Mas'ūdī*, Albany: State University of New York Press, 1975, 25.

89 Abbas, ed., *'Ahd Ardashīr*, 98&n16; Ibn 'Abd Rabbih al-Andalusī, *al-'Iqd al-farīd*, Cairo: al-Maṭba'a al-Azhariyya, 1928, 1: 18; in Arabic: "Wa-qāla 'Amrū b. al-'Ās: Lā sulṭān illā bi-al-rijāl wa-lā rijāl illā bi-māl wa-lā māl illā bi-'imāra wa-lā 'imāra illā bi-al-'adl." *Al-'Iqd al-farīd* was modeled on Ibn Qutayba's *Fountains of Information* (*'Uyūn al-akhbār*), but the attribution of this saying differs; cf. W. Werkmeister, *Quellenuntersuchungen zum Kitāb al-'Iqd al-Farīd des Andalusiers Ibn 'Abdrabbih (246/860–328/940): Ein Beitrag zur arabischen Literturgeschichte*, Berlin: Klaus Schwarz, 1983, 62–5. See Ibn 'Abd Rabbih, *The Unique Necklace*, vol. 1, trans. I. J. Boullata, Reading, UK: Garnet, 2006, 24; compare, "Among the duties of a ruler is to be just in his seen deeds. in order to preserve the well-being of his rule. If his administration is corrupt, his ruling power is gone"; ibid., 16.

90 Abū Zayd al-Balkhī, *Kitāb al-siyāsa*, trans. F. Rosenthal, "Abū Zayd al-Balkhī on Politics," in Bosworth, *The Islamic World*, 289, 293–4. The fact that philosophers traced this emphasis to Aristotle indicates that it had strong support in learned society; S. H. Nasr and O. Leaman (eds) *History of Islamic Philosophy*, London: Routledge, 1996, 2: 845.

91 Qudāma b. Ja'far, *Kitāb al-kharāj*, ed. and trans. A. Ben Shemesh, *Taxation in Islam*, vol. 2: *Qudāma b. Ja'far's Kitāb al-kharāj, Part Seven, and Excerpts from Abū Yūsuf's Kitāb al-kharāj*, Leiden: Brill, 1965, 21; Heck, *Construction*, 1–2; M. Ḥiyārī, "Qudāma b. Ǧa'fars Behandlung der Politik: Das Kapitel *As-siyāsa* aus seinem Vademecum für Sekretäre *Kitāb al-ḫarāǧ wa-ṣanā'at al-kitāba*," *Der Islam* 60, 1983: 91–103.

92 Qudāma b. Ja'far, *al-Siyāsa min kitāb al-kharāj wa-ṣinā'at al-kitāba*, ed. M. Ḥiyārī, Amman: al-Jāmi'a al-'Urduniyya, 1981, 50; the Arabic reads: "Lā mulk illā bi-dīn wa-shar' wa-lā dīn illā bi-mulk wa-dhabṭ." *Dhabṭ*, taxation (lit. "taking"), has also been translated as "administrative control"; Heck, *Construction*, 74–6.

93 Abū Ja'far Muḥammad b. Jarīr al-Ṭabarī, *Tā'rīkh al-rusūl wa'l-mulūk*, edited by M. J. de Goeje as *Annales Quos Scripsit Abu Djafar Mohammed ibn Djarir at-Tabari*, Leiden: Brill, 1879–1901, 1964–65; the Sasanians: ser. 1, vol. 2: 813–1072. Translations: T. Nöldeke (trans.) *Geschichte der Perser und Araber zur Zeit der Sasaniden, aus der Arabischen Chronik des Tabari*, Leiden: Brill, 1879, 1973; and

C. E. Bosworth (trans.) *The History of al-Ṭabarī*, vol. 5: *The Sāsānids, the Byzantines, the Lakhmids, and Yemen*, Albany: State University of New York Press, 1999, esp. 73, 107-12, 130–8, 157, 255–65, 404; Khalidi, *Arabic Historical Thought*, 78–9.

94 Abū Ja'far Muḥammad b. Jarīr al-Ṭabarī, *The History of al-Ṭabarī*, vol. 3, *The Children of Israel*, trans. W. M. Brinner, Albany: State University of New York Press, 1991, 25–7.

95 Abū al-Ḥasan 'Alī b. al-Ḥusayn al-Mas'ūdī, *Murūj al-dhahab wa-ma'ādin al-jawhar*, ed. B. de Maynard and P. de Courteille, rev. and corr. C. Pellat, 7 vols, Beirut: al-Jāmi'a al-Lubnāniyya, 1965–79.

96 De Lacy Evans O'Leary, *How Greek Science Passed to the Arabs*, London: Routledge and Kegan Paul, 1948, 155–81; A. M. H. Shboul, *al-Mas'ūdī and His World: a Muslim humanist and his interest in non-Muslims*, London: Ithaca Press, 1979, 102–13; EI2, s.v. "al-Mas'ūdī," 6: 784–89. Through al-Mas'ūdī we know about many lost works of the preceding century; most of his own works have also been lost.

97 Abū al-Ḥasan 'Alī b. al-Ḥusayn al-Mas'ūdī, *Kitāb al-tanbīh wa-al-ishrāf*, trans. B. Carra de Vaux as *Le livre de l'avertissement et de la revision*, Paris: Imprimerie nationale, 1896, 152.

98 Abū al-Ḥasan 'Alī b. al-Ḥusayn al-Mas'ūdī, *Les Prairies d'or*, trans. B. de Maynard and P. de Courteille, rev. and corr. C. Pellat, Paris: Société asiatique, 1962, 1: 198; al-Mas'ūdī, *Murūj al-dhahab*, 1: 261.

99 al-Mas'ūdī, *Prairies d'or*, 1: 218; al-Mas'ūdī, *Murūj al-dhahab*, 1: 289.

100 al-Mas'ūdī, *Prairies d'or*, 1: 222–24; al-Mas'ūdī, *Murūj al-dhahab*, 1: 293–94.

101 al-Mas'ūdī, *Prairies d'or*, 1: 236; al-Mas'ūdī, *Murūj al-dhahab*, 1: 311; the Arabic reads: "Al-mulk bi-al-jund wa-al-jund bi-al-māl wa-al-māl bi-al-kharāj wa-al-kharāj bi-al-'imāra wa-al-'imāra bi-al-'adl wa-al-'adl bi-islāḥ al-'ummāl wa-islāḥ al-'ummāl bi-istiqāmat al-wuzarā'."

102 Khalidi, *Islamic Historiography*, 79–80; S. M. Stern, "Al-Mas'udi and the Philosopher al-Farabi," in *Al-Mas'udi Millenary Commemoration Volume*, ed. S. M. Ahmad and A. Rahman, Calcutta: The Indian Society for the History of Science and The Institute of Islamic Studies, Aligarh Muslim University, 1960, 28–41; D. M. Dunlop, "A Source of al-Mas'udi: the Madinat al-fadila of al-Farabi," in ibid., 69–71.

103 Khalidi, *Islamic Historiography*, 67–77.

104 At least one contemporary historian, Ḥamza al-Isfahānī, saw the Buyid conquest of 945 as a deliverance from an impossible situation; D. Waines, "The Pre-Buyid Amirate: two views from the past," *IJMES* 8, 1977: 346. By the early Abbasid era Mesopotamia's land tax had fallen to about half its Sasanian total, apparently because population loss due to the plague prevented maintenance of the irrigation system; marshland spread in southern Iraq and reduced the cultivated area; R. M. Adams, *Land behind Baghdad: a history of settlement on the Diyala plains*, Chicago, IL: University of Chicago Press, 1965, 84–5; P. Christensen, *The Decline of Iranshahr: irrigation and environments in the history of the Middle East, 500 B.C. to A.D. 1500*, trans. S. Sampson, Odense, Denmark: University of Copenhagen Museum Tusculanum Press, 1993, 73–83, 88.

5 Politics in transition

1 In this period juristic, philosophical, and Near Eastern political thought wove together to create the characteristic form of Islamic politics; A. K. S. Lambton, *State and Government in Medieval Islam, an introduction to the study of Islamic political theory: the jurists*, Oxford: Oxford University Press, 1981. However, the separation between these strands was never as complete as such a schema implies.

2 R. P. Mottahedeh, *Loyalty and Leadership in an Early Islamic Society*, Princeton, NJ: Princeton University Press, 1980, 175–80; *CHIr*, 4: 57–89; S. Sabari, *Mouvements populaires à Bagdad à l'époque 'abbasside, IXe–XIe siècles*, Paris: Adrien Maisonneuve, 1981, 54–5, 72.

3 *Amīr al-'umarā'*; the origins of this office go back into the ninth century; É. Tyan, *Institutions du droit public musulman*, Paris: Recueil Sirey, 1954, 1: 533. Turkish bodyguard: M. S. Gordon, *The Breaking of a Thousand Swords: a history of the Turkish military of Samarra (A.H. 200–275/815–889 C.E.)*, Albany: State University of New York Press, 2001; on its Central Asian connections, C. I. Beckwith, "Aspects of the Early History of the Central-Asian Guard Corps in Islam," *AEuras* 4, 1984: 29–43.

4 Ibn al-Furāt; H. F. Amédroz (ed.), *The Historical Remains of Hilâl al-Ṣâbi', first part of his Kitab al-wuzara (Gotha MS 1756) and fragment of his History, 389–393 (BM Ms. Add. 19360)*, Beirut: Maṭba'a al-Abā' al-Yasu'iyīn, 1904, 258; tr. 345–46. Under his successor, 'Alī b. 'Īsā, "the Good

Vizier," the revenues of at least one province expanded 30 percent; according to Hilāl al-Sābi' this was because "the practice of justice became widespread and prosperity increased" (ibid.). Importance of the scribal corps and viziers: R. P. Mottahedeh, "Bureaucracy and the Patrimonial State in Early Islamic Iran and Iraq," *al-Abḥāth* 29, 1981: 25–36.

5 This is not to speak of the breaking away of territories, such as Umayyad Spain or parts of North Africa, that fell completely outside Abbasid control. In the ninth century, the Zanj, Khārijīs, and Qarmatians also rebelled but failed to obtain independent status. Without kinship ties between caliphs and governors, bureaucratic structures were apparently still too weak to hold the empire together; P. Crone, *Slaves on Horses: the evolution of the Islamic polity*, Cambridge: Cambridge University Press, 1980, 71.

6 By this time, at least the urban population was over half Muslim; R. W. Bulliet, *Conversion to Islam in the Medieval Period: an essay in quantitative history*, Cambridge: Harvard University Press, 1979, 83, 97, 109, 124. Literary development: R. N. Frye, "The New Persian Renaissance in Western Iran," in G. Makdisi (ed.) *Arabic and Islamic Studies in Honor of Hamilton A. R. Gibb*, Leiden: Brill, 1965, 225–31; R. N. Frye, *The Golden Age of Persia: the Arabs in the East*, London: Weidenfeld & Nicolson, 1975, 168–74; C. E. Bosworth, "The Interaction of Arabic and Persian Literature and Culture in the 10th and Early 11th Centuries," *al-Abḥāth* 27, 1978/9: 59–75.

7 Niẓām al-Mulk, cited in *CHIr* 4: 106; C. E. Bosworth, "The Heritage of Rulership in Early Islamic Iran and the Search for Dynastic Connections with the Past," *Iran* 11, 1973: 59–60; C. E. Bosworth, "The Armies of the Saffārids," *BSOAS* 31, 1968: 550.

8 See Ch. 2. Abū Ja'far Muḥammad b. Jarīr al-Ṭabarī, *Chronique d'Abou-Djafar Mohammed ben Djarir ben Yazid Tabari, tr. sur la version persane d'Abou-Ali Mohammed Bel'ami*, trans. H. Zotenberg, Paris: Imprimerie impériale, 1867–74, 2: 224–5. English trans. E. S. Waring, *A Tour to Sheeraz*, London: T. Cadell and W. Davies, 1807, 311–12; cited in W. Young (trans.) *The Wisdom of Naushirwan "The Just", King of Iran, commonly called Tauqiyat i Kisrawiya*, Lucknow: Newul Kishore Press, 1892, v–vi.

9 Al-Ṭabarī, *Chronique*, 2: 341. Bal'amī articulated what came to be the "official" history of the Muslim world; the multiple revisions of his work suggest that it became a vehicle for legitimating the new regional politics; E. L. Daniel, "Manuscripts and Editions of Bal'amī's *Tarjamah-i Tārīkh-i Ṭabarī*," *JRAS* 1990: 294–8, 300–2; A. C. S. Peacock, *Mediaeval Islamic Historiography and Political Legitimacy: Bal'amī's Tārīkhnāma*, London: Routledge, 2007, 167–71.

10 Abū Bakr Muḥammad b. Ja'far Narshakhī, *The History of Bukhara*, trans. R. N. Frye, Cambridge: Mediaeval Academy of America, 1954, 9; C. Schefer, *Chrestomathie persane*, Paris: 1883–5; Amsterdam: APA-Philo Press, 1976, 1: 17. The emergence of women as spokespersons for ideas of justice is very interesting; following Leila Ahmad, it might be hypothesized that they represent more egalitarian attitudes that appeared on the margins of Muslim society in opposition to a patriarchal "center" which was no longer much respected; *Women and Gender in Islam*, New Haven, CT: Yale University Press, 1992, 63–7.

11 Muḥammad ibn Ḥibbān al-Bustī, *Rawḍat al-'uqalā' wa nuzhat al-fuḍalā'*, ed. M. M. 'Abd al-Ḥamīd, Beirut: Dār al-Kutub al-'Ilmiyya, 1975, 268–9: "Wa-lā yadūmu mulku malik illā bi-a'wān tatī'uhū wa-lā yatī'uhū al-a'wān illā bi-wazīr wa-lā yatimmu dhālik illā an yakān al-wazīr wudūdan nasūhan wa-lā yūjadu dhālik min al-wazīr illā bi-al-'afāf wa-al-rā'y wa-lā yatimmu qiwām hu'lā' illā bi-al-māl wa-lā yūjad al-māl illā bi-salāḥ al-ra'iyya wa-lā taslaḥ al-ra'iyya illā bi-iqāma al-'adl fa-ka'anna thabāt al-mulk lā yakūn illā bi-luzūm al-'adl wa-zawāluhū lā yakūn illā bi-mufāraqatihi."

12 Moses: Muḥammad b. 'Abbās al-Khwarizmī (Jamāl al-Dīn Abī Bakr), *Kitāb mufīd al-'ulūm wa mubīd al-humūm*, ed. 'A. al-Ansarī, Sidon: Manshūrāt al-Maktaba al-Fikriyya, 1980, 417. Proper behavior: C.-H. de Fouchécour, *Moralia: les notions morales dans la littérature persane du 3e/9e au 7e/13e siècle*, Paris: Éditions Recherche sur les Civilisations, 1986, 375–8. Narshakhī, *History*, 3; J. S. Cowen, *Kalila wa Dimna: an animal allegory of the Mongol court*, New York, Oxford: Oxford University Press, 1989, 3.

13 B. Spuler, "The Evolution of Persian Historiography," in B. Lewis and P. M. Holt (eds) *Historians of the Middle East*, Historical Writing on the Peoples of Asia, 4, Oxford, New York: Oxford University Press, 1962, 129. Exceptions: J. S. Meisami, "Rulers and the Writing of History," in B. Gruendler and L. Marlow (eds) *Writers and Rulers: perspectives on their relationship from Abbasid to Safavid times*, Wiesbaden: Reichert, 2004, 74–5&n4. Dissemination: S. A. Arjomand, "Evolution of the Persianate Polity and Its Transmission to India," *Journal of Persianate Studies* 2, 2009: 115–36.

14 T. Nöldeke, *The Iranian National Epic, or, the Shahnamah*, trans. L. T. Bogdanov, Bombay: K. B. Cama Oriental Institute, 1930; Philadelphia, PA: Porcupine, 1979, 40–58. Earlier versions of the *Book of Kings* existed: see Ch. 4; J. S. Meisami, "Why Write History in Persian? historical writing in the Samanid period," in C. Hillenbrand (ed.) *Studies in Honour of Clifford Edmund Bosworth*, Leiden: Brill, 2000, 2: 357.

15 G. E. von Grunebaum, "Firdausi's Concept of History," in *60. Doğum Yılı Münasebetiyle Fuad Köprülü Armağanı*, Ankara: Ankara Üniversitesi Dil ve Tarih-Coğrafya Fakültesi, 1953, 177; A. Banani, "Ferdowsi and the Art of Tragic Epic," in *Islam and Its Cultural Divergence: studies in honor of Gustave E. von Grunebaum*, Urbana: University of Illinois Press, 1971, 5.

16 Firdausi, *The Epic of the Kings: Shah-nama, the national epic of Persia*, trans. R. Levy, London: Routledge and Kegan Paul, 1967, 105.

17 Firdausi, *Epic*, 270, 286.

18 Firdausi, *The Shahnama of Firdausi*, trans. A. G. Warner and E. Warner, London: Kegan Paul, Trench, Trübner and Co., 1905–25, 6: 274–83, 375; 7: 11, quotation on 226. See A. S. Shahbazi, *Ferdowsī: a critical biography*, Costa Mesa, CA: Harvard University and Mazda, 1991, 102–3; C.-H. de Fouchécour, "Une lecture du *Livre des Rois* de Ferdowsi," *StIr* 5, 1976: 171–202.

19 Narshakhī, *History*, 5.

20 The Umayyad caliph ʻAbd al-Malik was said to have rejected poetry written for him that contained crown imagery (I. Goldziher, "Islamisme et Parsisme," *Revue de l'histoire des religions* 43, 1901: 6), although his coins portrayed him wearing a crown (Tyan, *Institutions*, 1: 490).

21 W. Madelung, "The Assumption of the Title Shāhānshāh by the Būyids and 'The Reign of the Daylam (*Dawlat al-Daylam*)'," *JNES* 28, 1969: 86–93; J. S. Meisami, *Persian Historiography: to the end of the twelfth century*, Edinburgh: Edinburgh University Press, 1999, 41–3. The same traits legitimized the revolutionary Qarmatian *mahdī* in 928; W. Madelung, *Religious Trends in Early Islamic Iran*, Albany, NY: Persian Heritage Foundation, 1988, 96–7; W. W. Barthold, "Caliph and Sultan," trans. N. S. Doniach, *IQ* 7, 1963: 129.

22 K. Babayan, *Mystics, Monarchs, and Messiahs: cultural landscapes of early modern Iran*, Cambridge, MA: Harvard University Center for Middle Eastern Studies, 2002, 268; G. Makdisi, "Les rapports entre calife et sulṭân à l'époque saljûqide," *IJMES* 6, 1975: 228–32; H. F. Amédroz, "The Vizier Abu-l-Faḍl Ibn al 'Amīd from the 'Tajārib al-Umam' of Abu 'Ali Miskawaih," *Der Islam* 3, 1912: 342. Others tried to assimilate the Persians to the Arabs through descent from Abraham; Abū al-Ḥasan ʻAlī b. al-Ḥusayn al-Masʻūdī, *Kitāb al-tanbīh wa-al-ishrāf*, trans. B. Carra de Vaux as *Le livre de l'avertissement et de la revision*, Paris: Imprimerie nationale, 1897, 154.

23 Muḥammad b. Yaḥyá al-Sūlī, *Akhbār ar-Rāḍī billāh wa'l-Muttaqī billāh*, trans. M. Canard, Algiers: Imprimeries "La Typo-Litho" et Jules Carbonel Réunies, 1946–50, 1: 73; H. Busse, "The Revival of Persian Kingship under the Būyids," in D. S. Richards (ed.) *Islamic Civilisation 950–1150*, Oxford: Bruno Cassirer, 1973, 47–70.

24 Al-Masʻūdī, *Livre de l'avertissement*, 153; al-Bīrūnī is reported to have said the same thing; E. Yarshater (ed.) *Persian Literature*, [Albany, NY]: Bibliotheca Persica, 1988, 67. See B. Lewis, *Islam: from the Prophet Muhammad to the capture of Constantinople*, New York: Harper & Row, Harper Torchbooks, 1973, 2: 206–7.

25 V. Minorsky, "La domination des Dailamites," in *Iranica: twenty articles*, Publications of the University of Tehran, 775, Hertford, UK: Steven Austin, 1964, 12–30; *EI2*, s.v. "Daylam." Some local elite families probably did go back to late Sasanian times; Bosworth, "Heritage of Rulership," 55–7.

26 Frye, *Golden Age*, 209; *CHIr*, 4: 273–5. An argument that the Buyids were not Shiʻis: W. M. Watt, "The Significance of the Early Stages of Imami Shiʻism," in N. Keddie (ed.) *Religion and Politics in Iran: Shiʻism from quietism to revolution*, New Haven, CT: Yale University Press, 1983, 29. Buyid relations with Samanids and the caliphate: L. Treadwell, "*Shāhānshāh* and *al-Malik al-mu'ayyad*: the legitimation of power in Sāmānid and Būyid Iran," in *Culture and Memory in Medieval Islam: essays in honour of Wilferd Madelung*, London: IB Tauris, 2003, 318–37.

27 J. J. Donohue, *The Buwayhid Dynasty in Iraq, 334H./945 to 403H./1012: shaping institutions for the future*, Leiden: Brill, 2003, 118, 189–90; C. Cahen, "L'Évolution de l'iqtaʻ du IXe au XIIIe siècle: contribution à une histoire comparée des sociétés médiévales," *Annales: économies, sociétés, civilisations* 8, 1953: 34, 36; M. S. Khan, "The Effects of the *Iqṭāʻ* (Land-Grant) System under the Buwayhids," *IC* 58, 1984: 295–7.

28 M. A. Ahmad, *The Nature of Islamic Political Theory*, Karachi: Ma'aref, 1975, 119. Lambton states that the demand for justice inherent in these titles was now finding its way into Islamic

political thought; A. K. S. Lambton, "Concepts of Authority in Persia: Eleventh to Nineteenth Centuries A.D.," *Iran* 26, 1988: 99. In fact, it had already found its way there but was finding new expression.

29 L. Richter-Bernburg, "*Amīr-Malik-Shāhānshāh*: 'Aḍud ad-Daula's titulature re-examined," *Iran* 18, 1980: 87–8; the term "just amir" (*al-amīr al-'adl*) referred to "the office of upholding and guaranteeing equity among his subjects" (*CHIr*, 4: 280–85). In Twelver or Imāmī Shi'ī doctrine, however, the only just sultan was the true *imām*; A. A. Sachedina, *The Just Ruler* (al-sulṭān al-'ādil) *in Shī'ite Islam: the comprehensive authority of the jurist in Imamite jurisprudence*, Oxford: Oxford University Press, 1988.

30 H. Kennedy, *The Prophet and the Age of the Caliphates: the Islamic Near East from the sixth to the eleventh century*, London: Longman, 1986, 224. Buyid administration: H. Busse, *Chalif und Grosskönig: Die Buyiden im Iraq (945–1055)*, Beirut: Franz Steiner, 1969; tenth-century public works: A. Mez, *The Renaissance of Islam*, trans. S. Khuda Bakhsh and D. S. Margoliouth, London: Luzac, 1936, repr. 1957, 492–504.

31 Cited in J. Sadan, "A 'Closed-Circuit' Saying on Practical Justice," *JSAI* 10, 1987: 340.

32 J. L. Kraemer, *Humanism in the Renaissance of Islam: the cultural revival during the Buyid age*, Leiden: Brill, 1986; L. Marlow, *Hierarchy and Egalitarianism in Islamic Thought*, Cambridge: Cambridge University Press, 1997, 52; H. Daiber, "Political Philosophy," in S. H. Nasr and O. Leaman (eds) *History of Islamic Philosophy*, London: Routledge, 1996, 2: 842–3. *Denkard*: G. von Grunebaum, "Firdausī's Concept of History," *The American Anthropologist* 57.2 (81), 1955: 173; J. K. Choksy, *Conflict and Cooperation: Zoroastrian subalterns and Muslim elites in medieval Iranian society*, New York: Columbia University Press, 1997, 89, 99. *Epistles*: I. R. Netton, *Muslim Neoplatonists: an introduction to the thought of the Brethren of Purity*, Edinburgh: Edinburgh University Press, 1991; Lambton, *State and Government*, 294; H. Enayat, "An Outline of the Political Philosophy of the *Rasā'il* of the Ikhwān al-afā'," in S. H. Nasr (ed.) *Ismā'īlī Contributions to Islamic Culture*, Tehran: Imperial Iranian Academy of Philosophy, 1997, 35–41.

33 Ibn al-Haytham, *The Advent of the Fatimids: a contemporary Shi'i witness*, ed. and trans. W. Madelung and P. E. Walker, London: IB Tauris, 2000, 81; A. al-Azmeh, *Muslim Kingship: power and the sacred in Muslim, Christian, and Pagan polities*, London: IB Tauris, 1997, 190, 198, 206.

34 P. Sanders, "From Court Ceremony to Urban Language: ceremonial in Fatimid Cairo and Fuṭsṭā," in C. E. Bosworth *et al.* (ed.) *The Islamic World from Classical to Modern Times: essays in honor of Bernard Lewis*, Princeton, NJ: Darwin, 1989, 311–22; P. Sanders, *Ritual, Politics, and the City in Fatimid Cairo*, Albany: State University of New York Press, 1994.

35 Boaz Shoshan, "Fāṭimid Grain Policy and the Post of the Muḥtasib," *IJMES* 13, 1981: 183–5; Y. Lev, "The Suppression of Crime, the Supervision of Markets, and Urban Society in the Egyptian Capital during the Tenth and Eleventh Centuries," *MHR* 3, 1988: 90. The urban poor were the only group able to check the state's economic policies, through the threat of riot; M. A. Cook, "Economic Developments," in J. Schacht and C. E. Bosworth (ed.) *The Legacy of Islam*, 2nd ed., Oxford: Oxford University Press, 1979, 224.

36 K. M. Cuno, *The Pasha's Peasants: land, society, and economy in Lower Egypt, 1740–1858*, Cambridge: Cambridge University Press, 1992, 20; S. A. Assaad, *The Reign of al-Hakim bi Amr Allah (386/996–411/1021): a political study*, Beirut: Arab Institute for Research and Publishing, 1974, 78–83.

37 Qāḍī al-Nu'mān, trans. G. Salinger, "A Muslim Mirror for Princes," *MW* 46, 1956: 28, 33; Nāṣir-i Khusrau, *Naser-e Khosraw's Book of Travels (Safarnāma)*, trans. W. M. Thackston, Jr., New York: Bibliotheca Persica, 1986, 55–7.

38 P. J. Vatikiotis, "Al-Hakim bi-Amrillah: the god-king idea realised," *IC* 29, 1955: 1–8.

39 H. A. R. Gibb, "Government and Islam under the Early 'Abbasids: the political collapse of Islam," in *L'Élaboration de l'Islam*, Paris: Presses universitaires de France, 1961, 121; *CHIr*, 4: 87–8.

40 According to von Grunebaum, "It would seem that the Abbasids attempted upon occasion to exhibit different aspects of their kingship to the several sections of their subjects"; G. E. von Grunebaum, *Medieval Islam: a study in cultural orientation*, Chicago, IL: University of Chicago Press, 1946, 156. Caliphal troops: O. S. A. Ismail, "Mu'tasim and the Turks," *BSOAS* 29, 1966: 12–24; tribal legitimation would have been necessary whether these troops were ethnically Turkish or simply of nomadic origin. In the Byzantine and Sasanian empires, of course, religion and kingship were also in separate (though cooperating) hands.

41 Al-'Āmirī, "Al-I'lām bi-manāqib al-Islām," trans. F. Rosenthal, "State and Religion According to Abū l-Ḥasan al-'Āmirī," *IQ* 3, 1956: 47.

42 The usual description of this move as "the delegitimization of state power," implies that the only possible source of legitimation was the example of the Prophet, but many jurists and thinkers and the general population found other sources of legitimation convincing, such as royal behavior, election or choice, marriage, tribal kinship, inheritance, military success, cultural and/or religious patronage, or Sufi sheikhdom. A. J. Arberry, "An Arabic Treatise on Politics," *IQ* 2, 1955: 15; the mid-tenth-century treatise examined here combined Greek political philosophy with ideas from Persian and Arabic-Islamic sources.

43 Shaykh al-Ṭā'ifa al-Ṭūsī, *Al-Amālī*, quoted in Mullā Muḥammad Bāqir Majlisī, *'Ayn al-hayāt*, trans. W. C. Chittick, "Two Seventeenth-Century Persian Tracts on Kingship and Rulers," in S. A. Arjomand (ed.) *Authority and Political Culture in Shi'ism*, Albany: State University of New York Press, 1988, 287; see nn39 and 24.

44 'Alī b. Abī Ṭālib, *Classified Selections from Nahj al-Balāgha*, ed. F. Ebeid, trans. A Group of Moslem Specialists, [Cairo]: Dār al-Kutub al-Islāmiyya, 1989, 313–17; W. C. Chittick (ed. and trans.) *A Shi'ite Anthology*, London: Muhammadi Trust, 1980, 68–82; cf. Salinger, "Muslim Mirror," 30–1. This letter has been called a forgery, but it appeared in works written before this one with the same attribution; on the question of its authenticity compare W. al-Qāḍī, "An Early Fāṭimid Political Document," *SI* 48, 1978: 71–108; M.-T. Danishpazhouh, "An Annotated Bibliography on Government and Statecraft," in Arjomand, *Authority and Political Culture*, 215–16, no. 2; and M. Djebli, "Encore à propos de l'authenticité du *Nahj al-Balagha!*" *SI* 75, 1992: 33–56.

45 'Ali b. Abī Ṭālib, *Classified*, 307, 333–5.

46 "Siyāsat al-mulūk," trans. J. Sadan, "A New Source of the Buyid Period," *IOS* 9, 1979: 361n53.

47 Abū Sa'd Manṣūr b. al-Ḥusayn al-Ābī (d.1030), *Nathr al-durr*, ed. M. 'A. Qurna, Cairo: al-Hayā' al-Miṣriyya al-'Amma lil-Kitāb, 1980–90, 4: 233, 7: 81; trans. Sadan, "'Closed-Circuit' Saying," 337. The Arabic of Shapur's saying reads: "Wa-a'lam inna qiwām amrik bi-durūr al-kharāj wa-durūr al-kharāj bi-'imāra al-bilād wa-bulūgh al-ghāya fī dhālik bi-istiṣlāḥ ahlih bi-al-'adl 'alayh wa-al-mu'āwana lahum."

48 The "Book of Policy, for the Education of Rulers" ("Kitāb al-siyasa fī tadbir al-ri'āsa"), an expansion of Aristotle's letters to Alexander, was probably composed shortly before *The Secret of Secrets* (*Sirr al-asrār*); according to Grignaschi, it survives only as a sixteenth-century Ottoman paraphrase by Nevālī (Süleymaniye Kütüphanesi, ms. Hafiz Efendi 253), "'Siyâsatu-l-Âmmiyya'," 76, 226–31, 253. See A. S. Levend, "Siyaset-nameler," *TDAYB,* 1962: 176n6; J. Bielawski, "Lettres d'Aristote à Alexandre le Grand en version arabe," *RO* 28, 1964: 7–34. The Sasanian *Ayinnamag* was a similar compendium; M. Simidchieva, "*Siyāsat-nāme* Revisited: the question of authenticity," in B. G. Fragner *et al.* (eds) *Proceedings of the Second European Conference of Iranian Studies*, Rome: Istituto Italiano per il Medio ed Estremo Oriente, 1995, 666n8. Early translations of the *Sirr al-asrār*: M. Gaster, "The Hebrew Version of the 'Secretum Secretorum,' with an introduction and an English translation," *JRAS*, 1907: 879–912; 1908: 111–62, 1065–84; R. Steele (ed.) *Three Prose Version of the Secreta Secretorum*, London: Kegan Paul, Trench, Trübner, 1896; M. A. Manzalaoui (ed.), *Secretum Secretorum: nine English versions*, vol. 1, Oxford: Early English Text Society, 1997. Its place in the literature of science: W. Eamon, *Science and the Secrets of Nature: books of secrets in medieval and early modern culture*, Princeton, NJ: Princeton University Press, 1994, 39–53.

49 S. J. Williams, *The Secret of Secrets: the scholarly career of a pseudo-Aristotelian text in the Latin Middle Ages*, Ann Arbor: University of Michigan Press, 2003, 60–141. Bacon's descendant Francis Bacon must also have known this work, judging by his line, "The four pillars of government … are religion, justice, counsel, and treasure," quoted in B. Lewis, *A Middle East Mosaic: fragments of life, letters and history*, New York: Random House, 2000, 215.

50 D. M. Dunlop, "The Translations of al-Biṭrīq and Yahyā (Yuḥannā) b. al-Biṭrīq," *JRAS,* 1959: 140–50, discusses this translator but denies his authorship of *Sirr al-asrār* as a whole. Syriac involvement in translation of political literature: J. W. Watt, "Syriac and Syrians as Mediators of Greek Political Thought to Islam," *Mélanges de l'Université Saint-Joseph* 57, 2004: 121–49. A book by the physician Ḥunayn b. Isḥāq (d.78–9) contained excerpts from the letter or letters of Aristotle to Alexander, some of which were in the *Sirr al-asrār* (Bielawski, "Lettres," 11). The origins of the *Sirr* are studied by M. Grignaschi, who considers the attribution to Yuḥannā b. al-Biṭrīq merely a literary device: "Rasā'il Aristātālīsa"; "Roman épistolaire"; "'Siyâsatu-l-Âmmiyya'," 26; "L'Origine

et les métamorphoses du 'Sirr al-'asrār' (*Secretum Secretorum*)," *Archives d'histoire doctrinale et littéraire du moyen age*, 1976: 7–112; and "Remarques sur la formation et l'interpretation du *Sirr al-'asrār*," in W. F. Ryan and C. B. Schmitt (eds) *Pseudo-Aristotle, The 'Secret of Secrets': sources and influences*, London: Warburg Institute, 1982, 3–33. Also F. E. Peters, *Aristoteles Arabus: the Oriental translations and commentaries on the Aristotelian corpus*, Leiden: Brill, 1968, 67–71; M. Manzalaoui, "The Pseudo-Aristotelian *Kitāb sirr al-asrār*: facts and problems," *Oriens* 23/24, 1974: 147–257; Shaked, "From Iran to Islam: notes."

51 "Risāla fī siyāsat al-'Āmmiyya," trans. Grignaschi, "'Siyâsatu-l-Âmmiyya'," 258–60. The stories of Alexander also appear in the *Siyāsa* chapter of Qudāma b. Ja'far's *Kitāb al-kharāj*, and al-Ḥiyārī asserts that he got them from the *Sirr al-asrār* (Qudāma b. Ja'far, *al-Siyāsa*, 84–5; introduction by al-Ḥiyārī, 16–17). Since the *Sirr* was most likely compiled after Qudāma's death, however, he may have been using its lost source or an earlier compilation; the wording is similar but not identical to a passage of the *Sirr*, and he does not quote the Circle of Justice; 'A. Badawī (ed.) *Fontes Graecae Doctrinarum Politicarum Islamicarum, Testamenta Graeca (Pseudo-)Platonis, et Secretum Secretorum (Pseudo-) Aristotelis*, Cairo: Maṭba'a Dār al-Kutub al-Miṣriyya, 1954, 75–6.

52 *Secretum Secretorum*, ed. R. Steele, trans. I. Ali, *Opera hactenus inedita Rogeri Baconi*, vol. 5, Oxford: Clarendon Press, 1920, 224–7; Badawī, *Fontes*, 126–8; Gaster, "Hebrew," 901.

53 The Arabic reads: "Al-'ālam bustān siyājuhū al-dawla/Al-dawla sulṭān taḥjabuhū al-sunna/Al-sunna siyāsa [minhaj] yasūsuhā al-malik [imām]/Al-malik rā'in ya'ḍuduhā al-jaysh/Al-jaysh a'wān yakfaluhum al-māl/Al-māl rizq tajma'uhū al-ra'iyya/Al-ra'iyya 'abīd yata'abbaduhum [yashmāluhum/ yastamlakuhum] al-'adl/Al-'adl ma'lūf [ulfa] wa-huwa [bihi] ṣalāḥ [hayā'] al-'ālam." 'Alī's version: Steele, *Secretum Secretorum*, 227. Dragons (origin unknown) appear only in the Hebrew version, translated in Spain in the late twelfth or beginning of the thirteenth century. Grignaschi traced the eight sentences to Nevalī's sixteenth-century paraphrase of the "Kitāb al-siyāsa fī tadbīr al-ri'āsa," but they were not in Sālim's "Letters of Aristotle to Alexander"; "'Siyâsatu-l-Âmmiyya'," 253.

54 On the Platonic city in Arabic thought, al-Farābī, *Fuṣūl al-madanī: aphorisms of the statesman*, ed. and trans. D. M. Dunlop, Cambridge: Cambridge University Press, 1961, 53–5.

55 S. Redford, "Just Landscape in Medieval Anatolia," *Studies in the History of Gardens and Designed Landscapes* 20, 2000: 314–15; cf. A. M. Watson, *Agricultural Innovation in the Early Islamic World: the diffusion of crops and farming techniques, 700–1100*, Cambridge: Cambridge University Press, 1983, esp. 117–19.

56 The idea of the Circle of Justice retained its vitality in Spanish political thought after the Christian reconquista; the story of El Cid, for example, noted that King Alfonso "kept his kingdom so well, that rich and poor alike dwelt in peace and security … and in his days justice abounded in the land so, that if a woman had gone alone throughout the whole of his dominions, bearing gold and silver in her hand, she would have found none to hurt her, neither in the waste, nor in the peopled country"; R. Southey (trans.) *The Chronicle of the Cid*, New York: Heritage Press, 1958, 47. Even the late sixteenth-century thinker Juan de Mariana accepted the ideas of the Circle of Justice as the foundations of political economy; J. Laurès, *The Political Economy of Juan de Mariana*, New York: Fordham University Press, 1928, 77–9, 86, 114.

57 Sulaymān b. Ḥassān b. Juljul al-Andalūsī, *Les Générations des médecins et des sages (Ṭabaqāt al-'aṭibbā' wal-ḥukamā')*, ed. F. Sayyid, Cairo: Imprimerie de l'Institut français d'archéologie orientale, 1955, 26; see Badawī, *Fontes*, 36; Grignaschi, "'Siyâsatu-l-Âmmiyya'," 225; Peters, *Aristoteles*, 112; D. Gutas, "The Spurious and the Authentic in the Arabic Lives of Aristotle," in J. Kraye, W. F. Ryan, and C. B. Schmitt (eds) *Pseudo-Aristotle in the Middle Ages: the theology and other texts*, London: Warburg Institute, 1986, 23. Ibn Juljul stated that the lines were written on a *qubba* (dome), which Grignaschi ("Origine," 23n1; 61) translated as "sepulcre" or "tombe." By the thirteenth century, when this passage was repeated by Ibn Abī Usaybi'a, tombs were domed and the word dome signified a tomb; Ibn Abī Usaybi'a related that Aristotle desired to be buried in a costly building with the eight sentences written on its eight sides; Ibn Abī Usaybi'a, *'Uyūn al-anbā' fī Ṭabaqāt al-aṭibbā'*, ed. N. Riḍā, Beirut: Dār Maktabat al-Ḥayāh, 1980, 102–3. The dome, however, does not appear in the *Sirr al-asrār*: Ibn Juljul seems to have transferred to a concrete medium Aristotle's introductory remark on the Circle of Justice: "I have divided this figure according to the divisions of the heavenly spheres … like the continuation of the revolution of the heavens"; Steele, *Opera*, 226. On the heavenly dome see J. M. Bloom, "The *Qubbat al-khaḍrā'* and the Iconography of Height in Early Islamic Architecture," *ArsOr* 23, 1993: 136; on its relation to kingship see A. S. Melikian-Chirvani, "The Light of the World," in R. Hillenbrand (ed.) *The Art of the*

Saljūqs in Iran and Anatolia, Costa Mesa, CA: Mazda, 1994, 148–9. This dome (*qubba*) may then have been conflated with Aristotle's tomb (*qabr*), mentioned in another context on the first page of the *Sirr*, and called a pyramid (*ḥarām*) in later works, presumably to adjust for eight-sidedness (Seljuk tombs were often eight-sided with pyramidal roofs). Al-Harawī's twelfth-century treatise transferred the dome to a Persian setting; J. Sourdel-Thomine, "Les conseils du Šayḫ al-Harawī à un prince ayyūbide," *BEO* 17, 1961–2: 219, and *Laṭā'if al-Ḥikma* turned it into a crown; Sadan, "'Closed-Circuit' Saying," 332n17.

58 Ibn 'Abd al-Barr al-Namarī (979–1070), *Bahjat al-majālis wa-uns al-mujālis*, ed. M. M. al-Khawlī, Cairo: Dār al-Kutub al-'Arabī lil-Ṭabā'a wa-al-Nashr, 1967, 1: 334; Abū Bakr Muḥammad b. al-Ḥasan al-Murādī al-Haḍramī, *Kitāb al-siyāsa aw al-ishāra fī tadbīr al-imāra*, ed. S. al-Nasār, Casablanca: Dār al-Thiqāfa, 1981, 107.

59 Abū al-Wafā' al-Mubashshir b. Fātik, *Los Bocados de Oro (Mujtar al-Ḥikam)*, ed. 'A. Badawi, Beirut: Arab Institute for Research and Publishing, 1980, 222. Grignaschi asserts that al-Mubashshir's source was neither *The Secret of Secrets* nor its lost antecedent ("L'Origine," 61), but his version of the Circle matches one of those in *The Secret of Secrets*. Like *The Secret of Secrets*, Ibn Fātik's book was translated in the medieval period into several European languages and was printed in England by the pioneer printer Caxton. A fifteenth-century English translation displaced justice from its pivotal position as the well-being of the world: "The worlde is lyke a gardeyne wherof the dyches be lykened to realmes; and the realmes be maintened by the lawes whiche the kinge hath stablysshed, the kinge is mayntened by his knyghtes, the knyghtes bene gouerned by money, the money cometh of the people, the people is gouerned by iustice, and so is all the world"; C. F. Bühler (ed.) *The Dicts and Sayings of the Philosophers: the translations made by Stephen Scrope, William Worcester and an anonymous translator*, London: Oxford University Press, 1941, 177.

60 M. Arkoun, *Contribution à l'étude de l'humanisme arabe au IVe/Xe siècle: Miskawayh (320/325–421) = (932/936–1030), philosophe et historien*, Paris: J. Vrin, 1970; for his history see Abū 'Alī Aḥmad b. Muḥammad Miskawayh, *The Tajārib al-'umam or History of Ibn Miskawayh*, ed. L. Caetani, Leiden: Brill, 1909; B. H. Siddiqi, "Ibn Miskawaih's Theory of History," *Iqbal* 12, 1963/4: 71–80; Khalidi, *Arabic Historical Thought*, 173–4.

61 Abū 'Alī Aḥmad b. Muḥammad Miskawayh, *Al-Ḥikma al-khalida (Javidan khirad)*, ed. 'A. Badawī, Cairo: Dār al-Andalus, 1952; also M. Arkoun's introduction to Ibn-i Miskawayh, *Javidan khirad*, trans. T. M. Shushtari, ed. B. Thirvatian, Tehran: McGill University, Tehran Branch, 1976, 6.

62 Abū 'Alī Aḥmad b. Muḥammad Miskawayh, *An Unpublished Treatise of Miskawayh on Justice; or, Risāla fī māhiyat al-'adl li Miskawayh*, ed. and trans. M. S. Khan, Leiden: Brill, 1964, 28–31; M. Fakhry, "Justice in Islamic Philosophical Ethics: Miskawayh's mediating contribution," *Journal of Religious Ethics* 3, 1975: 247; A. al-Azmeh, *Arabic Thought and Islamic Societies*, London: Croom Helm, 1986, 35. See also Abū 'Alī Aḥmad b. Muḥammad Miskawayh, *Tahdhīb al-akhlāq wa-taṭhīr al-a'rāq*, trans. C. K. Zurayk as *The Refinement of Character*, Beirut: American University of Beirut, 1968, a Greek-influenced work of philosophical ethics, which discussed justice as a mean between two extremes.

63 M. A. Ansari, *The Ethical Philosophy of Miskawaih*, Aligarh: Aligarh Muslim University, 1964, 110–37; B. Bhat, *Abu Ali Miskawayh: a study of his historical and social thought*, New Delhi: Islamic Book Foundation, 1991, 158–9; Mottahedeh, *Loyalty*, 175–80; quotation from Fakhry, "Justice," 248.

64 J. Sadan, "'Community' and 'Extra-Community' as a Legal and Literary Problem," in J. L. Kraemer and I. Alon (eds) *Religion and Government in the World of Islam*, *IOS* 10, 1983: 102–15. Miskawayh saw the consequences of injustice in the Circle's pattern: "revenues were cut off, and the distant provinces reduced to ruin owing to the collapse of the capital. Political power came away empty-handed, the subjects were ruined, the house destroyed, food provisions failed and the army fell into disorder"; quoted in P. L. Heck, *The Construction of Knowledge in Islamic Civilization: Qudāma b. Ja'far and his* Kitāb al-Kharāj wa-Ṣinā'at al-Kitāba, Leiden: Brill, 2002, 224n78.

65 A. K. S. Lambton, "An Account of the *Tārīkhi Qumm*," *BSOAS* 12, 1948: 592–3.

66 Hasan Qummi, *Tarikh-i Qumm* (History of Qumm), cited in A. K. S. Lambton, *Landlord and Peasant in Persia*, rev. ed. London: Oxford University Press, 1969; repr. London: IB Tauris, 1991, xv; 34–40; 46–7; Cahen, "L'Évolution de l'iqta'," 28–35.

67 T. W. Arnold, *The Caliphate*, Oxford: Clarendon, 1924, 61–7. Religious thought apparently assented to caliphal subordination to avoid the dilemma of refusing to accept what would have become illegal orders from the divinely-appointed head of the Muslim community; I. M. Lapidus, "The Separation of State and Religion in the Development of Early Islamic Society," *IJMES* 6, 1975: 363–85.

68 On the ups and downs (or, rather, the downs and ups) of the relationship between caliph and sultan in Buyid times, A. H. Siddiqi, "Caliphate and Kingship in Medieval Persia," *IC* 9, 1935: 560–79; 10, 1936: 97–126, 260–79, 390–408; 11, 1937: 37–59, repr. as *Caliphate and Kingship in Medieval Persia*, Philadelphia, PA: Porcupine Press, 1977; M. Kabir, "The Relation of the Buwayhid Amirs with the 'Abbasid Caliphs," *JPHS* 2, 1954: 228–43; E. J. Hanne, *Putting the Caliph in His Place: power, authority, and the late Abbasid caliphate*, Madison, NJ: Fairleigh Dickinson University Press, 2007.

69 C. Cahen, "The Body Politic," in G. E. von Grunebaum (ed.) *Unity and Variety in Muslim Civilization*, Chicago, IL: University of Chicago Press, 1955, 151.

70 Abū al-Ḥasan 'Alī b. Muḥammad al-Māwardī, *al-Aḥkām al-Sulṭāniyya*, trans. W. H. Wahba as *The Ordinances of Government*, Reading, UK: Garnet Publishing, 1996, and by E. Fagnan as *Les statuts governementaux, ou Règles de droit public et administratif*, Algiers: Librairie de l'Université, 1915.

71 Al-Māwardī, *Ordinances*, 1; H. A. R. Gibb, "Al-Mawardi's Theory of the Caliphate," *IC* 11, 1937: 292–3; see also W. B. Hallaq, "Was the Gate of Ijtihad Closed?" *IJMES* 16, 1984: 13. This purpose was still valid even if al-Māwardī's was not the original proposal but a Shāfi'ī response to a Ḥanbalī proposal written about the same time, as proposed by D. P. Little, "A New Look at *al-Aḥkām al-sulṭāniyya*," *MW* 64, 1974: 1–15. It extended as well to the other offices discussed in these treatises: N. Hurvitz, "Competing Texts: the relationship between al-Mawardi's and Abu Ya'la's *al-Ahkam al-sultaniyya*," Occasional Publications, 8, Cambridge: Islamic Legal Studies Program of Harvard Law School, 2007.

72 H. Laoust, "La pensée et l'action politiques d'al-Mawardi (364–450/974–1058)," *REI* 36, 1968: 23; H. Mikhail, *Politics and Revelation: Mawardi and after*, Edinburgh: Edinburgh University Press, 1995, 47; al-Māwardī, *Ordinances*, 32–7.

73 Al-Māwardī, *Ordinances*, 16; cf. P. Crone, *God's Rule: six centuries of medieval Islamic political thought*, New York: Columbia University Press, 2004, 305–15, who lists providing security, maintaining the infrastructure, helping the poor, and supporting culture under the ruler's non-shar'ī duties.

74 Quoted in Q. Khan, *Al-Mawardi's Theory of the State*, Lahore: Bazm-i Iqbal, [1950s], 31; Mikhail, *Politics*, 33. This is an example of al-Azmeh's proposition that "*aḥkām* works are instruments of absolutist government which specify the pragmatic and ethical content of the *Fürstenspiegel* [advice works] as shar'ist"; al-Azmeh, *Muslim Kingship*, 100.

75 Al-Māwardī, *Ordinances*, 87–106, 170, 189–96.

76 Abū Yūsuf had considered ancient non-Arab customary practices not conflicting with Islam to have the force of law, and many pre-Islamic customs and ideas were incorporated in the *ḥadīth* of the early Muslims on which law was based; S. Vryonis, Jr., "Byzantium and Islam: seven–seventeenth century," *EEQ* 2.3, 1968/9: 223; W. M. Watt, *Muslim Intellectual: a study of al-Ghazali*, Edinburgh: Edinburgh University Press, 1963, 15. Ḥanafī law is thought to have legitimized the Near Eastern state in order to legalize ordinary people's transactions; B. Johansen, "Sacred and Religious Elements in Hanafite Law – function and limits of the absolute character of government authority," in E. Gellner and J.-C. Vatin (eds) *Islam et politique au Maghreb*, Paris: CNRS, 1981, 303.

77 See Abū al-Ḥasan 'Alī b. Muḥammad al-Māwardī, *Tashīl al-naẓar wa-ta'jīl al-afar fī akhlāq al-malik wa-siyāsat al-mulk*, ed. R. al-Sayyid, Beirut: Dār al-'Ulūm al-'Arabiyya, 1987, especially the enumeration of the king's helpers as care for the flock, army, money, and production (216–30); and ibid., *Durar al-sulūk fī siyāsat al-mulūk*, Riyadh: Dār al-Waṭan lil-Nashr, 1997.

78 Abū al-Ḥasan 'Alī b. Muḥammad al-Māwardī, *al-Tuḥfah al-mulukiyya fī al-ādāb al-siyāsiyya*, Alexandria: Mu'assasat Shabāb al-Jāmi'a, 1977, 71; ibid., *Qawānīn al-wizāra wa-siyāsat al-mulk*, ed. F. 'A. Aḥmad and M. S. Dāwūd, 3rd ed., Alexandria: Mu'assasat Shabāb al-Jāmi'a, 1991, 61.

79 The court was called *naẓr al-maẓālim*, "review of wrongs"; Laoust, "Pensée," 21–2; see H. 'Abd al-Mun'im, *Dīwān al-maẓālim*, Beirut: Dār al-Shurūq, 1983. For court procedures see al-Māwardī, *Ordinances*, 90; É. Tyan, *Histoire de l'organisation judiciaire en pays d'Islam*, Paris: Librairie du Recueil Sirey, 1938–43, 2: 141–289; R. Levy, *The Social Structure of Islam*, Cambridge: Cambridge University Press, 1957, 348–51; *EI2*, s.v. "maẓālim." Tyan considered cases involving the malfunctioning of public services as an artificial extension of *maẓālim* jurisdiction (Tyan, *Histoire*, 2: 182), but in reality such cases were the very essence of *maẓālim* justice, whose purpose was the protection of the weak and powerless in a system where power was concentrated at the top.

80 Al-Māwardī, *Ordinances*, 94; M. Khadduri and H. L. Liebesny (eds) *Law in the Middle East*, vol. 1: *Origin and Development of Islamic Law*, Washington, DC: Middle East Institute, 1955, 268; S. J. Staffa, *Conquest and Fusion: the social evolution of Cairo, AD 642–1850*, Leiden: Brill, 1977, 32.

81 Al-Māwardī, *Ordinances*, 88–93; H. F. Amédroz, "The Mazalim Jurisdiction in the Ahkam Sultaniyya of Mawardi," *JRAS* 1911: 659, conclusion from records of court decisions. See also S. B. Samadi, "Some Aspects of the Theory of the State and Administration under the Abbasids," *IC* 29, 1955: 142–3; examples in Tyan, *Histoire*, 2: 177–81. The special treasury, *bayt māl al-maẓālim*: D. Sourdel, *Le vizirat abbaside de 749 à 936 (132 à 324 de l'Hégire)*, 2 vols, Damascus: Institut français de Damas, 1959–60, 2: 595; Tyan, *Institutions*, 1: 422.

82 Sourdel, *Vizirat*, 2: 660–1; Tyan, *Histoire*, 2: 151; J. Dakhlia, *Le divan des rois: le politique et le religieux dans l'Islam*, Paris: Aubier, 1998, 72. Even the Saffarid rulers were careful to judge *maẓālim* cases in person and support public works and irrigation; *CHIr*, 4: 127–8. When the caliph al-Mustarshid drove the sultan's representatives out of Iraq, he sent his own representative to preside over the *maẓālim* court; C. Hillenbrand, *A Muslim Principality in Crusader Times: the early Artuqid state*, Istanbul: Nederlands Historisch-Archaeologisch Instituut, 1990, 67. The heir to the throne often gained recognition by hearing petitions and sitting in *maẓālim*; Ibn Hammad, trans. Dakhlia, *Divan*, 251. The caliph al-Mu'taḍid appointed a separate judge to hear complaints against court personnel (Tyan, *Histoire*, 2: 225); taxation cases were sometimes heard by finance administrators (Sourdel, *Vizirat*, 643); viziers and other appointees often presided. According to Ibn Khaldūn (cited in Dakhlia, *Divan*, 98), the "Rightly-Guided Caliphs" all judged cases in person, only gradually delegating this task to others.

83 The history of this court is contested; writers convey different, often conflicting, details. Pre-Islamic and Islamic examples: Mez, *Renaissance*, 233. 'Abd al-Malik: al-Māwardī, *Ordinances*, 88; P. Crone and M. Hinds, *God's Caliph: religious authority in the first centuries of Islam*, Cambridge: Cambridge University Press, 1986, 44–5; M. G. Morony, *Iraq after the Muslim Conquest*, Princeton, NJ: Princeton University Press, 1984, 86. Mu'āwiya: R. Hillenbrand, "*La Dolce Vita* in Early Islamic Syria: the evidence of later Umayyad palaces," *Art History* 5, 1982: 6. Abbasids: Abū Yūsuf, *Kitāb al-kharāj*, ed. and trans. A. Ben Shemesh, *Taxation in Islam*, vol. 3, *Abū Yūsuf's Kitāb al-kharāj*, Leiden: Brill, 1969, 107; C. E. Bosworth, "Administrative Literature," in M. J. L. Young, J. D. Latham, and R. B. Serjeant (eds) *Religion, Learning and Science in the Abbasid Period*, The Cambridge History of Arabic Literature, 3, Cambridge: Cambridge University Press, 1983–90, 165. Later Muslim society's increased demand for *maẓālim* courts may be related to the influence of the Turkish tradition of ruler's law (see Ch. 6); M. F. Köprülü, "Ortazaman Türk hukukî müessesesi," *Belleten* 2, 1938: 58–9; A. N. Poliak, "The Influence of Chingiz-Khan's Yāsa upon the General Organization of the Mamlūk State," *BSOAS* 10, 1942: 862. Court procedure: *EI2*, s.v. "Diwan"; Y. Tabbaa, *Constructions of Power and Piety in Medieval Aleppo*, University Park: Pennsylvania State University Press, 1997, 157–8; Heck, *Construction*, 86–7.

84 North Africa: Tyan, *Histoire*, 2: 161; J. F. P. Hopkins, *Medieval Muslim Government in Barbary: until the sixth century of the Hijra*, London: Luzac, 1958, 137–44; H. Yanagihashi, "The Judicial Functions of the *Sulṭān* in Civil Cases According to the Mālikīs up to the Sixth/Twelfth Century," *ILS* 3, 1996: 42. Spain: Tyan, *Histoire*, 2: 286–7; on Cordoba's lawcourts, C. Müller, *Gerichtspraxis im Stadtstaat Córdoba: Zum Recht der Gesellschaft in einer mālikitisch-islamischen Rechtstradition des 5./11. Jahrhunderts*, Leiden: Brill, 1999. Sicily: Ibn al-Athīr, trans. W. Granara, "*Jihād* and Cross-cultural Encounter in Muslim Sicily," *HMEIR* 3, 1996: 53. This court may have influenced European court practices; M. Amari, *Storia dei Musulmani de Sicilia*, 2nd ed., Rome: Catania, 1938, 3: 451–2; A. Ahmad, *A History of Islamic Sicily*, Edinburgh: Edinburgh University Press, 1975, 64–6. Women: al-Māwardī, *Ordinances*, 72 (admitting that most of the ulema rejected this view); Mez, *Renaissance*, 233&n8; H. F. Kasassbeh, *The Office of Qāḍī in the Early 'Abbāsid Caliphate (132–247/750–861)*, Jordan: Deanship of Research and Graduate Studies, Mu'tah University, 1994, 281; F. Mernissi, *The Forgotten Queens of Islam*, trans. M. J. Lakeland, Minneapolis: University of Minnesota Press, 1993, 42–3, where the main problem was that the woman judge had to appear in public. Ibn Qutayba, the first historian to quote the Circle of Justice, had served as a *maẓālim* judge; Heck, *Construction*, 46.

85 Donohue, *Buwayhid Dynasty*, 124; P. J. Vatikiotis, *The Faṭimid Theory of State*, Lahore: Institute of Islamic Culture, 1957; 2nd ed. 1981, 70–1. The image of the ruler as linch-pin of the universal order, inherent in the Circle of Justice, was compatible with the Shi'ī Fāṭimid understanding of the caliph's role; al-Qāḍī, "Early Fāṭimid," 102–3; P. J. Vatikiotis, "A Reconstruction of the Faṭimid Theory of State," *IC* 28, 1954: 399–409.

86 S. M. Imamuddin, "Administration under the Faṭimids," *JASP* 14, 1969: 263. According to al-Maqrīzī, some Faṭimid rulers and officials held *maẓālim* court as often as twice a week, and

earlier governors and rulers of Egypt had also performed this duty; A. Haji, "Institutions of Justice in Fatimid Egypt (358–567/969–1171)," in A. al-Azmeh (ed.) *Islamic Law: social and historical contexts*, New York: Routledge, 1988, 205–6. Ptolemaic, Roman, and Byzantine precedents: W. Björkman, "Die Bittschriften im *dīwān al-inšā*," *Der Islam* 18, 1929: 207–12.

87 Quotations from Salinger, "Muslim Mirror," 34, 31.

88 H. Massé, "Ibn el-Çaïrafi, code de la chancellerie d'état (période fâtimide)," *Bulletin de l'Institut français d'archéologie du Caire* 11, 1914: 113–15.

89 S. D. Goitein, "Petitions to Fatimid Caliphs from the Cairo Geniza," *Jewish Quarterly Review*, n.s. 45, 1954/5: 30–8; S. M. Stern, "Three Petitions of the Fāṭimid Period," *Oriens* 15, 1962: 172–209; S. D. Goitein, *Fāṭimid Decrees: original documents from the Fāṭimid chancery*, London: Faber & Faber, 1964; D. S. Richards, "A Fāṭimid Petition and 'Small Decree' from Sinai," *IOS* 3, 1973: 140–58; G. Khan, "A Petition to the Fāṭimid Caliph al-'Āmir," *JRAS* 1990: 44–54; G. Khan, "The Historical Development of the Structure of the Medieval Arabic Petition," *BSOAS* 53, 1990: 8–30; G. Khan, "A Copy of a Decree from the Archives of the Fāṭimid Chancery in Egypt," *BSOAS* 49, 1986: 439–53; G. Khan, *Arabic Legal and Administrative Documents in the Cambridge Genizah Collections*, Cambridge: Cambridge University Press, 1993, 321–76, 451. Petition topics: Stern, "Three Petitions," 175, 180, 184; Richards, "Fāṭimid Petition," 142–3; Stern, *Fāṭimid Decrees*, 83, 18–20, 72, 49; Khan, *Arabic Legal*, 321–60, 379–405.

90 Al-Māwardī, *Ordinances*, 87–90; Tyan, *Histoire*, 2: 268–9; Grignaschi, "Rasā'il Arisṭāṭālīsa," 10.

91 Hilāl al-Ṣābi', *Rusūm Dār al-Khilāfah: the rules and regulations of the 'Abbāsid court*, trans. E. A. Salem, Beirut: American University of Beirut, 1977.

92 Quotations from ibid., 10, 110.

93 This story, included in late editions of the *Thousand and One Nights*, is attributed to an editor familiar with the writings of Wahb b. Munabbih, a very early author of Persian Jewish background whose lost works are proposed as the story's source; Manzalaoui, "Pseudo-Aristotelian," 214–15. V. Chauvin, *La récension égyptienne des Mille et Une Nuits*, Brussels: Faculté de Philosophie et Lettres de L'Université de Liège, 1899, 61–2; M. J. de Hammer, *Contes inédits des Mille et Une Nuits*, trans. M. G.-S. Trébutien, Paris: Libraririe Orientale de Dondey-Dupré Père et Fils, 1828, 421–2 (672nd–673rd nights); M. al-'Adawī (ed.) *Kitāb alf layla wa-layla*, Bulaq: Maṭba'a 'Abd al-Raḥmān Rushdī Bey, 1862–3, 2: 393 (465th night). The Arabic reads: "Al-dīn bi-al-mulk wa-al-mulk bi-al-jund wa-al-jund bi-al-māl wa-al-māl bi-'imārat al-bilād wa-'imārat al-bilād bi-al-'adl fī-al-'ibād." This is the same version quoted by al-Ghazālī (see Ch. 6), and the story sounds like a summary of the one accompanying the Circle in his text; since this story was added later to the *Nights*, al-Ghazālī may be its actual source.

94 H. A. R. Gibb, "An Interpretation of Islamic History," *JWH* 1, 1953: 39–62, repr. in S. J. Shaw and W. K. Polk (eds) *Studies on the Civilization of Islam*, Boston, MA: Beacon Press, 1962, 14; ibid., "The Social Significance of the Shuubiya," in *Studia orientalia Ioanni Pedersen septuagenario A.D. VII id. nov. anno MCMLIII a collegis discipulis amicis dicata*, 105–14, Hauniae [Copenhagen]: E. Munksgaard, 1953; repr. in Shaw and Polk, *Studies on the Civilization of Islam*, 72. A different view of al-Māwardī's achievement: Q. Khan, *Al-Mawardi's Theory*. Lambton defined the problem as that of islamicizing the Sasanian ideal; A. K. S. Lambton, "Islamic Mirrors for Princes," in *La Persia nel medioevo: Atti del Convegno internazionale, Rome, 1970*, Rome: Accademia Nazionale dei Lincei, 1971, 424; but there was also a problem of integration.

95 See Richter-Bernburg, "*Amīr-Malik-Shāhānshāh*," 83.

96 Hilāl al-Ṣābi', *Rusūm*, 11.

97 Dakhlia, *Divan*, 166–7.

6 The Turks and Islamic civilization

1 Steppe empires: R. Grousset, *The Empire of the Steppes: a history of Central Asia*, trans. N. Walford, New Brunswick, NJ: Rutgers University Press, 1970; D. Sinor (ed.) *The Cambridge History of Early Inner Asia*, Cambridge: Cambridge University Press, 1990; S. Soucek, *A History of Inner Asia*, Cambridge: Cambridge University Press, 2000.

2 T. Tekin, *A Grammar of Orkhon Turkic*, Bloomington: Indiana University Research Center for the Language Sciences, 1968, 280.

3 P. B. Golden, "Imperial Ideology and the Sources of Political Unity amongst the Pre-Činggisid Nomads of Western Eurasia," *AEuras* 2, 1982: 46. Golden notes the similarity between this and

Chinese concepts of rule and provides evidence that the direction of borrowing at this time was from the steppe to China; ibid., 48.

4 Orkhon inscriptions, trans. Tekin, *Grammar*, 263, 261; see also 268, 275, 280, 291. The sovereign's jurisdiction was theoretically universal; see O. Turan, "The Ideal of World Domination among the Medieval Turks," *SI* 4, 1955: 79.

5 Orkhon inscriptions, trans. Tekin, *Grammar*, 263–4. Barfield differentiated Turco-Mongol tribes from Arab tribes by this organization, or "hierarchy"; T. J. Barfield, "Tribe and State Relations: the Inner Asian perspective," in P. S. Khoury and J. Kostiner (eds) *Tribes and State Formation in the Middle East*, Berkeley: University of California Press, 1990, 153–82.

6 Orkhon inscriptions, trans. Tekin, *Grammar*, 262, 266, 267-8; Golden, "Imperial Ideology," 51; L. Bazin, "Man and the Concept of History in Turkish Central Asia during the Eighth Century," *Diogenes*, no. 42, 1963: 96. See İ. Togan, "Patterns of Legitimization of Rule in the History of the Turks," in K. A. Ertürk (ed.) *Rethinking Central Asia: non-Eurocentric studies in history, social structure and identity*, Reading, UK: Ithaca, 1999, 39.

7 C. E. Bosworth, "Barbarian Incursions: the coming of the Turks into the Islamic world," in D. S. Richards (ed.) *Islamic Civilisation, 950–1150*, Oxford: Bruno Cassirer, 1973, 1–16; C. E. Bosworth, *The Ghaznavids: their empire in Afghanistan and eastern Iran, 944–1040*, 2nd ed., Beirut: Librairie du Liban, 1973.

8 R. P. Mottahedeh, "Some Attitudes towards Monarchy and Absolutism in the Eastern Islamic World of the Eleventh and Twelfth Centuries A.D.," *IOS* 10, 1983: 88. Abbasid literature characterized the Turks as superb warriors chosen by God for their military role in Muslim society; Abū 'Uthmān Amr b. Baḥr al-Jāḥiẓ, "The Merits of the Turks," trans. C. Pellat, *The Life and Works of Jāḥiẓ: translations of selected texts*, trans. D. M. Hawke, Berkeley: University of California Press, 1969, 91–7, excerpted in W. H. McNeill and M. R. Waldman (eds) *The Islamic World*, London: Oxford University Press, 1973, 113–17.

9 Abū Manṣūr al-Ḥusayn al-Tha'ālibī, *Histoire des Rois des Perses (Ghurar siyar al-mulūk)*, trans. H. Zotenberg, Paris: Imprimerie Nationale, 1900; Tehran: Maktabat al-Asadī, 1963, xix; garden on 723; Circle on 482; see 485, 499, 500, 509, 511, 529, 607. This text of the Circle of Justice is identical to Ibn Qutayba's. Another Tha'ālibī, the contemporary Abū Manṣūr 'Abd al-Malik, quoted the same version twice, once in a book of proverbs and once in a grammatical text; *al-Tamthīl wa'l-muḥāḍara*, ed. 'A. M. al-Ḥilw, Cairo: Dār Iyā' al-Kutub al-'Arabiyya, 1961, 136; *Thimār al-qulūb fi al-muḍāf wa'l-mansūb*, Cairo: Maṭba'at al-Ẓāhir, 1908, 140.

10 Sebüktegin, "Pandnama," trans. M. Nazim, "The *Pand-Namah* of Subuktigīn," *JRAS* 1933: 624, 625, 607. Bosworth doubted the ability of a "barbarian" to write such a testament; C. E. Bosworth, "Early Sources for the History of the First Four Ghaznavid Sultans (977–1041)," *IQ* 7, 1963: 19–20. Between an upbringing at the Samanid court in the chamberlain's household and access to a competent scribal cadre, however, Sebüktegin's authorship need not be denied.

11 Bayhaqī, "Tārīkh," trans. M. R. Waldman, *Toward a Theory of Historical Narrative: a case study in Perso-Islamicate historiography*, Columbus: Ohio State University Press, 1980, 153; C. E. Bosworth, "The Titulature of the Early Ghaznavids," *Oriens* 15, 1962: 216; M. Nazim, *The Life and Times of Sultān Mahmūd of Ghazna*, Lahore: Khalil, 1931, repr. 1973, 149, 134.

12 R. Hillenbrand, "The Architecture of the Ghaznavids and Ghurids," in C. Hillenbrand (ed.) *Studies in Honour of Clifford Edmund Bosworth*, vol. 2: *The Sultan's Turret: studies in Persian and Turkish culture*, Leiden: Brill, 2000, 2: 142, 147, 179, 201.

13 Abū al-Naṣr Muḥammad b. Muḥammad al-Jabbār al-'Utbī, *The Kitab-i-yamini: historical memoirs of the Amír Sabaktagin, and the Sultán Mahmúd of Ghazna*, trans. J. Reynolds, London: Oriental Translation Fund, 1858; Lahore: Qausain, 1975, 21, 150, 345, 470, 483. Poets such as 'Unsurī and Farrūkhī compared the Ghaznavids to the heroes and just rulers of the *Shāhnāma*; A. S. Melikian-Chirvani, "Le Livre des rois, miroir du destin," *StIr* 17, 1988: 12–20. On Maḥmūd's successors, C. E. Bosworth, *The Later Ghaznavids: Splendour and Decay: the dynasty in Afghanistan and Northern India, 1040–1186*, New York: Columbia University Press, 1977, 74, 86–7.

14 W. Barthold, *Turkestan Down to the Mongol Invasions*, ed. C. E. Bosworth, trans. Mrs. T. Minorsky, 3rd ed., E. J. W. Gibb Memorial Trust, London: Luzac, 1968, 291; Bosworth, *Ghaznavids*, 253; J. S. Meisami, *Persian Historiography: to the end of the twelfth century*, Edinburgh: Edinburgh University Press, 1999, 97–8. On the contradictory images of Maḥmūd see C. E. Bosworth,

"Mahmud of Ghazna in Contemporary Eyes and in Later Persian Literature," *Iran* 4, 1966: 85-92. Nishapur's real problem may have been that its walls were not strong enough to protect the city; J. Paul, "The Seljuq Conquest(s) of Nishapur: a reappraisal," *IranS* 38, 2005: 75–85.

15 Ibrāhīm: Al-Mervarrūdhī, *Ādāb al-harb wa'l-shujā'a*, trans. I. M. Shafi, "Fresh Light on the Ghaznavids," *IC* 12, 1938: 201; Sir J. Malcolm, *The History of Persia, from the most early period to the present time*, 2 vols, London: J. Murray and Longman, 1815, 1: 339; C. E. Bosworth, "The Imperial Policy of the Early Ghaznawids," *IS* 1, no. 3, 1962: 74–5. Poetry: J. S. Meisami, "Ghaznavid Panegyrics: some political implications," *Iran* 28, 1990: 35; J. W. Clinton, *The Divan of Manūchihrī Dāmghānī: a critical study*, Minneapolis, MN: Bibliotheca Islamica, 1972, 132, 138. Executions: Abū al-Faẓl Muḥammad Bayhaqī, *Tārīkh-i Bayhaqī*, ed. 'A. A. Fayyāz, Mashhad: Danishgāh-i Mashhad, 1971/1350, 221–36, "The Gibbeting of the Minister Hasanak," trans. J. E. Woods; Bayhaqī, "Tārīkh," trans. Waldman, 153–5.

16 Various regimes seem to have absorbed sedentary politics and the Circle of Justice with differing levels of thoroughness depending on how they immigrated into the Middle East, as organized tribal groups or as individuals; L. T. Darling, "Social Cohesion (*'Asabiyya*) and Justice in the Late Medieval Middle East," *CSSH* 47.2, 2007: 329–57.

17 C. E. Bosworth, "A Turco-Mongol Practice amongst the Early Ghaznavids," *CAJ* 7, 1962: 237–40; Bayhaqí, "Táríkhu-s Subuktigin," in H. M. Elliot and J. Dowson (ed. and trans.) *The History of India as Told by Its Own Historians*, London: Trübner, 1869; repr. New York: AMS Press, 1966, 2: 78.

18 R. N. Frye, *Bukhara: the medieval achievement*, Norman: University of Oklahoma Press, 1965, 123; Bosworth, *Ghaznavids*, 114, 167. On *ghazā* see L. T. Darling, "Contested Territory: Ottoman holy war in comparative perspective," *SI* 91, 2000: 133–63.

19 Yūsuf Khāṣṣ Ḥājib, *Wisdom of Royal Glory (Kutadgu bilig): a Turko-Islamic mirror for princes*, trans. R. Dankoff, Chicago, IL: University of Chicago Press, 1983, 107; Melikian-Chirvani, "Le livre des rois, miroir du destan," 26–9. Edib Ahmed, in *The Threshold of Reality (Atebetü'l-hakayık)*, called the Karakhanid Muḥammad Ispahsalar Beg "in justice and equity a real Anushirvan"; Edib Ahmed b. Mahmud Yükneki, *Atebetü'l-hakayık*, ed. R. R. Arat, Istanbul: Ateş, 1951, 84.

20 Yūsuf Khāṣṣ Ḥājib, *Wisdom*, 49, 106, 119, 121–2.

21 Ibid., 87, 142; see H. İnalcık, "Turkish and Iranian Political Theories and Traditions in *Kutadgu Bilig*," trans. D. A. Howard, in H. İnalcık, *The Middle East and the Balkans under the Ottoman Empire: essays on economy and society*, Bloomington: Indiana University Turkish Studies, 1993, 11–12; C. E. Bosworth, "The Heritage of Rulership in Early Islamic Iran and the Search for Dynastic Connections with the Past," *Iran* 11, 1973: 61–2; Golden, "Imperial Ideology," 41. The split seen by modern Turks between the Iranian concept of justice proceeding from the ruler and the Turkish idea that it proceeded from the law (*töre*) is overstated, since law itself proceeded from the king; cf. A. Uğur, *Osmanlı siyaset-nameler*, Istanbul: Milli Eğitim Bakanlığı, 2001, 88.

22 Dankoff, Introduction, *Wisdom*, 8–9; A. K. S. Lambton, "Changing Concepts of Justice and Injustice from the 5th/11th Century to the 8th/14th Century in Persia: the Saljuq Empire and the Ilkhanate," *SI* 68, 1988: 31.

23 A. C. S. Peacock, *Early Seljūq History: a new interpretation*, London: Routledge, 2010, 37–8, 54–5; O. Safi, *The Politics of Knowledge in Premodern Islam: negotiating ideology and religious inquiry*, Chapel Hill: University of North Carolina Press, 2006, 10, 12, 16, 218nn46, 57; C. Cahen, "Le Malik-Nâmeh et l'histoire des origins seljukides," *Oriens* 2, 1949: 42–3 (according to the *Malik-nâmeh* the Seljuks originated in the entourage of "Yabghu"; the *yabghu* was a ruler subordinate to the *khagan*); Sinor, *Early Inner Asia*, 362; A. K. S. Lambton, "Concepts of Authority in Persia: eleventh to nineteenth centuries A.D.," *Iran* 26, 1988: 99; 'Izz al-Dīn Ibn al-Athīr, *The Annals of the Saljuq Turks: selections from al-Kāmil fī'l-ta'rīkh of 'Izz al-Dīn Ibn al-Athīr*, trans. D. S. Richards, London: Routledge/Curzon, 2002, 31; İ. Kafesoğlu, *A History of the Seljuks: İbrahim Kafesoğlu's interpretation and the resulting controversy*, trans. G. Leiser, Carbondale: Southern Illinois University Press, 1988, 82; Golden, "Imperial Ideology," 66–7.

24 Bayhaqī, *Ta'rīkh*, trans. Bosworth, *Ghaznavids*, 256; Kafesoğlu, *History*, 82; Safi, *Politics*, 28; see Ibn al-Athīr, *Annals*, 26, 27n61; Tughril's title was *'ādil pādishāh*. To a later historian, Seljuk sovereignty meant that the ruler "forbade, he gave orders, he made grants, he levied taxes, he administered efficiently, he abolished things, he ordered affairs correctly, he abrogated them and he presided every Sunday and Wednesday over the investigation of *maẓālim*"; 'Imād al-Dīn al-Kātib al-Iṣfahān, *Zubdat al-nuṣra wa-nukhbat al-'uṣra*, trans. Bosworth, *Ghaznavids*, 267.

25 Khwāndamīr, *Habīb al-siyar*, trans. Julien Dumoret, "Histoire des Seldjoukides, extraite de l'ouvrage intitulé *Khélassat-oul-akhbar*, et traduite du persan de Khondémir," *JA* ser. 2, vol. 13, 1834: 242; see Kafesoğlu, *History*, 36. Tughril Beg appointed his half brother Ibrahim governor of Nishapur, but Ibrahim adopted a policy of tyranny until "the remonstrances of the inhabitants caused him to amend his ways"; Ḥamd Allāh Mustawfī Qazvīnī, *The Ta'rīkh-i-guzida or "Select History"*, abridged trans. E. G. Browne, Leiden: Brill; London: Luzac, 1913, 436.

26 Could they have construed themselves as *yabghus* to an Abbasid khaganate? See al-Mas'ūdī's characterization of the Khazar *khagan*: "His official function is that he be in the hands of another king and in his palace"; trans. Golden, "Imperial Ideology," 59, 67. See also A. Alföldi, "Türklerde çift krallık," in *İkinci Türk tarih kongresi (1937)*, Istanbul: Kenan, 1943, 507–10.

27 Ibn al-Athīr, *Annals*, 253, 182; Ibn al-Athīr thought the assassination was a plot by rival courtiers; ibid., 255. These courtiers are now thought to have arranged Niẓām al-Mulk's murder by an Isma'īlī assassin; A. A. Khismatulin, "To Forge a Book in the Medieval Ages: Nezām al-Molk's *Siyar al-moluk (Siyāsat-Nāma)*," *Journal of Persianate Studies* 1, 2008: 42; Safi, *Politics*, 74–9.

28 Hodgson, *Venture*, 2: 402-10; *EI2*, s.v. "Ghulām;" D. Ayalon, "The Mamlūks of the Seljuks: Islam's military might at the crossroads," *JRAS* 1996: 305–33. *The Book of Governance* suggests that by this time the army no longer consisted of nomads, since dismissed soldiers had no other means of support (i.e. were not herdsmen); it recommended bringing (more) Turks into the palace system as pages and bodyguards; Niẓām al-Mulk, *The Book of Government or Rules for Kings: The Siyar al-muluk or siyasat-nama*, trans. H. Darke, 2nd ed., London: Routledge & Kegan Paul, 1978, 102, 165–6; *CHIr*, 5: 81; S. R. A. Rizvi, "Political and Administrative Measures of Nizām al-Mulk Tūsī," *IS* 19, 1980: 112, 116.

29 S. Vryonis, "Seljuk Gulams and Ottoman Devshirmes," *Der Islam* 41, 1965: 227–31; C. Cahen, "L'Évolution de l'iqta' du IXe au XIIIe siècle: contribution à une histoire comparée des sociétés médiévales," *Annales: économies, sociétés, civilisations* 8, 1953: 39; A. K. S. Lambton, "Reflections on the *Iqṭā'*," in G. Makdisi (ed.) *Arabic and Islamic Stidies in Honor of Hamilton A. R. Gibb*, Leiden: Brill, 1965, 358–76. Land or revenue grants to government servants in lieu of salary are attested in the Near East from the third millennium BCE; M. deJ. Ellis, *Agriculture and the State in Ancient Mesopotamia: an introduction to problems of land tenure*, Philadelphia, PA: University Museum, 1976, 10, 20, 25.

30 C. Cahen, *Pre-Ottoman Turkey: a general survey of the material and spiritual culture and history c. 1071–1330*, trans. J. Jones-Williams, London: Sidgwick & Jackson, 1968, 152–3, 217–20, 224–9, 249–64; C. M. Brand, "The Turkish Element in Byzantium, eleventh–twelfth centuries," *Dumbarton Oaks Papers* 43, 1989: 1–25. On the early stages of conquest, Peacock, *Early Seljūq History*, 139–63.

31 S. Redford, "The Seljuks of Rum and the Antique," *Muqarnas* 10, 1993: 153–5; W. W. Barthold, "Caliph and Sultan," trans. N. S. Doniach, *IQ* 7, 1963: 130&n5. Some of the Seljuk sultans even inhabited ancient ruins; S. Redford, "Just Landscape in Medieval Anatolia," *Studies in the History of Gardens and Designed Landscapes* 20, 2000: 323. Verses from the *Shāhnāma* decorated palace walls: S. S. Blair, "The Ilkhanid Palace," *ArsOr* 23, 1993: 243. On Seljuk images of Solomon and ancient Persian kings: J. Zick-Nissen, "The Turquoise 'Jām' of King 'Jamshīd'," in R. Hillenbrand (ed.) *The Art of the Saljūqs in Iran and Anatolia*, Costa Mesa, CA: Mazda, 1994, 182.

32 M. F. Köprülü, *The Seljuks of Anatolia: their history and culture according to local Muslim sources*, ed. and trans. G. Leiser, Salt Lake City: University of Utah Press, 1992, 32–7.

33 Ibn al-Athīr, trans. M. H. M. Ahmad, "Some Notes on Arabic Historiography during the Zengid and Ayyubid Periods (512/1127–648/1250)," in B. Lewis and P. M. Holt, (eds) *Historians of the Middle East*, Historical Writing on the Peoples of Asia, 4, Oxford, New York: Oxford University Press, 1962, 81–92&n6. This hope was also expressed by Ibn Funduq; J. S. Meisami, "Rulers and the Writing of History," in B. Gruendler and L. Marlow, (eds) *Writers and Rulers: perspectives on their relationship from Abbasid to Safavid times*, Wiesbaden: Reichert, 2004, 82, 85. Cautionary use of the Persian tradition by the poet Khāqānī (d.1202): J. W. Clinton, "The *Madāen Qasida* of Xāqānī Sharvāni, I," *Edebiyat* 1, 1976: 153–70; cultural florescence: A. K. S. Lambton, "Aspects of Saljūq-Ghuzz Settlement in Persia," in Richards, *Islamic Civilisation*, 120-1.

34 Ibn al-Balkhī, *The Fārsnāma of Ibnu'l-Balkhī*, ed. G. Le Strange and R. A. Nicholson, E. J. W. Gibb Memorial Series, n.s. 1, London: Luzac, 1921, 1962, 5. This work's opening imitates Niẓām al-Mulk's *Siyāsat-nāma*: Meisami, *Persian Historiography*, 164–5.

35 Niẓāmī Ganjavī, *Kullīyāt-i Khamsa-yi Ḥakīm Niẓāmī Ganjavī*, Tehran: 'Alī Akbar 'Ilmī, 1331/1952; A. J. Arberry, *Classical Persian Literature*, New York: Macmillan, 1958, 126; *CHIr*, 5: 582–3;

J. S. Meisami, "Kings and Lovers: ethical dimensions of medieval Persian romance," *Edebiyat* 1, 1987: 3–7; Niẓāmī Ganjavī, *The Haft Paykar: a medieval Persian romance*, trans. J. S. Meisami, Oxford: Oxford University Press, 1995; E. Yarshater (ed.) *Persian Literature*, [Albany, NY]: Bibliotheca Persica, 1988, 168, 182–3; Nizāmī Ganjavī, *Makhzanol asrār, the treasury of mysteries*, trans. G. H. Darab, London: A. Probsthain, 1945, 217–19, 167–9, 157–60; a partial translation of the last story: E. G. Browne, *A Literary History of Persia*, Cambridge: Cambridge University Press, 1951, 2: 404. It may be related to the version in the *Thousand and One Nights*, which lacks the owls but includes Anushirvan (see Ch. 5).

36 P. E. Losensky, "*Fanā* and Taxes: a brief literary history of a Persian proverb," *Edebiyat* 7, 1996: 5; M. S. Southgate, *Iskandarnamah: a Persian medieval Alexander romance*, New York: Columbia University Press, 1978, 3, 181; J. Rypka, *History of Iranian Literature*, Dordrecht, Neth.: D. Reidel, 1968, 251; J. S. Cowen, *Kalila wa Dimna: an animal allegory of the Mongol court*, New York, Oxford: Oxford University Press, 1989, 9; A. Ateş, "Hicri VI–VIII. (XII–XIV.) asırlarda Anadolu'da Farsça eserler," *TM* 7–8, 1945: 111.

37 Advice literature, C.-H. de Fouchécour, *Moralia: les notions morales dans la littérature persane du 3e/9e au 7e/13e siècle*, Paris: Éditions Recherche sur les Civilisations, 1986. Seljuk adoption of the Near Eastern state: R. S. Humphreys, *Islamic History: a framework for inquiry*, rev. ed., Princeton, NJ: Princeton University Press, 1991, 148–68.

38 Persian political literature of the Seljuk period has not yet been examined by Turcologists or scholars of Inner Asian pastoral society with an eye to detecting such analogies. Mirrors for princes were one mechanism for integrating the varied cultures of the Muslim world.

39 Kai Kā'ūs ibn Iskandar, *A Mirror for Princes: the Qābūs nāma*, trans. R. Levy, New York: E. P. Dutton, 1951, 236. The frame story is usually taken literally, in view of Kai Ka'us's subordination to the Seljuks, but the diversity of occupations indicates that this work was designed for a much wider readership.

40 Kai Kā'ūs, *Mirror*, 222, 229; 213.

41 A. K. S. Lambton, "The Dilemma of Government in Islamic Persia: the *Siyāsat-nāma* of Niẓām al-Mulk," *Iran* 22, 1984: 64. On the book's authorship and organization see A. A. Khismatulin, "The Art of Medieval Counterfeiting: the *Siyar al-mulūk* (the *Siyāsat-nāma*) by Niẓām al-Mulk and the 'full' version of the *Naṣīḥat al-mulūk* by al-Ghazālī," *Manuscripta Orientalia* 14, 2008: 4–11; Khismatulin, "To Forge a Book"; M. Simidchieva, "*Siyāsat-nāme* Revisited: the question of authenticity," in B. G. Fragner, C. Fragner, G. Gnoll, R. Haag-Higuchi, M. Maggi and P. Orsatti (eds) *Proceedings of the Second European Conference of Iranian Studies*, Rome: Istituto Italiano per il Medio ed Estremo Oriente, 1995, 657–74. Questions not addressed by Khismatulin include who did write these works and what difference their authorship made. J. A. London, "'Speaking through the Voice of Another': forms of political thought and action in medieval Islamic contexts," PhD diss., University of Chicago, 2009, and Safi, *Politics*, assume Niẓām al-Mulk's authorship.

42 Niẓām al-Mulk, *Book of Government*, 12, 59. Lambton argues that the concept of the king as shepherd was "foreign to Niẓām al-Mulk," but since he and his father had worked for the Ghaznavids he was well acquainted with Turkish world views, and of course this concept also had a long history in Near Eastern thought. Lambton herself cites other references in his work to the shepherd; A. K. S. Lambton, "Justice in the Medieval Persian Theory of Kingship," *SI* 17, 1962: 102; A. K. S. Lambton, "Dilemma," 60; Niẓām al-Mulk, *Book of Government*, 39, 65.

43 Niẓām al-Mulk, *Book of Government*, 10–11; 59–60. Medieval Islamic art portrayed the ruler as the sun; his portrait appeared in the sun's place in zodiacal decorations on metalwork and woodcarvings; E. Baer, "The Ruler in Cosmic Setting: a note on medieval Islamic iconography," in *Essays in Islamic Art and Architecture in Honor of Katharina Otto-Dorn*, ed. A. Daneshvari, Malibu, CA: Undena, 1981, 13–19. Calling God "The Truth" also resonated with pre-Islamic religious concepts, this time ancient Persian ones.

44 Niẓām al-Mulk, *Book of Government*, 144, 10; Lambton, "Changing Concepts," 33–4. Marlow examines Niẓām al-Mulk's ideas on the social order; *Hierarchy*, 129–30.

45 Niẓām al-Mulk, *Book of Government*, 23, 32–4, 63; Lambton, "Justice," 104; Rizvi, "Political," 112.

46 Lambton, like Gibb, considered that Niẓām al-Mulk attempted such an assimilation but failed ("Dilemma," 64); for a counter-argument see S. R. A. Rizvi, *Nizam al-Mulk Tusi: his contribution to statecraft, political theory and the art of government*, Lahore, Muhammad Ashraf, 1978, 45–7. Al-Māwardī had recommended the ulema's active participation in government, especially in

guiding the ruler's behavior into the Straight Path; H. Mikhail, *Politics and Revelation: Mawardi and after*, Edinburgh: Edinburgh University Press, 1995, 48.

47 Abū Ḥāmid Muḥammad al-Ghazālī, *Ghazālī's Book of Counsel for Kings (Naṣīḥat al-mulūk)*, trans. F. R. C. Bagley, London: Oxford University Press, 1971.

48 Al-Ghazālī, *Naṣīḥat al-mulūk*, ed. J. Humā'ī, Tehran, 1361/1982; P. Crone, "Did al-Ghazālī Write a Mirror for Princes? On the authorship of *Naṣīḥat al-mulk*," *JSAI* 10, 1987: 167–91; de Fouchécour, *Moralia*, 391–3; C. Hillenbrand, "Islamic Orthodoxy or Realpolitik' al-Ghazālī's views on government," *Iran* 26, 1988: 92; Khismatulin, "Art of Medieval Counterfeiting," 19–27; Safi, *Politics*, 117. Older analyses assumed single authorship: A. K. S. Lambton, "The Theory of Kingship in the *Naṣīḥat ul-mulūk* of Ghazālī," *IQ* 1, 1954: 47–55. Hoğğa's work does not address this problem; M. Hoğğa, *Orthodoxie, subversion, et réforme en Islam: Gazālī et les Seljūqides*, Paris: J. Vrin, 1993.

49 Al-Ghazālī, *Counsel for Kings*, 45, 46, 59–60, 72, 74. Philosophers attributed most of these qualities to the ideal ruler; besides *ghazā*, the only specifically Islamic quality of kings was "frequent reading of the reports of the early Muslims," an islamicization of the ancient practice of reading the testaments of previous monarchs.

50 Ibid., 46, 55, 56; the Arabic reads: "Al-dīn bi'l-mulk wa'l-mulk bi'l-jund wa'l-jund bi'l-māl wa'l-māl bi-'imārat al-bilād wa-'imārat al-bilād bi'l-'adl"; Abū Ḥāmid al-Ghazālī, *Al-Tibr al-masbūk fī naṣīḥat al-mulūk*, ed. S. Khiḍr, [Cairo]: Maktabat al-Kullīyāt al-Azhariyya; Beirut: Dār Ibn Zaydūn, 1987, 52. The quotation of the Circle of Justice accompanied a story in which agents were sent out by Anushirvan in search of ruined villages in order to find an old brick to use as a medication; their failure to locate one proved the prosperity of the kingdom and the justice of its ruler.

51 Al-Ghazālī, *Counsel for Kings*, 65–70, 81–2; see also R. D. Marcotte, "Anūshirvān and Buzurgmihr – the Just Ruler and the Wise Counselor: two figures of Persian traditional moral literature," *RO* 51.2, 1998: 81–2. According to Dakhlia (*Divan*, 116–17), the concept of kingship as a reflection of the past, so prominent in the mirrors for princes, was essentially static, "a negation of History," but to me it confirms history's inexorable changes as well as its function as a source of models. On the vocabulary of ruins, Dakhlia, *Divan*, 157.

52 Al-Ghazālī, *Counsel for Kings*, 14–17, quotation on 29. A parallel Islamic *ḥadīth* held that the first to receive God's protection was the just *imām* (*imām 'ādil*); F. Rosenthal, "Political Justice and the Just Ruler," in J. L. Kraemer and I. Alon (eds) *Religion and Government in the World of Islam*, *IOS* 10, 1983: 96–7. Dankoff noted the similarity of these conclusions to those of Yūsuf Khāṣṣ Ḥājib; *Wisdom*, 27. In contrast to Crone's view of this section as more strictly Islamic than the second part, Lambton sees a Zoroastrian origin for the image of the tree of faith whose root is justice; Lambton, *State and Government*, 118&n49.

53 L. Binder, "Al-Ghazālī's Theory of Islamic Government," *MW* 45, 1955: 237–38; Lambton, "Concepts of Authority," 97; al-Ghazālī, *Faḍā'iḥ al-bāṭiniyya wa faḍā'il al-mustaẓhiriyya*, cited in Hoğğa, *Orthodoxie*, 70. Safi (*Politics*, 111) highlights changes in al-Ghazālī's political thought.

54 Abū Ḥāmid Muḥammad al-Ghazālī, *Critère de l'action* (*Mīzān al-a'mal*), trans. H. Hachem, Paris: G.-P. Maisonneuve, 1945, 62; this work is clearly indebted to Miskawayh. Bayhaqī drew the same analogy in the Ghaznavid context; quotations in Meisami, *Persian Historiography*, 82–3.

55 Abū Ḥāmid Muḥammad al-Ghazālī, *Kitāb al-iqtiṣād fī'l-i'tiqād*, trans. C. Hillenbrand, "Islamic Orthodoxy," 87. On the social hierarchy, H. Laoust, *La politique de Ġazālī*, Paris: Paul Geuthner, 1970, 74–5; the comment in the *Book of Government* on maintaining people in their ranks referred not to social classes but to ranks in government service; Niẓām al-Mulk, *Book of Government*, 9–10; cf. Lambton, "Dilemma," 59. On the need for kings, Lambton, "Changing Concepts," 43; F. M. Najjar, "*Siyasa* in Islamic Political Philosophy," in *Islamic Theology and Philosophy: studies in honor of George F. Hourani*, ed. M. E. Marmura, Albany: State University of New York Press, 1984, 98.

56 The Seljuk histories of Anatolia refer to surveys that left no land unsurveyed; Ö. L. Barkan, "Türkiye'de İmparatorluk devirlerinin büyük nüfus ve arazi tahrirleri ve hâkana mahsus istatistik defterleri," *İÜİFM* 2, 1940: 28. In an unsupported statement, Köprülü claimed that in Anatolia "the Seljuk government was careful to revive, as much as possible, villages that were damaged or dissolved as a result of warfare and anarchy, and lightened or forgave their taxes for a certain time and even distributed seed for sowing and animals to work the land"; M. F. Köprülü, *The Origins of the Ottoman Empire*, trans. and ed. G. Leiser, Albany: State University of New York Press, 1992, 55. On procedures resulting in the destruction of legal records, W. B. Hallaq, "The *Qāḍī*'s *Dīwān* (*Sijill*) before the Ottomans," *BSOAS* 61, 1998: 434–5.

57 Muntakhab al-Dīn Badī' Atābak al-Juvaynī, *Kitāb-i 'atabat al-kataba*, ed. M. Qazvīnī and 'A. Iqbāl, Tehran: Shirkat Sāmī Chāp, 1950; Bahā al-Dīn Muḥammad al-Baghdādī, *al-Tavassul ilá al-tarassul*, ed. A. Bahmanjār and M. Qazvīnī, Tehran: Shirkat al-Sahamī, 1937. Secretarial manuals: 'Abdallāh Marwārīd, *Staatsschreiben der Timuridenzeit: Das Šaraf-nāmä des 'Abdallāh Marwārīd in Kritischer Auswertung*, ed. H. R. Roemer, Wiesbaden: F. Steiner, 1952, 1–20.

58 Document trans. *CHIr*, 5: 209–10. This concept of justice also spread through literature; the translator of 'Utbī's history praised the ruler's construction efforts and his justice; in a "season of oppression and a time of tyranny the courts of his ardour and protection and the shelter of his favour and attention became a refuge for the weak, an asylum for the poor, a haven for the oppressed and a comforter for the wronged;" trans. Meisami, *Persian Historiography*, 257.

59 Document trans. *CHIr*, 5: 209; see also ibid., 5: 279; G. M. Kurpalidis, "The Seljuqids and the Sultan's Power," in B. Kellner-Heinkele (ed.) *Altaica Berolinensia: the concept of sovereignty in the Altaic world*, Wiesbaden: Harrassowitz, 1993, 134–5&n18. Local governments replicated the sultan's in miniature and had similar responsibilities; on their offices, H. Horst, *Die Staatsverwaltung der Grosselǧūqen und Ḫōrazmšāhs (1038–1231): Eine Untersuchung nach Urkundenformularen der Zeit*, Wiesbaden: F Steiner, 1964.

60 On *maẓālim*, Horst, *Staatsverwaltung*, 92–3; M. F. Köprülü, "Ortazaman Türk Hukukî Müesseseleri," *Belleten* 2, 1938: 65. On the governor, Lambton, "Administration of Sanjar's Empire," 376–7, 381; on the district head (*ra'īs*), ibid., 379, 383–8. Appointment orders quoted in Lambton, *Landlord*, 70–71; a diploma for a tribal supervisor (*shiḥna*) in Lambton, "Aspects of Saljūq-Ghuzz Settlement," 109.

61 On registers, al-Māwardī, *Ordinances*, 151, 215–18; Köprülü, *Seljuks of Anatolia*, 26, 35–7, 74nn39–40; on taxation procedures, *CHIr*, 5: 247–55. Similar registers were used to settle land disputes in Norman Sicily; D. Clementi, "Notes," in V. H. Galbraith, *The Making of Domesday Book*, Oxford: Clarendon, 1961, 55; K. Çiçek, "Osmanlılar'dan önce Akdeniz dünyasında yapılan tahrirler hakkında bazı gözlemler," *OTAM* 6, 1995: 51–89. J. Johns, *Arabic Administration in Norman Sicily: the royal dī wān*, Cambridge: Cambridge University Press, 2002, describes the system and its documents.

62 Document cited in A. K. S. Lambton, *Continuity and Change in Medieval Persia: aspects of administrative, economic and social history, 11th–14th century*, Albany, NY: Bibliotheca Persica, 1988, 163–4.

63 Document trans. *CHIr*, 5: 210. See B. Lewis, "Egypt and Syria," in P. M. Holt, A. K. S. Lambton and B. Lewis (eds) *The Cambridge History of Islam*, vol. 1A: *The Central Islamic Lands from pre-Islamic times to the First World War*, Cambridge: Cambridge University Press, 1970, 197; B. Spuler, "The Disintegration of the Caliphate in the East," in ibid., 159, 164&n23; E. Ashtor, *A Social and Economic History of the Near East in the Middle Ages*, Berkeley: University of California Press, 1976, 223, 244–5. On Anatolia, S. Redford, *Landscape and the State in Medieval Anatolia: Seljuk gardens and pavilions of Alanya, Turkey*, Oxford: Archaeopress, 2000, 62, 85; S. Redford., "Just Landscape," 314–15.

64 J. Paul, "*Inshā'* Collections as a Source on Iranian History," in B. G. Fragner, C. Fragner, G. Gnoli, R. Haag-Higuchi, M. Maggi and P. Orsatti (eds) *Proceedings of the Second European Conference of Iranian Studies*, Rome: Istituto Italiano per il Medio ed Estremo Oriente, 1995, 537–8. As all responsibility was considered to be personal rather than institutional, problems in the Middle East were invariably ascribed not to structural constraints but to the personal faults of officials, making them look more brutal and selfish than they actually were. This must be kept in mind to balance the modern assumption that problems must have vastly outnumbered complaints from a downtrodden and voiceless peasantry.

65 Al-Husaynī, cited in *CHIr*, 5: 86. Political connections: R. B. Cunningham and Y. K. Sarayrah, *Wasta: the hidden force in Middle Eastern society*, Westport, CT: Praeger, 1993.

66 Kafesoğlu, *History*, 90, 107; A. C. Schaendlinger, "Ämter und Funktionen im Reiche der Rūmseltschuken nach der 'Seltschukengeschichte des Ibn Bībī'," *WZKM* 62, 1969: 175; de Fouchécour, *Moralia*, 376, 380; Cahen, *Pre-Ottoman Turkey*, 228; A. K. S. Lambton, "The Administration of Sanjar's Empire as Illustrated in the *'Atabat al-Kataba*," *BSOAS* 20, 1957: 367–88; A. K. S. Lambton, *Continuity and Change*, 29, 80–1; C. L. Klausner, *The Seljuk Vezirate: a study of civil administration, 1055–1194*, Cambridge: Center for Middle Eastern Studies, 1973, 28. The fact that these systems provided inadequate security by today's standards should not blind us to their advance over other modes of governance of the time.

67 Klausner, *Seljuk Vezirate*, 23, 26–7; Kafesoğlu, *History*, 107; A. K. S. Lambton, "Quis Custodiet Custodes: some reflections on the Persian theory of government, (I)," *SI* 5, 1956: 133–4. The Seljuk *madrasas* increased the number of bureaucrats with religious training, but the idea that this

was their main purpose may be false; R. W. Bulliet, "Local Politics in Eastern Iran under the Ghaznavids and Seljuks," *IranS* 11, 1978: 51–3.

68 L. Marlow, "Kings, Prophets and the 'Ulamā' in Mediaeval Islamic Advice Literature," *SI* 81: 1995, 112. Western Muslim writers seem more interested than Iranian writers in integrating the Islamic and Near Eastern traditions, a conclusion Marlow supports while making a different point (ibid., 106). Some scholars expressed the opposite view, that shariah was the perfection of policy and thus the only guide; T. Khalidi, *Arabic Historical Thought in the Classical Period*, Cambridge: Cambridge University Press, 1994, 195. A. al-Azmeh, *Muslim Kingship: power and the sacred in Muslim, Christian, and Pagan polities*, London: IB Tauris, 1997, 105–6, focused on the attribution of the ideas more than the ideas themselves.

69 Al-Nasafī, trans. D. B. Macdonald, *The Development of Muslim Theology, Jurisprudence and Constitutional Theory*, 1903, repr. Lahore: Premier Book House, 1972, 314. Farīd al-Dīn 'Aṭṭār, *Pend-Nameh, ou, Le livre des conseils*, trans. S. de Sacy, Paris: Imprimerie Royale, 1819, 31.

70 Muḥammad b. al-Walīd al-Ṭurṭushī, *Flambeau of Kings (Sirāj al-mulūk)*, ed. J. al-Bayati, London: Riad El-Rayyes Books, 1990, 169–70; trans. B. Lewis, *Islam: from the Prophet Muhammad to the Capture of Constantinople*, New York: Harper & Row, Harper Torchbooks, 1973, 2: 134; Mikhail, *Politics*, 31; Khalidi, *Arabic Historical Thought*, 194; Manzalaoui, "Pseudo-Aristotelian," 158–9. Al-Ṭurṭushī retold the story of the owls and the ruined villages, transferred from Anūshirvān to the Abbasid caliph al-Ma'mūn; Bagley, Introduction, *Ghazālī's Book of Counsel*, xii, n2. He had actually met Niẓām al-Mulk and was a rival of al-Ghazālī; A. H. Dawood, "A Comparative Study of Arabic and Persian Mirrors for Princes from the Second to the Sixth Century A.H." PhD diss., University of London, 1965, 180–1.

71 Jirjis al-Makīn, *Universal History*, trans. E. A. W. Budge, *The Alexander Book in Ethiopia*, London: Oxford University Press, 1933, 233–4. Al-Makīn appended this discussion of *The Secret of Secrets* to the "Alexander romance," after the account of Alexander's burial and the eulogies of the sages.

72 H. A. R. Gibb, "The Career of Nūr-ad-Dīn," in K. M. Setton (ed.) *A History of the Crusades*, Madison: University of Wisconsin Press, 1969, 1: 513–27; W. M. Brinner, "Dar al-Sa'ada and Dar al-'Adl in Mamluk Damascus," in M. Rosen-Ayalon (ed.) *Studies in Memory of Gaston Wiet*, Jerusalem: Hebrew University, 1977, 235–47. A "House of Justice" in Aleppo was built or rebuilt by the Ayyubids; Y. Tabbaa, *Constructions of Power and Piety in Medieval Aleppo*, University Park: Pennsylvania State University Press, 1997, 63–4.

73 Anonymous, *The Sea of Precious Virtues (Baḥr al-favā'id): a medieval Islamic mirror for princes*, trans. J. S. Meisami, Salt Lake City: University of Utah Press, 1991, 295, 297.

74 Ibid., 140, 173.

75 Ibid., 21, 32, 301; Lambton, "Changing Concepts," 41.

76 Al-Harawī, *Al-Tadhkira al-harawiyya fī al-hiyal al-Ḥarbiyya*, ed. and trans. J. Sourdel-Thomine, "Les conseils du Šayḫ al-Harawī à un prince ayyūbide," *BÉO* 17, 1961–62: 219 (French translation), 263 (Arabic text); see also J. Sadan, "A 'Closed-Circuit' Saying on Practical Justice," *JSAI* 10, 1987: 335&n21.

77 Ẓahīr al-Dīn Nīshāpūrī, *The History of the Seljuq Turks, from The Jāmi' al-Tawārīkh: an Ilkhanid adaption of the Saljūq-nāma*, trans. K. A. Luther, ed. C. E. Bosworth, Richmond, Surrey, UK: Curzon Press, 2001; Persian text: Ẓahīr al-Dīn Nīshāpūrī, *The Saljūqnāma of Ẓahīr al-Dīn Nīshāpūrī*, ed. A. H. Morton, [Warminster]: E. J. W. Gibb Memorial Trust, 2004.

78 Muhammed b. Ali er-Râvendî, *Râhat-üs-sudûr ve Âyet-üs-sürûr*, trans. A. Ateş, Ankara: Türk Tarih Kurumu, 1957–1960, 1:68-82; trans. J. S. Meisami, "Rāvandī's *Rāḥat al-ṣudūr*: history or hybrid?" *Edebiyat* 5, 1994: 188, quotations on 206. See Meisami, *Persian Historiography*, 252. A twelfth-century Persian translation of *Kalila and Dimna* inserted the Circle into that book's political recommendations.

79 Kirmānī, *Al-Mukhtārāt min al-rasā'il*, 159, trans. D. Durand-Guédy, "Iranians at War under Turkish Domination: the example of pre-Mongol Isfahan," *IranS* 38, 2005:603; C. Lingwood, "Jami's 'Salaman va Absal' as an esoteric mirror for princes in its Aq-Qoyunlu context," PhD diss., University of Toronto, 2009, 106n49; S. A. Arjomand, "Medieval Persianate Political Ethic," *Studies on Persianate Societies* 1, 2003: 15; Lambton, "Changing Concepts," 45, 38; Lambton., "Islamic Mirrors for Princes," in *La Persia nel medioevo: atti del convegno internazionale, Rome, 1970*, Rome: Accademia Nazionale dei Lincei, 1971, 436–8; de Fouchécour, *Moralia*, 433; A. K. S. Lambton, "Reflections on the Role of Agriculture in Medieval Persia," in A. L. Udovitch (ed.) *The Islamic Middle East, 700–1900: studies in economic and social history*, Princeton, NJ: Darwin, 1981, 297.

80 The most famous of these refugees was the poet-mystic Jalāl al-Dīn Rūmī (1207–73). Sultan 'Alā' al-Dīn Kaykubād may have conducted a revenue survey of Anatolia, although no records of it remain; Cahen, *Pre-Ottoman Turkey*, 175. On the Mongols see Ch. 7.

81 C.-H. de Fouchécour, "*Ḥadāyeq al-siyar*, un miroir des princes de la cour de Qonya au VIIe–XIIIe siècle," *StIr* 1, 1972: 220–1, 224–5. Chapters on justice and injustice were mandatory in such works; Marlow, *Hierarchy*, 181–83. By this time, mirrors for princes had become so routine that they were used in fiction as plot devices (Fouchécour, *Moralia*, 431–2); in Varāvinī's tale, the *Marzbān-nāma*, written between 1210 and 1225, the presentation of a mirror for princes revealing the king's injustice opened the action; Sa'd al-Dīn Varāvinī, *The Tales of Marzuban*, trans. R. Levy, Bloomington: Indiana University Press, 1959, 6.

82 Najm al-Dīn Rāzī, *The Path of God's Bondsmen from Origin to Return*, trans. H. Algar, Delmar, NY: Caravan Books, 1982, 394–432, quotations on 413, 415; cf. Lambton, *Landlord*, xx,n1; Lambton, "Changing Concepts," 47; Lambton, "Theory of Kingship," 49n2; Lambton, "Justice," 110–15.

83 *Laṭā'if al-Ḥikma*, ed. G. H. Yūsufī, Tehran: Intishārāt-i Bunyād-i Farhang-i Īrān, 1972; Marlow, "Kings, Prophets," 115–17; Lambton, "Reflections," 297. *Laṭā'if al-Ḥikma* is usually attributed to the legal scholar Sirāj al-Dīn 'Urmawī, an Iranian emigré who became chief qadi for the Anatolian Seljuk sultan 'Izz al-Dīn II (1246–1261), but it may have been written by another Iranian emigré, the mystic Ahi Evren; M. Bayram, *Ahi Evren ve ahi teşkilâtının kuruluşu*, Konya: Bil-Tez, 1991, 88.

84 İ. Togan, *Flexibility and Limitation in Steppe Formations: the Kerait Khanate and Chinggis Khan*, Leiden: Brill, 1998, 36; A. Y. Ocak, *La révolte de Baba Resul ou la formation de l'hétérodoxie musulmane en Anatolie au XIIIe siècle*, Ankara: Türk Tarih Kurumu, 1989, 59, 72–4, 136; I. Mélikoff, "Un document akhi du XIIIe siècle," *Res Orientales* 6, 1994: 269; Mélikoff, *Abū Muslim, le "Porte-hache" du Khorassan, dans la tradition épique turco-iranienne*, Paris: Adrien Maisonneuve, 1962, 38, 64.

85 M. Chamberlain, *Knowledge and Social Practice in Medieval Damascus, 1190–1350*, Cambridge: Cambridge University Press, 1994, 49. As one Ayyubid aspirant to the throne proclaimed, "Kingship is not for inheritance but for the conqueror"; Aḥmad b. 'Alī al-Maqrīzī, *A History of the Ayyūbid Sultans of Egypt*, trans. R. J. C. Broadhurst, Boston, MA: Twayne, 1980, 135. On the Circle of Justice in the Delhi Sultanate, L. T. Darling, "'Do Justice, Do Justice, for That Is Paradise': Middle Eastern advice for Indian Muslim rulers," *CSSAAME* 22, 2002: 3–19.

86 Cahen, "L'évolution de l'*iqta'*," 46; al-Maqrīzī, *History*, 75–6, 231. A twelfth-century history of eastern Anatolia equated justice with remission of non-Islamic taxes and injustice with "murder, mulcting, and the imposition of illegal taxes"; C. Hillenbrand, *A Muslim Principality in Crusader Times: the early Artuqid state*, Istanbul: Nederlands Historisch-Archaeologisch Instituut, 1990, 109, 34, 42.

87 Bahā al-Dīn b. Shaddād, *The Life of Saladin, by Behâ ed-Dîn*, trans. C. W. Wilson and Lieutenant-Colonel Conder, London: Palestine Exploration Fund, 1897; repr. as *Saladin, or, what befell Sultan Yûsuf*, Lahore: Islamic Book Service 1976, 15. The *Shāhnāma* was translated into Arabic in Ayyubid times; C. E. Bosworth, "The Persian Contribution to Islamic Historiography in the Pre-Mongol Period," in R. G. Hovannisian and G. Sabagh (eds) *The Persian Presence in the Islamic World*, Cambridge: Cambridge University Press, 1998, 230n27. For Ayyubid-era petitions, G. Khan, *Arabic Legal and Administrative Documents in the Cambridge Genizah Collections*, Cambridge: Cambridge University Press, 1993, 361–76, 406–19.

88 Abd al-Raḥmān b. Naṣr al-Shayzarī, *Al-Nahj al-maslūk fi siyāsat al-mulūk*, Beirut: Dār al-Manār, 1994, 90–1, 248. See Abū al-Faḍl Ja'far ibn Shams al-Khilāfa, *Kitāb al-Ādāb*, ed. M. A. al-Khānjī, Cairo: Maṭba'at al-Sa'ādat, 1930, 27; this author's likely source was *al-Iqd al-farīd*, which has the same form of the saying, also attributed to 'Amr ibn al-'Ās (see Ch. 5).

89 Al-Maqrīzī, *History*, 233. Y. Tabbaa, "Circles of Power: palace, citadel, and city in Ayyubid Aleppo," *ArsOr* 23, 1993, 182–3; Y. Tabbaa, *Constructions of Power and Piety*, 63–6; S. M. Stern, "Petitions from the Ayyūbid Period," *BSOAS* 27, 1964, 14–16. Ibn Shaddād himself waited on Saladin for this purpose and was active in his administration of justice; in this way rulers could conveniently obey advice to associate with religious scholars rather than courtiers and scribes, whose faith might be less than orthodox.

90 Khan, *Arabic Legal*, 23; quotation from a document in S. M. Stern, "Two Ayyūbid Decrees from Sinai," in S. M. Stern (ed.) *Documents from Islamic Chanceries*, Columbia: University of South Carolina Press, 1965, 13.

91 For example, Ghiyāth al-Dīn, the Khwarazmian ruler of Iraq, was considered legitimate prey for his brother Jalāl al-Dīn because he could not control the district commanders, who ruled in his

name but refused to send any revenue, so "he, having no money to pay his Turkish mercenaries with, was constrained to let them plunder"; H. H. Howorth, *History of the Mongols, from the 9th to the 19th century*, London: Longmans, Green, 1888, 3: 3.

92 G. R. Aziz, *A Short History of the Khwarazmshahs*, Karachi: Pakistan Historical Society, 1978, 223–5; Aziz, "Literary and Cultural Activity in Khwarazm (11th–12th Century)," *JPHS* 22, 1974: 81–112.

93 Lambton, *State and Government*, 133–6; Lambton, "Quis, I," 140; Lambton, "Changing Concepts," 44; de Fouchécour, *Moralia*, 425–9. Arjomand argues that Rāzī aimed to subordinate the shariah's order to the political order; S. A. Arjomand, "Authority and Public Law in Sunni and Shi'ite Islam," R. D. Sharpe Lecture delivered at University of Chicago, March 1994, 26. He may, however, have been acknowledging a subordination that had already taken place.

94 Document from al-Baghdādī, *Al-Tavassul ilá al-tarassul*, trans. Lambton, *Landlord*, xxi. On the *maẓālim* court, Köprülü, "Ortazaman," 65.

95 Lambton, *State and Government*, 136–7; see Fakhr al-Dīn Rāzī, *Jāmi' al-'ulūm*, ed. M.Ḥ. Tasbīḥī, Tehran: Kitābkhānah Asadī, 1346/1967, 207. An identical version, possibly the source, appears in the fifteenth-century Jalāl al-Dīn Muḥammad b. Asad Davānī's *Akhlāq-i Jalālī*; Lucknow: Matba'-i Munshī Naval Kishūr, 1866, 331; see Ch. 7.

96 For this conflict see Barthold, *Turkestan*, 373–80, 403–27.

97 Sa'dī, *Morals Pointed and Tales Adorned: the Būstān of Sa'dī*, trans. G. M. Wickens, Toronto: University of Toronto Press, 1974, 10–11, 16, 17, 29, 30, 32, 42. S. Bağcı, "A New Theme of the Shirazi Frontispiece Miniatures: the *Dīvān* of Solomon," *Muqarnas* 12, 1995: 101–11.

98 N. O. Rabbat, "The Ideological Significance of the *Dār al-'Adl* in the Medieval Islamic Orient," *IJMES* 27, 1995: 4.

7 Mongols and Mamluks

1 U. Onon, trans., *The History and the Life of Chinggis Khan (The Secret History of the Mongols)*, Leiden: Brill, 1990, par. 74; F. W. Cleaves, ed. and trans., *The Secret History of the Mongols: for the first time done into English out of the original tongue and provided with an exegetical commentary*, vol. 1, Cambridge, MA: Harvard University Press, 1982, par. 74. These versions are hereafter cited together as Onon/Cleaves, followed by paragraph numbers. On Mongol history generally see R. Grousset, *The Empire of the Steppes: a history of Central Asia*, trans. N. Walford, New Brunswick, NJ: Rutgers University Press, 1970; D. O. Morgan, *The Mongols*, Oxford: Blackwell, 1986.

2 Onon/Cleaves, par. 202; İ. Togan, *Flexibility and Limitation in Steppe Formations: the Kerait Khanate and Chinggis Khan*, Leiden: Brill, 1998, 136–8; J. F. Fletcher, "The Mongols: ecological and social perspectives," *HJAS* 46 1986: 30. "Genghis" is the Italian spelling of the Mongol "Chinggis," Persian "Chingiz."

3 Onon/Cleaves, par. 113; quotation from Onon, 41; see Onon/Cleaves, par. 80.

4 O. Turan, "The Ideal of World Domination among the Medieval Turks," *SI* 4, 1955: 82; J. M. Smith, Jr., "The Mongols and World Conquest," *Mongolica* 5, 1994: 206–14. See Ch. 6.

5 "Success is regarded as the fundamental element for rulership": H. Franke, *From Tribal Chieftain to Universal Emperor and God: the legitimation of the Yüan dynasty*, Munich: Bayerischen Akademie der Wissenschaften, 1978, 16. Later ideology reversed the cause-and-effect relationship, making the leader's success the evidence of Heaven's choice; K. Sagaster, "Herrschaftsideologie und Friedensgedanke bei den Mongolen," *CAJ* 17, 1973: 223–42; A. K. S. Lambton, "Concepts of Authority in Persia: Eleventh to Nineteenth Centuries A.D.," *Iran* 26, 1988: 100.

6 Letter of Güyük Khan to Pope Innocent IV, trans. E. Voegelin, "The Mongol Orders of Submission to European Powers, 1245–1255," *Byzantion* 15, 1940–1: 403; W. Kotwicz, "Formules initiales des documents mongols aux XIIIe et XIVe ss.," *RO* 10, 1934: 132, 137. John of Plano Carpini reported in 1247 that the subjugation of the world was one of the *yāsā*s of Genghis Khān; B. Spuler, *History of the Mongols: based on Eastern and Western accounts of the thirteenth and fourteenth centuries*, trans. H. and S. Drummond, Berkeley: University of California Press, 1972, 81.

7 See Ch. 6. In legal terms, "It is the *yasa* and custom of the Mongols that whoever yields and submits to them is safe and free from the terror and disgrace of their severity"; 'Alā al-Dīn 'Atā-Malik Juvainī, *The History of the World-Conqueror*, trans. J. A. Boyle, Cambridge, MA: Harvard University Press, 1958; repr. as *Genghis Khan: the history of the World-Conqueror*, Manchester: Manchester University Press; Seattle: University of Washington Press, 1997, 1: 15.

8 Onon/Cleaves, on organization, pars. 186, 191, 198, 241–2, 265; on the personal guard, pars. 191–2, 224–34, 254; Rashīd al-Dīn [Rashiduddin] Faẓlullah, *Jami'u't-tawarikh: compendium of chronicles*, trans. W. M. Thackston, Cambridge, MA: Harvard University Department of Near Eastern Languages and Civilizations, 1998–9 (hereafter Rashīd al-Dīn/Thackston), 2: 272–84; Togan, *Flexibility*, 131–42; Kotwicz, "Formules," 151.

9 Onon/Cleaves, par. 278; quotation from Cleaves, 219; see al-'Umarī, cited in P. Ratchnevsky, *Genghis Khan: his life and legacy*, trans. T. N. Haining, Oxford: Blackwell, 1991, 82.

10 Juvainī, *History*, 1: 189; Onon/Cleaves, pars. 270, 278–81.

11 G. Vernadsky, "The Scope and Contents of Chingis Khan's *Yasa*," *HJAS* 3, 1938, 338; A. N. Poliak, "The Influence of Chingiz-Khan's Yāsa upon the General Organization of the Mamlūk State," *BSOAS* 10, 1942: 862; I. de Rachewiltz, "Some Remarks on the Ideological Foundations of Chingis Khan's Empire," *Papers on Far Eastern History* 7, 1973: 25.

12 Morgan and Aigle reached similar conclusions by different routes; D. O. Morgan, "The 'Great *Yāsā* of Chingiz Khān' and Mongol Law in the Īlkhānate," *BSOAS* 49, 1986: 170; Morgan, "The 'Great *Yasa* of Chinggis Khan' Revisited," in R. Amitai and M. Biran (eds) *Mongols, Turks, and Others: Eurasian nomads and the sedentary world*, Leiden: Brill, 2005, 301–4; D. Aigle, "Le grand *jasaq* de Gengis-Khan, l'empire, la culture mongole et la *shari'a*," *JESHO* 47, 2004: 31–79. Practices earlier ascribed to Mongol custom were later said to be parts of the *yāsā*; this could be a malicious error, as proposed by D. Ayalon, "The Great *Yāsa* of Chingiz Khān: a reexamination (A)," *SI* 33, 1971: 107 (speaking of al-Maqrīzī, who had ideological reasons for describing the *yāsā* as demonic), or it could be that Genghis Khān's customary practice came to be considered mandatory by later generations; M. G. S. Hodgson, *The Venture of Islam: Conscience and Faith in a World Civilization*, 3 vols, Chicago, IL: University of Chicago Press, 1974, 2: 406.

13 Juvainī, *History*, 1: 40. On the *yāsā* in Mongol politics, Juvainī, *History*, 1: 181–3, 240–4, 255–6. It was also called Genghis Khān's *sunna*, exemplary practice; D. Ayalon, "The Great *Yāsa* of Chingiz Khān: a reexamination (B)," *SI* 34, 1971: 173n3; D. Ayalon, "The Great *Yāsa* of Chingiz Khān: a reexamination (C2)," *SI* 38, 1973: 129–30.

14 Onon/Cleaves, par. 260; W. Barthold, *Turkestan Down to the Mongol Invasions*, ed. C. E. Bosworth, trans. Mrs. T. Minorsky, 3rd ed., E. J. W. Gibb Memorial Trust, London: Luzac, 1968, 394–400; Grousset, *Empire*, 238–42; see Ch. 6. Fletcher considered that terrorization and disdain for peasants motivated Mongol destructiveness; Fletcher, "Mongols," 42. But Genghis Khān's burning rage at Muḥammad Khwarazmshāh emerges vividly from Jūzjānī's narrative, which he obtained from an eyewitness; Minhaj-i Siraj Jūzjānī, *Ṭabaḳāt-i Nāṣirī: a general history of the Muhammedan dynasties of Asia*, trans. H. G. Raverty, London: Gilbert and Rivington, 1881–97; repr. Osnabrück: Biblio, 1991, 2: 1041.

15 Ratchnevsky, *Genghis Khan*, 131; see Barthold, *Turkestan*, 401–3. In contrast to Khwarazm, the provinces of Fars and Kirmān submitted voluntarily and remained unmolested in return for payments of tribute; Jūzjānī, *Ṭabaḳāt*, 2: 1119.

16 J. M. Smith, "Turanian Nomadism and Iranian Politics," *IranS* 11, 1978: 67. Many of the migrants were Turks absorbed into the Mongol enterprise. For Seljuk figures see A. C. S. Peacock, *Early Seljūq History: a new interpretation*, London: Routledge, 2010, 83–9.

17 Igor de Rachewiltz, "Yeh-lü Ch'u-ts'ai (1189–1243): Buddhist idealist and Confucian statesman," in A. F. Wright and D. Twitchett (eds) *Confucian Personalities*, Stanford, CA: Stanford University Press, 1962, 201; Ratchnevsky, *Genghis Khan*, 177.

18 Rashīd al-Dīn, cited in H. F. Schurmann, "Mongolian Tributary Practices of the Thirteenth Century," *HJAS* 19, 1956: 385. Scholars disagree about how literally to take this statement. Repeated tax levies were not totally arbitrary, but they were better suited to a pastoral economy than an agrarian one and were often not collected at times when crops were ripe; ibid., 359; J. M. Smith, Jr., "Mongol and Nomadic Taxation," *HJAS* 30, 1970: 62–74, 80–3.

19 V. Minorsky, trans. "Pūr-i Bahā and His Poems," in *Iranica: twenty articles*, Publications of the University of Tehran, 775, Hertford, UK: Steven Austin, 1964, 299–300.

20 Barthold, *Turkestan*, 467; I. P. Petrushevsky, "Rashīd al-Dīn's Conception of the State," *CAJ* 14, 1970: 149; A. P. Martinez, "Changes in Chancellery Languages and Language Changes in General in the Middle East, with particular reference to Iran in the Arab and Mongol periods," *AEuras* 7, 1987–91: 113; J. Aubin, *Émirs mongols et vizirs persans dans les remous de l'acculturation*, Paris: Association pour l'Avancement des Études Iraniennes, 1995; T. T. Allsen, *Mongol Imperialism: the policies*

of the Grand Qan Möngke in China, Russia, and the Islamic lands, 1251–1259, Berkeley: University of California Press, 1987, 146–7.

21 Quotations from Juvainī, *History*, 1: 107; 2: 576; and Rashīd al-Dīn/Thackston, 2: 411. See also Onon/Cleaves, par. 263, Juvainī, *History*, 1: 97, 2: 517, 598–602; T. T. Allsen, "Guard and Government in the Reign of the Grand Qan Möngke, 1251–59," *HJAS* 46, 1986: 495–512.

22 Juvainī, *History*, 1: 96, 108; its recovery was confirmed by a Chinese observer (Allsen, *Mongol Imperialism*, 89), although it suffered again at Timurid hands; G. Lane, *Early Mongol Rule in Thirteenth-Century Iran: a Persian renaissance*, London: Routledge/Curzon, 2003, 41. Nishapur, too, must have recovered significantly, or its restoration in 1270 after an earthquake would have been pointless; Minorsky, "Pūr-i Bahā," 294.

23 Onon/Cleaves, pars. 203, 222; Juvainī, *History*, 2: 493–505; de Rachewiltz, "Yeh-lü Ch'u-ts'ai," 201–5; Allsen, *Mongol Imperialism*, 82, 101, 130; Schurmann, "Mongolian Tributary Practices," 370. On Mongol censuses and taxation see Juvainī, *History*, 2: 517–21; Smith, "Mongol and Nomadic Taxation," 46–85; *CHIr*, 5: 529–37; T. T. Allsen, "Mongol Census Taking in Rus', 1245–1275," *Harvard Ukrainian Studies* 5, 1981: 32–53; Allsen, *Mongol Imperialism*, 144–88; A. K. S. Lambton, "Mongol Fiscal Administration in Persia," Pt 1, *SI* 64, 1986: 84–90.

24 Rashīd al-Dīn/Thackston, 2: 492–3. On Ṭūsī's career and changing beliefs, W. Madelung, "Naṣīr ad-Dīn Ṭūsī's Ethics between Philosophy, Shi'ism, and Sufism," in R. G. Hovannisian (ed.) *Ethics in Islam*, Malibu, CA: Undena, 1985, 85–101.

25 Naṣīr al-Dīn Ṭūsī, *Zīj-i Ilkhānī*, trans. A. J. Arberry in *Classical Persian Literature*, New York: Macmillan, 1958, 259–60; *EIr*, s.v. "Andarz"; J. A. Boyle, "The Longer Introduction to the *Zīj-i Ilkhānī* of Naṣīr ad-Dīn Ṭūsī," *JSS* 8, 1963: 245–7.

26 Naṣīr ad-Dīn Ṭūsī, *The Nasirean Ethics*, trans. G. M. Wickens, London: G. Allen & Unwin, 1964, 95–9, 100–1 (emphasis the translator's). Ṭūsī's list of classes put "men of the pen" (ulema and scribes) above warriors, who had come first for the Sasanians, and merchants above farmers, whom the Sasanians had considered more important because they sustained the rest. Justice and tranquillity were prerequisites for prosperity, as demonstrated at the death of Sultan Abū Sa'īd, when the ensuing disorder prevented the cultivation of the land and actually caused a famine; A. K. S. Lambton, *Continuity and Change in Medieval Persia: aspects of administrative, economic and social history, 11th–14th century*, Albany, NY: Bibliotheca Persica, 1988, 166. Renaissance Europe had a similar concept, there called "equality": Patricia Springborg, *Western Republicanism and the Oriental Prince*, Austin: University of Texas Press, 1992, 201–3.

27 Naṣīr al-Dīn Ṭūsī, "Faṣl," ed. and trans. M. Minovi and V. Minorsky, "Naṣīr al-Dīn Ṭūsī on Finance," *BSOAS* 10, 1940–2: 778, quotation on 769. See Ş. Yaltkaya, "İlhanîler devri idarî teşkilâtına dair Nasîr-ed-Din Tûsî'nin bir eseri," *THİTM* 2, 1932–9: 7–16; de Fouchécour, *Moralia*, 436–37; Ṭūsī, *Nasirean Ethics*, 230. Like al-Ghazālī, Ṭūsī wrote a variety of works discussing ethics from philosophical, administrative, and religious viewpoints; *EIr*, s.vv. "Andarz," "Akhlāq."

28 A. K. S. Lambton, "Changing Concepts of Justice and Injustice from the 5th/11th Century to the 8th/14th Century in Persia: the Saljuq Empire and the Ilkhanate," *SI* 68, 1988: 53–5; quotations, trans. de Fouchécour, *Moralia*, 438; John Walbridge, "The Political Thought of Qṭub al-Dīn al-Shīrāzī," in C. E. Butterworth (ed.) *The Political Aspects of Islamic Philosophy: essays in honor of Muhsin S. Mahdi*, Cambridge: Harvard University Press, 1992, 370–1; Bar Hebraeus, *The Chronography of Gregory Abû'l Faraj*, trans. E. A. W. Budge, London: Oxford University Press, 1932, 1: 403.

29 D. O. Morgan, "Mongol or Persian: the government of Ilkhānid Iran," *HMEIR* 3, 1996: 68. A list of viziers is in B. Spuler, *Die Mongolen in Iran: Politik, Verwaltung und Kulture der Ilchanzeit 1220–1350*, Berlin: Akademie-Verlag, 1968: 285–8; and the description of a just vizier in Ḥāfiẓ-i Abrū, *Chronique des Rois Mongols en Iran*, ed. and trans. K. Bayani, Paris: Adrien-Maisonneuve, 1936–8, 2:34. The Qazvīnī family also had a tradition of bureaucratic service stretching back to Abbasid times. Repeated purges of expert officials may have contributed to the later Mongols' reputed governmental incapacity; A. K. S. Lambton, "Mongol Fiscal Administration in Persia (Part II)," *SI* 65, 1987: 104, 117.

30 J. Aubin, "Réseau pastoral et réseau caravanier: les grand'routes du Khurassan à l'époque mongole," in *Le monde iranien et l'Islam*, Geneva: Librairie Droz, 1971, 1: 126–7; J. Aubin, "Le patronage culturel en Iran sous les Ilkhans: une grande famille de Yazd," in idem, *Le monde iranien et l'Islam: sociétés et cultures*, Paris: Société d'Histoire de l'Orient, 1975, 3: 113–18.

31 Rashīd al-Dīn/Thackston, 3: 538; Howorth, *History*, 3: 220, citing Vaṣṣāf; A. Z. V. Togan, "Mogollar devrinde Anadolu'nun iktisadî vaziyeti," *THİTM* 1, 1931: 28–9; trans. G. Leiser, "Economic Conditions in Anatolia in the Mongol Period," *AI* 25, 1991: 220; A. P. Martinez, "Bullionistic Imperialism: the Īl-Xānid mint's exploitation of the Rum-Saljuqid currency, 654–695 H./1256–1296 A. D.," *ArchOtt* 13, 1993–4: 218n4; Kerîmüddin Mahmud Aksarayî, *Müsāmeret ül-ahbār: Moğollar zamanında Türkiye Selçukları tarihi*, ed. O. Turan, Ankara: Türk Tarih Kurumu, 1944, 79–81; trans. M. Öztürk, Ankara: Türk Tarih Kurumu, 2000, 60–2.

32 *CHIr*, 5: 339, 342, 623; Lambton, *Continuity*, 183.

33 Juvainī, *History*, 1: 24; see 1: 196, 253, 362; 2: 571–2, 604, 607. Juvainī has often been seen as secretly anti-Mongol because quotations from the *Shāhnāma* in his history placed the Mongols in the role of adversary and he praised the Khwarazmians, for whom his family had worked; J. A. Boyle, introduction to Juvainī, *History*, xlii–xlvii; E. A. Polyakova, "The Development of a Literary Canon in Medieval Persian Chronicles: the triumph of etiquette," *IranS* 17, 1984: 245–7; T. Fitzherbert, "Portrait of a Lost Leader: Jalal al-Din Khwarazmshah and Juvaini," in J. Raby and T. Fitzherbert (eds) *The Court of the Il-khans, 1290–1340*, Oxford: Oxford University Press, 1996, 70. Yet he could not praise the pagan Mongols without elevating a Muslim regime at least as high. Moreover, comparing Genghis Khan with the Turanian prince Afrasiyab meant including him in Iran's heroic past; A. S. Melikian-Chirvani, "Conscience du passé et résistance culturelle dans l'Iran mongol," in D. Aigle (ed.) *L'Iran face à la domination mongole*, Tehran: Institut Français de Recherche en Iran, 1997, 139–48. Juvainī also compared the Mongol rulers to Sasanian monarchs and described their rule in Iran as motivated by concern for the welfare of their state, in which he held an important position all his life. As he said himself, "my dance is to the tune of the times"; Juvainī, *History*, 1: 11. Some have seen this as "nauseating flattery" (e.g. Ayalon, "Great *Yāsa* [A]," 133), but perhaps it was meant as positive reinforcement; on the ruler's image as a model for virtue see J. S. Meisami, *Medieval Persian Court Poetry*, Princeton, NJ: Princeton University Press, 1987, 43. Like other Iranian intellectuals, Juvainī doubtless wished to restore a Muslim regime, but this occurred through the Ilkhanids' conversion, in which he probably played an important part; A. S. Melikian-Chirvani, "Le livre des rois, miroir du destan. II: Takht-e Soleymān et la symbolique du *Shāh-nāme*," *StIr* 20, 1991: 71.

34 Juvainī, *History*, 1: 24; 2: 555, 557, 569, 596.

35 Ibid., 1: 4, 23–34, 189–90, 196, 199, 204–7; 2: 552. Juvainī referred to rolls on which the "Great Book of Yasas" was written, which he had not actually seen, but which, he said, were exhibited at the accession of a new ruler; ibid., 1: 25; 2: 573&n72.

36 On the Maragha observatory and the one built by the Timurid prince Ulugh Beg, A. Sayılı, *The Observatory in Islam and its place in the general history of the observatory*, Ankara: Türk Tarih Kurumu, 1960.

37 A. S. Melikian-Chirvani, "Le *Shāh-nāme*, la gnose soufie et le pouvoir mongol," *JA* 272, 1984: 256–7. Pictures of the site and of the tile decorations: L. Komaroff and S. Carboni (eds) *The Legacy of Genghis Khan: courtly art and culture in Western Asia, 1256–1353*, New York and New Haven, CT: Metropolitan Museum of Art and Yale University Press, 2002, 44, 52, 74, 84–103. The original throne of Solomon (identified with Jamshīd) was presumed to be in Persepolis; S. Bağcı, "A New Theme of the Shirazi Frontispiece Miniatures: the *Dīwān* of Solomon," *Muqarnas* 12, 1995: 107. Construction of the palace was begun by Abāqā and continued by the Muslim khan Aḥmad Tegüder, to whose patronage the motif of Alexander is attributed; Juvainī may have suggested the motifs and chosen the quotations. A poem compared Juvainī to Alexander's mystical advisor Khiẓr, placing Aḥmad Tegüder in the role of Alexander; Melikian-Chirvani, "Livre des rois, II," 124–33.

38 Petrushevsky, "Rashīd al-Dīn's Conception," 148–50.

39 T. T. Allsen, "Changing Forms of Legitimation in Mongol Iran," in G. Seaman and D. Marks (eds) *Rulers from the Steppe: state formation on the Eurasian periphery*, Los Angeles: Ethnographics Press, University of Southern California, 1991, 230. Now that the Perso-Arabic tradition included also Turco-Mongol precedents, the term "Perso-Islamic" becomes more appropriate.

40 Rashīd al-Dīn, *The Successors of Genghis Khan*, trans. J. A. Boyle, New York: Columbia University Press, 1971 (hereafter Rashīd al-Dīn/Boyle), 61, 187, 218; Rashīd al-Dīn/Thackston, 3: 560, 563, 628. Justice: Rashīd al-Dīn/Thackston, 3: 756; P. Christensen, *The Decline of Iranshahr: irrigation and environments in the history of the Middle East, 500 B.C. to A.D. 1500*, trans. S. Sampson, Odense, Denmark: University of Copenhagen Museum Tusculanum Press, 1993, 70, 94. The history's

composition: A. Z. V. Togan, "The Composition of the History of the Mongols by Rashīd al-Dīn," *CAJ* 7, 1962: 60–72; T. T. Allsen, *Culture and Conquest in Mongol Eurasia,* Cambridge: Cambridge University Press, 2001, 83–102. The work highlights parallels with the *Shāhnāma*; A. Soudavar, "The Saga of Abu-Sa'id Bahador Khan," in Raby and Fitzherbert, *Court of the Il-khans*, 173–6, 181, 185.

41 Rashīd al-Dīn, *Jāmi' al-Tawārikh*, trans. A. P. Martinez, "Some Notes on the Īl-Xānid Army," *AEuras* 6, 1986: 203; cf. Rashīd al-Dīn/Thackston, 3: 652.

42 Rashīd al-Dīn Faẓlullāh, *Mukātabāt-i Rashīdī*, ed. M. Shafī', Lahore: Kulliyat-i Panjāb, 1945, 120; trans. Petrushevsky, "Rashīd al-Dīn's Conception," 154–5. The Arabic "Lā taḥaṣṣil al-salṭana illā bi'l-jund/Wa-lā al-jund illā bi'l-māl/Wa-lā al-māl illā bi'l-ra'iyya/Wa-lā ra'iyya illā bi'l-'adl"; and the Persian reads: "Bādshāhī ḥāṣil namī shüd illā bi-lashkar/Va lashkar ba-māl tuvān jam' āvard/Va māl az ra'iyat ḥāṣil kardū/Va ra'iyat rā bi-'adl nigāh tuvān dāsht." A. H. Morton analyzed this book as a forgery of the Timurid period; "The Letters of Rashīd al-Dīn: Ilkhānid fact or Timurid fiction?" in R. Amitai-Preiss and D. O. Morgan (eds) *The Mongol Empire and Its Legacy*, Leiden: Brill, 1999, 155–99. It may, however, have been based partly on existing documents, and all the information in it is not necessarily false. Rashīd al-Dīn's commitment to the concept of the Circle of Justice is clear from his history.

43 On the Rashidian quarter, Lambton, *Continuity*, 145–6, 324; K. Jahn, "Tebriz: Doğu ile Batı arasında bir ortaçağ kültür merkezi," trans. İ. Aka, *TAD* 13, 1979–80: Çeviriler 59–78; B. Hoffman, "Rašīdaddīn Faḍlallāh as the Perfect Organizer: the case of the endowment slaves and gardens of the Rab'-i Rašīdī," in Fragner, *Second European Conference of Iranian Studies*, 287–96. On coinage, A. P. Martinez, "The Third Portion of the History of Ǧāzān Xān in Rašīdu'd-Dīn's *Ta'rīx-e Mobārak-e Ǧāzānī*," pt. 2 (hereafter Rashīd al-Dīn/Martinez 2), *AEuras* 8, 1992–4: 201n79; A. P. Martinez, "Regional Mint Outflows and the Dynamics of Bullion Flows through the Īl-Xānate," *JTS* 8, 1984: 173; A. P. Martinez, "Bullionistic Imperialism," 178; 248–9n50.

44 Rashīd al-Dīn, *Jāmi' al-tawārikh*, trans. A. P. Martinez, "The Third Portion of the History of Ǧāzān Xān in Rašīdu'd-Dīn's *Ta'rīx-e Mobārak-e Ǧāzānī*," pt. 1, *AEuras* 6, 1986: 65–7 (hereafter Rashīd al-Dīn/Martinez 1); cf. Rashīd al-Dīn/Thackston, 3: 673. Lambton asserts that no census was carried out (*Continuity,* 140, 202, 211), but see Lambton, *Landlord*, 83.

45 Ghāzān's edicts and letters at the conquest of Damascus in 1300 conflated Islamic and Near Eastern concepts of justice; L. Guo, *Early Mamluk Syrian Historiography: al-Yūnīnī's Dhayl mir'āt al-zamān*, Leiden: Brill, 1998, 1: 140, 183.

46 Rashīd al-Dīn/Thackston, 708–13 (tax edict); 700–8, 713–14, 736–42, 754–9; B. F. Manz, *The Rise and Rule of Tamerlane*, Cambridge: Cambridge University Press, 1989, 5–6. Rashīd al-Dīn owned a Persian translation of a Chinese administrative manual; Allsen, *Culture*, 78.

47 Rashīd al-Dīn/Thackston, 730–5; Rashīd al-Dīn/Martinez 1, 87n9; 88–108; Lambton, *Landlord*, 89–91; quotation trans. D. O. Morgan, "The Mongol Armies in Persia," *Der Islam* 56, 1979: 93. Some doubt whether this order was implemented, for example R. Amitai, "Turko-Mongolian Nomads and the *Iqṭā'* System in the Islamic Middle East (ca. 1000–1400 AD)," in A. M. Khazanov and A. Wink (eds) *Nomads in the Sedentary World*, Richmond, UK: Curzon, 2001, 152–71; but for its later effect, see L. T. Darling, "The Development of Ottoman Governmental Institutions in the Fourteenth Century: a reconstruction," in *Living in the Ottoman Ecumenical Community: essays in honour of Suraiya Faroqhi*, ed. V. Costantini and M. Koller, Leiden: Brill, 2008, 23–5.

48 Rashīd al-Dīn/Thackston, 3: 689–762; C. D'Ohsson, *Histoire des Mongols, depuis Tchinguiz-Khan jusqu'à Timour Bey ou Tamerlan*–La Haye and Amsterdam: Frères Van Cleef, 1835, 4: 370–477, trans. Howorth, *History*, 3: 498–530; Spuler, *History*, 148–64.

49 D'Ohsson, trans. Howorth, *History*, 3: 523; cf. Rashīd al-Dīn/Thackston, 3: 692.

50 Rashīd al-Dīn/Martinez 1, 103; Rashīd al-Dīn/Thackston, 3: 712, 757.

51 Rashīd al-Dīn/Martinez 1, 72. "What better witness could there be than a register, which has no vested interests?" (Rashīd al-Dīn/Thackston, 3: 675).

52 Christensen, *Decline*, 40–4 and tables 4, 5, and 6, figures from Ibn Khurdādhbih (*Kitāb al-masālik wa'l-mamālik*) and Ḥamd-Allāh Mustawfī Qazvīnī (*Nuzhat al-qulūb*); Spuler, *Mongolen*, 322, 325–6; R. M. Adams, *Land behind Baghdad: a history of settlement on the Diyala plains*, Chicago, IL: University of Chicago Press, 1965, 97–111; J. Donohue, "Land Tenure in Hilāl al-Ṣabī's *Kitāb al-wuzarā'*," in T. Khalidi (ed.) *Land Tenure and Social Transformation in the Middle East*, Beirut: American University of Beirut, 1984, 123.

53 M. F. Köprülü, *Les origines de l'empire ottoman*, Paris, E. de Boccard, 1935; *The Origins of the Ottoman Empire*, trans. and ed. G. Leiser, Albany: State University of New York Press, 1992, 59; *CHIr*, 5: 496–8, figures from Qazvīnī, Yāqūt (*Mu'jam al-Buldān*), and Māzāndarānī (*Risāla-yi Falakiyya*); Lambton, *Continuity*, 219.

54 Rashīd al-Dīn/Thackston, 3: 683; Lambton, *Continuity*, 170, 177, 183. Khuzistan: Lambton, *Landlord*, 95.

55 Ibn Baṭṭuṭa, trans. Spuler, *History*, 206; Ayalon, "Great *Yāsa* (B)," 171–2; Morgan, "'Great *Yāsā* of Chingiz Khān'," 170, 172; Ayalon, "Great *Yāsa* (A)," 138.

56 Qirṭāy al-'Izzī al-Khaznadārī, "A Visit to the Mongols," trans. B. Lewis, *Islam: from the Prophet Muhammad to the capture of Constantinople*, New York: Harper & Row, Harper Torchbooks, 1973, 1: 89–96; see Mīr Khvānd, cited in Vernadsky, "Scope," 352.

57 Rashīd al-Dīn/Thackston, 3: 689–90; Lambton, "Quis, I," 144–5; Lambton, *Continuity*, 90–6. On the Mongol assembly (*yārghū*), which examined misbehaving officials, rebellious vassals, and members of the royal house, Juvainī, *History*, 1: 242, 2: 579–83, 589, 605; Rashīd al-Dīn/Thackston, 2: 393, 406–9; Morgan, "'Great *Yāsā* of Chingiz Khān'," 175; Lambton, *Continuity*, 87; Aigle, "Grand *jasaq*," 52, 62. Provincial *maẓālim* courts also existed; one was in Ardabil, another in Khurasan; Ḥāfiẓ-i Abrū, *Chronique*, 2: 43. *Maẓālim* cases were later returned to military jurisdiction, but one document suggests that a mixed court handled cases between officials and peasants, deciding on "shariah and justice and according to custom" (Lambton, *Continuity*, 95). Ibn Taymiya made this court his excuse for invalidating the Islam of the Ilkhanids; E. Sivan, *Radical Islam: medieval theology and modern politics*, New Haven, CT Yale University Press, 1985, 97–8.

58 E. Ashtor, *A Social and Economic History of the Near East in the Middle Ages*, Berkeley: University of California Press, 1976, 320; M. W. Dols, *The Black Death in the Middle East*, Princeton, NJ: Princeton University Press, 1977, 255–80.

59 Melikian-Chirvani, "Conscience du passé," 168. R. Hillenbrand, "The Iskandar Cycle in the Great Mongol *Šāhnāma*," in Bridges and Bürgel, *Problematics of Power*, 208, 212; O. Grabar and S. Blair, *Epic Images and Contemporary History: the illustrations of the Great Mongol Shahnama*, Chicago, IL: University of Chicago Press, 1980, 19; Soudavar, "Saga," 125, 133, 144, 158. Ghāzān was also portrayed as Anushirvan the Just (ibid., 127).

60 Vaṣṣāf, *Tārīkh*, 491, trans. Spuler, *History of the Mongols*, 166–7. See Lambton, "Changing Concepts," 58; Aubin, "Patronage culturel en Iran," 113; Lambton, "Reflections," 303; *CHIr*, 5: 495; Ḥāfiẓ-i Abrū, *Chronique*, 128.

61 On Vaṣṣāf, *CHIr*, 5: 501; Lambton, "Mongol Fiscal Administration, II," 104, 117, 121, 122. On the inscriptions, Khwāndamīr, *Habibu's-Siyar*, Tome Three: *The Reign of the Mongol and the Turk*, trans. W. M. Thackston, Cambridge, MA: Harvard University Department of Near Eastern Languages and Civilizations, 1994, 1: 95–6; P. Wittek, "Ankara'da bir İlhanî kitabesi," *THİTM* 1, 1931: 162–6; W. Barthold, "İlhanlılar devrinde malî vaziyet," *THİTM* 1, 1931: 138; W. Hinz, "Steuerinschriften aus dem Mittelalterlichen vorderen Orient," *Belleten* 13, 1949: 746; Schurmann, "Mongolian Tributary Practices," 388.

62 J. Aubin, "Le *quriltai* de Sultân-Maydân (1336)," *JA* 274, 1991: 175–97; C. Melville, *The Fall of Amir Chupan and the Decline of the Ilkhanate, 1327–37: a decade of discord in Mongol Iran*, Bloomington: Indiana University Research Institute for Inner Asian Studies, 1999.

63 Hodgson, *Venture*, 2: 406; Lambton, "Changing Concepts," 51. On Öljeitü's titles, Rashīd al-Dīn/Thackston, 1: 3n4; Abū Bakr al-Quṭb al-Ahrī, *Ta'rīkh-i Shaikh Uwais (History of Shaikh Uwais): an important source for the history of Ādharbaijān in the fourteenth century*, ed. and trans. J. B. van Loon, 's-Gravenhage: Mouton, 1954, 51, 54.

64 N. M. Titley, *Persian Miniature Painting and Its Influence on the Art of Turkey and India: the British Library collections*, London: The British Library, 1983, 42, 165.

65 Ibn-i Yamīn, trans. E. G. Browne, *A Literary History of Persia*, Cambridge: Cambridge University Press, 1951, 3: 214. On court poets, ibid., 3: 160.

66 Ubayd Zākānī, *The Ethics of the Aristocrats and other satirical works*, trans. H. Javadi, Piedmont, CA: Jahan Books, 1985, 39–40.

67 Ḥāfiẓ-i Abrū, *Chronique*, 152; Khwāndamīr, *Habibu's-Siyar*, 1: 134.

68 S. Album, "Power and Legitimacy: the coinage of Mubāriz al-Dīn Muḥammad ibn al-Muẓaffar at Yazd and Kirmān," in J. Aubin (ed.) *Le monde iranien et l'Islam: sociétés et cultures*, Geneva: Librairie Droz, 1974, 2: 159–60. Few scribes besides Rashīd al-Dīn received more than a bare mention;

exceptions in Khwāndamīr, *Habibu's-siyar*, 1: 135–140; al-Ahrī, *Ta'rīkh*, 75; Ḥāfiẓ-i Abrū, *Chronique*, 128, 144, 154; Qazwīnī, *Ta'rīkh-i-guzida*, 156, 164–5, 178–9.

69 M. Nabipour, *Die beiden persischen Leitfäden des Falak 'Alā-ye Tabrīzī über das staatliche Rechnungswesen im 14. Jahrhundert*, Göttingen: Georg-August-Universität, 1973; N. Göyünç, "Das sogenannte Ǧāme'o'l-Ḥesāb das 'Emād as-Sarāwī," PhD diss., Georg-August-Universität, 1962; W. Hinz, *Die Resalä-ye Falakiyyä des 'Abdollah ibn Moḥammad ibn Kiya al-Mazandarani: ein persischer Leitfaden des staatlichen Rechnungswesens (um 1363)*, Wiesbaden: Franz Steiner, 1952. On these manuals, P. Remler, "New Light on Economic History from Ilkhanid Accounting Manuals," *IranS* 13, 1980: 162–63; O. Güvemli, *Türk Devletleri Muhasebe Tarihi*, vol. 1, *Osmanlı İmparatorluğu'na kadar*, Istanbul: Muhasebe Öğretim Üyeleri Bilim ve Dayanışma Vakfi, 1995. Similar works written under the Jalayirid and Timurid regimes have been lost (Togan, "Economic Conditions," 216).

70 Quotations from Ḥāfiẓ-i Abrū, *Chronique* 153; Khwāndamīr, *Habibu's-siyar*, 1: 136. See al-Ahrī, *Ta'rīkh*, 13; Soudavar, "Saga," 169; *CHIr*, 6: 7–9; Dawlatshāh Samarqandī, "Tadhkirat al-shu'arā," in *A Century of Princes: sources on Timurid history and art*, trans. W. M. Thackston, Cambridge: Aga Khan Program for Islamic Architecture, 1989, 12–13; J. E. Woods, "Timur's Genealogy," in M. M. Mazzaoui and V. B. Moreen (eds) *Intellectual Studies on Islam: essays written in honor of Martin B. Dickson*, Salt Lake City: University of Utah Press, 1990, 108.

71 Muḥammad b. Hindūshāh Nakhjavānī, *Dastūr al-kātib fī ta'yīn al-marātib*, trans. Rashīd al-Dīn/Martinez 1, 57–8n3, and Lambton, "Mongol Fiscal Administration, 1," 86n3; see Lambton, *Continuity*, 61–2. Titles of Shaykh Uvays: J. E. Woods, *The Aqquyunlu: clan, confederation, empire*, rev. ed., Salt Lake City: University of Utah Press, 1999, 5; other quotations: Arjomand, "Authority and Public Law," 31; *EI2*, s.v. "Ḳānūnnāme."

72 Khwāndamīr, *Habibu's-Siyar*, 1: 288. B. F. Manz, "Tamerlane and the Symbolism of Sovereignty," *IranS* 21.1/2, 1988: 105–22; idem, "Mongol History Rewritten and Relived," *RMMM* 89–90, 2000: 138, 141, 143; *CHIr*, 6: 44, 83–91, 95, 133; T. W. Lentz and G. D. Lowry, *Timur and the Princely Vision: Persian art and culture in the fifteenth century*, Washington, DC: Smithsonian Institution, Arthur M. Sackler Gallery, and Los Angeles County Museum of Art, 1989, 32–41; 92–4; L. Golombek and D. Wilber, *The Timurid Architecture of Iran and Turan*, Princeton, NJ: Princeton University Press, 1988, 2: 16.

73 Sharaf al-Dīn 'Alī Yazdī, *Political and Military Institutes of Tamerlane*, trans. Major Davy, Delhi: Idarah-i Adabiyat-i Delli, 1972, 131, modernized text; Sharaf al-Dīn 'Alī Yazdī, *Temur tuzuklari*, Tashkent: Ghafur Ghulom, 1996. This work was compiled in seventeenth-century India but claimed to be based on an older text; the argument against its authenticity starts from its recording Tīmūr's death in the first person, but that may well be a literary device; cf. Arberry, *Classical Persian Literature*, 364; I. A. Khan, "The Turko-Mongol Theory of Kingship," *Medieval India: a miscellany* 2, 1972: 10.

74 R. Hillenbrand, "The Uses of Space in Timurid Painting," in L. Golombek and M. Subtelny (eds) *Timurid Art and Culture: Iran and Central Asia in the fifteenth century*, Leiden: Brill, 1992, 92–5 (my thanks to R. Dankoff for help in relocating this reference); P. Soucek, "The Manuscripts of Iskandar Sultan: structure and content," in ibid., 116–31; M. Bernardini, "Aspects littéraires et idéologiques des relations entre aristocratie et architecture à l'époque timouride," in ibid., 36; Eleanor Sims, "Ibrahim-Sultan's Illustrated *Zafarnama* of 1436 and Its Impact in the Muslim East," in ibid., 132–43; *EIr*, s.v. "Andarz;" *CHIr*, 6: 845–67; B. W. Robinson, *Fifteenth-Century Persian Painting: problems and issues*, New York: New York University Press, 1991, 29–30, 38; Lentz and Lowry, *Timur*, 52, 114, 126, 262, 284, 296; Arberry, *Classical Persian Literature*, 448; M. S. Simpson, *Sultan Ibrahim Mirza's Haft Awrang: a princely manuscript from sixteenth-century Iran*, New Haven, CT: New Haven, CT: Yale University Press, 1997, 86; Jāmī, *Masnavī-i haft awrang*, ed. M. Mudarris Gilani, Tehran: Kitābfurūshī-i Sa'dī, 1982. For paintings of Anushirvan and Sultan Sanjar see K. Adahl, *A Khamsa of Nizami of 1439: origin of the miniatures – a presentation and analysis*, Uppsala: Almqvist & Wiksell International, 1981, 38, 68; for fifteenth-century examples in the manuscripts of a single library see I. Stchoukine, *Les peintures des manuscrits de la "Khamseh" de Niẓāmī au Topkapı Sarayı Müzesi d'Istanbul*, Paris: Paul Geuthner, 1977, 29, 36, 41, 49, 55, 63, 68, 71, 81, 83, 86, 89, 91, 94, 95, 98, 100, 101; of these paintings, eight are of Anushirvan, fourteen of Sanjar.

75 Quotations from A. K. Sanjian, trans., *Colophons of Armenian Manuscripts, 1301–1480: a source for Middle Eastern history*, Cambridge: Harvard University Press, 1969, 146, 178; Khwāndamīr,

Habibu's-siyar, 2: 314, 331. See Manz, "Mongol History," 143–46; *CHIr*, 6: 136; M. Haider, "The Sovereign in the Timurid State (XIVth–XVth Centuries)," *Turcica* 8, 1976: 64, 73; Lentz and Lowry, *Timur*, 80. The Chinese emperor was portrayed as evaluating Shāhrūkh's reign by asking about the price of grain, the extent of welfare, and the safety of the roads; Ghiyathuddin Naqqash, "Report to Mirza Baysunghur on the Timurid Legation to the Ming Court at Peking," trans. Thackston, *Century of Princes*, 289.

76 Dawlatshāh, "Tadhkirat al-shu'arā," 20; Titley, *Persian Miniature Painting*, 19; M. E. Subtelny, *Le monde est un jardin: aspects de l'histoire culturelle de l'Iran médiéval*, Paris: Association pour l'Avancement des Études Iraniennes, 2002, 40. Others ascribed the stability of his reign to his outstanding wife Gawhar Shad and his excellent administrators rather than his own good administration; *CHIr*, 6: 104.

77 Khwāndamīr, *Habibu's-siyar*, 2: 386; Dawlatshāh, "Tadhkirat al-shu'arā," 48, 51; see B. O'Kane, *Timurid Architecture in Khurasan*, N.p.: Mazdâ/Undena, 1987, 7; *CHI*, 6:130; Lentz and Lowry, *Timur*, 251. The illustrations in Baysunghur's *Shāhnāma* focused on "the responsibilities and preoccupations of rulers" and "legitimacy and the continuity of princely government;" his brother Ibrahim's copy emphasized his "dynastic preoccupations" and his cousin Muḥammad Jūkī's a "romantic and unearthly fantasy"; Eleanor Sims, "The Illustrated Manuscripts of Firdausī's *Shahnama* Commissioned by Princes of the House of Tīmūr," *ArsOr* 22, 1992: 44–5, 48, 56.

78 Sultan-Husayn Mirza, "Apologia," trans. Thackston, *Century of Princes*, 374–5; Dawlatshāh, "Tadhkirat al-Shu'arā," 61; see Lentz and Lowry, *Timur*, 254; O'Kane, *Timurid Architecture*, 5; Timurid dams and canals: ibid., 15; on these policies' results, B. F. Manz, "Administration and the Delegation of Authority in Temür's Dominions," *CAJ* 20, 1976: 197, 202; *CHIr*, 6: 133–34; M. E. Subtelny, "Centralizing Reform and Its Opponents in the Late Timurid Period," *IranS* 21.1/2, 1988: 126, 135–9, 151.

79 Mīr Khvānd, Muhammad b. Khāvandshāh, *Tārīkh ravzat al-safā*, Tehran: Markaz-i Khayyām Pīrūz, 1959, 1: 735; *The Rauzat-us-Safa, or, Garden of Purity*, pt 1, vol. 2, trans. E. Rehatsek, London: Royal Asiatic Society, 1891; Delhi: Idarah-i Adabiyat-i Delli, 1900, 328. The original quotation, written in Arabic in a Persian work, reads in the standard way, but Rehatsek's translation, "a kingdom cannot subsist except by men, and men cannot subsist except by property, and property cannot subsist except by civilization, and civilization cannot subsist except by justice," seems designed to appeal to British views on property and the role of the state.

80 A. K. S. Lambton, "Early Timurid Theories of State: Ḥāfiẓ Abrū and Niẓām al-Dīn Šāmī," *BEO* 30, 1978: 3–5; Lambton, "Reflections on the Role of Agriculture," 305; M. E. Subtelny, "A Medieval Persian Agricultural Manual in Context: the *Irshād al-Zirā'a* in late Timurid and early Safavid Khorasan," *StIr* 22, 1993: 201–4.

81 M. E. Subtelny, "A Late Medieval Persian *Summa* on Ethics: Kashifi's *Akhlāq-i Muḥsinī*," *IranS* 36, 2003: 607. Ḥusayn Vā'iz Kāshifī, *Akhlāḳ-i Muḥsinī*, Lucknow: Matbaa-yi Tij Kumar, 1957, 34, 187, trans. Subtelny, *Le monde*, 60, 62; Ḥusayn Vā'iz Kāshifī, *Akhlāḳ-i Muḥsinī, or The Morals of the Beneficent*, trans. H. G. Keene, Hertford: Stephen Austin, 1850; London: W. H. Allen, 1867, 42; Kāshifī, *Akhlāq-i Muḥsinī*, 217, trans. M. E. Subtelny, *Timurids in Transition: Turko-Persian politics and acculturation in medieval Iran*, Leiden: Brill, 2007, 36. See Lambton, "Justice," 94, 117–18.

82 Illustration and translation in Lentz and Lowry, *Timur*, 12; also the frontispiece for Ibn Khaldūn, *The Muqaddimah: an introduction to history*, trans. F. Rosenthal, New York: Pantheon Books, 1958, vol. 2. The Arabic text was identical to one of those in *The Secret of Secrets*, where it also rounded off the counsels of Alexander.

83 'L. Golombek, "Discourses of an Imaginary Arts Council in Fifteenth-Century Iran," in Golombek and Subtelny, *Timurid Art and Culture*, 15nn50&51; J. Aubin, "Un soyurghal Qara-Qoyunlu concernant le bulūk de Bawānāt-Harāt-Marwast," in Stern, *Documents from Islamic Chanceries*, 162. Descriptions of Karakoyunlu rulers: Sanjian, *Colophons*, 139, 141, 145; 258, 198; also 204, 259, 264; B. Hoffmann, "Turkmen Princes and Religious Dignitaries: a sketch in group profiles," in Golombek and Subtelny, *Timurid Art and Culture*, 24, 27n6; V. Minorsky, "Jihān-Shāh Qara-Qoyunlu and His Poetry," *BSOAS* 16, 1954: 274–7, 293.

84 Woods, *Aqquyunlu*, 56. "Eğer nöker ve il ve reayet olmayıcak olursa padişahlık mümkün değüldür;" Yazıcıoğlu, "Tārīkh-i Āl-i Selçūq," MS Topkapı Sarayı Kütüphanesi, Revan 1390, f. 16a; thanks to S. Yıldız for access to a copy of this manuscript, now published: Yazıcızâde Ali, *Tevârîh-i Âl-i Selçuk*, ed. A. Bakır, Istanbul: Çamlıca, 2009, 35.

85 Woods, *Aqquyunlu*, 9, 17–19, 54–6, 89, 106–10, 140.

86 Jalāl al-Dīn Muḥammad b. Asad Davānī, *The English Translation of "The Akhlak-i-Jalali", A Code of Morality in Persian*, trans. S. H. Deen, Lahore: Sheikh Mubarak Ali, 1939, v; an older and less complete translation is *Practical Philosophy of the Muhammadan People*, trans. W. F. Thompson, London: Oriental Translation Fund, 1839. Davānī's other works on justice: M.-T. Danishpazhouh, "An Annotated Bibliography on Government and Statecraft," in S. A. Arjomand (ed.) *Authority and Political Culture in Shi'ism*, Albany: State University of New York Press, 1988, 221–2. E. Rosenthal (*Political Thought*, 211–23) analyzes Davānī's Islamicization of Ṭūsī's political thought.

87 Davānī, *English Translation*, v, 194–5, 208.

88 Būdāq Munshī Qazvīnī, trans. Woods, *Aqquyunlu*, 109; Faḍlullāh b. Rūzbihān Khunjī Isfahānī, *Muslim Conduct of State, based upon the Sulūk-ul-mulūk*, trans. M. Aslam, Lahore: University of Islamabad Press, 1974, 217, 229; Lambton, *State and Government*, 186–96.

89 Jalāl al-Dīn Muḥammad b. Asad Davānī, *Akhlāq -i Jalālī,* Lucknow: Matba'-i Munshī Naval Kishūr, 1866, 331, translation mine with emendations from R. M. Eaton, *The Rise of Islam and the Bengal Frontier, 1204–1760*, Berkeley: University of California Press, 1993, 29. The Persian reads: "'Ālam bustān ast ki ābyār-i ān dawlat ast/Dawlat sulṭān ast ki ḥājib-i ān sharī'at ast/Sharī'at siyāsat ast ki nigahdār-i ān mulk ast/Mulk madīna ast ki padīdāranda-i ān lashkar ast/Lashkar rā māl kifālat kunad/Māl az ra'iyyat ḥāṣil shawad/Ra'iyyat rā 'adl banda sāzad/'Adl madār-i ṣalāḥ-i 'ālam ast." This part of the text was omitted from Thompson's translation but included in Deen's. Davānī stated that he took it from "the book 'Sirr-ul-Asrar'," with an introduction by the translator "who had been ordered by Caliph Mamoon to translate it from Hebrew into Arabic diction"; *English Translation*, 244. Today's Hebrew version, however, was made later, in the early twelfth century; Davānī may have had before him not today's *Sirr* but some earlier version. The wording is the same as the Circle added to Rāẓī's book, and this version does seem appropriate to the violent Khwarazmshahs, who appeared just only in comparison with the Mongols (Ch. 6). The fact that Davānī cited it from the *Sirr* rather than Rāẓī, however, supports Lambton's argument that the Circle was not originally in Rāẓī's book (with which he was surely familiar) but was added by a copyist at a later date, perhaps from Davānī's.

90 As Davānī defines a city, it "does not imply houses and walls, rather,. it means a public congregation that admits of a proper regulation of affairs" (*English Translation*, 163). Fleischer states that Davānī islamicized the concept of law by inserting the term "shariah"; Cornell Fleischer, "Royal Authority, Dynastic Cyclism, and 'Ibn Khaldûnism' in Sixteenth-Century Ottoman Letters," *JAAS* 18, 1983: 201. But see al-'Abbāsī (d.1310) below for the same term over a century earlier.

91 *CHIr*, 6:500, 510; for bestowal documents, V. Minorsky, "A *Soyūrghāl* of Qāsim b. Jahāngīr Aq-qoyunlu (903/1498)," *BSOAS* 9, 1937–9: 933–4, 952–4; Woods, *Aqquyunlu*, 108&n97, 109, 137–40; Lambton, *Landlord*, 101; W. Hinz, "Das Steuerwesen Ostanatoliens im 15. und 16. Jahrhundert," *ZDMG* 100, 1950: 177–201. Uzun Hasan reportedly wanted to abolish the Mongol trade tax (*tamgha*) as unislamic, but resistance from military leaders who benefitted from it was too great; *CHIr*, 507.

92 Faḍlullāh b. Rūzbihān Khunjī Isfahānī, *Sulūk al-mulūk*, trans. Lambton, "Changing Concepts of Authority," 65, alterations mine; Faḍlullāh b. Rūzbihān Khunjī Iṣfahānī, "Mihmān-nāma-i Bukhārā," trans. Lambton, "Changing Concepts of Authority," 70n8. M. Alam, "State Building under the Mughals: religion, culture and politics," *Cahiers d'Asie centrale* 3/4, 1997: 115.

93 For this debate al-Mawardī's *Book of Government* was translated into Turkish; Danishpazhouh, "Annotated Bibliography," 218n1. Heroic epics, historical or fictional, contributed to the discourse on justice; on lost and surviving epics, I. Mélikoff, *Abū Muslim, le "Porte-hache" du Khorassan, dans la tradition épique turco-iranienne*, Paris: Adrien Maisonneuve, 1962, 77–9. Historians focusing on military and political conflict rather than ideology paint this as a period of mindless violence; cf. R. M. Savory, "The Struggle for Supremacy in Persia after the Death of Tīmūr," *Der Islam* 40, 1965: 35–65.

94 V. Minorsky, "The Aq-qoyunlu and Land Reforms," *BSOAS* 17, 1955: 449–62; Subtelny, "Centralizing Reform," 129–30; Faḍlullāh b. Rūzbihān Khunjī Isfahānī, *Persia in A.D. 1478–1490: an abridged translation of Tārīkh-i 'Ālam-Ārā-yi Amīnī*, trans. V. Minorsky, London: Royal Asiatic Society, 1957, 41, 75, 77–78, 85, 93; M. Aslam, "Faḍl-Ullah bin Rūzbihān al-Iṣfahānī," *JAS Pakistan* 10, 1965: 126–7.

95 Minorsky, "Aq-qoyunlu and Land Reforms," 459–61; Woods, *Aqquyunlu*, 145; 167.

96 Lambton, *State and Government*, 138; E. Rosenthal, *Political Thought*, 43, 46, 49; L. S. Northrup, *From Slave to Sultan: the career of al-Manṣūr Qalāwūn and the consolidation of Mamluk rule in Egypt and Syria (678–689A.H./1279–1290A.D.)*, Stuttgart: Franz Steiner, 1998, 174–6. P. M. Holt, "The Position and Power of the Mamlūk Sultan," *BSOAS* 38, 1975: 240. How the ruler gained power had become irrelevant; what counted was his justice once in power; R. S. Humphreys, *Islamic History: a framework for inquiry*, rev. ed., Princeton, NJ: Princeton University Press, 1991, 140; L. T. Darling, "Medieval Egyptian Society and the Concept of the Circle of Justice," *MSR* 10.2, 2006: 1–17.

97 Taqī al-Dīn b. Taimiyya, *Ibn Taimiyya on Public and Private Law in Islam*, trans. O. A. Farrukh, Beirut: Khayats, 1966, 187–8, 33, 71, 19. George Makdisi classifies this book as a work of *adab*; G. Makdisi, *The Rise of Humanism in Classical Islam and the Christian West: with special reference to scholasticism*, Edinburgh: Edinburgh University Press, 1990, 341. See Najjar, "*Siyasa,*" 100; Lambton, *State and Government*, 150; H. Enayat, *Modern Islamic Political Thought*, Austin: University of Texas Press, 1982, 12. Ibn Taimiyya's "*hadīth*" were not in the canonical collections: H. Ennaïfer, "La pensée sociale dans les écrits musulmans modernes," trans. S. Ghrab, in *Foi et justice: un défi pour le christianisme et pour l'islam*, Paris: Centurion, 1993, 169.

98 Badr al-Din Muḥammad b. Ibrahim b. Jamā'a, *Taḥrīr al-aḥkām fī tadbīr ahl al-Islām*, trans. E. Rosenthal, *Political Thought*, 50; Lambton, *State*, 140.

99 Badr al-Din Muḥammad b. Ibrahim b. Jamā'a, *Taḥrīr al-aḥkām fi tadbīr ahl al-Islām*, ed. H. Kofler, "Handbuch des islamischen Staats- und Verwaltungsrechtes von Badr-al-Dīn ibn Ǧamā'ah," *Islamica* 6, 1934, 363; partial trans. E. Rosenthal, *Political Thought*, 50; and partial trans. Lambton, *State and Government*, 143&n16. The Arabic reads: "Al-sulṭān binā' asāsuhū al-jund wa'l-jund jaysh yajma'uhum al-māl wa'l-māl rizq tajlibuhū al-'imāra wa'l-'imāra 'amal yanmū bi'l-'adl wa-qāla al-ḥukamā' al-'ālam bustān siyājuhu al-dawla wa'l-dawla sulṭān ya'ḍuduhū al-jaysh wa'l-jaysh jund yajma'uhum al-māl wa'l-māl rizq tajma'uhū al-ra'īya wa'l-ra'īya 'abīd yunshi'uhum al-'adl."

100 On Ibn Abī Usaybi'a and Aristotle's tomb see Ch. 5, n. 57.

101 Muḥammad b. Ibrāhīm b. Yaḥyá al-Waṭwaṭ, *Ghurar al-khaṣā'ieq al-wāḍiḥah wa-'urar al-naqā'iṣ al-fāḍiḥah*, Bulaq: al-Maṭba'a al-Miṣriyya, 1867, 33. The Arabic reads: "Fa-al-'adl qawām al-dunyā wa'l-dīn/Wa-sabab salāḥ al-makhlūqīn."

102 It is estimated that prior to the nineteenth century, perhaps one-third of Cairo's (male?) population was literate; N. Hanna, "Culture in Ottoman Egypt," in C. F. Petry and M. W. Daly (eds) *The Cambridge History of Egypt*, vol. 2, M. W. Daly (ed.) *Modern Egypt, from 1517 to the end of the twentieth century*, Cambridge: Cambridge University Press, 1998, 100–6. Cairo libraries: O. Weintritt, "Concepts of History as Reflected in Arabic Historiographical Writing in Ottoman Syria and Egypt (1517–1700)," in T. Philipp and U. Haarmann (eds) *The Mamluks in Egyptian Politics and Society*, Cambridge: Cambridge University Press, 1998, 199–200; public education: Jonathan Berkey, *The Transmission of Knowledge in Medieval Cairo: a social history of Islamic education*, Princeton, NJ: Princeton University Press, 1992, 201–3.

103 Shihāb al-Dīn Aḥmad b. 'Abd al-Wahhab al-Nuwayrī, *Nihāyat al-Arab fi funūn al-adab*, Cairo: Dār al-Kutub, 1964, 6: 35, quotes *al-'Iqd al-farīd*, the version most commonly quoted by Egyptian authors; Shihāb al-Dīn Muḥammad al-Ibshīhī, *Al-Mustaṭraf fī kull fann mustaẓraf*, Beirut: Dār al-Kutub al-'Ilmiyya, 1983, 1: 228.

104 Ḥasan ibn 'Alī al-'Abbāsī, *Āthār al-uwal fī tartīb al-duwal*, Beirut: Dār al-Jīl, 1989, 71: "Al-'ālam bustān siyājuhu al-dawla/Al-dawla sulṭān taḥfadhuhā al-sunna/Al-sunna sharī'a yaḥūtuhā al-malik/Al-malik rā'in ta'ḍaduhū al-jund/Al-jund a'wān yakfaluhum al-māl/Al-māl rizq tajma'uhū al-ra'iyya/Al-ra'iyya ḳhuddām yata'abbaduhum al-'adl/Al-'adl ma'lūf bihi salāḥ al-'ālam." Al-Munāwī in sixteenth-century Egypt described the eight sentences as being written on a wheel or ball which Aristotle turned to demonstrate their continuousness and interrelatedness; al-'Abbasī was perhaps that author's source; J. Sadan, "A 'Closed-Circuit' Saying on Practical Justice," *JSAI* 10, 1987: 335&n20; *EI2*, s.v. "al-Munāwī". Abū 'Abd Allāh Muḥammad b. 'Alī ibn al-Azraq, *Badā'i' al-silk fī Ṭabā'i' al-milk*, ed. 'A. S. al-Nashshār, Baghdad: Wizārat al-I'lām, 1977–8, 1: 229; his version reads: "Al-'ālam bustān siyājuhu al-dawla/Wa'l-dawla sulṭān taḥyā bihi al-nufūs/Al-sunna siyāsa yasūsuhā al-malik/Al-malik niẓām ya'ḍaduhū al-jund/Al-jund a'wām yakfaluhum al-māl/Al-māl rizq tajma'uhū al-ra'iyya/Al-ra'iyya 'abīd yaktanafuhum al-'adl/Al-'adl ma'lūf wa-bihi qawām al-'ālam."

105 Qalāwūn, memoranda, trans. P. Lewicka, "What a King Should Care About: two memoranda of the Mamluk Sultan on running the state's affairs," *Studia Arabistyczne i Islamistyczne* 6, 1998: 5–45;

cited in Northrup, *From Slave*, 257; Sato T., *State and Rural Society in Medieval Islam: sultans, muqta's and fallahun*, Leiden: Brill, 1997, 108–9. Sultanic charity: Ulrich Haarmann, "*Rather the Injustice of the Turks than the Righteousness of the Arabs* – changing 'ulamā attitudes towards Mamluk rule in the late fifteenth century," *SI* 68, 1988: 70; A. Sabra, *Poverty and Charity in Medieval Islam: Mamluk Egypt, 1250–1517*, Cambridge: Cambridge University Press, 2000, 139, 141, 143, 153–65. Later sultans' failure to provide public relief led to great loss of life in 1394–96, 1402–5, and throughout the fifteenth century.

106 Al-Qalqashandī, trans. É. Tyan, *Histoire de l'organisation judiciaire en pays d'Islam*, Paris: Recueil Sirey, 1938–43, 2: 147; see ibid., 2: 184–5, 194, 199; I. Perho, "The Sultan and the Common People," *Studia Orientalia* 82, 1997: 145, 148; Holt, "Position and Power," 247.

107 Houses of Justice: J. S. Nielsen, *Secular Justice in an Islamic State: maẓālim under the Baḥrī Mamlūks, 662/1264–789/1387*, Istanbul: Nederlands Historisch-Archaeologisch Instituut, 1985, 51; N. O. Rabbat, "The Ideological Significance of the *Dār al-'Adl* in the Medieval Islamic Orient," *IJMES* 27, 1995: 14, 18; diagrams: ibid., 8–11. Stables: W. Björkman, "Die Bittschriften im *dīwān al-inšā*," *Der Islam* 18, 1929: 115; Tyan, *Histoire*, 2: 247–50; Nielsen, *Secular Justice*, 56–58. Relations between qadis and *maẓālim* courts: J. H. Escovitz, *The Office of Qāḍī al-Quḍāt in Cairo under the Baḥrī Mamlūks*, Berlin: Klaus Schwarz, 1984, 154, 159, 187, 212.

108 J. S. Nielsen, "*Maẓālim* and *Dār al-'Adl* under the Early Mamluks," *MW* 66, 1976: 130; Nielsen, *Secular Justice*, 52, 61, 123. Ceremonies: S. M. Stern, "Petitions from the Mamlūk Period (Notes on the Mamlūk Documents from Sinai)," *BSOAS* 29, 1966: 265–6. Complaints against high officials sometimes employed less formal but more effective channels, such as the sultan's wife; Nielsen, "*Maẓālim* and *Dār al-'Adl*," 120.

109 Perho, "Sultan," 148–9; Miura T., "The Structure of the Quarter and the Role of the Outlaws – the Ṣāliḥīya quarter and the Zu'r in the Mamlūk period," in *Urbanism in Islam: the proceedings of the International Conference on Urbanism in Islam*, Tokyo: Research Project "Urbanism in Islam" and Middle East Culture Center in Japan, 1989, 3: 420, 423–4; B. Shoshan, *Popular Culture in Medieval Cairo*, Cambridge: Cambridge University Press, 1993, 52, 54, 56. Grocers: B. Shoshan, "Grain Riots and the 'Moral Economy': Cairo, 1350–1517," *Journal of Interdisciplinary History* 10, 1980: 465; these measures were also used during the Fatimid period; Y. Lev, "The Suppression of Crime, the Supervision of Markets, and Urban Society in the Egyptian Capital during the Tenth and Eleventh Centuries," *MHR* 3, 1988: 85. Quotation: I. M. Lapidus, *Muslim Cities in the Later Middle Ages*, Cambridge, MA: Harvard University Press, 1967, 147; Shoshan, "Grain Riots," 461, 470.

110 Perho, "Sultan," 149–50; C. F. Petry, "'Quis Custodiet Custodes?' Revisited: the prosecution of crime in the late Mamluk Sultanate," *MSR* 3, 1999: 30; W. Tucker, "Environmental Hazards, Natural Disasters, Economic Loss, and Mortality in Mamluk Syria," *MSR* 3, 1999: 122&n118.

111 C. F. Petry, *Twilight of Majesty: the reigns of the Mamlūk Sultans al-Ashraf Qāytbāy and Qānṣūh al-Ghawrī in Egypt*, Seattle: University of Washington Press, 1993, 79, 106; C. F. Petry, *Protectors or Praetorians? the last Mamlūk Sultans and Egypt's waning as a great power*, Albany: State University of New York Press, 1994, 155–8, 164, 161; idem, "Royal Justice in Mamlūk Cairo: contrasting motives of two sultans," in *Saber Religioso y Poder Político*, 197–211; Muḥammad b. 'Abd al-Wahhāb al-A'raj, *Taḥrīr al-sulūk f ī tadbīr al-mulūk*, ed. F. 'Abd al-Mun'im, Alexandria: Mu'assasat Shabāb al-Jāmi'ah, 1982. Al-Ghūrī's motive as piety: R. Irwin, "The Privatization of 'Justice' under the Circassian Mamluks," *MSR* 6, 2002: 69.

112 Muhammad b. Ahmad b. Iyas, *An Account of the Ottoman Conquest of Egypt in the Year A.H. 922 (A.D. 1516)*, trans. W. H. Salmon, London: Royal Asiatic Society, 1921; repr. Westport, CT: Hyperion Press, 1981, 5–6, 26, 44, 57, 58, 76, 78–80, 93–5, 112–13. A. Akgündüz, ed., *Osmanlı kanunnameleri ve hukukî tahlilleri*, Istanbul: Fey Vakfı, 1990–6, 6: 83; M. Winter, "Attitudes toward the Ottomans in Egyptian Historiography during Ottoman Rule," in H. Kennedy (ed.) *The Historiography of Islamic Egypt (c. 950–1800)*, Leiden: Brill, 2001, 201. A similar episode in eighteenth-century Tunisia: J. Dakhlia, *Le Divan des rois: Le politique et le religieux dans l'Islam*, Paris: Aubier, 1998, 91–2.

113 Al-Nuwayrī, trans. G. Frantz-Murphy, *The Agrarian Administration of Egypt from the Arabs to the Ottomans*, Supplément aux Annales Islamologiques, 9, Cairo: Institut Français d'Archéologie Orientale, 1986, 11–13, 52. Al-Nābulusī, trans. C. A. Owen, "Scandal in the Egyptian Treasury: a portion of the *Luma' al-Qawānīn* of 'Uthmān ibn Ibrāhīm al-Nābulusī," *JNES* 14, 1955: 80; see C. Cahen, "Abū 'Amr 'Uthmān b. Ibrāhīm al-Nābulusī, Kitāb Luma' al-Qawānīn al-Muḍiyya f ī

Dawāwīn al-Diyār al-Miṣriyya," *BEO* 16, 1958–60: 119–34; idem, "Quelques aspects de l'administration égyptienne médiévale vus par un de ses fonctionnaires," *Bulletin de la Faculté des Lettres de Strasbourg* 36.4, February 1948: 97–108. Localities surveyed: H. Halm, *Ägypten nach den mamlukischen Lehensregistern*, Beihefte zum Tübinger Atlas des Vorderen Orients, Reihe B, no. 38, Wiesbaden: Ludwig Reichert, 1979.

114 The thirty-year period coincided with the solar/lunar year cycle which generated an extra lunar year every thirty-three solar years; it also coincided with the conjunction of the two unlucky planets Saturn and Mars in the sign of Cancer once every thirty years, presaging disturbances and poor conditions; Frantz-Murphy, *Agrarian*, 56; M. Brett, "The Way of the Peasant," *BSOAS* 47, 1984: 51; Ibn Khaldūn, *Muqaddimah*, 2: 213.

115 Frantz-Murphy, *Agrarian*, 69–70; H. Rabie, *The Financial System of Egypt, A.H. 564–741/A.D. 1169–1341*, London: Oxford University Press, 1972, 52–5; P. M. Holt, "The Sultanate of al-Manṣūr Lāchīn (696–9/1296–9)," *BSOAS* 36, 1973, 527–9; A. Levanoni, *A Turning Point in Mamluk History: The Third Reign of al-Nāṣir Muḥammad Ibn Qalāwūn (1310–1341)*, Leiden: Brill, 1995, 31–53. Ashtor, *Social and Economic*, 315; Petry, *Protectors or Praetorians?* 106. Other instances of this type of survey (*rawk*): Halm, *Ägypten*, 1: 10–31.

116 Procedures: S. al-Droubi, *A Critical Edition of and Study on Ibn Faḍl Allāh's Manual of Secretaryship "Al-Ta'rīf bi'l-Muṣṭalaḥ al-Sharīf"*, al-Karak: Mu'tah University, 1992, 68–79; *EI2*, s.v. "Maẓālim;" Stern, "Petitions from the Mamlūk Period," 240–1, 251; on Qalqashandī's 14-volume administrative manual *ṣubḥ al-a'shā*: W. Björkman, *Beiträge zur Geschichte der Staatskanzlei im islamschen Ägypten*, Hamburg: Friederichsen, De Gruyter & Co., 1928; petition topics: Stern, "Petitions from the Mamlūk Period," 245, 250; D. S. Richards, "A Mamlūk Petition and a Report from the *Dīwān al-Jaysh*," *BSOAS* 40, 1977: 3.

117 Al-Qalqashandī, trans. Tyan, *Histoire*, 2: 174; Ayalon, "Great *Yāsa* (C2)," 108–9, 123n5; Lewis, *Islam*, 2: 43. Ayalon dismisses al-Maqrīzī as a source for the *yāsā's* contents ("Great *Yāsa* [A]," 105, 115), but he cannot be dismissed as a witness to its prestige; his very vehemence against it indicates its respected position in Mamluk society. Pun between *yāsa* and *siyāsa*: Ayalon, "Great *Yāsa* (B)," 178–9; idem, "Great *Yāsa* (C2)," 109–11; Aigle, "Grand *jasaq*," 38; al-Maqrīzī's use of it: Tyan, *Histoire*, 2: 174; D. Ayalon, "The Great *Yāsa* of Chingiz Khān: A Reexamination (C1)", *SI* 36, 1972: 118, 121, 124; idem, "Great *Yāsa* (C2)," 110–12; Nielsen, *Secular Justice*, 104.

118 Abū al-Maḥāsin Yūsuf b. Taghrībirdī, *al-Nujūm al-zāhira fī mulūk Miṣr wa'l-Qāhira*, trans. W. Popper, *History of Egypt, 1382–1469 A.D.*, Berkeley, University of California Press, 1909–36, 6: 356, cited by Irwin, "Privatization of 'Justice'," 70&n33, see 64–6; Shams al-Dīn Muḥammad al-Sakhāwī, *Al-Ḍaw' al-lāmi' li-ahl al-qarn al-tāsi'*, trans. Berkey, *Transmission*, 149; Albrecht Fuess, "Legends Against Injustice: thoughts on the relationship between the Mamluk military elite and their Arab subjects," paper presented at the Middle East Studies Association Convention, Anchorage, Alaska, 9 November 2003.

119 Ayalon, "Great *Yāsa* (C1)," 128–32; J. M. Rogers, "Evidence for Mamlūk-Mongol Relations, 1260–1360," in A. Raymond, M. Rogers, and M. Wahba (eds) *Colloque international sur l'histoire du Caire*, Gräfenhainichen: Ministry of Culture of the Arab Republic of Egypt, 1969, 386–7; E. Atıl, *Renaissance of Islam: art of the Mamluks*, Washington, DC: Smithsonian Institution Press, 1981, 250, 252; Komaroff and Carboni, *Legacy*, 207–9; B. Flemming, "Literary Activities in Mamluk Halls and Barracks," in Rosen-Ayalon, *Studies in Memory of Gaston Wiet*, 251–7; A. Bodrogligeti, "Notes on the Turkish Literature at the Mameluke Court," *AOH* 14, 1962: 273–82; E. Atıl, "Mamluk Painting in the Late Fifteenth Century," *Muqarnas* 2, 1984, 160–6; J. P. Berkey, "Culture and Society during the Late Middle Ages," in C. F. Petry and M. W. Daly (eds) *The Cambridge History of Egypt*, vol. 1: *Islamic Egypt, 640–1517*, ed. C. F. Petry, Cambridge: Cambridge University Press, 1998, 395; J. M. Bloom, "Mamluk Art and Architectural History: a review article," *MSR* 3, 1999: 47. See B. Flemming, "Šerif, Sultan Gavrī, und die 'Perser'," *Der Islam* 45, 1969: 81–93; B. Flemming, "Aus den Nachtgesprächen Sultan Gauris," in *Folia Rara: Wolfgang Voigt LXV. Diem Natalen Celebranti*, ed. H. Franke, W. Heissig and W. Treve (eds), Wiesbaden: Franz Steiner, 1976, 22–8.

120 D. Haldane, *Mamluk Painting*, Warminster, UK: Aris & Phillips, 1978, 8–11, 3; R. Irwin, "The Political Thinking of the 'Virtuous Ruler,' Qānṣūh al-Ghawrī," *MSR* 12, 2008: 43–7. Abū al-Qāsim b. Raḍwān al-Māliqī, *al-Shuhub al-lāmi'a fī al-siyāsa al-nāfi'a*, ed. 'A. S. al-Nashshār, Casablanca: Dār al-Thaqāfa, 1984, 87; Mūsā b. Yūsuf Abū Hammū, *Wāsiṭat al-sulūk fī siyāsat al-mulūk*, Tunis: Maṭba'a al-Kawla al-Tūnisiyya, 1279/1862–3, 118. Abū Hammū's secretary Yaḥyá b. Khaldūn, the brother of the famous historian, wrote a panegyric centering his regime within the

world of the mirrors for princes; Dakhlia, *Divan*, 37–8. On Ibn Riḍwān and Abū Hammū see further 'I. al-'Allām, *Al-Sulṭa wa'l-siyāsa fī al-adab al-sulṭānī*, Casablanca: Ifrīqīyah al-Sharq, 1991. Moroccan sultans participated in the delivery of justice in conjunction with the shariah courts; D. S. Powers, *Law, Society, and Culture in the Maghrib, 1300–1500*, Cambridge: Cambridge University Press, 2002, 34, 86, 196.

121 Ibn Khaldūn described his work in the *maẓālim* court in his autobiography: "I made the utmost effort to enforce God's law, as I had been charged to do. I considered the plaintiff and the accused equally, without any concern for their status or power in society; I gave assistance to any weaker party, to level out power inequalities; I refused mediation or petitions on either party's behalf"; 'Abd al-Rahmān b. Khaldūn, *Le Voyage d'Occident et d'Orient*, trans. A. Cheddadi, Paris: Sindbad, 1980, 154–5, trans. Morimoto K., "What Ibn Khaldūn Saw: the judiciary of Mamluk Egypt," *MSR* 6, 2002: 112.

122 'Abd al-Rahmān b. Khaldūn, *Kitāb al-'ibar*, Cairo: al-Maṭba'a al-Miṣriyya bi-Bulāq, 1867, 1: 32–3; Ibn Khaldūn, *Muqaddimah*, 3: 81–2; Ibn Khaldūn, *The Muqaddimah*, abridged by N. J. Dawood, Princeton, NJ: Princeton University Press, 1967 (hereafter Ibn Khaldūn/Dawood), 40–1; on Bahrām and the owls see Ch. 5. This quotation suggests that the sources of the Circle hypothesized by Grignaschi (see Ch. 5) had disappeared by Ibn Khaldūn's day. On Ibn Khaldūn's sources see W. J. Fischel, *Ibn Khaldūn in Egypt: his public functions and his historical research (1382–1406), a study in Islamic historiography*, Berkeley: University of California Press, 1967, 109–19.

123 Lambton, *State and Government*, 163; Rosenthal, *Political Thought*, 92; quotations from Ibn Khaldūn, *Muqaddimah*, 1: 284, 313, 340-1; 2: 3, 5, 104–6, 139; Ibn Khaldūn/Dawood, 108, 134–35, 189–90, 238–9. Ibn Khaldūn saw justice as a necessary quality in any ruler, Muslim or not, although the justice of religious law was preferable; Ibn Khaldūn, *Muqaddimah*, 1: 386–7, 448–9; Ibn Khaldūn/Dawood, 154–5, 171; M. Mahdi, *Ibn Khaldūn's Philosophy of History: a study in the philosophic foundation of the science of culture*, Chicago, IL: University of Chicago Press, 1964, 242n4, 265.

124 M. Brett, "The Way of the Nomad," *BSOAS* 58, 1995: 265–7; Hodgson, *Venture*, 2: 55n9 and 478n12. A comparison with societies lacking this scribal development: L. T. Darling, "Social Cohesion (*'Asabiyya*) and Justice in the Late Medieval Middle East," *CSSH* 49, 2007: 329–57.

8 Early modern empires

1 The early modern Middle East: D. E. Streusand, *Islamic Gunpowder Empires: Ottomans, Safavids, and Mughals*, Boulder, CO: Westview, 2010; S. F. Dale, *The Muslim Empires of the Ottomans, Safavids, and Mughals*, Cambridge: Cambridge University Press, 2010; L. T. Darling, "Rethinking Europe and the Islamic World in the Age of Exploration," *JEMH* 2, 1998: 221–46. The Mughal Empire will not be discussed here.

2 Ottoman history generally: H. İnalcık, *The Ottoman Empire: the classical age, 1300–1600*, trans. N. Itzkowitz and C. Imber, London: Weidenfeld & Nicolson, 1973; S. J. Shaw and E. K. Shaw, *The History of the Ottoman Empire and Modern Turkey*, 2 vols, Cambridge: Cambridge University Press, 1976; C. Finkel, *Osman's Dream*, London: John Murray; New York: Basic Books, 2005.

3 Periodization: L. T. Darling, "Another Look at Periodization in the Ottoman Empire," *TSAB* 26, 2002: 19–28; legitimation: S. Faroqhi, "Die Legitimation des Osmanensultans: Zur Beziehung von Religion, Kunst und Politik im 16. und 17. Jahrhundert," *Zeitschrift für Turkeistudien* 2, 1989: 49–67.

4 Aşıkpaşazade, *'Āshıkpashazādeh ta'rīkhī: a history of the Ottoman Empire to A.H. 833 (AD 1478)*, ed. 'Ālī Bey, Istanbul: Matbaa-ı 'Āmire, 1914; repr. Westmead, UK: Gregg International, 1970, 14, 30. Anatolia before 1299: C. Kafadar, *Between Two Worlds: the construction of the Ottoman state*, Berkeley: University of California Press, 1995, 132, 140; L. T. Darling, "Persianate Sources on Anatolia and the Early History of the Ottomans," *Studies on Persianate Societies* 2, 2004: 126–44.

5 Ahmedî, *İskendernâme*, trans. K. Silay, "Aḥmedī's History of the Ottoman Dynasty," *JTS* 16, 1992 (hereafter Ahmedi/Silay): 145, trans. 135.

6 M. F. Köprülü, *The Seljuks of Anatolia: their history and culture according to local Muslim sources*, ed. and trans. G. Leiser, Salt Lake City: University of Utah Press, 1992; O. Turan, "Selçuk Türkiyesi din tarihine dair bir kaynak: *fusṭāṭ ul-'adāle fī kavā'id us-salṭana*," in *Fuad Köprülü armağanı*, Istanbul: Ankara Üniversitesi Dil ve Tarih-Coğrafya Fakültesi, 1953, 585–6; İ. H. Uzunçarşılı, *Anadolu beylikleri ve Akkoyunlu, Karakoyunlu devletleri*, Ankara: Türk Tarih Kurumu, 1937, 209–15; Rukneddin

Abū Bakr b. al-Zakī, *Ravzat al-kuttāb va ḥadīḳat al-albāb*, ed. A. Sevim, Ankara: Türk Tarih Kurumu, 1972; İ. H. Uzunçarşılı and E. Z. Karal, *Osmanlı tarihi*, Ankara: Türk Tarih Kurumu, 1947–62, 1: 27; Kerîmüddin Mahmud Aksarayı, *Müsāmeret ül-ahbār: Mogollar zamanında Türkiye Selçukları tarihi*, ed. O. Turan, Ankara: Türk Tarih Kurumu, 1944, 84, 244, 327; trans. M. Öztürk, Ankara: Türk Tarih Kurumu, 2000, 64, 197, 264; O. Turan, *Türkiye Selçukluları hakkında resmī vesikalar*, Ankara: Türk Tarih Kurumu, 1958, 147, 183; Ḥasan b. 'Abdi'l-Mu'min el-Hōyī [Khuī], *Gunyetu'l-kātib ve munyetu'ṭ-ṭālib, Rusūmu-r-resā'il ve nucūmu'l-fażā'il*, ed. A. S. Erzi, Ankara: Türk Tarih Kurumu, 1963, 40, 42. Persianate officials in Anatolia: Aksarâyî, *Müsāmeret ül-ahbār*, 149, 181, 258 (trans. Öztürk, 118, 144–5, 208).

7 I. Beldiceanu-Steinherr, *Recherches sur les actes des règnes des sultans Osman, Orkhan et Murad I*–Monachii: Societatea Academica Romana, 1967; P. Wittek, "Notes sur la tughra ottomane," *Byzantion* 20, 1950, 282; İ. H. Uzunçarşılı, "Gazi Orhan Bey vakfiyesi," *Belleten* 5, 1941: 277–88 & plates 86–7.

8 Ebü'l-Hayr Rūmī, *Saltuk-name: the legend of Sarı Saltuk*, ed. F. İz, Sources of Oriental Languages and Literatures, 4, Cambridge, MA: Orient Press, 1974–84; İnalcık, *Classical Age*, 66; I. Mélikoff, "Qui était Sarı Saltuk? Quelques remarques sur les manuscrits du Saltukname," in C. Heywood and C. Imber (eds) *Studies in Ottoman History in Honour of Professor V. L. Ménage*, Istanbul: Isis, 1994, 231–8; A. Y. Ocak, *Sarı Saltık: popüler İslâm'ın Balkanlar'daki destanî öncüsü*, Ankara: Türk Tarih Kurumu, 2002.

9 E. Birnbaum, *The Book of Advice by King Kay Kā'us ibn Iskander: the earliest Old Ottoman Turkish version of his Ḳābūsnāme*, Cambridge, MA: Harvard University Printing Office, 1981; M. F. Köprülü, *Türk edebiyatı tarihi*, Istanbul: Milli Matbaa, 1926; repr. Istanbul: Ötüken, 1984, 340–2; A. S. Levend, "Ümmet çağında ahlâk kitaplarımız," *TDAYB*, 1963: 107–9; A. Ateş, "Hicri VI–VIII. (XII–XIV.) asırlarda Anadolu'da Farsça eserler," *TM* 7–8, 1945: 105, 111, 120, 123; P. Fodor, "State and Society, Crisis and Reform, in 15th–17th century Ottoman mirrors for princes," *AOH* 40, 1986: 220–21; B. Flemming, "Šerif, Sultan Gavrī, und die 'Perser'," *Der Islam* 45, 1969: 86.

10 Ateş, "Farsça eserler," 111; Y. Oğuzoğlu, *Osmanlı devlet anlayışı*, Istanbul: Eren, 2000, 185–92. Fifteenth-century versions of Osman's advice to Orhan on justice have both a tribal and a Near Eastern flavor; see H. Algul, "Osman Gazi'nin oğlu Orhan Gazi'ye nasihatlar," in *Osman Gazi ve dönemi*, Bursa: Bursa Kültür Sanat ve Turizm Vakfi, 1996, 99–104.

11 Comparison of military slave systems: S. Vryonis, "Seljuk Gulams and Ottoman Devshirmes," *Der Islam* 41, 1965: 224–52. Prisoners of war and sons of neighboring rulers also entered the Ottoman service cadre; M. T. Gökbilgin, "XVI. asır başlarında Osmanlı devleti hizmetindekin Akkoyunlu ümerası," *TM* 9, 1951: 36. To view the *devşirme* only in the context of shariah laws on slavery and booty is too narrow; it was also the Ottoman version of ancient practices of incorporation long employed on the Turks themselves. They were everyone's military slaves for centuries and used that position as a stepping stone to power; slavery meant something different to them than to us.

12 H. İnalcık, "Ottoman Methods of Conquest," *SI* 2, 1954: 114. Imperial orders protecting peasants and townsmen: M. Kiel, *Art and Society of Bulgaria in the Turkish Period*, Assen, Netherlands: Van Gorcum, 1985, 159, 164, 166; mandating strict adherence to tax registers: A. Singer, *Palestinian Peasants and Ottoman Officials: rural administration around sixteenth-century Jerusalem*, Cambridge: Cambridge University Press, 1994, 46.

13 H. İnalcık, "Timariotes chrétiens en Albanie au XV. siècle d'après un registre de timars ottoman," *Mitteilungen des österreichischen Staatsarchiv* 4, 1951: 120; L. T. Darling, "The Development of Ottoman Governmental Institutions in the Fourteenth Century: a reconstruction," in *Living in the Ottoman Ecumenical Community: essays in honour of Suraiya Faroqhi*, ed. V. Costantini and M. Koller, Leiden: Brill, 2008, 23–7. The *timar* system: İnalcık's works, especially *Classical Age* and H. İnalcık with D. Quataert (eds) *An Economic and Social History of the Ottoman Empire*, Cambridge: Cambridge University Press, 1994, 1: 103–78. It was this centralized control over landholding, learned in exile among the Ottomans, that Uzun Hasan's grandson and Bayezid II's son-in-law, Sultan Ahmad, attempted unsuccessfully to introduce among the Akkoyunlu in 1497; J. E. Woods, *The Aqquyunlu: Clan, Confederation, Empire: a study in 15th/9th century Turko-Iranian politics*, rev. ed. Salt Lake City: University of Utah Press, 1999, 158; see Ch. 7.

14 Tahrir Defteri 548, in Ö. L. Barkan, *XV. ve XVIıncı asırlarda Osmanlı İmparatorluğunda zirai ekonominin hukuku ve mali esasları*, vol. 1: *Kanunlar*, Istanbul: Türkiyat Enstitüsü, 1943 (hereafter *Kanunlar*), 63n3, trans. R. Murphey, "The Conceptual and Pragmatic Uses of the 'Summary' (*Idjmal*) Register in Sixteenth-Century Ottoman Administrative Practice, *AOtt* 14, 1995–6: 112.

15 H. İnalcık, *Hicrî 835 tarihli sûret-i defter-i sancak-ı Arvanid*, Ankara: Türk Tarih Kurumu, 1954; J. Káldy-Nagy, "The Administration of the *Sanjāq* Registrations in Hungary," *AOH* 21, 1968: 181–223; I. Beldiceanu-Steinherr and N. Beldiceanu, "Règlement ottoman concernant le recensement (première moitié du XVIe siècle)," *Südost-Forschungen* 37, 1978: 6; Singer, *Palestinian Peasants*, 37; see 121, 127.

16 Byzantine influences: H. W. Lowry, *The Nature of the Early Ottoman State*, Albany: State University of New York Press, 2003; Seljuk influences: M. F. Köprülü, "Bizans müesseselerinin Osmanlı müesseselerine te'siri hakkında bazı mülâhazalar," *THİTM* 1, 1931: 165–313; Istanbul: Ötüken, 1980; *Some Observations on the Influence of Byzantine Institutions on Ottoman Institutions*, trans. G. Leiser, Istanbul: Türk Tarih Kurumu, 1999.

17 Ahmedî, "Dastān ve tevārīh-i Āl-i Osman," in *Osmanlı tarihleri*, ed. Ç. N. Atsız, Istanbul: Türkiye Yayınevi, 1949, 3–35; C. Sawyer, "Sword of Conquest, Dove of the Soul: political and spiritual values in Aḥmadī's *Iskandarnāma*," in M. Bridges and J. C. Bürgel (eds) *The Problematics of Power: Eastern and Western representations of Alexander the Great*, Bern: Peter Lang, 1996, 135–48; E. J. W. Gibb, *A History of Ottoman Poetry*, London: Luzac, 1900, 1: 272, 284. Other Anatolian versions of Alexander's tale: A. S. Levend, *Türk edebiyatı tarihi*, Ankara: Türk Tarih Kurumu, 1973, 136. Ahmedî's version circulated throughout the Middle East and was read by the Mamluks and Shaybanids; E. Atıl, *Renaissance of Islam: art of the Mamluks*, Washington, DC: Smithsonian Institution Press, 1981, 252–3; E. Birnbaum. "The Ottomans and Chagatay Literature," *CAJ* 20, 1976: 163.

18 Ahmedi/Silay, 145; translation 135; cf. Ahmedî, "Dastān," 6; N. Azamat, ed., *Anonim tevârîh-i Âl-i Osman, F. Giese neşri*, Istanbul: Marmara Üniversitesi Edebiyat Fakültesi, 1992, 3. Lowry stresses Ahmedî's contrast between *ghazā* as war against non-Muslims and Bâyezîd's conquest of Muslim territories, but that argument would appeal only to the Ottomans' Muslim followers; Lowry, *Nature*, 18–21. The range of meanings of claims to *ghazā*: Kafadar, *Between Two Worlds*, 62–90, 109–14; L. T. Darling, "Contested Territory: Ottoman holy war in comparative perspective," *SI* 91, 2000: 133–63; cf. Pál Fodor, "Aḥmedī's Dāsitān as a Source of Early Ottoman History," *AOH* 38, 1984: 41–54.

19 Lowry (*Nature*, 17) makes the same point on other grounds. The critique of Ottoman governmental decline usually attributed to the seventeenth century was an intellectual staple of the early sixteenth; C. H. Fleischer, "From Şeyhzade Korkud to Mustafa Âlî: cultural origins of the Ottoman *nasihatname*," in H. W. Lowry and R. S. Hattox (eds) *IIIrd Congress on the Social and Economic History of Turkey*, Istanbul: İsis, 1990, 73, 77. Here it appears in the early fifteenth century, when the great days of the empire were yet to come, reinforcing scholars' conclusion that "decline consciousness" was unrelated to actual decline; R. Murphey, "Mustafa Ali and the Politics of Cultural Despair," *IJMES* 21, 1989: 243–55; C. Kafadar, "The Question of Ottoman Decline," *HMEIR* 4, 1997–8: 43.

20 F. Giese, *Die altosmanischen anonymen Chroniken = [Tevarih-i Al-i 'Osman]: in Text und Übersetzung*, pt 2, Abhandlung für die Kunde des Morgenlandes 17, no. 1, 27–33, trans. B. Lewis, *Islam: from the Prophet Muhammad to the capture of Constantinople*, New York: Harper & Row, Harper Torchbooks, 1973, 1: 138–9; this passage also castigates the "Persian" Candarlı viziers and the Karamanlıs who, disgracefully, "compiled account books." Quotation: Ahmedî, "Dastān," 22; Aḥmedi/Silay, 155, trans. 143 (Rum = Byzantine Anatolia). Ahmedî was not the only writer to describe Bâyezîd as a lover of justice: *İA*, s.v. "Bayezid I."

21 H. İnalcık, "Byzantium and the Origins of the Crisis of 1444 under the Light of Turkish Sources," in *Actes du XIIe congrès international d'études byzantines*, Belgrade, 1964; Nendeln, Liechtenstein: Kraus Reprint, 1978, 2: 160; O. Aslanapa, *Turkish Art and Architecture*, London: Faber & Faber, 1971, 200; E. G. Browne, *A Literary History of Persia*, Cambridge: Cambridge University Press, 1951, 3: 400–1; Marthe Bernus-Taylor, "Le décor du 'Complexe Vert' à Bursa, reflet de l'art timouride," *Cahiers d'Asie Centrale* 3/4, 1997: 257; *EI2*, s.v. "Othmanli," 211.

22 A. Z. V. Togan, "Mogollar devrinde Anadolu'nun iktisadî vaziyeti," *THİTM* 1, 1931: 28–9; trans. G. Leiser, "Economic Conditions in Anatolia in the Mongol Period," *AI* 25, 1991: 216–17; M. Nabipour, *Die beiden persischen Leitfäden des Falak 'Alā-ye Tabrīzī über das staatliche Rechnungswesen im 14. Jahrhundert*, Göttingen: Georg-August-Universität, 1973, 7; N. Göyünç, "Das sogenannte Ǧāme' o'l-Ḥesāb das 'Emād as-Sarāwī," PhD diss., Georg-August-Universität, 1962, 1; N. Göyünç, "İmâd es-Serâvî ve Eseri," *TD* 15, 1965: 73–4.

23 İnalcık, "Ottoman Methods of Conquest," 110–11; İnalcık, *Economic and Social History*, 1: 132–9; Káldy-Nagy, "Administration," 181–223; R. Murphey, "Ottoman Census Methods in the

Mid-Sixteenth Century: three case histories," *SI* 71, 1990: 119; Ö. L. Barkan, "Türkiye'de İmparatorluk devirlerinin büyük nüfus ve arazi tahrirleri ve hâkana mahsus istatistik defterleri," *İÜİFM* 2, 1940: 39–40. A bibliography of published registers and studies: A. Gürbüz, *XV.–XVI. yüzyıl Osmanlı sancak çalışmaları: değerlendirme ve bibliografik bir deneme*, Istanbul: Dergâh, 2001.

24 D. A. Howard, "The Ottoman *Timar* System and Its Transformation, 1563–1656," PhD diss., Indiana University, 1987, 24–5. Provincial codes: Barkan, *Kanunlar*; A. Akgündüz (ed.) *Osmanlı kanunnameleri ve hukukî tahlilleri*, Istanbul: Fey Vakfı, 1990–6, vols 5 and 6.

25 Şeyhoğlu Muṣṭafā, *Kenzü'l-küberâ ve mehekkü'l-ulemâ*, ed. K. Yavuz, Ankara: Atatürk Kültür, Dil ve Tarih Yüksek Kurumu, 1991, 45, 47, 49, 64, 70, twins on 71; Köprülü, *Türk edebiyatı tarihi*, 350; A. Uğur, *Osmanlı siyâset-nâmeleri*, Istanbul: Milli Eğitim Bakanlığı, 2001, 55&n11. The anonymous *Kenzü's-sa'adet* is still unpublished; E. Blochet, *Catalogue des manuscrits turcs*, Paris: Bibliothèque Nationale, 1932, Supplément, no. 210. Anatolian literature: Uzunçarşılı, *Anadolu beylikleri*, 213, 215; Uzunçarşılı and Karal, *Osmanlı tarihi*, 1: 62.

26 Ahmed ibn Hüsameddin el-Amâsî, *Mir'at ul-mulûk*, MS Süleymaniye Esad Efendi 1890, fols. 67b–68a; the saying is in Arabic within the Turkish text. In al-Ghazālī's version the tile was a brick, but Amâsî's Circle is the same as al-Ghazālī's; Abū Ḥāmid al-Ghazālī, *Al-Tibr al-masbūk fī nasīhat al-mulūk*, ed. S. Khiḍr, Beirut: Dār Ibn Zaydūn, 1987, 52; Abū Ḥāmid Muḥammad al-Ghazālī, *Ghazālī's Book of Counsel for Kings (Naṣīḥat al-mulūk)*, trans. F. R. C. Bagley, London: Oxford University Press, 1971, 55–6. Interestingly, mosques and tombs were first lavishly tiled during Mehmed I's reign by tile-makers from Tabriz; G. Necipoğlu, "From International Timurid to Ottoman: a change of taste in sixteenth-century ceramic tiles," *Muqarnas* 7, 1990: 136–7. Uğur lists Amâsî's other sayings on justice; *Osmanlı siyaset-nameler*, 72–5. Levend incorrectly dates this text to the seventeenth century despite its dedication to Mehmed I and its copy date of 943/1536; A. S. Levend, "Siyaset-nameler," *TDAYB* 1962: 186, followed by Uğur, *Osmanlı siyaset-nameler*, 56; cf. Fleischer, "From Şeyhzade Korkud," 69n8.

27 H. İnalcık and M. Oğuz (eds) *Gazavāt-i Sultān Murād b. Mehemmed Hān*, Ankara: Türk Tarih Kurumu, 1978. İ. H. Ertaylan, *Ahmed-i Dā'ī: hayatı ve eserleri*, Istanbul: İstanbul Üniversitesi Edebiyat Fakültesi, 1952, 3–28, 157–60, 129; W. Björkman, "Die Anfänge der türkischen Briefsammlungen," *Orientalia Suecana* 5, 1956: 20–9; İ. Ç. Derdiyok, "Eski Türk edebiyatı'nda mektup yazma kuralları hakkında bilgi veren en eski eser: Ahmed Dâ'i'nin Teressül'ü," *Toplumsal Tarih* 1.6, June 1994: 56–9; Ş. Tekin, "Fatih Sultan Mehmed devrine âit bir inşâ mecmuası," *JTS* 20, 1996: 282–90. Other scribal handbooks, J. Matuz, "Über die Epistolographie und Inšā'-Literatur des Osmanen," *Deutscher Orientalistentag* 17, 1968, *ZDMG* Supplementa, I, pt. 2, Wiesbaden, 1970, 581; Blochet, *Catalogue*, ancien fonds nos 221–31, Supplément nos 101–23; Köprülü, *Türk edebiyatı tarihi*, 359, 368.

28 Uzunçarşılı, *Anadolu beylikleri*, 219–23; S. Bağcı, "From Translated Word to Translated Image: the illustrated *Şehnâme-i Türkî* copies," *Muqarnas* 17, 2000: 165–6. Blochet, *Catalogue*, Supplément no. 530; F. E. Karatay (ed.), *Topkapı Sarayı Müzesi Kütüphanesi Türkçe yazmalar kataloğu*, Istanbul: Topkapı Sarayı Müzesi, 1961, 487; Murad II, *Fatih Sultan Mehmed'e nasihatler*, Istanbul: Tercüman, 1976. For Ahmed-i Dā'ī's poem see H. İnalcık, "Osmanlı Pâdişahı," *AÜSBFD* 13.4, 1958: 79. These works' celebration of the bureaucratic state competed with the legitimacy derived from the Central Asian tribal background, as in Yazıcıoğlu's *Oğuznâme*.

29 F. Babinger, *Mehmed the Conqueror and His Time*, ed. W. C. Hickman, trans. R. Manheim, Princeton, NJ: Princeton University Press, 1978, 494. Rome as the new "Red Apple": H. İnalcık, "The Policy of Mehmed II toward the Greek Population of Istanbul and the Byzantine Buildings of the City," *Dumbarton Oaks Papers* 23/24, 1969/70: 233.

30 Sinan Paşa, *Ahlakname/Nasihatname*, MS Süleymaniye Laleli 1611/2, fol. 231b; pub. as *Maarifname*, ed. İ. H. Ertaylan, Istanbul: İstanbul Üniversitesi Edebiyat Fakültesi, 1961, 250–1.

31 Quotation: Giacomo Tedaldi, in J. R. M. Jones (ed.) *The Siege of Constantinople 1453: seven contemporary accounts*, Amsterdam: Adolf M. Hakkert, 1972, 9. Babinger, *Mehmed the Conqueror*, 377–80, 497–507; S. Bağcı, "An Iranian Epic and an Ottoman Painter: Nakkaş Osman's "new" visual interpretation of the Shâhnâmah," in S. Prätor and C. K. Neumann (eds) *Frauen, Bilder und Gelehrte: Studien zu Gesellschaft und Künsten im Osmanischen Reich, Festschrift Hans Georg Majer*, Istanbul: Simurg, 2002, 2: 433.

32 Babinger, *Mehmed the Conqueror*, 471–72; Ateş, "Farsça eserler," 102; Köprülü, *Türk edebiyatı tarihi*, 363, 375–6, 380; Browne, *Literary History of Persia*, 3: 423; H. Sohrweide, "Dichter und Gelehrte aus dem Osten im osmanischen Reich (1453–1600): ein Beitrag zur türkisch-persischen

Kulturgeschichte," *Der Islam* 46, 1970: 263–302; Birnbaum, "Ottomans and Chagatay Literature," 159–66&n7; Levend, "Ümmet çağında ahlâk," 410. At this time, the Ottomans learned of *The Wisdom of Royal Glory* (Köprülü, *Türk edebiyatı tarihi*, 368) and translated the *Zāfarnāma*, Buzurgmihr's advice to Anushirvan; C. Schefer, *Chrestomathie persane*, Paris: E. Leroux, 1883–5, repr. Amsterdam: APA-Philo 1976, 1: 4.

33 G. Necipoğlu, *Architecture, Ceremonial, and Power: the Topkapı Palace in the fifteenth and sixteenth centuries*, Cambridge: MIT Press, 1991, 45–6, 57, 64–68, 84–6, 201, 203–4; council hall: M. Ârif, "Kânûnnâme-i Âl-ı Osmân," *TOEM*, suppl. 3, 1330/1912: 23; miniatures: İnalcık, *Classical Age*, plates 6 and 9; diagram: İ. H. Uzunçarşılı, *Osmanlı devletinin merkez ve bahriye teşkilâtı*, Ankara: Türk Tarih Kurumu, 1948, 267; sultans attending council meetings and hearing complaints: İnalcık, *Classical Age*, 90–1.

34 H. İnalcık, "Adâletnâmeler," *Belgeler* 2, nos. 3–4, 1965: 51; Doris Behrens-Abouseif, *Egypt's Adjustment to Ottoman Rule: institutions, waqf and architecture in Cairo (16th and 17th centuries)*, Leiden: Brill, 1994, 63–4; Howard, "Ottoman *Timar* System," 83; B. McGowan, "Ottoman Political Communication," in H. D. Lasswell, D. Lerner, and H. Speier (eds) *Propaganda and Communication in World History*, Honolulu: East–West Center and University Press of Hawaii, 1979, 1: 445, 461.

35 N. Beldiceanu (ed.) *Code de lois coutumières de Meḥmed II: Kitāb-i qavānīn-i ʻörfiyye-i ʻOsmānī*, Wiesbaden: Harrassowitz, 1967; R. Anhegger and H. İnalcık (eds) *Ḳānūnnāme-i sulṭānī ber mūceb-i örf-i ʻOsmānī*, Ankara: Türk Tarih Kurumu, 1956; A. Özcan, *Kanûnnâme-i Âl-i Osman (tahlil ve karşılaştırmalı metin)*, Istanbul: Kitabevi, 2003; Ârif, "Kanunname-i Âl-ı Osman"; A. Özcan, "Fatih'in teşkilât kanunnâmesi ve nizam-ı âlem için kardeş katlı meselesi," *TD* 33, 1980–1: 7–56.

36 H. İnalcık, "Osmanlı hukukuna giriş: örfi-sultani hukuk ve Fatih'in kanunları," *AÜSBFD* 13.2, 1958: 102–26; H. İnalcık, "Suleiman the Lawgiver and Ottoman Law," *AO* 1, 1969: 105–38; *EI2*, s.v. "Ḳānūn." F. Acun, "Ottoman Administrative Priorities: revenue maximisation in the province of Karahisar-ı Şarki," in M. Köhbach, G. Procházka-Eisl, and C. Römer (eds) *Acta Viennensia Ottomanica*, Vienna: Institut für Orientalistik, 1999, 7–12; L. T. Darling, *Revenue-Raising and Legitimacy: tax collection and finance administration in the Ottoman Empire, 1560–1660*, Leiden: Brill, 1996, 144–6, 261–3, 270, 273, 276. Quotation: İstanbul Üniversitesi Kütüphanesi, MS T1807 (1095/1683–84), trans. U. Heyd, "*Ḳānūn* and *Sharīʻa* in Old Ottoman Criminal Justice," *Proceedings of the Israel Academy of Sciences and Humanities* 3.1, 1967: 3.

37 U. Heyd, *Studies in Old Ottoman Criminal Law*, ed. V. L. Ménage, Oxford: Clarendon, 1973, 216; N. Calder, "Legitimacy and Accommodation in Safavid Iran: the juristic theory of Muḥammad Bāqir al-Sabzavārī (d.1090/1679)," *Iran* 25, 1987: 103. Chamberlains and Mamluks judging shariah cases: Ch. 7; R. Irwin, "The Privatization of 'Justice' under the Circassian Mamluks," *MSR* 6, 2002: 65.

38 Quotation: Babinger, *Mehmed the Conqueror*, 459. İnalcık, "Policy of Mehmed II," 237, 239; Ö. L. Barkan and E. H. Ayverdi (eds) *İstanbul vakıflar tahrir defteri: 953 (1546) târîhli*, Istanbul: Vakıflar Genel Müdürlüğü, 1970.

39 Bertrandon de la Brocquière, "The Travels of Bertrandon de la Brocquiere," in T. Wright (ed.) *Early Travels in Palestine*, London: Henry G. Bohn, 1848, 348; Babinger, *Mehmed the Conqueror*, 5, 27. The Muscovites also cited Mehmed's justice admiringly: I. Peresvetov, "Ivan Peresvetov's Recommendations," in G. Vernadsky, R. T. Fisher, Jr., A. D. Ferguson, A. Lossky and S. Pushkarev (eds) *A Source Book for Russian History from Early Times to 1917*, New Haven, CT: Yale University Press, 1972, 163.

40 Konstantin Mihailovič, *Memoirs of a Janissary*, trans. B. Stolz, Ann Arbor: Department of Slavic Languages and Literatures, University of Michigan, 1975, 29, 153. Official injustice seems to have been proportional to distance from the capital; H. Gerber, *State, Society, and Law in Islam: Ottoman law in comparative perspective*, Albany: State University of New York Press, 1994, 21.

41 V. Grecu (ed.) *Istoria Turco-Bizantina*, Bucharest, 1958, 178; cited in Heyd, *Old Ottoman Criminal Law*, 227, quoted in İnalcık, *Classical Age*, 89.

42 L. T. Darling, "Political Change and Political Discourse in the Early Modern Mediterranean World," *Journal of Interdisciplinary History* 38, 2008: 505–31. On Safavid political history, R. Savory, *Iran under the Safavids*, Cambridge: Cambridge University Press, 1980.

43 Darling, "Rethinking," 232–46.

44 O. Özel, "Limits of the Almighty: Mehmed II's 'land reform' revisited," *JESHO* 42, 1999: 226–46, and works cited there.

45 İnalcık, "Policy of Mehmed II," 245–6. On extraordinary taxes, L. T. Darling, "Avarız in 1501," in N. Göyünç, J.-L. Bacqué-Grammont, and Ö, Ergenç (eds) *Halil İnalcık armağanı*, Istanbul: Eren, forthcoming.

46 Bayezid tried to learn Uighur Turkish; Köprülü, *Türk edebiyatı tarihi*, 374–6; Birnbaum, "Ottomans and Chagatay Literature," 165–7&n27. He also invited Michelangelo to Istanbul; E. Atıl, "Art of the Book," in E. Atıl, *Turkish Art*, Washington and New York: Smithsonian Institution and Harry N. Abrams, 1980, 164. The Ottomans were translating Timurid literature as soon as two years after its composition; G. Hagen, "Translations and Translators in a Multilingual Society: a case study of Persian-Ottoman translations, late fifteenth to early seventeenth century," *Eurasian Studies* 2, 2003: 101. On Jami's mirror for princes, C. Lingwood, "Jami's 'Salaman va Absal' as an esoteric mirror for princes in its Aq-Qoyunlu context," PhD diss., University of Toronto, 2008, 61. On the literature of Bayezid's reign, Levend, *Türk edebiyatı tarihi*, 107–8, 110; M. Rogers, "The Chester Beatty Süleymânnâme Again," in R. Hillenbrand (ed.) *Persian Painting from the Mongols to the Qajars: studies in honour of Basil W. Robinson*, London: IB Tauris, 2000, 187; G. Fehérvári, "An Illustrated Turkish Khamsa of Nizāmī," in G. Fehér (ed.) *Fifth International Congress of Turkish Art*, Budapest: Akadémiai Kiadó, 1978, 323; Blochet, *Catalogue*, ancien fonds nos. 309–11; A. S. Levend, "Aḥmed Rızvān'ın İskender-nāmesi," *Türk Dili* 1, 1951: 143–51; E. Sims, "Two Turkish Paintings in a Mid-Fifteenth Century Persian Nizami in the Topkapı Sarayı Library," in H. G. Majer (ed.) *VI. Internationaler Kongress für Turkische Kunst*, Munich: Institut für Geschichte und Kultur des Nahen Orients sowie Turkologie, 1979, 93; A. Yoltar-Yıldırım, "A 1498–99 *Khusraw va Shīrīn*: turning the pages of an Ottoman illustrated manuscript," *Muqarnas* 22, 2005: 95–109.

47 İnalcık, "Suleiman the Lawgiver," 110, 123–4. Some argue that Bayezid's was the first legal compilation; B. Tezcan, "The 'Kânûnnâme of Mehmed II:' a different perspective," in K. Çiçek (ed.) *The Great Ottoman-Turkish Civilisation*, Ankara: Yeni Türkiye, 2000, 3: 662n2.

48 Tursun Beg, *The History of Mehmed the Conqueror*, ed. H. İnalcık and R. Murphey, Minneapolis: Bibliotheca Islamica, 1978, 18–23, text 12a, 10b, 13a, 14a, 13b. H. İnalcık, "The Nature of Traditional Society: Turkey," in R. E. Ward and D. A. Rostow (eds) *Political Modernization in Japan and Turkey*, Princeton, NJ: Princeton University Press, 1964, 42–3; B. Lewis, *Istanbul and the Civilization of the Ottoman Empire*, Norman: University of Oklahoma Press, 1963, 38–9, 50; K. İnan, "The Incorporation of Writings on the Periphery in Ottoman Historiography: Tursun Bey's comparison of Mehmed II and Bayezid II," *IJTS* 9, 2003: 109, 111, 113.

49 *Bâyezîdnâme*, partial trans. I. Nyitrai, "Sultan Bayezid II as the Only Legitimate Pretender to the Ottoman Throne (a Persian *Šāhnāme* dated from 1486)," in Köhbach, Procházka-Eisl and Römer, *Acta Viennensia Ottomanica*, 263. Bayezid's library included several versions of Alexander's tale in Persian and Turkish (ibid., 265).

50 Fleischer, "From Şeyhzade," 70–3; N. al-Tikriti, "Şehzade Korkud [*c.*1468–1513]," in K. Çiçek (ed.) *Pax Ottomana: studies in memoriam Prof. Dr. Nejat Göyünç*, Haarlem, Ankara: SOTA-Yeni Türkiye, 2001, 672.

51 Lawcodes: A. S. Tveritinova, *Kniga Zakonov Sultana Selima I*, Moscow: Rlavnaya Redaktsiya Bostochnoi, Lyteraturyi, 1969; Y. Yücel and S. Pulaha, *I. Selim kānūnnāmesi (Tirana ve Leningrad nüshaları (1512–1520))*, Ankara: Türk Tarih Kurumu, 1995; E. Z. Karal, "Yavuz Sultan Selim'in oğlu Şehzade Süleyman'a Manisa Sancağını idare etmesi için gönderdiği siyasetnâme," *Belleten* 6, 1942: 37–44; İnalcık, "Suleiman the Lawgiver," 120–1. Surveys codified provincial laws and incorporated the codes of former rulers such as Uzun Hasan, the Serbian despot Stefan Dushan, and the Mamluk sultans; Barkan, *Kanunlar*, 130–9; Akgündüz, *Osmanlı kanunnameleri*, 3: 227, 243–300, 487–94, 500; D. A. Howard, "Historical Scholarship and the Classical Ottoman Ḳānūnnāmes," *AOtt* 14, 1995–6: 91; H. W. Lowry, "The Ottoman Liva Kanunnames Contained in the Defter-i Hakani," *OA* 2, 1981: 56–73. Petitions: İnalcık, "Suleiman the Lawgiver," 138; ibid., "Adâletnâmeler," 51.

52 R. A. Abou El-Haj, "Aspects of the Legitimation of Ottoman Rule as Reflected in the Preambles to Two Early Liva Kanunameler," *Turcica* 21–3, 1991: 371–83, quotation on 376; B. Flemming, "Public Opinion under Sultan Süleymân," in H. İnalcık and C. Kafadar (eds) *Süleymân the Second and His Time*, Istanbul: Isis, 1993, 54.

53 Idris Bitlisi, "Kânûn-ı Şehinşâhî," in Akgündüz, *Osmanlı kanunnameleri*, 3: 13, 11, 22–4, 27, 29–33, Circle on 32; the circularity of Idris's Circle was broken, but the subsequent discussion showed that he understood the concept in its entirety.

54 N. M. Titley, *Persian Miniature Painting and Its Influence on the Art of Turkey and India: the British Library collections,* London: The British Library, 1983, 134–5; E. Grube, "Herat, Tabriz, Istanbul – the development of a pictorial style," in R. Pinder-Wilson (ed.) *Paintings from Islamic Lands,* Oxford: Bruno Cassirer, 1969, 107; T. W. Lentz and G. D. Lowry, *Timur and the Princely Vision: Persian art and culture in the fifteenth century,* Washington, DC: Smithsonian Institution, Arthur M. Sackler Gallery, and Los Angeles County Museum of Art, 1989, 105. Early sixteenth-century Ottoman miniatures show influences from Central Asia and eastern Anatolia; Aslanapa, *Turkish Art,* 314; F. Çağman, "The Miniatures of the Divan-ı Hüseyni and the Influence of Their Style," in Fehér, *Fifth International Congress,* 237, 242. They have also been compared to Romanesque art brought from Spain by Jews fleeing the inquisition; F. Çağman and Z. Tanındı, *The Topkapı Saray Museum: the albums and illustrated manuscripts,* trans. and ed. J. M. Rogers, London: Thames & Hudson, 1986, 12.

55 İ. Kafesoğlu, "Büyük Selçuklu veziri Nizâmü'l-Mülk'un eseri Siyâsetnâme ve Türkçe tercümesi," *TM* 12, 1955: 233n9; R. Milstein, K. Rührdanz, and B. Schmitz, *Stories of the Prophets: illustrated manuscripts of Qisas al-Anbiya',* Costa Mesa, CA: Mazda, 1999, 34.

56 V. Minorsky, "The Poetry of Shāh Ismā'īl I," *BSOAS* 19, 1940–2: 1042a, 1046a, 1047a; I. Mélikoff, "The Worship of Shah Isma'il in Turkey in Past and Present Time," *Journal of Azerbaijani Studies* 1, 1998: 65; K. Babayan, "The Safavid Synthesis: from Qizilbash Islam to Imamite Shi'ism," *IranS* 27, 1994: 143. Safavid document forms demonstrated continuity with Akkoyunlu practice; B. G. Fragner, "Shah Ismail's Fermans and Sanads: tradition and reform in Persophone administration and chancellery affairs," *Journal of Azerbaijani Studies* 1, 1998: 43, 46.

57 Quotation from Mullā Muḥammad Bāqir Sabzavārī (d.1679), trans. H. Enayat, *Modern Islamic Political Thought,* Austin: University of Texas Press, 1982, 173. R. Tapper, "Shāhsevan in Ṣafavid Persia," *BSOAS* 37, 1974: 327; W. Floor, *A Fiscal History of Iran in the Safavid and Qajar Periods, 1500–1925,* New York: Bibliotheca Persica Press, 1998, 215.

58 K. Babayan, *Mystics, Monarchs, and Messiahs: cultural landscapes of early modern Iran,* Cambridge, MA: Harvard University Center for Middle Eastern Studies, 2002, 323–4; A. Banani, "Reflections on the Social and Economic Structure of Safavid Persia at Its Zenith," *IranS* 11, 1978: 96; A. K. S. Lambton," Quis Custodiet Custodes: some reflections on the Persian theory of government, I," *SI* 5, 1956: 131; S. A. Arjomand, *The Shadow of God and the Hidden Imam: religion, political order, and societal change in Shi'ite Iran from the beginning to 1890,* Chicago, IL: University of Chicago Press, 1984, 61, 176, 177, 179, 180.

59 M. B. Dickson and S. C. Welch, *The Houghton Shahnameh,* Cambridge, MA: Harvard University Press, 1981; S. C. Welch, *A King's Book of Kings: the Shah-nameh of Shah Tahmasp,* New York: Metropolitan Museum of Art, 1972, 18–21; J. M. Bloom, "Epic Images Revisited: an Ilkhanid legacy in early Safavid painting," in A. J. Newman (ed.) *Society and Culture in the Early Modern Middle East: studies on Iran in the Safavid period,* Leiden: Brill, 2003, 245, 247. This masterpiece has now been destroyed by art collectors. Other copies: A. J. Newman, *Safavid Iran: rebirth of a Persian Empire,* London: IB Tauris, 2006, 18, 34–5, 48, 59, 79, 90, 102.

60 S. C. Welch, "The *Shāhnāmeh* (Book of Kings) of Shah Tahmasp," in T. Falk (ed.) *Treasures of Islam,* London: Sotheby's/Philip Wilson, 1985, 69; Babayan, *Mystics, Monarchs,* xxx, 297, 318, 326, 327. This work was commissioned for Tahmasp as a young prince; perhaps he saw it as a training manual for Selim II. Interest in these epics revived under Shāh 'Abbās I (1587–1629) but declined again after his death; J. Calmard, "Popular Literature under the Safavids," in A. J. Newman (ed.) *Society and Culture in the Early Modern Middle East: studies on Iran in the Safavid period,* Leiden: Brill, 2003, 333, 335. New forms of the epics appeared late in the Safavid period; W. Hanaway, Introduction to *Love and War: adventures from the Firuz Shāh Nāma of Sheikh Bighami,* Delmar, NY: Scholars' Facsimiles and Reprints, 1974, 9. Artists' dispersal: Dickson, *Houghton Shahnama,* 45–46, 230; Robinson, "Survey," 50, 54, 58, 60, 64–66, 68–69; K, Rührdanz, "About a Group of Truncated *Shāhnāmas*: a case study in the commercial production of illustrated manuscripts in the second part of the sixteenth century," *Muqarnas* 14, 1997: 118–34.

61 R. D. McChesney, "Four Sources on Shah 'Abbas's Building of Isfahan," *Muqarnas* 5, 1988: 110–14; A. Welch, "Worldly and Otherworldly Love in Safavi Painting," in R. Hillenbrand (ed.) *Persian Painting from the Mongols to the Qajars: studies in honour of Basil W. Robinson,* London: IB Tauris, 2000, 301; Ebba Koch, "Diwan-i 'Amm and Chihil Sutun: the audience halls of Shah Jahan," *Muqarnas* 11, 1994: 152; S. S. Blair, "The Ilkhanid Palace," *Ars Orientalis* 23, 1993: 244; G. Necipoğlu, "Framing the Gaze in Ottoman, Safavid, and Mughal Palaces,"

ArsOr 23, 1993: 308–9. Open palaces may simply have been cheaper to build; *CHIr* 6: 774–84, 795–807.

62 Lambton, "Quis," 126–27; A. Black, *The History of Islamic Political Thought: from the Prophet to the present*, Edinburgh: Edinburgh University Press, 2001, 224. Calmard, "Popular Literature," 333–5. R. M. Savory, "The *Qizilbāsh*, Education and the Arts," *Turcica* 6, 1975: 168–76; J. R. I Cole, "Ideology, Ethics, and Philosophical Discourse in Eighteenth Century Iran," *IranS* 22.1, 1989: 15, 20; Browne, *Literary History of Persia*, 4: 227–70, 424, 445; Jan Rypka, *History of Iranian Literature*, Dordrecht, Neth.: D. Reidel, 1968, 293–4, 445.

63 V. Minorsky (trans.) *Tadhkirat al-mulūk: a manual of Ṣafavid administration*, Cambridge, UK: E. J. W. Gibb Memorial Trust, 1943; repr. 1980, 41, 110, quotation on 45.

64 R. Savory, "Notes on the Safavid State," *IranS*, 1, 1968: 99. Minorsky (trans.) *Tadhkirat al-mulūk*, 50–1, 119–20, 197; Arjomand, *Shadow of God*, 195; *EI2*, s.v. "Maḥkama," 5: 16; W. Floor, "The Secular Judicial System in Safavid Persia," *StIr* 29, 2000: 13–14, 24, 46; ibid., *Safavid Government Institutions*, Costa Mesa, CA: Mazda, 2001, 31; A. K. S. Lambton, "The Office of Kalântar under the Safawids and Afshars," in *Mélanges d'orientalisme offerts à Henri Massé*, Tehran: Imprimerie de l'Université, 1963, 212–14; J. R. Perry, "Justice for the Underprivileged: the ombudsman tradition of Iran," *JNES* 37, 1978: 209; W. C. Chittick, "Two Seventeenth-Century Persian Tracts on Kingship and Rulers," in S. A. Arjomand (ed.) *Authority and Political Culture in Shi'ism*, Albany: State University of New York Press, 1988, 286, 291.

65 Proverb quoted by several Safavid poets; P. E. Losensky, "Fanā and Taxes: a brief literary history of a Persian proverb," *Edebiyat* 7, 1996: 13–16.

66 *CHIr* 6: 493; 554–5; quotations from documents in B. G. Martin, "Seven Ṣafawid Documents from Azarbayjan," in S. M. Stern (ed.) *Documents from Islamic Chanceries*, Columbia, SC: University of South Carolina Press, 1965, 190–1, 198–9.

67 A. K. S. Lambton, "The Tribal Resurgence and the Decline of the Bureaucracy in the Eighteenth Century," in T. Naff and R. Owen (eds) *Studies in Eighteenth Century Islamic History*, Carbondale: Southern Illinois University Press, 1977, 108–29; A. Seyf, "Despotism and the Disintegration of the Iranian Economy, 1500–1800," in E. Kedourie and S. G. Haim (eds) *Essays on the Economic History of the Middle East*, London: Frank Cass, 1988, 6, 9–10; Minorsky (trans.) *Tadhkirat al-mulūk*, 23. The per-capita tax yield was only one-fifth that of France; ibid., 186.

68 Few Savafid documents remain, because the Afghans dumped the archives in the river; Banani, "Reflections," 92. Surviving documents, H. Busse, *Untersuchungen zum Islamischen Kanzleiwesen an Hand Turkmenischer und Safawidischer Urkunden*, Cairo: Kommissionsverlag Sirovič Bookshop, 1959, and sources listed in Banani, "Reflections," 106. Nādir Shāh: Sir J. Malcolm, *The History of Persia, from the most early period to the present time*, London: John Murray and Longman, 1815, 2: 87, 99, 108, quotation on 107; Seyf, "Despotism," 13, 14; Lambton, "Tribal Resurgence," 110, 128.

69 A. D. Tushingham, "The *Takht-i marmar* (Marble Throne) in Teheran," in C. J. Adams (ed.) *Iranian Civilization and Culture: essays in honour of the 2,500th anniversary of the founding of the Persian Empire*, Montreal: McGill University Institute of Islamic Studies, 1972, 125–6; Perry, "Justice," 212 (the spokesman's title was *vakil al-ra'āyā*).

70 J. R. Perry, *Karim Khan Zand: a history of Iran, 1747–1779*, Chicago, IL: University of Chicago Press, 1979, 214, 233, 237, 289; Malcolm, *History*, 2: 146, quotation on 150–1.

71 A. G. Frank, *ReOrient: global economy in the Asian age*, Berkeley: University of California Press, 1998.

72 R. Touchan, Ü. Akkemik, M. K. Hughes, and N. Erkan, "May-June Precipitation Reconstruction of Southwestern Anatolia, Turkey, during the Last 900 Years from Tree Rings," *Quaternary Research* 68, 2007: 200; Ö. L. Barkan, "Research on the Ottoman Fiscal Surveys," in M. A. Cook (ed.) *Studies in the Economic History of the Middle East: from the rise of Islam to the present day*, London: Oxford University Press, 1970, 163–71.

73 C. H. Fleischer, "The Lawgiver as Messiah: the making of the imperial image in the reign of Süleymân," in G. Veinstein (ed.) *Soliman le magnifique et son temps*, Paris: La Documentation Française, 1992, 159–77; Necipoğlu, *Architecture, Ceremonial, and Power*, 252–3; Ö. L. Barkan, *Süleymaniye Cami ve imareti inşaatı (1550–1557)*, 2 vols, Ankara: Türk Tarih Kurumu, 1972; Darling, "Another Look," 19–28.

74 M. Akdağ, *Türk halkının dirlik ve düzenlik kavgası (= Celali ısyanları)*, Ankara: Bilgi, 1975; H. İnalcık, "Military and Fiscal Transformation in the Ottoman Empire, 1600–1700," *AO* 6, 1980: 292–7; J. A. Goldstone, *Revolution and Rebellion in the Early Modern World*, Berkeley: University of

California Press, 1991, 378–9, 385; K. Barkey, *Bandits and Bureaucrats: the Ottoman route to state centralization*, Ithaca: Cornell University Press, 1994, 237–42.

75 Letter trans. T. S. Halman, "The Empire of Poetry: Süleyman the Magnificent as poet," in H. C. Güzel, C. Oğuz, O. Karatay, and M. Ocak (eds) *The Turks*, Ankara: Yeni Türkiye, 2002, 3: 907; İnalcık, "Suleiman the Lawgiver," 110; Fleischer, "Lawgiver as Messiah," 164, 173; G. Necipoğlu, "A Kânûn for the State, a Canon for the Arts: conceptualizing the classical synthesis of Ottoman art and architecture," in Veinstein, *Soliman le magnifique*, 212.

76 Quotation trans. W. G. Andrews, "Literary Art of the Golden Age: the age of Süleymân," in İnalcık and Kafadar, *Süleymân the Second*, 354. İnalcık, *Classical Age*, plate 10; compare with the image of Sanjar in Titley, *Persian Miniature Painting*, plate 2, or M. Lukens-Swietochowski, "The School of Herat from 1450 to 1506," in B. Gray (ed.) *The Arts of the Book in Central Asia: 14th–16th centuries*, Boulder, CO: Shambhala-UNESCO, 1979, plates 74–5.

77 G. İnal, "The Ottoman Interpretation of Firdausi's Shahnama," in Majer, *VI. Internationaler Kongress für Turkische Kunst*, 52. Bağcı, "From Translated Word," 166; ibid., "Iranian Epic," 425–7; Titley, *Persian Miniature Painting*, 135.

78 C. Woodhead, "An Experiment in Official Historiography: The Post of Şehnāmeci in the Ottoman Empire, c. 1555–1605," *WZKM* 75, 1983: 157–82; E. G. Sims, "The Turks and Illustrated Historical Texts," in Fehér, *Fifth International Congress*, 748–9; Levend, *Türk edebiyatı tarihi*, 111; Köprülü, *Türk edebiyatı tarihi*, 374; Atıl, *Turkish Art*, 165–6; cf. A. S. Levend, *Ǧazavāt-nāmeler ve Mihaloğlu Ali Bey'in Ǧazavāt-nāmesi*, Ankara: Türk Tarih Kurumu, 1956. The first two official Ottoman court historians or *şehnameci*s came from Iran with the exiled prince Alqās Mīrzā; Sohrweide, "Dichter und Gelehrte," 269.

79 Eyyûbî, *Menâḳib-i Sulṭan Süleyman (Risâle-i Pâdişâh-nâme)*, ed. M. Akkuş, Ankara: Kültür Bakanlığı, 1991, 5, 8, 112–21; quotation trans. R. Murphey, "Süleyman I and the Conquest of Hungary: Ottoman manifest destiny or a delayed reaction to Charles V's universalist vision?" *JEMH* 5, 2001: 200. E. Atıl, *Süleymanname: the illustrated history of Süleyman the Magnificent*, Washington, DC: National Gallery of Art, New York: H. N. Abrams, 1986.

80 M. A. Aynî, *Türk ahlâkcıları*, Istanbul: Marifet, 1939, 206; Alaeddin Ali Çelebi (d.1543), *Humâyûnnâme*, Bulaq: Dār al-Ṭibā'a al-'Āmire, 1838; H. Yılmaz, "The Sultan and the Sultanate: Envisioning Rulership in the Age of Süleymān the Lawgiver (1520–1566)," PhD diss., Harvard University, 2005, 45–7, 70–2. Süleymanic-era literature: Köprülü, *Türk edebiyatı tarihi*, 377–400.

81 Many copies were made of this book, parts of it were translated in Europe, and it became the foundation of Ottoman ethics textbooks; *EI2*, s.v. "Ḳınalızâde"; B. Tezcan, "The Definition of Sultanic Legitimacy in the Sixteenth Century Ottoman Empire: the *Ahlâk-ı Alâ'î* of Kınalızâde Alî Çelebi (1510–1572)," MA Thesis, Princeton University, 1996, 25–30; B. Tezcan, "Ethics as a Domain to Discuss the Political: Kınalızade Ali Efendi's *Ahlâk-ı Alâî*," in *Learning and Education in the Ottoman World*, ed. A. Çaksu, Istanbul: IRCICA, 2001, 109–20.

82 Kınalızâde 'Alī Çelebi, *Ahlâk-ı 'Alâ'î*, Bulaq: n.p., 1248/1832–3, 3: 49, trans. Fleischer, "Royal Authority," 201, alterations mine; the Turkish reads: "Cihân bir bâğdır dîvârî devlet; Devletin nâẓimî şerî'atdır; Şerî'ata olamaz hîç ḥâris illâ melik; Melik ẓabṭ eylemez illâ leşker; Leşkerî cem' edemez illâ mâl; Mâlî cem' eyleyin ra'îyetdir; Ra'îyetî kûl eder pâdişâh 'âleme 'adıl; 'Adıldır mûcib-i salâh-ı cihân." See ibid., 3: 7–16.

83 Kınalızâde, *Ahlâk-ı 'Alâ'î*, 2: 105–6; see C. H. Fleischer, *Bureaucrat and Intellectual in the Ottoman Empire: the historian Mustafa Âli (1541–1600)*, Princeton, NJ: Princeton University Press, 1986, 291. On walled gardens, W. G. Andrews, *Poetry's Voice, Society's Song: Ottoman lyric poetry*, Seattle: University of Washington Press, 1985, 151–5; Necipoğlu, *Architecture, Ceremonial, and Power*, 184–9. Lütfî Pâşâ, *History of the Ottoman Dynasty*, said of Selim's conquests that he "hewed a garden from a disorderly world" (quoted in Fleischer, "Lawgiver as Messiah," 163). On the garden, the garden as palace, and the world as a garden tended by the world-conquering sultan, W. G. Andrews, "Speaking of Power: the 'Ottoman kaside'," in *Qasida Poetry in Islamic Asia and Africa*, vol. 1: *Classical Traditions and Modern Meanings*, ed. S. Sperl and C. Shackle, Leiden: Brill, 1996, 293.

84 Akdağ, *Türk halkının dirlik*, 503–4; H. İnalcık, "State, Sovereignty and Law during the Reign of Süleymân," in İnalcık and Kafadar, *Süleymân the Second*, 62–4; İnalcık, "Adâletnâmeler"; İnalcık, "Suleiman the Lawgiver," 134–6. Justice decrees were issued until the nineteenth century against oppressive officials, corrupt ulema, and the depredations of bandits, nomads, and warlords;

Y. Özkaya, "XVIIIinci yüzyılda çıkarılan adalet-nâmelere göre Türkiye'nin iç durumu," *Belleten* 38, 1974: 445–91.

85 İnalcık, "Adâletnâmeler," 51, 87, 88–91; S. Faroqhi, "Sainthood as Means of Self-Defense in Seventeenth-Century Ottoman Anatolia," in G. M. Smith and C. W. Ernst (eds) *Manifestations of Sainthood in Islam*, Istanbul: İsis Press, 1993, 202–3; S. Faroqhi, "Political Activity among Ottoman Taxpayers and the Problem of Sultanic Legitimation (1570–1630)," *JESHO* 35, 1992: 10–13; M. Winter, "Attitudes toward the Ottomans in Egyptian Historiography during Ottoman Rule," in *The Historiography of Islamic Egypt (c. 950–1800)*, ed. H. Kennedy, Leiden: Brill, 2001, 293.

86 İnalcık, "State, Sovereignty," 77–8; Lowry, "Ottoman Liva Kanunnames;" K. Çiçek, "The Earliest Population and Fiscal Surveys (Tahrir Defterleri) for the Anatolian Provinces of the Ottoman Empire," *OTAM* 7, 1996: 45–98; N. Göyünç, "Provincial Organization of the Ottoman Empire in Pre-Tanzimat Period," in Çiçek, *Great Ottoman-Turkish Civilisation*, 3: 521; S. J. Shaw, *The Financial and Administrative Organization and Development of Ottoman Egypt, 1517–1798*, Princeton, NJ: Princeton University Press, 1962: 17–19, 31–5. Preamble, probably composed by Celâlzâde: Akgündüz, *Osmanlı kanunnameleri*, 6: 83, 6:101n1; the *kanunname* itself: ibid., 6: 86–176; see İnalcık, "Adâletnâmeler," 61–3.

87 İnalcık, "Suleiman the Lawgiver," 112, 115–20; Karal, "Yavuz Sultan Selim'in oğlu," 37–44; Akgündüz, *Osmanlı kanunnameleri*, 4: 296–360; quotation on 296; cf. Heyd, *Old Ottoman Criminal Law*, 176–7.

88 H. İnalcık, "Islamization of Ottoman Laws on Land and Land Tax," in *Festgabe an Josef Matuz: Osmanistik – Turkologie – Diplomatik*, ed. C. Fragner and K. Schwarz, Berlin: Klaus Schwarz, 1992, 101–18; M. E. Düzdağ, *Şeyhülislâm Ebussuûd Efendi fetvaları ışığında 16. asır Türk hayatı*, Istanbul: Enderun, 1983; C. Imber, *Ebu's-su'ud: the Islamic legal tradition*, Edinburgh: Edinburgh University Press, 1997.

89 Minkârizâde Dede Efendi, or Dede Cöngi Efendi (d.1565), "Siyaset-i şer'iye," in Akgündüz, *Osmanlı kanunnameleri*, 4: 127–73; Heyd, *Old Ottoman Criminal Law*, 198&n4, 201–3, 216; *EI2*, s.v. "Siyasa"; Yılmaz, "The Sultan and the Sultanate," 73–6. The Arab ulema generally championed the shariah against the *kanun*, condemning *kanun* in terms of the Mongol *yāsā*; M. Winter, "The Islamic Profile and the Religious Policy of the Ruling Class in Ottoman Egypt," *IOS* 10, 1983: 135; M. Winter, "The Ottoman Occupation," in *Islamic Egypt, 640–1517*, ed. C. F. Petry, v.1 of Petry and Daly, *Cambridge History of Egypt*, 509–10.

90 H. Gerber, "*Sharia, Kanun* and Custom in the Ottoman Law: the court records of 17th-century Bursa," *IJTS* 2.1, 1981: 138–39; Gerber, *State, Society*, 113; Heyd, "*Ḳanun* and *Sharī'a*," 8–9, Heyd, *Old Ottoman Criminal Law*, 32, 173–4, 183, 209–12, 216. For counts and maps of major mosques and *medreses* in Anatolia, S. Faroqhi, "A Map of Anatolian Friday Mosques, 1520–1535," *OA* 4, 1984: 161–73, and 5, 1985: the map; no page number.

91 D. A. Howard, "The 'Ruling Institution', Genre, and the Story of the Decline of the Ottoman Empire," Grand Rapids, MI, unpublished paper, 1992; R. Murphey, "Süleymân's Eastern Policy," in İnalcık and Kafadar, *Süleymân the Second*, 244&n49. Survey registers: *Başbakanlık Osmanlı arşivi rehberi*, Ankara: T.C. Başbakanlık Devlet Arşivleri Genel Müdürlüğü, 1992, 190–221.

92 Quotation from Anonymous, *Kitâb-i müstetâb*, ed. Y. Yücel, Ankara: Türk Tarih Kurumu, 1983, 14, trans. Howard, "Ottoman *Timar* System," 25. *Kânûns* regulating statesmen's titles and status order: Akgündüz, *Osmanlı kanunnameleri*, 4: 432–50. On the military, J. Káldy-Nagy, "The 'Strangers' (*Ecnebiler*) in the 16th Century Ottoman Military Organization," in *Between the Danube and the Caucasus*, ed. G. Kara, Budapest: Akadémiai Kiadó, 1987, 165–9; P. Fodor, "Making a Living on the Frontiers: Volunteers in the Sixteenth-Century Ottoman Army," in P. Fodor, *In Quest of the Golden Apple: imperial ideology, politics, and military administration in the Ottoman Empire*, Istanbul: İsis, 2000, 275–304. Judges: Flemming, "Public Opinion," 56. Scribes: C. H. Fleischer, "Between the Lines: Realities of Scribal Life in the Sixteenth Century," in Heywood and Imber, *Studies in Ottoman History in Honour of Professor V. L. Ménage*, 59. See Goldstone, *Revolution*; G. Hagen, "Legitimacy and World Order," in *Legitimizing the Order: the Ottoman rhetoric of state power*, ed. H. T. Karateke and M. Reinkowski, Leiden: Brill, 2005, 62–3.

93 Uğur, *Osmanlı siyaset-nameler*, 47–54; Levend, "Siyaset-nameler," 185; Karatay, *Topkapı Sarayı*, 489–95; H. İnalcık, "Sultan Süleymân: the man and the statesman," in Veinstein, *Soliman le magnifique*, 90–1.

94 İ. H. Uzunçarşılı, "Onaltıncı asır ortalarında yaşamış olan iki büyük şahsiyet: Tosyalı Celâl Zâde Mustafa ve Salih Çelebiler," *Belleten* 22, no. 87, 1958: 391–441 (this work discussed on 411).

95 Celâlzâde Mustafâ, *Mevāhibü'l-hallāk fī merātibü'l-ahlak*, MS Süleymaniye Bağdatlı Vehbi 763, fol. 218b; the Turkish reads: "Pâdişâh çobâna benzer ki asker ile anakût gelir asker a'vândır ki mâl ile beslenir mâl berrdir adet ra'iyet anı cem' eder ra'iyet savâddır ki 'adl ile kullanır 'adl esâsdır ki 'âlemin kavmı anıgeledir." See Fleischer, "Royal Authority," 201.

96 Darling, *Revenue-Raising*, 52–67; cf. R. Huang, "Fiscal Administration during the Ming Dynasty," in *Chinese Government in Ming Times: seven studies*, ed. C. O. Hucker, New York: Columbia University Press, 1969, 105, 126–7.

97 M. Akdağ, "Celâli isyanlarından büyük kaçgunluk, 1603–1606," *TAD* 2, 1964: 1–49; M. Akdağ, "Medreseli isyanları," *İÜİFM* 11, 1949–50: 361–87; M. Akdağ, *Türk halkının dirlik*, 153–254; M. A. Cook, *Population Pressure in Rural Anatolia, 1450–1600*, London: Oxford University Press, 1972, 10–11; S. Faroqhi, "The Peasants of Saideli in the Late Sixteenth Century," *AO* 8, 1983: 215–50; O. Özel, "The Transformation of Provincial Administration in Anatolia: observations on Amasya from 15th to 17th centuries," in *The Ottoman Empire: myths, realities and 'black holes': contributions in honour of Colin Imber*, ed. E. Kermeli and O. Özel, Istanbul: İsis Press, 2006, 68; Faroqhi, "Political Activity," 27–9, 36, 38; A. Singer, "Peasant Migration: law and practice in early Ottoman Palestine," *NPT* no. 8, Fall 1992: 55–6, 62; A. Singer *Palestinian Peasants*, 69, 125–6; O. Özel, "Population Changes in Ottoman Anatolia during the 16th and 17th Centuries: the 'demographic crisis' reconsidered," *IJMES* 36, 2004: 187. The attractions of urban life or status as a state servant also formed motives for leaving the land.

98 U. Heyd, *Ottoman Documents on Palestine, 1552–1615: a study of the firman according to the mühimme defteri*, Oxford: Clarendon, 1960, 93. Barkey, *Bandits and Bureaucrats*, does not address petitioning the sultan, although it discusses the courts; 86, 89, 103–7, 148–75.

99 Lüṭfî Pâshâ, *Das Aṣafnâme des Luṭfî Pascha*, ed. R. Tschudi, Leipzig: W. Drugulin, 1910 (hereafter Luṭfî Pâshâ/Tschudi); transliteration, Akgündüz, *Osmanlı kanunnameleri*, 4: 258–76; modern Turkish translation, Lüṭfi Paşa, *Asafnâme*, ed. A. Uğur, Ankara: Kültür ve Turizm Bakanlığı, 1982.

100 Lüṭfî Pâshâ/Tschudi, 35; trans. B. Lewis, "Ottoman Observers of Ottoman Decline," *IS* 1, 1962: 73; cf. Fodor, "State and Society," 223. In a new scholarly edition of the text this quotation reads: "Saltanat hazine ile olur. Ve cem'-i hazine tedbir ile olur, zulm ü sitemle olmaz"; M. S. Kütükoğlu, "Lüṭfî Paşa Âsafnâmesi (yeni bir metin tesisi denemesi)," in *Prof. Dr. Bekir Kütükoğlu'na Armağan*, Istanbul: Edebiyat Fakültesi, 1991, 91: "The sultanate endures by the treasury, and collection for the treasury succeeds by good management; it will not survive with oppression and wrong."

101 R. C. Jennings, "Kadi, Court, and Legal Procedure in 17th C. Ottoman Kayseri," *SI* 48, 1978: 133–72; Gerber, *State, Society*, 16, 40; Darling, *Revenue-Raising*, 201–3; İ. Ortaylı, "On the Role of the Ottoman Kadı in Provincial Administration," *Turkish Public Administration Annual* 3, 1976: 1–21; quotation from Singer, *Palestinian Peasants*, 45.

102 Ahmedi/Silay, 143; H. İnalcık, "A Report on the Corrupt Ḳāḍıs under Bayezid II," in *Studia Ottomanica: Festgabe für György Hazai zum 65. Geburtstag*, ed. B. Kellner-Heinkele and P. Zieme, Wiesbaden: Harrassowitz, 1997, 76–7; Faroqhi, "Political Activity," 17–23; Gerber, *State, Society*, 158–61; İnalcık, "Adâletnâmeler," 77; B. Ergene, *Local Court, Provincial Society and Justice in the Ottoman Empire: legal practice and dispute resolution in Çankırı and Kastamonu (1652–1744)*, Leiden: Brill, 2003, 109–15; A. Mumcu, *Osmanlı Devletinde Rüşvet (özellikle adlî rüşvet)*, Istanbul: İnkilâp, 1985.

103 There is no count of these judgeships, but for the growth of towns see L. T. Erder and S. Faroqhi, "The Development of the Anatolian Urban Network during the Sixteenth Century," *JESHO* 23, 1980: 265–303. For sixteenth-century instructions to new qadis, Ahmed Lütfi Bey, *Mir'at-ı adâlet*, trans. E. Beylem as *Osmanlı Adalet Düzeni*, Istanbul: Fatih, 1979, 55–9.

104 Ergene, *Local Court*, 45, 105; Singer, *Palestinian Peasants*, 17; Gerber, *State, Society*, 138–9. Court use by different social groups: B. A. Ergene, "Social Identity and Patterns of Interaction in the Sharia Court of Kastamonu (1740–44)," *ILS* 15, 2008: 20–54.

105 H. Ongan, *Ankara'nın iki numaralı şer'iye sicili*, Ankara: Türk Tarih Kurumu, 1974, nos 1752, 1754, 1528, 747; İnalcık, *Classical Age*, 74, 89–93; Gerber, *Islamic Law and Culture*, 58; G. Üçel-Aybet, "An Analytical Study of the Administrative and Social Policy of the Ottoman State (16th and 17th Centuries)," in *Comité international d'études pré-ottomanes et ottomanes: VIth symposium*, ed. J.-L. Bacqué-Grammont and E. van Donzel, Istanbul: Divit, 1987, 167. Necipoğlu, *Architecture, Ceremonial, and Power*, 80; M. S. Kütükoğlu, "Minyatürlerde divân-ı humâyûn ve arz odası," *TED* no. 16, 1998: 58–68.

106 H. İnalcık, "Osmanlı bürokrasisinde ahkâm ve muâmelât," *OA* 1, 1980: 1–14; ibid., "Şikâyet hakkı: 'Arẓ-ı Ḥâl ve 'Arẓ-ı Maḥżar'lar," *OA* 7–8, 1988: 33–54. See Darling, *Revenue-Raising*, 246–80; S. Faroqhi, "Crime, Women, and Wealth in the Eighteenth-Century Anatolian Countryside," in *Women in the Ottoman Empire: Middle Eastern women in the early modern era*, ed. M. C. Zilfi, Leiden: Brill, 1997, 6–27; M. Ursinus, *Grievance Administration (Şikayet) in an Ottoman Province: the Kaymakam of Rumelia's "Record book of complaints" of 1781–1783*, London: RoutledgeCurzon, 2005; L. T. Darling, "Murder and Mayhem in Ottoman Rumeli: local political relations in eighteenth-century Macedonia," in *Popular Protest and Public Participation in the Ottoman Empire*, ed. E. Gara, E. Kabadayı, and C. Neumann, Istanbul: Bilgi University Press, 2011, pages 177–95; Darling, *Revenue-Raising*, 248–60; Singer, *Palestinian Peasants*, 123; V. Ostapchuk, "The Ottoman Black Sea Frontier and the Relations of the Porte with the Polish-Lithuanian Commonwealth and Muscovy, 1622–1628," PhD diss., Harvard University, 1989, 260–3.

107 L. T. Darling, "The Finance Scribes and Ottoman Politics," in Farah, *Decision Making*, 95–7. S. Faroqhi, "Political Initiatives 'From the Bottom Up' in the Sixteenth and Seventeenth-Century Ottoman Empire: some evidence for their existence," in H. G. Majer (ed.) *Osmanistische Studien zur Wirtscharts- und Sozialgeschichte in Memoriam Vančo Boškov*, Wiesbaden: Harrassowitz, 1986, 27–30, stresses the active role of provincial notables in petitioning rulers ("from the middle up?").

108 F. Zarinebaf-Shahr, "Women, Law and Imperial Justice in Ottoman Istanbul in the Late Seventeenth Century," in A. E. Sonbol (ed.) *Women, the Family, and Divorce Laws in Islamic History*, Syracuse, NY: Syracuse University Press, 1996, 86–8; 10 to 20 percent of cases in the shariah court involved women, and 8 to 9 percent of petitions to the imperial court were from women. F. Zarinebaf-Shahr, "Ottoman Women and the Tradition of Seeking Justice in the Eighteenth Century," in Zilfi, *Women in the Ottoman Empire*, 256; Faroqhi, "Crime, Women, and Wealth," 27.

109 M. M. İlhan, "The Ottoman Archives and Their Importance for Historical Studies: with special reference to Arab provinces," *Belleten* 55, 1991: 447; Başbakanlık Osmanlı Arşivi, Kamil Kepeci Tasnifi, Register No. 2576, 1633–43, 100; Maliyeden Müdevver Tasnifi, Register No. 2765, 1644, 203.

110 Darling, *Revenue-Raising*, 160, 246, 280; Faroqhi, "Political Initiatives," 30–1.

111 J. C. Scott, "Everyday Forms of Peasant Resistance," *Journal of Peasant Studies* 13.2, 1985/6: 5–35; J. C. Scott, *Weapons of the Weak: everyday forms of peasant resistance*, New Haven, CT: Yale University Press, 1985. A. Matkovski, "La résistance des paysans macédoniens contre l'attachement à la glèbe pendant la domination ottomane," in *Actes du Ier congrès international des études balkaniques et sud-est européennes*, Sofia: Academie Bulgare des Sciences, 1969, 3: 703–8. Singer, *Palestinian Peasants*, 41, 107, 114, 125; Darling, *Revenue-Raising*, 196, 224, 226, 262, 267, 273, 275; G. Veinstein, "La voix du maître à travers les firmans de Soliman le Magnifique," in Veinstein, *Soliman le magnifique*, 140; B. A. Ergene, "On Ottoman Justice: Interpretations in Conflict (1600–1800)," *ILS* 8, 1991: 67.

112 B. Lewis, "Some Reflections on the Decline of the Ottoman Empire," *SI* 9, 1957: 111–27.

113 Hodgson, *Venture*, 3: 176–222.

114 İnalcık and Quataert, *Economic and Social History*, vol. 2. The legal meaning of injustice: A. Mumcu, *Osmanlı hukukunda zulüm kavramı: deneme*, 2nd ed., Ankara: Birey ve Toplum, 1985. Apocalypticism: C. H. Fleischer, "Mahdi and Millennium: messianic dimensions in the development of Ottoman imperial ideology," in Çiçek, *Great Ottoman-Turkish Civilisation*, 3: 52; sense of decline: C. Kafadar, "The Myth of the Golden Age: Ottoman historical consciousness in the post-Süleymânic era," in İnalcık and Kafadar, *Süleymân the Second*, 38–9.

115 Darling, *Revenue-Raising*, 246; H. İslamoğlu-İnan, *State and Peasant in the Ottoman Empire: agrarian power relations and regional economic development in Ottoman Anatolia during the sixteenth century*, Leiden: Brill, 1994, 208&n9, 224; F. Tabak, *The Waning of the Mediterranean, 1550–1870: a geohistorical approach*, Baltimore, MD: Johns Hopkins University Press, 2008. Climate change: P. I. Kuniholm, "Archaeological Evidence and Non-Evidence for Climatic Change," *Philosophical Transactions of the Royal Society of London* A330, 1990: 645–55; Touchan, Akkemik, Huges and Erkan, "May-June Precipitation," 200; Ü. Akkemik, N. Dağdeviren, and A. Aras, "A Preliminary Reconstruction (A.D. 1635–2000) of Spring Precipitation using Oak Tree Rings in the Western Black Sea Region of Turkey," *International Journal of Biometeorology* 49, 2005: 297–302.

116 C. Kafadar, "When Coins Turned into Drops of Dew and Bankers Became Robbers of Shadows: the boundaries of Ottoman economic imagination at the end of the sixteenth century," PhD diss., McGill University, 1986; İnalcık, "Military and Fiscal Transformation," 311–37; L. T. Darling,

"Ottoman Fiscal Administration: decline or adaptation'" *JEEH* 26, 1997: 157–79; Ş. Pamuk, *A Monetary History of the Ottoman Empire*, Cambridge: Cambridge University Press, 2000, 112–58.

117 Ş. Pamuk, "The Price Revolution in the Ottoman Empire Reconsidered," *IJMES* 33, 2001: 79–82. Evidence on the *timar* system's survival from complaint registers: Gerber, *State, Society*, 165–70.

118 Barkey, *Bandits and Bureaucrats*, 160–1, 167; Özel, "Changes in Settlement Patterns," 176–78; Akdağ, *Türk halkının dirlik*; M. Cezar, *Osmanlı tarihinde levendler*, Istanbul: Çelikcilt, 1965; W. J. Griswold, *The Great Anatolia Rebellion, 1000–1020/1591–1611*, Berlin: Klaus Schwarz, 1983; S. Faroqhi, "Crisis and Change, 1590–1699," in İnalcık and Quataert, *Economic and Social History*, 2: 467; S. Faroqhi, "Seeking Wisdom in China: an attempt to make sense of the Celali rebellions," in *Ẓafarnāme: memorial volume of Felix Tauer*, ed. R. Veselý and E. Gombár, Prague: enigma corporation, 1996, 102–3. Nobody yet has researched the surplus population of young women; shariah court records should provide some information.

119 L. P. Peirce, *The Imperial Harem: women and sovereignty in the Ottoman Empire*, New York: Oxford University Press, 1993, P. Fodor, "Sultan, Imperial Council, Grand Vizier: changes in the Ottoman ruling elite and the formation of the grand vizieral *telhīṣ*," *AOH* 47, 1994: 67–85.

120 Uğur, *Osmanlı siyaset-nameler*; O. M. Çolak, "İstanbul kütüphanelerinde bulunan siyasetnâmeler bibliografyası," *TALID* 1.2, 2003: 339–78; Levend, "Siyaset-nameler"; O. Köksal, "XVII. yüzyılda Osmanlı devleti'nde ıslahat ihtiyacının algılanışı ve ıslahat temayülleri," in K. Çiçek (ed.) *Osmanlı*, Ankara: Yeni Türkiye, 1999, 7: 162–9; H. Yılmaz, "Osmanl tarihçiliğinde Tanzimat öncesi siyaset düşüncesine yaklaşımlar," *TALID* 1.2, 2003: 231–98. Abou-El-Haj argued for a study of advice writers in historical context; R. A. Abou-El-Haj, "The Expression of Ottoman Political Culture in the Literature of Advice to Princes (Nasihatnameler), Sixteenth to Twentieth Centuries," in *Sociology in the Rubric of Social Science: Professor Ramkrishna Mukherjee felicitation volume*, ed. R. K. Bhattacharya and A. K. Ghosh, Calcutta: Anthropological Survey of India, 1995, 284–5. Pending such a study, I limit my discussion to how these authors quote the Circle of Justice.

121 Muṣṭafâ 'Âlî, *Nuṣḥat al-salaṭīn*, ed. and trans. A. Tietze, *Muṣṭafā 'Ālī's Counsel for Sultans of 1581: edition, translation, notes*, Philosophisch-Historische Klasse, 137, 158, Vienna: Österreischschen Akademie der Wissenschaften, 1979, 1982, 1: 17, 18 (text: 89, 90); R. 'A. Abou-El-Haj, *Formation of the Modern State: the Ottoman Empire, sixteenth to eighteenth centuries*, Albany: State University of New York Press, 1991. On Muṣṭafâ 'Âlî and his works: Fleischer, *Bureaucrat and Intellectual*. 'Âlî used the advice format to comment directly on current problems; this development began earlier with the *Asafnâme* of Lüṭfî Paşa. 'Âlî's complaining tone contrasts with the dispassionate air of an earlier secretary's petition to Sultan Süleyman; Fleischer, "Between the Lines," 53.

122 Âlî, *Nuṣḥat al-salaṭīn*, 1: 19 (text: 91); Muṣṭafâ 'Âlî, *Hālāt'ül-Ḳāhire*, ed, and trans. A. Tietze, *Muṣṭafā Ālī's Description of Cairo of 1599: text, transliteration, translation, notes*, Philosophisch-Historische Klasse, 120, Vienna: Österreichischen Akademie der Wissenschaften, 1975, 80 (text: 172).

123 Muṣṭafâ 'Âlî, *Künh al-ahbār*, in J. Schmidt, *Pure Water for Thirsty Muslims: a study of Muṣṭafa 'Ālī of Gallipoli's Künhü' l-ahbār*, Leiden: Het Oosters Instituut, 1991, 132, 133, 150, 152, 155–65, 201. This is the "alternative" interpretation of justice discussed by Ergene, "On Ottoman Justice," 57n13.

124 Âlî, *Nuṣḥat al-salaṭīn*, 1: 37, 41 (text: 121, 126); Howard, "Ottoman *Timar* System," 179–82. According to Fleischer, 'Âlî equated the Ottoman *kanun* with the *yāsā* of Genghis Khan and considered that the Ottoman Empire could have been a universal dominion like that of the Mongols or Alexander the Great; *Bureaucrat and Intellectual*, 275, 280, 284.

125 Ḥasan Kāfī Efendī al-Āqḥiṣārī, *Uṣūl al-ḥikam fī niẓām al-'alam*, ed. N. R. al-Hmoud, Amman: Publication of the University of Jordan, 1986 (hereafter Āqḥiṣārī/Hmoud), 22; Ḥasan Kāfī al-Aqḥiṣārī, *Uṣūl al-ḥikam fi niẓām al-'alam*, ed. I. Ṣ. al-'Amdū, Kuwait: Dhāt al-Salāsil, 1987 (hereafter Aqḥiṣārī/'Amdū), 122–3; Turkish trans., M. İpşirli, "Hasan Kâfi el-Akhisarî ve devlet düzenine ait eseri *Usûlü'l-hikem fî nizâmi'l-âlem*," *TED* 10–11, 1979–80: 254; French trans., M. Garcin de Tassy, "Principes de Sagesse, touchant l'art de gouverner," *JA* 4, 1824: 220. The Arabic original quotes the standard four-line form attributed to Ardashir. The Turkish translation elaborates on it, defining its terms within the Ottoman administrative context. Where the Arabic has "sulṭān," for example, the Turkish adds "pādişāhlık," and where the Arabic has "rijāl" (men), the Turkish adds, "ya'nī asker" (i.e., soldiers).

126 Aqḥiṣārī/Hmoud, 22; Aqḥiṣārī/'Amdū, 122–3; İpşirli, "Hasan Kâfi el-Akhisarî," 254; Garcin de Tassy, "Principes de Sagesse," 220. For a partial study of this and related texts see Hagen, "Legitimacy and World Order," 55–83.

127 İnalcık, "Military and Fiscal Transformation," 288–9; Barkey, *Bandits and Bureaucrats*. Faroqhi suggests that bandits and Celalis desired to belong to the state because, once adrift from village and army, they had no other strong social or religious ties; Faroqhi, "Seeking Wisdom in China," 121.

128 See H. İnalcık, "The Heyday and Decline of the Ottoman Empire," in *CHI*, 346; A.-K. Rafeq, "The Local Forces in Syria in the Seventeenth and Eighteenth Centuries," in V. J. Parry and M. E. Yapp (eds) *War, Technology and Society in the Middle East*, London: Oxford University Press, 1975, 277–307; B. Tezcan, "Searching for Osman: a reassessment of the deposition of the Ottoman sultan Osman II (1618–1622)," PhD diss., Princeton University, 2001, 240–58.

129 Anonymous, *Kitāb-i müsteṭāb*, ed. Y. Yücel, *Osmanlı devlet teşkilâtına dair kaynaklar*, Ankara: Türk Tarih Kurumu, 1983/88, 1–40, esp. 2–3, 12, 15–16, 24, 31; Circle of Justice on 18; cf. Akgündüz, *Osmanlı kanunnameleri*, 9: 593–685.

130 Koçi Bey, *Koçi Bey risalesi*, ed. Y. Kurt, Ankara: Ecdad, 1994, 62, 65 (text: 55–6, 59). On Ottoman state structure in Koçi Bey's *Risale*, Abou-El-Haj, *Formation*, esp. 29–35, 79–89. On Koçi Bey and the decline paradigm, Lewis, "Ottoman Observers," 75–8.

131 Quotation: Koçi Bey, trans. Rosenthal, *Political Thought*, 227. Koçı Bey, *Koçi Bey risalesi*, ed. A. K. Aksüt, Istanbul: Vakıt, 1939, 79, 121; F. R. Unat, "Sadrazam Kemankeş Kara Mustafa Paşa Lâyihası," *TV* 1, 1941–2: 452, 467 (this work is also Koçi Bey's *Risale*; see D. A. Howard, "Ottoman Historiography and the Literature of 'Decline' of the Sixteenth and Seventeenth Centuries," *JAH* 22, 1988: 64–5n32). For contemporary assessments of İbrahim's reign see R. Murphey, "Ottoman Historical Writing in the Seventeenth Century: a survey of the general development of the genre after the reign of Sultan Ahmed I (1603–1617)," *AOtt* 13, 1993–94: 290–4.

132 Haci Halife Kâtip Çelebi, *Düstûru'l-amel li-ıslahi'l-halel*, in Ayn Ali Efendi, *Kavânîn-i Âl-i Osman der hülâsa-i mezâmin-i defter-i dîvân*, ed. M. T. Gökbilgin, Istanbul: Enderun, 1979, 124; Ayn Ali Efendi, *Bozuklukların düzeltilmesinde tutulacak yollar (Düstûru'l-amel li-ıslahi'l-halel)*, ed. and trans. A. Can, Ankara: Kültür ve Turizm Bakanlığı, 1982, 22. See Ayn-i Ali Efendi, *The Balance of Truth*, trans. G. L. Lewis, London: George Allen and Unwin, 1957, 33–4. After retiring from government service, Kâtip Çelebi wrote a history, a geography, and a bibliography; see *Kâtip Çelebi: Hayatı ve Eserleri Hakkında İncelemeler*, Ankara: Türk Tarih Kurumu, 1985.

133 Quotation from Kâtip Çelebi, *Takvimü't-tevarih*, Istanbul: İbrahim Müteferrika, 1733, 246, trans. Hagen, "Legitimacy and World Order," 71. Fleischer, "Royal Authority," 199.

134 Kâtip Çelebi, *Fezleke*, Istanbul: Ceride-i Havadis Matbaası, 1869–70, 384–5, cited in Lewis, "Ottoman Observers," 81.

135 Gerber, *State, Society*, 170. We do not yet know whether peasants experienced lighter taxes or greater justice as a result of Köprülü's policies; the *avarız* did decrease, but that is assumed to result from population decline rather than policy change; B. McGowan, *Economic Life in Ottoman Europe: taxation, trade and the struggle for land, 1600–1800*, Cambridge: Cambridge University Press, and Paris: Éditions de la Maison des Sciences de l'Homme, 1981, 112–14.

136 Al-Ḥasan al-Yūsī, *Rasā'il Abī 'Alī al-Ḥasan Mas'ūd al-Yūsī*, Casablanca: Dār al-Thaqāfa, 1981, 1: 241–2, trans. J. Dakhlia, *Le Divan des rois: Le politique et le religieux dans l'Islam*, Paris: Aubier, 1998, 145. J. Berque, *Al-Yousi: problèmes de la culture marocaine au XVIIème siècle*, Paris: Mouton, 1958, 92; J. Berque, *Ulémas, fondateurs, insurgés du Maghreb: XVIIe siècle*, Paris: Sindbad, 1982, 245–6. Another letter al-Yūsī wrote to Mulay Ismail was entitled, "Exhortation to Kings to Do Justice"; H. Munson, Jr., *Religion and Power in Morocco*, New Haven, CT: Yale University Press, 1993, 27; see also 29. Mulay Ismail reputedly created a regime in which "a woman could walk alone from the Sahara to the Mediterranean, decked out in her finest gold, and never be molested," but he exiled al-Yūsī; M. E. Combs-Schilling, *Sacred Performances: Islam, sexuality, and sacrifice*, New York: Columbia University Press, 1989, 178.

137 Eyyubî Efendi, *Eyyubî Efendi kanûnnâmesi: tahlil ve metin*, ed. A. Özcan, Istanbul: Eren, 1994; Hezarfen Hüseyin Efendi, *Telhîsü'l-beyân fî kavânîn-i Âl-i Osmân*, ed. S. İlgürel, Ankara: Türk Tarih Kurumu, 1998. For unpublished advice works from Mehmed IV's reign, Uğur, *Osmanlı siyaset-nameler*, 61–2, 65; Çolak, "Siyasetnâmeler bibliografyası," 339–78.

138 Tevki'î Abdürrahman Paşa, "Osmanlı kanunnameleri," *MTM* 1.3, 1913/1331: 49–112, 304–48, 497–544; Tevki'î Abdurrahman Paşa, *Osmanlı Devleti'nde Teşrifat ve Törenler: Tevki'î Abdurrahman Paşa Kānûn-Nâmesi*, trans. Sadık Müfit Bilge, Istanbul: Kitabevi, 2011; S. Albayrak, *Budin kanunnamesi ve Osmanlı toprak meselesi*, Istanbul: Tercüman, 1973; C. Woodhead, "After Celalzade: the Ottoman *nişancı* c. 1560–1700," in A. Christmann and R. Gleave (eds) *Studies in Islamic Law: a*

festschrift for Colin Imber, Oxford: Oxford University Press for the University of Manchester, 2007, 308–9. Ahmed I's lawcode: Akgündüz, *Osmanlı kanunnameleri*, 9: 491–554.

139 Tevki'î, "Osmanlı kanunnameleri," 528; Ergene, *Local Court*, 173n6.

140 H. G. Majer, *Das osmanische "Registerbuch der Beschwerden" (Şikāyet Defteri) vom Jahre 1675*, Vienna: Österreichischen Akademie der Wissenschaften, 1984, esp. 23. Ergene, *Local Court*, 49–51, 104–5; S. Demirci, "Complaints about *Avârız* Assessment and Payment in the *Avârız*-Tax System, an aspect of the relationship between centre and periphery: a case study of Kayseri, 1618–1700," *JESHO* 46, 2003: 437–74; Gerber, *State, Society*, 155–61. In Morocco, too, an observer reported seeing assemblies of women crying at the door of the *divan* for justice; Dakhlia, *Divan*, 265.

141 E. Yi, *Guild Dynamics in Seventeenth-Century Istanbul: fluidity and leverage*, Leiden: Brill, 2004, 188, 197–206. On bread, grain, and related taxation, L. Güçer, *XVI–XVII. asırlarda Osmanlı İmparatorluğunda hububat meselesi ve hububattan alınan vergiler*, Istanbul: Sermet Matbaası, 1964.

142 M. L. Meriwether, "Urban Notables and Rural Resources in Aleppo, 1770–1830," *IJTS* 4.1, 1987: 59; A. Raymond, "Quartiers et mouvements populaires au Caire au XVIIIème siècle," in P. M. Holt (ed.) *Political and Social Change in Modern Egypt: historical studies from the Ottoman conquest to the United Arab Republic*, London: Oxford University Press, 1968, 109, 113; R. Murphey, "Provisioning Istanbul: the state and subsistence in the early modern Middle East," *Food and Foodways* 2, 1988: 217–63; J. Grehan, "Street Violence and Social Imagiation in Late-Mamluk and Ottoman Damascus (ca. 1500–1800)," *IJMES* 35, 2003: 224–6.

143 Müneccimbaşı Ahmet Dede, *Saha'ifü'l-ahbar*, Istanbul: Matbaa-ı 'Âmire, 1285/1868, characterization as *naṣīḥa*, 3: 749; Müneccimbaşı Ahmet Dede, *Müneccimbaşı tarihi (Sahaif-ül-ahbar fî vekayi-ül-a'sâr)*, trans. İ. Erünsal, 2 vols, Istanbul, Tercüman, 1970–4. This work uses several sources now lost to us.

144 Muṣṭafâ Na'ima, *Tarih-i Na'ima: ravzatü'l-Hüseyn fī hulâsat-i ahbari'l-hafikayn*, Istanbul: Matbaa-ı 'Amire, 1281–3/1864–6; ed. M. İpşirli, Ankara: Türk Tarih Kurumu, 2007. Naima brought this history only to 1659 before he died. Fraser's English translation covers only the years 1591–1624, despite its title: Naima, *Annals of the Turkish Empire from 1591 to 1659 of the Christian Era*, trans. C. Fraser, London: John Murray, 1832; repr. New York: Arno Press, 1973.

145 Na'ima, *Tarih*, 1864, 40; 2007, 30. Kınalızâde, of course, borrowed the Circle from Dāvānī, not Ibn Khaldūn; Fleischer, "Royal Authority," 201.

146 L. V. Thomas, *A Study of Naima*, ed. N. Itzkowitz, New York: New York University Press, 1972, 102–6. Ágoston attributes the Ottomans' late seventeenth-century military difficulties to the Europeans' shift from siege warfare, at which the Ottomans excelled, to field battles, for which neither their training nor their weaponry was suited at that date; G. Ágoston, *Guns for the Sultan: military power and the weapons industry in the Ottoman Empire*, Cambridge: Cambridge University Press, 2005, 201. Marsigli particularly noted Ottoman problems with coordination in the field; L. F. Marsigli, *Stato Militare dell'Impero Ottomanno*, Graz: Akademische Druck u. Verlagsanstalt, 1972, 2: 131. Eugene of Savoy may have played a part in the Ottomans' major losses: N. Itzkowitz, *Ottoman Empire and Islamic Tradition*, Chicago, IL: University of Chicago Press, 1972, 102–3.

147 R. A. Abou-El-Haj, *The 1703 Rebellion and the Structure of Ottoman Politics*, Istanbul: Nederlands Historisch-Archaeologisch Instituut, 1984; Defterdar Sarı Mehmed Paşa, *Zübde-i vekayiât*, ed. A. Özcan, Ankara: Türk Tarih Kurumu, 1995.

148 Sarı Memed Pasha, the Defterdār, *Ottoman Statecraft: the book of counsel for vezirs and governors*, trans. W. L. Wright, Jr., Princeton, NJ: Princeton University Press, 1935; Westport, CT: repr. Greenwood Press, 1971, 64 (p. 5, fol. 3v). Translation amended; Wright translated the Arabic word *rijāl* in this statement not as "men" but as "men of substance"; in other contexts this word clearly means soldiers, and this quotation also goes on to speak of "armies experienced in wars" rather than rich men. On ethical and advice works from this era, Levend, "Ümmet Cağında Ahlak Kitaplarımız," 102; Levend, "Siyaset-nameler," 187–8.

149 Sarı Mehmed, *Ottoman Statecraft*, 76 (p. 20, fol. 11r.). Translation amended; Wright again translated *rijāl* as "men of substance" rather than soldiers.

150 Sarı Mehmed, *Ottoman Statecraft*, 117, cited in İnalcık, "State, Sovereignty," 89, from Uzunçarşılı, *Osmanlı tarihi*, 2: 420.

151 F. Zarinebaf, J. Bennet, and J. L. Davis, *A Historical and Economic Geography of Ottoman Greece: the southwestern Morea in the 18th century*, [Princeton, NJ]: The American School of Classical Studies at Athens, 2005; F. Zarinebaf-Shahr, "Tabriz under Ottoman Rule (1725–1730)," PhD diss., University

of Chicago, 1991. A late eighteenth-century recommendation for a survey: Cezzâr Ahmed Pasha, *Ottoman Egypt in the Eighteenth Century: the Nizâmnâme-i Mısır of Cezzâr Ahmed Pasha*, ed. and trans. S. J. Shaw, Cambridge: Center for Middle Eastern Studies, Harvard University, 1962, 37.

152 Sarı Mehmed, *Ottoman Statecraft*, 119–20 (p.75, fol.38v). Here, too, Wright translated *rijāl* as "men of consequence," apparently believing that they rather than "troops" formed the basis of the sultan's power; Wright's translation may reflect his own society more than Sarı Mehmed's.

153 A. Ö. Evin, "The Tulip Age and Definitions of 'Westernization'," in O. Okyar and H. İnalcık (eds) *Türkiye'nin sosyal ve ekonomik tarihi (1071–1920)*, Ankara: Meteksan, 1980, 131–5, 143; A. Salzmann, "The Age of Tulips: confluence and conflict in early modern consumer culture (1550–1730)," in D. Quataert (ed.) *Consumption Studies and the History of the Ottoman Empire, 1550–1922: an introduction*, Albany: State University of New York Press, 2000, 83–106; C. Erimtan, "The Perception of Saadabad: the 'Tulip Age' and Ottoman-Safavid rivalry," in D. Sajdi (ed.) *Ottoman Tulips, Ottoman Coffee: leisure and lifestyle in the eighteenth century*, London: Tauris Academic Studies, 2007, 41–62; S. Hamadeh, "Ottoman Expressions of Early Modernity and the 'Inevitable' Question of Westernization," *Journal of the Society of Architectural Historians* 63, March 2004: 40–5.

154 S. Hamadeh, *The City's Pleasures: Istanbul in the eighteenth century*, Seattle: University of Washington Press, 2008; Evin, "Tulip Age," 134–9; W. Heinz, "Die Kultur der Tulpenzeit des Osmanischen Reiches," *WZKM* 61, 1967: 62–116; T. Artan, "Architecture as a Theatre of Life: profile of the eighteenth-century Bosphorus," PhD diss., MIT, 1989; T. Artan, "Noble Women Who Changed the Face of the Bosphorus and … the Palaces of the Sultanas," *İstanbul* 1.1, Winter 1993: 87–97. The darker side: F. Zarinebaf, *Crime and Punishment in Istanbul, 1650–1850*, Berkeley: University of California Press, 2010.

155 B. Lewis, "Ibn Khaldun in Turkey," in M. Sharon (ed.) *Studies in Islamic History and Civilization in Honour of Professor David Ayalon*, Jerusalem, Cana, and Leiden: Brill, 1986, 527–30, repr. in *Islam in History: Ideas, People, and Events in the Middle East*, New ed., Chicago and La Salle, Open Court, 1993, 235; A. Şen, *İbrahim Müteferrika ve Usûlü'l-hikem fî nizâmi'l-ümem*, Ankara: Türkiye Diyanet Vakfi, 1995, 123–91.

156 D. Sajdi, "Decline, Its Discontents and Ottoman Cultural History: by way of introduction," in Sajdi, *Ottoman Tulips, Ottoman Coffee*, 34.

157 M. M. Aktepe, *Patrona İsyanı (1730)*, Istanbul: Edebiyat Fakültesi, 1958; R. W. Olson, "The Esnaf and the Patrona Halil Rebellion of 1730: a realignment in Ottoman politics?" *JESHO* 17, 1974: 329–44; R. W. Olson, "Some Comments on Eighteenth Century Ottoman Historiography," in R. Olson and S. A. Ani (eds) *Islamic and Middle Eastern Societies: a festschrift in honor of Professor Wadie Jwaideh*, Brattleboro, VT: Amana Books, 1987, 137–51; A. Matkovski, "L'insurrection de Patrona Halil à Istanbul (28 septembre 1730) et sa répercussion en Macédoine," *Balcanica* 13–14, 1982–3: 105–15.

158 S. Faroqhi, "Presenting the Sultans' Power, Glory and Piety: a comparative perspective," in Z. T. Ertuğ (ed.) *Prof. Dr. Mübahat S. Kütükoğlu'na armağan*, Istanbul: Edebiyat Fakültesi, 2006, 179–80. Mahmud's second grand vizier, İbrahim Paşa, made himself popular by hearing petitions and lowering food prices, while his third, Topal Osman Paşa, was said to use justice as a cover for jealous violence; M. L. Shay, *The Ottoman Empire from 1720 to 1734 as revealed in despatches of the Venetian baili*, Westport, CT: Greenwood Press, 1978, 31, 34.

159 Grehan, "Street Violence," 218–19; G. E. el-Shayyal, "Some Aspects of Intellectual and Social Life in Eighteenth-century Egypt," in Holt, *Political and Social Change*, 122–3.

160 Grehan, "Street Violence," 227–9; Grehan, *Everyday Life and Consumer Culture in 18th-Century Damascus*, Seattle: University of Washington Press, 2007, 86–91; D. Douwes, *The Ottomans in Syria: a history of justice and oppression*, London: IB Tauris, 2000, 159–60; B. Marino, "L'approvisionnement en céréales des villes de la Syrie Ottomane (XVIe–XVIIIe siècles)," in B. Marino and C. Virlouvet (eds) *Nourrir les cités de Méditerranée: antiquite-temps modernes*, Paris: Maisonneuve et Larose, 2003, 503. On Istanbul's bread and grain supply, O. Yıldırım, "Bread and Empire: the workings of grain provisioning in Istanbul during the eighteenth century," in ibid., 251–72.

161 B. Masters, "The View from the Province: Syrian chroncles of the eighteenth century," *JAOS* 114, 1994: 357; M. R. Hickok, "Homicide in Ottoman Bosnia," in F. Anscombe (ed.) *The Ottoman Balkans, 1750–1830*, Princeton, NJ: Markus Wiener, 2006, 38. Aḥmad b. 'Abd al-Mun'īm al-Damanhūrī (d.1778), *Al-Naf' al-ghazīr f ī salāḥ al-sulṭān wa'l-wazīr*, Alexandria: Mu'assasat Shabāb al-Jāmi'a, 1992, 52; Muḥammad Saghīr b. Yūsuf, *Mashra' al-mulkī* (1763–64), trans. Dakhlia, *Divan*, 139–40.

162 B. McGowan, "The Age of the Ayans, 1699–1812," in İnalcık and Quataert, *Economic and Social History*, 2: 639–44, 653; L. T. Darling, "Public Finances: the role of the Ottoman centre," in S. N. Faroqhi (ed.) *The Cambridge History of Turkey*, vol. 3, *The Later Empire, 1603–1839*, Cambridge: Cambridge University Press, 2006, 126; V. H. Aksan, "Whatever Happened to the Janissaries' Mobilization for the 1768–1774 Russo-Ottoman War," *War in History* 5, 1998: 25–8; Özkaya, "İç Durumu," 489.

163 T. Güran, "The State Role in the Grain Supply of Istanbul: the grain administration, 1793–1839," *IJTS* 3, 1984: 27–41; E. Özveren, "Black Sea and the Grain Provisioning of Istanbul in the *Longue Durée*," in Marino and Virlouvet, *Nourrir les cités*, 223–49; Yıldırım, "Bread and Empire," 256–61; L. M. Şaşmazer, "Policing Bread Price and Production in Ottoman Istanbul, 1793–1807," *TSAB* 24.1, Spring 2000: 25, 27, 30–3.

164 V. H. Aksan, "Ottoman Political Writing, 1768–1808," *IJMES* 25, 1993, 53–69. Nehîfi Mehmed Efendi, *Nehcü's-sülûk fî siyâseti'l-mülûk*, Istanbul: Ali Riza Efendi, 1869, trans. H. Algül, [Istanbul]: Tercüman, 1974; 'Abd al-Raḥmān b. Naṣr al-Shayzarī, *Al-Nahj al-maslūk fī siyāsat al-mulūk*, Beirut: Dār al-Manār, 1994. Nehîfi's work was printed several times in the nineteenth century, suggesting that for the Ottomans it had more than historical value; these editions include Cairo, 1841; Cairo, 1856; Istanbul, 1869; Istanbul, 1869 (a different edition); and Cairo, 1908.

165 Na'ima, *Tarih*, trans. Thomas, *Study*, 45–8. Naima explained that this work was not the book of the same name by the famous Sufi author al-Suhrawardī, but Nehîfi, confused by his contorted explanation, apparently thought it was, and subsequent editors have followed his error. Thomas did not, but he attributed the work to al-Shirāzī rather than al-Shayzarī; Thomas, *Study*, 78.

166 Nehîfî, *Nehcü's-sülûk*, 21 (trans. 54). Nehîfî Mehmed Efendi, also wrote a book of advice to viziers that, among other things, explained how to deal with petitions and how to investigate the conditions of the realm to eliminate oppression of the common people; Uğur, *Osmanlı siyaset-nameler*, 110–13.

167 F. Sarıcaoğlu, *Kendi kaleminden bir padişahın portresi: Sultan I. Abdülhamid (1774–1789)*, Istanbul: Tarih ve Tabiat Vakfı, 2001, 250, trans. Finkel, *Osman's Dream*, 382. Douwes even saw the Circle as having been broken at this point; Douwes, *Ottomans*, 217.

168 V. H. Aksan, "Feeding the Ottoman Troops on the Danube, 1768–1774," *War and Society* 13, 1995: 1–14; repr. in V. H. Aksan, *Ottomans and Europeans: Contacts and Conflicts*, Istanbul: İsis, 2004, 215; D. R. Khoury, "The Ottoman Centre versus Provincial Power-Holders: an analysis of the historiography," in *The Cambridge History of Turkey*, 3: 52–5; on a new *maẓālim* court in Egypt, H. A. R. Gibb and H. Bowen, *Islamic Society and the West: a study of the impact of Western civilization on Moslem culture in the Near East*, London: Oxford University Press, 1957, v. 1, pt. 2: 130.

169 J.-P. Thieck, "Décentralisation ottomane et affirmation urbaine à Alep à la fin du XVIIIème siècle," in M. Zakaria (eds) *Mouvements communautaires et espaces urbaines au Machreq*, Beirut: Centre d'études et de recherches sur le Moyen-Orient contemporain (CERMOC), 1985, 117–68, cited in Khoury, "The Ottoman Centre," 153; M. R. Hickok, *Ottoman Military Administration in Eighteenth-Century Bosnia*, Leiden: Brill, 1997, 101, 104, 107, 115–16.

170 Finkel, *Osman's Dream*, 387; McGowan, "Age of the Ayans," 658–709; İnalcık, "Centralization and Decentralization"; Darling, "Public Finances," 124. Quotation: Gerber, *Islamic Law and Culture*, 66.

171 Hickok, "Homicide," 43–4; see K. Çiçek, "A Quest for Justice in a Mixed Society: the Turks and the Greek Cypriots before the sharia court of Nicosia," in Çiçek, *Great Ottoman-Turkish Civilisation*, 2: 474; S. H. Winter, "Shiite Emirs and Ottoman Authorities: the campaign against the Hamadas of Mt. Lebanon, 1693–1694," *AOtt* 18, 2000: 221.

172 Winter, "Shiite Emirs," 222; G. Veinstein, "İnalcık's Views on the Ottoman Eighteenth Century and the Fiscal Problem," *Oriente Moderno*, n.s. 18/79, 1999: 8–9; İnalcık, "Military and Fiscal Transformation"; B. W. McGowan, "The Study of Land and Agriculture in the Ottoman Provinces within the context of an expanding world economy in the 17th and 18th centuries," *IJTS* 2.1, 1981: 59–60; Khoury, "Ottoman Centre," 135–7, 155.

173 McGowan, "Age of the Ayans," 711; Ş. Mardin, "Power, Civil Society and Culture in the Ottoman Empire," *CSSH* 11, 1969: 263, 267; Darling, *Revenue-Raising*, 273–4; G. Veinstein, "On the *Çiftlik* Debate," in Ç. Keyder and F. Tabak (eds) *Landholding and Commercial Agriculture in the Middle East*, Albany: State University of New York Press, 1991, 52; A. Anastasopoulos, "Lighting the Flame of Disorder: *ayan* infighting and state intervention in Ottoman Karaferye, 1758–59,"

IJTS 8, 2002: 86–7; N. Çevikel, "Muslim-Non-Muslim Relations in the Ottoman Province of Cyprus (1750–1800)," in Çiçek, *Great Ottoman-Turkish Civilisation*, 2: 428; see also Cezzâr, *Ottoman Egypt*; F. Adanır, "Semi-Autonomous Provincial Forces in the Balkans and Anatolia," in Faroqhi, *Cambridge History of Turkey*, 3: 178–79; Hickok, *Ottoman Military Administration*, 129, 134, 151, 156.

9 Modernization and revolution

1 The term "modernization" seems a more neutral alternative to "reform," which assumes that things are wrong and need to be fixed, or "Westernization," the conscious imitation of European culture. By it I mean not some autonomous or utopian process but the accumulation of changes in economy and society associated with the Industrial Revolution, especially the aspects that have proven to be more or less universal. The distinction between technical and political modernization is also made in B. Lewis, *What Went Wrong? Western impact and Middle Eastern response*, Oxford: Oxford University Press, 2002, 135, despite his "impact and response" view of modernization.

2 J. L. Gelvin, *The Modern Middle East: a history*, New York, Oxford: Oxford University Press, 2005; D. Quataert, *The Ottoman Empire, 1700–1922*, Cambridge: Cambridge University Press, 2000.

3 H. İnalcık, "The Nature of Traditional Society: Turkey," in R. E. Ward and D. A. Rostow (eds) *Political Modernization in Japan and Turkey*, Princeton, NJ: Princeton University Press, 1964, 49. The Iraqi historian 'Alī al-'Umarī of Mosul echoed this idea in describing the Ottoman sultan's indispensability; trans. P. Kemp, "Mosuli Sketches of Ottoman History," *MES* 17, 1981: 317.

4 Mehmed Emin, "Ahvâl-ı Bosna," trans. A. S. Aličič, "*Ahvali Bosna* od Muhameda Emina Iseviča (poc. XIXe v.): Uvod, Prevod s Turskog i Napomene," *POF* 32–3, 1982–3: 197; this analysis was also made in the Arab provinces after 1860. R. Zens, "Pasvanoğlu Osman Paşa and the Paşalık of Belgrade, 1791–1807," *IJTS* 8, 2002: 93.

5 "Sened-i İttifak," in Ahmed Cevdet, *Tarih-i Cevdet*, Istanbul: Matbaa-ı Osmaniye, 1309/1891–2, 9: 281; S. J. Shaw and E. K. Shaw, *The History of the Ottoman Empire and Modern Turkey*, Cambridge: Cambridge University Press, 1976, 2: 2; K. H. Karpat, "The Land Regime, Social Structure, and Modernization in the Ottoman Empire," in W. R. Polk and R. L. Chambers (eds) *Beginnings of Modernization in the Middle East: the nineteenth century*, Chicago, IL: University of Chicago Press, 1968, 79. This document had a centralizing effect, as K. Barkey argues: *Empire of Difference: the Ottomans in comparative perspective*, Cambridge: Cambridge University Press, 2008, 218–24. See 'Alī al-'Umarī's treatise as described by D. R. Khoury, *State and Provincial Society in the Ottoman Empire: Mosul, 1540–1834*, Cambridge: Cambridge University Press, 1997, 173–8.

6 F. J. Anscombe, "Islam and the Age of Ottoman Reform," *Past & Present* no. 208, August 2010: 159–89.

7 Censuses are now discussed as aspects of what Foucault called "governmentality," but they were old techniques of Ottoman and Middle Eastern imperial control and the provision of justice whose meanings were still current (especially for those subject to them), though they acquired new modern meanings; M. Foucault, "Governmentality," in G. Burchell, C. Gordon and P. Miller (eds) *The Foucault Effect: studies in governmentality*, London: Harvester/Wheatsheaf, 1991, 87–104; L. Hudson, "Late Ottoman Damascus: investments in public space and the emergence of popular sovereignty," *Critique* 15, 2006: 151–69.

8 M. Çadırcı, "Tanzimat," in Çiçek, *Great Ottoman-Turkish Civilisation*, 3: 582; M. A. Yalçınkaya, "The Provincial Reforms of the Early Tanzimat Period as Implemented in the Kaza of Avrethisarı," *OTAM* 6, 1995: 359.

9 B. Lewis, *The Emergence of Modern Turkey*, Oxford: Oxford University Press, 1961, 94–7; R. H. Davison, *Reform in the Ottoman Empire, 1856–1876*, Princeton, NJ: Princeton University Press, 1963, 41. Rudolph Peters ignored the *maẓālim* role of the councils and criticized them for being administrative bodies rather than independent judiciaries; R. Peters, "Islamic and Secular Criminal Law in Nineteenth Century Egypt: the role and function of the qadi," *ILS* 4, 1997: 75. Still, he identified the principle behind them: "Petitions to the Khedive or higher judicial bodies were an important corrective against failures at a lower level. They were taken seriously and resulted in special investigations after which subjects often would get the rights that had been denied to them"; R. Peters, "Administrators and Magistrates: the development of a secular judiciary in Egypt, 1853–1871," *WI* 39, 1999: 395.

10 L. S. Diba, "Images of Power and the Power of Images: intention and response in early Qajar painting (1785–1834)," in L. S. Diba and M. Ekhtiar (eds) *Royal Persian Paintings: the Qajar epoch, 1785–1925*, New York: IB Tauris and Brooklyn Museum of Art, 1998, 36; A. K. S. Lambton, "The Persian 'Ulamā and Constitutional Reform," in *Le shî'isme imâmite: colloque de Strasbourg*, Paris: Presses Universitaires de France, 1970, 246.

11 Sir J. Malcolm, *The History of Persia, from the most early period to the present time*, London: John Murray and Longman, 1815, 2: 312, 434–5, quotation on 304; G. R. G. Hambly, "Aqa Mohammad Khan and the Establishment of the Qajar Dynasty," *Journal of the Royal Central Asian Society* 50, 1963: 163.

12 Diploma of Fatḥ 'Alī Shāh, 1800, trans. A. K. S. Lambton, "Quis Custodiet Custodes: some reflections on the Persian theory of government (conclusion)," *SI* 6, 1956: 143; titles: E. Abrahamian, "Oriental Despotism: the case of Qajar Iran," *IJMES* 5, 1974: 9; quotation: Ḥasan-e Fasā'ī, *History of Persia under Qājār Rule: translated from the Persian of Ḥasan-e Fasā'i's* Fārsnāma-ye Nāṣerī, trans. H. Busse, New York: Columbia University Press, 1972, 81.

13 J. Lerner, "Sasanian and Achaemenid Revivals in Qajar Art," in V. S. Curtis, R. Hillenbrand, and J. M. Rogers (eds) *The Art and Archaeology of Ancient Persia: new light on the Parthian and Sasanian Empires*, London: IB Tauris with the British Institute of Persian Studies, 1998, 164; A. K. S. Lambton, *Qajar Persia: eleven studies*, London: IB Tauris, 1987, 92; Diba, "Images," 33–4; quotation: A. D. Tushingham, "The *Takht-i marmar* (Marble Throne) in Teheran," in C. J. Adams (ed.) *Iranian Culture and Civilization: essays in honour of the 2,500th anniversary of the founding of the Persian Empire*, Montreal: McGill University Institute of Islamic Studies, 1972, 126.

14 Abrahamian, "Oriental Despotism," 18–19, 25, 26; W. Floor, "Change and Development in the Judicial System of Qajar Iran (1800–1925)," in C. E. Bosworth and C. Hillenbrand (eds) *Qajar Iran: political, social and cultural change, 1800–1925*, Costa Mesa, CA: Mazda, 1983, 118.

15 Faṭh 'Ali Khān Sabā-yi Kāshānī, *Shāhānshāhnāma*, cited in Diba, "Images," 36; *Tuḥfat al-mulūk*, cited in A. R. Sheikholeslami, *The Structure of Central Authority in Qajar Iran, 1871–1896*, Atlanta, GA: Scholars Press, 1997, 4; M.-T. Danishpazhouh, "An Annotated Bibliography on Government and Statecraft," in S. A. Arjomand (ed.) *Authority and Political Culture in Shi'ism*, Albany: State University of New York Press, 1988, 224–5.

16 Quotations: 'Alī b. Abī Ṭālib, *Nahjul Balagha, peak of eloquence*, trans. S. A. Reza, Elmhurst: Tahrike Tarsile Quran, 1984, 540–1, quoted in A. Amanat, *Pivot of the Universe: Nasir al-Din Shah Qajar and the Iranian monarchy, 1831–1896*, Berkeley: University of California Press, 1990, 71–2. Thanks to the Jesuit-Krauss-McCormick Library in Chicago for helping me locate this edition.

17 Abd al-Raḥmān al-Jabartī, *'Abd al-Raḥmān al-Jabartī's History of Egypt: 'ajā'ib al-āthār fī'l-tarājim wa'l-akhbār*, ed. T. Philipp and M. Perlmann, trans. D. Crecelius, B. 'Abd al-Malik, C. Wendell, M. Fishbein, T. Philipp and M. Perlmann, Stuttgart: Franz Steiner, 1994, 1: 10, 13; 3: 1.

18 Al-Jabartī, *History*, 1: 41; K. M. Cuno, *The Pasha's Peasants: land, society, and economy in Lower Egypt, 1740–1858*, Cambridge: Cambridge University Press, 1992, 45. Sonbol saw the decline in Egypt in the late eighteenth-century as moral or symbolic, not economic or social, since courts operated normally; A. E. Sonbol, *The New Mamluks: Egyptian society and modern feudalism*, Syracuse: Syracuse University Press, 2000, 2, 15–19.

19 Al-Jabartī, *History*, 3: 505, 506, quotations: 5, 36; Peters, "Administrators," 395; A. L. S. Marsot, *Egypt in the Reign of Muhammad Ali*, Cambridge: Cambridge University Press, 1984, 47; G. Delanoue, *Moralistes et politiques musulmans dans l'Égypte du XIXe siècle, 1798–1882*, Cairo: Institut Français d'Archéologie Orientale, 1982, 1: 57–8.

20 A. L. S. Marsot, "Religion or Opposition? urban protest movements in Egypt," *IJMES* 16, 1984: 544; H. Dodwell, *The Founder of Modern Egypt: a study of Muhammad 'Ali*, Cambridge: Cambridge University Press, 1931, 1967, 21, 201; Marsot, *Egypt*, 102.

21 Aḥmad al-Nāṣirī al-Salāwī, *Kitāb al-istiqçâ: chronique de la dynastie alaouie de Maroc*, trans. E. Fumey, *Archives marocaines* 9, 1906: 386; cited in J. Dakhlia, *Le divan des rois: le politique et le religieux dans l'Islam*, Paris: Aubier, 1998, 104. The Moroccan sultan's delegates in city and countryside received complaints, solved problems, and mediated disputes; A. Claisse, "Makhzen Traditions and Administrative Channels," in I. W. Zartman (ed.) *The Political Economy of Morocco*, New York: Praeger, 1987, 42.

22 Letter from the ulema of Tlemcen, trans. C. R. Pennell, *Tyranny, Just Rule & Moroccan Political Thought*, University of Nairobi Department of History, Staff Seminar Paper no. 8, 1986/7, May 1987, 23.

23 Muḥammad b. 'Abd al-Qādir, *Tuḥfat al-zā'ir fī tārīkh al-Jazā'ir wa-al-Amīr 'Abd al-Qādir*, trans. R. Danziger, *Abd al-Qadir and the Algerians: resistance to the French and internal consolidation*, New York: Holmes & Meier, 1977, 72; R. R. Laremont, *Islam and the Politics of Resistance in Algeria, 1783–1992*, Trenton, NJ: Africa World Press, 2000, 36. See Danziger, *Abd al-Qadir*, 192; D. Commins, "'Abd al-Qādir al-Jazā'irī and Islamic Reform," *MW* 78, 1988: 127.

24 Ahmad b. Abi Diyaf, *Consult Them in the Matter: a nineteenth-century Islamic argument for constitutional government*, trans. L. C. Brown, Fayetteville: University of Arkansas Press, 2005, 36, 75, 107–15, 126–9, quotations on 38, 115.

25 M. Ben Smail and L. Valensi, "Le règne de Hammouda Pacha dans la chronique d'Ibn Abi-ḍ-Ḍiyaf," *Cahiers de Tunisie* 19, no. 73–4, 1971: 95–107; Dakhlia, *Divan*, 171, 174–7; R. Brunschvig, "Justice religieuse et justice laïque dans la Tunisie des Deys et des Beys jusqu'au milieu du XIXe siècle," *SI* 23, 1965: 17–70.

26 FO 195/100 Blunt to Ponsonby 30 January 183, trans. B Özdemir, *Ottoman Reforms and Social Life: reflections from Salonica, 1830–1850*, Istanbul: İsis, 2003, 179.

27 Gelvin calls this "defensive developmentalism"; *Modern Middle East*, 73–87. Standard modernization narratives: Lewis, *Emergence*; J. H. Thompson and R. D. Reischauer (eds) *Modernization of the Arab World*, Princeton, NJ: Van Nostrand, 1966; C. E. Black and L. C. Brown (eds) *Modernization in the Middle East: the Ottoman Empire and Its Afro-Asian successors*, Princeton, NJ: Darwin, 1992.

28 Sadık Rifat Paşa, *Müntahabat-ı âsar*, trans. Lewis, *Emergence*, 129. On local origins of modernization: J. Hanssen, T. Philipp, and S. Weber (eds) *The Empire in the City: Arab provincial capitals in the late Ottoman Empire*, Beirut: Ergon, 2002; N. Lafi (ed.) *Municipalités méditerranéennes: Les réformes urbaines ottomanes au miroir d'une histoire comparée (Moyen-Orient, Maghreb, Europe méridionale)*, Berlin: Klaus Schwarz, 2005.

29 Sadık Rifat Paşa, *Müntahabat-ı âsar*, quoted in 'Abdurrahman Şeref, *Tarih musahabeleri*, Istanbul: Matbaa-i Âmire, 1339/1920, 125; Ş. Mardin, *The Genesis of Young Ottoman Thought: a study in the modernization of Turkish political ideas*, Princeton, NJ: Princeton University Press, 1962; Syracuse: Syracuse University Press, 2000, 180; Ş. Mardin, "The Mind of the Turkish Reformer, 1700–1900," *Western Humanities Review* 14, 1960: 426.

30 'Ali Paşa's memorandum to a subordinate, trans. E. Z. Karal, "Ali Paşanın Trablusgarp Valisine bir Tahriratı," *Tarih Vesikaları* 1, 1941/2: 297; compare 'Ali's political testament, E. D. Akarlı, *Belgelerle Tanzimat: Osmanlı sadrıazamlarından Âli ve Fuad Paşaların siyasî vasiyyetnâmeleri*, Istanbul: Boğaziçi Üniversitesi Matbaası, 1978; trans. F. M. Andic and S. Andic, *The Last of the Ottoman Grandees: the life and political testament of Âli Paşa*, Istanbul: İsis Press, 1996.

31 Gülhâne Ḥaṭṭ-ı Şerif, quoted in Ahmed Lütfi, *Tarih-i Lütfî*, Istanbul: Matbaa-yi Âmire, 1873–1912, 6: 62, trans. M. Ma'oz in *Ottoman Reform in Syrian and Palestine, 1840–1861: the impact of the Tanzimat on politics and society*, Oxford: Clarendon, 1968, 69; cf. Shaw and Shaw, *History*, 2: 60; J. C. Hurewitz, "The Hatti Şerif of Gülhane, 3 November 1839," in J. C. Hurewitz, *Diplomacy in the Near and Middle East: a documentary record*, Princeton, NJ: D. Van Nostrand, 1956, 1: 114; or K. F. Khater, *Sources in the History of the Modern Middle East*, Boston, MA: Houghton Mifflin, 2004, 12–13. Türköne characterized the rescript as a justice decree (*adâletnâme*); M. Türköne, "The Tanzimat Charter and Mehmed Sadık Rıfat Pasha," in Çiçek, *Great Ottoman-Turkish Civilisation*, 3: 99.

32 Ḥaṭṭ-ı Şerif, quoted in Lütfî, *Tarih*, 6: 63; H. İnalcık, "Tanzimat'ın Uygulanması ve Sosyal Tepkileri," *Belleten* 28, 1964: 630, 660–71; B. Abu-Manneh, "The Islamic Roots of the Gülhane Rescript," *WI* 34, 1994: 174, 196

33 *Takvim-i Vekayı*, no. 198, trans. Abu-Manneh, "Islamic Roots," 196; S. Deringil, "The Invention of Tradition as Public Image in the Late Ottoman Empire, 1808 to 1908," *CSSH* 35, 1993: 10. Rather than erecting statues of its promulgator to commemorate the issuance of the Rescript, the Ottomans proposed to set up a stone bearing a full copy of the edict, as in the days of Hammurabi; K. Kreiser, "Public Monuments in Turkey and Egypt, 1840–1916," *Muqarnas* 14, 1997: 103.

34 Ḥaṭṭ-ı Şerif, quoted in Lütfî, *Tarih*, 6: 64; H. İnalcık, "Application of the Tanzimat and Its Social Effects," *AOtt* 5, 1973: 97–128, rpt. in *The Ottoman Empire: conquest, organization and economy*, London: Variorum, 1978, XVI, 3; R. Kaynar, *Mustafa Reşit Paşa ve Tanzimat*, Ankara: Türk Tarih Kurumu, 1954, 183.

35 M. İpşirli, "Osmanlılarda Cuma Selâmlığı (halk-hükümdar münâsebetleri açısından önemi)," in *Prof. Dr. Bekir Kütükoğlu'na armağan*, Istanbul: İstanbul Üniversitesi Edebiyat Fakültesi, 1991, 466–70.

36 İnalcık, "Application," 7, 10–11; E. R. Toledano, "The Legislative Process in the Ottoman Empire in the Early *Tanzimat* Period: a footnote," *IJTS* 1.2, 1980: 100; E. Thompson, "Ottoman Political Reform in the Provinces: the Damascus Advisory Council in 1844–45," *IJMES* 25, 1993: 460–1, 468–70; A. Naff, "A Social History of Zahle, the Principal Market Town in Nineteenth-Century Lebanon," PhD diss., UCLA, 1972, 428; Yalçınkaya, "Provincial," 364–71.

37 Lütfî, *Tarih*, 5: 109, Turkish trans. E. Z. Karal, *Osmanlı İmparatorluğunda İlk Nüfus Sayımı, 1831*, Ankara: T. C. Başvekâlet İstatistik Umum Müdürlüğü, 1943, 9; English trans. C. Issawi, *The Economic History of Turkey, 1800–1914*, Chicago, IL: University of Chicago Press, 1980, 21. Censuses: K. M. Cuno and M. J. Reimer, "The Census Registers of Nineteenth-Century Egypt: a new source for social historians," *BRIJMES* 24, 1997: 196–8; censuses from 1843–4, 1847–8, 1856, and 1870: Karal, *Nüfus*, 10; Ma'oz, *Ottoman Reform*, 82; C. Küçük, "Tanzimat'ın ilk yıllarında Erzurum'un cizye geliri ve reâya nüfusu," *TD* 31, 1977: 219–30; 1866–73 (Danube and Iraq): K. H. Karpat, "Ottoman Population Records and the Census of 1881/82–1893," *IJMES* 9, 1978: 245; 1874: Karpat, "Ottoman Population," 247; 1878 (Istanbul only): Karal, *Nüfus*, 10; 1881: Karpat, "Ottoman Population," 249–56; 1866, 1881, and 1895: F. M. Göçek and M. Ş. Hanioğlu, "Western Knowledge, Imperial Control, and the Use of Statistics in the Ottoman Empire," in J. L. Warner (ed.) *Cultural Horizons: a festschrift in honor of Talat S. Halman*, Syracuse: Syracuse University Press, 2001, 114–15; 1885 and 1907: A. Duben and C. Bahar, *Istanbul Households: marriage, family and fertility, 1880–1940*, Cambridge: Cambridge University Press, 1991, 15. See K. Hayashi and M. Aydın (eds) *The Ottoman State and Societies in Change: a study of the nineteenth-century temettuat registers*, London: Kegan Paul, 2004; F. Adanır, "The Ottoman Peasantries, c.1360–c.1860," in T. Scott (ed.) *The Peasantries of Europe: from the fourteenth to the eighteenth centuries*, London: Longman, 1998, 309&n245. Total population: Issawi, *Turkey*, 17.

38 Edict of Sultan Abdülmecid, trans. E. D. Akarlı, *The Long Peace: Ottoman Lebanon, 1861–1920*, Berkeley: University of California Press, 1993, 34; decrees of 1850 for Aleppo, trans. A. Vrolijk, "No Conscripts for the *Nizâm*: the 1850 events in Aleppo as reflected in documents from Syrian and Dutch archives," *JTS* 26, 2002: 318, 322.

39 S. J. Shaw, "The Nineteenth-Century Ottoman Reforms and Revenue System," *IJMES* 6, 1975: 421; Ç. Keyder, "Introduction: large-scale commercial agriculture in the Ottoman Empire'" in Ç. Keyder and F. Tabak (eds) *Landholding and Commercial Agriculture in the Middle East*, Albany: State University of New York Press, 1991, 10.

40 Ş. Mardin, "Center-Periphery Relations: a key to Turkish politics?" *Daedalus* 102.1, 1973: 180; Issawi, *Turkey*, 353; S. J. Shaw, "Some Aspects of the Aims and Achievements of the Nineteenth-Century Ottoman Reformers," in Polk and Chambers, *Beginnings of Modernization*, 33.

41 Lewis, *Emergence*, 110–21; Shaw and Shaw, *History*, 2: 76–82; İnalcık, "Application," 8, 17; R. Kasaba, "A Time and a Place for the Nonstate: social change in the Ottoman Empire during the 'long nineteenth century'," in J. S. Migdal, A. Kohli, and V. Shue (eds) *State Power and Social Forces: Domination and Transformation in the Third World*, Cambridge: Cambridge University Press, 1994, 215, 217.

42 Ubicini, cited in M. Palairet, "Farm Productivity under Ottoman Rule and Self-government in Bulgaria c. 1860–1890," in S. J. Kirschbaum (ed.) *East European History*, Columbus, OH: Slavica, 1988, 90, 100; D. Quataert, "The Commercialization of Agriculture in Ottoman Turkey, 1800–1914," *IJTS* 1.2, 1980: 41; C. Clay, "Labour Migration and Economic Conditions in Nineteenth Century Anatolia," *MES* 34, 1998: 1–32. A similar decline in Bulgaria is attributed to the social organization of production (Palairet, "Farm," 108–12); in Syria to climatic conditions; L. S. Schilcher, "The Great Depression (1873–1896) and the Rise of Syrian Arab Nationalism," *NPT* 5–6, 1991: 175–8.

43 Ahmed Cevdet Paşa, *Tezâkir-i Cevdet*, Ankara: Türk Tarih Kurumu, 1953, 1: 18–22, cited in Issawi, *Turkey*, 350; M. Ma'oz, "The Impact of Modernization on Syrian Politics and Society during the Early *Tanzimat* Period," in Polk and Chambers, *Beginnings of Modernization*, 346–7; A. Salzmann, "Citizens in Search of a State: the limits of political participation in the late Ottoman Empire," in M. Hanagan and C. Tilly (eds) *Extending Citizenship, Reconfiguring States*, Lanham: Rowman and Littlefield, 1999, 56–7.

44 *Gülhâne Ḥaṭṭ-ı Şerif*, quoted in Lütfî, *Tarih*, 6: 61; trans. Kaynar, *Mustafa*, 183; trans. Hurewitz, "Hatti Şerif," 114. M. Reinkowski, "The State's Security and the Subjects' Prosperity: notions of order in Ottoman bureaucratic correspondence (19th century)," in H. T. Karateke and M. Reinkowski (eds) *Legitimizing the Order: the Ottoman rhetoric of state power*, Leiden: Brill, 2005, 195–212.

45 *Ḥaṭṭ-ı hümâyûn*, trans. Hurewitz, "Sultan Abdümecid's Hatti hümayun," in ibid., *Diplomacy in the Near and Middle East: a documentary record, 1646–1914*, Princeton, NJ: D. Van Nostrand, 1956, 150.

46 D. Quataert, "The Age of Reforms, 1812–1914," in H. İnalcık with D. Quataert (eds) *An Economic and Social History of the Ottoman Empire*, Cambridge: Cambridge University Press, 1994, 889; Ş. Pamuk, "Prices in the Ottoman Empire, 1469–1914," *IJMES* 36, 2004: 455, 456, 459; İnalcık, "Application," 30–31; H. İnalcık, *Tanzimat ve Bulgar Meselesi*, Ankara: Türk Tarih Kurumu, 1943; Edmund Burke III, "Rural Collective Action and the Emergence of Modern Lebanon: a comparative historical perspective," in N. Shehadi and D. H. Mills (eds) *Lebanon: a history of conflict and consensus*, London: Centre for Lebanese Studies and IB Tauris, 1988, 23.

47 *Al-dawla al-miṣriyya al-'ādila*, see J. M. Rood, "Mehmed Ali as Mutinous Khedive: the roots of rebellion," *IJTS* 8, 2002: 125; Marsot, *Egypt*, 172; A. L. S. Marsot, "Muhammmad Ali's Internal Policies," in *L'Égypte au XIXe siècle*, Paris: CNRS, 1982, 158–9. The elimination of tax farming hurt small investors who sub-farmed smaller revenue sources under larger tax farmers; while rich men at the top of the system received compensation, sub-farmers got nothing and lost their source of income as well; Sonbol, *New Mamluks*, 44; cf. for a later period M. G. Majd, "Small Landowners and Land Distribution in Iran, 1962–71," *IJMES* 32, 2000: 123–53. Forced labor was abolished when year-round agriculture was instituted; N. Brown, "The Ignorance and Inscrutability of the Egyptian Peasantry," in F. Kazemi and J. Waterbury (eds) *Peasants and Politics in the Modern Middle East*, Miami: Florida International University Press, 1991, 216.

48 Cuno and Reimer, "Census," 195, 213. Douwes noticed no essential differences between the Ottomans' rule in Syria and Muḥammad 'Alī's except for the latter's more effective use of force; D. Douwes, *The Ottomans in Syria: a history of justice and oppression*, London: IB Tauris, 2000, 192–4, 204–5, 207, 216.

49 *Siyāsatnāme 'an bayān al-'amaliyya*, cited in R. A. Hamed, "The *Siyasatname* and the Institutionalization of Central Administration under Muhammad 'Ali," in N. Hanna (ed.) *The State and Its Servants: administration in Egypt from Ottoman times to the present*, Cairo: American University in Cairo Press, 1995, 83. To curb officials' abuse of authority, Muḥammad 'Alī issued a memorandum on agriculture and administration, *Lāyihat zirāat al-fallāh wa-tadbīr aḥkām al-siyāsa bi-qasd al-najāh*; Marsot, "Muhammmad Ali's Internal Policies," 163.

50 R. Peters, "'For His Correction and as a Deterrent Example for Others': Meḥmed 'Ali's first criminal legislation (1829–1830)," *ILS* 6, 1999: 170–2. Muḥammad 'Alī's justice was not exemplary but rationalized, connecting severity of crime and amount of punishment.

51 B. Cannon, *Politics of Law and the Courts in Nineteenth-Century Egypt*, Salt Lake City: University of Utah Press, 1988, 24; Peters, "Administrators and Magistrates," 392. Most of the Council's decrees were issued under 'Abbās (1848–1854); Sa'īd (1854–1863) added to them; Isma'īl (1863–1879) recodified them. The centralizing trend was partly reversed under Isma'īl, who appointed village courts to hear local petitions, but since nobody outside Cairo was familiar with the new laws, peasants had difficulty obtaining justice from village judges, Cannon, *Politics of Law*, 29, 83, 353.

52 Peters, "Islamic and Secular," 75; Peters compared the councils unfavorably to the shariah courts, but that is the wrong comparison. K. Fahmy, "The Police and the People in Nineteenth-Century Egypt," *WI* 39, 1999: 344, 350, 361; Cannon, *Politics of Law*, 34. A new school for judges was opened in Istanbul to standardize training in court practice; J. Akiba, "A New School for Qadis: education of the sharia judges in the Late Ottoman Empire," *Turcica* 35, 2003: 125–63.

53 Fahmy, "Police," 376; M. Ener, *Managing Egypt's Poor and the Politics of Benevolence, 1800–1952*, Princeton, NJ: Princeton University Press, 2003, 49–75; J. T. Chalcraft, *The Striking Cabbies of Cairo and Other Stories: crafts and guilds in Egypt, 1863–1914*, Albany: State University of New York Press, 2004, 74; higher taxation produced a greater demand for official rectitude (ibid., 77).

54 R. R. al-Ṭahṭāwī, *An Imam in Paris: account of a stay in France by an Egyptian cleric (1826–1831)*, trans. D. L. Newman, London: Saqi Books, 2004, 194–213; quotation on 194; see R. R. al-Ṭahṭāwī , *al-A'māl al-kāmilah li-Rifā'ah Rāfi' al-Ṭahṭāwī*, ed. M. 'Imārah, Beirut: al-Mu'assasa al-'Arabiyya li'l-Dirāsāt wa-al-Nashr, 1973, vol. 2. On al-Ṭahṭāwī and contemporary thinkers, A. Hourani, *Arabic Thought in the Liberal Age, 1798–1939*, London: Oxford University Press, 1970.

55 Al-Ṭahṭāwī, *Imam*, 206; see Rifā'a Rāfi' al-Ṭahṭāwī, *Takhlīs al-ibrīz ilà talkhīs Bārīz*, quoted in R. Khūrī, *Modern Arab Thought: channels of the French Revolution to the Arab East*, trans. I. 'Abbas, rev. and ed. C. Issawi, Princeton, NJ: Kingston Press, 1983, 103. The same point appears in al-Ṭahṭāwī 's later advice work, *Manāhij al-albāb al-miṣriyya f ī mabāhij al-ādāb al-'aṣriyya* [The Paths of Egyptian

Minds through the Joys of Modern Manners], quoted in Delanoue, *Moralistes*, 2: 433; J. R. Cole, "Rifā'a al-Ṭahṭāwī and the Revival of Practical Philosophy," *MW* 70, 1980: 30–2.

56 Al-Ṭahṭāwī, *al-A'māl al-kāmilah*, 1: 519; Cole, "Rifā'a al-Ṭahṭāwī," 29, 32, 43.

57 *Qānūn al-muntakhabāt*, trans. J. Chalcraft, "Engaging the State: peasants and petitions in Egypt on the eve of colonial rule," *IJMES* 37, 2005: 306. Delanoue, *Moralistes*, 2: 468, 477; J. S. Ismael and T. Y. Ismael, "Cultural Perspectives on Social Welfare in the Emergence of Modern Arab Social Thought," *MW* 85, 1995: 90; Marsot, *Egypt*, 122, 135, 162. At the end of his reign, Muḥammad 'Alī reduced the personal tax for the poor, which previously had been the same as for the rich; 'Ali al-Giritli, *Tārīkh al-sinā'a fī Miṣr*, trans. C. Issawi, *The Economic History of the Middle East, 1800–1914: a book of readings*, Chicago, IL: University of Chicago Press, 1966; Midway Reprint, 1975, 396.

58 W. R. Polk, *The Opening of South Lebanon, 1788–1840: a study of the impact of the West on the Middle East*, Cambridge, MA: Harvard University Press, 1963, 45, 111.

59 K. S. Salibi, *The Modern History of Lebanon*, New York: Praeger, 1965, 23. Inscription trans. W. O. Douglas, *Strange Lands and Friendly People*, New York: Harper & Brothers, 1951, 211. The comparison with Topkapı comes from personal observation. Bashīr II's installation document ordered him "to preserve order, to protect the common people, to extirpate those who exceed their limits, to pay taxes, to avoid oppression"; trans. Ussama Makdisi, "Ottoman Orientalism," *AHR* 107, 2002: 776.

60 C. H. Churchill, *The Druzes and the Maronites under Turkish Rule, from 1840–60*, London: B. Quaritch, 1862; repr. New York: Arno Press, 1973, 122–3; quoted in Salibi, *Modern History of Lebanon*, 81; Antun Dahir al-Aqîqi, "The Aqîqi Manuscript," trans. M. H. Kerr, *Lebanon in the Last Years of Feudalism, 1840–1868: a contemporary account by Antun Dahir al-Aqiqi, and other documents*, Beirut: American University of Beirut, 1959, 38; Naff, "Social," 563; M. L. Gross, "Ottoman Rule in the Province of Damascus, 1860–1909," PhD diss., Georgetown University, 1979, 110.

61 Al-Aqîqi, "Manuscript," 53; cf. U. Makdisi, "Corrupting the Sublime Sultanate: the revolt of Tanyus Shahin in nineteenth-century Ottoman Lebanon," *CSSH* 42, 2000: 193, 196. List of demands addressed to the patriarch: trans. Kerr, *Lebanon*, 97–8; A. Havemann, "The Impact of Peasant Resistance on Nineteenth-Century Mount Lebanon," in Kazemi and Waterbury, *Peasants*, 91. Peasants' appeal against an oppressive landlord for violating the governor's justice: B. Doumani, *Rediscovering Palestine: merchants and peasants in Jabal Nablus, 1700–1900*, Berkeley: University of California Press, 1995, 172, 175–6.

62 L. T. Darling, *Revenue-Raising and Legitimacy: Tax Collection and Finance Administration in the Ottoman Empire, 1560–1660*, Leiden: Brill, 1996, 131, 228; Douwes, *Ottomans*, 188–210. On these techniques as new and modern processes instituted by the Egyptian occupation, J. Hanssen, "Practices of Integration: center-periphery relations in the Ottoman Empire," in Hanssen *et al.*, *Empire in the City*, 51.

63 Hanssen, "Practices of Integration," 56–63; see Nablus in Doumani, *Rediscovering*, 241.

64 Probably the best known such figure was Bū Ziyān (1849); P. von Sivers, "The Realm of Justice: apocalyptic revolts in Algeria (1849–1879)," *Humaniora Islamica* 1, 1973: 52; J. Clancy-Smith, "La révolte de Bû Ziyân en Algérie, 1849," *RMMM* nos. 91–4, 2000: 185.

65 Ibn Abi Diyaf, *Consult Them*, 48, 53, 128-9; Ibn Abi Diyaf, *Itḥāf al-zamān bi-akhbār mulūk Tūnis wa-'ahd al-amān*, cited in Dakhlia, *Divan*, 301. On the unpublished Hanafi commentary, Ibn Abi Diyaf, *Consult Them*, 129, 147n2.

66 L. C. Brown, *The Tunisia of Ahmad Bey, 1847–1855*, Princeton, NJ: Princeton University Press, 1974, 95, 314. Quotations from Muḥammad al-Kardūdī al-Fāsī, *Kashf al-ghumma*, MS D1281, Bibliothèque Générale, Rabat, trans. A. K. Bennison, "The 'New Order' and Islamic Order: the introduction of the *Niẓāmī* army in the western Maghrib and its legitimation, 1830–73," *IJMES* 36, 2004: 604.

67 Letter from the Miad to the Bey, 1854, trans. E. Hermassi, *Leadership and National Development in North Africa: a comparative study*, Berkeley: University of California Press, 1972, 53; Brown, *Tunisia*, 197.

68 B. Slama, *L'insurrection de 1864 en Tunisie*, Tunis: Maison Tunisienne de l'Édition, 1967, 6; L. Valensi, *Tunisian Peasants in the Eighteenth and Nineteenth Centuries*, Cambridge: Cambridge University Press, and Paris: Éditions de la Maison des Sciences de l'Homme, 1985, 238–9. On the constitution and revolt, Ibn Abi Diyaf, *Consult Them*, 7–11, 19, 27. The ulema of the Zaytūna *madrasa* also helped develop reform ideas for Tunisia; A. S. Tamimi, *Rachid Ghannouchi: a democrat within Islamism*, Oxford: Oxford University Press, 2001, 39.

69 S. Marsans-Sakly, "The Networks of Tunisia's 1864 Revolt," paper presented at the American Historical Association Convention, Chicago, 4 January 2003, 6; see also S. Marsans-Sakly, "The Revolt of 1864 in Tunisia: History, Power, and Memory," PhD diss., New York University, 2010; Slama, *Insurrection*, 37–8 & n3, 92; A. H. Green, A. S. Gamal, and R. Mortel, "A Tunisian Reply to a Wahhabi Proclamation: texts and contexts," in *In Quest of an Islamic Humanism: Arabic and Islamic studies in memory of Mohamed al-Nowaihi*, ed. A. H. Green, Cairo: American University in Cairo Press, 1984, 160–1; Edmund Burke III, "Understanding Arab Protest Movements," *Maghreb Review* 11.1, 1986: 34.

70 Slama, *Insurrection*, 174; Von Sivers, "Realm of Justice," 45.

71 H. Farman Farmayan, "The Forces of Modernization in Nineteenth Century Iran: a historical survey," in Polk and Chambers, *Beginnings of Modernization*, 120–4; Malcolm, *History*, 2: 402, 404, 473; Fraser, quoted in Lambton, *Landlord*, 136–7; V. Martin, *The Qajar Pact: bargaining, protest and the state in nineteenth-century Persia*, London: IB Tauris, 2005. On the popular view of the ruler's responsibility for prosperity, Ḥasan-e Fasāʾī, *History*, 279–80.

72 Malcolm, *History*, 2: 444, quotation on 429–30; *CHIr*, 7: 151; R. Loeffler, "Tribal Order and the State: the political organization of Boir Ahmad," *IranS* 11, 1978: 148. M. Dorraj, *From Zarathustra to Khomeini: populism and dissent in Iran*, Boulder, CO: Lynne Reinner, 1990, 88–9; Martin, *Qajar Pact*, 9.

73 N. R. Keddie, with a section by Y. Richard, *Roots of Revolution: an interpretive history of modern Iran*, New Haven, CT: Yale University Press, 1981, 48; K. Greussing, "The Babi Movement in Iran, 1844–52: from merchant protest to peasant revolution," in J. M. Bak and G. Benecke (eds) *Religion and Rural Revolt*, Manchester, UK and Dover, NH: Manchester University Press, 1982, 261, 264–5.

74 J. R. I. Cole, "Iranian Millenarianism and Democratic Thought in the 19th Century," *IJMES* 24, 1992: 7, 15, 16; Babayan, *Mystics, Monarchs*, 488.

75 Edmund Burke III, "Changing Patterns of Peasant Protest in the Middle East, 1750–1950," in Kazemi and Waterbury, *Peasants*, 30.

76 Amanat, *Pivot*, 10; Diba, "Images," 36. Nāṣir al-Dīn's reign has been depicted as an alternation between modernization and conservatism, or secularism and religion, or provincialism and centralization; here it will be considered in terms of the ideology of justice and its delivery.

77 Quotation: Ḥasan-e Fasāʾī, *History*, 375; A. R. Sheikholeslami, "The Patrimonial Structure of Iranian Bureaucracy in the Late Nineteenth Century," *IranS* 11, 1978: 221; A. R. Sheikholeslami, *Structure*, 67, 83. A later grand vizier decreed that "kingship has no children. Rather, soldiers are the Shah's children, and subjects are his relatives," trans. Sheikholeslami, *Structure*, 47.

78 Lambton, *Qajar Persia*, 209; A. Ghani, "Disputes in a Court of *Sharia*, Kunar Valley, Afghanistan, 1885–1890," *IJMES* 15, 1983: 353. For the contrast between British and Iranian ideologies, see the case of grain sales during a famine: Martin, *Qajar Pact*, 46, n. 62.

79 Lambton, *Qajar Persia*, 292; S. A. Arjomand, *The Turban for the Crown: the Islamic Revolution in Iran*, New York, Oxford: Oxford University Press, 1988, 31–2; F. Kashani-Sabet, *Frontier Fictions: shaping the Iranian nation, 1804–1946*, Princeton, NJ: Princeton University Press, 1999, 86; E. Yarshater, "Observations on Nâsir al-Dîn Shah," in Bosworth and Hillenbrand, *Qajar Iran*, 6–7.

80 Muʿayyir al-Mamālik, *Yāddashthā'yī az zindigānī-i khuṣūṣī-i Nāṣir al-Dīn*, trans. Lambton, *Qajar Persia*, 95. On Nāṣir al-Dīn's notes, Yarshater, "Observations on Nâsir al-Dîn Shah," 6–7, 10–11.

81 Calendar quoted in Ḥasan-e Fasāʾī, *History*, 362. Floor, "Change and Development," 121; a microfilm of about 800 petition summaries is at Tehran University.

82 Ḥasan-e Fasāʾī, *History*, 381; Amanat, *Pivot*, 393–4. Some scholars decry these measures as "traditional" and "conservative;" others find them admirable, vehicles of reform. Either way, they are evidence of how the idea of the Circle of Justice pervaded Iranian political behavior.

83 F. Adamiyyat and H. Natiq, *Afkar-i ijtimaʿi va siyasi va iqtisadi dar athar-i muntashir nashuda-yi dawra-yi Qajar*, cited in Floor, "Change and Development," 122; M. E. Nezam-Mafi, "The Council for the Investigation of Grievances: a case study of nineteenth century Iranian social history," *IranS* 22, 1989: 59–60; I. Schneider, *The Petitioning System in Iran: state, society and power relations in the late 19th century*, Wiesbaden: Harrassowitz, 2006, esp. 85, 99–102. By the 1890s provincial councils of justice also began to appear; Martin, *Qajar Pact*, 64.

84 Mustashar al-Dawla, Yūsuf b. Kāẓim, *The Essence of Modernity: Mirza Yusof Khan Mustashar ad-Dowla Tabrizi's treatise on codified law (Yak kalima)*, trans. A. A. Seyed-Gohrab and S. McGlinn, Amsterdam and West Lafayette, Indiana: Rozenberg and Purdue University Press, 2007, 3–4, 9–14, 19–20. F. Zarinebaf (personal communication) identified the constitution discussed in this

book as the French Constitution of 1831. B. Alavi, "Critical Writings on the Renewal of Islam," in Bosworth and Hillenbrand, *Qajar Iran*, 249; Farman Farmayan, "Forces," 139.

85 Malcolm, *History*, 2: 439; V. Martin, *Islam and Modernism: the Iranian Revolution of 1906*, Syracuse, NY: Syracuse University Press, 1989, 9–10; Lambton, *Qajar Persia*, 292; Floor, "Change and Development," 113; Sheikholeslami, *Structure*, 56; H. Algar, *Religion and State in Iran, 1785–1906: the role of the ulama in the Qajar period*, Berkeley: University of California Press, 1969, 165.

86 Ḥasan-e Fasāʾī, *History*, 349, 352–4, 357, 375, 386–7, 396, 398, 403–12; see also Busse's introduction, xvii–xviii.

87 Malkum Khan, *Majmu'ah-yi asar*, ed. M.-M. Tabataba'i, Tehran: Kitābkhānah Danish 1327/1948–9, 94, trans. S. Bakhash, *Iran: monarchy, bureaucracy and reform under the Qajars: 1858–1896*, Oxford: St. Antony's College, 1978, 11; see Amanat, *Pivot*, 275, 358–64; H. Algar, *Mīrzā Malkum Khān: a study in the history of Iranian modernism*, Berkeley: University of California Press, 1973, 30. On Mirza Husayn, Floor, "Change and Development," 122; Bakhash, *Iran*, 82–3.

88 FO 60/267, Enclosure, quoted in Amanat, *Pivot*, 387.

89 C. Masroori, "Mirza Yaʿqub Khan's Call for Representative Government, Toleration and Islamic Reform in Nineteenth-Century Iran," *MES* 37, 2001: 93. M. Bayat-Philipp, "Mirza Aqa Khan Kirmani: a nineteenth century Persian nationalist," in E. Kedourie and S. G. Haim (eds) *Towards a Modern Iran: studies in thought, politics and society*, London: Frank Cass, 1980, 80. See the treatise quoted in Kashani-Sabet, *Frontier Fictions*, 95–6. The interest in pre-Islamic Iran began early; a student sent abroad to study became in 1845 the first to recommend abandoning Islam and basing the kingdom on pre-Islamic precedents; Farman Farmayan, "Forces," 125–6.

90 N. R. Keddie, *Historical Obstacles to Agrarian Change in Iran*, Claremont, 1950, and "Report on Bushire," A and P 1880, 73, quoted in C. Issawi, *The Economic History of Iran, 1800–1914*, Chicago, IL: University of Chicago Press, 1971, 55, 230. On land sales, *CHIr*, 7: 468, 495–6.

91 Lambton, *Qajar Persia*, 295.

92 E. B. Eastwick, *Journal of a Diplomat's Three Years' Residence in Persia*, London: Smith, Elder & Co., 1864, 1: 288–90; Amanat, *Pivot*, 379–82; Kashani-Sabet, *Frontier Fictions*, 81–2. The term "welfare" (*refāh*) entered the discourse in the 1890s in a newspaper description of a reforming governor; Martin, *Qajar Pact*, 64.

93 Mīrzā Rezā Kirmanī, trans. E. G. Browne, *The Persian Revolution of 1905–1909*, London: Frank Cass/Cambridge University Press, 1910; repr. New York: Barnes and Noble, 1966, 66–72; *CHIr*, 7: 197; J. Foran, *Fragile Resistance: social transformation in Iran from 1500 to the Revolution,* Boulder, CO: Westview, 1993, 142; Martin, *Islam and Modernism*, 30.

94 Cartoons: *Tamaddun*, repr. in Kashani-Sabet, *Frontier Fictions*, 120; quotation: *Tamaddun*, trans. Kashani-Sabet, *Frontier Fictions*, 106, a statement usually attributed to Aristotle. Al-Ghazālī's *Naṣīḥat al-mulūk* also imaged justice as a tree.

95 BBA, İrade D31753 Leff. 3, n.d., trans. Makdisi, "Ottoman Orientalism," 781; "Francīs Fathallāh al-Marrāsh, 1836–1873," in Khūrī, *Modern Arab Thought*, 114–15.

96 Hanssen emphasized the development of sectarian arguments in "Practices of Integration," 57, 61, 62; see Chalcraft, *Striking Cabbies*, 201; Gross, "Ottoman," 30; Naff, "Social," 432. The rising mercantile and intellectual middle class acted as spokesmen for the common people; wealthy peasants and village notables performed the same role in Egypt; N. J. Brown, "Peasants and Notables in Egyptian Politics," *MES* 26, 1990: 147–51.

97 Quataert, "Commercialization," 43; Akarlı, *Long Peace*, 61; Gross, "Ottoman," 208–10, 237.

98 Ş. Mardin, "The Just and the Unjust," *Daedalus* 120.3, Summer 1991: 121. The 1876 Constitution guaranteed the right of petition; the parliament had a special petitions committee to handle complaints; Article 14, in "The First Ottoman Constitutional Regime, the Constitution of December 1876, selected articles," in R. G. Landen (ed.) *The Emergence of the Modern Middle East: selected readings*, New York: Van Nostrand Reinhold, 1970, 100.

99 Ottoman printing: J. Strauss, "'*Kütüp ve resail-i mevkute*': printing and publishing in a multi-ethnic society," in E. Özdalga (ed.) *Late Ottoman Society: the intellectual legacy*, London: RoutledgeCurzon, 2005, 225–53. This literature became available to the public in the new reading rooms and libraries.

100 H. Z. Ülken, "Tanzimattan sonra fikir hareketleri," in H.-A. Yücel (ed.) *Tanzimat I: yüzüncü yıldönümü münasebetile*, Istanbul: Maarif, 1940, 774; *EI2*, s.v. "Kınalızade," 101; Mardin, *Genesis*, 197–8&n6; Delanoue, *Moralistes*, 2: 412; B. Lewis, "Ibn Khaldun in Turkey," in *Islam in History: ideas, people, and events in the Middle East*, new ed., revised and expanded, Chicago and La Salle,

Open Court, 1993, 235; M. A. Mehmet, "La crise ottomane dans la vision de Hasan Kiafi Akhisri (1544–1616)," *Revue des études sud-est européenes* 13, 1975: 388n27; N. Berkes, *The Development of Secularism in Turkey*, Montreal: McGill University Press, 1964; New York: Routledge, 1998, 160–9; R. Abou-El-Haj, "Theorizing in Historical Writing beyond the Nation-State: Ottoman society in the middle period," in I. Baldauf and S. Faroqhi (eds) *Armağan: festschrift für Andreas Tietze*, Prague: enigma corporation, 1994, 8. Ibn Khaldūn's work strongly influenced the nineteenth century's greatest historian, Cevdet; B. Atalay, "Ottoman State and Ahmet Cevdet Pasha's History," in Çiçek, *Great Ottoman-Turkish Civilisation*, 3: 393.

101 Mehmed Said Efendi, *Ahlâk-ı Hamida*, Istanbul: Elcevaip Matbaası, 1882, trans. J. A. Decourdemanche as *La morale musulmane, ou, l'Akhlaqi-Hamidé*, Paris: E. Leroux, 1888; see A. S. Levend, "Siyaset-nameler," *TDAYB* 1962: 184, 188; A. S. Levend, "Ümmet çağında ahlâk kitaplarımız," *TDAYB* 1963: 99. Mehmed Nüsret Paşa, "Muqaddima," in Mehmed Nüsret Paşa (trans.) *Nüsret el-Ḥamîd 'ala siyâset el-'abîd tercüme-i Sulûk el-mâlik fî tedbir el-memâlik*, by Shihāb al-Dīn Aḥmad b. Muḥammad b. Abī al-Rabī' (d.885), Istanbul: Matba'a-i 'Amire, 1296/1878, 5–6; the wording of this Circle is identical to that of Kınalızâde, probably its source; see Berkes, *Development*, 238. Ahmed Lütfi Bey, *Mir'at-ı adâlet*, trans. E. Beylem as *Osmanlı adalet düzeni*, Istanbul: Fatih, 1979. Ş. Mardin, "The Nakşibendi Order in Turkish History," in R. Tapper (ed.) *Islam in Modern Turkey: religion, politics and literature in a secular state*, London: IB Tauris, 1991, 139; Mardin, *Genesis*, 199.

102 Namık Kemal, "Wa-shāwirhum f ī 'l-'amr," *Hürriyet*, 20 July 1868: 1; Mardin, *Genesis*, 82, 99, 306.

103 Quotations from Şinasi, trans. Lewis, *Emergence*, 134; and M. Colombe, "Une letter d'un prince égyptien du XIXe siècle au sultan ottoman Abd al-Aziz," *Orient* 2, 1958: 32; trans. Ş. Mardin, "The Mind of the Turkish Reformer, 1700–1900," *Western Humanities Review* 14, 1960: 429. Mardin, *Genesis*, 133, 165, 366, 376; V. Fontanier, *Voyage en Orient*, Paris, 1829, 1: 322, cited in Mardin, *Genesis*, 165n108; B. Lewis, "Some English Travellers in the East," *MES* 4, 1968: 303, 306; Namık Kemal, "Usul-u meşveret hakkında mektuplar," *Hürriyet*, 14 September 1868: 6; Lewis, *Emergence*, 167; Ş. Mardin, "Freedom in an Ottoman Perspective," in M. Heper and A. Evin (eds) *State, Democracy and the Military: Turkey in the 1980s*, Berlin: Walter de Gruyter, 1988, 25. Ibn Abi Diyaf, "Dhayl," citing Abū 'Abd Allāh Ḥusayn Khojā's *Bashā'ir ahl al-imān bi-futuhat al-'Uthmān* on the laws of the Ottoman state, said that *kānūn* made the ulema and janissaries a check on the sultan; *Consult Them*, 80.

104 Kamil Pasha's 1881 speech, trans. H. K. Bayur, *Sadrazam Kâmil Paşa: siyasî hayatı*, Ankara: Sanat, 1954, 78.

105 Shiblī Shumayyil, "Shakwa wa amāl marfū'ah ilā jalālat al-Sulṭān al-Mu'aẓẓam 'Abd al-Ḥamīd Khān," trans. C. E. Farah, "Reformed Ottomanism and Social Change," in *La vie sociale dans les province arabes à l'époque ottomane*, ed. A. Temimi, Zaghouan: CEROMDI, 1988, 3: 141. Shiblī Shumayyil, "True Socialism," trans. S. A. Hanna, in S. A. Hanna and G. H. Gardner, *Arab Socialism: a documentary survey*, Salt Lake City: University of Utah Press, 1969, 292–6.

106 Ḥusayn al-Marṣafī, *Risālat al-kalim al-thamān*, Cairo: al-Maṭba'a al-Sharafiyya, 1881, 35, trans. Delanoue, *Moralistes*, 2: 374. Sadullah Paşa, a Turkish visitor to the 1878 Paris exposition, created a Circle featuring technological development as the product of freedom: "Without freedom, there can be no security, without security, no endeavour; without endeavour, no prosperity; without prosperity, no happiness"; Sa'dullah Paşa, *1878 Paris Ekspozisyonu*, quoted in Ebüzziya Tevfik, *Numune-i edebiyat-ı osmaniye*, 3rd ed., Istanbul, Matbaa-i Ebüzziya, 1306/1885, 288, trans. B. Lewis, *The Middle East and the West*, London/Bloomington: Indiana University Press, 1964, 47, and cited in *EI*, s.v. "Hurriyya," 3: 592b.

107 Al-Afghānī, "Islamic Socialism," trans. Sami A. Hanna, "Al-Afghāni: a pioneer of Islamic socialism," *MW* 57, 1967: 30–1; repr. in Hanna and Gardner, *Arab Socialism*, 273–4. Quotation: Al-Afghānī, "Al-Ḥukūma al-istibdādiyya," trans. L. M. Kenny, "Al-Afghani on Types of Despotic Government," *JAOS* 86, 1966: 25. On Abū Dharr, A. J. Cameron, *Abû Dharr al-Ghifârî: an examination of his image in the hagiography of Islam*, London: Royal Asiatic Society, 1973.

108 Mahmud Nedim, *Ayine-yi devlet*, Istanbul: Karabet, 1909, 43, 45; see B. Abu-Manneh, "The Sultan and the Bureaucracy: the anti-Tanzimat concepts of Grand Vizier Mahmud Nedim Paşa," *IJMES* 22, 1990: 257. Abduh: M. H. Kerr, *Islamic Reform: the political and legal theories of Muḥammad 'Abduh and Rashīd Rıḍā*, Berkeley: University of California Press, 1966, 137. Muṣṭafā Kāmil's speech in Alexandria, 1900, cited in N. Safran, *Egypt in Search of Political Community: an analysis of the intellectual and political evolution of Egypt, 1804–1952*, Cambridge, MA: Harvard

University Press, 1961, 87. Circle of injustice: L. Wedeen, *Ambiguities of Domination: politics, rhetoric, and symbols in contemporary Syria*, Chicago, IL: University of Chicago Press, 1999, 135, fig. 14.

109 L. C. Brown, "The Tunisian Path to Modernization," in M. Milson (ed.) *Society and Political Structure in the Arab World*, New York: Humanities Press, 1973, 205. Brown calls the complaint box "a fitting symbol for a Weberian model of rational bureaucracy," but we can see in it a modern version of *maẓālim* – recall the Mongol box on a string and Nāṣir al-Dīn's "Chest of Justice." Khayr al-Dīn al-Tūnisī, *The Surest Path: the political treatise of a nineteenth-century Muslim statesman*, trans. L. C. Brown, Cambridge: Center for Middle Eastern Studies of Harvard University, 1967, 71, 81; L. C. Brown, *Religion and State: the Muslim approach to politics*, New York: Columbia University Press, 2000, 94. The Moroccan al-Kattānī urged in 1908, "From oppression ruin and from justice prosperity"; Muḥammad b. Ja'far, *Salwat al-anfās wa muḥadathāt al-akyās bi-man uqbira min al-'ulamā' wa'l-sultanā' bi-Fās*, Fez: Aḥmad al-Azraq, 1899, 1: 205, trans. H. Munson, Jr., *Religion and Power in Morocco*, New Haven, CT: Yale University Press, 1993, 91.

110 English trans.: Khayr al-Dīn, *Surest Path*, 74, 81, 97; French: *Réformes nécessaires aux états musulmans*, Paris: Imprimerie Administrative de Paul Dupont, 1868; or *Essai sur les réformes nécessaires aux états musulmans*, ed. M. Morsy, Paris: Édisud, 1987. Arabic: Khayr al-Dīn, *Aqwām al-masālik fī ma'rifat aḥwāl al-mamālik*, Tunis: Bayt al- Ḥikma, 2000, 1: 120. See Dakhlia, *Divan*, 63–4.

111 B. Tlili, "Éléments pour une approche de la pensée socio-économique de Khérédine (1810–1889)," *ROMM* 10, 1971: 135, compares Khayr al-Dīn's ideas to saint-simonianism: L. Anderson, *The State and Social Transformation in Tunisia and Libya, 1830–1980,* Princeton, NJ: Princeton University Press, 1986, 42–54. According to Charles Tilly, the loose fiscal relationships common to empires were unable to meet the national state's need for a more intense government involvement in the building up of the country; C. Tilly, *Coercion, Capital, and European States,* AD *990–1990,* Cambridge: Basil Blackwell, 1990, 15–25.

112 Khayr al-Dīn, *Mémoires*, in M.-S. Mzali and J. Pignon, *Khereddine, homme d'état: Mémoires,* [Tunis]: Maison Tunisienne de l'Édition, 1971, 1:35, trans. Tlili, "Éléments," 147.

113 Clician Vassif Effendi, *Son Altesse, Midhat-Pacha, Grand Vizir*, cited in S. Shamir, "The Modernization of Syria: problems and solutions in the early period of Abdülhamid," in Polk and Chambers, *Beginnings of Modernization*, 359. A. H. Midhat, *The Life of Midhat Pasha*, London: John Murray, 1903; New York: Arno Press, 1973, 35–8, 49–51; Gross, "Ottoman," 284; S. Shamir, "Midhat Pasha and the Anti-Turkish Agitation in Syria," *MES* 10, 1974: 126–7; Shamir, "Modernization," 374.

114 *Muhākamat Midhat Bāshā*, trans. K. Hatātā, Cairo, n.d., 199–200, trans. I. 'Abbas, "The Trial of Midhat Pasha," in Khūrī, *Modern Arab Thought*, 199. Bulgaria: M. Todorova, "Midhat Paşa's Governorship of the Danube Province," in C. H. Farah (ed.) *Decision Making and Change in the Ottoman Empire*, Kirksville, MO: Thomas Jefferson University Press, 1993, 119.

115 A. Rubin, "Legal Borrowing and Its Impact on Ottoman Legal Culture in the Late Nineteenth Century," *Continuity and Change* 22, 2007: 280–5; *Mecelle-i ahkâm-ı adliyye*, 16 vols, Istanbul: Mecelle Mazbatası, 1869–76; W. E. Grigsby (trans.) *The Medjelle or Ottoman Civil Law*, London: Stevens, 1895. The expansion of education was, ironically, a prerequisite for the spread of nationalist ideologies; E. Ö. Evered, *Empire and Education under the Ottomans: politics, reform and resistance from the Tanzimat to the Young Turks*, London: IB Tauris, 2012.

116 Chalcraft, *Striking Cabbies*, 67, 75–6, 80, 82, 89; in the third quarter of the nineteenth century, petitions increased sixteenfold. Numerous petitions from cabdrivers and their families preceded the cab strike of 1907; J. Chalcraft, "The Cairo Cab Drivers and the Strike of 1907," in Hanssen, Philipp, and Weber, *Empire in the City*, 188–9.

117 The Ottoman Constitution: http://www.bilkent.edu.tr/~genckaya/documents1.html, accessed 3 May 2012. R. Devereux, *The First Ottoman Constitutional Period: a study of the Midhat Constitution and Parliament,* Baltimore: Johns Hopkins Press, 1963, 31–79, 248; Davison, *Reform*, 370–80; Berkes, *Development*, 226–48, 250.

118 R. A. Hinnebusch, *Authoritarian Power and State Formation in Ba'thist Syria: army, party, and peasant*, Boulder, CO: Westview, 1990, 32; C. Issawi (ed.) *The Fertile Crescent, 1800–1914*, New York: Oxford University Press, 1988, 24–5, 285–6, 289, 329, 365; Issawi, *Turkey*, 202–4, 226; Issawi, *Iran*, 208, 378; Issawi, *Middle East*, 73, 84, 167–8, 264, 366, 387; K. H. Karpat, "Some Historical and Methodological Considerations Concerning Social Stratification in the Middle East," in C. A. O. van Nieuwenhuijze (ed.) *Commoners, Climbers and Notables: a sampler of studies on*

social ranking in the Middle East, Leiden: Brill, 1977, 96–8; H. Gerber, *The Social Origins of the Modern Middle East*, Boulder, CO: Lynne Reinner, 1987, 67–90; M. R. El-Ghonemy, *The Political Economy of Rural Poverty: the case for land reform*, London: Routledge, 1990, 159–60. Quataert, "Age of Reforms," 856–61; rural economy; 861–75. M. A. Ghalwash, "Land Acquisition by the Peasants of Mid-Nineteenth Century Egypt: the *ramya* system," *SI* 88, 1998: 134, 137. On the land laws themselves, D. Jorgens, "A Comparative Examination of the Provisions of the Ottoman Land Code and Khedive Sa'id's Law of 1858," and H. İslamoğlu, "Property as a Contested Domain: a reevaluation of the Ottoman Land Code of 1858," both in R. Owen (ed.) *New Perspectives on Property and Land in the Middle East*, Cambridge: Center for Middle Eastern Studies of Harvard University, 2000, 93–119 and 3–61 respectively. On similar processes in Europe, J. Blum, *The End of the Old Order in Rural Europe*, Princeton, NJ: Princeton University Press, 1978, 437.

119 C. Issawi, "Shifts in Economic Power," in Issawi, *Middle East*, 509 (see Hinnebusch, *Authoritarian Power*, 27); L. S. Schilcher, "Violence in Rural Syria in the 1880s and 1890s: state centralization, rural integration, and the world market," in Kazemi and Waterbury, *Peasants*, 52–3; G. Corm, "Systèmes de pouvoir et changements sociaux et régionaux au Machrek arabe," in J.-C. Santucci and H. El Malki (eds) *État et développement dans le monde arabe: crises et mutations au Maghreb*, Paris: CNRS, 1990, 41–2; L. Addi, "Forme néo-patrimoniale de l'état et secteur public en Algérie," in Santucci and El Malki, Etat et development, 79; J. A. Reilly, "Property, Status, and Class in Ottoman Damascus: case studies from the nineteenth century," *JAOS* 112, 1992: 9–21; H. Gülalp, "Universalism versus Particularism: Ottoman historiography and the 'grand narrative'," *NPT* 13, 1994: 163–4. This change was actually quite gradual; the law legitimized and generalized what was already happening. Production for the market became widespread in the century before 1858, and in periods of governmental weakness or preoccupation, tax farmers and other landholders behaved like owners who could do whatever they wanted with their land and labor force. K. M. Cuno, "The Origins of Private Ownership of Land in Egypt: a reappraisal," *IJMES* 12, 1980: 247; Burke, "Understanding Arab Protest Movements," 336.

120 J. Bowring, *Report on the Commercial Statistics of Syria,* London: W. Clowes for H.M. Stationery Office, 1840, quoted in Issawi, *Fertile Crescent*, 55; FO 78/3070, "Report on Syria," quoted in Issawi, *Fertile Crescent*, 57; FO 78/490, "Report on Agriculture of Bursa, 1841," quoted in Issawi, *Turkey*, 222; FO 83/346, "Report," quoted in Issawi, *Turkey*, 223; FO 78/289, James Brant, "Report of a Journey through a Part of Armenia and Asia Minor, 1836," quoted in Issawi, *Turkey*, 224; J. Fraser, cited in N. R. Keddie, *Historical Obstacles to Agrarian Change in Iran,* Claremont, 1950, excerpted in Issawi, *Iran*, 54; Lambton, *Landlord*, 137.

121 Burke, "Changing Patterns," 25; H. İnalcık, "The Emergence of Big Farms, *Çiftliks*: state, landlords, and tenants," in Keyder and Tabak, *Landholding and Commercial Agriculture*, 17-34; F. Tabak, "Agrarian Fluctuations and Modes of Labor Control in the Western Arc of the Fertile Crescent, c. 1700–1850," in ibid., 148–54; H. İslamoğlu, "Modernities Compared: state transformations and constitutions of property in the Qing and Ottoman Empires," *JEMH* 5, 2001: 374.

122 FO 195/527 November 6, 1857, quoted in G. Augustinos, "Europeans, Ottoman Reformers, and the *Reaya*: a question of historical focus," in R. Frucht (ed.) *Labyrinth of Nationalism, Complexities of Diplomacy: essays in honor of Charles and Barbara Jelavich*, Columbus, OH: Slavica Publishers, 1992, 244; B. Özdemir, "Being a Part of the Cinderella Service: Consul Charles Blunt at Salonica in the 1840s," in C. Imber, K. Kiyotaki, and R. Murphey (eds) *Frontiers of Ottoman Studies: state, province and the West*, London: IB Tauris, 2005, 2: 245; Hourani, "Ottoman Reform," 65; Gross, "Ottoman," 146n81.

123 Burke, "Changing Patterns," 32; İnalcık, *Tanzimat*; A. Richards, "Primitive Accumulation in Egypt, 1798–1882," *Review: Fernand Braudel Center* 1.2, Fall 1977: 47–9.

124 AD 2343/286, Cousse to HC, 24 April 1919, official sermon, quoted in J. L. Gelvin, *Divided Loyalties: nationalism and mass politics in Syria at the close of empire*, Berkeley: University of California Press, 1998, 190.

125 Quotations from Muḥammad 'Abdūh, *The Nature of Despotism and the Perniciousness of Enslavement*, in Z. K. I. Babakhan, *Islam and Muslims in the Land of Soviets*, trans. R. Dixon, Moscow: Progress, 1980, 96; and FO 141/380, September 22, 1904; thanks to Ziad Fahmy for this petition from el-Kafr el-Gedid. I. Khuri-Makdisi, *The Eastern Mediterranean and the Making of Global Radicalism, 1860–1914*, Berkeley: University of California Press, 2010, 103. Chalcraft (*Striking Cabbies*, 77) understood from the rapidity of response that petitions were taken more seriously in the

bureaucracy than ever before. See Brown, *Peasant Politics*, 171–74; Chalcraft, "Engaging the State," 304, 309, 312, 313, 318; Edmund Burke III, "Islam and Social Movements: methodological reflections," in E. Burke III and I. M. Lapidus (eds) *Islam, Politics, and Social Movements*, Berkeley: University of California Press, 1988, 28–31.

126 Hasan-e Fasā'ī, *History*, 376; J. R. I. Cole, *Colonialism and Revolution in the Middle East: social and cultural origins of Egypt's 'Urabi movement*, Princeton, NJ: Princeton University Press, 1993, 191, 167; Chalcraft, "Engaging the State," 320n5; Gross "Ottoman," 208–10, 237–8, 248; V. Martin, "Women and Popular Protest: women's demonstration in nineteenth-century Iran," in S. Cronin (ed.) *Subalterns and Social Protest: history from below in the Middle East and North Africa*, London: Routledge, 2008, 55; Shoko Okazaki, "The Great Persian Famine of 1870–71," *BSOAS* 49, 1986: 183–92; Shaw and Shaw, *History*, 2: 156; Quataert, "Commercialization," 52. Drought of 1873–4: P. I. Kuniholm, "Archaeological Evidence and Non-Evidence for Climatic Change," *Philosophical Transactions of the Royal Society of London* A330, 1990: 650; R. D'Arrigo and H. M. Cullen, "A 350-Year (AD 1628–1980) Reconstruction of Turkish Precipitation," *Dendrochronologia* 19, 2001: 173; Ü. Akkemik and A. Aras, "Reconstruction (1689–1994 AD) of April–August Precipitation in the Southern Part of Central Turkey," *International Journal of Climatology* 25, 2005: 546.

127 Village headman: M. Sharubim, *al-Kāfi f ī tā'rīkh Miṣr al-qadīm wa-al-hadīth,* Bulaq: al-Maṭba'a al-Kubrá al-Amiriyya, 1898–1900, 4: 237, trans. Cole, *Colonialism*, 262; also 88, 219, 263; Gabriel Baer, *Studies in the Social History of Modern Egypt*, Chicago, IL: University of Chicago Press, 1969, 100; cf. P. M. Holt, *The Mahdist State in the Sudan, 1881–1898: a study of its origins, development and overthrow*, Oxford: Clarendon, 1958, 242–3. Petition from Egyptian notables, cited in A. Schölch, *Egypt for the Egyptians! the socio-political crisis in Egypt 1878–1882*, London: Ithaca Press for the Middle East Centre, St. Antony's College, Oxford, 1981, 170–1&n49.

128 *Le Tunisien*, cited in Byron Cannon, "Rural Social Justice Rhetoric and the Young Tunisian Movement, 1907–1912," *RHM* 17, nos. 59–60, 1990: 64; Y. Ben-Bassat, "In Search of Justice: petitions sent from Palestine to Istanbul from the 1870s onwards," *Turcica* 41, 2009: 89–114; Schilcher, "Violence," 61–4; H. Batatu, *Syria's Peasantry, the Descendants of Its Lesser Rural Notables, and Their Politics*, Princeton, NJ: Princeton University Press, 1999, 113–15; L. Anderson, "Nineteenth-Century Reform in Ottoman Libya," IJMES 16, 1984: 333; A. Sainte-Marie, "La commune d'Azeffoun à la fin du XIXème siècle," *Revue algérienne des sciences juridiques, economiques, et politiques* 9, 1974: 446, 450; Quataert, "Age of Reforms," 876; Burke, "Changing Patterns," 32; Chalcraft, "Engaging the State," 323, n. 42; Cole, *Colonialism*, 209, 233.

129 Al-Kawākibī, *Umm al-qurā*, cited in J. G. Rahme, "'Abd al-Raḥmān al-Kawākibī's Reformist Ideology, Arab Pan-Islamism, and the Internal Other," *JIS* 10, 1999: 163–5; "'Abd al-Raḥmān al-Kawākibī, 1849–1902," in Khūrī, *Modern Arab Thought*, 137–8; H. Ennaïfer, "La pensée sociale dans les écrits musulmans modernes," trans. S. Ghrab, in *Foi et justice: un défi pour le christianisme et pour l'islam*, ed. J.-P. Gabus, Paris: Centurion, 1993, 174.

130 D. Quataert, "Machine Breaking and the Changing Carpet Industry of Western Anatolia, 1860–1908," *JSH* 19, 1985–6: 483, D. Quataert, "Rural Unrest in the Ottoman Empire, 1830–1914," in Kazemi and Waterbury, *Peasants*, 45; G. Denoeux, *Urban Unrest in the Middle East: a comparative study of informal networks in Egypt, Iran, and Lebanon*, Albany: State University of New York Press, 1993, 88. E. Zürcher, *Turkey: a modern history*, London: IB Tauris, 2004, 80–99; F. Ahmad, *The Young Turks: the Committee of Union and Progress in Turkish politics, 1908–1914*, Oxford: Clarendon, 1969, 1–13; A. Kansu, *The Revolution of 1908 in Turkey*, Leiden: Brill, 1997.

131 Lambton, *Qajar Persia*, 297–8, 299–300; M. Moaddel, "Shi'i Political Discourse and Class Mobilization in the Tobacco Movement of 1890–92," in J. Foran (ed.) *A Century of Revolution: social movements in Iran*, Minneapolis: University of Minnesota Press, 1994, 15, 17; M. Bayat, *Iran's First Revolution: Shi'ism and the Constitutional Revolution of 1905–1909*, New York: Oxford University Press, 1991, 19; N. R. Keddie, *Religion and Rebellion in Iran: the Tobacco Protest of 1891–1892*, London: Frank Cass, 1966. Deindustrialization by Russia and Britain is also part of this story: A. Ashraf, "Historical Obstacles to the Development of a Bourgeoisie in Iran," in M. A. Cook (ed.) *Studies in the Economic History of the Middle East: from the rise of Islam to the present day*, London: Oxford University Press, 1970, 326. E. Abrahamian, "The Causes of the Constitutional Revolution in Iran," *IJMES* 10, 1979: 395; E. Abrahamian, "The Crowd in the Persian Revolution 1," *IranS* 2, 1969: 140.

132 Mīrzā Muḥammad Nāẓim al-Islām Kirmānī, *Tārīkh-i bīdārī-yi Irāniyān,* 1953, 374, trans. N. Sohrabi, "Revolution and State Culture: the Circle of Justice and constitutionalism in 1906 Iran," in G. Steinmetz (ed.) *State/Culture: state-formation after the cultural turn*, Ithaca: Cornell University Press, 1999, 265. Abrahamian, "Causes," 401; Bayat, *Iran's First Revolution*, 22.

133 Abrahamian, "Crowd in the Persian Revolution," 184; Algar, *Religion and State*, 247–8; Martin, *Islam and Modernism*, 74–5. Quotation from Mohammad Ṭabāṭabā'ī in Mīrzā Muḥammad Nāẓim al-Islām Kirmānī, *Tārīkh-i bīdārī-yi Irāniyān*, Tehran: Intishārāt-i Bunyad-i Farhang-i Iran, 1967, 2: 213, trans. Bayat, *Iran's First Revolution*, 127.

134 Browne, *Persian Revolution*, 121; Sohrabi, "Revolution," 265–6; E. Abrahamian, "The Crowd in Iranian Politics, 1905–1953," *Past & Present* 41, 1968: 196; P. Paidar, *Women and the Political Process in Twentieth-Century Iran*, Cambridge: Cambridge University Press, 1995, 54. Quotation from Mohammad Ṭabāṭabā'ī, sermon, in Kirmānī, *Tārīkh-i bīdārī-yi Irāniyān*, 1967, 2: 213, trans. Bayat, *Iran's First Revolution*, 127.

135 J. R. Perry, "Justice for the Underprivileged: the ombudsman tradition of Iran," *JNES* 37, 1978: 213. *Akhtar* 11, 4 Sept. 1895, trans. M. R. Afshari, "The *Pīshivarān* and Merchants in Precapitalist Iranian Society: an essay on the background and causes of the Constitutional Revolution," *IJMES* 15, 1983: 150.

136 Sohrabi, "Revolution," 265–70, 282–4; J. Afary, *The Iranian Constitutional Revolution, 1906–1911: grassroots democracy, social democracy, and the origins of feminism*, New York: Columbia University Press, 1996, 53, 151; Arjomand, *Turban for the Crown*, 47–8, 57. M. Bayat, "The Cultural Implications of the Constitutional Revolution," in Bosworth and Hillenbrand, *Qajar Iran*, 69; Bayat, *Iran's First Revolution*, 159.

137 Afary, *Iranian Constitutional Revolution*, 87, 90; Abrahamian, "Crowd in Iranian Politics," 197; Abrahamian, "Crowd in the Persian Revolution," 142; Bayat, *Iran's First Revolution*, 103.

138 Abrahamian, "Crowd in the Persian Revolution," 143; Afary, *Iranian Constitutional Revolution*, 154, 165; Arjomand, *Turban for the Crown*, 47.

139 Abrahamian, "Crowd in the Persian Revolution," 135–6, 140-2; Paidar, Women, 55; Algar, *Religion and State*, 254; Lambton, *Qajar Persia*, 327. Merchants and landowners on the local councils, for example in Gilan, opposed agrarian reform as well; J. Afary, "Peasant Rebellions of the Caspian Region during the Iranian Constitutional Revolution, 1906–1909," *IJMES* 23, 1991: 152.

10 The Middle East in the twentieth century

1 For the history of the twentieth-century Middle East, see W. L. Cleveland, *A History of the Modern Middle East*, Boulder, CO: Westview Press, 1994; 4th ed. 2009; J. L. Gelvin, *The Modern Middle East: a history*, New York, Oxford: Oxford University Press, 2005.

2 M. Halpern, *The Politics of Social Change in the Middle East and North Africa*, Princeton, NJ: Princeton University Press, 1963, 93.

3 The model for this terminology is Hodgson's medieval "military patronage state," in which a military elite maintained its ascendancy by cultural and political patronage; M. G. S. Hodgson, *The Venture of Islam: conscience and history in a world civilization*, 3 vols, Chicago, IL: University of Chicago Press, 1974, 2: 402–10; see Ch. 6. In modern times, landowners and businessmen dispensed new forms of social and political patronage; J. Waterbury, "An Attempt to Put Patrons and Clients in Their Place," in E. Gellner and J. Waterbury (eds) *Patrons and Clients in Mediterranean Societies*, London: Duckworth, 1977, 329–42.

4 Albert Hourani, *Arabic Thought in the Liberal Age, 1798–1939*, London: Oxford University Press, 1970, 344; see Ch. 9 for the development of this bourgeoisie.

5 Z. Gökalp, *The Principles of Turkism*, trans. R. Devereux, Leiden: Brill, 1968, 116. This definition echoed the *Tanẓimat* criminal code of 1840; R. A. Miller, *Legislating Authority: sin and crime in the Ottoman Empire and Turkey*, New York: Routledge, 2005, 28.

6 A. Şerif, *Anadolu'da tanın*, ed. M. Ç. Börekçi, Istanbul: Kavram, 1977, 46–7, republished Ankara: Türk Tarih Kurumu, 1999, 1: 33–4, trans. F. Ahmad, "The Agrarian Policy of the Young Turks, 1908–1918," in J.-L. Bacqué-Grammont and P. Dumont (ed.) *Économie et sociétés dans l'empire ottoman (fin du XVIIIe siècle–début du XXe siècle)*, Paris: CNRS, 1983, 275–6.

7 Mustafa Kemal Atatürk, *Thus Spoke Atatürk: his sayings, thoughts and memoirs*, ed. and trans. H. Melzig, Istanbul: Kenan, 1943, 8. He also echoed an old Mamluk idea: "Sovereignty is acquired by force, by power and by violence"; Mustafa Kemal Atatürk, *A Speech Delivered by*

Mustafa Kemal Atatürk, 1927 [Nutuk], Ankara: Ministry of Education of the Turkish Republic/ Başbakanlık Basımevi, 1981, 576; see also 437.

8 Ahmad, "Agrarian Policy," 288; Ç. Keyder, *State and Class in Turkey: a study in capitalist development*, London: Verso, 1987, 69, 78–83; F. W. Frey, *The Turkish Political Elite*, Cambridge, MA: MIT Press, 1965, 81, 83, 146. Although "agriculture" as an occupational grouping was statistically underrepresented among parliamentary delegates, large landlords were overrepresented and the peasants, 65 percent of the population, not at all; ibid., 181.

9 É. Copeaux, "Les prédécesseurs médiévaux d'Atatürk: Bilge kaghan et le sultan Alp Arslan," *RMMM* 89–90, 2000: 228.

10 D. A. Rustow, "Ataturk's Political Leadership," in R. B. Winder (ed.) *Near Eastern Round Table, 1967–68*, New York: Near East Center and the Center for International Studies, 1969, 150; D. Ergil, *Social History of the Turkish National Struggle, 1919–22: the unfinished revolution*, Lahore: Sind Sagar Academy, 1977, 121–2; E. Z. Karal, "The Principles of Kemalism," in A. Kazancıgil and E. Özbudun (eds) *Atatürk: founder of a modern state*, Hamden, CT: Archon Books, 1981, 20; Keyder, *State and Class*, 95–7, 107–10; see Atatürk's speech in J. M. Landau (ed.) *Atatürk and the Modernization of Turkey*, Boulder, CO: Westview, 1984, 39.

11 M. E. Meeker, *A Nation of Empire: the Ottoman legacy of Turkish modernity*, Berkeley: University of California Press, 2002, 328; N. Yalman, "On Land Disputes in Eastern Turkey," in G. L. Tikku (ed.) *Islam and Its Cultural Divergence: studies in honor of Gustave E. von Grunebaum*, Urbana: University of Illinois Press, 1971, 198, 208; Z. Lockman, "Imagining the Working Class: culture, nationalism, and class formation in Egypt, 1899–1914," *Poetics Today* 15, 1994: 166–8.

12 I. M. Smilianskaya, "Razlozhenie feodalnikh otmoshenii v Sirii i Livane v Serredine XIX v." [The Disintegration of Feudal Relations in Syria and Lebanon in the Middle of the Nineteenth Century], trans. Issawi, *Middle East*, 239; T. Petran, *Syria*, London: Ernest Benn, 1972, 69–70; E. Thompson, *Colonial Citizens: republican rights, paternal privilege, and gender in French Syria and Lebanon*, New York: Columbia University Press, 2000, 54; R. A. Hinnebusch, *Authoritarian Power and State Formation in Ba'thist Syria: army, party, and peasant*, Boulder, CO: Westview, 1990, 32.

13 M. Deeb, *Party Politics in Egypt: the Wafd and its rivals, 1919–1939*, London: Ithaca Press for The Middle East Centre, St. Antony's College, Oxford, 1979, 151; M. Ener, *Managing Egypt's Poor and the Politics of Benevolence, 1800–1952*, Princeton, NJ: Princeton University Press, 2003, 125–31.

14 M. R. Afshari, "The Historians of the Constitutional Movement and the Making of the Iranian Populist Tradition," *IJMES* 25, 1993: 483; A. K. S. Lambton, *Landlord and Peasant in Persia*, London: Oxford University Press, 1953; repr. London: IB Tauris, 1991, 190, 294; R. W. Cottam, *Nationalism in Iran: updated through 1978*, Pittsburgh, PA: University of Pittsburgh Press, 1979, 34, 49; N. R. Keddie, with a section by Y. Richard, *Roots of Revolution: an interpretive history of modern Iran*, New Haven, CT: Yale University Press, 1981, 87, 96, 104–5; M. R. Ghods, "Government and Society in Iran, 1926–34," *MES* 27, 1991: 222.

15 Iran: F. Kazemi, "Peasant Uprisings in Twentieth-Century Iran, Iraq, and Turkey," in F. Kazemi and J. Waterbury (eds) *Peasants and Politics in the Modern Middle East*, Miami: Florida International University Press, 1991, 105–6; S. Cronin, "Resisting the New State: the rural poor, land and modernity in Iran, 1921–1941," in S. Cronin (ed.) *Subalterns and Social Protest: history from below in the Middle East and North Africa*, London: Routledge, 2008, 148–51, 161–2. Egypt: F. Abaza, *al-Ḍāḥik al-bākī*, Cairo: Maṭba'at al-Hilāl, 1933, 74–6, trans. G. Baer, *Studies in the Social History of Modern Egypt*, Chicago, IL: University of Chicago Press, 1969, 101–2, quotation on 102; also quoted in A. M. al-'Aqqād, *al-Dīmūqrāṭiyya fī al-Islām*, trans. N. Safran, *Egypt in Search of Political Community: an analysis of the intellectual and political evolution of Egypt, 1804–1952*, Cambridge, MA: Harvard University Press, 1961, 197–8; R. C. Schulze, "Colonization and Resistance: the Egyptian peasant rebellion, 1919," in Kazemi and Waterbury, *Peasants*, 188–95; M. R. El-Ghonemy, *The Political Economy of Rural Poverty: the case for land reform*, London: Routledge, 1990, 159.

16 Morocco: W. H. Lewis, "Rural Administration in Morocco," *MEJ* 14, 1960: 52; E. Gellner, "Patterns of Rural Rebellion in Morocco: tribes as minorities," *Archives européennes de sociologie* 3, 1962: 297; E. Hermassi, *Leadership and National Development in North Africa: a comparative study*, Berkeley: University of California Press, 1972, 147. Syria: J. L. Gelvin, "The Social Origins of Popular Nationalism in Syria: evidence for a new framework," *IJMES* 26, 1994: 656; E. Thompson, "The Climax and Crisis of the Colonial Welfare State in Syria and Lebanon during World

War II," in S. Heydemann (ed.) *War, Institutions, and Social Change in the Middle East*, Berkeley: University of California Press, 2000, 60–1; Egypt: N. J. Brown, *Peasant Politics in Modern Egypt: the struggle against the state*, New Haven, CT: Yale University Press, 1990, 167–70.

17 Thompson, *Colonial Citizens*, 104, 163–7; Thompson "Climax and Crisis," 80–2; Iran: S. A. Arjomand, *The Turban for the Crown: the Islamic Revolution in Iran*, New York, Oxford: Oxford University Press, 1988, 67–8.

18 'Ali 'Abd al-Rāziq, "L'Islam et les bases du pouvoir," trans. L. Bercher, *REI* 7, 1930: 353–91; 8, 1934: 163–222; L. Binder, *Islamic Liberalism: a critique of development ideologies*, Chicago, IL: University of Chicago Press, 1988, 131; S. T. Ali, *A Religion, Not a State: Ali 'Abd al-Raziq's Islamic justification of political secularism*, Salt Lake City: University of Utah Press, 2009. D. Semah, *Four Egyptian Literary Critics*, Leiden: Brill, 1974, 111, 112–13; P. Cachia, *Ṭāhā Ḥusayn: his place in the Egyptian literary renaissance,* London: Luzac, 1956, 60.

19 M. al-Ghazzāli, *Min huna na'mal*, 1951, trans. I. R. al-Faruqi as *Our Beginning in Wisdom*, Washington, DC: American Council of Learned Societies, 1953, 129. See R. P. Mitchell, *The Society of the Muslim Brothers*, New York: Oxford University Press, 1969, 210, 220–1; J. Beinin, "Islamic Responses to the Capitalist Penetration of the Middle East," in B. F. Stowasser (ed.) *The Islamic Impulse*, London: Croom Helm, 1987, 95; A. A. Musallam, "Sayyid Queqb and Social Justice, 1945–1948," *JIS* 4, 1993: 55. A similar analysis by a Marxist: T. Sonn, "Bandali al-Jawzi's *Min tārīkh al-ḥarakāt al-fikriyyāt fi'l-Islām*: the first Marxist interpretation of Islam," *IJMES* 17, 1985: 92, 104.

20 S. Quṭb, *Al-'Adāla al-ijtimā'iyya fi'l-Islām*, trans. J. B. Hardie, *Social Justice in Islam*, Washington, DC: American Council of Learned Societies, 1953; A. J. Bergesen (ed.) *The Sayyid Qutb Reader: selected writings on politics, religion, and society*, New York, London: Routledge, 2008. State persecution motivated Quṭb to drop social justice and preach the elimination of the regime, for which he was executed. Beinin points out the similarity of Quṭb's notion of "mutual social responsibility" to E. P. Thompson's concept of the moral economy; Beinin, "Islamic Responses," 95, 99. A. A. Maududi, *Come Let Us Change This World*, trans. K. Siddique, Karachi: Salma Siddique, 1971, 10, 29, 37.

21 Safran, *Egypt*, 203; quotations from Ṭ. Ḥussein, *The Sufferers: stories and polemics*, trans. M. El-Zayyat, Cairo: American University in Cairo Press, 1993, 1, 4. Similarly, the Christian Farah Antun argued for social justice and a fairer distribution of wealth; D. M. Reid, *The Odyssey of Farah Antun: a Syrian Christian's quest for secularism*, Minneapolis and Chicago, IL: Bibliotheca Islamica, 1975, 114–16.

22 Quotations: K. M. Khālid, *Min huna nabda'*, 1950, trans. I. R. al-Faruqi as *From Here We Start*, Washington, DC: American Council of Learned Societies, 1953, 67–8, 75, 129–30; Beinin, "Islamic Responses," 92.

23 When Amir Habibullah became Afghanistan's king in the early twentieth century, he took responsibility for maintaining order and providing justice, employing the concepts of the ruler as God's vicegerent, the Shadow of God on earth, a shepherd, nourisher, guide and protector of his subjects; S. Nawid, "The State, the Clergy, and British Imperial Policy in Afghanistan during the Nineteenth and Early Twentieth Centuries," *IJMES* 29, 1997: 597–8, citing M. T. Afghani, *Toḥfat al-amir fi bayan-i soluk wa al-tadbir*, Kabul: Government Printing House, 1910, published by King Habibullah.

24 Kuwait: U. Rabi, "The Kuwaiti Royal Family in the Postliberation Period: reinstitutionalizing the 'first among equals' system in Kuwait," in J. Kostiner (ed.) *Middle East Monarchies: the challenge of modernity*, Boulder, CO: Lynne Reinner, 2000, 152. Yemen: B. Messick, *The Calligraphic State: textual domination and history in a Muslim society*, Berkeley: University of California Press, 1993, 174–5.

25 A. Layish, "Saudi Arabian Legal Reform as a Mechanism to Moderate Wahhabi Doctrine," *JAOS* 107, 1987: 280, 285; J. Schacht, *An Introduction to Islamic Law*, Oxford: Clarendon, 1962, 1984, 87. In Saudi Arabia ruler's law was not called *ḳānūn* but *niẓām*, order. A. Al-Yassini, *Religion and State in the Kingdom of Saudi Arabia*, Boulder, CO: Westview, 1985, 75&n43. Women's *maẓālim* sessions: R. Lacey, *The Kingdom*, New York: Harcourt Brace Jovanovich, 1981, 311; S. Mackey, *Saudis: inside the desert kingdom*, New York: Penguin/Signet, 1990, 138.

26 Al-Yassini, *Religion*, 77; D. E. Long, "The Board of Grievances in Saudi Arabia," *MEJ* 27, 1973: 74. In the same year people began to send petitions to the Sultan of Oman, who had ousted the ulema rulers of the interior, but "were immediately discouraged from doing so," which raised

complaints about the injustice of secular rule; D. F. Eickelman, "From Theocracy to Monarchy: authority and legitimacy in Inner Oman, 1935–1957," *IJMES* 17, 1985: 17.

27 Al-Yassini, *Religion*, 114, 117; Syria: Thompson, *Colonial Citizens*, 158. J. Kostiner and J. Teitelbaum, "State-Formation and the Saudi Monarchy," in Kostiner, *Middle East Monarchies*, 137; K. A. Chaudhry, "Economic Liberalization in Oil-Exporting Countries: Iraq and Saudi Arabia," in I. Harik and D. J. Sullivan (eds) *Privatization and Liberalization in the Middle East*, Bloomington: Indiana University Press, 1992, 147, 151, 159; H. F. Eilts, "Saudi Arabia: traditionalism versus modernism – a royal dilemma?" in P. J. Chelkowski and R. J. Pranger (eds) *Ideology and Power in the Middle East: Studies in Honor of George Lenczowski*, Durham, NC: Duke University Press, 1988, 59–60; M. C. Hudson, *Arab Politics: the search for legitimacy*, New Haven, CT: Yale University Press, 1977, 396. Quotation from "The Permanent Constitution of the Yemeni Arab Republic," San'a, 27 March 1964, pub. *al-Thawra*, 2 April 1964, in *Arab Political Documents, 1964*, Beirut: Political Studies and Public Administration Department of the American University of Beirut, 1964, 121.

28 Hussein, King of Jordan, *Uneasy Lies the Head*, New York: Bernard Geis Associates, 1962, 65–6. His visits dwindled in the 1970s and petitioning decreased in favor of more "modern" forms of intervention; R. B. Cunningham and Y. K. Sarayrah, *Wasta: the hidden force in Middle Eastern society*, Westport, CT: Praeger, 1993, 144–5.

29 Hussein, *Uneasy Lies the Head*, 67–8, 99, 235, 247; U. Dann, *King Hussein and the Challenge of Arab Radicalism: Jordan, 1955–1967*, New York: Oxford University Press, in cooperation with The Moshe Dayan Center, 1989, 9; L. L. Layne, *Home and Homeland: the dialogics of tribal and national identities in Jordan*, Princeton, NJ: Princeton University Press, 1994, 148; A. Susser, "The Jordanian Monarchy: the Hashemite success story," in Kostiner, *Middle East Monarchies*, 99. In the 1970s Jordanians began to agitate for political rights, and in the 1990s Hussein began to grant them, but his successor Abdullah reversed that policy; S. Glain, "Kingdom of Corruption," *The Nation*, 30 May 2005: 22–3.

30 Hassan II, *Le Maroc en Marche: discours de Sa Majeste Hassan II depuis son avenement au trone*, Mohammedia, Morocco: Offset de Fedala, 1965/6 475–6; D. F. Eickelman, *Knowledge and Power in Morocco: the education of a twentieth-century notable*, Princeton, NJ: Princeton University Press, 1985, 88–90; I. W. Zartman, *Destiny of a Dynasty: the search for institutions in Morocco's developing society*, Columbia, SC: University of South Carolina Press, 1964, 39. As these requests extended even to official appointments, the French colonial authorities eliminated the Feast of Students. Governors also held *maẓālim* court in provincial capitals; K. L. Brown, *People of Sale: tradition and change in a Moroccan city, 1830–1930*, Cambridge, MA: Harvard University Press, 1976, 166.

31 M. Morsy, "Arbitration as a Political Institution: an interpretation of the status of monarchy in Morocco," in A. S. Ahmed and D. M. Hart (eds) *Islam in Tribal Societies: from the Atlas to the Indus*, London: Routledge & Kegan Paul, 1984, 44, 55–8; R. Bourqia, "The Cultural Legacy of Power in Morocco," in R. Bourqia and S. G. Miller (eds) *In the Shadow of the Sultan: culture, power, and politics in Morocco*, Cambridge, MA: Harvard University Center for Middle Eastern Studies, 1999, 249; quotation: Muḥammad b. Ja'far al-Kattānī, *Salwat al-anfas*, Fez: Aḥmad al-Azraq, 1899, 1989, 205, trans. H. Munson, Jr., *Religion and Power in Morocco*, New Haven, CT: Yale University Press, 1993, 91.

32 Hassan II, *Maroc*, 34, 241, 338, 443–4; Hassan II, *The Challenge: the memoirs of King Hassan II of Morocco*, trans. A. Rhodes, London: Macmillan, 1978, 94; J. Waterbury, *The Commander of the Faithful: the Moroccan political elite – a study in segmented politics*, New York: Columbia University Press, 1970, 156.

33 Waterbury, *Commander*, 148, 154, 158; Hassan II, *La mémoire d'un roi: entretiens avec Eric Laurent*, Paris: Plon, 1993, 139–40; A. Claisse, "Makhzen Traditions and Administrative Channels," in I. W. Zartman (ed.) *The Political Economy of Morocco*, New York: Praeger, 1987, 46–7, 52; Hermassi, *Leadership*, 193. Unlike other Middle Eastern countries, Morocco experienced no land reform in the 1960s; ibid., 181–2.

34 Hassan II, *Challenge*, 91, 94; Waterbury, *Commander*, 403, 17, 152–7; I. W. Zartman, "King Hassan's New Morocco," in Zartman, *Political Economy*, 1; A. Doumou, ed. *The Moroccan State in Historical Perspective, 1850–1985*, trans. A. K. Armah, Dakar, Senegal: CODESRIA, 1990, 5.

35 Hassan II, *Maroc*, 358; see 476, 479, 504. This definition became popular beyond Morocco, as an Egyptian interviewee in 2008 told a reporter: "If democracy brings us food we can afford, and a

government that really cares about its people, then this is what we want"; quoted in M. Slackman, "Don't Leave Home Without a Cultural Compass," *New York Times*, 11 June 2008: A8.

36 A. Marashi, *Nationalizing Iran: culture, power, and the state, 1870–1940*, Seattle: University of Washington Press, 2008, 52–3, 124–32; Arjomand, *Turban*, 68, 80; E. Abrahamian, *Iran: between two revolutions*, Princeton, NJ: Princeton University Press, 1982, 189, 192; S. Mackey, *The Iranians: Persia, Islam and the soul of a nation*, New York: Penguin/Dutton, 1996, 169, 177; Cronin, "Resisting," 145. In that period the police reprimanded those who wrote to the Shah; E. A. Bayne, *Persian Kingship in Transition: conversation with a monarch whose office is traditional and whose goal is modernization*, New York: American Universities Field Staff, 1968, 132. For the Testament of Ardashīr see Ch. 3.

37 M. R. Pahlavi, *Mission for My Country*, London: Hutchinson & Co., 1961, 31. Historians educated during his reign were apparently steeped in this symbolism, for they often look at the whole modern era through that lens. Fortunately, in the case of Muḥammad Reẓa himself, his own extensive writings indicate the role the concept had for him.

38 M. R. Pahlavi, *The White Revolution*, 2nd ed., Tehran: The Imperial Pahlavi Library/Kayhan Press, 1967, 21, 35, 136, 141–9; quotation of justice proverb on 143, new Circle on 171. Houses of Equity (*khānahā-ye enṣāf*): J. R. Perry, "Justice for the Underprivileged: the ombudsman tradition of Iran," *JNES* 37, 1978: 215; M. M. J. Fischer, "Legal Postulates in Flux: justice, wit, and hierarchy in Iran," in D. H. Dwyer (ed.) *Law and Islam in the Middle East*, New York: Bergin & Garvey, 1990, 137–8; M. R. Pahlavi, *Answer to History*, New York: Stein & Day, 1980, 109–10.

39 Dependence on resources rather than taxes is said to insulate the rentier state from popular criticism; H. Mahdavy, "Patterns and Problems of Economic Development in Rentier States: the case of Iran," in M. A. Cook (ed.) *Studies in the Economic History of the Middle East: from the rise of Islam to the present day*, London: Oxford University Press, 1970, 428–67; H. Beblawi and G. Luciani, Introduction to H. Beblawi and G. Luciani (eds) *The Rentier State*, London: Croom Helm, 1987, 4–14. Some rentier states, however, had reasons other than financial need to be responsive to their populations.

40 Quotation: G. E. Goodell, *The Elementary Structures of Political Life: rural development in Pahlavi Iran*, New York: Oxford University Press, 1986, 28; this sense comes through in the shah's writings as well. K. McLachlan, *The Neglected Garden: the politics and ecology of agriculture in Iran*, London: IB Tauris, 1988, 2; M. Amjad, *Iran: from royal dictatorship to theocracy*, Westport, CT: Greenwood Press, 1989, 94; K. Ehsani, "Rural Society and Agricultural Development in Post-Revolution Iran: the first two decades," *Critique* 15, 2006: 84.

41 A. Ashraf, "Historical Obstacles to the Development of a Bourgeoisie in Iran," in Cook, *Studies*, 331; P. W. English, *City and Village in Iran: settlement and economy in the Kirman Basin*, Madison: University of Wisconsin Press, 1966, 66; N. R. Keddie, "The Iranian Village before and after Land Reform," *JContempH* 3.3, 1968: 75, 79, 82n14, 84; N. R. Keddie, "Stratification, Social Control, and Capitalism in Iranian Villages Before and After Land Reform," in R. Antoun and I. Harik (eds) *Rural Politics and Social Change in the Middle East*, Bloomington: Indiana University Press, 1972, 391, 394; R. M. Savory, "Social Development in Iran during the Pahlavi Era," in G. Lenczowski (ed.) *Iran under the Pahlavis*, Stanford, CA: Hoover Institution Press, 1978, 110; A. Najmabadi, *Land Reform and Social Change in Iran*, Salt Lake City: University of Utah Press, 1987, 9–11, 25–8, 86; Abrahamian, *Iran*, 430, 439; J. Foran, *Fragile Resistance: social transformation in Iran from 1500 to the Revolution*, Boulder, CO: Westview, 1993, 318; E. J. Hooglund, *Land and Revolution in Iran, 1960–1980*, Austin: University of Texas Press, 1982, 50, 59, 62–79; M. G. Majd, *Resistance to the Shah: landowners and ulama in Iran*, Gainesville: University Press of Florida, 2000, 331, 337, 346–7; M. G. Majd, "Small Landowners and Land Distribution in Iran, 1962–71," *IJMES* 32, 2000: 124.

42 Khomeini, personal interview, 10 January 1967, cited in J. A. Bill, *The Politics of Iran: groups, classes, and modernization*, Columbus, OH: Charles E. Merrill, 1972, 24; J. Amuzegar, *The Dynamics of the Iranian Revolution: the Pahlavis' triumph and tragedy*, Albany: State University of New York Press, 1991, 125–9, 148–9, 151–3; Abrahamian, *Iran*, 427, 429; Hooglund, *Land*, 80, 111, 119, 137; Cottam, *Nationalism*, 291, 312; H. Katouzian, "The Aridisolatic Society: a model of long-term social and economic development in Iran," *IJMES* 15, 1983: 273.

43 G. Bechor, "'To Hold the Hand of the Weak': the emergence of contractual justice in the Egyptian civil law," *ILS* 8, 2001: 188, quotations on 190, 191.

44 M. Aflaq, *Choice of Texts from the Ba'th Party Founder's Thought*, [Baghdad]: Arab Ba'th Socialist Party, 1977, 43.

45 A. Rabo, "Nation-State Building in Syria: Ba'th and Islam – conflict or accommodation?" in K. Ferdinand and M. Mozaffari (eds) *Islam: state and society*, London and Riverdale: Curzon Press/ Riverdale, 1988, 124.

46 K. El-Menoufi, "The Orientation of Egyptian Peasants toward Political Authority between Continuity and Change," *MES* 18, 1982: 88–9; I. Harik, *The Political Mobilization of Peasants: a study of an Egyptian community*, Bloomington: Indiana University Press, 1974, 173, 176, 191. A myth of total state tyranny and exploitation paralleled the myth of justice among both elites, for whom it sustained British rule as a milder form of exploitation, and peasants, for whom it justified resistance to the state's demands and refusal to cooperate with its initiatives.

47 Quotation from Ba'th Party Constitution, article 42, trans. J. F. Devlin, *The Ba'th Party: a history from its origins to 1966*, Stanford, CA: Hoover Institution Press, 1976, 34; see K. S. Abu Jaber, *The Arab Ba'th Socialist Party: history, ideology, and organization*, Syracuse: Syracuse University Press, 1966, 105; R. Mabro, *The Egyptian Economy, 1952–1972*, Oxford: Clarendon, 1974, 128.

48 G. A. Nasser, speech on 22 July 1961, trans. M. H. Kerr, "The Emergence of a Socialist Ideology in Egypt," *MEJ* 16, 1962: 143.

49 D. Warriner, *Land Reform and Development in the Middle East: a study of Egypt, Syria, and Iraq*, 2nd ed., London: Oxford University Press, 1962, 14; A. Hottinger, "How the Arab Bourgeoisie Lost Power," *JContempH* 3.3, 1968: 111. For figures, often contradictory, see Sir M. Darling, "Land Reform in Italy and Egypt," *Year Book of Agricultural Co-operation*, 1956, 14–17; R. H. Dekmejian, *Egypt Under Nasir: a study in political dynamics*, Albany: State University of New York Press, 1971, 123; S. Radwan, *Agrarian Reform and Rural Poverty, Egypt, 1952–1975*, Geneva: International Labour Office, 1977, 35, 46; R. H. Adams, Jr., *Development and Social Change in Rural Egypt*, Syracuse, NY: Syracuse University Press, 1986, 13, 17; El-Menoufi, "Orientation," 82–4. Studies providing long-term series of figures and comparing landholding, income disparities, and social services across Middle Eastern countries and with developed and underdeveloped economies are rare; most studies give apparently random figures or compare unlikes.

50 R. Saad, *Social History of an Agrarian Reform Community in Egypt*, Cairo Papers in Social Science, 11, Cairo: American University in Cairo Press, 1998, 55, 69–70. Y. M. Sadowski, *Political Vegetables? businessman and bureaucrat in the development of Egyptian agriculture*, Washington, DC: The Brookings Institution, 1991, 66.

51 L. Binder, *The Ideological Revolution in the Middle East*, New York: J. Wiley and Sons, 1964, 218; Radwan, *Agrarian Reform*, 38; R. Owen, "Large Landowners, Agricultural Progress and the State in Egypt, 1800–1970: an overview with many questions," in A. Richards (ed.) *Food, States, and Peasants: analyses of the agrarian question in the Middle East*, Boulder, CO: Westview, 1986, 82; P. O'Brien, *The Revolution in Egypt's Economic System: from private enterprise tosSocialism, 1952–1965*, London: Oxford University Press, 1966, 293, 295, 300; G. S. Saab, *The Egyptian Agrarian Reform, 1952–1962*, London: Oxford University Press, 1967, 122, 126.

52 Radwan, *Agrarian Reform*, 46; Adams, *Development*, 113; G. Lewy, *Religion and Revolution*, New York: Oxford University Press, 1974, 451.

53 Quotation from National Charter, trans. E. S. Farag, in *Nasser Speaks: basic documents*, London: Morssett Press, 1972, 70; see "President Nasser's Speech to the National Assembly (Excerpts)," Cairo, 25 March 1964, *Egyptian Gazette*, 27 March 1964, trans. *Arab Political Documents, 1964*, 108; *Nasser's Speeches* 1: 150, 4: 743, 751, 768, cited by Binder, *Ideological Revolution*, 223.

54 "Formulas for Change, the evolution of Nasserism, 1952–1962," trans. R. G Landen (ed.) *The Emergence of the Modern Middle East: selected readings*, New York: Van Nostrand Reinhold, 1970, 307; N. Rejwan, *Nasserist Ideology: its exponents and critics*, New York: John Wiley and Sons, 1974, 195, 248. The reciprocity implied in the National Charter is also noted by A. E. Sonbol, *The New Mamluks: Egyptian society and modern feudalism*, Syracuse, NY: Syracuse University Press, 2000, 122.

55 G. A. Nasser, "Speech delivered at Damascus on February 24, 1961," trans. *Speeches and Press-Interviews*, Cairo: United Arab Republic Information Department, 1961, 53; O'Brien, *Revolution*, 283.

56 G. A. Nasser, "Speech delivered on February 22, 1961 (20:30 hrs.)," trans. ibid., *Speeches and Press-Interviews*, 39. A letter Nasser wrote to King Hussein in 1958 had a similar message: "Domestically

we seek democracy, not only in general elections, but also including participation in a national economic revolution to increase production and achieve equality in distribution," trans. Binder, *Ideological Revolution*, 208. B. Dajani, "The National Charter and Socio-Economic Organization in the United Arab Republic," *MEEP* 8, 1961: 52–3.

57 "President Nasser's Speech," 25 March 1964, *Arab Political Documents, 1964*, 109–10; "Speech by President Nasser Commemorating Victory Day at Port Said (Excerpts)," 21 December 1965, *Egyptian Gazette*, 22 December 1965, trans. *Arab Political Documents, 1965*, 469; M. R. El-Ghonemy, *Affluence and Poverty in the Middle East*, London: Routledge, 1998, 22; R. S. Humphreys, *Between Memory and Desire: the Middle East in a troubled age*, Berkeley: University of California Press, 1999, 40.

58 The other was its inadequacy in the face of the Palestinian problem; Hudson, *Arab Politics*, 21, 28, 244.

59 H. Ammar, *Growing Up in an Egyptian Village: Silwa, Province of Aswan*, New York: Octagon Books, 1966, 108–9; J. B. Mayfield, *Rural Politics in Nasser's Egypt: a quest for legitimacy*, Austin: University of Texas Press, 1971, 148; H. Fakhouri, *Kafr el-Elow, an Egyptian Village in Transition*, New York: Holt, Rinehart and Winston, 1972, 106; Adams, *Development*, 155; K. J. Beattie, *Egypt During the Nasser Years: ideology, politics, and civil society*, Boulder, CO: Westview, 1994, 163; Sonbol, *New Mamluks*, 137. On Kamshish see H. Ansari, *Egypt, The Stalled Society*, Albany: State University of New York Press, 1986, 28, 57, 147; Harik, *Political Mobilization*, 92, 172–3.

60 National Charter, trans. Rejwan, *Nasserist Ideology*, 226; Dekmejian, *Egypt*, 90; Sonbol, *New Mamluks*, 149; Lewy, *Religion*, 452.

61 Humphreys, *Between Memory and Desire*, 41; J. Beinin, "Islam, Marxism, and the Shubra al-Khayma Textile Workers: Muslim Brothers and Communists in the Egyptian trade union movement," in E. Burke III, and I. M. Lapidus (eds) *Islam, Politics, and Social Movements*, Berkeley: University of California Press, 1988, 219; A. El-Kosheri Mahfouz, *Socialisme et pouvoir en Égypte*, Paris: R. Pichon et R. Durand-Auzias, 1972, 92; Mitchell, *Society*, 287–91; I. M. Husaini, *The Moslem Brethren: the greatest of modern Islamic movements*, Beirut: Khayat's, 1956, 51–3; Mayfield, *Rural Politics*, 53; A. L. Marsot, "Religion or Opposition? urban protest movements in Egypt," *IJMES* 16, 1984: 546.

62 M. al-Sibāʿī, *Ishtirākiyyat al-Islām*, 2nd ed., Cairo: al-Dār al-Qawmiyya, 1960, trans. G. H. Gardner and S. A. Hanna, in S. A. Hanna and G. H. Gardner, *Arab Socialism: a documentary survey*, Salt Lake City: University of Utah Press, 1969, 66; S. A. Hanna and G. H. Gardner, "Al-Takāful al-ijtimāʿī: mutual or joint responsibility," al-Sibāʿī, in Hanna and Gardner, *Arab Socialism*, 149–71; Rejwan, *Nasserist Ideology*, 39; Enayat, *Modern Islamic Political Thought*, 144–51; Y. M. Sadowski, "Political Power and Economic Organization in Syria: the course of state intervention, 1946–1958," PhD diss., University of California-Los Angeles, 1984, 41; Beinin, "Islam, Marxism," 219.

63 M. Qaḍḍafi, *Kitāb al-akhḍar* (1979), trans. H. M. Christman, *Qaddafi's Green Book: an unauthorized edition*, Buffalo, NY: Prometheus Books, 1988.

64 Popular song, trans. D. Blundy and A. Lycett, *Qaddafi and the Libyan Revolution*, London: Weidenfeld and Nicolson, 1987, 20; quotation from M. al-Qaddafi, "A Visit to Fezzan," trans. I. W. Zartman, *Man, State, and Society in the Contemporary Maghrib*, New York: Praeger, 1973, 131.

65 Libya, Revolutionary Command Council, "Constitutional Declaration of December 1969," trans. M. A. El-Khawas, *Qaddafi: his ideology in theory and practice*, Brattleboro, VT: Amana Books, 1986, 63; J. Bearman, *Qadhafi's Libya*, London: Zed Books, 1986, 58–9.

66 M. al-Qaddafi, speech at Sebha, 22 September 1969, quoted in Bearman, *Qadhafi's Libya*, 128.

67 Quotations: "The Constitution of the Arab Resurrection Socialist Party," trans. L. Binder, *MEJ* 13, 1959: 195–200, repr. in Hanna and Gardner, *Arab Socialism*, 306; speech of M. Aflaq, 27 January 1947, trans. in Arab Ba'th Socialist Party, *A Survey of the Ba'th Party's Struggle, 1947–1974*, [S.I.]: Unity Freedom Socialism, 1978, 19 (see also14); "The Programme Approved by the Extraordinary Regional Congress of the Ba'th Party in Damascus (Excerpts)," Damascus, 22 July 1965, *al-Ba'th*, 23 July 1965, trans. *Arab Political Documents, 1965*, 260. Abu Jaber, *Arab Ba'th*, 104, 107; Rabo, "Nation-State Building," 118.

68 A. Hourani, "Ottoman Reform and the Politics of Notables," in W. R. Polk and R. L. Chambers (eds) *Beginnings of Modernization in the Middle East*, Chicago, IL: University of Chicago Press, 1968, 41–68; M. Ma'oz, "Society and State in Modern Syria," in M. Milson (ed.) *Society and Political Structure in the Arab World*, New York: Humanities Press, 1973, 30; Sadowski, "Political Power," 43–4.

69 "Cabinet Statement of Mr. Salahuddin Bitar's Government (Excerpts)," Damascus, 23 May 1964, *Al-Ahrar*, 24 May 1964, trans. *Arab Political Documents, 1964*, 188. S. Heydemann, *Authoritarianism in Syria: institutions and social conflict, 1946–1970*, Ithaca, NY: Cornell University Press, 1999, 21.
70 Devlin, *Ba'th*, 33; Abu Jaber, *Arab Ba'th*, 112–13; Heydemann, *Authoritarianism*, 21, 125.
71 S. M. Dabbagh, "Agrarian Reform in Syria," *MEEP* 1, 1962: 13; R. Springborg, "Baathism in Practice: agriculture, politics, and political culture in Syria and Iraq," *MES* 17, 1981: 197; F. Metral, "State and Peasants in Syria: a local view of a government irrigation project," *Peasant Studies* 11.2, Winter 1984: 71; Sadowski, "Political Power," 41; N. Sato, "'We Are No More in Bondage, We Are Peasants': memory and the construction of identity in the Syrian Jazirah," *Journal of Mediterranean Studies* 7, 1997: 201. A similar reform began in Algeria in 1972; S. Bedrani, "Algérie: une nouvelle politique envers la paysannerie'" *RMMM* 45, 1987: 57. The amount of land distributed in Syria is contested: Dabbagh says 56 percent ("Agrarian Reform," 10); Heydemann says 40 percent (*Authoritarianism*, 163); and H. Batatu says 20 percent (*Syria's Peasantry, the Descendants of Its Lesser Rural Notables, and Their Politics*, Princeton, NJ: Princeton University Press, 1999, 75, 169). See also R. A. Hinnebusch, *Peasant and Bureaucracy in Ba'thist Syria: the political economy of rural development*, Boulder, CO: Westview Press, 1989, 222–51.
72 Hinnebusch, *Peasant*, 22; S. Bitar, "The Rise and Decline of the Baath," *MEI* July 1971: 16; I. Rabinovich, *Syria under the Ba'th, 1963–66: the army-party symbiosis*, Jerusalem: Israel Universities Press, New York: Halsted Press/John Wiley & Sons, 1972, 211; M. Aflaq, "Some Theoretical Points of Departure," introduction to the ideological report of the Sixth National Congress of the Ba'th, quoted in Rabinovitch, *Syria*, 244–5, 255.
73 R. A. Fernea, "State and Tribe in Southern Iraq: the struggle for hegemony before the 1958 revolution," in R. A. Fernea and W. R. Louis (eds) *The Iraqi Revolution of 1958: the old social classes revisited*, London: IB Tauris, 1991, 143; E. Penrose and E. F. Penrose, *Iraq: international relations and national development*, London: Ernest Benn, Boulder, CO: Westview, 1978, 152, 171; F. I. Qubain, *The Reconstruction of Iraq: 1950–1957*, New York: Frederick A. Praeger, 1958, 121; Warriner, *Land Reform*, 2, 124, 131; M. Khadduri, *Republican 'Iraq: a study in 'Iraqi politics since the Revolution of 1958*, London: Oxford University Press, 1969, 8, 154–5, 248.
74 Abd al-Karīm Qassem, speech published in *Al-Fajr al-Jadīd*, 24 February 1963, trans. H. Batatu, *The Old Social Classes and the Revolutionary Movements of Iraq: a study of Iraq's old landed and commercial classes and of its Communists, Ba'thists, and Free Officers*, Princeton, NJ: Princeton University Press, 1978, 839, see also 836; Iraq, *The Principles of the July 14 Revolution in the Speeches of the Leader*, trans. ibid., 842. See survey of Baghdad migrants (1957), quoted in Penrose and Penrose, *Iraq*, 165.
75 Penrose and Penrose, *Iraq*, 241–8; Khadduri, *Republican Iraq*, 151–2; E. Davis, *Memories of State: politics, history, and collective identity in modern Iraq*, Berkeley: University of California Press, 2005, 144.
76 Abd al-Raḥmān al-Bazzāz, press conference (23 September 1965), quoted in Khadduri, *Republican Iraq*, 256.
77 Ṭariq 'Azīz, "The July 17th, 1968, Revolution: a new kind of revolution," in *The Revolution of the New Way*, [Milan]: Arab Ba'th Socialist Party, 1977, 13–15. Gilsenan found the same connection in Lebanon between order, things being in their right relations and place (*niẓām*), and "the proper actions of those in power and of their subordinates, the appropriate practices of hierarchy"; M. Gilsenan, "*Nizam Ma Fi*: discourses of order, disorder and history in a Lebanese context," in J. P. Spagnolo (ed.) *Problems of the Modern Middle East in Historical Perspective: essays in honour of Albert Hourani*, Reading, UK: Ithaca Press, for the Middle East Centre, St. Antony's College, Oxford, 1992, 88–9.
78 "Speech of President 'Aref of Iraq at the Opening of the Palestine Liberation Office in Baghdad (Excerpts)," 1 May 1965, trans. *Arab Political Documents, 1965*, 158.
79 Stele: A. Baram, *Culture, History and Ideology in the Formation of Ba'thist Iraq, 1968–89*, New York: St. Martin's, 1991, 28; Assembly House: A. Baram, "Mesopotamian Identity in Ba'thi Iraq," *MES* 19, 1983: 431.
80 *Al-Thawra*, 20 September 1987, reproduced in Baram, *Culture*, fig. 20.
81 F. Matar, *Saddam Hussein: the man, the cause and the future*, London: Third World Centre, 1981, 256; P. Marr, "Iraq: its revolutionary experience under the Ba'th," in Chelkowski and Pranger, *Ideology and Power*, 200–1; S. al-Khalil (K. Makiya), *Republic of Fear: the inside story of Saddam's Iraq*, Berkeley: University of California Press; New York: Pantheon, 1989, 94; J. Miller and L. Mylroie, *Saddam Hussein and the Crisis in the Gulf*, New York: Times Books, Random House, 1990, 118.

82 Baram, *Culture*, 48, 50, 74; Matar, *Saddam Hussein*, 170; D. M. Reid, "The Postage Stamp: a window on Saddam Hussein's Iraq," *MEJ* 47, 1993: 79 and plate 1: 6; 84 and plate 2: 15; quotation: L. Yahia and K. Wendl, *I Was Saddam's Son*, New York: Arcade, 1997, 29.
83 Saddam Hussein, *Saddam Hussein on Current Events in Iraq*, trans. K. Kishtainy, London: Longman, 1977, viii, 52; Miller and Mylroie, *Saddam Hussein*, 117; see also M. Khadduri, *Socialist Iraq: a study in Iraqi politics since 1968*, Washington, DC: Middle East Institute, 1978, 75n39; Matar, *Saddam Hussein*, 165–7, 221; Saddam Hussein, speech of 31 July 1979, trans. *Saddam Hussein*, 170–1; quotation by Saddam Hussein: trans. Matar, 223.
84 *Kifāḥ al-sijjīh al-thawra*, Year 2, No. 30, 30 May 1954, 7, trans. Batatu, *Old Social Classes*, 697; E. Davis and N. Gavrielides, "Statecraft, Historical Memory, and Popular Culture in Iraq and Kuwait," in E. Davis and N. Gavrielides (eds) *Statecraft in the Middle East: oil, historical memory, and popular culture*, Miami: Florida International University Press, 1991, 117; G. Corm, "Systèmes de pouvoir et changements sociaux et régionaux au Machrek arabe," in J.-C. Santucci and H. El Malki (eds) *État et développement dans le monde arabe: crises et mutations au Maghreb*, Paris: CNRS, 1990, 48–54.
85 Rachid al-Ghannouchi, cited in J. M. Davis, *Between Jihad and Salaam: profiles in Islam*, New York: St. Martin's, 1997, 84.
86 The archetypal example is B. Lewis, *What Went Wrong? Western impact and Middle Eastern response*, Oxford: Oxford University Press, 2002.
87 M. LeVine, *Why They Don't Hate Us: lifting the veil on the axis of evil*, Oxford: Oneworld, 2005, 133, quoting from a 2003 World Bank report, "Overview: creating 100 million jobs for a fast-growing work force." This progress turned around after 1980 (LeVine, 134).
88 R. Mabro and P. O'Brien, "Structural Changes in the Egyptian Economy, 1937–1965," in Cook, *Studies*, 412, 425; G. A. Amin, *The Modernization of Poverty: a study in the political economy of growth in nine Arab countries, 1945–1970*, Leiden: Brill, 1974, 11; G. A. Amin, *Egypt's Economic Predicament: a study in the interaction of external pressure, political folly and social tension in Egypt, 1960–1990*, Leiden: Brill, 1995, 114; Radwan, *Agrarian Reform*, 46; El-Ghonemy, *Political Economy*, 234; T. Mitchell, "The Object of Development: America's Egypt," in J. Crush (ed.) *Power of Development*, London: Routledge, 1995, 132; A. Richards, "Economic Imperatives and Political Systems," *MEJ* 47, 1993: 223; Economic and Social Commission for Western Asia, *Arab Women in ESCWA Member States: Statistics, Indicators and Trends*, New York: United Nations, 1994, 57–61, 77–82, 148–50; R. Bush, *Economic Crisis and the Politics of Reform in Egypt*, Boulder, CO: Westview, 1999, 14; S. J. A. Shukri, *Social Changes and Women in the Middle East: state policy, education, economics and development*, Aldershot, UK: Ashgate, 1999, 47.
89 D. Brumberg, "Survival Strategies vs. Democratic Bargains: the politics of economic reform in contemporary Egypt," in H. J. Barkey (ed.) *The Politics of Economic Reform in the Middle East*, New York: St. Martin's, 1992, 74; S. Heydemann, "Taxation without Representation: authoritarianism and economic liberalization in Syria," in E. Goldberg, R. Kasaba, and J. S. Migdal (eds) *Rules and Rights in the Middle East: democracy, law, and society*, Seattle: University of Washington Press, 1993, 69–101, esp. 75; S. E. Ibrahim, "Civil Society and Prospects of Democratization in the Arab World," in S. E. Ibrahim, *Egypt, Islam and Democracy: critical essays*, 2nd ed., Cairo: American University in Cairo Press, 2002, 252. A non-historical explanation: L. Sadiki, "Popular Uprisings and Arab Democratization," *IJMES* 32, 2000: 75–80; a contrary view: J. Crystal, "Authoritarianism and Its Adversaries in the Arab World," *World Politics* 46, 1994: 280.
90 Amin, *Modernization of Poverty*, 42; amounts spent rose to 50 percent of the budget in Iraq, 90 percent in Egypt and Syria. K. H. al-Naqeeb, "Social Origins of the Authoritarian State in the Arab East," in Davis and Gavrielides, *Statecraft*, 56; El-Ghonemy, *Affluence*, 64; Ibrahim, "Civil Society," 250.
91 H. Ait Amara, "The State, Social Classes and Agricultural Policies in the Arab World," in Beblawi and Luciani, *The Rentier State*, 139; Mitchell, "Object of Development," 132; Richards, "Economic Imperatives," 226; R. Kasaba and F. Tabak, "Fatal Conjuncture: the decline and fall of the modern agrarian order during the Bretton Woods era," in P. McMichael (ed.) *Food and Agrarian Orders in the World-Economy*, Westport, CT: Greenwood, 1995, 79–93. On the "rentier state" see n39.
92 Bush, *Economic Crisis*, 64; Amin, *Egypt's Economic Predicament*, ix, 122–30. That these problems were not Middle Eastern in origin was demonstrated by the film *Bamako*, which traced their effects in Africa. The West had an ideological prejudice against state action in the economy and worked

hard to discourage it; Amin, *Egypt's Economic Predicament*, 73&n6. As late as 2001, the disastrous effects of these policies for 90 percent of the population appeared to be accidental, but it subsequently became clear that the policy and all its side effects, including malnutrition and starvation, massacres of protesters and economic migrants, and the continued reduction of political as well as human rights, were engineered by economists and their political allies. On this development, R. H. Bates, ed., *Toward a Political Economy of Development: a rational choice perspective*, Berkeley: University of California Press, 1988; D. Harvey, *A Brief History of Neoliberalism*, Oxford: Oxford University Press, 2005; and N. Klein, *The "Shock" Doctrine: the rise of disaster capitalism*, New York: Metropolitan Books, Henry Holt, 2007. On the period 1980–2004 see LeVine, *Why They Don't Hate Us*.

93 Mitchell, "Object of Development," 135; D. Weiss, "Ibn Khaldun on Economic Transformation," *IJMES* 27, 1995: 27, 35; S. J. Glain, *Mullahs, Merchants, and Militants: the economic collapse of the Arab world*, New York: St. Martin's, 2004, 15, 65, 122; LeVine, *Why They Don't Hate Us*, 134, 221. Galal Amin also noticed the historical parallel; Amin, *Egypt's Economic Predicament*, 103–4, 115–18.

94 D. Eickelman, *The Middle East and Central Asia: an anthropological approach*, third ed., Upper Saddle River, NJ: Prentice Hall, 1998, 331–4. Around 1975 the percentage of the population engaged in agriculture showed large decreases: in Egypt and Saudi Arabia it went below 50 percent at this time, in Syria below 25 percent; Economic and Social Commission for Western Asia, *Arab Women*, 269–82. See M. M. Hafez, *Why Muslims Rebel: repression and resistance in the Islamic world*, Boulder, CO: Lynne Reinner, 2003.

95 Hudson, *Arab Politics*, 396–8; R. K. Hunaidi, untitled paper, in *The Middle East: a new look*, New York: International Advisory Council Symposium, 15 June 2000, 12; Eickelman, *Middle East*, 331–4.

96 For simplicity's sake, "Islamists" refers here to all advocates of political Islam, from centrist groups working through existing political institutions to violent radicals using terror tactics. M. Y. Geyikdağı, *Political Parties in Turkey: the role of Islam*, New York: Praeger, 1984, 99; L. C. Brown, *Religion and State: the Muslim approach to politics*, New York: Columbia University Press, 2000, 125; I. M. Lapidus, "Islamic Revival and Modernity: the contemporary movements and the historical paradigms," *JESHO* 40, 1997: 445; L. T. Fawaz, *An Occasion for War: civil conflict in Lebanon and Damascus in 1860*, Berkeley: University of California Press, 1994, 5.

97 Y. Y. Haddad, *Contemporary Islam and the Challenge of History*, Albany: State University of New York Press, 1982, 33–45.

98 F. Fernández-Armesto, *Sadat and His Statecraft*, London: Kensal, 1982, 108–9; M. N. Cooper, *The Transformation of Egypt*, Baltimore, MD: The Johns Hopkins University Press, 1982, 107; R. A. Hinnebusch, "The National Progressive Unionist Party: the nationalist-left opposition in post-populist Egypt," *ASQ* 3, 1979: 326; Mitchell, "Object of Development," 132; R. Springborg, "Patrimonialism and Policy Making in Egypt: Nasser and Sadat and the tenure policy for reclaimed lands," *MES* 15, 1979: 65–6; I. Ibrahim, "Religion and Politics under Nasser and Sadat," in Stowasser, *Islamic Impulse*, 129; Saad, *Social History*, 95–110; Bush, *Economic Crisis*, 16–17.

99 Amin, *Egypt's Economic Predicament*, 115, 119; quotation from Marsot, "Religion or Opposition?" 548. According to Naomi Klein, the "trickle-down" theory of economic development, in all the instances in which it was tried, did not work, not even in the United States, where in 2005 the income of a CEO averaged 411 times that of a worker; *"Shock" Doctrine*, 214–15, 444–5.

100 Cooper, *Transformation*, 106, 107, 125; Hinnebusch, "National Progressive Unionist Party," 329; Ibrahim, "Religion and Politics," 129.

101 Cooper, *Transformation*, 236; Ansari, *Egypt*, 185–7; H. Alderman, "Food Subsidies and State Policies in Egypt," in Richards, *Food, States, and Peasants*, 191; Sadowski, *Political Vegetables?* 160; quotations from Sadiki, "Popular Uprisings," 77; Fernández-Armesto, *Sadat*, 155.

102 H. Hanafi, "The Relevance of the Islamic Alternative in Egypt," *ASQ* 4.1–2, Spring 1980: 62; Hinnebusch, *Authoritarian Power*, 202; Sadowski, *Political Vegetables?* 133; S. E. Ibrahim, "Governance and Structural Adjustment: the Egyptian case," in S. E. Ibrahim, *Egypt, Islam*, 145, 153; Amin, *Egypt's Economic Predicament*, 122, 124; Bush, *Economic Crisis*, 1, 96, 113–29; G. Abdel-Khalek, *Stabilization and Adjustment in Egypt: reform or de-industrialization?* Cheltenham, UK: Edward Elgar, 2001, 86; M. Kassem, *Egyptian Politics: the dynamics of authoritarian rule*, Boulder, CO: Lynne Reinner, 2004, 15.

103 R. R. Laremont, *Islam and the Politics of Resistance in Algeria, 1783–1992*, Trenton, NJ: Africa World Press, 2000, 163; M. Tessler, "Tunisia at the Crossroads," *Current History* 84, May 1985: 218; D. Seddon, "Politics and the Price of Bread in Tunisia," in Richards, *Food, States, and Peasants*, 215; W. D. Swearingen, "Agricultural Policies and the Growing Food Security Crisis," in J. P. Entelis and P. C. Naylor (eds) *State and Society in Algeria*, Boulder, CO: Westview, 1992, 117; R. Leveau, "Stabilité du pouvoir monarchique et financement de la dette," *Maghreb-Machrek* 118, Oct.–Dec. 1987: 10; O. Schlumberger, "Transition to Development?" in G. Joffé (ed.) *Jordan in Transition*, London: Hurst & Company, 2002, 234.

104 B. Amrani, "Catastrophe Nationale," *Jeune Afrique* no. 1794, 25–31 May 1995: 34. For Moroccan government investments see S. M. Nsouli, S. Eken, K. Enders, V.-C. Thai, J. Decressin, and F. Cartiglia, with J. Bungay, *Resilience and Growth through Sustained Adjustment: the Moroccan experience*, Occasional Paper 117, Washington, DC: International Monetary Fund, 1995, 18; D. Seddon, "Riot and Rebellion in North Africa: political responses to economic crisis in Tunisia, Morocco and Sudan," in B. Berberoglu (ed.) *Power and Stability in the Middle East*, London: Zed, 1989, 128, 132; Berberoglu, "Politics," 209–10; D. Vanderwalle, "Ben Ali's New Era: pluralism and economic privation in Tunisia," in Barkey, *Politics*, 108; Leveau, "Stabilité," 5; M. Tessler, "The Origins of Popular Support for Islamist Movements: a political economy analysis," in J. P. Entelis (ed.) *Islam, Democracy, and the State in North Africa*, Bloomington: Indiana University Press, 1997, 95–9.

105 A. Bligh, *The Political Legacy of King Hussein*, Brighton: Sussex Academic Press, 2002, 201; H. El-Said, "The Political Economy of Reform in Jordan: breaking resistance to reform?" in Joffé, *Jordan in Transition*, 262, 265; C. R. Ryan, *Jordan in Transition: from Hussein to Abdullah*, Boulder, CO: Lynne Rienner, 2002, 61–2.

106 H. Roberts, "The FLN: French conceptions, Algerian realities," in E. G. H. Joffé (ed.) *North Africa: nation, state, and region*, London: Routledge, 1993, 111; S. Mezhoud, "*Glasnost* the Algerian Way: the role of Berber nationalists in political reform," in Joffé, *North Africa*, 148; M. Stone, *The Agony of Algeria*, New York: Columbia University Press, 1997, 63–6; J. P. Entelis, "Introduction: state and society in transition," in Entelis and Naylor, *State and Society*, 1–2; E. Hermassi and D. Vanderwalle, "The Second Stage of State Building," in I. W. Zartman and W. M. Habeeb (eds) *Polity and Society in Contemporary North Africa*, Boulder, CO: Westview, 1993, 22; K. Pfeifer, "Algeria's Implicit Stabilization Program," in Barkey, *Politics*, 175.

107 J. P. Entelis, "Islam, Democracy, and the State: the reemergence of authoritarian politics in Algeria," in J. Ruedy (ed.) *Islamism and Secularism in North Africa*, New York: St. Martin's, 1994, 237; Stone, *Agony*, 63, 99; J. M. Abun-Nasr, "Militant Islam: a historical perspective," in E. Gellner (ed.) *Islamic Dilemmas: reformers, nationalists and industralization: the southern shore of the Mediterranean*, Berlin: Mouton, 1985, 88–9; S. E. Marshall, "Islamic Revival in the Maghreb: the utility of tradition for modernizing elites," *Studies in Comparative International Development* 14.2, 1979: 102; L. Anderson, *The State and Social Transformation in Tunisia and Libya, 1830–1980*, Princeton, NJ: Princeton University Press, 1986, 245; Sadiki, "Popular Uprisings," 83; Vanderwalle, "Ben Ali's New Era," 108, 117.

108 A. Drysdale, "The Asad Regime and Its Troubles," *MERIP Reports* no. 110, November/December 1982: 3; F. H. Lawson, "Social Bases for the Hamah Revolt," *MERIP Reports* no. 110, November-December 1982: 24, 27–8; U. F. Abd-Allah, *The Islamic Struggle in Syria*, Berkeley, CA: Mizan, 1983, 141–63; Rabo, "Nation-State Building," 124; quotation: "The Proclamation of the Islamic Revolution of Syria," quoted in Abd-Allah, *Islamic Struggle*, 214.

109 Lawson, "Social Bases," 24–8; Batatu, *Syria*, 269.

110 V. Perthes, *The Political Economy of Syria under Asad*, London: IB Tauris, 1995, 48; E. Zisser, *Asad's Legacy: Syria in transition*, London: Hurst, 2001, 189–90; M. Kedar, *Asad in Search of Legitimacy: message and rhetoric in the Syrian press under Ḥāfiẓ and Bashār*, Brighton, Portland: Sussex Academy Press, 2005, 231–2; W. W. Harris, "The Crisis of Democracy in Twentieth-Century Syria and Lebanon," in W. W. Harris (ed.) *Challenges to Democracy in the Middle East*, Princeton, NJ: Markus Weiner, 1997, 13; Zisser, *Asad's Legacy*, 194; H. G. Lobmeyer, "*Al-dimuqratiyya hiyya al-hall?* the Syrian opposition at the end of the Asad era," in E. Kienle (ed.) *Contemporary Syria: liberalization between cold war and cold peace*, London: British Academic Press, 1994, 81; cartoon: L. Wedeen, *Ambiguities of Domination: politics, rhetoric, and symbols in contemporary Syria*, Chicago, IL: University of Chicago Press, 1999, 115.

111 R. Springborg, "Infitah, Agrarian Transformation, and Elite Consolidation in Contemporary Iraq," *MEJ* 40, 1986: 33–4, 36–9, 48; Miller and Mylroie, *Saddam Hussein*, 118.

112 Miller and Mylroie, *Saddam Hussein*, 130–2, quotation: 130.

113 The Malian film *Bamako*: n92; Egypt: Ibrahim, "Governance and Structural Adjustment," 160; Iran: Amuzegar, *Dynamics*, 283.

114 Pfeifer, "Algeria's Implicit Stabilization," 154; A. E. Sonbol, "Egypt," in *The Politics of Islamic Revivalism: diversity and unity*, ed. S. T. Hunter, Bloomington: Indiana University Press, 1988, 25; S. E. Ibrahim, "Anatomy of Egypt's Militant Islamic Groups: methodological notes and preliminary findings," *IJMES* 12, 1980: 423–53; ibid., "Religion and Politics," 130; Geyikdağı, *Political*, 156.

115 Algeria: Laremont, *Islam*, 187; Iraq: H. Ennaïfer, "La pensée sociale dans les écrits musulmans modernes," trans. S. Ghrab, in *Foi et justice: un défi pour le christianisme et pour l'islam*, ed. J.-P. Gabus, Paris: Centurion, 1993, 183–4. Like Sayyid Quṭb, Baqir al-Sadr began to espouse the overthrow of the regime and was imprisoned and executed, leaving behind a radicalized extremist movement. Ennaïfer ("Pensée," 170) sees the problem of justice in the Arab world as inextricably linked to the fight against tyranny (foreign or home-grown), which long obscured the issue of social justice.

116 L. W. Snider, "The Lebanese Forces: their origins and role in Lebanon's politics," *MEJ* 38, 1984: 1, 18–24; H. Jaber, *Hezbollah: born with a vengeance*, New York: Columbia University Press, 1997, 147–8; F. Ajami, *The Vanished Imam: Musa al Sadr and the Shia of Lebanon*, Ithaca, NY: Cornell University Press, 1986, 136; A. R. Norton, "Shi'ism and Social Protest in Lebanon," in J. R. I. Cole and N. R. Keddie (ed.) *Shi'ism and Social Protest*, New Haven, CT: Yale University Press, 1986, 166; A. Gemayel, *Peace and Unity: major speeches 1982–1984*, Gerrards Cross: Colin Smythe, 1984, 70, 71, 144.

117 P. D. Gaffney, *The Prophet's Pulpit: Islamic preaching in contemporary Egypt*, Berkeley: University of California Press, 1994, 180; see also 128.

118 S. Abed-Kotob, "The Accommodationists Speak: goals and strategies of the Muslim Brotherhood of Egypt," *IJMES* 27, 1995: 326–7; G. Denoeux, *Urban Unrest in the Middle East: a comparative study of informal networks in Egypt, Iran, and Lebanon*, Albany: State University of New York Press, 1993, 154; D. J. Sullivan, *Private Voluntary Organizations in Egypt: Islamic development, private initiative, and state control*, Gainesville: University Press of Florida, 1994, 65; Sonbol, *New Mamluks*, 181–90; Lapidus, "Islamic Revival," 447. Many besides the Muslim Brotherhood took an active part in the debate on justice. Adel Eid: A. M. Lesch, "The Muslim Brotherhood in Egypt: reform or revolution?" in M. C. Moen and L. S. Gustafson (eds) *The Religious Challenge to the State*, Philadelphia, PA: Temple University Press, 1992, 200; Hasan Hanafi: R. Matthee, "The Egyptian Opposition on the Iranian Revolution," in Cole and Keddie, *Shi'ism*, 248. Those identifying the main problem as political dominance by the West and the Middle Eastern governments' complicity in it turned to violence as their last resort against a powerful state.

119 G. Abdo, *No God but God: Egypt and the triumph of Islam*, Oxford: Oxford University Press, 2000, 96–7; Ibrahim, "Governance," 167.

120 M. Harbi, "Un ouvrage du cheikh Abdellatif b. Ali al-Soltani: 'Le mazdakisme est à l'origine du socialisme'," *Sou'al* 5, 1985: 135–7; M. Harbi, "Chapître-Pamphlet de Abdessalam Yassine contre le roi Hassan II," *Sou'al* 5, 1985: 151–3; Munson, *Religion*, 169.

121 Rachid Ghannouchi, trans. A. S. Tamimi, *Rachid Ghannouchi: a democrat within Islamism*, Oxford: Oxford University Press, 2001, 52.

122 I. W. Zartman, "The Challenge of Democratic Alternatives in the Maghrib," in Ruedy, *Islamism and Secularism*, 215; Entelis, "Islam, Democracy," 237; Laremont, *Islam*, 181, 185, 187; H. Roberts, *The Battlefield Algeria, 1988–2002: studies in a broken polity*, London: Verso, 2003, 337–8. FIS funding came mainly from foreign sources, notably Saudi Arabia, but the violence was a response to political repression at home; Hafez, *Why Muslims Rebel*, xvi, 1–2.

123 *The Constitution of the Republic of Turkey, 1982*, Ankara: Prime Ministry Directorate General of Press and Information, 1982, 5. Roderic Davison traced this concept back to the Tanzimat proclamations; R. H. Davison, "The Turkish Constitution of 1982 as a Reflection and a Reminder of Turkish History," *Türk Kültürü Araştırmaları* 27, 1989: 75; cf. Ch. 9.

124 Anonymous, quoted in J. B. White, *Islamist Mobilization in Turkey: a study in vernacular politics*, Seattle: University of Washington Press, 2000, 129.

125 N. Erbakan, *Adil ekonomik düzen*, Ankara: Semih Ofset Matbaacılık, 1991, 5; in the Turkish state budget less money was spent on the Turkish people than on interest on the national debt. D. Shankland, "Old Ideas in New Forms: millennial movements in the Republic of Turkey," in

F. Bowie with C. Deacy (eds) *The Coming Deliverer: millennial themes in world religions*, Cardiff: University of Wales Press, 1997, 229–30; D. Shankland, *Islam and Society in Turkey*, Huntingdon, England: Eothen Press, 1999, 213; R. Boztemur, "Political Islam in Secular Turkey in 2000: change in the rhetoric towards westernization, human rights and democracy," *IJTS* 7, 2001: 129–30.

126 M. Howe, *Turkey Today: a nation divided over Islam's revival*, Boulder, CO: Westview, 2000, 27, 29; Shankland, *Islam and Society*, 105; White, *Islamist Mobilization*, 18, 54; Y. Navaro-Yashin, "Uses and Abuses of 'State and Civil Society' in Contemporary Turkey," *NPT* 18, Spring 1998: 12–13.

127 Ş. Mardin, "Some Notes on Normative Conflicts in Turkey," in P. L. Berger (ed.) *The Limits of Social Cohesion: conflict and mediation in pluralist societies*, Boulder, CO: Westview, 1998, 227; White, *Islamist Mobilization*, 11; Shankland, *Islam and Society*, 105; quotation: Y. Navaro-Yashin, *Faces of the State: secularism and public life in Turkey*, Princeton, NJ: Princeton University Press, 2002, 141.

128 Once in power, some Islamist governments succumbed to the coercive logic of the state, turning "mutual social responsibility" into enforced compliance, which made people lose faith, not in Islam, but in the state as an instrument; C. Tripp, *Islam and the Moral Economy: the challenge of capitalism*, Cambridge: Cambridge University Press, 2006, 99–102.

129 J. B. White, "The Islamist Paradox," in D. Kandiyoti and A. Saktanber (eds) *Fragments of Culture: the everyday of modern Turkey*, London: IB Tauris, 2002, 212; Mardin, "Some Notes," 230; Navaro-Yashin, *Faces*, 192. M. Özel (ed.) *Mustafa Kemal Atatürk*, Ankara: T. C. Kültür Bakanlığı, 1996, 1998, 2001, "Kütahya'da tren ıstasyonda vatandaşların dileklerinin alıp inciliyor (24 Ocak 1933)," 116; M. Taylor, personal communication.

130 Yassini, *Religion*, 126; F. Ajami, *The Arab Predicament: Arab political thought and practice since 1967*, Cambridge: Cambridge University Press, 1981, 72.

131 M. al-Rasheed, "God, the King and the Nation: political rhetoric in Saudi Arabia in the 1990s," *MEJ* 50, 1996: 362–3. M. Fandy, "CyberResistance: Saudi opposition between globalization and localization," *CSSH* 41, 1999: 134; T. Asad, "The Limits of Religious Criticism in the Middle East: notes on Islamic public argument," in T. Asad, *Genealogies of Religion: discipline and reasons of power in Christianity and Islam*, Baltimore, MD: Johns Hopkins Press, 1993, 223&n40; G. Krämer, "Good Counsel to the King: the Islamist opposition in Saudi Arabia, Jordan, and Morocco," in Kostiner, *Middle East Monarchies*, 263–4.

132 J. Teitelbaum, "Saudi Arabia," in *Middle East Contemporary Survey*, vol. 16, 1992, ed. A. Ayalon, Boulder, CO: Westview, 1995, 670–2, 690–2; J. Teitelbaum, *Holier than Thou: Saudi Arabia's Islamic opposition*, Washington, DC: Washington Institute for Near East Policy, 2000, xiii; Fandy, "CyberResistance," 140; al-Rasheed, "God," 370; L. Anderson, "Dynasts and Nationalists: why monarchies survive," in Kostiner, *Middle East Monarchies*, 59: "For what is a king without subjects?"

133 J. D. Green, *Revolution in Iran: the politics of countermobilization*, New York: Praeger, 1982, 64.

134 Cottam, *Nationalism*, 323; El-Ghonemy, *Affluence*, 51; Mehrchid, "Ali Shariati: une théologìe de la liberation?" *Soual* no. 5, April 1985: 97; A. Ashraf, "State and Agrarian Relations Before and After the Iranian Revolution, 1960–1990," in Kazemi and Waterbury, *Peasants and Politics*, 289; A.-R. Nobari, "An Exile's Dream for Iran: an interview with the Shi'ite leader Ayatollah-Khomaini," in A.-R. Nobari (ed.) *Iran Erupts: Independence: news and analysis of the Iranian national movement*, Stanford, CA: Iran–America Documentation Group, 1978, 12. In this interview Khomeini put the figure for food imports at 93 percent, but that was 93 percent of the amount that would have been required for consumption on the level of the wealthy nations; the 70-percent figure reflects Iran's actual consumption level. A.-H. Banisadr and P. Vieille, "Iran and the Multinationals," in ibid., 30; M. Kamrava, *Revolution in Iran: the roots of turmoil*, London: Routledge, 1990, 106.

135 D. Harney, *The Priest and the King: an eyewitness account of the Iranian Revolution*, London: British Academic Press, 1998, 184n27.

136 J. Āl-e Ahmad, *Plagued by the West (=Gharbzadegi)*, trans. P. Sprachman, Delmar, NY: Caravan Books, 1981; K. Farmanfarmaian, "Planning, Development and Revolution: reflections on Iran, 1958–1978," in W. G. Miller and P. H. Stoddard (eds) *Perspectives on the Middle East 1983: proceedings of a conference*, Washington, DC: Middle East Institute in cooperation with The Fletcher School of Law and Diplomacy, 1983, 77–8.

137 M. J. Fischer, *Iran: from religious dispute to revolution*, Cambridge, MA: Harvard University Press, 1980, 181; M. Hegland, "Two Images of Husain: accommodation and revolution in an Iranian village," in N. R. Keddie (ed.) *Religion and Politics in Iran: Shi'ism from quietism to revolution*, New

Haven, CT: Yale University Press, 1983, 220; S. Akhavi, "Shariati's Social Thought," in ibid., 136; Ennaïfer, "Pensée," 186; Mehrchid, "Ali Shariati," 102–7; H. Algar, "Social Justice in the Ideology and Legislation of the Islamic Revolution of Iran," in L. O. Michalak and J. W. Salacuse (eds) *Social Legislation in the Contemporary Middle East*, Berkeley: Institute of International Studies, 1986, 30; E. Abrahamian, *Radical Islam: the Iranian Mojahedin*, London: IB Tauris, 1989, 112; E. Abrahamian, "'Ali Shari'ati: ideologue of the Iranian Revolution," in Burke and Lapidus, *Islam, Politics*, 290-1; quotations: 295.

138 M. Bayat, "Mahmud Taleqani and the Iranian Revolution," in M. Kramer (ed.) *Shi'ism, Resistance, and Revolution*, Boulder, CO: Westview, 1987, 68; S. Bakhash, "Islam and Social Justice in Iran," in ibid., 96; R. Mottahedeh, *The Mantle of the Prophet: religion and politics in Iran*, New York: Pantheon, 1985, 308; Green, *Revolution*, 54; J. de Groot, *Religion, Culture and Politics in Iran: from the Qajars to Khomeini*, London: IB Tauris, 2007, 198–9.

139 R. W. Cottam, "The Iranian Revolution," in Cole and Keddie, *Shi'ism*, 61, 81; D. R. Heisey and J. D. Trebing, "Authority and Legitimacy: a rhetorical case study of the Iranian Revolution," *Communication Monographs* 53, 1986: 302–3; Harney, *Priest*, 186n3; Abrahamian, *Iran*, 532–3. The role of the United States in these events is unclear as of this writing.

140 R. Khomeini, "Islamic Government," in R. Khomeini, *Islam and Revolution: writings and declarations*, trans. H. Algar, London: KPI, 1981, 25–166; E. Abrahamian, *Khomeinism: essays of the Islamic Republic*, Berkeley: University of California Press, 1993, 10.

141 "Constitution of the Islamic Republic of Iran," *MEJ* 34, 1980: 184–204 or http://www.iranonline.com/iran/iran-info/Government/constitution.html, 3 May 2012. F. Halliday, "Theses on the Iranian Revolution," *Race & Class* 21, 1979: 87; S. Bakhash, *The Reign of the Ayatollahs: Iran and the Islamic Revolution*, New York: Basic Books, 1984, 212–15; Bakhash, "Islam and Social Justice," 96; N. R. Keddie, "Islamic Revivalism Past and Present, with emphasis on Iran," in B. M. Rosen (ed.) *Iran since the Revolution: internal dynamics, regional conflict, and the superpowers*, New York: Columbia University Press, 1985, 11–13; A. Schirazi, *Islamic Development Policy: the agrarian question in Iran*, trans. P. J. Ziess-Lawrence, Boulder, CO: Lynne Reinner, 1993, 309–11.

142 Keddie, *Roots*, 272; R. Ahmad, "Expecting Mahdi, Encountering Zarathustra: politics of representing the pre-Islamic legacy in post-Islamic Revolutionary Persian novels," paper presented at Colloquium Series, Department of Near Eastern Studies, University of Arizona, 4 December 2009. The first generation of scholars and officials who wrote after 1980 on the revolution, on the reign of the Shah, or on the Constitutional Revolution had been imbued with the ideology of the Circle of Justice and saw the history of those periods through its lens.

143 R. Loeffler, "Economic Changes in a Rural Area since 1979," in N. R. Keddie and E. Hooglund (eds) *The Iranian Revolution and the Islamic Republic*, rev. ed., Syracuse, NY: Syracuse University Press, 1986, 93; E. Ferdows, "The Reconstruction Crusade and Class Conflict in Iran," *MERIP Reports*, no. 113, Mar.–Apr. 1983: 12; M. Mujaheri, *Islamic Revolution: future path of the nations*, Tehran: The External Liaison Section of the Central Office of Jihad-e Sazandegi, 1982, 145–6; the figures in the chart do not match those in the text and the dates are not comparable. For some different statistics from other periods see Algar, "Social Justice," 39; Amjad, *Iran*, 151; Schirazi, *Islamic Development*, 159, 306–7, but see 311; M. Azkia, "Rural Society and Revolution in Iran," in E. Hooglund (ed.) *Twenty Years of Islamic Revolution: political and social transition in Iran since 1979*, Syracuse, NY: Syracuse University Press, 2002, 96–119; Ehsani, "Rural Society," 89. The Turkish state had a similar program, called Yol-Su-Elektrik, that finished in the 1990s.

144 Schirazi, *Islamic Development*, 80, 98, 296–97, 320; Algar, "Social Justice," 49, 56–7; on the labor law see Schirazi, *Islamic Development*, 186–95.

145 Bakhash, "Islam," 96, 109; Bakhash, *Reign*, 212–18; Keddie, "Islamic Revivalism," 11–13. In some places sharecropping was even revived; Schirazi, *Islamic Development*, 235; A. Rahnema and F. Nomani, *The Secular Miracle: religion, politics and economic policy in Iran*, London: Zed, 1990, 132; S. Karimi, "Economic Policies and Structure Changes since the Revolution," in Keddie and Hooglund, *Iranian Revolution*, 35; H. Afshar, "The Iranian Theocracy," in H. Afshar (ed.) *Iran: A Revolution in Turmoil*, London: Macmillan, 1985, 236–8.

146 A.-H. Banisadr, *The Fundamental Principles and Precepts of Islamic Government*, trans. M. R. Ghanoonparvar, Lexington, KY: Mazda, 1981, 98–9; Bakhash, *Reign*, 218; quotation: *Kauthar: An Anthology of the Speeches of Imam Khomeini (s.a.) Including an Account of the Events of the Islamic Revolution, 1962–1978*, vol. 2, Tehran: Institute for the Compilation and Publication of the Works of Imam Khomeini, 1995, 360.

147 S. Behdad, "The Post-Revolutionary Economic Crisis," in S. Rahnema and S. Behdad (eds) *Iran after the Revolution: crisis of an Islamic state*, London: IB Tauris, 1995, 99, 116, 122; S. Behdad, "A Disputed Utopia: Islamic economics in revolutionary Iran," *CSSH* 36, 1994: 811; Abrahamian, *Khomeinism*, 138–9; V. Moghadam, "Islamic Populism, Class, and Gender in Postrevolutionary Iran," in J. Foran (ed.) *A Century of Revolution: social movements in Iran*, Minneapolis: University of Minnesota Press, 1994, 191; H. Omid, *Islam and the Post-Revolutionary State in Iran*, New York: St. Martin's, 1994, 219. During the 1990s, many of the surviving large capitalist farms collapsed; the peasant economy of the village was replaced by the development of small to medium farmer capitalism, in which less than half the village population made its living by farming; A. I. Ajami, "From Peasant to Farmer: a study of agrarian transformation in an Iranian village, 1967–2002," *IJMES* 37, 2005: 337–41.

148 Abrahamian, *Radical Islam*, 207; Ministry quotation: Schirazi, *Islamic Development*, 272; new Circle: R. K. Ramazani, quoted in Mackey, *Iranians*, 379. The Iranian philosopher Soroush also concluded that the justice of democracy demanded a degree of prior economic justice; A. Soroush, *Reason, Freedom & Democracy in Islam*, trans. and ed. M. Sadri and A. Sadri, Oxford: Oxford University Press, 2000, 45, 147.

149 Quotations: S. Akhavi, "Introduction: Ideology and the Iranian Revolution," in *Iran since the Revolution: Internal Dynamics, Regional Conflict, and the Superpowers*, ed. B. M. Rosen, Boulder, CO: Social Science Monographs, New York: Columbia University Press, 1985, xviii; R. Loeffler, *Islam in Practice: religious beliefs in a Persian village*, Albany: State University of New York, 1988, 226, 238; see also Loeffler, *Islam*, 133, 229, 232, 233–4, 236; Bakhash, *Reign*, 248–9; Bakhash, "Islam," 96.

150 M. Gerhardt, "Sport and Civil Society in Iran," in Hooglund, *Twenty Years of Islamic Revolution*, 51–3; *Salam*: D. Menashri, "The Persian Monarchy and the Islamic Republic," in Kostiner, *Middle East Monarchies*, 226; D. Menashri, *Post-Revolutionary Politics in Iran: religion, society and power*, London: Frank Cass, 2001, 119; quotation: D. Menashri, "Persian Monarchy," 226.

151 Batebi was far from the only victim of regime embarrassment; in 1992 the Egyptian government arrested Sheikh Gaber, a young Islamist leader, and killed, wounded, or arrested over 600 of his followers, apparently on the grounds that he had succeeded in cleaning up Cairo's Western Munira slum neighborhood and bringing in social services where it had failed; S. E. Ibrahim, "The Changing Face of Egypt's Islamic Activism" (Cairo, 6 May 1995), in Ibrahim, *Egypt, Islam*, 88.

152 See A. Batebi, "Letter to the Head of the Judiciary," http://www.abfiran.org/english/document-201-392.php, accessed 3 May 2012. For the controversial photograph see http://www.economist.com/node/11707464‘source=hptextfeature&story_id=11707464, accessed 3 May 2012; see also *http://en.wikipedia.org/wiki/Batebi*, accessed 3 May 2012.

Bibliography

This bibliography contains only works mentioned in the notes. The notes usually include only original publication information, but the bibliography lists reprints of books and articles. Names of modern authors are abbreviated, but names of pre-modern authors are not. Titles in Middle Eastern languages are capitalized as in French. Titles and authors' names are alphabetized disregarding diacritical marks. They are spelled or transliterated mainly as on the publication, but in cases of disagreement they are spelled as found in US library catalogues. The particle "al-" before a name is disregarded in alphabetizing, but when it is spelled "El-" as part of the name, only the punctuation is disregarded. The word *ibn,* "son of," is not abbreviated in the text, but it is in the bibliography except when it comes at the beginning of a name.

Literary sources for the Circle of Justice and related statements

Abbas, I. (ed.) *'Ahd Ardashīr*, Beirut: Dar Sader, 1967.

al-'Abbāsī, Ḥasan b. 'Alī, *Āthār al-auwal fī tartīb al-duwal*, Beirut: Dār al-Jīl, 1989.

al-Ābī, Abū Sa'd Manṣūr b. al-Ḥusayn, *Nathr al-durr*, ed. M. 'A. Qurna, 7 vols in 8, Cairo: al-Hayā' al-Miṣriyya al-'Āmma lil-Kitāb, 1980–90.

Abū Bakr b. al-Zakī, Rukneddin, *Ravzat al-kuttāb va ḥadīḳat al-albāb*, ed. A. Sevim, Ankara: Türk Tarih Kurumu, 1972.

Abū Hammū, Mūsā b. Yūsuf, *Wāsiṭat al-sulūk fī siyāsat al-mulūk*, Tunis: Maṭba'a al-Kawla al-Tūnisiyya, 1279/1862–3.

Abū Yūsuf, *Kitāb al-kharāj*, ed. and trans. A. Ben Shemesh, *Taxation in Islam*, vol. 3, *Abū Yūsuf's Kitāb al-kharāj*, Leiden: Brill, 1969.

al-'Adawī, M. (ed.) *Kitāb alf layla wa-layla*, Bulaq: Maṭba'a 'Abd al-Raḥmān Rushdī Bey, 1862.

Aflaq, M. *Choice of Texts from the Ba'th Party Founder's Thought*, [Baghdad]: Arab Ba'th Socialist Party, 1977.

Agence France-Presse, news release, Amman, Jordan, 30 July 2001.

Ahmedī, "Dastān ve tevārīh-i Āl-i Osman," in *Osmanlı tarihleri*, ed. Ç. N. Atsız, 3–35, Istanbul: Türkiye Basımevi, 1949.

——. *İskendernâme*, trans. K. Silay, "Aḥmedī's History of the Ottoman Dynasty," *JTS* 16, 1992: 129–200.

al-Ahrī, Abū Bakr al-Quṭbī, *Ta'rīkh-i Shaikh Uwais (History of Shaikh Uwais): an important source for the history of Ādharbaijān in the fourteenth century*, trans. J. B. van Loon, 's-Gravenhage: Mouton, 1954.

Akgündüz, A. (ed.) *Osmanlı kanunnameleri ve hukukî tahlilleri*, 9 vols, Istanbul: Fey Vakfı, 1990–6.

Akhisari, see al-Āqḥiṣārī, İpşirli, and Garcin de Tassy.

Akhtar, Istanbul, vol. 11, 4 September 1895.

Aksarayı, Kerîmüddin Mahmud, *Müsāmeret ül-Ahbār: Moğollar zamanında Türkiye Selçukları tarihi*, ed. O. Turan, Ankara: Türk Tarih Kurumu, 1944; *Selçukī Devletleri Tarihi*, trans. N. Gençosman, Ankara: Recep Ulusoğlu, 1943; *Müsāmeret ül-Ahbār*, trans. M. Öztürk, Ankara: Türk Tarih Kurumu, 2000.

'Alī b. Abī Ṭālib, *Nahjul Balagha, Peak of Eloquence,* trans. S. A. Reza, Elmhurst, Tahrike Tarsile Quran, 1984; *Classified Selections from Nahj al-Balāgha,* ed. F. Ebeid, trans. A Group of Moslem Specialists, [Cairo]: Dār al-Kutub al-Islāmiyyah, 1989.

al-'Allām, 'Izz al-Dīn, *Al-Sulṭa wa-al-siyāsa fī al-adab al-sulṭānī,* Casablanca: Ifrīqiyya al-Sharq, 1991.

al-Amāsī, Ahmed b. Hüsameddin, *Mir'at ul-Muluk,* MS Süleymaniye Esad Efendi 1890.

al-Āqḥiṣārī, Ḥasan Kāfī, *Uṣūl al-Ḥikam fī Niẓām al-'Ālam,* ed. N. R. al-Hmoud, Amman: University of Jordan, 1986; *Uṣūl al-Ḥikam fī Niẓām al-'Ālam,* ed. I.Ṣ. al-'Amdu, Kuwait: Dhāt al-Silāsil, 1987.

al-A'raj, Muḥammad b. 'Abd al-Wahhāb, *Taḥrīr al-sulūk fī tadbīr al-mulūk,* ed. F. 'Abd al-Mun'im, Alexandria: Mu'assasat Shabāb al-Jāmi'ah, 1982.

American University of Beirut, *Arab Political Documents 1964,* Beirut: Political Studies and Public Administration Department of the American University of Beirut, 1964.

——. *Arab Political Documents 1965,* Beirut: Political Studies and Public Administration Department of the American University of Beirut, 1965.

Arab Ba'th Socialist Party, *A Survey of the Ba'th Party's Struggle, 1947–1974,* [S.I.]: Unity Freedom Socialism, 1978.

'Aṭṭār, Farīd al-Dīn, *Pend-Nameh, ou, Le livre des conseils,* trans. S. de Sacy, Paris: Imprimerie Royale, 1819.

'Aziz, T. "The July 17th, 1968, Revolution: a new kind of revolution," in *The Revolution of the New Way,* 9–33, [Milan]: Arab Ba'th Socialist Party, 1977.

Badawī, 'A. (ed.) *Fontes Graecae Doctrinarum Politicarum Islamicarum, Testamenta Graeca (Pseudo-)Platonis, et Secretum Secretorum (Pseudo-) Aristotelis,* Cairo: Maṭba'a Dār al-Kutub al-Miṣriyya, 1954.

Badr al-Dīn Muḥammad b. Ibrāhīm b. Jamā'a, *Taḥrīr al-aḥkām fī tadbīr ahl al-Islām,* ed. H. Kofler, "Handbuch des islamischen Staats- und Verwaltungsrechtes von Badr-al-Dīn ibn Ǧamā'ah," *Islamica* 6, 1934: 349–414; 7, 1935: 1–64; Schlussheft, 1938: 18–129.

Bal'amī, Abū 'Alī Muḥammad, *Chronique d'Abou-Djafar Mohammed ben Djarir ben Yazid Tabari, tr. sur la version persane d'Abou-Ali Mohammed Bel'ami,* trans. H. Zotenberg, 4 vols, Oriental Translation Fund Publications, 70, Paris: Imprimerie impériale, 1867–74.

Banisadr, A.-H. *The Fundamental Principles and Precepts of Islamic Government,* trans. M. R. Ghanoonparvar, Lexington, KY: Mazda, 1981.

Bar Hebraeus, *The Chronography of Gregory Abû'l Faraj,* trans. E. A. W. Budge, 2 vols, London: Oxford University Press, 1932.

Batebi, A. "Letter to the Head of the Judiciary," *http://www.abfiran.org/english/document-201-392.php,* accessed 26 July 2007.

Beldiceanu, N. (ed.) *Code des lois coutumières de Meḥmed II: Kitāb-i qavānīn-i 'örfiyye-i 'osmānī,* Wiesbaden: Harrassowitz, 1967.

Bell, H. I. "Translations of the Greek Aphrodito Papyri in the British Museum," *Der Islam* 2, 1911: 269–83, 372–84; 3, 1912: 133–40, 369–73; 4, 1913: 87–96.

Bielawski, J. (trans.) *Lettre d'Aristote à Alexandre sur la politique envers les cités,* Wroclaw: Polskiej Akademii Nauk, 1970.

Binder, L. (trans.) "The Constitution of the Arab Resurrection Socialist Party," *MEJ* 13, 1959: 195–200, repr. in S. A. Hanna and G. H. Gardner, *Arab Socialism: A Documentary Survey,* 305–12, Salt Lake City: University of Utah Press, 1969.

Birnbaum, E. *The Book of Advice by King Kay Kā'us ibn Iskander: the earliest Old Ottoman Turkish version of his Ḳābūsnāme,* Sources on Oriental Languages and Literatures, 6, Cambridge, MA: Harvard University Printing Office, 1981.

Björkman, W. "Die Bittschriften im *dīwān al-inšā,*" *Der Islam* 18, 1929: 207–12.

Bosworth, C. E. "An Early Arabic Mirror for Princes: Ṭāhir Dhū'l-Yamīnain's epistle to his son 'Abdallāh (206/821)," *JNES* 29, 1970: 25–41.

Boyce, M. (trans.) *The Letter of Tansar,* Rome: Istituto Italiano per il Medio ed Estremo Oriente, 1968.

Boyle, J. A. "The Longer Introduction to the *Zīj-i Ilkhānī* of Naṣīr ad-Dīn Ṭūsī," *JSS* 8, 1963: 244–54.

Budge, E. A. W. (trans.) *The Alexander Book in Ethiopia,* London: Oxford University Press, 1933.

Bühler, C. F. (ed.) *The Dicts and Sayings of the Philosophers: the translations made by Stephen Scrope, William Worcester and an anonymous translator,* London: Oxford University Press, 1941.

Cahen, C. "Abū 'Amr 'Uthmān b. Ibrāhīm al-Nābulusī, *Kitāb luma' al-qawānīn al-muḍiyya fī dawāwīn al-diyār al-Miṣriyya*," *BEO* 16, 1958–60: 119–34.

Celalzade Mustafa, *Mevāhibü'l-hallāk fī merātibü'l-ahlak*, MS Süleymaniye Bağdatlı Vehbi 763.

Chittick, W. C. (ed. and trans.) *A Shi'ite Anthology*, London: Muhammadi Trust, 1980.

Chittick, W. C. "Two Seventeenth-Century Persian Tracts on Kingship and Rulers," in S. A. Arjomand (ed.) *Authority and Political Culture in Shi'ism*, 267–304, Albany: State University of New York Press, 1988.

Cleaves, F. W. (ed. and trans.) *The Secret History of the Mongols: for the first time done into English out of the original tongue and provided with an exegetical commentary*, Cambridge, MA: Harvard University Press, 1982.

Clinton, J. W. *The Divan of Manūchihrī Dāmghānī: a critical study*, Minneapolis: Bibliotheca Islamica, 1972.

Clinton, J. W. "The *Madāen Qasida* of Xāqānī Sharvāni, I," *Edebiyat* 1, 1976: 153–70.

Clouston, W. A. (ed.) *Arabian Poetry for English Readers*, trans. J. D. Carlyle, Glasgow: M'Laren and Son, 1881.

Colombe, M. "Une letter d'un prince égyptien du XIXe siècle au sultan ottoman Abd al-Aziz," *Orient* 2, 1958: 23–38.

Cooper, J. S. *Presargonic Inscriptions*, Sumerian and Akkadian Royal Inscriptions, 1, New Haven, CT: American Oriental Society, 1986.

Cowen, J. S. *Kalila wa Dimna: an animal allegory of the Mongol court*, New York, Oxford: Oxford University Press, 1989.

al-Damanhūrī, Aḥmad b. 'Abd al-Mun'im, *Al-Naf' al-ghazīr fī salāḥ al-sulṭān wa-al-wazīr*, Alexandria: Mu'assasat Shabāb al-Jāmi'a, 1992.

Davānī, Jalāl al-Dīn Muḥammad b. Asad, *Akhlāq-i Jalālī*, Lucknow: Matba'-i Munshī Naval Kishūr, 1866; *Practical Philosophy of the Muhammadan People,* trans. W. F. Thompson, London: Oriental Translation Fund, 1839; *The English Translation of "The Akhlak-i-Jalali", a code of morality in Persian*, trans. S. H. Deen, Lahore: Sheikh Mubarak Ali, 1939.

Dawlatshāh Samarqandī, "Tadhkirat al-shu'arā," in W. M. Thackston (trans.) *A Century of Princes: sources on Timurid history and art*, 11–62, Cambridge: Aga Khan Program for Islamic Architecture, 1989.

de Ménasce, J. P. (trans.) *Le troisième livre du Denkart*, Paris: C. Klincksieck, 1973.

de Montchrétien, A. *Traicté de l'œconomie politique*, Paris: Librairie Plon, 1889.

Dickson, M. B. and Welch, S. C. (eds) *The Houghton Shahnameh*, Cambridge, MA: Harvard University Press, 1981.

al-Dīnawarī, Abū Ḥanīfa, *Kitāb al-akhbār al-ṭiwāl*, ed. V. Guirgass, Leiden: Brill, 1888.

Douglas, W. O. *Strange Lands and Friendly People*, New York: Harper & Brothers, 1951.

Edzard, D. O. *Gudea and His Dynasty*, Royal Inscriptions of Mesopotamia, Early Periods, 3/1, Toronto: University of Toronto Press, 1997.

Eilers, W. "Le texte cunéiforme du Cylindre de Cyrus," *Commémoration Cyrus, Hommage universel: actes du congrès de Shiraz 1971*, AcIr 1–3, ser. 1, vols 1–3, 2: 25–34, Leiden: Brill, 1974.

Erbakan, N. *Adil ekonomik düzen*, Ankara: Semih, 1991.

Eyyubî Efendi, *Eyyubî Efendi Kanûnnâmesi: tahlil ve metin*, ed. A. Özcan, Istanbul: Eren, 1994.

Faḍlullāh b. Rūzbihān Khunjī Isfahānī, *Persia in A.D. 1478–1490: an abridged translation of Tārīkh-i 'Ālam-Ārā-yi Amīnī*, trans. V. Minorsky, London: Royal Asiatic Society, 1957.

——. *Muslim Conduct of State, based upon the Sulūk-ul-mulūk*, trans. M. Aslam, Lahore: University of Islamabad Press, 1974.

Finkelstein, J. J. "Ammisaduqa's Edict and the Babylonian 'Law Codes'," *JCS* 15, 1961: 91–104.

——. "Some New *Misharum* Material and Its Implications," *Studies in Honor of Benno Landsberger on His Seventy-Fifth Birthday*, Oriental Institute Assyriological Studies, 16, 233–46, Chicago, IL: University of Chicago Press, 1965.

——. "The Edict of Ammisaduqa, a New Text," *RA* 63, 1969: 45–64.

Firdausi, *The Shahnama of Firdausi*, trans. A. G. Warner and E. Warner, 9 vols, London: Kegan Paul, Trench, Trübner, 1905–25.

Frame, G. *Rulers of Babylonia: from the second dynasty of Isin to the end of Assyrian domination (1157–612 BC)*, Royal Inscriptions of Mesopotamia, Babylonian Periods, 2, Toronto: University of Toronto Press, 1995.

Frantz-Murphy, G. "A Comparison of the Arabic and Earlier Egyptian Contract Formularies, Part II: terminology in the Arabic warranty and the idiom of clearing/cleaning," *JNES* 44, 1985: 99–114.

——. *The Agrarian Administration of Egypt from the Arabs to the Ottomans*, Supplément aux Annales Islamologiques, 9, Cairo: Institut Français d'Archéologie Orientale, 1986.

Frayne, D. R. (ed.) *Old Babylonian Period (2003–1595 BC)*, Royal Inscriptions of Mesopotamia, Early Periods, 4, Toronto: University of Toronto Press, 1990.

——. (ed.) *Sargonic and Gutian Periods (2334–2113 BC)*, Royal Inscriptions of Mesopotamia, Early Periods, 2, Toronto: University of Toronto Press, 1993.

——. (ed.) *Ur III Period (2112–2004 BC)*, Royal Inscriptions of Mesopotamia, Early Periods, 3/2, Toronto: University of Toronto Pres, 1997.

——. (ed.) *Presargonic Period (2700–2350 BC)*, Royal Inscriptions of Mesopotamia, Early Periods, 1, Toronto: University of Toronto Press, 2008.

Garcin de Tassy, M. "Principes de sagesse, touchant l'art de gouverner," *JA* 4, 1824: 213–26, 283–90.

Gaster, M. "The Hebrew Version of the 'Secretum Secretorum,' with an introduction and an English translation," *JRAS* 1907: 879–912; 1908: 111–162, 1065–1084.

Gelb, I. J. and Kienast, B. *Die Altakkadischen Königsinschriften des dritten Jahrtausends vor Chr.*, Freiburger Altorientalische Studien, 7, Stuttgart: Franz Steiner, 1990.

al-Ghazālī, Abū Ḥāmid Muḥammad, *Critère de l'action (Mīzān al-a'mal)*, trans. H. Hachem, Paris: G.-P. Maisonneuve, 1945.

——. *Naṣīḥat al-mulūk*, ed. J. Humā'ī, Tehran: Babak, 1361/1982; *Ghazālī's Book of Counsel for Kings (Naṣīḥat al-Mulūk)*, trans. F. R. C. Bagley, London: Oxford University Press, 1964, repr. 1971.

——. *Al-Tibr al-masbūk fi naṣīḥat al-mulūk*, ed. Sāmī Khiḍr, [Cairo]: Maktabat al-Kullīyāt al-Azhariyya; Beirut: Dār Ibn Zaydūn, 1987.

al-Ghazzālī, M. *Min huna na'mal,* trans. I. R. al-Faruqi as *Our Beginning in Wisdom*, Washington, DC: American Council of Learned Societies, 1953.

Ghiyathuddin Naqqash, "Report to Mirza Baysunghur on the Timurid Legation to the Ming Court at Peking," in W. M. Thackston (trans.) *A Century of Princes: sources on Timurid history and art*, 279–97, Cambridge: Aga Khan Program for Islamic Architecture, 1989.

Giese, F. (ed. and trans.) *Die altosmanischen anonymen Chroniken = [Tevarih-i Al-i 'Osman]: in Text und Übersetzung,* pt. 2, *Übersetzung*, Abhandlung für die Kunde des Morgenlandes 17, no. 1, 2–170, Leipzig: F. A. Brockhaus, 1925; repr. Nendeln: Kraus Reprint, 1966.

Grayson, A. K. *Assyrian Royal Inscriptions*, 2 vols, Records of the Ancient Near East, 1 and 2, Wiesbaden: Harrassowitz, 1972–6.

——. *Assyrian Rulers of the Third and Second Millennia BC (to 1115 BC)*, The Royal Inscriptions of Mesopotamia, Assyrian Periods, 1, Toronto: University of Toronto Press, 1987.

——. *Assyrian Rulers of the Early First Millennium BC, I (1114–859 BC)*, Royal Inscriptions of Mesopotamia, Assyrian Periods, 2, Toronto: University of Toronto Press, 1991.

——. *Assyrian Rulers of the Early First Millennium BC, II (858–745 BC)*, Royal Inscriptions of Mesopotamia, Assyrian Periods, 3, Toronto: University of Toronto Press, 1996.

Green, A. H., Gamal, A. S. and Mortel, R. "A Tunisian Reply to a Wahhabi Proclamation: texts and contexts," in A. H. Green (ed.) *In Quest of an Islamic Humanism: Arabic and Islamic studies in memory of Mohamed al-Nowaihi*, 155–77, Cairo: The American University in Cairo Press, 1984.

Grignaschi, M. "Les 'Rasā'il 'Āristāṭālīsa 'ilā-l-Iskandar' de Sālim Abū-l-'Alā' et l'activité culturelle à l'époque omayyade," *BEO* 19, 1965–6: 7–83.

——. "Quelques spécimens de la littérature sassanide conservés dans les bibliothèques d'Istanbul," *JA* 254, 1966: 1–142.

——. "La 'Siyâsatu-l-Âmmiyya' et l'influence iranienne sur la pensée politique islamique," *Monumentum H. S. Nyberg*, AcIr 4–7, ser. 2, vols 1–4, 3: 33–287, Leiden: Brill, 1975.

——. "L'Origine et les métamorphoses du 'Sirr al-'asrār' *(Secretum Secretorum)*," *Archives d'histoire doctrinale et littéraire du moyen age* 43, 1976: 7–112.

Grohmann, A. *Arabic Papyri in the Egyptian Library*, 6 vols, Cairo: Egyptian Library Press, 1934–62.

Gurney, O. R. "The Sultantepe Tablets (continued): IV. the Cuthaean legend of Naram-Sin," *Anatolian Studies* 5, 1955: 93–113.

Hâfiẓ-i Abrû, *Chronique des Rois Mongols en Iran*, ed. and trans. K. Bayani, 2 vols, Paris: Adrien-Maisonneuve, 1936.

Hammer, M. J. de, *Contes inédits des Mille et Une Nuits*, trans. M. G.-S. Trébutien, Paris: Dondey-Dupré Père et Fils, 1828.

al-Harawī, *Al-tadhkira al-harawiyya fi al-hiyal al-ḥarbiyya*, ed. and trans. J. Sourdel-Thomine, "Les conseils du Šayḫ al-Harawī à un prince ayyūbide," *BEO* 17, 1961–62: 205–66.

Ḥasan-e Fasā'ī, *History of Persia under Qājār Rule: translated from the Persian of Ḥasan-e Fasā'i's* Fārsnāma-ye Nāṣerī, trans. H. Busse, New York: Columbia University Press, 1972.

Hassan II, *Le Maroc en Marche: discours de Sa Majeste Hassan II depuis son avenement au trone*, Mohammedia, Morocco: Offset de Fedala, 1965/6.

——. *The Challenge: the memoirs of King Hassan II of Morocco*, trans. A. Rhodes, London: Macmillan, 1978.

——. *La mémoire d'un roi: entretiens avec Eric Laurent*, Paris: Plon, 1993.

Heyd, U. *Ottoman Documents on Palestine, 1552–1615: a study of the firman according to the mühimme defteri*, Oxford: Clarendon, 1960.

Hilāl al-Ṣābi', *The Historical Remains of Hilal al-Sâbi', first part of his Kitab al-Wuzara (Gotha Ms. 1756) and fragment of his History 389–393 (BMMs. Add. 19360)*, ed. and trans. H. F. Amédroz, Beirut: Maṭba'a al-Aba' al-Yesu'iyīn, 1904.

——. *Rusūm Dār al-Khilāfah: the rules and regulations of the 'Abbāsid court*, trans. E. A. Salem, Beirut: American University of Beirut, 1977.

Hinz, W. "Steuerinschriften aus dem Mittelalterlichen vorderen Orient," *Belleten* 13, 1949: 745–69.

Ḥiyari, M. "Qudāma b. Ǧa'fars Behandlung der Politik: Das Kapitel *As-siyāsa* aus seinem Vademecum für Sekretäre *Kitāb al-ḫarāǧ wa-ṣanā'at al-kitāba*," *Der Islam* 60, 1983: 91–103.

Howorth, H. H. *History of the Mongols, from the 9th to the 19th Century*, 4 vols, London: Longmans, Green, and CO., OR Green, 1876–1927.

Humback, H. and Skjaervø, P. O. *The Sassanian Inscription of Paikuli*, 3 vols, Wiesbaden: Ludwig Reichert, 1983.

Hurewitz, J. C. *Diplomacy in the Near and Middle East: a documentary record*, 2 vols, Princeton, NJ: D. Van Nostrand, 1956.

Hurowitz, V. A. "Advice to a Prince: a message from Ea," *State Archives of Assyria Bulletin* 12, 1998: 39–53.

Hussein, King of Jordan, *Uneasy Lies the Head*, New York: Bernard Geis Associates, 1962.

Hussein, S. *Saddam Hussein on Current Events in Iraq*, trans. K. Kishtainy, London: Longman, 1977.

Ibn 'Abd al-Barr al-Namarī, *Bahjat al-majālis wa-uns al-mujālis*, ed. M. M. al-Khawlī, 2 vols, Cairo: Dār al-Kutub al-'Arabī lil-Ṭabā'a wa-al-Nashr, 1967.

Ibn 'Abd Rabbih al-Andalusī, *Al-'Iqd al-farīd*, 4 vols, Cairo: al-Maṭba'a al-Azhariyya, 1928; *The Unique Necklace*, trans. I. J. Boullata, vol. 1, Reading, UK: Garnet, 2006.

Ibn Abi Diyaf, Ahmad, *Consult Them in the Matter: a nineteenth-century Islamic argument for constitutional government*, trans. L. C. Brown, Fayetteville: University of Arkansas Press, 2005.

Ibn Abī Usaybi'a, *'Uyūn al-anbā' fī ṭabaqāt al-aṭibbā'*, ed. N. Riḍā, Beirut: Dār Maktabat al-Ḥayāh, 1980.

Ibn al-'Arabī, Muhyī al-Dīn, *Les illuminations de La Mecque = The Meccan Illuminations: textes choisis = selected texts*, trans. M. Chodkiewicz, Paris: Sindbad, 1988.

Ibn al-Athīr, 'Izz al-Dīn, *The Annals of the Saljuq Turks: Selections from* al-Kāmil fī'l-Tārīkh *of 'Izz al-Dīn Ibn al-Athīr*, trans. D. S. Richards, London: Routledge/Curzon, 2002.

Ibn al-Azraq, Abū 'Abd Allāh Muḥammad b. 'Alī, *Badā'i' al-silk fī Ṭabā'i' al-milk*, ed. 'A. S. al-Nashshār, 2 vols, Baghdad: Wizārat al-I'lām, 1977–8.

Ibn al-Balkhī, *The Fārsnāma of Ibnu'l-Balkhī*, ed. G. Le Strange and R. A. Nicholson, E. J. W. Gibb Memorial Series, n.s. 1, London: Luzac, 1921, repr. 1962.

Ibn al-Muqaffa', 'Abdallāh, Al-adab *al-kabīr*, in M. Kurd Ali (ed.) *Rasā'il al-bulaghā'*, 55–114, Cairo: Dār al-Kutub al-'Arabīyya al-Kubrá, 1913.

Ibn Ḥibbān al-Bustī, Muḥammad, *Rawḍat al-'uqalā' wa nuzhat al-fuḍalā'*, ed. M. M. 'Abd al-Ḥamīd, Beirut: Dār al-Kutub al-'Ilmiyya, 1975.

Ibn Iyās, Muḥammad b. Aḥmad, *An Account of the Ottoman Conquest of Egypt in the Year A.H. 922 (A.D. 1516)*, trans. W. H. Salmon, London: Royal Asiatic Society, 1921; repr. Westport, CT: Hyperion, 1981.

Ibn Juljul al-Andalūsī, Sulaymān b. Ḥassān, *Les Générations des médecins et des sages (Ṭabaqāt al-'aṭibbā' wal-ḥukamā')*, ed. F. Sayyid, Cairo: Imprimerie de l'Institut français d'archéologie orientale, 1955.

Ibn Khaldūn, 'Abd al-Rahmān, *Kitāb al-'ibār*, 8 vols, Cairo: al-Maṭba'a al-Miṣriyya bi-Bulāq, 1867.

——. *The Muqaddimah: An Introduction to History*, trans. F. Rosenthal, 3 vols, Bollingen Series 43, New York: Pantheon, 1958; abridged by N. J. Dawood, Princeton, NJ: Princeton University Press, 1967.

——. *Le Voyage d'Occident et d'Orient*, trans. A. Cheddadi, Paris: Sindbad, 1980.

Ibn Qutayba Abdallāh b. Muslim, *Kitāb 'uyūn al-akhbār*, 10 pts. in 4 vols, Cairo: Dār al-Kutub al-Mieqrī yya, 1925–30; J. Horovitz (trans.) "Ibn Quteiba's 'Uyun al-Akhbar," *IC* 4, 1930: 171–98, 331–62, 487–540; 5, 1931: 1–27, 194–224.

Ibn Raḍwān al-Māliqī, Abū al-Qāsim, *Al-shuhub al-lāmi'a fi al-siyāsa al-nāfi'a*, ed. 'A. S. al-Nashshār, Casablanca: Dār al-Thaqāfa, 1984.

Ibn Shaddād, Bahā al-Dīn, *The Life of Saladin, by Behâ ed-Dîn*, trans. C. W. Wilson and Lieutenant-Colonel Conder, London: Palestine Exploration Fund, 1897; repr. as *Saladin, or, What Befell Sultan Yûsuf*, Lahore: Islamic Book Service 1976.

Ibn Taimiyya, Taqī al-Dīn, *Ibn Taimiyya on Public and Private Law in Islam*, trans. O. A. Farrukh, Beirut: Khayats, 1966.

al-Ibshīhī, Shihāb al-Dīn Muḥammad, *Al-Mustaṭraf fī kull fann mustaẓraf*, 2 vols, Beirut: Dār al-Kutub al-'Ilmiyya, 1983.

İnalcık, H. "Adâletnâmeler," *Belgeler* 2, nos. 3–4, 1965: 49–145 and plates.

İpşirli, M. "Hasan Kâfi el-Akhisarî ve Devlet Düzenine ait Eseri *Usûlü'l-Hikem fî Nizâmi'l-Âlem*," *TED* 10–11, 1979–80: 239–78.

al-Jabartī, 'Abd al-Raḥmān, *'Abd al-Raḥmān al-Jabartī's History of Egypt: 'ajā'ib al-āthār fī'l-tarājim wa'l-akhbār*, ed. T. Philipp and M. Perlmann, trans. D. Crecelius, B. 'Abd al-Malik, C. Wendell, M. Fishbein, T. Philipp and M. Perlmann, 5 vols in 3, Stuttgart: Franz Steiner, 1994.

Jacobsen, T. *The Harps that Once …: Sumerian poetry in translation*, New Haven, CT: Yale University Press, 1987.

Juvaini [Juvaynī], 'Ala al-Din 'Ata-Malik, *The History of the World-Conqueror*, trans. J. A. Boyle, 2 vols, Cambridge, MA: Harvard University Press, 1958; repr. as *Genghis Khan: the history of the World-Conqueror*, 1 vol., introduction and bibliography by D. O. Morgan, Manchester: Manchester University Press, and Seattle: University of Washington Press, 1997.

Kai Kā'ūs b. Iskandar, *A Mirror for Princes: the Qābūs Nāma*, trans. R. Levy, New York: E. P. Dutton, 1951.

Kāshifī, Ḥusayn Vā'iz, *Akhlāḳ-i Muḥsinī*, Lucknow: Matbaa-yi Tij Kumar, 1957; trans. H. G. Keene (trans.) *Akhlāḳ-i Muḥsinī, or, the morals of the Beneficent*, Hertford: Stephen Austin, 1850; repr. London: W. H. Allen, 1867.

Kâtip Çelebi, Haci Halife, *Düstûru'l-amel li-ıslahi'l-halel*, in Ayn-i Ali Efendi, *Kavânîn-i Âl-i Osman der hülâsa-i mezâmin-i defter-i dîvân*, ed. M. T. Gökbilgin, 119–40, Istanbul: Enderun, 1979; *Bozuklukların düzeltilmesinde tutulacak yollar (düstûru'l-amel li-ıslahi'l-halel)*, trans. A. Can, Ankara: Kültür ve Turizm Bakanlığı, 1982.

Keith-Falconer, G. N. trans. *Kalilah and Dimnah, or, the fables of Bidpai*, Cambridge, 1985; repr. Amsterdam: Philo, 1970.

Kemal, Namık, "Wa-shāwirhum fī 'l-'amr," *Hürriyet*, 20 July 1868: 1.

Kemp, P. "Mosuli Sketches of Ottoman History," *MES* 17, 1981: 310–33.

Kenny, L. M. "Al-Afghani on Types of Despotic Government," *JAOS* 86, 1966: 19–27.

Kent, R. G. *Old Persian: grammar, texts, lexicon*, 2nd ed. New Haven, CT: American Oriental Society, 1953.

Khālid, K. M. *Min huna nabda'*, trans. I. R. al-Faruqi, as *From Here We Start*, Washington, DC: American Council of Learned Societies, 1953.

Khayr al-Dīn al-Tūnisī, *Aqwām al-Masālik fi Ma'rifat Aḥwāl al-Mamālik* (1868), Tunis: Bayt al-Ḥikma, 2000; French trans. *Réformes nécessaires aux états musulmans*, Paris: Imprimerie Administrative de Paul Dupont, 1868; *Essai sur les réformes nécessaires aux états musulmans*, ed. M. Morsy, Paris: Édisud, 1987; introduction trans. L. C. Brown as *The Surest Path: The Political Treatise of a Nineteenth-Century Muslim Statesman*, Cambridge, MA: Center for Middle Eastern Studies of Harvard University, 1967.

Khoury, R. G. *Chrestomathie de papyrologie arabe: Documents relatifs à la vie privée, sociale et administrative dans les premiers siècles islamiques, préparée par Adolf Grohmann*, Leiden: Brill, 1993.

Khūrī, R. *Modern Arab Thought: channels of the French Revolution to the Arab East*, trans. I. 'Abbas, rev. and ed. C. Issawi, Princeton, NJ: Kingston Press, 1983.

al-Khwarizmi, Muḥammad b. al-'Abbās (Jamāl al-Dīn Abī Bakr), *Kitāb mufīd al-'ulūm wa-mubīd al-humūm*, ed. 'A. al-Ansarī, Sayda: Manshūrāt al-Maktaba al-Fikriyya, 1980.

Kınalızade 'Ali Çelebi, *Ahlāk-i 'Alā'ī*, Bulāq: Matba'at Bulāq, 1228/1832–3.

Kirmānī, Mīrzā Muḥammad Nāẓim al-Islām, *Tārīkh-i Bīdārī-yi Īrāniyān*, 2 vols, Tehran: Intishārāt-i Bunyād-i Farhang-i Īrān, 1967.

Klein, J. *Three Šulgi Hymns: Sumerian royal hymns glorifying King Šulgi of Ur*, Ramat-Gan, Israel: Bar-Ilan University Press, 1981.

Koçi Bey, *Koçi Bey Risalesi*, ed. A. K. Aksüt, Istanbul: Vakıt, 1939; ed. Y. Kurt, Ankara: Ecdad, 1994.

Kütükoğlu, M. S. "Lütfi Paşa Âsafnâmesi (Yeni Bir Metin Tesisi Denemesi)," in *Prof. Dr. Bekir Kütükoğlu'na Armağan*, 49–99, Istanbul: Edebiyat Fakültesi, 1991.

Lambert, W. G. (ed.) *Babylonian Wisdom Literature*, Oxford: Clarendon, 1960.

Luckenbill, D. D. *Ancient Records of Assyria and Babylonia*, 2 vols, Chicago, IL: University of Chicago Press, 1926–7.

Lüṭfi Pâshâ, *Das Aṣafnâme des Luṭfî Pascha*, ed. R. Tschudi, Leipzig: W. Drugulin, 1910; A. Uğur (trans.) *Asafnâme*, Ankara: T. C. Kültür ve Turizm Bakanlığı, 1982.

McNeill, W. H. and Waldman, M. R. (eds) *The Islamic World*, London: Oxford University Press, 1973, 113–17.

Madan, D. M. (ed.) *The Complete Text of the Pahlavi Dinkard*, Bombay: Society for the Promotion of Researches into the Zoroastrian Religion, 1911.

al-Makīn, Jirjis, *Universal History*, trans. Sir E. A. W. Budge, as *The Alexander Book in Ethiopia*, London: Oxford University Press, 1933.

Malcolm, J. *The History of Persia, from the most early period to the present time*, 2 vols, London: John Murray and Longman, 1815.

Manzalaoui, M. A. (ed.) *Secretum Secretorum: nine English versions*, Oxford: Early English Text Society, 1977.

Margoliouth, D. S. "Omar's Instructions to the Kadi," *JRAS* 1910: 307–26.

Martinez, A. P. "The Third Portion of the History of Ğāzān Xān in Rašīdu'd-Dīn's *Ta'rīx-e Mobārak-e Ğāzānī*," *AEuras* 6, 1986: 41–128; 8, 1992–4: 99–206.

Masroori, C. "Mirza Ya'qub Khan's Call for Representative Government, Toleration and Islamic Reform in Nineteenth-Century Iran," *MES* 37.1, 2001: 89–100.

Massé, H. "Ibn el-Çaïrafi, code de la chancellerie d'état (Période fâtimide)," *Bulletin de l'Institut français d'archéologie orientale* 11, 1914: 65–120.

al-Mas'ūdī, Abū al-Ḥasan 'Alī b. al-Ḥusayn, *Murūj al-dhahab wa-ma'ādin al-jawhar*, ed. B. de Maynard and P. de Courteille, rev. and corr. C. Pellat, 7 vols, Beirut: al-Jāmi'a al-Lubnānīyya, 1965–79; *Les Prairies d'or*, trans. B. de Maynard and P. de Courteille, rev. and corr. C. Pellat, 5 vols, Paris: Société asiatique, 1962; *The Meadows of Gold: the Abbasids*, trans. and ed. P. Lunde and C. Stone London: Kegan Paul International, 1989.

——. *Kitāb al-tanbīh wa-al-ishrāf*, trans. B. Carra de Vaux as *Le livre de l'avertissement et de la revision*, Paris: Imprimerie nationale, 1896.

Maududi, A. A. *Come Let Us Change This World*, trans. K. Siddique, Karachi: Salma Siddique, 1971.

al-Māwardī, Abū al-Ḥasan ʻAlī b. Muḥammad, *al-Aḥkām al-Sulṭānīyya, The Ordinances of Government*, trans. W. H. Wahba Reading, UK: Garnet, 1996; *Les statuts governementaux, ou Règles de droit public et administratif*, trans. E. Fagnan Algiers: Librairie de l'Université, 1915.

——. *Durar al-sulūk fī siyāsat al-mulūk*, ed. F. A. Ahmad, Riyadh: Dār al-Waṭan lil-Nashr, 1997.

——. *Qawānīn al-wizāra wa-siyāsat al-mulk*, ed. F. ʻA. Aḥmad and M. S. Dāwūd, 3rd ed., Alexandria: Mu'assasat Shabāb al-Jāmiʻa, 1991.

——. *Tashīl al-naẓar wa-taʻjīl al-Ẓafar fī akhlāq al-malik wa-siyāsat al-mulk*, ed. R. al-Sayyid, Beirut: Dār al-Ulūm al-ʻArabiyya lil-Ṭabāʻa wa-al-Nashr, 1987.

——. *al-Tuḥfa al-mulukiyya fī al-Ādāb al-siyāsiyya*, Alexandria: Mu'assasat Shabāb al-Jāmiʻa, 1977.

Mehmed Nüsret Paşa, "Muqaddima," in Shihāb al-Dīn Aḥmad b. Muḥammad b. Abī al-Rabīʻ, *Nüsret el-Ḥamîd ʻala siyâset el-ʻabîd tercüme-i Sulûk el-mâlik fî tedbir el-memâlik*, trans. Mehmed Nüsret Paşa, Istanbul: Matbaa-yi Âmire, 1296/1878–9.

Meisami, J. S. (trans.) *The Sea of Precious Virtues (Baḥr al-Favā'id): a medieval Islamic mirror for princes*, Salt Lake City: University of Utah Press, 1991.

Minorsky, V. (trans) *Tadhkirat al-Mulūk: a manual of Ṣafavid administration*, Cambridge, UK: E. J. W. Gibb Memorial Trust, 1943; repr. 1980.

Minovi, M. and Minorsky, V. "Naṣīr al-Dīn Ṭūsī on Finance," *BSOAS* 10, 1940–2: 755–89.

Mīr Khvānd, Muhammad b. Khāvandshah, *Tārīkh ravzat al-safā*, 10 vols, Tehran: Markaz-i Khayyām Pī rūz, 1959–60; part 1, vol. 2, *The Rauzat-us-safa, or, Garden of Purity*, trans. E. Rehatsek, E. J. W. Gibb Memorial Series, London: Royal Asiatic Society, 1891; repr. Delhi: Idara-yi Adabiyat-i Delli, 1900.

al-Mubashshir b. Fātik, Abū al-Wafā', *Los Bocados de Oro (Mujtar al-Ḥikam)*, ed. ʻA. Badawī, Beirut: Arab Institute for Research and Publishing, 1980.

Muṣṭafā ʻĀlī, *Muṣṭafā ʻĀlī's Description of Cairo of 1599: text, transliteration, translation, notes*, [*Ḥālāt'ül-kāhire*], ed. and trans. A. Tietze Philosophisch-Historische Klasse, 120, Vienna: Österreichischen Akademie der Wissenschaften, 1975.

——. *Muṣṭafā ʻĀlī's Counsel for Sultans of 1581: edition, translation, notes*, [*Nusḥat al-salaṭīn*], ed. and trans. A. Tietze, 2 vols, Philosophisch-Historische Klasse, 137, 158, Vienna: Österreischschen Akademie der Wissenschaften, 1979, 1982.

Na'ima, Mustafā, *Tarih-i Na'ima: ravzatül-Hüseyn fī hulâsati ahbari'l-hafikayn*, Istanbul: Matbaa-yi Âmire, 1281–83/1864–66; *Tarih-i Na'ima: ravzatül-Hüseyn fī hulâsati ahbari'l-hafikayn*, ed. M. İpşirli, Ankara: Türk Tarih Kurumu, 2007; *Annals of the Turkish Empire from 1591 to 1659 of the Christian Era*, trans. C. Fraser, London: John Murray, 1832; repr. New York: Arno Press, 1973.

Najm al-Dīn Rāzī, *The Path of God's Bondsmen from Origin to Return*, trans. H. Algar, Delmar, NY: Caravan Books, 1982.

Narshakhī, Abū Bakr Muḥammad b. Ja'far, *The History of Bukhara*, trans. R. N. Frye, Cambridge, MA: Mediaeval Academy of America, 1954.

Nasser, G. A. *Speeches and Press-Interviews*, Cairo: United Arab Republic Information Department, 1961.

——. *Nasser Speaks: basic documents*, trans. E. S. Farag, London: Morssett, 1972.

Nazim, M. "The *Pand-Namah* of Subuktigīn," *JRAS* 1933: 605–28.

Nedim, Mahmud, *Ayine-yi Devlet*, Istanbul: Karabet Matbaası, 1909.

Nīshāpūrī, Ẓahīr al-Dīn, *The Saljūqnāma of Ẓahīr al-Dīn Nīshāpūrī*, ed. A. H. Morton Warminster: E. J. W. Gibb Memorial Trust, 2004; *The History of the Seljuq Turks, from the Jāmiʻ al-Tawārīkh: an Ilkhanid adaption of the* Saljūq-nāma, trans. K. A. Luther, ed. C. E. Bosworth, Richmond, Surrey, UK: Curzon, 2001.

Nizam al-Mulk, *The Book of Government or Rules for Kings: the Siyar al-muluk or siyasat-nama*, trans. Hubert Darke, 2nd ed. London: Routledge & Kegan Paul, 1978.

Nizāmī Ganjavī, *Kullīyāt-i Khamsa-yi Hakīm Nizāmī Ganjavī*, Tehran: ʻAlī Akbar ʻIlmī, 1331/1952; *Makhzanol Asrār, The Treasury of Mysteries*, trans. G. H. Darab, London: Arthur Probsthain, 1945; *The Haft Paykar: a medieval Persian romance*, trans. J. S. Meisami, Oxford: Oxford University Press, 1995.

Nöldeke, T. (ed.) *The Iranian National Epic, or, the Shahnamah*, trans. L. T. Bogdanov, Bombay: K. R. Cama Oriental Institute, 1930; repr. Philadelphia, PA: Porcupine Press, 1979.

al-Nuwayrī, Shihāb al-Dīn Aḥmad b. 'Abd al-Wahhab, *Nihāyat al-Arab fi funūn al-adab*, 33 vols, Cairo: Dār al-Kutub, 1964–97.

Nyitrai, I. "Sultan Bayezid II as the Only Legitimate Pretender to the Ottoman Throne (a Persian *Šāhnāme* dated from 1486)," in M. Köhbach, G. Procházka-Eisl, and C. Römer (eds) *Acta Viennensia Ottomanica*, 261–6, Vienna: Institut für Orientalistik, 1999.

Onon, U. (trans.) *The History and the Life of Chinggis Khan (The Secret History of the Mongols)* Leiden: Brill, 1990.

Pahlavi, M. R. *Mission for My Country*, London: Hutchinson, 1961.

——. *The White Revolution*, 2nd ed. Tehran: The Imperial Pahlavi Library/Kayhan Press, 1967.

——. *Answer to History*, New York: Stein & Day, 1980.

Pritchard, J. B. (ed.) *Ancient Near Eastern Texts relating to the Old Testament*, 2nd ed. Princeton, NJ: Princeton University Press, 1955.

al-Qaddafi, M. "A Visit to Fezzan," in I. W. Zartman (ed.) *Man, State, and Society in the Contemporary Maghrib*, 131–6, New York: Praeger, 1973.

al-Qāḍī, W. "An Early Faṭimid Political Document," *SI* 48, 1978: 71–108.

Qudāma b. Ja'far, *Kitāb al-kharāj*, ed. and trans. A. Ben Shemesh, *Taxation in Islam*, vol. 2: *Qudāma b. Ja'far's Kitāb al-kharāj, Part Seven, and Excerpts from Abū Yūsuf's Kitāb al-kharāj*, Leiden: Brill, 1965.

——. *al-Siyāsa min kitāb al-kharāj wa-ṣinā'at al-kitāba*, ed. M. Ḥiyari, Amman: al-Jāmi'a al-'Urduniyya, 1981.

Rashīd al-Dīn Faḍlullāh, *Mukātabāt-i Rashīdī*, ed. Muhammad Shafī', Lahore: Kulliat-i Panjāb, 1945.

——. *The Successors of Genghis Khan*, trans. J. A. Boyle, New York: Columbia University Press, 1971.

——. *Jami'u't-tawarikh: compendium of chronicles*, trans. W. M. Thackston, Sources of Oriental Languages and Literatures, 45, Cambridge, MA: Harvard University Department of Near Eastern Languages and Civilizations, 1998–9.

er-Râvendî, Muhammed b. Ali, *Râhat-üs-sudûr ve âyet-üs-sürûr*, trans. A. Ateş, 2 vols, Ankara: Türk Tarih Kurumu, 1957–60.

Rawlinson, G. *The Seventh Great Oriental Monarchy*, London: Longmans, Green, 1876, repr. Tehran: Imperial Organization for Social Services, 1976.

Rāzī, Fakhr al-Dīn, *Jāmi' al-'ulūm*, ed. M. H. Tasbīhī, Tehran: Kitābkhānah Asadī, 1346/1967.

Sa'dī, *Morals Pointed and Tales Adorned: the Būstān of Sa'dī*, trans. G. M. Wickens, Toronto: University of Toronto Press, 1974.

Sa'dullah Paşa, *1878 Paris ekspozisyonu*, quoted in Ebüzziya Tevfik, *Numune-i edebiyat-ı Osmaniye*, 3rd ed., Istanbul, Matbaa-i Ebüzziya, 1306/1885, 288, trans. B. Lewis, *The Middle East and the West*, 47, London/Bloomington: Indiana University Press, 1964.

al-Salāwī, Aḥmad al-Nāṣirī, *Kitāb al-istiqçâ: chronique de la dynastie alaouie de Maroc*, trans. E. Fumey, *Archives marocaines* 9, 1906: 1–399; 10, 1907: 1–424.

Salinger, G. "A Muslim Mirror for Princes," *MW* 46, 1956: 24–39.

Sanjana, B., Kohiyar, R. E and Darab, D. (eds and trans.) *The Dinkard*, 19 vols, Bombay: Duftur Ashkara, 1874–1928.

Sarı Meḥmed Pasha, The Defterdār, *Ottoman Statecraft: the book of counsel for vezirs and governors*, trans W. L. Wright, Jr. Princeton, NJ: Princeton University Press, 1935; repr. Westport, CT: Greenwood, 1971.

Schefer, C. *Chrestomathie persane*, Paris: E. Leroux, 1883–5, repr. Amsterdam: APA-Philo 1976.

Schmitt, R. *The Bisitun Inscriptions of Darius the Great: Old Persian text*, Corpus Inscriptionum Iranicarum, pt. 1, vol. 1, London: School of Oriental and African Studies, 1991.

Şeref, 'Abdurrahman, *Tarih Musahabeleri*, Istanbul: Matba'a-i 'Âmire, 1339/1920.

Şerif, A. *Anadolu'da tanın*, ed. M. Ç. Börekçi, 2 vols, Ankara: Türk Tarih Kurumu, 1999.

Serjeant, R. B. "The Caliph 'Umar's Letters to Abū Mūsā al-Ash'arī and Mu'āwiya," *JSS* 29, 1984: 65–79, repr. in *Customary and Shari'ah Law in Arabian Society* Hampshire, UK: Variorum, 1991, II.

Seux, M.-J. *Épithetes royales akkadiennes et sumériennes*, Literature ancien de la proche orient, Paris: Letouzey et Ané, 1967.

Şeyhoğlu Mustafâ, *Kenzü'l-küberâ ve mehekkü'l-ulemâ: inceleme, metin, indeks*, ed. K. Yavuz, Ankara: Atatürk Kültür, Dil ve Tarih Yüksek Kurumu, 1991.

al-Shayzarī, 'Abd al-Raḥmān b. Naṣr, *Al-Nahj al-maslūk fi siyāsat al-mulūk,* Beirut: Dār al-Manār, 1994; *Nehcü's-sülûk fî siyâseti'l-mülûk,* trans. Ahmed [Mehmed Efendi] Nahîfî, Istanbul: Ali Riza Efendi, 1869; *Nehcü's-sülûk fî siyâseti'l-mülûk*, trans. H. Algül, 1001 Temel Eser, Istanbul: Tercüman, 1974.

al-Sibā'ī, M. *Ishtirākiyyat al-Islām*, Caro: Dār al-Qawmiyya lil-Tiba'a wa-al-Nashr, 1961: "Islamic Socialism," trans. G. H. Gardner and S. A. Hanna *MW* 56, 1966: 71–86, repr. in S. A. Hanna and G. H. Gardner, *Arab Socialism: a documentary survey*, 64–79, Salt Lake City: University of Utah Press, 1969.

——. "Al-Takāful al-ijtimā'ī (mutual or joint responsibility)," from *Ishtirākiyyat al-Islām*, trans. S. A. Hanna, in S.A. Hanna and G. H. Gardner, *Arab Socialism: a documentary survey*, 149–71, Salt Lake City: University of Utah Press, 1969.

Sinan Paşa, *Ahlakname, Nasihatname*, MS Süleymaniye Laleli 1611/2; İ *Maarifname*, ed. H. Ertaylan, Istanbul: İstanbul Üniversitesi Edebiyat Fakültesi, 1961.

Slackman, M. "Don't Leave Home without a Cultural Compass," *New York Times*, 11 June 2008: 8.

Sommerfeld, W. "Die Kurigalzu-Text MAH 15922," *Archiv für Orientforschung* 32, 1985: 3–22.

Sourdel-Thomine, J. "Les conseils du Šayḫ al-Harawī à un prince ayyūbide," *BEO* 17, 1961–2: 205–66.

Southey, R. (trans.) *The Chronicle of the Cid*, New York: Heritage Press, 1958.

Southgate, M. S. *Iskandarnamah: a Persian medieval Alexander romance*, New York: Columbia University Press, 1978.

Spuler, B. *History of the Mongols: based on Eastern and Western accounts of the thirteenth and fourteenth centuries*, trans. H. and S. Drummond, Berkeley: University of California Press, 1972.

Steele, R. (ed.) *Three Prose Versions of the Secreta Secretorum*, London: Kegan Paul, Trench, Trübner, 1896.

——. *Opera hactenus inedita Rogeri Baconi,* vol. 5: *Secretum Secretorum*, English trans. I. Ali, Oxford: Clarendon Press, 1920.

Steible, H. *Die Neusumerischen Bau- und Weihinschriften*, 2 vols, Freiburger Altorientalische Studien, 9, Stuttgart: Franz Steiner, 1991.

Stern, S. M. "Three Petitions of the Fatimid Period," *Oriens* 15, 1962: 172–209.

——. "Petitions from the Ayyūbid Period," *BSOAS* 27, 1964: 1–32.

——. "Two Ayyūbid Decrees from Sinai," in S. M. Stern (ed.) *Documents from Islamic Chanceries*, 9–38, Columbia: University of South Carolina Press, 1965.

Subtelny, M. E. *Le monde est un jardin: aspects de l'histoire culturelle de l'Iran médiéval*, Paris: Association pour l'Avancement des Études Iraniennes, 2002.

Sultan-Husayn Mirza, "Apologia," in *A Century of Princes: sources on Timurid history and art*, trans. W. M. Thackston, 373–76, Cambridge: Aga Khan Program for Islamic Architecture, 1989.

al-Ṭabarī, Abū Ja'far Muḥammad b. Jarīr, *Annales Quos Scripsit Abu Djafar Mohammed ibn Djarir at-Ṭabari* [*Tā'rīkh al-rusūl wa-al-mulūk*], ed. M. J. de Goeje, 16 vols, Leiden: Brill, 1879–1901; repr. 1964–65; translation: *The History of al-Ṭabarī*, ed. E. Yarshater, 40 vols, Albany: State University of New York Press, 1987–99.

——. *The History of al-Ṭabarī,* vol. 3, *The Children of Israel*, trans. W. M. Brinner, Albany: State University of New York Press, 1991.

——. *The History of al-Ṭabarī,* vol. 5: *The Sāsānids, the Byzantines, the Lakhmids, and Yemen*, trans. C. E. Bosworth, Albany: State University of New York Press, 1999; *Geschichte der Perser und Araber zur Zeit der Sasaniden, aus der Arabischen Chronik des Tabari*, trans. T. Nöldeke, Leiden: Brill, 1879; repr. 1973.

——. *The History of al-Ṭabarī,* vol. 15: *The Crisis of the Early Caliphate*, trans. R. S. Humphreys, Albany: State University of New York Press, 1988.

——. *The History of al-Ṭabarī,* vol. 18, *Between Civil Wars: The Caliphate of Mu'āwiyah*, trans. M. G. Morony, Albany: State University of New York Press, 1987.

——. *The History of al-Ṭabarī,* vol. 26, *The Waning of the Umayyad Caliphate*, trans. C. Hillenbrand, Albany: State University of New York Press, 1989.

——. *The History of al-Ṭabarī: The Early 'Abbāsī Empire*, trans. J. A. Williams, 2 vols, Albany: State University of New York Press, 1988–9.

——. *The History of al-Ṭabarī*, vol. 29, *Al-Manṣūr and al-Mahdī*, trans. H. Kennedy, Albany: State University of New York Press, 1990.

——. *The History of al-Ṭabarī*, vol. 32, *The Reunification of the 'Abbasid Caliphate*, trans. C. E. Bosworth, Albany: State University of New York Press, 1987.

——. *The History of al-Ṭabarī*, vol. 34, *The Revolt of the Zanj*, trans. D. Waines, Albany: State University of New York Press, 1992.

Tadmor, H. *The Inscriptions of Tiglath-Pileser III, King of Assyria*, Jerusalem: Israel Academy of Sciences and Humanities, 1994.

al-Ṭahṭāwī, Rifā'a Rāfi', *al-A'māl al-Kāmilah li-Rifā'ah Rāfi' al-Ṭahṭāwī*, ed. M. 'Imārah, 5 vols, Beirut: al-Mu'assasa al-'Arabiyya li'l-Dirāsāt wa-al-Nashr, 1973.

——. *An Imam in Paris: account of a stay in France by an Egyptian cleric (1826–1831)*, intro. and trans. D. L. Newman, London: Saqi Books, 2004.

Tekin, T. *A Grammar of Orkhon Turkic*, Bloomington: Indiana University Research Center for the Language Sciences, 1968.

al-Tha'ālibī, Abū Manṣūr 'Abd al-Malik b. Muḥammad b. Ismā'īl, *Thimār al-qulūb fi al-muḍāf wa-al-mansūb*, ed. M. A. Ibrahim, Cairo: Maṭba'at al-Ẓāhir, 1908.

——. *al-Tamthīl wa-al-muḥāḍara*, ed. A. M. al-Ḥilw Cairo: Dār Ihyā' al-Kutub al-'Arabiyya, 1961.

al-Tha'ālibī, Abū Manṣūr al-Ḥusayn, *Histoire des rois des Perses (Ghurar siyar al-mulūk)*, trans. H. Zotenberg, Paris: Imprimerie Nationale, 1900; repr. Tehran: Maktabat al-Asadī, 1963.

Tursun Beg, *The History of Mehmed the Conqueror*, ed. H. İnalcık and R. Murphey, Minneapolis: Bibliotheca Islamica, 1978.

al-Turtushī, Muḥammad b. al-Walīd, *Sirāj al-mulūk (Flambeau of Kings)*, ed. J. al-Bayati, London: Riad El-Rayyes, 1990.

Ṭūsī, Naṣīr ad-Dīn, *The Nasirean Ethics*, trans. G. M. Wickens, London: George Allen & Unwin, 1964.

'Ubayd Zākānī, *The Ethics of the Aristocrats and other satirical works*, trans. H. Javadi, Piedmont, CA: Jahan Books, 1985.

Unat, F. R. "Sadrazam Kemankeş Kara Mustafa Paşa Lâyihası," *Tarih Vesikaları* 1.6, 1941–2: 443–80.

'Urmawī, Sirāj al-Dīn (attributed), *Latā'if al-Ḥikma*, ed. G. H. Yūsufī, Tehran: Intishārāt-i Bunyād-i Farhang-i Īrān, 1972.

al-'Utbi, Abu al-Nasr Muhammad b. al-Jabbar, *The Kitab-i-Yamini: historical memoirs of the Amír Sabaktagin, and the Sultán Mahmúd of Ghazna*, trans. J. Reynolds London: Oriental Translation Fund, 1858; repr. ed., Lahore: Qausain, 1975.

G. Vernadsky, R. T. Fisher, Jr., A. D. Ferguson, A. Lossky, and S. Pushkarev (eds) "Ivan Peresvetov's Recommendations," in *A Source Book for Russian History from Early Times to 1917*, 162–4, New Haven, CT: Yale University Press, 1972.

Waring, E. S. *A Tour to Sheeraz*, London: T. Cadell and W. Davies, 1807.

al-Waṭwāṭ, Muḥammad b. Ibrāhīm b. Yaḥyá, *Ghurar al-khaṣā'iṣ al-wāḍiḥah wa-'urar al-naqā'iṣ al-fāḍiḥah*, Bulaq: al-Maṭba'a al-Miṣriyya, 1867.

West, E. W. (ed. and trans.) *Pahlavi Texts*, pt. 3, Sacred Books of the East, 24, Oxford: Clarendon Press, 1885.

Williams, J. A. (ed.) *Themes of Islamic Civilization*, Berkeley: University of California Press, 1971.

Yaltkaya, Ş. "İlhanîler devri idarî teşkilâtına dair Nasîr-ed-Dini Tûsî'nin bir eseri," *THİTM* 2, 1932–9: 7–16.

Yazıcıoğlu, "Tārīh-i Āl-i Selçūk," MS Topkapı Sarayı Kütüphanesi, Revan 1390; Yazıcızâde Ali, *Tevârîh-i Âl-i Selçuk*, ed. A. Bakır, Istanbul: Çamlıca, 2009.

Young, W. (trans.) *The Wisdom of Naushirwan "The Just", King of Iran, commonly called Tauqiyat i Kisrawiya*, Lucknow: Newul Kishore Press, 1892.

Yücel, Y. (ed.) *Kitâb-i müstetâb*, in *Osmanlı devlet teşkilâtına dair kaynaklar*, 1–40, Ankara: Türk Tarih Kurumu, 1988.

Yūsuf Khāṣṣ Ḥājib, *Uigurische Sprachmonumente und das Kudatku bilik: uigurischer Text mit Transscription und Übersetzung nebst einem uigurisch-deutschen Wörterbuche und lithografirten Facsimile aus dem Originaltexte des Kudatku bilik*, ed. and trans. Á. Vámbéry, Innsbruck: Wagner Universitäts-Buchdruckerei, 1870;

Wisdom of Royal Glory (Kutadgu Bilig): a Turko-Islamic mirror for princes, trans. R. Dankoff, Chicago, IL: University of Chicago Press, 1983.

Other primary sources

Abbas, I. (ed.) *'Abd al-Ḥamīd bin Yaḥyá al-Kātib wa-mā tabaqqā min rasā'ilihī wa-rasā'il Sālim Abi al-'Alā'*, Amman: Dār al-Shurūq, 1988.

Abbott, N. *The Ḳurrah Papyri from Aphrodito in the Oriental Institute*, Studies in Ancient Oriental Civilization, 15, Chicago, IL: University of Chicago Press, 1938.

'Abd al-Hamīd, "Risāla ilá al-kuttāb," in M. Kurd Ali (ed.) *Rasā'il al-bulaghā'*, 172–6, Cairo: Dār al-Kutub al-'Arabīyya al-Kubrá, 1913.

'Abd al-Raziq, 'A. "L'Islam et les bases du pouvoir," trans. L. Bercher, *REI* 7, 1930: 353–391; 8, 1934: 163–222.

Akarlı, E. D. (ed.) *Belgelerle Tanzimat: Osmanlı sadrıazamlarından Âli ve Fuad paşaların siyasî vasiyyetnâmeleri*, Istanbul: Boğaziçi Üniversitesi Matbaası, 1978.

Alaeddin Ali Çelebi, *Humâyûnnâme*, Bulaq: Dār al-Ṭibā'a al-'Āmire, 1838.

Albayrak, S. *Budin kanunnāmesi ve Osmanlı toprak meselesi*, 1001 Temel Eser, Istanbul: Tercuman, 1973.

Āl-e Ahmad, J. *Plagued by the West (=Gharbzadegi)*, trans. P. Sprachman, Delmar, NY: Caravan Books, 1981.

Andic, F. M. and Andic, S. *The Last of the Ottoman Grandees: the life and political testament of Âli Paşa*, Istanbul: İsis, 1996.

Anhegger, R. and İnalcık, H. *Ḳānūnnāme-i Sulṭānī ber Mūceb-i örf-i 'osmānī*, Ankara: Türk Tarih Kurumu, 1956.

Arberry, A. J. *The Koran Interpreted*, New York: Macmillan, 1955.

Ârif, M. (ed.) "Kanunname-i Âl-ı Osman," *TOEM*, Supplement 3, 1330/1912.

Aşıkpaşazade, *'Āshiqpashazādeh ta'rīkhī: a history of the Ottoman Empire to A.H. 833 (AD 1478)*, ed. 'Ālī Bey, Istanbul: Matbaa-ı 'Āmire, 1914; repr. Westmead, UK: Gregg International, 1970.

Atatürk, M. K. *Thus Spoke Atatürk: his sayings, thoughts and memoirs*, ed. and trans. H. Melzig, Istanbul, Kenan Printing-House, 1943.

——. *A Speech Delivered by Mustafa Kemal Atatürk, 1927 [Nutuk]*, Ankara: Ministry of Education of the Turkish Republic/Başbakanlı Basımevi, 1981.

Azamat, N. (ed.) *Anonim tevârîh-i Âl-i Osman, F. Giese neşri*, Istanbul: Marmara Üniversitesi Edebiyat Fakültesi, 1992.

al-Baghdādī, Bahā al-Dīn Muḥammad, *Al-Tavassul ilà al-tarassul*, ed. A. Bahmanjār and M. Qazvīnī, Tehran: Shirkat al-Sahami, 1937.

Bahār, M. T. (ed.) *Tārīkh-i Sistān*, Tehran: Zavvār, 1935; *The Tārikh-e Sistān*, trans. M. Gold, Rome: Istituto Italiano per il Medio ed Estremo Oriente, 1976.

Barkan, Ö. L. *XV. ve XVIıncı Asırlarda Osmanlı İmparatorluğunda zirai ekonominin hukuku ve mali esasları*, Vol. 1: *Kanunlar*, Istanbul: Türkiyat Enstitüsü, 1943.

——, *Süleymaniye Cami ve imareti inşaatı (1550–1557)* 2 vols, Ankara: Türk Tarih Kurumu, 1972.

Başbakanlık Osmanlı arşivi rehberi, Ankara: T.C. Başbakanlık Devlet Arşivleri Genel Müdürlüğü, 1992.

Bayhaqī, Abū al-Faẓl Muḥammad, *Tārīkh-i Bayhaqī*, ed. 'A. A. Fayyāz, Mashhad: Danishgah-I Mashhad, 1971/1350.

Bayne, E. A. *Persian Kingship in Transition: conversation with a monarch whose office is traditional and whose goal is modernization*, New York: American Universities Field Staff, 1968.

Beldiceanu-Steinherr, I. *Recherches sur les actes des règnes des sultans Osman, Orkhan et Murad I*, Societas Academic Dacoromana, Acta Historica, 7, Monachii: Societatea Academica Romana, 1967.

Ben Smail, M. and Valensi, L. "Le règne de Hammouda Pacha dans la chronique d'Ibn Abi-ḍ-Ḍiyaf," *Cahiers de Tunisie* vol 19. no. 73–74, 1971: 87–108.

Bertrandon de la Brocquière, "The Travels of Bertrandon de la Brocquiere," in T. Wright (ed.) *Early Travels in Palestine*, 283–382, London: Henry G. Bohn, 1848.

Barkan, Ö. L. and Ayverdi, E. H. (eds) *İstanbul vakıflar tahrir defteri: 953 (1546) Târîhli*, Istanbul: Baha Matbaası, 1970.

Cevdet, A. *Tarih-i Cevdet*, 12 vols in 6, Istanbul: Matbaa-ı Osmaniye, 1309/1892.

——. *Tezakir-i Cevdet*, 4 vols, Ankara: Türk Tarih Kurumu, 1953.

Cezzâr Aḥmed Pasha, *Ottoman Egypt in the Eighteenth Century: the Niẓâmnâme-i Mıṣır of Cezzâr Aḥmed Pasha*, ed. and trans. S. J. Shaw, Cambridge, MA: Center for Middle Eastern Studies of Harvard University, 1962.

The Ottomon Constitution of 1876 in the Ottoman Empire: http://www.bilkent.edu.tr/~genckaya/documents1.html, accessed 22 February 2005 and 5 December 2011.

"Constitution of the Islamic Republic of Iran," *MEJ* 34, 1980: 184–204; http://www.iranonline.com/iran/iran-info/Government/constitution.html, accessed 5 December 2011.

The Constitution of the Republic of Turkey, 1982, Ankara: Prime Ministry Directorate General of Press and Information, 1982; http://www.anayasa.gov.tr/images/loaded/pdf_dosyalari/THE_CONSTITUTION_OF_THE_REPUBLIC_OF_TURKEY.pdf, accessed 5 December 2011.

al-Droubi, S. *A Critical Edition of and Study on Ibn Faḍl Allāh's Manual of Secretaryship "Al-ta'rīf bi'l-muṣṭalaḥ al-sharīf,"* al-Karak: Mu'tah University, 1992.

Eastwick, E. B. *Journal of a Diplomate's Three Years' Residence in Persia*, 2 vols, London: Smith, Elder, 1864.

Ebü'l-Hayr Rūmī, *Saltuk-name: the legend of Sarı Saltuk*, ed. F. İz, 7 vols, Sources of Oriental Languages and Literatures, 4, Cambridge, MA: Orient, 1974–84.

Edib Ahmed b. Mahmud Yükneki, *Atebetü'l-hakayık*, ed. R. R. Arat, Istanbul: Ateş, 1951.

Emin, Mehmed, *see* Mehmed Emin.

Eyyûbî, *Menâḳib-i Sulṭan Süleyman (risâle-i pâdişâh-nâme)*, ed. M. Akkuş, Ankara: T. C. Kultur Bakanlığı, 1991.

Fales, F. M. *Censimenti e catasti di epoca neo-assira*, Rome: Centro per le Antichità e la Storia dell'Arte del Vicino Oriente, 1973.

al-Farābī, *Fuṣūl al-Madanī: Aphorisms of the Statesman*, ed. and trans. D. M. Dunlop, Cambridge: Cambridge University Press, 1961.

Farber, W. "Die Vergöttlichung Narām-Sîns," *Orientalia* 52, 1983: 67–72.

Firdausi, *The Epic of the Kings: Shah-nama, the national epic of Persia*, trans. R. Levy, London: Routledge & Kegan Paul, 1967.

——. *The Shahnama of Firdausi*, trans. A. G. Warner and E. Warner, 9 vols, London: Kegan Paul, Trench, Trübner and Co., 1905-25.

Frankena, R. (ed.) *Briefe aus dem British Museum (LIH und CT2–33)*, Altbabylonische Briefe im Umschrift und Übersetzung, 2, Leiden: Brill, 1966.

Gemayel, A. *Peace and Unity: major speeches 1982–1984*, Gerrards Cross: Colin Smythe, 1984.

Gibb, E. J. W. *A History of Ottoman Poetry*, 6 vols, London: Luzac, 1900, repr. 1958.

Gibb, H. A. R., Kramers, J. H., Lévi-Provonçal, E. Schacht, J., Lewis, B., and Pellat, C. (eds) *The Encyclopaedia of Islam*, 2nd ed., Leiden: Brill, 1954–2004.

Glain, S. "Kingdom of Corruption," *The Nation*, 30 May 2005: 22–3.

Gökalp, Z. *The Principles of Turkism*, trans. R. Devereux, Leiden: Brill, 1968.

Göyünç, N. "Das sogenannte Ǧāme'o'l-Ḥesāb das 'Emād as-Sarāwī," PhD diss., Georg-August-Universität, 1962.

Guo, L. *Early Mamluk Syrian Historiography: al-Yūnīnī's Dhayl Mir'āt al-Zamān*, 2 vols, Leiden: Brill, 1998.

Hallock, R. T. *Persepolis Fortification Tablets*, Oriental Institute Publications, 92, Chicago, IL: University of Chicago Press, 1969.

Hezarfen Hüseyin, *Telhîsü'l-beyân fî kavânîn-i Âl-i Osmân*, ed. Sevim İlgürel, Ankara: Türk Tarih Kurumu, 1998.

Hinke, W. J. *A New Boundary Stone of Nebuchadrezzar I from Nippur, with a concordance of proper names and a glossary of the kudurru inscriptions thus far published*, The Babylonian Expedition of the University of Pennsylvania, Series D: Researches and Treatises, 4, Philadelphia, PA: University of Pennsylvania, 1907.

Hinz, W. *Die Resalä-ye Falakiyyä des 'Abdollah ibn Moḥammad ibn Kiya al-Mazandarani: ein persischer Leitfaden des staatlichen Rechnungswesens (um 1363)*, Wiesbaden: Franz Steiner, 1952.

Horst, H. *Die Staatsverwaltung der Grosselǧūqen und Ḫōrazmšāhs (1038–1231): Eine Untersuchung nach Urkundenformularen der Zeit*, Wiesbaden: Franz Steiner, 1964.

el-Hōyī [Khūī], Ḥasan b. 'Abdi'l-Mu'min, *Gunyetu'l-kātib ve munyetü'ṭ-Ṭālib, rusūmu-r-resā'il ve nucūmu'l-fazā'il*, ed. A. S. Erzi, Ankara: Türk Tarih Kurumu, 1963.

Ibn al-Haytham, Ja'far b. Aḥmad, *The Advent of the Fatimids: A Contemporary Shi'i Witness*, ed. and trans. W. Madelung and P. E. Walker, London: IB Tauris, 2000.

Ibn al-Muqaffa', 'Abdallāh *Risāla fi al-saḥāba*, in M. Kurd Ali (ed.) *Rasā'il al-bulaghā'*, 120–31, Cairo: Dār al-Kutub al-'Arabīyya al-Kubrá, 1913; C. Pellat (ed. and trans.) *"Conseilleur" du Calife (Kitāb al-Saḥāba)*, Paris: G.-P. Maisonneuve et Larose, 1976.

Ibn al-Nadīm, Mueqammad b. Isḥāq, *The Fihrist of al-Nadīm: a tenth-century survey of Muslim culture*, ed. and trans. B. Dodge, 2 vols, New York: Columbia University Press, 1970.

Ibn Qutayba, 'Abdallah b. Muslim, *al-Ma'ārif: Ibn Coteiba's Handbuch der Geschichte*, ed. F. Wüstenfeld, Göttingen: Vandenhoeck and Ruprecht, 1850.

Ibn Taghrībirdī, Abū al-Maḥāsin Yūsuf, *al-Nujūm al-zāhira fi mulūk Miṣr wa'l-Qāhira*, trans. W. Popper, *History of Egypt, 1382–1469 A.D.*, 8 vols, University of California Publications in Semitic Philology, 13–14, 17–19, 22–24, Berkeley, University of California Press, 1909–36.

İnalcık, H. *Hicrî 835 tarihli sûret-i defter-i sancak-ı Arvanid*, Ankara: Türk Tarih Kurumu, 1954.

Isidore of Charax, *Parthian Stations, by Isidore of Charax: an account of the overland trade route between the Levant and India in the first century B.C.*, ed. and trans. W. H. Schoff, 1914; repr. Chicago, IL: Ares, 1976.

Issawi, C. (ed.) *The Economic History of the Middle East, 1800–1914: a book of readings*, Chicago, IL: University of Chicago Press, 1966; Midway Reprint, 1975.

——. (ed.) *The Economic History of Iran, 1800–1914*, Chicago, IL: University of Chicago Press, 1971.

——. (ed.) *The Economic History of Turkey, 1800–1914*, Chicago, IL: University of Chicago Press, 1980.

——. (ed.) *The Fertile Crescent, 1800–1914*, New York: Oxford University Press, 1988.

Jāmī, *Masnavī-i haft awrang*, ed. M. Mudarris Gilani, Tehran: Kitābfurūshī-i Sa'dī, 1982.

Johns, C. H. W. *An Assyrian Doomsday Book: or, liber censualis of the district round Harran, in the seventh century* BC, Assyriologische Bibliothek, 17, Leipzig: J. C. Hinrichs, 1901.

al-Juvaynī, Muntakhab al-Dīn Badī' Atābak, *Kitāb-i 'atabat al-kataba*, ed. M. Qazvīnī and 'A. Iqbāl, Tehran: Shirkat Sāmī Chāp, 1950.

Juzjānī, Minhaj-i Siraj, *ṭabaḳāt-i Nāṣirī: a general history of the Muhammedan dynasties of Asia*, trans. H. G. Raverty, London: Gilbert and Rivington, 1881–97; repr. Osnabrück: Biblio, 1991.

Karal, E. Z. "Ali Paşanın Trablusgarp Valisine bir Tahriratı," *TV* 1, 1941/42: 297–302.

——. "Yavuz Sultan Selim'in oğlu Şehzade Süleyman'a Manisa Sancağını idare etmesi için gönderdiği siyasetnâme," *Belleten* 6, 1942: 37–44.

——. *Osmanlı İmparatorluğunda ilk nüfus sayımı, 1831*, Ankara: T. C. Başvekâlet İstatistik Umum Müdürlüğü, 1943.

Kâtip Çelebi, and Haci Halife, *The Balance of Truth*, trans. G. L. Lewis, London: George Allen & Unwin, 1957.

Kâtip Çelebi: hayatı ve eserleri hakkında incelemeler, Ankara: Türk Tarih Kurumu, 1985.

Kauthar: an anthology of the speeches of Imam Khomeini (s.a.) including an account of the events of the Islamic Revolution, 1962–1978, vol. 2, Tehran: Institute for the Compilation and Publication of the Works of Imam Khomeini, 1995.

Kemal, Namık, "Usul-u Meşveret Hakkinda Mektuplar," *Hürriyet*, 14 September 1868: 6.

Kerr, M. H. (trans.) *Lebanon in the Last Years of Feudalism, 1840–1868: a contemporary account by Antun Dahir al-Aqiqi, and other documents*, Beirut: American University of Beirut, 1959.

Khan, G. *Arabic Papyri: selected material from the Khalili collection*, Oxford: Nour Foundation and Oxford University Press, 1992.

——. *Arabic Legal and Administrative Documents in the Cambridge Genizah Collections*, Cambridge: Cambridge University Press, 1993.

Khomeini, Ruhollah, *Islam and Revolution: writings and declarations*, trans. H. Algar, London: KPI, 1981.

Khwāndamīr (Khvand Mir), Ghiyāth al-Dīn, *Khulāsat al-akhbār*, trans. J. Dumoret, "Histoire des Seldjoukides, extraite de l'ouvrage intitulé *Khélassat-oul-akhbar*, et traduite du persan de Khondémir," *JA*, ser. 2, vol. 13, 1834: 240–56.

——. *Habibu's-siyar, Tome Three: the reign of the Mongol and the Turk*, trans. W. M. Thackston, 3 vols, Cambridge, MA: Harvard University Department of Near Eastern Languages and Civilizations, 1994.

König, F. W. *Die elamischen Königsinschriften*, Archiv für Orientforschung, Beiheft 16, Graz: Archiv für Orientforschung, 1965.

Kraemer, C. J., Jr. *Excavations at Nessana*, vol. 3, *non-literary papyri*, Princeton, NJ: Princeton University Press, 1958.

Landen, R. G. (ed.) *The Emergence of the Modern Middle East: selected readings*, New York: Van Nostrand Reinhold, 1970.

Levend, A. S. *Ǧazavāt-nāmeler ve Mihaloğlu Ali Bey'in Ǧazavāt-nāmesi*, Ankara: Türk Tarih Kurumu, 1956.

Lüṭfî, Ahmed, *Tariḥ-i Lüṭfî*, 8 vols in 3, Istanbul: Mahmud Bey Matbaası, 1302/1885–6.

Lütfi Bey, Ahmed, *Mir'at-i adâlet*, trans. E. Beylem, *Osmanlı adalet düzeni*, Istanbul: Fatih, 1979.

Majer, H. G. *Das osmanische "Registerbuch der Beschwerden" (Şikāyet Defteri) vom Jahre 1675*, Vienna: Österreichischen Akademie der Wissenschaften, 1984.

al-Maqrīzī, Aḥmad b. 'Alī, *A History of the Ayyūbid Sultans of Egypt*, trans. R. J. C. Broadhurst, Boston, MA: Twayne, 1980.

Marsigli, L. F. *Stato Militare dell'Impero Ottomanno*, 2 vols in 1, Graz: Akademische Druck u. Verlagsanstalt, 1972.

Martin, B. G. "Seven Ṣafawid Documents from Azarbayjan," in S. M. Stern (ed.) *Documents from Islamic Chanceries*, 171–206, Columbia, SC: University of South Carolina Press, 1965.

Marwārīd, 'Abdallāh b. Muḥammad, *Staatsschreiben der Timuridenzeit: Das Šaraf-nāmä des 'Abdallāh Marwārīd in kritischer Auswertung*, ed. H. R. Roemer, Wiesbaden: Franz Steiner, 1952.

Mecelle Mazbatası, *Mecelle-i ahkâm-ı 'adliyye*, 16 vols, Istanbul, 1869–76; *The Medjelle or Ottoman Civil Law*, trans. W. E. Grigsby, London: Stevens, 1895.

Mehmed Emin, "Ahvâl-ı Bosna," trans. A. S. Alicič, "*Ahvali Bosna* od Muhameda Emina Iseviča (poc. XIXe v.): Uvod, Prevod s Turskog i Napomene," *POF* 32–3, 1982–3: 163–98.

Mehmed Said Efendi, *Ahlâk-ı Hamida,* Istanbul: Elcevaip Matbaası, 1881; *La morale musulmane, ou, l'Akhlaqi-Hamidé*, trans. J. A. Decourdemanche, Paris: E. Leroux, 1888.

Mélikoff, I. *Abū Muslim, le "Porte-hache" du Khorassan, dans la tradition épique turco-iranienne*, Paris: Adrien Maisonneuve, 1962.

Melville-Jones, J. R. *The Siege of Constantinople 1453: seven contemporary accounts*, Amsterdam: Adolf M. Hakkert, 1972.

Mihailovič, Konstantin, *Memoirs of a Janissary*, trans. B. Stolz, historical commentary by S. Soucek, Ann Arbor: Department of Slavic Languages and Literatures, University of Michigan, 1975.

Miskawayh, Abū 'Alī Aḥmad b. Muḥammad, *The Tajārib al-'umam or History of Ibn Miskawayh*, ed. L. Caetani, E. J. W. Gibb Memorial Series, vol. 7, no. 1, Leiden: Brill, 1909–17.

——. *Al-Ḥikma al-khalida (Javidan khirad)*, ed. 'A. Badawī, Cairo: Dār al-Andalus, 1952; *Javidan khirad*, ed. B. Sarvatian, trans. T. M. Shushtari, introd. M. Arkoun, Tehran: McGill University, Tehran Branch, 1976.

——. *An Unpublished Treatise of Miskawayh on Justice; or, Risāla fī māhiyat al-'adl lī Miskawayh*, ed. and trans. M. S. Khan, Leiden: Brill, 1964.

——. *Tahdhīb al-akhlāq wa-taṭhīr al-a'rāq*, trans. C. K. Zurayk as *The Refinement of Character*, Beirut: American University of Beirut, 1968.

Moran, W. L. (ed. and trans.) *The Amarna Letters*, Baltimore: Johns Hopkins, 1992.

Müneccimbaşı Ahmet Dede, *Saha'ifü'l-ahbar*, trans. Ahmed Nedīm, 3 vols, Istanbul: Matbaa-i 'Âmire, 1285/1868; *Müneccimbaşı tarihi (Sahaif-ül-ahbar fî vekayi-ül-a'sâr)*, trans. İ. Erünsal, 2 vols, 1001 Temel Eser, 37, Istanbul: Tercüman, 1970–4.

Murad II, Sultan, *Fatih Sultan Mehmed'e nasihatler*, trans. A. Uçman, 1001 Temel Eser, 76, Istanbul: Tercüman Gazetesi, 1976.

al-Murādī al-Ḥaḍramī, Abū Bakr Muḥammad b. al-Ḥasan, *Kitāb al-siyāsa aw al-ishāra fī tadbīr al-imāra*, ed. S. al-Nashshār, Casablanca: Dār al-Thaqāfa, 1981.
Mustashar al-Dawla, Yūsuf b. Kāzim, *The Essence of Modernity: Mirza Yusof Khan Mustashar ad-Dowla Tabrizi's treatise on codified law (Yak Kalima)*, trans. A. A. Seyed-Gohrab and S. McGlinn, Amsterdam and West Lafayette, IN: Rozenberg and Purdue University Press, 2007.
Mzali, M.-S. and Pignon, J. *Khereddine, homme d'état: mémoires*, 2 vols, Tunis: Maison Tunisienne de l'Édition, 1971.
Nabipour, M. *Die beiden persischen Leitfäden des Falak 'Alā-ye Tabrīzī über das staatliche Rechnungswesen im 14. Jahrhundert*, Göttingen: Georg-August-Universität, 1973.
Nahîfî, *see* al-Shayzarī.
Nasir-i Khusrau, *Naser-e Khosraw's Book of Travels (Safarnāma)*, trans. W. M. Thackston, Jr., New York: Bibliotheca Persica, 1986.
Ongan, H. *Ankara'nın iki numaralı şer'iye sicili*, Ankara: Türk Tarih Kurumu, 1974.
Owen, C. A. "Scandal in the Egyptian Treasury: a portion of the *Luma' al-Qawānīn* of 'Uthmān ibn Ibrāhīm al-Nābulusī," *JNES* 14, 1955: 70–95.
Özcan, A. *Kanûnnâme-i Âl-i Osman: (tahlil ve karsilastirmali metin)*, Istanbul: Kitabevi, 2003.
Özkaya, Y. "XVIIIinci yüzyılda çıkarılan adalet-nâmelere göre Türkiye'nin iç durumu," *Belleten* 38, 1974: 445–91.
Parpola, S. *The Correspondence of Sargon II, Part I: letters from Assyria and the West*, State Archives of Assyria, 1, Helsinki: Helsinki University Press, 1987.
Pellat, C. "Une charge contre les secrétaires d'état attribuée à Ǧāḥiẓ," *Hespéris* 43, 1956: 29–50.
——. *The Life and Works of Jāḥiẓ: translations of selected texts*, trans. D. M. Hawke, Berkeley: University of California Press, 1969.
——. (trans.) *Le livre de la couronne, attribué à Ǧaḥiẓ*, Paris: Société d'Édition "Les Belles Lettres," 1954.
Perikhanian, A. (trans.) *The Book of a Thousand Judgements (a Sasanian law-book)*, trans. from Russian by N. Garsoian, Costa Mesa, CA: Mazda, 1997.
al-Qaḍḍāfī, M. *Kitāb al-akhḍar* (1979), trans. H. M. Christman as *Qaddafi's Green Book: an unauthorized edition*, Buffalo, NY: Prometheus Books, 1988.
Qazwīnī, Ḥamd Allāh Mustawfī, *The Ta'rīkh-i-guzida or "Select History"*, abridged trans. E. G. Browne, E. J. W. Gibb Memorial Series, vol. 23, pt. 2, Leiden: Brill; London: Luzac, 1913.
Qutb, S. *Al-'Adāla al-ijtimā'iyya fī'l-Islām*, Cairo: Maktabat Miṣr wa Maṭba'atuhā, 1949; *Social Justice in Islam*, trans. J. B. Hardie. Washington, DC: American Council of Learned Societies, 1953.
——. *The Sayyid Qutb Reader: selected writings on politics, religion, and society*, ed. A. J. Bergesen, New York, London: Routledge, 2008.
Said, Mehmed, *Ahlâk-ı Hamida*, Istanbul: Elcevaip Matbaası, 1882; trans. J. A. Decourdemanche as *La morale musulmane, ou, l'Akhlaqi-Hamidé*, Paris: Ernest Leroux, 1888.
Sanjian, A. K. (trans.) *Colophons of Armenian Manuscripts, 1301–1480: a source for Middle Eastern history*, Cambridge, MA: Harvard University Press, 1969.
Sarı Mehmed Paşa, the Defterdar, *Zübde-i vekayiât*, ed. A. Özcan, Ankara: Türk Tarih Kurumu, 1995.
Sarıcaoğlu, F. *Kendi kaleminden bir padişahın portresi: Sultan I. Abdülhamid (1774–1789)* Istanbul: Tarih ve Tabiat Vakfı, 2001.
Şen, A. *İbrahim Müteferrika ve Usûlü'l-hikem fî nizâmi'l-umem* Ankara: Türkiye Diyanet Vakfı, 1995.
Soroush, A. *Reason, Freedom & Democracy in Islam*, trans. and ed. M. Sadri and A. Sadri, Oxford: Oxford University Press, 2000.
Stern, S. M. *Fatimid Decrees: original documents from the Fatimid chancery*, London: Faber & Faber, 1964.
al-Ṣūlī, Muḥammad b. Yaḥyá, *Akhbār ar-Rāḍī billāh wa'l-Muttaqī billāh*, trans. M. Canard, 2 vols, Algiers: Imprimeries "La Typo-Litho" et Jules Carbonel réunies, 1946–50.
Tafazzolī, A. *Mēnō-ye Xerad*, Tehran, Tus, 1364/1985.
Tardy, J. "Traduction d'*al-adab al-kabīr* d'Ibn al-Muqaffa'," *AI* 27, 1993: 181–223.
Tekin, Ş. "Fatih Sultan Mehmed devrine âit bir inşâ mecmuası," *JTS* 20, 1996: 267–315.

Tevki'i Abdürrahman Paşa, "Osmanlı Kanunnameleri," *MTM* 1, 1913/1331: 49–112, 304–348, 497–544; *Osmanlı Devleti'nde Teşrifat ve Törenler: Tevki'î Abdurrahman Paşa Kānûn-Nâmesi* trans. Sadık Müfit Bilge, Istanbul: Kitabevi, 2011.

Turan, O. *Türkiye Selçukluları hakkında resmī vesikalar*, Ankara: Türk Tarih Kurumu, 1958.

Tvertinova, A. S. *Kniga Zakonov Sultana Selima I. (Sultan I. Selim'in kanun-namesi)* Moscow: Nauka, 1969.

Ursinus, M. *Grievance Administration (Şikayet) in an Ottoman Province: the Kaymakam of Rumelia's "Record book of complaints" of 1781–1783*, London: RoutledgeCurzon, 2005.

Uzunçarşılı, İ. H. "Gazi Orhan Bey vakfiyesi," *Belleten* 5, 1941: 277–88 and plates 86–87.

van Soldt, W. H. (trans.) *Letters in the British Museum, Part 2*, Altbabylonische Briefe im Umschrift und Übersetzung, 2, Leiden: Brill, 1994.

Varāvīnī, Sa'd al-Dīn, *The Tales of Marzuban*, trans. R. Levy, Bloomington: Indiana University Press, 1959.

Waldman, M. R. *Toward a Theory of Historical Narrative: a case study in Perso-Islamicate historiography*, Columbus: Ohio State University Press, 1980.

Wittek, P. "Ankara'da bir İlhanî kitabesi," *THİTM* 1, 1931: 161–64 and plates 1–4.

Yahia, L. and Wendl, K. *I Was Saddam's Son*, New York: Arcade, 1997.

al-Ya'qūbī, Aḥmad b. Abī Ya'qūb, *Tā'rīkh Aḥmad ibn Abī Ya'qūb,* ed. M. T. Houtsma as *Ibn Wādhih qui dicitur al-Ja'qubī Historiae*, 2 vols, Leiden: Brill, 1883.

Yazdī, Sharaf al-Dīn 'Alī, *Political and Military Institutes of Tamerlane*, trans. W. Davy, 1783; Delhi: Idarah-i Adabiyat-i Delli, 1972; *Temur Tuzukları*, trans. B. A. Ahmedov, Tashkent: Ghafur Ghulom, 1991.

Yücel, Y. and Pulaha, S. (eds) *I. Selim kānūnnāmeleri (1512–1520)* Ankara: Türk Tarih Kurumu, 1995.

Reference works and textbooks

Ateş, A. "Hicri VI–VIII. (XII–XIV.) asırlarda Anadolu'da Farsça eserler," *TM* 7–8, 1945: 94–135.

Aynî, M. A. *Türk ahlâkcıları*, Istanbul: Marifet, 1939.

Blochet, E. *Catalogue des manuscrits turcs*, 2 vols, Paris: Bibliothèque Nationale, 1932.

Çağman, F. and Tanındı, Z. *The Topkapı Saray Museum: the albums and illustrated manuscripts*, trans. and ed. J. M. Rogers, London: Thames & Hudson, 1986.

Cleveland, W. L. *A History of the Modern Middle East*, Boulder, CO: Westview, 1994.

Çolak, O. M. "İstanbul kütüphanelerinde bulunan siyasetnâmeler bibliografyası," *TALID* 1, no. 2, 2003: 339–78.

Dale, S. F. *The Muslim Empires of the Ottomans, Safavids, and Mughals*, Cambridge: Cambridge University Press, 2010.

Danishpazhouh, M.-T. "An Annotated Bibliography on Government and Statecraft," in S. A. Arjomand (ed.) *Authority and Political Culture in Shi'ism*, 213–39, Albany: State University of New York Press, 1988.

Elliot, H. M. and Dowson, J. (ed. and trans.) *The History of India as Told by Its Own Historians*, 10 vols, London: Trübner, 1869; repr. New York: AMS Press, 1966.

Finkel, C. *Osman's Dream*, London: John Murray, 2005; New York: Basic Books, 2006.

Gelb, I. J., Jacobsen, T., Landsberger, B., and Oppenheim, A. L. (eds) *The Assyrian Dictionary*, Chicago, IL: Oriental Institute, 1956–2010.

Gelvin, J. L. *The Modern Middle East: a history*, New York, Oxford: Oxford University Press, 2005.

Gibb, H. A. R., Kramers, J. H., Lévi-Provonçal, E., Schacht, J., Lewis, B. and Pellat, C. (eds) *Encyclopaedia of Islam*, Leiden: Brill, 1913–38; 2nd ed. Leiden: Brill, 1954–.

Gürbüz, A. *XV.–XVI. yüzyıl Osmanlı sancak çalışmaları: değerlendirme ve bibliografik bir deneme*, Istanbul: Dergâh, 2001.

Hodgson, M. G. S. *The Venture of Islam: conscience and history in a world civilization*, 3 vols, Chicago, IL: Chicago, IL: University of Chicago Press, 1974.

Humphreys, R. S. *Islamic History: a framework for inquiry*, rev. ed., Princeton, NJ: Princeton University Press, 1991.

İlhan, M. M. "The Ottoman Archives and Their Importance for Historical Studies: with special reference to Arab provinces," *Belleten* 55, 1991: 415–71 and plates.
İnalcık, H. *The Ottoman Empire: the classical age, 1300–1600*, trans. N. Itzkowitz and C. Imber, London: Weidenfeld & Nicolson, 1973, repr. London: Phoenix, 1994; New York: Routledge, 2001.
Itzkowitz, N. *Ottoman Empire and Islamic Tradition*, Chicago, IL: University of Chicago Press, 1972.
Karatay, F. E. (ed.) *Topkaı Sarayı Müzesi Kütüphanesi Türkçe yazmalar kataloğu*, Istanbul: Topkapı Sarayı Müzesi, 1961.
Khater, A. F. *Sources in the History of the Modern Middle East*, Boston, MA: Houghton Mifflin, 2004.
Köprülü, M. F. *Türk edebiyatı tarihi*, Istanbul: Milli Matbaa, 1926; repr. Istanbul: Ötüken, 1984.
——. "Anadolu Selçuklulari tarihi'nin yerli kaynaklari," *Belleten* 7 (1943): 379–458; *The Seljuks of Anatolia: their history and culture according to local Muslim sources,* ed. and trans. G. Leiser, Salt Lake City: University of Utah Press, 1992.
Lowry, H. W. "The Ottoman Liva Kanunnames Contained in the Defter-i Hakani," *OA* 2, 1981: 43–74.
Morgan, D. O. *The Mongols*, Oxford: Basil Blackwell, 1986.
Olmstead, A. T. *History of Assyria*, Chicago, IL: University of Chicago Press, 1923.
Oppenheim, A. L. *Ancient Mesopotamia: portrait of a dead civilization*, rev. ed. completed by E. Reiner, Chicago, IL: University of Chicago Press, 1977.
Quataert, D. *The Ottoman Empire, 1700–1922*, Cambridge: Cambridge University Press, 2000.
Roux, G. *Ancient Iraq*, London: George Allen & Unwin, 1964; 2nd ed. Harmondsworth, UK: Penguin, 1980.
Sasson, J. M. (ed.) *Civilizations of the Ancient Near East*, 4 vols, New York: Simon & Schuster Macmillan, 1995.
Savory, R. M. *Iran under the Safavids*, Cambridge: Cambridge University Press, 1980.
Shaw, S. J. and Shaw, E. K. *The History of the Ottoman Empire and Modern Turkey*, 2 vols, Cambridge: Cambridge University Press, 1976–7.
Storey, C. A. *Persian Literature: a bio-bibliographical survey,* vol. 1, pt. 1: *Qur'anic Literature: History*, London: Luzac, 1927.
Streusand, D. E. *Islamic Gunpowder Empires: Ottomans, Safavids, and Mughals*, Boulder, CO: Westview, 2010.
Uğur, A. *Osmanlı siyâset-nâmeleri*, Istanbul: Milli Eğitim Bakanlığı, 2001.
Ullmann, M. *Wörterbuch der klassischen arabischen Sprache*, Wiesbaden: Harrassowitz, 1978.
Yatshatar, E. (ed.) *Encyclopaedia Iranica*, London: Routledge & Kegan Paul, 1982.
——. *Persian Literature*, [Albany, NY]: Bibliotheca Persica, 1988.

Studies

'Abd al-Mun'im, Ḥ. *Dīwān al-maẓālim*, Beirut: Dār al-Shurūq, 1983.
Abd-Allah, U. F. *The Islamic Struggle in Syria*, Berkeley, CA: Mizan, 1983.
Abdel-Khalek, G. *Stabilization and Adjustment in Egypt: reform or de-industrialization?* Cheltenham, UK: Edward Elgar, 2001.
Abdo, G. *No God but God: Egypt and the triumph of Islam*, Oxford: Oxford University Press, 2000.
Abed-Kotob, S. "The Accommodationists Speak: goals and strategies of the Muslim Brotherhood of Egypt," *IJMES* 27, 1995: 321–39.
Abou-El-Haj, R. A. *The 1703 Rebellion and the Structure of Ottoman Politics*, Istanbul: Nederlands Historisch-Archaeologisch Instituut, 1984.
——. *Formation of the Modern State: the Ottoman Empire, sixteenth to eighteenth centuries*, Albany: State University of New York Press, 1991.
——. "Aspects of the Legitimation of Ottoman Rule as Reflected in the Preambles to Two Early Liva Kanunameler," *Turcica*, 21–23 (1991): 371–83.
——. "Theorizing in Historical Writing beyond the Nation-State: Ottoman society in the middle period," in I. Baldauf and S. Faroqhi (eds) *Armağan: Festschrift für Andreas Tietze*, 1–18, Prague: enigma corporation, 1994.

——. "The Expression of Ottoman Political Culture in the Literature of Advice to Princes (Nasihatnameler), sixteenth to twentieth centuries," in R. K. Bhattacharya and A. K. Ghosh (eds) *Sociology in the Rubric of Social Science: Professor Ramkrishna Mukherjee felicitation volume*, 282–92, Calcutta: Anthropological Survey of India, 1995.

Abrahamian, E. "The Crowd in Iranian Politics, 1905–1953," *Past & Present* 41, 1968: 184–210.

——. "The Crowd in the Persian Revolution 1," *IranS* 2, 1969: 128–50.

——. "Oriental Despotism: the case of Qajar Iran," *IJMES* 5, 1974: 3–31.

——. "The Causes of the Constitutional Revolution in Iran," *IJMES* 10, 1979: 381–414.

——. *Iran: between two revolutions*, Princeton, NJ: Princeton University Press, 1982.

——. *Radical Islam: the Iranian Mojahedin*, London: IB Tauris, 1989.

——. *Khomeinism: essays of the Islamic Republic*, Berkeley: University of California Press, 1993.

Abu Jaber, Kamel S. *The Arab Ba'th Socialist Party: history, ideology, and organization*, Syracuse: Syracuse University Press, 1966.

Abu-Manneh, B. "The Sultan and the Bureaucracy: the anti-Tanzimat concepts of Grand Vizier Mahmud Nedim Paşa," *IJMES* 22, 1990: 257–74.

——. "The Islamic Roots of the Gülhane Rescript," *WI* 34, 1994: 173–203.

Abun-Nasr, J. M. "Militant Islam: a historical perspective," in E. Gellner (ed.) *Islamic Dilemmas: Reformers, Nationalists and Industralization: the southern shore of the Mediterranean*, 73–93, Berlin: Mouton Publishers, 1985.

Acun, F. "Ottoman Administrative Priorities: revenue maximisation in the province of Karahisar-ı Şarki," in M. Köhbach, G. Procházka-Eisl, and C. Römer (eds) *Acta Viennensia Ottomanica*, 7–12, Vienna: Institut für Orientalistik, 1999.

Adahl, K. *A Khamsa of Nizami of 1439: origin of the miniatures–a presentation and analysis*, Uppsala: Almqvist & Wiksell International, 1981.

Adamiyyat, F. and Natiq, H. *Afkār-i ijtimāʿī va siyāsī va iqtiṣādī dar asār-i muntashir nashuda-yi davra-yi Qajar*, Tehran: Intishārāt-i Āgāh, 1977.

Adams, R. H. Jr. *Development and Social Change in Rural Egypt*, Syracuse: Syracuse University Press, 1986.

Adams, R. M. "Agriculture and Urban Life in Early Southwestern Iran," *Science* n.s. 136, no. 3511, April 13, 1962: 109–22.

——. *Land behind Baghdad: a history of settlement on the Diyala plains*, Chicago, IL: University of Chicago Press, 1965.

Adanır, F. "The Ottoman Peasantries, *c.*1360–*c.*1860," in T. Scott (ed.) *The Peasantries of Europe: from the fourteenth to the eighteenth centuries*, 269–310, London: Longman, 1998.

——. "Semi-Autonomous Provincial Forces in the Balkans and Anatolia," in S. N. Faroqhi (ed.) *The Cambridge History of Turkey*, vol. 3, *The Later Ottoman Empire, 1603–1839*, 157–206, Cambridge: Cambridge University Press, 2006.

Addi, L. "Forme néo-patrimoniale de l'état et secteur public en Algérie," in J.-C. Santucci and H. El Malki (eds) *État et développement dans le monde arabe: crises et mutations au Maghreb*, 79–97, Paris: CNRS, 1990.

Afary, J. "Peasant Rebellions of the Caspian Region during the Iranian Constitutional Revolution, 1906–1909," *IJMES* 23, 1991: 137–61.

——. *The Iranian Constitutional Revolution, 1906–1911: grassroots democracy, social democracy, and the origins of feminism*, New York: Columbia University Press, 1996.

Afshar, H. "The Iranian Theocracy," in H. Afshar (ed.) *Iran: a revolution in turmoil*, 220–43, London: Macmillan, 1985.

Afshari, M. R. "The *Pīshivarān* and Merchants in Precapitalist Iranian Society: An Essay on the Background and Causes of the Constitutional Revolution," *IJMES* 15, 1983: 133–55.

——. "The Historians of the Constitutional Movement and the Making of the Iranian Populist Tradition," *IJMES* 25, 1993: 477–94.

Ágoston, G. *Guns for the Sultan: military power and the weapons industry in the Ottoman Empire* Cambridge: Cambridge University Press, 2005.

Ahmad, A. *A History of Islamic Sicily*, Edinburgh: Edinburgh University Press, 1975.

Ahmad, F. "The Agrarian Policy of the Young Turks, 1908–1918," in J.-L. Bacqué-Grammont and P. Dumont (eds) *Économie et sociétés dans l'empire ottoman (fin du XVIIIe siècle–début du XXe siècle)*, 275–88, Paris: CNRS, 1983.

——. *The Young Turks: the Committee of Union and Progress in Turkish politics, 1908–1914*, Oxford: Clarendon, 1969.

Ahmad, K. and Hassan, A. "Distributive Justice: the Islamic perspective," *Intellectual Discourse* 8, 2000: 159–72.

Ahmad, L. *Women and Gender in Islam*, New Haven, CT: Yale University Press, 1992.

Ahmad, M. *The Nature of Islamic Political Theory*, Karachi: Ma'aref, 1975.

Ahmad, M. H. M. "Some Notes on Arabic Historiography during the Zengid and Ayyubid Periods (512/1127–648/1250)," in B. Lewis and P. M. Holt (eds) *Historians of the Middle East*, Historical Writing on the Peoples of Asia, 4, 79–97, Oxford, New York: Oxford University Press, 1962.

Ahmad, R. "Expecting Mahdi, Encountering Zarathustra: Politics of Representing the Pre-Islamic Legacy in Post-Islamic Revolutionary Persian Novels," paper presented at Colloquium Series, Department of Near Eastern Studies, University of Arizona, December 4, 2009.

Ahrweiler, H. *L'idéologie politique de l'Empire byzantin*, Paris: Presses universitaires de France, 1975.

Aigle, D. "Le grand *jasaq* de Gengis-Khan, l'empire, la culture mongole et la *shari'a*," *JESHO* 47, 2004: 31–79.

Ait Amara, H. "The State, Social Classes and Agricultural Policies in the Arab World," in H. Beblawi and G. Luciani (eds) *The Rentier State*, 138–58, London: Croom Helm, 1987.

Ajami, A. I. "From Peasant to Farmer: a study of agrarian transformation in an Iranian village, 1967–2002," *IJMES* 37, 2005: 327–49.

Ajami, F. *The Arab Predicament: Arab political thought and practice since 1967*, Cambridge: Cambridge University Press, 1981.

——. *The Vanished Imam: Musa al Sadr and the Shia of Lebanon*, Ithaca, NY: Cornell University Press, 1986.

Akarlı, E. D. *The Long Peace: Ottoman Lebanon, 1861–1920*, Berkeley: University of California Press, 1993.

Akdağ, M. "Medreseli isyanları," *İÜIFM* 11, 1949–50: 361–87.

——. "Celâli isyanlarından büyük kaçgunluk, 1603–1606," *TAD* 2, 1964: 1–49.

——. *Türk halkının dirlik ve düzenlik kavgası*, Ankara: Bilgi Yayınları, 1975.

Akhavi, S. "Introduction: ideology and the Iranian Revolution," in B. M. Rosen (ed.) *Iran since the Revolution: internal dynamics, regional conflict, and the superpowers*, xi–xx, Boulder, CO: Social Science Monographs, New York: Columbia University Press, 1985.

——. "Shariati's Social Thought," in N. R. Keddie (ed.) *Religion and Politics in Iran: Shi'ism from quietism to revolution*, 125–44, New Haven, CT: Yale University Press, 1983.

Akiba, J. "A New School for Qadis: education of the sharia judges in the late Ottoman Empire," *Turcica* 35, 2003: 125–63.

Akkemik, Ü. and Aras, A. "Reconstruction (1689–1994 AD) of April–August Precipitation in the Southern Part of Central Turkey," *International Journal of Climatology* 25, 2005: 537–48.

Akkemik, Ü., Dağdeviren, N. and Aras, A. "A Preliminary Reconstruction (A.D. 1635–2000) of Spring Precipitation using Oak Tree Rings in the Western Black Sea Region of Turkey," *International Journal of Biometeorology* 49, 2005: 297–302.

Aksan, V. H. "Ottoman Political Writing, 1768–1808," *IJMES* 25, 1993: 53–69; repr. in V. H. Aksan, *Ottomans and Europeans: contacts and conflicts*, Istanbul: İsis, 2004, 25–44.

——. "Feeding the Ottoman Troops on the Danube, 1768–1774," *War and Society* 13, 1995: 1–14; repr. in V. H. Aksan, *Ottomans and Europeans: contacts and conflicts*, Istanbul: İsis, 2004, 209–22.

——. "Whatever Happened to the Janissaries? mobilization for the 1768–1774 Russo-Ottoman War," *War in History* 5, 1998: 23–36; repr. in V. H. Aksan, *Ottomans and Europeans: contacts and conflicts*, Istanbul: İsis, 2004, 223–38.

Aktepe, M. M. *Patrona İsyanı (1730)*, Istanbul: Edebiyat Fakültesi, 1958.

Alavi, B. "Critical Writings on the Renewal of Islam," in C. E. Bosworth and C. Hillenbrand (eds) *Qajar Iran: political, social and cultural change, 1800–1925*, 243–54, Costa Mesa, CA: Mazda, 1983.

Album, S. "Power and Legitimacy: the coinage of Mubāriz al-Dīn Muḥammad ibn al-Muẓaffar at Yazd and Kirmān," in J. Aubin (ed.) *Le monde iranien et l'Islam: sociétés et cultures*, 4 vols, 2: 157–71, Geneva: Droz, 1974.

Alderman, H. "Food Subsidies and State Policies in Egypt," in A. Richards (ed.) *Food, States, and Peasants: analyses of the agrarian question in the Middle East*, 183–200, Boulder, CO: Westview, 1986.

Alföldi, A. "Türklerde çift krallık," in *İkinci Türk tarih kongresi (1937)*, 507–19, Istanbul: Kenan, 1943.

Algar, H. *Religion and State in Iran, 1785–1906: the role of the ulama in the Qajar period*, Berkeley: University of California Press, 1969.

——. *Mīrzā Malkum Khān: a study in the history of Iranian modernism*, Berkeley: University of California Press, 1973.

——. "Social Justice in the Ideology and Legislation of the Islamic Revolution of Iran," in L. O. Michalak and J. W. Salacuse (eds) *Social Legislation in the Contemporary Middle East*, 17–60, Berkeley: Institute of International Studies, 1986.

Algul, H. "Osman Gazi'nin oğlu Orhan Gazi'ye nasihatlar," in *Osman Gazi ve dönemi*, 99–104, Bursa: Bursa Kültür Sanat ve Turizm Vakfi, 1996.

Ali, S. T. *A Religion, Not a State: Ali 'Abd al-Raziq's Islamic justification of political secularism*, Salt Lake City: University of Utah Press, 2009.

Allsen, T. T. "Mongol Census Taking in Rus', 1245–1275," *Harvard Ukraininan Studies* 5, 1981: 32–53.

——. "Guard and Government in the Reign of the Grand Qan Möngke, 1251–59," *HJAS* 46, 1986: 495–512.

——. *Mongol Imperialism: the policies of the Grand Qan Möngke in China, Russia, and the Islamic Lands, 1251–1259*, Berkeley: University of California Press, 1987.

——. "Changing Forms of Legitimation in Mongol Iran," in G. Seaman and D. Marks (eds) *Rulers from the Steppe: state formation on the Eurasian periphery*, 223–41, Los Angeles: Ethnographics Press, University of Southern California, 1991.

——. *Culture and Conquest in Mongol Eurasia*, Cambridge: Cambridge University Press, 2001.

Amanat, A. *Pivot of the Universe: Nasir al-Din Shah Qajar and the Iranian monarchy, 1831–1896*, Berkeley: University of California Press, 1997.

Amari, M. *Storia dei Musulmani de Sicilia*, 2nd ed., 5 vols in 8, Rome: Catania, 1938.

Amédroz, H. F. "The Mazalim Jurisdiction in the Ahkam Sultaniyya of Mawardi," *JRAS* 1911: 635–74.

——. "The Vizier Abu-l-Faḍl Ibn al 'Amīd from the 'Tajārib al-Umam' of Abu 'Ali Miskawaih," *Der Islam* 3, 1912: 323–57.

Amin, G. A. *The Modernization of Poverty: a study in the political economy of growth in nine Arab countries, 1945–1970*, Leiden: Brill, 1974.

——. *Egypt's Economic Predicament: a study in the interaction of external pressure, political folly and social tension in Egypt, 1960–1990*, Leiden: Brill, 1995.

Amitai, R. "Turko-Mongolian Nomads and the *Iqṭā'* System in the Islamic Middle East (*c.*1000–1400 AD)," in A. M. Khazanov and A. Wink (eds) *Nomads in the Sedentary World*, 152–71, Richmond, UK: Curzon, 2001.

Amjad, M. *Iran: from royal dictatorship to theocracy*, Westport, CT: Greenwood, 1989.

Ammar, H. *Growing Up in an Egyptian Village: Silwa, Province of Aswan*, New York: Octagon Books, 1966.

Amrani, B. "Catastrophe Nationale," *Jeune Afrique* no. 1794, 25–31 May 1995: 34–35.

Amuzegar, J. *The Dynamics of the Iranian Revolution: the Pahlavis' triumph and tragedy*, Albany: State University of New York Press, 1991.

Anastasopoulos, A. "Lighting the Flame of Disorder: *ayan* infighting and state intervention in Ottoman Karaferye, 1758–59," *IJTS* 8, 2002: 73–88.

Anderson, L. "Nineteenth-Century Reform in Ottoman Libya," *IJMES* 16, 1984: 325–48.

——. *The State and Social Transformation in Tunisia and Libya, 1830–1980*, Princeton, NJ: Princeton University Press, 1986.
——. "Dynasts and Nationalists: why monarchies survive," in J Kostiner (ed.) *Middle East Monarchies: The Challenge of Modernity*, 53–69, Boulder, CO: Lynne Reinner, 2000.
Andre-Salvini, B. and Salvini, M. "Ein König von Dér," *Altorientalische Forschungen* 24, 1997: 39–43.
Andrews, W. G. *Poetry's Voice, Society's Song: Ottoman lyric poetry*, Seattle: University of Washington Press, 1985.
——. "Literary Art of the Golden Age: the age of Süleymân," in H. İnalcık and C. Kafadar (eds) *Süleymân the Second and His Time*, 353–68, Istanbul: İsis, 1993.
——. "Speaking of Power: The 'Ottoman Kaside'," in S. Sperl and C. Shackle (eds) *Qasida Poetry in Islamic Asia and Africa*, vol. 1: *Classical Traditions and Modern Meanings*, 281–300, Leiden: Brill, 1996.
Ansari, H. *Egypt, the Stalled Society*, Albany: State University of New York Press, 1986.
Ansari, M. A. H. *The Ethical Philosophy of Miskawaih*, Aligarh: Aligarh Muslim University, 1964.
Anscombe, F. J. "Islam and the Age of Ottoman Reform," *Past & Present*, no. 208, August 2010: 159–89.
Aperghis, G. G. *The Seleukid Royal Economy: the finances and financial administration of the Seleukid Empire*, Cambridge: Cambridge University Press, 2004.
Arazi, A. and El'ad, 'A. "'L'épître à l'armée': al-Ma'mūn et la seconde da'wa," *SI* 67, 1988: 27–70.
Arberry, A. J. "An Arabic Treatise on Politics," *IQ*, 2, 1955: 9–22.
——. *Classical Persian Literature*, New York: Macmillan, 1958.
Arjomand, S.A. *The Shadow of God and the Hidden Imam: religion, political order, and societal change in Shi'ite Iran from the beginning to 1890*, Chicago, IL:Chicago, IL: University of Chicago Press, 1984.
——. *The Turban for the Crown: the Islamic Revolution in Iran*, New York, Oxford: Oxford University Press, 1988.
——. "Authority and Public Law in Sunni and Shi'ite Islam," R. D. Sharpe Lecture presented at University of Chicago, March 1994.
——. "Medieval Persianate Political Ethic," *Studies on Persianate Societies* 1, 2003: 3–30.
——. "Evolution of the Persianate Polity and Its Transmission to India," *Journal of Persianate Studies* 2, 2009: 115–36.
Arkoun, M. *Contribution à l'étude de l'humanisme arabe au IVe/Xe siècle: Miskawayh (320/325–421)=(932/936–1030), philosophe et historien*, Paris: J. Vrin, 1970.
Arnold, T. W. *The Caliphate*, Oxford: Clarendon, 1924.
Artan, T. "Architecture as a Theatre of Life: profile of the eighteenth-century Bosphorus," PhD diss. MIT, 1989.
Artan, T. "Noble Women Who Changed the Face of the Bosphorus and … the Palaces of the Sultanas," *İstanbul,* 1.1, Winter 1993: 87–97.
Asad, T. "The Limits of Religious Criticism in the Middle East: notes on Islamic public argument," in T. Asad, *Genealogies of Religion: discipline and reasons of power in Christianity and Islam*, 200–38, Baltimore, OH: Johns Hopkins Press, 1993.
Ashraf, A. "Historical Obstacles to the Development of a Bourgeoisie in Iran," in M. A. Cook (ed.) *Studies in the Economic History of the Middle East: from the rise of Islam to the present day*, 308–32, London: Oxford University Press, 1970.
——. "State and Agrarian Relations before and after the Iranian Revolution, 1960–1990," in F. Kazemi and J. Waterbury (eds) *Peasants and Politics in the Modern Middle East*, 277–311, Miami: Florida International University Press, 1991.
Ashtor, E. *A Social and Economic History of the Near East in the Middle Ages*, Berkeley: University of California Press, 1976.
Aslam, M. "Faḍl-Ullah bin Rūzbihān al-Işfahānī," *JAS Pakistan* 10, 1965: 121–34.
Aslanapa, O. *Turkish Art and Architecture*, London: Faber and Faber, 1971.
Assaad, S. A. *The Reign of al-Hakim bi Amr Allah (386/996–411/1021): a political study*, Beirut: Arab Institute for Research and Publishing, 1974.

Atalay, B. "Ottoman State and Ahmet Cevdet Pasha's History," in K. Çiçek (ed.) *The Great Ottoman-Turkish Civilisation*, 4 vols, 3: 389–404, Ankara: Yeni Türkiye, 2000.

Atıl, E. "The Art of the Book," in E. Atıl (ed.) *Turkish Art*, 137–238, New York: Smithsonian Institution and H. N. Abrams, 1980.

——. *Renaissance of Islam: art of the Mamluks*, Washington, DC: Smithsonian Institution, 1981.

——. "Mamluk Painting in the Late Fifteenth Century," *Muqarnas* 2, 1984: 159–71.

——. *Süleymanname: the illustrated history of Süleyman the Magnificent*, Washington, DC: National Gallery of Art, New York: H. N. Abrams, 1986.

——(ed.) *Turkish Art*, Washington and New York: Smithsonian Institution and H. N. Abrams, 1980.

Aubin, J. "Un soyurghal Qara-Qoyunlu concernant le bulūk de Bawānāt-Harāt-Marwast," in S. M. Stern (ed.) *Documents from Islamic Chanceries*, 159–70, Columbia: University of South Carolina Press, 1965.

——. "Réseau pastoral et réseau caravanier: les grand'routes du Khurassan à l'époque mongole," in *Le monde iranien et l'Islam: sociétés et cultures*, 4 vols, 1: 105–30, Geneva: Droz, 1971.

——. "Le patronage culturel en Iran sous les Ilkhans: une grande famille de Yazd," in J. Aubin, *Le monde iranien et l'Islam: sociétés et cultures*, 4 vols, 3: 107–18, Paris: Société d'Histoire de l'Orient, 1975.

——. "Le *quriltai* de Sultân-Maydân (1336)," *JA* 274, 1991: 175–97.

——. *Émirs mongols et vizirs persans dans les remous de l'acculturation*, Paris: Association pour l'Avancement des Études Iraniennes, 1995.

Augustinos, G. "Europeans, Ottoman Reformers, and the *Reaya*: a question of historical focus," in R. Frucht (ed.) *Labyrinth of Nationalism, Complexities of Diplomacy: essays in honor of Charles and Barbara Jelavich*, 234–48, Columbus, OH: Slavica, 1992.

Ayalon, D. "The Great *Yāsa* of Chingiz Khān: a reexamination," (A) *SI* 33, 1971: 97–140; (B) 34, 1971: 151–80; (C1) 36, 1972: 113–58; (C2) 38, 1973: 107–58.

——. "The Mamlūks of the Seljuks: Islam's military might at the crossroads," *JRAS* (1996): 305–33.

Ayoub, M. "The Islamic Concept of Justice," in N. H. Barazangi, M. R. Zaman, and O. Afzal (eds) *Islamic Identity and the Struggle for Justice*, 19–26, Gainesville: University Press of Florida, 1996.

Azarnoush, M. "From Persepolis to al-Fustat: continuation of Achaemenid architectural concepts," in B. G. Fragner, C. Fragner, G. Gnoli, R. Haag-Higuchi, M. Maggi, and P. Orsatti (eds) *Proceedings of the Second European Conference of Iranian Studies*, 47–52, Rome: Istituto Italiano per il Medio ed Estremo Oriente, 1995.

Aziz, G. R. "Literary and Cultural Activity in Khwarazm (11th–12th Century)," *JPHS* 22 (1974): 81–112.

——. *A Short History of the Khwarazmshahs*, Karachi: Pakistan Historical Society, 1978.

Azkia, M. "Rural Society and Revolution in Iran," in E. Hooglund (ed.) *Twenty Years of Islamic Revolution: Political and Social Transition in Iran since 1979*, 96–119, Syracuse: Syracuse University Press, 2002.

al-Azmeh, A. *Arabic Thought and Islamic Societies*, London: Croom Helm, 1986.

——. *Muslim Kingship: power and the sacred in Muslim, Christian, and Pagan polities*, London: IB Tauris, 1997.

Babakhan, Ziyauddin Khan b. Ishan, *Islam and Muslims in the Land of Soviets*, trans. R. Dixon, Moscow: Progress, 1980.

Babayan, K. "The Safavid Synthesis: from Qizilbash Islam to Imamite Shi'ism," *IranS* 27, 1994: 135–61.

——. *Mystics, Monarchs, and Messiahs: cultural landscapes of early modern Iran*, Cambridge, MA: Harvard University Center for Middle Eastern Studies, 2002.

Babinger, F. *Mehmed the Conqueror and His Time*, ed. W. C. Hickman, trans. R. Manheim, Princeton, NJ: Princeton University Press, 1978.

Back, M. *Die Sassanidischen Staatsinschriften: Studien zur Orthographie und Phonologie des Mittelpersischen*, AcIr 18, ser. 3, vol. 8, Leiden: Brill, 1978.

Baer, E. "The Ruler in Cosmic Setting: a note on medieval Islamic iconography," in A. Daneshvari (ed.) *Essays in Islamic Art and Architecture in Honor of Katharina Otto-Dorn*, 13–19, Malibu, CA: Undena, 1981.

Baer, G. *Studies in the Social History of Modern Egypt*, Chicago, IL: University of Chicago Press, 1969.

Bagby, I. A. "The Issue of *Maslaḥah* in Classical Islamic Legal Theory," *IJIAS* 2, 1985: 1–11.

Bağcı, S. "A New Theme of the Shirazi Frontispiece Miniatures: the *Dīvān* of Solomon," *Muqarnas* 12, 1995: 101–11.

——. "From Translated Word to Translated Image: the illustrated *Şehnâme-i Türkî* copies," *Muqarnas* 17, 2000: 162–76.

——. "An Iranian Epic and an Ottoman Painter: Nakkaş Osman's 'new' visual interpretation of the Shâhnâmah," in S. Prätor and C. K. Neumann (eds) *Frauen, Bilder und Gelehrte: Studien zu Gesellschaft und Künsten im Osmanischen Reich, Festschrift Hans Georg Majer*, 2 vols, Istanbul: Simurg, 2002, 2: 421–39.

Bailey, H., Avery, P. W., Fisher, W. B., Gershevitch, I., Yarshater, E. (eds) *The Cambridge History of Iran*, 7 vols, Cambridge: Cambridge University Press, 1968–91.

Bakhash, S. *Iran: monarchy, bureaucracy and reform under the Qajars: 1858–1896*, Oxford: St. Antony's College, 1978.

——. *The Reign of the Ayatollahs: Iran and the Islamic Revolution*, New York: Basic Books, 1984.

——. "Islam and Social Justice in Iran," in M. Kramer (ed.) *Shi'ism, Resistance, and Revolution*, 95–115, Boulder, CO: Westview, 1987.

Banani, A. "Ferdowsi and the Art of Tragic Epic," in *Islam and Its Cultural Divergence: studies in honor of Gustave E. von Grunebaum*, Urbana: University of Illinois Press, 1971.

——. "Reflections on the Social and Economic Structure of Safavid Persia at Its Zenith," *IranS* 11, 1978: 83–116.

Banisadr, A.-H. and Vieille, P. "Iran and the Multinationals," in A.-R. Nobari (ed.) *Iran Erupts: Independence: news and analysis of the Iranian national movement*, 24–33, Stanford: Iran–America Documentation Group, 1978.

Baram, A. "Mesopotamian Identity in Ba'thi Iraq," *MES* 19, 1983: 426–55.

——. *Culture, History and Ideology in the Formation of Ba'thist Iraq, 1968–89*, New York: St. Martin's, 1991.

Barfield, T. J. "Tribe and State Relations: the Inner Asian perspective," in P. S. Khoury and J. Kostiner (ed.) *Tribes and State Formation in the Middle East*, 153–82, Berkeley: University of California Press, 1990.

Barkan, Ö. L. "Türkiye'de imparatorluk devirlerinin büyük nüfus ve arazi tahrirleri ve Hâkana mahsus istatistik defterleri," *İÜİFM* 2, 1940: 20–59, 214–47.

——. *XV ve XVIinci asırlaarda Osmanlı imparatorlluğunda ziraî ekonominin hukukî ve malî esasları, I. Kanunlar*, Istanbul: Türkiyat Enstitüsü, 1943.

——. "Research on the Ottoman Fiscal Surveys," in M. A. Cook (ed.) *Studies in the Economic History of the Middle East: from the rise of Islam to the present day*, 163–71, London: Oxford University Press, 1970.

Barker, E. (ed. and trans.) *Social and Political Thought in Byzantium: from Justinian I to the last Palaeologus*, Oxford: Clarendon, 1957.

Barkey, K. *Bandits and Bureaucrats: the Ottoman route to state centralization*, Ithaca: Cornell University Press, 1994.

——. *Empire of Difference: the Ottomans in comparative perspective*, Cambridge: Cambridge University Press, 2008.

Barthold, W. W. "İlhanlılar Devrinde Malî Vaziyet," *THİTM* 1, 1931: 135–60.

——. "Caliph and Sultan," trans. N. S. Doniach, *IQ* 7, 1963: 117–35.

——. *Turkestan Down to the Mongol Invasions*, ed. C. E. Bosworth, trans. Mrs. T. Minorsky, 3rd ed., E. J. W. Gibb Memorial Trust, London: Luzac, 1968.

Bashear, S. *Arabs and Others in Early Islam*, Princeton, NJ: Darwin, 1997.

Batatu, H. *The Old Social Classes and the Revolutionary Movements of Iraq: a study of Iraq's old landed and commercial classes and of its Communists, Ba'thists, and Free Officers*, Princeton, NJ: Princeton University Press, 1978.

——. *Syria's Peasantry, the Descendants of Its Lesser Rural Notables, and Their Politics*, Princeton, NJ: Princeton University Press, 1999.

Bates, R. H. (ed.) *Toward a Political Economy of Development: a rational choice perspective*, Berkeley: University of California Press, 1988.

Bayat-Philipp, M. "Mirza Aqa Khan Kirmani: a nineteenth century Persian nationalist," in E. Kedourie and S. G. Haim (eds) *Towards a Modern Iran: studies in thought, politics and society*, 64–95, London: Frank Cass, 1980.

Bayat, M. "The Cultural Implications of the Constitutional Revolution," in C. E. Bosworth and C. Hillenbrand (eds) *Qajar Iran: Political, Social and Cultural Change, 1800–1925*, 65–75, Costa Mesa, CA: Mazda Publishers, 1983.

——. "Mahmud Taleqani and the Iranian Revolution," in M. Kramer (ed.) *Shi'ism, Resistance, and Revolution*, 67–94, Boulder, CO: Westview, 1987.

——. *Iran's First Revolution: Shi'ism and the Constitutional Revolution of 1905–1909*, New York: Oxford University Press, 1991.

Bayram, M. *Ahi Evren ve ahi teşkilâtı'nın kuruluşu*, Konya: Bil-Tez, 1991.

Bayur, H. K. *Sadrazam Kâmil Paşa: siyasî hayatı*, Ankara: Sanat, 1954.

Bazin, L. "Man and the Concept of History in Turkish Central Asia during the Eighth Century," *Diogenes*, no. 42, 1963: 81–97.

Bearman, J. *Qadhafi's Libya*, London: Zed Books, 1986.

Beattie, K. J. *Egypt during the Nasser Years: ideology, politics, and civil society*, Boulder, CO: Westview 1994.

Beaulieu, P.-A. *The Reign of Nabonidus, King of Babylon (556–539 BC)*, Yale Near East Researches, 10, New Haven, CT: Yale University Press, 1989.

Beblawi, H. and Luciani, G. Introduction to H. Beblawi and G. Luciani (eds) *The Rentier State*, 1–21, London: Croom Helm, 1987.

Bechor, G. "'To Hold the Hand of the Weak': the emergence of contractual justice in the Egyptian civil law," *ILS* 8, 2001: 179–200.

Beckwith, C. I. "Aspects of the Early History of the Central-Asian Guard Corps in Islam," *AEuras* 4, 1984: 29–43.

Bedrani, S. "Algérie: une nouvelle politique envers la paysannerie?" *RMMM* 45, 1987: 55–66.

Behdad, S. "A Disputed Utopia: Islamic economics in revolutionary Iran," *CSSH* 36, 1994: 775–813.

——. "The Post-Revolutionary Economic Crisis," in S. Rahnema and S. Behdad (eds) *Iran after the Revolution: crisis of an Islamic state*, 97–128, London: IB Tauris, 1995.

Behrens-Abouseif, D. *Egypt's Adjustment to Ottoman Rule: institutions waqf and architecture in Cairo (16th and 17th centuries)* Leiden: Brill, 1994.

Beinin, J. "Islam, Marxism, and the Shubra al-Khayma Textile Workers: Muslim Brothers and Communists in the Egyptian trade union movement," in E. Burke III and I. M. Lapidus (eds) *Islam, Politics, and Social Movements*, 207–27, Berkeley: University of California Press, 1988.

——. "Islamic Responses to the Capitalist Penetration of the Middle East," in B. F. Stowasser (ed.) *The Islamic Impulse*, 87–105, London: Croom Helm, 1987.

Beldiceanu-Steinherr, I. and Beldiceanu, N. "Règlement ottoman concernant le recensement (première moitié du XVIe siècle)," *Südost-Forschungen* 37, 1978: 1–40.

Ben-Bassat, Y. "In Search of Justice: petitions sent from Palestine to Istanbul from the 1870s onwards," *Turcica* 41, 2009: 89–114.

Bennison, A. K. "The 'New Order' and Islamic Order: the introduction of the *Niẓāmī* army in the western Maghrib and its legitimation, 1830–73," *IJMES* 36, 2004: 591–612.

Berkes, N. *The Development of Secularism in Turkey*, Montreal: McGill University Press, 1964; repr. New York: Routledge, 1998.

Berkey, J. P. *The Transmission of Knowledge in Medieval Cairo: a social history of Islamic education*, Princeton, NJ: Princeton University Press, 1992.

Bernardini, M. "Aspects littéraires et idéologiques des relations entre aristocratie et architecture à l'époque timouride," in L. Golombek and M. Subtelny (eds) *Timurid Art and Culture: Iran and Central Asia in the fifteenth century*, 36–43, Leiden: Brill, 1992.

Bernus-Taylor, M. "Le décor du 'Complexe Vert' à Bursa, reflet de l'art timouride," *Cahiers d'Asie Centrale* 3/4, 1997: 251–66.

Berque, J. *Al-Yousi: Problèmes de la culture marocaine au XVIIème siècle*, Paris: Mouton, 1958.

——. *Ulémas, fondateurs, insurgés du Maghreb: XVIIe siècle*, Paris: Sindbad, 1982.

Bhat, B. *Abu Ali Miskawayh: a study of his historical and social thought*, New Delhi: Islamic Book Foundation, 1991.
Biddle, D. W. "The Development of the Bureaucracy of the Islamic Empire during the Late Umayyad and Early Abbasid Period," PhD diss., University of Texas at Austin, 1972.
Bielawski, J. "Lettres d'Aristote à Alexandre le Grand en version arabe," *RO* 28, 1964: 7–34.
Bill, J. A. *The Politics of Iran: groups, classes, and modernization*, Columbus, OH: C. E. Merrill, 1972.
Billows, R. A. *Kings and Colonists: aspects of Macedonian imperialism*, Leiden: Brill, 1995.
Binder, L. "Al-Ghazālī's Theory of Islamic Government," *MW* 45, 1955: 229–41.
——. *The Ideological Revolution in the Middle East*, New York: John Wiley and Sons, 1964.
——. *Islamic Liberalism: a critique of development ideologies*, Chicago, IL: University of Chicago Press, 1988.
Birnbaum, E. "The Ottomans and Chagatay Literature," *CAJ* 20, 1976: 157–90.
Bitar, S. "The Rise and Decline of the Baath," *Middle East International*, June 1971: 12–15; July 1971: 13–16.
Björkman, W. *Beiträge zur Geschichte der Staatskanzlei im islamschen Ägypten*, Hamburg: Friederichsen, De Gruyter & Co., 1928.
——. "Die Anfänge der türkischen Briefsammlungen," *Orientalia Suecana* 5, 1956: 20–9.
Black, A. *The History of Islamic Political Thought: from the Prophet to the present*, Edinburgh: Edinburgh University Press, 2001.
Black, C. E. and Brown, L. C. (eds) *Modernization in the Middle East: the Ottoman Empire and its Afro-Asian successors*, Princeton, NJ: Darwin, 1992.
Blair, S. S. "The Ilkhanid Palace," *ArsOr* 23, 1993: 239–46.
Bligh, A. *The Political Legacy of King Hussein*, Brighton: Sussex Academic Press, 2002.
Bloom, J. M. "The *Qubbat al-Khaḍrā'* and the Iconography of Height in Early Islamic Architecture," *ArsOr* 23, 1993: 135–42.
——. "Mamluk Art and Architectural History: a review article," *MSR* 3, 1999: 31–58.
——. "Epic Images Revisited: an Ilkhanid legacy in early Safavid painting," in A. J. Newman (ed.) *Society and Culture in the Early Modern Middle East: studies on Iran in the Safavid period*, 237–48, Leiden: Brill, 2003.
Blum, J. *The End of the Old Order in Rural Europe*, Princeton, NJ: Princeton University Press, 1978.
Boardman, J., Lewis, D. M. and Ostwald, M. (eds) *Cambridge Ancient History*, Vol. 4: *Persia, Greece and the Western Mediterranean, c. 525 to 479 B.C.*, 2nd ed., Cambridge: Cambridge University Press, 1988.
Bodrogligeti, A. "Notes on the Turkish Literature at the Mameluke Court," *AOH* 14, 1962: 273–82.
Boissier, A. "Document cassite," *RA* 29, 1932: 93–104.
Bonebakker, S. A. "*Adab* and the Concept of Belles-Lettres," in *Abbasid Belles-Lettres*, ed. J. Ashtiany, T. M. Johnstone, J. D. Latham, R. B. Serjeant, and G. R. Smith, The Cambridge History of Arabic Literature, 2, 16–30, Cambridge: Cambridge University Press, 1990.
Bonner, M. *Aristocratic Violence and Holy War: studies in the jihad and the Arab-Byzantine frontier*, New Haven, CT: American Oriental Society, 1996.
Bosworth, C. E. "The Imperial Policy of the Early Ghaznawids," *IS* 1.3, 1962: 49–82; repr. in C. E. Bosworth, *The Medieval History of Iran, Afghanistan and Central Asia*, London: Variorum, 1977, XI.
——. "The Titulature of the Early Ghaznavids," *Oriens* 15, 1962: 210–33; repr. in C. E. Bosworth, *The Medieval History of Iran, Afghanistan and Central Asia*, London: Variorum, 1977, X.
——. "A Turco-Mongol Practice amongst the Early Ghaznavids'" *CAJ* 7, 1962: 237–40; repr. in C. E. Bosworth, *The Medieval History of Iran, Afghanistan and Central Asia*, London: Variorum, 1977, XII.
——. "Early Sources for the History of the First Four Ghaznavid Sultans (977–1041)," *IQ* 7, 1963: 3–22; repr. in C. E. Bosworth, *The Medieval History of Iran, Afghanistan and Central Asia*, London: Variorum, 1977, XIII.
——. "Mahmud of Ghazna in Contemporary Eyes and in Later Persian Literature," *Iran* 4, 1966: 85–92; repr. in C. E. Bosworth, *The Medieval History of Iran, Afghanistan and Central Asia*, London: Variorum, 1977, XVI.
——. "The Armies of the Saffārids," *BSOAS* 31, 1968: 550; repr. in C. E. Bosworth, *The Medieval History of Iran, Afghanistan and Central Asia,* London: Variorum, 1977, XVII.

——. "The Tahirids and Arabic Culture," *JSS* 14, 1969: 45–79; repr. in C. E. Bosworth, *Medieval Arabic Culture and Administration*, London: Variorum, 1982, II.

——. "Barbarian Incursions: the coming of the Turks into the Islamic world," in D. H. Richards (ed.) *Islamic Civilisation, 950–1150*, Oxford: Bruno Cassirer, 1973; repr. in C. E. Bosworth, *The Medieval History of Iran, Afghanistan and Central Asia*, London: Variorum, 1977, XXIII.

——. *The Ghaznavids: their empire in Afghanistan and eastern Iran, 944–1040*, Edinburgh: Edinburgh University Press, 1963; 2nd ed. Beirut: Librairie du Liban, 1973.

——. "The Heritage of Rulership in Early Islamic Iran and the Search for Dynastic Connections with the Past," *IranS* 11, 1978: 7–34; repr. in C. E. Bosworth, *The Medieval History of Iran, Afghanistan and Central Asia*, London: Variorum, 1977, VII.

——. *The Later Ghaznavids: Splendour and Decay: the dynasty in Afghanistan and northern India, 1040–1186*, New York: Columbia University Press, 1977.

——. "The Interaction of Arabic and Persian Literature and Culture in the 10th and Early 11th Centuries," *al-Abḥāth* 27, 1978/79: 59–75; repr. in C. E. Bosworth, *Medieval Arabic Culture and Administration*, London: Variorum, 1982, VIII.

——. "Administrative Literature," in M. J. L. Young, J. D. Latham, and R. B. Serjeant (eds) *Religion, Learning and Science in the Abbasid Period*, The Cambridge History of Arabic Literature, 3, 155–67, Cambridge: Cambridge University Press, 1990.

——. "The Persian Contribution to Islamic Historiography in the Pre-Mongol Period," in R. G. Hovannisian and G. Sabagh (eds) *The Persian Presence in the Islamic World*, 218–36, Cambridge: Cambridge University Press, 1998.

Bourqia, R. "The Cultural Legacy of Power in Morocco," in R. Bourqia and S. G. Miller (eds) *In the Shadow of the Sultan: culture, power, and politics in Morocco*, 243–58, Cambridge, MA: Harvard University Center for Middle Eastern Studies, 1999.

Bouvat, L. *Les Barmécides d'après les historiens arabes et perses*, Paris: Ernest Leroux, 1912.

Boyce, M. "Middle Persian Literature," in B. Spuler and I Gershevitch (eds) *Handbuch der Orientalistik*, sect. 1, vol. 4, pt. 2, fasc. 1, 31–66, Leiden: Brill, 1968.

Boztemur, R. "Political Islam in Secular Turkey in 2000: change in the rhetoric towards westernization, human rights and democracy," *IJTS* 7, 2001: 125–37.

Brand, C. M. "The Turkish Element in Byzantium, Eleventh-Twelfth Centuries," *Dumbarton Oaks Papers* 43, 1989: 1–25.

Brett, M. "The Way of the Peasant," *BSOAS* 47, 1984: 44–56.

——. "The Way of the Nomad," *BSOAS* 58, 1995: 251–69.

Briant, P. *Rois, tributs et paysans: Études sur les formations tributaires du Moyen-Orient ancient*, Paris: Annales littéraires de l'Université de Besançon, 1982.

——. *Histoire de L'empire perse de Cyrus à Alexandre*, Paris: Fayard, 1996.

Brinkman, J. A. "Provincial Administration in Babylonia under the Second Dynasty of Isin," *JESHO* 6, 1963: 233–43.

——. "The Monarchy in the Time of the Kassite Dynasty," in P. Garelli (ed.) *Le palais et la royauté (archéologie et civilisation)*, Rencontre assyriologique internationale, 19th, Paris, 1971, 395–408, Paris: Paul Geuthner, 1974.

Brinner, W. M. "Dar al-Sa'ada and Dar al-'Adl in Mamluk Damascus," in M. Rosen-Ayalon (ed.) *Studies in Memory of Gaston Wiet*, 235–47, Jerusalem: Hebrew University, 1977.

Brown, K. L. *People of Sale: tradition and change in a Moroccan city, 1830–1930*, Cambridge, MA: Harvard University Press, 1976.

Brown, L. C. "The Tunisian Path to Modernization," in M. Milson (ed.) *Society and Political Structure in the Arab World*, 183–230, New York: Humanities Press, 1973.

——. *The Tunisia of Ahmad Bey, 1847–1855*, Princeton, NJ: Princeton University Press, 1974.

——. *Religion and State: the Muslim approach to politics*, New York: Columbia University Press, 2000.

Brown, N. J. *Peasant Politics in Modern Egypt: the struggle against the state*, New Haven, CT: Yale University Press, 1990.

——. "Peasants and Notables in Egyptian Politics," *MES* 26, 1990: 145–60.

——. "The Ignorance and Inscrutability of the Egyptian Peasantry," in F. Kazemi and J. Waterbury (eds) *Peasants and Politics in the Modern Middle East*, 203–21, Miami: Florida International University Press, 1991.

Browne, E. G. "Some Account of the Arabic Work Entitled 'Nihāyetu'l-irab fi akhbāri'l-furs wa'l-'Arab,' particularly of that part which treats of the Persian kings," *JRAS* 1900: 195–259.

——. *The Persian Revolution of 1905–1909*, London: Frank Cass/Cambridge University Press, 1910; repr. New York: Barnes and Noble, 1966.

——. *A Literary History of Persia*, 4 vols, Cambridge: Cambridge University Press, 1951.

Brumberg, D. "Survival Strategies vs. Democratic Bargains: the politics of economic reform in contemporary Egypt," in H. J. Barkey (ed.) *The Politics of Economic Reform in the Middle East*, 73–104, New York: St. Martin's, 1992.

Brunschvig, R. "Justice religieuse et justice laïque dans la Tunisie des Deys et des Beys jusqu'au milieu du XIXe siècle," *SI* 23, 1965: 17–70.

Bulliet, R. W. "Local Politics in Eastern Iran under the Ghaznavids and Seljuks," *IranS* 11, 1978: 35–56.

——. *Conversion to Islam in the Medieval Period: an essay in quantitative history*, Cambridge, MA: Harvard University Press, 1979.

Burke, E., III, "Understanding Arab Protest Movements," *Maghreb Review* 11.1, 1986: 27–32; repr. in *ASQ* 8, 1986: 333–45.

——. "Islam and Social Movements: methodological reflections," in E. Burke III and I. M. Lapidus (eds) *Islam, Politics, and Social Movements*, 17–35, Berkeley: University of California Press, 1988.

——. "Rural Collective Action and the Emergence of Modern Lebanon: a comparative historical perspective," in N. Shehadi and D. H. Mills (eds) *Lebanon: a history of conflict and consensus*, 14–30, London: Centre for Lebanese Studies and IB Tauris, 1988.

——. "Changing Patterns of Peasant Protest in the Middle East, 1750–1950," in F. Kazemi and J. Waterbury (eds) *Peasants and Politics in the Modern Middle East*, 24–37, Miami: Florida International University Press, 1991.

Bush, R. *Economic Crisis and the Politics of Reform in Egypt*, Boulder, CO: Westview, 1999.

Busse, H. *Untersuchungen zum Islamischen Kanzleiwesen an Hand Turkmenischer und Safawidischer Urkunden*, Cairo: Kommissionsverlag Sirovič Bookshop, 1959.

——. *Chalif und Grosskönig: Die Buyiden im Iraq (945–1055)* Wiesbaden: Franz Steiner, 1969.

——. "The Revival of Persian Kingship under the Būyids," in D. S. Richards (ed.) *Islamic Civilisation 950–1150*, 47–70, Oxford: Bruno Cassirer, 1973.

Butterworth, C. E. "State and Authority in Arabic Political Thought," in G. Salamé (ed.) *The Foundations of the Arab State*, 91–111, London: Croom Helm, 1987

Cachia, P. *Ṭāhā Ḥusayn: his place in the Egyptian literary renaissance*, London: Luzac, 1956.

Çadırcı, M. "Tanzimat," in K. Çiçek (ed.) *The Great Ottoman-Turkish Civilisation*, 4 vols, 3: 573–89, Ankara: Yeni Türkiye, 2000.

Çağman, F. "The Miniatures of the Divan-ı Hüseyni and the Influence of Their Style," in G. Fehér (ed.) *Fifth Interntional Congress of Turkish Art*, 231–60, Budapest: Akadémiai Kiadó, 1978.

Cahen, C. "Quelques aspects de l'administration égyptienne médiévale vus par un de ses fonctionnaires," *Bulletin de la Faculté des Lettres de Strasbourg* 36.4, February 1948: 97–108.

——. "Le Malik-Nameh et l'histoire des origins seljukides," *Oriens* 2, 1949: 31–65.

——. "L'Évolution de l'iqta' du IXe au XIIIe siècle: contribution à une histoire comparée des sociétés médiévales," *Annales: économies, sociétés, civilisations* 8, 1953: 25–52.

——. "The Body Politic," in G. E. von Grunebaum (ed.) *Unity and Variety in Muslim Civilization*, 132–63, Chicago, IL: University of Chicago Press, 1955.

——. *Pre-Ottoman Turkey: a general survey of the material and spiritual culture and history c. 1071–1330*, trans. J. Jones-Williams, London: Sidgwick & Jackson, 1968.

——. "History and Historians," in *Religion, Learning and Science in the Abbasid Period*, ed. M. J. L. Young, J. D. Latham, and R. B. Serjeant, The Cambridge History of Arabic Literature, 3, 188–233, Cambridge: Cambridge University Press, 1990.

Cahill, N. "The Treasury at Persepolis," *American Journal of Archaeology* 89, 1985: 373–89.

Calder, N. "Legitimacy and Accommodation in Safavid Iran: the juristic theory of Muḥammad Bāqir al-Sabzavārī (d. 1090/1679)," *Iran* 25, 1987: 91–105.

Calmard, J. "Popular Literature under the Safavids," in A J. Newman (ed.) *Society and Culture in the Early Modern Middle East: studies on Iran in the Safavid period*, 315–39, Leiden: Brill, 2003.

Cameron, A. J. *Abû Dharr al-Ghifârî: an examination of his image in the hagiography of Islam*, London: Royal Asiatic Society, 1973.

Cameron, G. G. *Persepolis Treasury Tablets*, Oriental Institute Publications, 65, Chicago, IL: University of Chicago Press, 1948.

——. "Persepolis Treasury Tablets Old and New," *JNES* 17, 1958: 161–76.

Canby, J. V. *The "Ur-Nammu" Stela*, Philadelphia, PA: University of Pennsylvania Museum of Archaeology and Anthropology, 2001.

Cannon, B. *Politics of Law and the Courts in Nineteenth-Century Egypt*, Salt Lake City: University of Utah Press, 1988.

——. "Rural Social Justice Rhetoric and the Young Tunisian Movement, 1907–1912," *RHM* 17, no. 59–60, 1990: 63–71.

Cardescia, G. (ed. and trans.) *Les archives des Murasû, une famille d'hommes d'affaires babyloniens à l'époque perse (455–403 av. J.-C.)* Paris: Imprimerie nationale, 1951.

Çevikel, N. "Muslim-Non-Muslim Relations in the Ottoman Province of Cyprus (1750–1800)," in K. Çiçek (ed.) *The Great Ottoman-Turkish Civilisation* 4 vols, 2: 428–37, Ankara: Yeni Türkiye, 2000.

Cezar, M. *Osmanlı tarihinde levendler*, Istanbul: Çelikcilt, 1965.

Chalcraft, J. T. "The Cairo Cab Drivers and the Strike of 1907," in J. Hanssen, T. Philipp, and S. Weber (eds) *The Empire in the City: Arab provincial capitals in the late Ottoman Empire*, 173–98, Beirut: Ergon Verlag Würzburg, 2002.

——. *The Striking Cabbies of Cairo and Other Stories: crafts and guilds in Egypt, 1863–1914*, Albany: State University of New York Press, 2004.

——. "Engaging the State: peasants and petitions in Egypt on the eve of colonial rule," *IJMES* 37, 2005: 303–25.

Chamberlain, M. *Knowledge and Social Practice in Medieval Damascus, 1190–1350*, Cambridge: Cambridge University Press, 1994.

Charlesworth, A. and Randall, A. J. "Comment: Morals, Markets and the English Crowd in 1766," *Past & Present* 114, 1987: 200–13.

Charpin, D. "Immigrés, refugiés et déportés en Babylonie sous Hammu-rabi et ses successeurs," in D. Charpin and F. Joannès (eds) *La circulation des biens, des personnes et des idées dans le Proche-orient ancien*, 207–18, Paris: Éditions Recherche sur les Civilisations, 1992.

Chaudhry, K. A. "Economic Liberalization in Oil-Exporting Countries: Iraq and Saudi Arabia," in I. Harik and D. J. Sullivan (eds) *Privatization and Liberalization in the Middle East*, 145–66, Bloomington: Indiana University Press, 1992.

Chauvin, V. *La récension égyptienne des Mille et Une Nuits*, Brussels: Faculté de Philosophie et Lettres de L'Université de Liège, 1899.

Choksy, J. K. "Sacral Kingship in Sasanian Iran," *Bulletin of the Asia Institute* n.s. 2, 1988: 35–52.

——. *Conflict and Cooperation: Zoroastrian subalterns and Muslim elites in medieval Iranian society*, New York: Columbia University Press, 1997.

Christensen, A. E. *L'Empire des Sassanides: le peuple, l'état, la cour*, Copenhagen: B. Lunos, 1907.

——. "La légende du sage Buzurjmihr," *AcOr* 8, 1930: 81–128.

——. *L'Iran sous les Sassanides*, 2nd ed. Osnabrück: O. Zeller, 1971.

Christensen, P. *The Decline of Iranshahr: irrigation and environments in the history of the Middle East, 500 B.C. to A.D. 1500*, trans. S. Sampson, Odense, Denmark: University of Copenhagen Museum Tusculanum Press, 1993.

Churchill, C. H. *The Druzes and the Maronites under Turkish Rule, from 1840–60*, London: B. Quaritch, 1862; repr. New York: Arno, 1973.

Çiçek, K. "Osmanlılar'dan önce Akdeniz dünyasında yapılan tahrirler hakkında bazı gözlemler," *OTAM* 6, 1995: 51–89.
——. "The Earliest Population and Fiscal Surveys (Tahrir Defterleri) for the Anatolian Provinces of the Ottoman Empire," *OTAM* 7, 1996: 45–98.
——. "A Quest for Justice in a Mixed Society: the Turks and the Greek Cypriots before the sharia court of Nicosia," in K. Çiçek (ed.) *The Great Ottoman-Turkish Civilisation*, 4 vols, 2: 472–91, Ankara: Yeni Türkiye, 2000.
Claisse, A. "Makhzen Traditions and Administrative Channels," in I. W. Zartman (ed.) *The Political Economy of Morocco*, 34–58, New York: Praeger, 1987.
Clancy-Smith, J. "La révolte de Bû Ziyân en Algérie, 1849," *RMMM* nos. 91–4, 2000: 181–208.
Clay, C. "Labour Migration and Economic Conditions in Nineteenth Century Anatolia," *MES* 34.4, 1998: 1–32.
Cobb, P. M. *White Banners: contention in 'Abbāsid Syria, 750–880*, Albany: State University of New York Press, 2001.
Cole, J. R. I. "Rifā'a al-Ṭahṭāwī and the Revival of Practical Philosophy," *MW* 70, 1980: 29–46.
——. "Ideology, Ethics, and Philosophical Discourse in Eighteenth Century Iran," *IranS* 22.1, 1989: 8–34.
——. "Iranian Millenarianism and Democratic Thought in the 19th Century," *IJMES* 24, 1992: 1–26.
——. *Colonialism and Revolution in the Middle East: social and cultural origins of Egypt's 'Urabi movement*, Princeton, NJ: Princeton University Press, 1993.
Colledge, M. A. R. *The Parthians*, New York: Praeger, 1967.
——. *Parthian Art*, London: Paul Elek, 1977.
Combs-Schilling, M. E. *Sacred Performances: Islam, sexuality, and sacrifice*, New York: Columbia University Press, 1989.
Commins, D. "'Abd al-Qādir al-Jazā'irī and Islamic Reform," *MW* 78, 1988: 121–31.
Cook, J. M. *The Persian Empire*, New York: Schocken, 1983.
Cook, M. A. *Population Pressure in Rural Anatolia, 1450–1600*, London: Oxford University Press, 1972.
——. "Economic Developments," in J. Schacht and C. E. Bosworth (eds) *The Legacy of Islam*, 2nd ed., 210–43, Oxford: Oxford University Press, 1979.
——. *Commanding Right and Forbidding Wrong in Islamic Thought*, Cambridge: Cambridge University Press, 2000.
Cooper, M. N. *The Transformation of Egypt*, Baltimore, MD: The Johns Hopkins University Press, 1982.
Copeaux, É. "Les prédécesseurs médiévaux d'Atatürk: Bilge kaghan et le sultan Alp Arslan," *RMMM* nos. 89–90, 2000: 217–43.
Corm, G. "Systèmes de pouvoir et changements sociaux et régionaux au Machrek arabe," in J.-C. Santucci and H. El Malki (eds) *État et développement dans le monde arabe: Crises et mutations au Maghreb*, 39–54, Paris: CNRS, 1990.
Cottam, R. W. *Nationalism in Iran: updated through 1978*, Pittsburgh: University of Pittsburgh Press, 1964, 1979.
——. "The Iranian Revolution," in J. R. I. Cole and N. R. Keddie (eds) *Shi'ism and Social Protest*, 55–87, New Haven, CT: Yale University Press, 1986.
Crone, P. *Slaves on Horses: the evolution of the Islamic polity*, Cambridge: Cambridge University Press, 1980.
——. "Did al-Ghazālī Write a Mirror for Princes? on the authorship of *Naṣīḥat al-mulūk*," *JSAI* 10, 1987: 167–91.
——. "Kavād's Heresy and Mazdak's Revolt," *Iran* 29, 1991: 21–42.
——. *God's Rule: six centuries of medieval Islamic political thought*, New York: Columbia University Press, 2004.
——. and Hinds, M. *God's Caliph: religious authority in the first centuries of Islam*, Cambridge: Cambridge University Press, 1986.
Cronin, S. "Resisting the New State: the rural poor, land and modernity in Iran, 1921–1941," in S. Cronin (ed.) *Subalterns and Social Protest: history from below in the Middle East and North Africa*, 141–70, London: Routledge, 2008.

Crystal, J. "Review: authoritarianism and its adversaries in the Arab world," *World Politics* 46, 1994: 262–89.

Cunningham, R. B. and Sarayrah, Y. K. *Wasta: the hidden force in Middle Eastern society*, Westport, CT: Praeger, 1993.

Cuno, K. M. "The Origins of Private Ownership of Land in Egypt: a reappraisal," *IJMES* 12, 1980: 245–75.

——. *The Pasha's Peasants: land, society, and economy in Lower Egypt, 1740–1858*, Cambridge: Cambridge University Press, 1992.

——. and Reimer, M. J. "The Census Registers of Nineteenth-Century Egypt: a new source for social historians," *BRIJMES* 24, 1997: 193–216.

Curtis, J. E. and Reade, J. E. (eds) *Art and Empire: treasures from Assyria in the British Museum*, London: British Museum, 1995.

Dabbagh, S. M. "Agrarian Reform in Syria," *MEEP* 9, 1962: 1–15.

Daiber, H. "Political Philosophy," in S. H. Nasr and O. Leaman (eds) *History of Islamic Philosophy*, 2: 841–85, London: Routledge, 1996.

Dajani, B. "The National Charter and Socio-Economic Organization in the United Arab Republic," *MEEP* 8, 1961: 33–54.

Dakhlia, J. *Le Divan des rois: le politique et le religieux dans l'Islam*, Paris: Aubier, 1998.

Dandamayev, M. A. "Achaemenid Babylonia," in I. M. Diakonoff (ed.) *Ancient Mesopotamia, Socio-Economic History: a collection of studies by Soviet scholars*, USSR Academy of Sciences, Institute of the Peoples of Asia, 296–311, Moscow: "Nauka" Publishing House, 1969.

——. and Lukonin, V. G. *The Cultural and Social Institutions of Ancient Iran*, trans. P. L. Kohl and D. J. Dadson, Cambridge: Cambridge University Press, 1989.

Daniel, E. L. *The Political and Social History of Khurasan under Abbasid rule, 747–820*, Minneapolis: Bibliotheca Islamica, 1979.

——. "Manuscripts and Editions of Bal'amī's *Tarjamah-i Tārīkh-i Ṭabarī*," *JRAS* 1990: 282–321.

Dann, U. *King Hussein and the Challenge of Arab Radicalism: Jordan, 1955–1967*, New York: Oxford University Press, in cooperation with The Moshe Dayan Center, 1989.

Danziger, R. *Abd al-Qadir and the Algerians: resistance to the French and internal consolidation*, New York: Holmes & Meier, 1977.

Darling, L. T. "The Finance Scribes and Ottoman Politics," in C. E. Farah (ed.) *Decision Making and Change in the Ottoman Empire*, 89–100, Kirksville, MO: Thomas Jefferson University Press, 1993.

——. *Revenue-Raising and Legitimacy: Tax Collection and Finance Administration in the Ottoman Empire, 1560–1660*, Leiden: Brill, 1996.

——. "Ottoman Fiscal Administration: decline or adaptation?" *JEEH* 26, 1997: 157–79.

——. "Rethinking Europe and the Islamic World in the Age of Exploration," *JEMH* 2, 1998: 221–46.

——. "Contested Territory: Ottoman holy war in comparative perspective," *SI* 91, 2000: 133–63.

——. "'Do Justice, Do Justice, for That is Paradise': Middle Eastern advice for Indian Muslim rulers," *CSSAAME* 22, 2002: 3–19.

——. "Another Look at Periodization in the Ottoman Empire," *TSAB* 26, 2002: 19–28.

——. "Persian Sources on Anatolia and the Early History of the Ottomans," *Studies on Persianate Societies* 2, 2004: 126–44.

——. "Medieval Egyptian Society and the Concept of the Circle of Justice," *MSR* 10, no. 2, 2006: 1–17.

——. "Public Finances: the role of the Ottoman centre," in S. N. Faroqhi (ed.) *The Cambridge History of Turkey*, vol. 3, *The Later Ottoman Empire, 1603–1839*, 118–31, Cambridge: Cambridge University Press, 2006.

——. "Social Cohesion *('Asabiyya)* and Justice in the Late Medieval Middle East," *CSSH* 49, 2007: 329–57.

——. "The Development of Ottoman Governmental Institutions in the Fourteenth Century: a reconstruction," in *Living in the Ottoman Ecumenical Community: essays in honour of Suraiya Faroqhi*, ed. V. Costantini and M. Koller, 17–34, Leiden: Brill, 2008.

——. "Political Change and Political Discourse in the Early Modern Mediterranean World," *Journal of Interdisciplinary History* 38, 2008: 505–31.

——. "Avarız in 1501," in N. Göyünç, J.-L. Bacqué-Grammont, and Ö. Ergenç (eds) *Halil İnalcık Armağanı*, Istanbul: Eren, forthcoming.

——. "Murder and Mayhem in Ottoman Rumeli: local political relations in eighteenth-century Macedonia," in E. Gara, E. Kabadayı, and C. Neumann (eds) *Popular Protest and Public Participation in the Ottoman Empire*, Istanbul, 177–95.

Darling, Sir M. "Land Reform in Italy and Egypt," *Year Book of Agricultural Co-operation,* 1956: 1–26.

D'Arrigo, R. and Cullen, H. M. "A 350-Year (AD 1628–1980) Reconstruction of Turkish Precipitation," *Dendrochronologia* 19, 2001: 169–77.

Daryaee, T. "National History or Keyanid History? the nature of Sasanid Zoroastrian historiography," *IranS* 28, 1995: 129–41.

——. "The Use of Religio-Political Propaganda on the Coinage of Xusrō II," *American Journal of Numismatics* 9, 1997: 41–53.

Davis, E. *Memories of State: politics, history, and collective identity in modern Iraq*, Berkeley: University of California Press, 2005.

Davis, E. and Gavrielides, N. "Statecraft, Historical Memory, and Popular Culture in Iraq and Kuwait," in E. Davis and N. Gavrielides (eds) *Statecraft in the Middle East: oil, historical memory, and popular culture*, 116–148, Miami: Florida International University Press, 1991.

Davis, J. *Libyan Politics: an account of the Zuwaya and their government*, London: IB Tauris, 1987.

Davis, J. M. *Between Jihad and Salaam: profiles in Islam*, New York: St. Martin's, 1997.

Davison, R. H. *Reform in the Ottoman Empire, 1856–1876*, Princeton, NJ: Princeton University Press, 1963.

——. "The Turkish Constitution of 1982 as a Reflection and a Reminder of Turkish History," in *Türk Kültürü Araştırmaları* 27, 1989: 63–77.

Dawood, A. H. "A Comparative Study of Arabic and Persian Mirrors for Princes from the Second to the Sixth Century A.H." PhD diss., University of London, 1965.

de Fouchécour, C.-H. "*Ḥadāyeq al-Siyar*, un Miroir des Princes de la cour de Qonya au VIIe-XIIIe siècle," *StIr* 1, 1972: 219–28.

——. "Une lecture du *Livre des Rois* de Ferdowsi," *StIr* 5, 1976: 171–202.

——. *Moralia: Les notions morales dans la littérature persane du 3e/9e au 7e/13e siècle*, Paris: Éditions Recherche sur les Civilisations, 1986.

de Groot, J. *Religion, Culture and Politics in Iran: from the Qajars to Khomeini*, London: IB Tauris, 2007.

de Ménasce, J. P. "Le protecteur des pauvres dans l'Iran sassanide," in *Mélanges d'orientalisme offerts à Henri Massé*, 282–7, Tehran: Imprimerie de l'Université, 1963.

de Rachewiltz, I. "Some Remarks on the Ideological Foundations of Chingis Khan's Empire," *Papers on Far Eastern History* 7, 1973: 21–36.

——. "Yeh-lü Ch'u-ts'ai (1189–1243): Buddhist idealist and Confucian statesman," in *Confucian Personalities,* ed. A. F. Wright and D. Twitchett, 189–216, Stanford: Stanford University Press, 1962.

Deeb, M. *Party Politics in Egypt: the Wafd and its rivals, 1919–1939*, London: Ithaca Press for The Middle East Centre, St. Antony's College, Oxford, 1979.

Dekmejian, R. H. *Egypt under Nasir: a study in political dynamics*, Albany: State University of New York Press, 1971.

Delanoue, G. *Moralistes et politiques musulmans dans l'Égypte du XIXe siècle, 1798–1882*, 2 vols, Cairo: Institut Français d'Archéologie Orientale, 1982.

Demirci, S. "Complaints about *Avânz* Assessment and Payment in the *Avânz*-Tax System, an aspect of the relationship between centre and periphery: a case study of Kayseri, 1618–1700," *JESHO* 46, 2003: 437–74.

Denoeux, G. *Urban Unrest in the Middle East: a comparative study of informal networks in Egypt, Iran, and Lebanon*, Albany: State University of New York Press, 1993.

Derdiyok, İ. Ç. "Eski Türk edebiyatı'nda mektup yazma kuralları hakkında bilgi veren en eski eser: Ahmed Dâ'i'nin *Teressül*'ü," *Toplumsal Tarih* 1.6, June 1994: 56–59.

Deringil, S. "The Invention of Tradition as Public Image in the Late Ottoman Empire, 1808 to 1908," *CSSH* 35, 1993: 3–29.

Devereux, R. *The First Ottoman Constitutional Period: a study of the Midhat constitution and parliament*, Baltimore: Johns Hopkins Press, 1963.

Devlin, J. F. *The Ba'th Party: a history from its origins to 1966*, Stanford: Hoover Institution Press, 1976.

Diba, L. S. "Images of Power and the Power of Images: intention and response in early Qajar painting (1785–1834)," in L. S. Diba and M. Ekhtiar (eds) *Royal Persian Paintings: the Qajar epoch, 1785–1925*, 30–49, New York: IB Tauris and Brooklyn Museum of Art, 1998.

Djebli, M. "Encore à propos de l'authenticité du *Nahj al-Balagha!*" *SI* 75, 1992: 33–56.

Dodwell, H. *The Founder of Modern Egypt: a study of Muhammad 'Ali*, Cambridge: Cambridge University Press, 1931, repr. 1967.

D'Ohsson, C. *Histoire des Mongols, depuis Tchinguiz-Khan jusqu'à Timour Bey ou Tamerlan*, 4 vols, La Haye and Amsterdam: Frères Van Cleef, 1835.

Dols, M. W. *The Black Death in the Middle East*, Princeton, NJ: Princeton University Press, 1977.

Donner, F. M. *The Early Islamic Conquests*, Princeton, NJ: Princeton University Press, 1981.

——. "The Formation of the Islamic State," *JAOS* 106.2, 1986: 283–96.

——. *Narratives of Islamic Origins: the beginnings of Islamic historical writing*, Princeton, NJ: Darwin, 1998.

——. "From Believers to Muslims: confessional self-identity in the early Islamic community," *Al-Abhath* 50–51, 2002–3: 9–53.

Donohue, J. J. "Land Tenure in Hilāl al-Ṣābī's *Kitāb al-wuzarā'*," in T. Khalidi (ed.) *Land Tenure and Social Transformation in the Middle East*, 121–9, Beirut: American University of Beirut, 1984.

——. *The Buwayhid Dynasty in Iraq, 334H./945 to 403H./1012: shaping institutions for the future*, Leiden: Brill, 2003.

Dorraj, M. *From Zarathustra to Khomeini: populism and dissent in Iran*, Boulder, CO: Lynne Reinner, 1990.

Doumani, B. *Rediscovering Palestine: merchants and peasants in Jabal Nablus, 1700–1900*, Berkeley: University of California Press, 1995.

Doumou, A. (ed.) *The Moroccan State in Historical Perspective, 1850–1985*, trans. A. K. Armah, Dakar, Senegal: CODESRIA, 1990.

Douwes, D. *The Ottomans in Syria: a history of justice and oppression*, 154–83, London: IB Tauris, 2000.

Downey, G. "The Seleucids: the theory of monarchy," in *The Greek Political Experience: studies in honor of William Kelly Prentice*, 162–72, repr. ed., New York: Russell and Russell, 1969.

Drysdale, A. "The Asad Regime and Its Troubles," *MERIP Reports* no. 110, November/December 1982: 3–20.

Duben, A. and Bahar, C. *Istanbul Households: marriage, family and fertility, 1880–1940*, Cambridge: Cambridge University Press, 1991.

Dunlop, D. M. "A Source of al-Mas'udi: the Madinat al-fadila of al-Farabi," in S. M. Ahmad and A. Rahman (eds) *Al-Mas'udi Millenary Commemoration Volume*, 69–71, Calcutta: The Indian Society for the History of Science and The Institute of Islamic Studies, Aligarh Muslim University, 1960.

——. "The Translations of al-Biṭrīq and Yaḥyā (Yuḥannā) b. al-Biṭrīq," *JRAS* 1959: 140–50.

Durand-Guédy, D. "Iranians at War under Turkish Domination: the example of pre-Mongol Isfahan," *IranS* 38, 2005: 587–606.

Duri, A. A. *The Rise of Historical Writing among the Arabs*, ed. and trans. L. I. Conrad, Princeton, NJ: Princeton University Press, 1983.

Düzdağ, M. E. *Şeyhülislâm Ebussuûd Efendi Fetvaları Işığında 16. Asır Türk Hayatı*, Istanbul: Enderun, 1983.

Dvornik, F. *Origins of Intelligence Services: the ancient Near East, Persia, Greece, Roman, Byzantium, the Arab Muslim empires, the Mongol empire, China, Muscovy*, New Brunswick, NJ: Rutgers University Press, 1974.

Eamon, W. *Science and the Secrets of Nature: books of secrets in medieval and early modern culture*, Princeton, NJ: Princeton University Press, 1994.

Eaton, R. M. *The Rise of Islam and the Bengal Frontier, 1204–1760*, Berkeley: University of California Press, 1993.

Economic and Social Commission for Western Asia, *Arab Women in ESCWA Member States: statistics, indicators and trends*, New York: United Nations, 1994.

Ehsani, K. "Rural Society and Agricultural Development in Post-Revolution Iran: the first two decades," *Critique* 15, 2006: 79–96.

Eickelman, D. F. "From Theocracy to Monarchy: authority and legitimacy in inner Oman, 1935–1957," *IJMES* 17, 1985: 3–24.

——. *Knowledge and Power in Morocco: the education of a twentieth-century notable*, Princeton, NJ: Princeton University Press, 1985.

——. *The Middle East and Central Asia: an anthropological approach*, 3rd ed. Upper Saddle River, NJ: Prentice Hall, 1998.

Eilts, H. F. "Saudi Arabia: traditionalism versus modernism – a royal dilemma?" in P. J. Chelkowski and R. J. Pranger (eds) *Ideology and Power in the Middle East: studies in honor of George Lenczowski*, 56–88, Durham: Duke University Press, 1988.

Eisenstadt, S. N. *The Political Systems of Empires*, London, New York: Free Press of Glencoe, 1963.

El-Ghonemy, M. R. *The Political Economy of Rural Poverty: the case for land reform*, London: Routledge, 1990.

——. *Affluence and Poverty in the Middle East*, London: Routledge, 1998.

El-Khawas, M. A. *Qaddafi: his ideology in theory and practice*, Brattleboro, VT: Amana Books, 1986.

El-Kosheri Mahfouz, A. *Socialisme et pouvoir en Égypte*, Paris: R. Pichon et R. Durand-Auzias, 1972.

Ellis, M. deJ. *Agriculture and the State in Ancient Mesopotamia: an introduction to problems of land tenure*, Philadelphia, PA: University Museum, 1976.

El-Menoufi, K. "The Orientation of Egyptian Peasants toward Political Authority between Continuity and Change," *MES* 18, 1982: 82–93.

El-Said, H. "The Political Economy of Reform in Jordan: breaking resistance to reform?" in G. Joffé (ed.) *Jordan in Transition*, 254–77, London: Hurst & Company, 2002.

Enayat, H. *Modern Islamic Political Thought*, Austin: University of Texas Press, 1982.

——. "An Outline of the Political Philosophy of the *Rasā'il* of the Ikhwān al-Ṣafā'," in S. H. Nasr (ed.) *Ismā'īlī Contributions to Islamic Culture*, 23–49, Tehran: Imperial Iranian Academy of Philosophy, 1997.

Ener, M. *Managing Egypt's Poor and the Politics of Benevolence, 1800–1952*, Princeton, NJ: Princeton University Press, 2003.

English, P. W. *City and Village in Iran: settlement and economy in the Kirman Basin*, Madison: University of Wisconsin Press, 1966.

Ennaïfer, H. "La pensée sociale dans les écrits musulmans modernes," trans. S. Ghrab, in *Foi et justice: un défi pour le christianisme et pour l'islam*, ed. J.-P. Gabus, 168–88, Paris: Centurion, 1993.

Entelis, J. P. "Introduction: state and society in transition," in J. P. Entelis and P. C. Naylor (eds) *State and Society in Algeria*, 1–30, Boulder, CO: Westview, 1992.

——. "Islam, Democracy, and the State: the reemergence of authoritarian politics in Algeria," in J. Ruedy (ed.) *Islamism and Secularism in North Africa*, 219–51, New York: St. Martin's, 1994.

Erder, L. T. and Faroqhi, S. "The Development of the Anatolian Urban Network during the Sixteenth Century," *JESHO* 23, 1980: 265–303.

Ergene, B. A. "On Ottoman Justice: interpretations in conflict (1600–1800)," *ILS* 8, 2001: 52–87.

——. *Local Court, Provincial Society and Justice in the Ottoman Empire: legal practice and dispute resolution in Çankırı and Kastamonu (1652–1744)* Leiden: Brill, 2003.

——. "Social Identity and Patterns of Interaction in the Sharia Court of Kastamonu (1740–44)," *ILS* 15, 2008: 20–54.

Ergil, D. *Social History of the Turkish National Struggle, 1919–22: the unfinished revolution*, Lahore: Sind Sagar Academy, 1977.

Erimtan, C. "The Perception of Saadabad: the 'Tulip Age' and Ottoman–Safavid rivalry," in D. Sajdi (ed.) *Ottoman Tulips, Ottoman Coffee: leisure and lifestyle in the eighteenth century*, 41–62, London: Tauris Academic Studies, 2007.

Ertaylan, İ. H. *Ahmed-i Dā'ī: hayatı ve eserleri*, Istanbul: İstanbul Üniversitesi Edebiyat Fakültesi, 1952.

Escovitz, J. H. *The Office of* Qāḍī al-Quḍāt *in Cairo under the Baḥrī Mamlūks*, Berlin: Klaus Schwarz, 1984.

Evered, E. Ö. *Empire and Education under the Ottomans: politics, reform and resistance from the Tanzimat to the Young Turks*, London: IB Tauris, 2012.

Evin, A. Ö. "The Tulip Age and Definitions of 'Westernization'," in O. Okyar and H. İnalcık (eds) *Türkiye'nin sosyal ve ekonomik tarihi (1071–1920)*, 131–45, Ankara: Meteksan, 1980.

Fahmy, K. "The Police and the People in Nineteenth-Century Egypt," *WI* 39, 1999: 340–77.

Fakhouri, H. *Kafr el-Elow, an Egyptian village in transition*, New York: Holt, Rinehart and Winston, 1972.

Fakhry, M. "Justice in Islamic Philosophical Ethics: Miskawayh's mediating contribution," *Journal of Religious Ethics* 3, 1975: 243–54.

Fandy, M. "CyberResistance: Saudi opposition between globalization and localization," *CSSH* 41, 1999: 124–47.

Farah, C. E. "Reformed Ottomanism and Social Change," in A. Temimi (ed.) *La vie sociale dans les province arabes à l'époque ottomane*, 3 vols in 2, 3: 139–50, Zaghouan: CEROMDI, 1988.

Farman Farmayan, H. "The Forces of Modernization in Nineteenth Century Iran: a historical survey," in W. R. Polk and R. L. Chambers (eds) *Beginnings of Modernization in the Middle East: the nineteenth century*, 119–51, Chicago, IL: University of Chicago Press, 1968.

Farmanfarmaian, K. "Planning, Development and Revolution: Reflections on Iran, 1958–1978," in W. G. Miller and P. H. Stoddard (eds) *Perspectives on the Middle East 1983: proceedings of a conference*, 72–82, Washington, DC: Middle East Institute in cooperation with The Fletcher School of Law and Diplomacy, 1983.

Faroqhi, S. "The Peasants of Saideli in the Late Sixteenth Century," *AOtt* 8, 1983: 215–50.

——. "A Map of Anatolian Friday Mosques, 1520–1535," *OA* 4, 1984: 161–73, map in 5, 1985: no page number.

——. "Political Initiatives 'From the Bottom Up' in the Sixteenth and Seventeenth-Century Ottoman Empire: some evidence for their existence," in H. G. Majer (ed.) *Osmanistische Studien zur Wirtscharts- und Sozialgeschichte in Memoriam Vančo Boškov*, 24–33, Wiesbaden: Harrassowitz, 1986.

——. "Die Legitimation des Osmanensultans: Zur Beziehung von Religion, Kunst und Politik im 16. und 17. Jahrhundert," *Zeitschrift für Turkeistudien* 2, 1989: 49–67.

——. "Political Activity among Ottoman Taxpayers and the Problem of Sultanic Legitimation (1570–1630)," *JESHO* 35 (1992): 1–39.

——. "Sainthood as Means of Self-Defense in Seventeeth-Century Ottoman Anatolia," in G. M. Smith and C. W. Ernst (ed.) *Manifestations of Sainthood in Islam*, 193–208, Istanbul: İsis, 1993.

——. "Crisis and Change, 1590–1699," in H. İnalcık with D. Quataert (eds) *An Economic and Social History of the Ottoman Empire*, 2: 411–636, Cambridge: Cambridge University Press, 1994.

——. "Seeking Wisdom in China: An Attempt to Make Sense of the Celali Rebellions," in R. Veselý and E. Gombár (eds) *Ẓafar nāme: Memorial Volume of Felix Tauer*, 101–24, Prague: enigma corporation, 1996.

——. "Crime, Women, and Wealth in the Eighteenth-Century Anatolian Countryside," in M. C. Zilfi (ed.) *Women in the Ottoman Empire: Middle Eastern women in the early modern era*, 6–27, Leiden: Brill, 1997.

——. "Presenting the Sultans' Power, Glory and Piety: a comparative perspective," in Z. T. Ertuğ (ed.) *Prof. Dr. Mübahat S. Kütükoğlu'na armağan*, 169–206, Istanbul: İstanbul Üniversitesi Edebiyat Fakültesi, 2006.

Faruqhi, A. A. *Early Muslim Historiography: a study of early transmitters of Arab history from the rise of Islam up to the end of the Umayyad period, 612–750 A.D.* Delhi: Idara-i Adabiyat-i Dihli, 1979.

Fawaz, L. T. *An Occasion for War: civil conflict in Lebanon and Damascus in 1860*, Berkeley: University of California Press, 1994.

Fehérvári, G. "An Illustrated Turkish Khamsa of Nizāmī," in G. Fehér (ed.) *Fifth Interntional Congress of Turkish Art*, 323–37, Budapest: Akadémiai Kiadó, 1978.

Fensham, F. C. "Widow, Orphan, and the Poor in Ancient Near Eastern Legal and Wisdom Literature," *JNES* 21, 1962: 129–39.

Ferdows, E. "The Reconstruction Crusade and Class Conflict in Iran," *MERIP Reports*, no. 113, Mar.–Apr. 1983: 11–15.

Fernández-Armesto, F. *Sadat and His Statecraft*, London: Kensal Press, 1982.

Fernea, R. A. "State and Tribe in Southern Iraq: the struggle for hegemony before the 1958 revolution," in R. A. Fernea and W. R. Louis (eds) *The Iraqi Revolution of 1958: the old social classes revisited,* 142–53, London: IB Tauris, 1991.

Fındıkoğlu, Z. F. "Türkiye'de Ibn Haldunizm," in *Fuad Köprülü Armağanı, 60. doğum yılı münasebetiyle: mélanges Fuad Köprülü*, 153–63, Ankara: Dil ve Tarih-Coğrafya Fakültesi, 1953.

Fischel, W. J. *Ibn Khaldūn in Egypt: his public functions and his historical research (1382–1406), a study in Islamic historiography*, Berkeley: University of California Press, 1967.

Fischer, M. M. J. *Iran: from religious dispute to revolution*, Cambridge, MA: Harvard University Press, 1980.

——. "Legal Postulates in Flux: justice, wit, and hierarchy in Iran," in D. H. Dwyer (ed.) *Law and Islam in the Middle East*, 115–42, New York: Bergin and Garvey, 1990.

Fish, T. "Some Aspects of Kingship in the Sumerian City and Kingdom of Ur," *Bulletin of the John Rylands Library* 34, 1951/2: 37–43.

Fisher, A. "The Life and Family of Süleymân I," in H. İnalcık and C. Kafadar (eds) *Süleymân the Second and His Time*, 1–20, Istanbul: İsis Press, 1993.

Fitzherbert, T. "Portrait of a Lost Leader: Jalal al-Din Khwarazmshah and Juvaini," in J. Raby and T. Fitzherbert (eds) *The Court of the Il-khans, 1290–1340*, 63–77, Oxford: Oxford University Press, 1996.

Fleischer, C. H. "Royal Authority, Dynastic Cyclism, and 'Ibn Khaldûnism' in Sixteenth-Century Ottoman Letters," *JAAS* 18, 1983: 198–220.

——. *Bureaucrat and Intellectual in the Ottoman Empire: the historian Mustafa Âli (1541–1600)* Princeton, NJ: Princeton University Press, 1986.

——. "From Şeyhzade Korkud to Mustafa Âlî: cultural origins of the Ottoman *nasihatname*," in H. W. Lowry and R. S. Hattox (eds) *IIIrd Congress on the Social and Economic History of Turkey*, 67–77, Istanbul: İsis, 1990.

——. "The Lawgiver as Messiah: the making of the imperial image in the reign of Süleymân," in G. Veinstein (ed.) *Soliman le magnifique et son temps*, 159–77, Paris: La Documentation Française, 1992.

——. "Between the Lines: realities of scribal life in the sixteenth century," in C. Heywood and C. Imber (eds) *Studies in Ottoman History in Honour of Professor V. L. Ménage*, 45–61, Istanbul: İsis, 1994.

——. "Mahdi and Millennium: messianic dimensions in the development of Ottoman imperial ideology," in K. Çiçek (ed.) *The Great Ottoman-Turkish Civilisation,* 4 vols, 3: 42–54, Ankara: Yeni Türkiye, 2000.

Flemming, B. "Serif, Sultan Gavrī und die 'Perser'," *Der Islam* 45, 1969: 81–93.

——. "Aus den Nachtgesprächen Sultan Gauris," in H. Franke, W. Heissig and W. Treue (eds) *Folia Rara: Wolfgang Voigt LXV. Diem Natalen Celebranti*, 22–8, Wiesbaden: Franz Steiner, 1976.

——. "Literary Activities in Mamluk Halls and Barracks," in M. Rosen-Ayalon (ed.) *Studies in Memory of Gaston Wiet*, 249–60, Jerusalem: Hebrew University, 1977.

——. "Public Opinion under Sultan Süleymân," in H. İnalcık and C. Kafadar (eds) *Süleymân the Second and His Time*, 49–58, Istanbul: İsis, 1993.

Fletcher, J. F. "The Mongols: ecological and social perspectives," *HJAS* 46, 1986: 11–50; repr. in B. F. Manz (ed.) *Studies on Chinese and Islamic Inner Asia*, Aldershot, UK: Variorum, 1995, IX.

Floor, W. "Change and Development in the Judicial System of Qajar Iran (1800–1925)," in C. E. Bosworth and C. Hillenbrand (eds) *Qajar Iran: political, social and cultural change, 1800–1925*, 113–47, Edinburgh: Edinburgh University Press, 1983.

——. *A Fiscal History of Iran in the Safavid and Qajar Periods, 1500–1925*, New York: Bibliotheca Persica, 1998.

——. "The Secular Judicial System in Safavid Persia," *StIr* 29, 2000: 9–60.

——. *Safavid Government Institutions*, Costa Mesa, CA: Mazda, 2001.

Fodor, P. "Aḥmedī's Dāsitān as a Source of Early Ottoman History," *AOH* 38, 1984: 41–54.
——. "State and Society, Crisis and Reform, in 15th–17th century Ottoman mirrors for princes," *AOH* 40, 1986: 217–40.
——. "Making a Living on the Frontiers: volunteers in the sixteenth-century Ottoman army," in P. Fodor, *In Quest of the Golden Apple: imperial ideology, politics, and military administration in the Ottoman Empire*, 275–304, Istanbul: İsis, 2000.
——. "Sultan, Imperial Council, Grand Vizier: changes in the Ottoman ruling elite and the formation of the grand vizieral *telhīṣ*," *AOH* 47, 1994: 67–85.
Foran, J. *Fragile Resistance: social transformation in Iran from 1500 to the Revolution*, Boulder, CO: Westview, 1993.
Foucault, M. "Governmentality," in G. Burchell, C. Gordon and P. Miller (eds) *The Foucault Effect: studies in governmentality*, 87–104, London: Harvester/Wheatsheaf, 1991.
Fragner, B. G. "Shah Ismail's Fermans and Sanads: tradition and reform in Persophone administration and chancellery affairs," *Journal of Azerbaijani Studies* 1, 1998: 35–46.
Frank, A. G. *ReOrient: global economy in the Asian age*, Berkeley: University of California Press, 1998.
Franke, H. *From Tribal Chieftain to Universal Emperor and God: the legitimation of the Yüan dynasty*, Philosophisch-Historische Klasse, Sitzungsberichte, 2, Munich: Bayerischen Akademie der Wissenschaften, 1978.
Frey, F. W. *The Turkish Political Elite*, Cambridge: MIT Press, 1965.
Friedlander, I. "The Heterodoxies of the Shi'ites in the Presentation of Ibn Hazm," *JAOS* 28, 1907: 1–80.
Frye, R. N. *The Heritage of Persia*, London: Weidenfeld and Nicolson, 1962.
——. *Bukhara: the medieval achievement*, Norman, OK: University of Oklahoma Press, 1965.
——. "The New Persian Renaissance in Western Iran," in G. Makdisi (ed.) *Arabic and Islamic Studies in Honor of Hamilton A. R. Gibb*, 225–31, Leiden: Brill, 1965.
——. *The Golden Age of Persia: the Arabs in the East*, London: Weidenfeld & Nicolson, 1975.
——. *The History of Ancient Iran*, Munich: C. H. Beck, 1984.
——. "Pre-Islamic and Early Islamic Cultures in Central Asia," in R. L. Canfield (ed.) *Turko-Persia in Historical Perspective*, 35–52, Cambridge: Cambridge University Press, 1991.
Fuess, A. "Legends against Injustice: thoughts on the relationship between the Mamluk military elite and their Arab subjects," paper presented at the Middle East Studies Association, Anchorage, Alaska, 9 November 2003.
Gabrieli, F. "L'opera di Ibn al-Muqaffa'," *Rivista degli studi orientali* 13, 1931–32: 197–247.
Gaffney, P. D. *The Prophet's Pulpit: Islamic preaching in contemporary Egypt*, Berkeley: University of California Press, 1994.
Galbraith, V. H. *The Making of Domesday Book*, Oxford: Clarendon, 1961.
Gellner, E. "Patterns of Rural Rebellion in Morocco: tribes as minorities," *Archives européennes de sociologie* 3, 1962: 297–311.
Gelvin, J. L. "The Social Origins of Popular Nationalism in Syria: evidence for a new framework," *IJMES* 26, 1994: 645–61.
——. *Divided Loyalties: nationalism and mass politics in Syria at the close of empire*, Berkeley: University of California Press, 1998.
Gerber, H. "*Sharia, Kanun* and Custom in the Ottoman Law: the court records of 17th-century Bursa," *IJTS* 2.1, 1981: 131–47.
——. *The Social Origins of the Modern Middle East*, Boulder, CO: Lynne Reinner, 1987.
——. *State, Society, and Law in Islam: Ottoman law in comparative perspective*, Albany: State University of New York Press, 1994.
——. *Islamic Law and Culture, 1600–1840*, Leiden: Brill, 1999.
Gerhardt, M. "Sport and Civil Society in Iran," in E. J. Hooglund (ed.) *Twenty Years of Islamic Revolution: political and social transition in Iran since 1979*, 36–55, Syracuse: Syracuse University Press, 2002.
Geyikdağı, M. Y. *Political Parties in Turkey: the role of Islam*, New York: Praeger, 1984.

Ghalwash, M. A. "Land Acquisition by the Peasants of Mid-Nineteenth Century Egypt: the *ramya* system," *SI* 88, 1998: 121–39.

Ghani, A. "Disputes in a Court of *Sharia*, Kunar Valley, Afghanistan, 1885–1890," *IJMES* 15, 1983: 353–67.

Ghirshman, R. *Iran: Parthians and Sasanians*, trans. S. Gilbert and J. Emmans, [London]: Thames and Hudson, 1962.

Ghods, M. R. "Government and Society in Iran, 1926–34," *MES* 27, 1991: 219–30.

Gibb, H. A. R. "Al-Mawardi's Theory of the Caliphate," *IC* 11, 1937: 291–302; repr. in S. J. Shaw and W. R. Polk (eds) *Studies on the Civilization of Islam*, 151–65, Boston, MA: Beacon Press, 1962.

——. "The Evolution of Government in Early Islam," *SI* 4, 1955: 1–17, repr. in S. J. Shaw and W. R. Polk (eds) *Studies on the Civilization of Islam*, 34–45, Boston, MA: Beacon Press, 1962.

——. "Government and Islam under the Early 'Abbasids: the political collapse of Islam," in *L'Élaboration de l'Islam: Colloque de Strasbourg, 12–13–14 juin 1959,* 115–27, Paris: Presses universitaires de France, 1961.

——. "An Interpretation of Islamic History," *JWH* 1 (1953): 39–62; repr. in S. J. Shaw and W. R. Polk (eds) *Studies on the Civilization of Islam*, 3–33, Boston, MA: Beacon Press, 1962.

——. "The Career of Nūr-ad-Dīn," in K. M. Setton (ed.) *A History of the Crusades*, 4 vols, 1: 513–27, Madison: University of Wisconsin Press, 1969.

——. "The Social Significance of the Shuubiya," in *Studia orientalia Ioanni Pedersen septuagenario A.D. VII id. nov. anno MCMLIII a collegis discipulis amicis dicata,* 105–14, Hauniae [Copenhagen]: E. Munksgaard, 1953; repr. in S. J. Shaw and W. R. Polk (eds) *Studies on the Civilization of Islam*, 62–73, Boston, MA: Beacon Press, 1962.

——. "Tā'rīkh," in *The Encyclopaedia of Islam: a dictionary of the geography, ethnography and biography of the Muhammadan peoples*, ed. M. T. Houtsma, T. W. Arnold, R. Hartmann, and H. A. R. Gibb, Leyden, Brill; London, Luzac, 1913–36; Supplement, 1938, 233–45; repr. in S. J. Shaw and W. R. Polk (eds) *Studies on the Civilization of Islam*, 108–37, Boston, MA: Beacon Press, 1962.

Gibb, H. A. R. and Bowen, H. *Islamic Society and the West: a study of the impact of Western civilization on Moslem culture in the Near East*, 1 vol. in 2 pts, London: Oxford University Press, 1957.

Gibbon, E. *The History of the Decline and Fall of the Roman Empire*, new ed., London: Lackington, Harding, Hughes, Mavor, and Jones, 1820.

Gignoux, P. "Church-State Relations in the Sasanian Period," in H.I.H. Prince T. Mikasa (ed.) *Monarchies and Socio-Religious Traditions in the Ancient Near East*, 72–80, Wiesbaden: Harrassowitz, 1984.

Gilsenan, M. "*Nizam Ma Fi*: discourses of order, disorder and history in a Lebanese Context," in J. P. Spagnolo (ed.) *Problems of the Modern Middle East in Historical Perspective: essays in honour of Albert Hourani,* 79–104, Reading: Ithaca Press, for the Middle East Centre, St. Antony's College, Oxford, 1992.

Glain, S. J. *Mullahs, Merchants, and Militants: the economic collapse of the Arab world*, New York: St. Martin's, 2004.

Gnoli, G. "Note su xšāyaθiya-e xšaça," in *Ex Orbe Religionum: studia Geo Widengren oblata,* 2 vols, 2: 88–97, Leiden: Brill, 1972.

——. *The Idea of Iran: an essay on its origin*, Rome: Istituto Italiano per il Medio ed Estremo Oriente, 1989.

Göçek, F. M. and Hanioğlu, M. Ş. "Western Knowledge, Imperial Control, and the Use of Statistics in the Ottoman Empire," in J. L. Warner (ed.) *Cultural Horizons: a festschrift in honor of Talat S. Halman*, 105–16, Syracuse: Syracuse University Press, 2001.

Goitein, S. D. "Petitions to Fatimid Caliphs from the Cairo Geniza," *Jewish Quarterly Review*, n.s. 45, 1954/55: 30–8.

Gökbilgin, M. T. "XVI. asır başlarında osmanlı devleti hizmetindekin Akkoyunlu ümerası," *TM* 9, 1946/51: 35–46.

Golden, P. B. "Imperial Ideology and the Sources of Political Unity amongst the Pre-Činggisid Nomads of Western Eurasia," *AEuras* 2, 1982: 37–76.

Goldstone, J. A. *Revolution and Rebellion in the Early Modern World*, Berkeley: University of California Press, 1991.

Goldziher, I. "'Arab and 'Ajam," in S. M. Stern (ed.) *Muslim Studies*, trans. C. R. Barber and S. M. Stern, 2 vols, 1: 98–136, London: George Allen & Unwin, 1889–90.

——. "Du sens propre des expressions Ombre de Dieu, Khalife de Dieu, pour designer les chefs d'Islam," *Revue de l'histoire des religions* 35, 1897: 331–8.

——. "Islamisme et Parsisme," *Revue de l'histoire des religions* 43, 1901: 1–29.

Golombek, L. "Discourses of an Imaginary Arts Council in Fifteenth-Century Iran," in L. Golombek and M. Subtelny (eds) *Timurid Art and Culture: Iran and Central Asia in the fifteenth century*, 1–17, Leiden: Brill, 1992.

——. and Wilber, D. *The Timurid Architecture of Iran and Turan*, 2 vols, Princeton, NJ: Princeton University Press, 1988.

Goodell, G. E. *The Elementary Structures of Political Life: rural development in Pahlavi Iran*, New York: Oxford University Press, 1986.

Goodenough, E. R. "The Political Philosophy of Hellenistic Kingship," *Yale Classical Studies* 1, 1928: 55–102.

Gopnik, H. "Death and Taxes in the Neo-Assyrian Reliefs," in S. E. Orel (ed.) *Death and Taxes in the Ancient Near East*, 61–86, Lewiston: Edwin Mellen, 1992.

Gordon, M. S. *The Breaking of a Thousand Swords: a history of the Turkish military of Samarra (A.H. 200–275/815–889 C.E.)* Albany: State University of New York Press, 2001.

Göyünç, N. "Das sogenannte Ǧāme'o'l-Ḥesāb das 'Emād as-Sarāwī," PhD diss., Georg-August-Universität, 1962.

——. "İmâd es-Serâvî ve Eseri," *Tarih Dergisi* 15 no. 20, 1965: 73–86.

——. "Provincial Organization of the Ottoman Empire in Pre-Tanzimat Period," in K. Çiçek (ed.) *The Great Ottoman-Turkish Civilisation*, 4 vols, 3: 519–32, Ankara: Yeni Türkiye, 2000.

Grabar, O. *The Formation of Islamic Art*, New Haven, CT: Yale University Press, 1973.

——. "Al-Mushatta, Baghdād, and Wāsiṭ," in J. Kritzek & R. B. Winder (eds) *The World of Islam: studies in honor of P. K. Hitti*, 99–108, London: Macmillan & Co., 1959.

——. "Umayyad 'Palace' and the 'Abbasid 'Revolution'," *SI* 18, 1963: 5–18.

——. *Sasanian Silver: late antique and early mediaeval arts of luxury from Iran*, Ann Arbor: University of Michigan Museum of Art, 1967.

——. "Notes sur les cérémonies umayyades," in M. Rosen-Ayalon (ed.) *Studies in Memory of Gaston Wiet*, 51–60, Jerusalem: Institute of Asian and African Studies, Hebrew University of Jerusalem, 1977.

——. and Blair, S. *Epic Images and Contemporary History: the illustrations of the Great Mongol Shahnama*, Chicago, IL: University of Chicago Press, 1980.

Granara, W. "*Jihād* and Cross-cultural Encounter in Muslim Sicily," *HMEIR* 3, 1996: 42–61.

Green, J. D. *Revolution in Iran: the politics of countermobilization*, New York: Praeger, 1982.

Grehan, J. "Street Violence and Social Imagiation in Late-Mamluk and Ottoman Damascus (ca. 1500–1800)," *IJMES* 35, 2003: 215–36.

——. *Everyday Life and Consumer Culture in 18th-Century Damascus*, Seattle: University of Washington Press, 2007.

Greussing, K. "The Babi Movement in Iran, 1844–52: from merchant protest to peasant revolution," in J. M. Bak and G. Benecke (eds) *Religion and Rural Revolt*, 256–69, Manchester, UK and Dover, NH: Manchester University Press, 1982.

Grignaschi, M. "Le roman épistolaire classique conservé dans la version arabe de Sālim Abū-l-'Alā'," *Le Muséon* 80, 1967: 211–64.

——. "La Nihāyatu-l-'Arab fī Aḫbāri-l-Furs wa-l-'Arab," *BEO* 22, 1969: 15–67; 26, 1973: 83–184.

——. "Remarques sur la formation et l'interpretation du *Sirr al-'asrār*," in W. F. Ryan and C. B. Schmitt (eds) *Pseudo-Aristotle, the 'Secret of Secrets': sources and influences*, 3–33, London: Warburg Institute, 1982.

——. "Un roman épistolaire gréco-arabe: la correspondence entre Aristote et Alexandre," in M. Bridges and J. C. Bürgel (eds) *The Problematics of Power: Eastern and Western representations of Alexander the Great*, 109–23, Bern: Peter Lang, 1996.

Griswold, W. J. *The Great Anatolia Rebellion, 1000–1020/1591–1611*, Berlin: Klaus Schwarz, 1983.

Gross, M. L. "Ottoman Rule in the Province of Damascus, 1860–1909," PhD diss., Georgetown University, 1979.

Grousset, R. *The Empire of the Steppes: a history of Central Asia*, trans. N. Walford, New Brunswick, NJ: Rutgers University Press, 1970.

Grube, E. J. "Herat, Tabriz, Istanbul–the development of a pictorial style," in R. Pinder-Wilson (ed.) *Paintings from Islamic Lands*, 85–109, Oxford: Bruno Cassirer, 1969.

Güçer, L. *XVI–XVII. asırlarda Osmanlı İmparatorluğunda hububat meselesi ve hububattan alınan vergiler*, Istanbul: İstanbul Üniversitesi İktisat Fakültesi,1964.

Gülalp, H. "Universalism versus Particularism: Ottoman historiography and the 'grand narrative'," *NPT* 13, 1994: 151–69.

Güran, T. "The State Role in the Grain Supply of Istanbul: the grain administration, 1793–1839," *IJTS* 3, 1984: 27–41.

Gutas, D. *Greek Thought, Arabic Culture: the Graeco-Arabic translation movement in Baghdad and early 'Abbāsid society (2nd–4th/8th–10th centuries)* London: Routledge, 1998.

Gutas, D. "The Spurious and the Authentic in the Arabic Lives of Aristotle," in J. Kraye, W. F. Ryan, and C. B. Schmitt (eds) *Pseudo-Aristotle in the Middle Ages: the Theology and other texts*, 15–36, London: Warburg Institute, 1986.

Güvemli, O. *Türk devletleri muhasebe tarihi,* vol. 1, *Osmanlı İmparatorluğu'na kadar*, Istanbul: Muhasebe Öğretim Üyeleri Bilim ve Dayanışma Vakfı, 1995.

Haarmann, U. "*Rather the Injustice of the Turks than the Righteousness of the Arabs*–changing 'ulamā attitudes towards Mamluk rule in the late fifteenth century," *SI* 68, 1988: 61–77.

Haddad, Y. Y. *Contemporary Islam and the Challenge of History*, Albany: State University of New York Press, 1982.

Hadi Hussain, M. and Kamali, A.-H. *The Nature of the Islamic State*, Karachi: National Book Foundation, 1977.

Hafez, M. M. *Why Muslims Rebel: repression and resistance in the Islamic world*, Boulder, CO: Lynne Reinner, 2003.

Hagen, G. "Translations and Translators in a Multilingual Society: a case study of Persian-Ottoman translations, late fifteenth to early seventeenth century," *Eurasian Studies* 2, 2003: 95–134.

——. "Legitimacy and World Order," in H. T. Karateke and M. Reinkowski (eds) *Legitimizing the Order: the Ottoman rhetoric of state power*, 55–83, Leiden: Brill, 2005.

Hägg, T. "The Oriental Reception of Greek Novels: a survey with some preliminary considerations," *Symbolae Osloenses* 61, 1986: 99–131.

Haider, M. "The Sovereign in the Timurid State (XIVth–XVth Centuries)," *Turcica* 8, 1976: 61–82.

Haji, A. "Institutions of Justice in Fatimid Egypt (358–567/969–1171)," in A. al-Azmeh (ed.) *Islamic Law: social and historical contexts*, 198–214, New York: Routledge, 1988.

Haldane, D. *Mamluk Painting*, Warminster, UK: Aris & Phillips, 1978.

Hallaq, W. B. "Was the Gate of Ijtihad Closed?" *IJMES* 16, 1984: 3–41.

——. "Model *Shurūṭ* Works and the Dialectic of Doctrine and Practice," *ILS* 2, 1995: 109–34.

——. "The *Qāḍī*'s *Dīwān (Sijill)* before the Ottomans," *BSOAS* 61, 1998: 415–36.

Halliday, F. "Theses on the Iranian Revolution," *Race & Class* 21, 1979: 81–90.

Halm, H. *Ägypten nach den mamlukischen Lehensregistern*, 2 vols, Beihefte zum Tübinger Atlas des Vorderen Orients, Reihe B (Geisteswissenschaft), No. 38, Wiesbaden: L. Reichert, 1979.

Halman, T. S. "The Empire of Poetry: Süleyman the Magnificent as poet," in H. C. Güzel, C. Oğuz, O. Karatay, and M. Ocak (eds) *The Turks*, 6 vols, 3: 907–11, Ankara: Yeni Türkiye, 2002.

Halpern, M. *The Politics of Social Change in the Middle East and North Africa*, Princeton, NJ: Princeton University Press, 1963.

Hamadeh, S. "Ottoman Expressions of Early Modernity and the 'Inevitable' Question of Westernization," *Journal of the Society of Architectural Historians* 63, March 2004: 32–51.

——. *The City's Pleasures: Istanbul in the eighteenth century*, Seattle: University of Washington Press, 2008.

Hambly, G. R. G. "Aqa Mohammad Khan and the Establishment of the Qajar Dynasty," *Journal of the Royal Central Asian Society* 50, 1963: 161–74.

Hamed, R. A. "The *Siyasatname* and the Institutionalization of Central Administration under Muhammad 'Ali," in N. Hanna (ed.) *The State and Its Servants: Administration in Egypt from Ottoman Times to the Present*, 75–86, Cairo: American University in Cairo Press, 1995.

Hanafi, H. "The Relevance of the Islamic Alternative in Egypt," *ASQ* 4.1–2, Spring 1980: 54–74.

Hanaway, W. Introduction to *Love and War: adventures from the Firuz Shāh Nāma of Sheikh Bighami*, 1–24, Delmar, NY: Scholars' Facsimiles and Reprints, 1974.

Hanna, N. "Culture in Ottoman Egypt," in C. F. Petry and M. W. Daly (eds) *The Cambridge History of Egypt*, vol. 2, *Modern Egypt, from 1517 to the End of the Twentieth Century*, ed. M. W. Daly, 87–112, Cambridge: Cambridge University Press, 1998.

Hanna, S. A. "Al-Afghāni: a pioneer of Islamic socialism," *MW* 57, 1967: 24–32.

Hanne, E. J. *Putting the Caliph in His Place: power, authority, and the late Abbasid caliphate*, Madison, NJ: Fairleigh Dickinson University Press, 2007.

Hanssen, J. "Practices of Integration – Center-Periphery Relations in the Ottoman Empire," in J. Hanssen, T. Philipp and S. Weber (eds) *The Empire in the City: Arab provincial capitals in the late Ottoman Empire*, 49–74, Beirut: Ergon, 2002.

——. Philipp, T. and Weber, S. (eds) *The Empire in the City: Arab provincial capitals in the late Ottoman Empire*, Beirut: Ergon Verlag Würzburg, 2002.

Harbi, M. "Chapître-Pamphlet de Abdessalam Yassine contre le roi Hassan II," *Sou'al* 5, 1985: 151–7.

——. "Un ouvrage du cheikh Abdellatif b. Ali al-Soltani: "Le mazdakisme est à l'origine du socialisme"," *Sou'al* 5, 1985: 135–9.

Harik, I. *The Political Mobilization of Peasants: a study of an Egyptian community*, Bloomington: Indiana University Press, 1974.

Harmatta, J. "Parthia and Elymais in the 2nd Century B.C.," *Acta Antiqua Academiae Scientiarum Hungaricae* 29, 1981: 189–217.

Harney, D. *The Priest and the King: an eyewitness account of the Iranian Revolution*, London: British Academic Press, 1998.

Harper, P. O. and Meyers, P. *Silver Vessels of the Sasanian Period*, vol. 1: *Royal Imagery*, New York: Metropolitan Museum of Art, 1981.

Harris, W. W. "The Crisis of Democracy in Twentieth-Century Syria and Lebanon," in W. W. Harris (ed.) *Challenges to Democracy in the Middle East*, 1–28, Princeton, NJ: Markus Weiner, 1997.

Harvey, D. *A Brief History of Neoliberalism*, Oxford: Oxford University Press, 2005.

Havemann, A. "The Impact of Peasant Resistance on Nineteenth-Century Mount Lebanon," in F. Kazemi and J. Waterbury (eds) *Peasants and Politics in the Modern Middle East*, 85–100, Miami: Florida International University Press, 1991.

Hawting, G. R. *The First Dynasty of Islam: the Umayyad caliphate*, AD *661–750*, London: Croom Helm, 1986.

Hayashi, K. and Aydın, M. (eds) *The Ottoman State and Societies in Change: a study of the nineteenth-century temettuat registers*, London: Kegan Paul, 2004.

Heck, P. L. *The Construction of Knowledge in Islamic Civilization: Qudāma b. Ja'far and his* Kitāb al-kharāj wa-ṣinā'at al-kitāba, Leiden: Brill, 2002.

Hegland, M. "Two Images of Husain: accommodation and revolution in an Iranian village," in N. R. Keddie (ed.) *Religion and Politics in Iran: Shi'ism from quietism to revolution*, 218–35, New Haven, CT: Yale University Press, 1983.

Heinz, W. "Die Kultur der Tulpenzeit des Osmanischen Reiches," *WZKM* 61, 1967: 62–116.

Heisey, D. R. and Trebing, J. D. "Authority and Legitimacy: a rhetorical case study of the Iranian Revolution," *Communication Monographs* 53, 1986: 295–310.

Helms, M. W. *Craft and the Kingly Ideal: art, trade and power*, Austin: University of Texas Press, 1993.

Hermassi, E. *Leadership and National Development in North Africa: a comparative study*, Berkeley: University of California Press, 1972.

——. and Vanderwalle, D. "The Second Stage of State Building," in I W. Zartman and W. M. Habeeb (eds) *Polity and Society in Contemporary North Africa*, 19–41, Boulder, CO: Westview, 1993.

Herrenschmidt, C. "Désignation de l'empire et concepts politiques de Darius Ier d'après ses inscriptions en vieux-perse," *StIr* 5, 1976: 33–65.

Heyd, U. "*Ḳanun* and *Sharī'a* in Old Ottoman Criminal Justice," *Proceedings of the Israel Academy of Sciences and Humanities* 3.1, 1967: 1–18.

——. *Studies in Old Ottoman Criminal Law*, ed. V. L. Ménage, Oxford: Clarendon, 1973.

Heydemann, S. "The Political Logic of Economic Rationality: selective stabilization in Syria," in H. J. Barkey (ed.) *The Politics of Economic Reform in the Middle East*, 11–39, New York: St. Martin's, 1992.

——. "Taxation without Representation: authoritarianism and economic liberalization in Syria," in E. Goldberg, R. Kasaba, and J. S. Migdal (eds) *Rules and Rights in the Middle East: democracy, law, and Society*, 69–101, Seattle: University of Washington Press, 1993.

——. *Authoritarianism in Syria: institutions and social conflict, 1946–1970*, Ithaca, NY: Cornell University Press, 1999.

Hickok, M. R. *Ottoman Military Administration in Eighteenth-Century Bosnia*, Leiden: Brill, 1997.

——. "Homicide in Ottoman Bosnia," in F. Anscombe (ed.) *The Ottoman Balkans, 1750–1830*, 35–59, Princeton, NJ: Markus Wiener, 2006.

Hillenbrand, C. "Islamic Orthodoxy or Realpolitik? al-Ghazālī's views on government," *Iran* 26, 1988: 81–94.

——. *A Muslim Principality in Crusader Times: the early Artuqid state*, Istanbul: Nederlands Historisch-Archaeologisch Instituut, 1990.

Hillenbrand, R. "The Architecture of the Ghaznavids and Ghurids," in C. Hillenbrand (ed.) *Studies in Honour of Clifford Edmund Bosworth*, vol. 2: *The Sultan's Turret: studies in Persian and Turkish culture*, 124–206 and plates, Leiden: Brill, 2000.

——. "*La Dolce Vita* in Early Islamic Syria: the evidence of later Umayyad palaces," *Art History* 5, 1982: 1–35.

——. "The Iskandar Cycle in the Great Mongol *Šāhnāma*," in M. Bridges and J. C. Bürgel (eds) *The Problematics of Power: Eastern and Western representations of Alexander the Great*, 203–30, Bern: Peter Lang, 1996.

——. "The Uses of Space in Timurid Painting," in L. Golombek and M. Subtelny (eds) *Timurid Art and Culture: Iran and Central Asia in the fifteenth century*, 76–102, Leiden: Brill, 1992.

Hinnebusch, R. A. "The National Progressive Unionist Party: the nationalist-left opposition in post-populist Egypt," *ASQ* 3.4, 1981: 325–51.

——. *Peasant and Bureaucracy in Ba'thist Syria: the political economy of rural development*, Boulder, CO: Westview, 1989.

——. *Authoritarian Power and State Formation in Ba'thist Syria: army, party, and peasant*, Boulder, CO: Westview, 1990.

Hinz, W. "Das Steuerwesen Ostanatoliens im 15. und 16. Jahrhundert," *ZDMG* 100, 1950: 177–201.

Hocart, A. M. *Kings and Councillors: an essay in the comparative anatomy of human society*, ed. R. Needham, Chicago, IL: University of Chicago Press, 1970.

Hoffmann, B. "Turkmen Princes and Religious Dignitaries: a sketch in group profiles," in L. Golombek and M. Subtelny (eds) *Timurid Art and Culture: Iran and Central Asia in the fifteenth century*, 23–28, Leiden: Brill, 1992.

——. "Rašīdaddīn Faḍlallāh as the Perfect Organizer: the case of the endowment slaves and gardens of the Rab'-i Rašīdī," in B. G. Fragner, C. Fragner, G. Gnoli, R. Haag-Higuchi, M. Maggi, and P. Orsatti (eds) *Proceedings of the Second European Conference of Iranian Studies*, 287–96, Rome: Istituto Italiano per il Medio ed Estremo Oriente, 1995.

Hoğğa, M. *Orthodoxie, subversion, et réforme en Islam: Gazālī et les Seljūqides*, Paris: J. Vrin, 1993.

Holloway, S. W. *Aššur is King! Aššur is King! religion in the exercise of power in the Neo-Assyrian Empire*, Leiden: Brill, 2002.

Holt, P. M. *The Mahdist State in the Sudan, 1881–1898: a study of its origins, development and overthrow*, Oxford: Clarendon, 1958.

——. "The Position and Power of the Mamlūk Sultan," *BSOAS* 38, 1975: 237–49.

——. "The Sultanate of al-Maneqūr Lāchīn (696–9/1296–9)," *BSOAS* 36, 1973: 521–32.

Holt, P. M, Lambton, A. K. S. and Lewis, B. (eds) *The Cambridge History of Islam*, 4 vols, Cambridge: Cambridge University Press, 1970.

Hooglund, E. J. *Land and Revolution in Iran, 1960–1980*, Austin: University of Texas Press, 1982.
Hooke, S. H. (ed.) *Myth, Ritual, and Kingship: essays on the theory and practice of kingship in the ancient Near East and in Israel*, Oxford: Clarendon, 1958.
Hopkins, J. F. P. *Medieval Muslim Government in Barbary: until the sixth century of the Hijra*, London: Luzac, 1958.
Hottinger, A. "How the Arab Bourgeoisie Lost Power," *JContempH* 3.3, 1968: 111–28.
Hourani, A. "Ottoman Reform and the Politics of Notables," in W. R. Polk and R. L. Chambers (eds) *Beginnings of Modernization in the Middle East*, 41–68, Chicago, IL: University of Chicago Press, 1968.
——. *Arabic Thought in the Liberal Age, 1798–1939*, London: Oxford University Press, 1970.
Howard, D. A. "Historical Scholarship and the Classical Ottoman Ḳānūnnāmes," *AOtt* 14, 1995–6: 79–110.
——. "The Ottoman *Timar* System and Its Transformation, 1563–1656," PhD diss., Indiana University, 1987.
——. "Ottoman Historiography and the Literature of 'Decline' of the Sixteenth and Seventeenth Centuries," *JAH* 22, 1988: 52–77.
——. "The 'Ruling Institution,' Genre, and the Story of the Decline of the Ottoman Empire," Grand Rapids, MI: unpublished paper, 1992.
Howe, M. *Turkey Today: a nation divided over Islam's revival*, Boulder, CO: Westview, 2000.
Hruška, B. "Die Reformtexte Urukaginas: der verspätete Versuch einer Konsolidierung des stadtstaates von Lagas," in P. Garelli (ed.) *Le palais et la royauté (archéologie et civilisation)*, Rencontre assyriologique internationale, 19th, Paris, 1971, 151–61, Paris: Paul Geuthner, 1974.
Huang, R. "Fiscal Administration during the Ming Dynasty," in C. O. Hucker (ed.) *Chinese Government in Ming Times: seven studies*, 73–128, 248–58, New York: Columbia University Press, 1969.
Huart, C. *Ancient Persia and Iranian Civilization*, trans. M. R. Dobie, New York: A. A. Knopf, 1927.
Hudson, L. "Late Ottoman Damascus: investments in public space and the emergence of popular sovereignty," *Critique* 15, 2006: 151–69.
Hudson, M. C. *Arab Politics: the search for legitimacy*, New Haven, CT: Yale University Press, 1977.
Humphreys, R. S. *Between Memory and Desire: the Middle East in a troubled age*, Berkeley: University of California Press, 1999.
Hunaidi, R. K. Untitled Paper, in *The Middle East: a new look*, New York: International Advisory Council Symposium, 15 June 2000, 12.
Hurvitz, N. "Competing Texts: the relationship between al-Mawardi's and Abu Ya'la's *al-Ahkam al-sultaniyya*," Occasional Publications, 8, Cambridge, MA: Islamic Legal Studies Program of Harvard Law School, 2007.
Husaini, I. M. *The Moslem Brethren: the greatest of modern Islamic movements*, Beirut: Khayat's, 1956.
——. *The Life and Works of Ibn Qutayba*, Beirut: American Press, 1950.
Hussein [Ḥusayn], T. *The Sufferers: stories and polemics*, trans. M. El-Zayyat, Cairo: American University in Cairo Press, 1993.
Ibrahim, I. "Religion and Politics under Nasser and Sadat, 1952–1981," in *The Islamic Impulse*, ed. B. F. Stowasser, 121–34, London: Croom Helm, 1987.
Ibrahim, S. E. "Anatomy of Egypt's Militant Islamic Groups: methodological notes and preliminary findings," *IJMES* 12, 1980: 423–53.
——. "The Changing Face of Egypt's Islamic Activism" (6 May 1995), repr. in *Egypt, Islam and Democracy: critical essays*, 2nd ed., 69–79, Cairo: American University in Cairo Press, 2002.
——. "Civil Society and Prospects of Democratization in the Arab World," in R. G. Norton (ed.) *Civil Society in the Middle East*, 27–54, Leiden: Brill, 1995–6; repr. in *Egypt, Islam and Democracy: critical essays*, 2nd ed., 245–66, Cairo: American University in Cairo Press, 2002.
——. "Governance and Structural Adjustment: the Egyptian case," in *Egypt, Islam and Democracy: critical essays*, 2nd ed., 135–81, Cairo: American University in Cairo Press, 2002.
Imamuddin, S. M. "Administration under the Fatimids," *JAS Pakistan* 14, 1969: 253–69.
Imber, C. *Ebu's-su'ud: The Islamic Legal Tradition*, Edinburgh: Edinburgh University Press, 1997.

İnal, G. "The Ottoman Interpretation of Firdausi's Shahnama," in H. G. Majer (ed.) *VI. Internationaler Kongress für Turkische Kunst*, 52, Munich: Geschichte und Kulture des Nahen Orients sowie Turkologie, 1979.

İnalcık, H. *Tanzimat ve Bulgar Meselesi*, Ankara: Türk Tarih Kurumu, 1943.

——. "Timariotes chrétiens en Albanie au XV. siècle, d'après un registre de timars ottoman," *Mitteilungen des österreichischen Staatsarchiv* 4, 1951: 118–38.

——. "Ottoman Methods of Conquest," *SI* 2, 1954: 104–29, repr. in H. İnalcık, *The Ottoman Empire: Conquest, Organization and Economy*, London: Variorum, 1978, I.

——. "Osmanlı hukukuna giriş: örfi-sultani hukuk ve Fatih'in kanunları," *AÜSBFD* 13.2, 1958: 102–26.

——. "Osmanlı pâdişahı," *AÜSBFD* 13.4, 1958: 68–79.

——. "Byzantium and the Origins of the Crisis of 1444 under the Light of Turkish Sources," in *Actes du XIIe congrès international d'études byzantines*, 2 vols, 2: 159–63, Belgrade, 1964; repr. Nendeln, Liechtenstein: Kraus Reprint, 1978.

——. "Tanzimat'ın Uygulanması ve Sosyal Tepkileri," *Belleten* 28, 1964: 612–90.

——. "The Nature of Traditional Society: Turkey," in R. E. Ward and D. A. Rostow (eds) *Political Modernization in Japan and Turkey*, 42–63, Princeton, NJ: Princeton University Press, 1964; repr. in *The Ottoman Empire: conquest, organization and economy*, London: Variorum, 1978, XV.

——. "*Kutadgu Bilig*' de Türk ve İran Siyaset Nazariye ve Gelenekleri," in *Reşit Rahmeti Arat Için*, Ankara: Türk Kültürünü Araştırma Enstitüsü, 1966, 259–75; "Turkish and Iranian Political Theories and Traditions in *Kutadgu Bilig*," trans. D. A. Howard, in İnalcık, H., *The Middle East and the Balkans under the Ottoman Empire: Essays on Economy and Society*, 1–18, Bloomington: Indiana University Turkish Studies, 1993.

——. "The Policy of Mehmed II toward the Greek Population of Istanbul and the Byzantine Buildings of the City," *Dumbarton Oaks Papers* 23/24, 1969/70: 231–49, repr. in H. İnalcık, *The Ottoman Empire: conquest, organization and economy*, London: Variorum, 1978, VI.

——. "Suleiman the Lawgiver and Ottoman Law," *AOtt* 1, 1969: 105–38, repr. in H. İnalcık, *The Ottoman Empire: conquest, organization and economy*, London: Variorum, 1978, VII.

——. "The Heyday and Decline of the Ottoman Empire," in P. M. Holt, A. K. S. Lambton and B. Lewis (eds) *The Cambridge History of Islam*, vol. 2A, Cambridge: Cambridge University Press, 1970.

——. "Application of the Tanzimat and Its Social Effects," *AOtt* 5, 1973: 97–128, repr. in *The Ottoman Empire: conquest, organization and economy*, London: Variorum, 1978, XVI.

——. "Military and Fiscal Transformation in the Ottoman Empire, 1600–1700," *AOtt* 6, 1980: 283–337.

——. "Osmanlı bürokrasisinde ahkâm ve muâmelât," *OA* 1, 1980: 1–14.

——. "Şikâyet hakkı: 'arz-i hâl ve 'arz-i mahzar'lar," *Osmanlı Araştımaları* 7–8, 1988: 33–54; repr. in H. İnalcık, *Osmanlı devlet, hukuk, adâlet,* 49–74, Istanbul: Eren, 2000.

——. "The Emergence of Big Farms, *Çiftliks*: state, landlords, and tenants," in Ç. Keyder and F. Tabak (eds) *Landholding and Commercial Agriculture in the Middle East*, 17–34, Albany: State University of New York Press, 1991.

——. "Islamization of Ottoman Laws on Land and Land Taxation," in C. Fragner and K. Schwarz (ed.) *Festgabe an Josef Matuz: Osmanistik-Turkologie-Diplomatik*, 100–16, Berlin: Klaus Schwarz, 1992; repr. in H. İnalcık, *Essays in Ottoman History*, 155–69, Istanbul: Eren, 1998. ILL

——. "Sultan Süleymân: the man and the statesman," in G. Veinstein (ed.) *Soliman le magnifique et son temps*, 89–103, Paris: La Documentation Française, 1992.

——. "State, Sovereignty and Law during the Reign of Süleymân," in H. İnalcık and C. Kafadar (eds) *Süleymân the Second and His Time*, 59–92, Istanbul: İsis Press, 1993.

——. "A Report on the Corrupt Ḳāeqīs under Bayezid II," in B. Kellner-Heinkele and P. Zieme (eds) *Studia Ottomanica: Festgabe für György Hazai zum 65. Geburtstag*, 75–86, Wiesbaden: Harrassowitz, 1997.

——. "The Origin and Definition of the Circle of Justice (Dâire-i Adâlet)," in M. Demirci (ed.) *Selçuklu'dan Osmanlı'ya bilim, kültür ve sanat: Prof. Dr. Mikâil Bayram'a armağan*, 23–26, Konya: Kömen Yayınevi, 2009.

İnalick, H., and Oğuz, M. (eds) *Gazavāt-i Sultān Murād b. Mehemmed Hān*, Ankara: Türk Tarih Kurumu, 1978.

İnalick, H., and Quataert, D. (eds) *An Economic and Social History of the Ottoman Empire*, 2 vols, Cambridge: Cambridge University Press, 1994.

İnan, K. "The Incorporation of Writings on the Periphery in Ottoman Historiography: Tursun Bey's comparison of Mehmed II and Bayezid II," *IJTS* 9, 2003: 105–17.

Inostranzev, K. *Iranian Influence on Moslem Literature*, trans. G. K. Nariman, Bombay: D. B. Taraporevala Sons, 1918.

İpşirli, M. "Osmanlılarda Cuma Selâmlığı (halk-hükümdar münâsebetleri açısından önemi)," in *Prof. Dr. Bekir Kütükoğlu'na Armağan*, 459–71, Istanbul: İstanbul Üniversitesi Edebiyat Fakültesi, 1991.

Irwin, R. "The Privatization of 'Justice' under the Circassian Mamluks," *MSR* 6, 2002: 63–70.

——. "The Political Thinking of the 'Virtuous Ruler,' Qāneqūh al-Ghawrī," *MSR* 12, 2008: 37–49.

İslamoğlu, H. "Property as a Contested Domain: a reevaluation of the Ottoman Land Code of 1858," in R. Owen (ed.) *New Perspectives on Property and Land in the Middle East*, 3–61, Cambridge, MA: Center for Middle Eastern Studies of Harvard University, 2000.

——. "Modernities Compared: state transformations and constitutions of property in the Qing and Ottoman Empires," *JEMH* 5, 2001: 353–86.

İslamoğlu-İnan, H. *State and Peasant in the Ottoman Empire: agrarian power relations and regional economic development in Ottoman Anatolia during the sixteenth century*, Leiden: Brill, 1994.

Ismael, J. S. and Ismael, T. Y. "Cultural Perspectives on Social Welfare in the Emergence of Modern Arab Social Thought," *MW* 85, 1995: 82–106.

Ismail, O. S. A. "Mu'tasim and the Turks," *BSOAS* 29, 1966: 12–24.

Jaber, H. *Hezbollah: born with a vengeance*, New York: Columbia University Press, 1997.

Jacobsen, T. and Lloyd, S. *Sennacherib's Aqueduct at Jerwan*, Oriental Institute Publications, 24, Chicago, IL: University of Chicago Press, 1935.

Jahn, K. "Tebriz: doğu ile batı arasında bir ortaçağ kültür merkezi," trans. İ. Aka, *TAD* 13, 1979–80: Çeviriler 59–78.

Jennings, R. C. "Kadi, Court, and Legal Procedure in 17th C. Ottoman Kayseri," *SI* 48, 1978: 133–72.

——. *Christians and Muslims in Ottoman Cyprus and the Mediterranean World, 1571–1640*, New York: New York University Press, 1993.

Johansen, B. "Sacred and Religious Element in Hanafite Law–function and limits of the absolute character of government authority," in E. Gellner and J.-C. Vatin (eds) *Islam et politique au Maghreb*, 281–303, Paris: CNRS, 1981.

Johns, J. *Arabic Administration in Norman Sicily: the royal dīwān*, Cambridge: Cambridge University Press, 2002.

Jorgens, D. "A Comparative Examination of the Provisions of the Ottoman Land Code and Khedive Sa'id's Law of 1858," in R. Owen (ed.) *New Perspectives on Property and Land in the Middle East*, 93–119, Cambridge, MA: Center for Middle Eastern Studies of Harvard University, 2000.

Kabir, M. "The Relation of the Buwayhid Amirs with the 'Abbasid Caliphs," *JPHS* 2, 1954: 228–43.

Kafadar, C. "'When Coins Turned into Drops of Dew and Bankers Became Robbers of Shadows': the boundaries of Ottoman economic imagination at the end of the sixteenth century," PhD diss., McGill University, 1986.

——. "The Myth of the Golden Age: Ottoman historical consciousness in the post-Süleymânic era," in H. İnalcık and C. Kafadar (eds) *Süleymân the Second and His Time*, 37–48, Istanbul: İsis Press, 1993.

——. *Between Two Worlds: the construction of the Ottoman state*, Berkeley: University of California Press, 1995.

——. "The Question of Ottoman Decline," *HMEIR* 4, 1997–98: 30–75.

Kafesoğlu, İ. "Büyük Selçuklu veziri Nizâmü'l-Mülk'un eseri Siyâsetnâme ve Türkçe tercümesi," *TM* 12, 1955: 231–56.

——. *A History of the Seljuks: İbrahim Kafesoğlu's interpretation and the resulting controversy*, trans. G. Leiser, Carbondale: Southern Illinois University Press, 1988.

Káldy-Nagy, J. "The Administration of the *Sanjāq* Registrations in Hungary," *AOH* 21, 1968: 181–223.

——. "The 'Strangers' *(Ecnebiler)* in the 16th Century Ottoman Military Organization," in G. Kara (ed.) *Between the Danube and the Caucasus*, 165–9, Budapest: Akadémiai Kiadó, 1987.
Kallek, C. "Yaḥyā ibn Ādam's *Kitāb al-kharādj*: religious guidelines for public finance," *JESHO* 44, 2001: 103–22.
Kamali, M. H. *Freedom, Equality and Justice in Islam*, Cambridge: The Islamic Texts Society, 2002.
Kamrava, M. *Revolution in Iran: the roots of turmoil*, London: Routledge, 1990.
Kanga, M. F. "Kingship and Religion in Iran," *Commémoration Cyrus, Hommage universel: actes du congrès de Shiraz 1971*, AcIr 1–3, ser. 1, vols 1–3, 3: 221–31, Leiden: Brill, 1974.
Kansu, A. *The Revolution of 1908 in Turkey*, Leiden: Brill, 1997.
Karal, E. Z. "The Principles of Kemalism," in A. Kazancıgil and E. Özbudun (eds) *Atatürk: founder of a modern state*, Hamden, CT: Archon Books, 1981, 11–35.
Karateke, H. T. "Legitimizing the Ottoman Sultanate: a framework for historical analysis," in H. T. Karateke and M. Reinkowski (eds) *Legitimizing the Order: the Ottoman rhetoric of state power*, 13–52, Leiden: Brill, 2005.
Karimi, S. "Economic Policies and Structure Changes since the Revolution," in N. R. Keddie and E. Hooglund (eds) *The Iranian Revolution and the Islamic Republic*, rev. ed., 32–54, Syracuse: Syracuse University Press, 1986.
Karpat, K. H. "The Land Regime, Social Structure, and Modernization in the Ottoman Empire," in W. R. Polk and R. L. Chambers (eds) *Beginnings of Modernization in the Middle East: the nineteenth century*, 69–90, Chicago, IL: University of Chicago Press, 1968.
——. "Some Historical and Methodological Considerations concerning Social Stratification in the Middle East," in C. A. O. van Nieuwenhuijze (ed.) *Commoners, Climbers and Notables: a sampler of studies on social ranking in the Middle East*, 83–106, Leiden: Brill, 1977.
——. "Ottoman Population Records and the Census of 1881/82–1893," *IJMES* 9, 1978: 237–74.
Kasaba, R. "A Time and a Place for the Nonstate: social change in the Ottoman Empire during the 'long nineteenth century'," in J. S. Migdal, A. Kohli, and V. Shue (eds) *State Power and Social Forces: domination and transformation in the Third World*, 207–30, Cambridge: Cambridge University Press, 1994.
Kasaba, R. and Tabak, F. "Fatal Conjuncture: the decline and fall of the modern agrarian order during the Bretton Woods era," in P. McMichael (ed.) *Food and Agrarian Orders in the World-Economy*, 79–93, Westport, CT: Greenwood, 1995.
Kasassbeh, H. F. *The Office of Qāḍī in the Early 'Abbāsid Caliphate (132–247/750–861)*, Jordan: Publications of the Deanship of Research and Graduate Studies, Mu'tah University, 1994.
Kashani-Sabet, F. *Frontier Fictions: shaping the Iranian nation, 1804–1946*, Princeton, NJ: Princeton University Press, 1999.
Kassem, M. *Egyptian Politics: the dynamics of authoritarian rule*, Boulder, CO: Lynne Reinner, 2004.
Katouzian, H. "The Aridisolatic Society: a model of long-term social and economic development in Iran," *IJMES* 15, 1983: 259–81.
Kaynar, R. *Mustafa Reşit Paşa ve Tanzimat*, Ankara: Türk Tarih Kurumu, 1954.
Kazemi, F. "Peasant Uprisings in Twentieth-Century Iran, Iraq, and Turkey," in F. Kazemi and J. Waterbury (eds) *Peasants and Politics in the Modern Middle East*, 101–24, Miami: Florida International University Press, 1991.
Kedar, M. *Asad in Search of Legitimacy: message and rhetoric in the Syrian press under Ḥāfiẓ and Bashār*, Brighton, Portland: Sussex Academy Press, 2005.
Keddie, N. R. *Religion and Rebellion in Iran: the tobacco protest of 1891–1892*, London: Frank Cass, 1966.
——. "The Iranian Village before and after Land Reform," *JContempH* 3.3, 1968: 69–91.
——. "Stratification, Social Control, and Capitalism in Iranian Villages before and after Land Reform," in R. Antoun and I. Harik (eds) *Rural Politics and Social Change in the Middle East*, 364–402, Bloomington: Indiana University Press, 1972.
——. "Islamic Revivalism Past and Present, with Emphasis on Iran," in B. M. Rosen (ed.) *Iran since the Revolution: internal dynamics, regional conflict, and the superpowers*, 3–19, New York: Columbia University Press, 1985.

——. with a section by Richard, Y. *Roots of Revolution: an interpretive history of modern Iran*, New Haven, CT: Yale University Press, 1981.

Kennedy, H. *The Prophet and the Age of the Caliphates: the Islamic Near East from the sixth to the eleventh century*, London: Longman, 1986.

——. "The Barmakid Revolution in Islamic Government," in C. Melville (ed.) *History and Literature in Iran: Persian and Islamic studies in honour of P. W. Avery*, 89–98, London: British Academic Press of IB Tauris, 1990, repr. 1998.

Kerr, M. H. "The Emergence of a Socialist Ideology in Egypt," *MEJ* 16, 1962: 127–44.

——. *Islamic Reform: the political and legal theories of Muḥammad 'Abduh and Rashīd Rıḍā*, Berkeley: University of California Press, 1966.

Keyder, Ç. *State and Class in Turkey: a study in capitalist development*, London: Verso, 1987.

——. "Introduction: Large-Scale Commercial Agriculture in the Ottoman Empire" in Ç. Keyder and F. Tabak (eds) *Landholding and Commercial Agriculture in the Middle East*, 1–13, Albany: State University of New York Press, 1991.

Khadduri, M. *Republican 'Iraq: a study in 'Iraqi politics since the revolution of 1958*, London: Oxford University Press, 1969.

——. *Socialist Iraq: a study in Iraqi politics since 1968*, Washington, DC: Middle East Institute, 1978.

——. and Liebesny, H. L. (eds) *Law in the Middle East*, vol. 1: *Origin and Development of Islamic Law*, Washington, DC: Middle East Institute, 1955.

Khalidi, T. *Islamic Historiography: the histories of Mas'ūdī*, Albany, NY: State University of New York Press, 1975.

——. *Arabic Historical Thought in the Classical Period*, Cambridge: Cambridge University Press, 1994.

Khan, G. "A Copy of a Decree from the Archives of the Fāṭimid Chancery in Egypt," *BSOAS* 49, 1986: 439–53.

——. "The Historical Development of the Structure of the Medieval Arabic Petition," *BSOAS* 53, 1990: 8–30.

——. "A Petition to the Fatimid Caliph al-'Amir," *JRAS* 1990: 44–54.

Khan, I. A. "The Turko-Mongol Theory of Kingship," *Medieval India: a miscellany* 2, 1972: 8–18.

Khan, M. H. "Mediaeval Muslim Political Theories of Rebellion against the State," *IC* 18, 1944: 36–44.

Khan, M. S. "The Effects of the *Iqṭā'* (Land-Grant) System under the Buwayhids," *IC* 58, 1984: 289–305.

Khan, Q. *Al-Mawardi's Theory of the State*, Lahore: Bazm-i Iqbal, [1950s].

Khismatulin, A. A. "The Art of Medieval Counterfeiting: the *Siyar al-Mulūk* (the *Siyāsat-Nāma*) by Nieqām al-Mulk and the 'full' version of the *Naṣīḥat al-Mulūk* by al-Ghazālī," *Manuscripta Orientalia* 14, 2008: 3–31.

——. "To Forge a Book in the Medieval Ages: Nezām al-Molk's *Siyar al-Moluk (Siyāsat-Nāma)*," *Journal of Persianate Studies* 1, 2008: 30–66.

Khoury, D. R. *State and Provincial Society in the Ottoman Empire: Mosul, 1540–1834*, Cambridge: Cambridge University Press, 1997.

——. "The Ottoman Centre versus Provincial Power-Holders: an analysis of the historiography," in S. N. Faroqhi (ed.) *The Cambridge History of Turkey*, vol. 3. *The Later Ottoman Empire, 1603–1839*, 135–56, Cambridge: Cambridge University Press, 2006.

Khuri-Makdisi, I. *The Eastern Mediterranean and the Making of Global Radicalism, 1860–1914*, Berkeley: University of California Press, 2010.

Kiel, M. *Art and Society of Bulgaria in the Turkish Period*, Assen, Neth.: Van Gorcum, 1985.

King, L. W. (ed.) *Babylonian Boundary-Stones and Memorial-Tablets in the British Museum*, London: Trustees of the British Museum, 1912.

Kister, M. J. "The Social and Political Implications of Three Traditions in the *Kitāb al-Kharādj* of Yahya b. Adam," *JESHO* 3, 1960: 326–34.

Klausner, C. L. *The Seljuk Vezirate: a study of civil administration, 1055–1194*, Cambridge: Center for Middle Eastern Studies, 1973.

Klein, N. *The "Shock" Doctrine: the rise of disaster capitalism*, New York: Metropolitan Books, Henry Holt, 2007.

Koch, E. "Diwan-i 'Amm and Chihil Sutun: the audience halls of Shah Jahan," *Muqarnas* 11, 1994: 143–65.

Köksal, O. "XVII. yüzyılda Osmanlı devleti'nde ıslahat ihtiyacının algılanışı ve ıslahat temayülleri," in K. Çiçek, G. Eren, C. Oguz and H. İnalcık (eds) *Osmanlı*, 12 vols, 7: 162–9, Ankara: Yeni Türkiye, 1999.

Komaroff, L. and Carboni, S. (eds) *The Legacy of Genghis Khan: courtly art and culture in western Asia, 1256–1353*, New York and New Haven, CT: Metropolitan Museum of Art and Yale University Press, 2002.

Köprülü, M. F. "Bizans müesseselerinin Osmanlı müesseselerine te'siri hakkında bazı mülâhazalar," *THİTM* 1, 1931: 165–313, repr. Istanbul: Ötüken, 1980; *Some Observations on the Influence of Byzantine Institutions on Ottoman Institutions*, trans. G. Leiser Istanbul: Türk Tarih Kurumu, 1999.

——. *Les origines de l'empire ottoman*, Paris, E. de Boccard, 1935; *Osmanlı devletin kuruluşu*, Ankara, Türk Tarih Kurumu, 1959; *The Origins of the Ottoman Empire*, trans. and ed. G. Leiser, Albany: State University of New York Press, 1992.

——. "Ortazaman Türk hukukî müesseseleri," *Belleten* 2, 1938: 39–72.

Kostiner, J. and Teitelbaum, J. "State-Formation and the Saudi Monarchy," in J. Kostiner (ed.) *Middle East Monarchies: the challenge of modernity*, 131–49, Boulder, CO: Lynne Reinner, 2000.

Kotwicz, W. "Formules initiales des documents mongols aux XIIIe et XIVe ss.," *Rocznik Orientalistyczny* 10, 1934: 131–57.

Kracke, E. A., Jr. "Early Visions of Justice for the Humble in East and West," *JAOS* 96, 1976: 492–8.

Krader, L. *The Asiatic Mode of Production: sources, development and critique in the writings of Karl Marx*, Assen: Van Gorcum, 1975.

Kraemer, J. L. *Humanism in the Renaissance of Islam: the cultural revival during the Buyid age*, Leiden: Brill, 1986.

Krämer, G. "Good Counsel to the King: the Islamist opposition in Saudi Arabia, Jordan, and Morocco," in J. Kostiner (ed.) *Middle East Monarchies: the challenge of modernity*, 257–87, Boulder, CO: Lynne Reinner, 2000.

Kramer, S. N. *The Sumerians: their history, culture, and character*, Chicago, IL: University of Chicago Press, 1963.

——. "The Ur-Nammu Code: who was its author?" *Orientalia* n.s. 52, 1983: 453–56.

Kraus, F. R. *Ein Edikt des Königs Ammi-Saduqa von Babylon*, Leiden: Brill, 1958.

Kreiser, K. "Public Monuments in Turkey and Egypt, 1840–1916," *Muqarnas* 14, 1997: 103–17.

Krynen, J. *Idéal du prince et pouvoir royale en France à la fin du moyen age (1380–1440)* Paris: A. et J. Picard, 1981.

Küçük, C. "Tanzimat'ın İlk Yıllarında Erzurum'un Cizye Geliri ve Reâya Nüfusu," *TD* 31, 1977: 199–234.

Kuhrt, A. "Berossus' *Babyloniaka* and Seleucid Rule in Babylonia," in A. Kuhrt and S. Sherwin-White (eds) *Hellenism in the East: the interaction of Greek and non-Greek civilizations from Syria to Central Asia after Alexander*, 32–56, London: Duckworth, 1987.

——. "Usurpation, Conquest and Ceremonial: from Babylon to Persia," in D. Cannadine and S. Price (eds) *Rituals of Royalty: power and ceremonial in traditional societies*, 20–55, Cambridge: Cambridge University Press, 1987.

——. *The Ancient Near East, c.3000–330 BC*, 2 vols, London: Routledge, 1994.

——. and Sherwin-White, S. "Aspects of Seleucid Royal Ideology: The Cylinder of Antiochus I from Borsippa," *Journal of Hellenic Studies* 111, 1991: 71–86.

Kuniholm, P. I. "Archaeological Evidence and Non-Evidence for Climatic Change," *Philosophical Transactions of the Royal Society of London* A330, 1990: 645–55.

Kuran, T. "On the Notion of Economic Justice in Contemporary Islamic Thought," *IJMES* 21, 1989: 171–91.

Kurpalidis, G. M. "The Seljuqids and the Sultan's Power," in B. Kellner-Heinkele (ed.) *Altaica Berolinensia: The Concept of Sovereignty in the Altaic World*, 133–8, Wiesbaden: Harrassowitz, 1993.

Kütükoğlu, M. S. "Minyatürlerde Divân-ı Humâyûn ve Arz Odası," *TED*, no. 16, 1998: 47–68.
Lacey, R. *The Kingdom*, New York: Harcourt Brace Jovanovich, 1981.
Lafi, N. (ed.) *Municipalités méditerranéennes: les réformes urbaines ottomanes au miroir d'une histoire comparée (Moyen-Orient, Maghreb, Europe méridionale)* Berlin: Klaus Schwarz, 2005.
Lafont, B. "Le roi de Mari et les prophètes du dieu Adad," *RA* 78, 1984: 7–18.
Lambton, A. K. S. "An Account of the *Tārīkhi Qumm*," *BSOAS* 12, 1948: 586–96.
——. "The Theory of Kingship in the *Naṣīḥat ul-Mulūk* of Ghazālī," *IQ* 1, 1954: 47–55; repr. in Lambton, A. K. S., *Theory and Practice in Medieval Persian Government*, London: Variorum, 1980, V.
——. "Quis Custodiet Custodes: some reflections on the Persian theory of government, I," *SI* 5, 1956: 125–48; repr. in Lambton, A. K. S., *Theory and Practice in Medieval Persian Government*, London: Variorum, 1980, II.
——. "Quis Custodiet Custodes: some reflections on the Persian theory of government (conclusion)," *Studia Islamica* 6, 1956: 125–46; repr. in Lambton, A. K. S., *Theory and Practice in Medieval Persian Government*, London: Variorum, 1980, III.
——. "The Administration of Sanjar's Empire as Illustrated in the *'Atabat al-Kataba*," *BSOAS* 20, 1957: 367–88; repr. in Lambton, A. K. S., *Theory and Practice in Medieval Persian Government*, London: Variorum, 1980, XII.
——. "Justice in the Medieval Persian Theory of Kingship," *SI* 17, 1962: 91–119; repr. in Lambton, A. K. S., *Theory and Practice in Medieval Persian Government*, London: Variorum, 1980, IV.
——. "The Office of Kalântar under the Safawids and Afshars," in *Mélanges d'orientalisme offerts à Henri Massé*, 206–18, Tehran: Imprimerie de l'Université, 1963.
——. "Reflections on the *Iqtā'*," in G. Makdisi (ed.) *Arabic and Islamic Studies in Honor of Hamilton A. R. Gibb*, 358–76, Brill, 1965, repr. in A. K. S. Lambton, *Theory and Practice in Medieval Persian Government*, London: Variorum, 1980, X.
——. *Landlord and Peasant in Persia*, rev. ed. London: Oxford University Press, 1969; repr. London: IB Tauris, 1991.
——. "The Persian 'Ulamā and Constitutional Reform," in *Le shî'isme imâmite: colloque de Strasbourg*, 245–69, Paris: Presses Universitaires de France, 1970.
——. "Islamic Mirrors for Princes," in *La Persia nel medioevo: atti del convegno internazionale, Rome, 1970*, 419–42, Rome: Accademia Nazionale dei Lincei, 1971; repr. in A. K. S. Lambton, *Theory and Practice in Medieval Persian Government*, London: Variorum, 1980, VI.
——. "Aspects of Saljūq-Ghuzz Settlement in Persia," in D. S. Richards (ed.) *Islamic Civilisation: 950–1150*, 105–25, Oxford: Bruno Cassirer, 1973; repr. in A. K. S. Lambton, *Theory and Practice in Medieval Persian Government*, London: Variorum, 1980, IX.
——. "Islamic Political Thought," in J. Schacht and C. E. Bosworth (eds) *The Legacy of Islam*, 2nd ed., 404–24, Oxford: Oxford University Press, 1979, c1974; repr. in A. K. S. Lambton, *Theory and Practice in Medieval Persian Government*, London: Variorum, 1980, I.
——. "The Tribal Resurgence and the Decline of the Bureaucracy in the Eighteenth Century," in T. Naff and R. Owen (eds) *Studies in Eighteenth Century Islamic History*, 108–29, Carbondale: Southern Illinois University Press, 1977.
——. "Early Timurid Theories of State: Ḥāfieq Abrū and Niẓām al-Dīn Šāmī," *BEO* 30, 1978: 1–9.
——. "Reflections on the Role of Agriculture in Medieval Persia," in A. L. Udovitch (ed.) *The Islamic Middle East, 700–1900: studies in economic and social history*, 283–312, Princeton, NJ: Darwin, 1981.
——. *State and Government in Medieval Islam, an introduction to the study of Islamic political theory: the jurists*, Oxford: Oxford University Press, 1981.
——. "The Dilemma of Government in Islamic Persia: the *Siyāsat-nāma* of Nizām al-Mulk," *Iran* 22, 1984: 55–66.
——. "Mongol Fiscal Administration in Persia," pt. 1, *SI* 64, 1986: 79–99; pt. 2, *SI* 65, 1987: 97–123.
——. *Qajar Persia: eleven studies*, London: IB Tauris, 1987.
——. "Changing Concepts of Justice and Injustice from the 5th/11th Century to the 8th/14th Century in Persia: the Saljuq Empire and the Ilkhanate," *SI* 68, 1988: 27–60.

——. "Concepts of Authority in Persia: eleventh to nineteenth centuries A.D.," *Iran* 26, 1988: 95–103.
——. *Continuity and Change in Medieval Persia: aspects of administrative, economic and social history, 11th–14th century*, Albany, NY: Bibliotheca Persica, 1988.
——. "Introduction," in K. Ferdinand and M. Mozaffari (eds) *Islam: state and society*, 1–10, London: Curzon/Riverdale; MD: Riverdale, 1988.
Lammens, H. "Le chantre des Omiades: Notes biographiques et littéraires sur le poète arabe Aḫṭal," *JA*, ser. 9, vol. 4, 1894: 94–176, 193–241, 381–459.
Landau, J. M. (ed.) *Atatürk and the Modernization of Turkey*, Boulder, CO: Westview, 1984.
Lane, G. *Early Mongol Rule in Thirteenth-Century Iran: a Persian Renaissance*, London: Routledge/Curzon, 2003.
Laoust, H. "La pensée et l'action politiques d'al-Mawardi (364–450/974–1058)," *REI* 36, 1968: 11–92.
——. *La politique de Ġazālī*, Paris: Paul Geuthner, 1970.
Lapidus, I. M. *Muslim Cities in the Later Middle Ages*, Cambridge, MA: Harvard University Press, 1967.
——. "The Separation of State and Religion in the Development of Early Islamic Society," *IJMES* 6, 1975: 363–85.
——. "The Arab Conquests and the Formation of Islamic Society," in G. H. A. Juynboll (ed.) *Studies on the First Century of Islamic Society*, 49–72, Carbondale: Southern Illinois University Press, 1982.
——. "Tribes and State Formation in Islamic History," in P. S. Khoury and J. Kostiner (eds) *Tribes and State Formation in the Middle East*, 25–47, Berkeley: University of California Press, 1990.
——. "Islamic Revival and Modernity: the contemporary movements and the historical paradigms," *JESHO* 40, 1997: 444–60.
Laremont, R. R. *Islam and the Politics of Resistance in Algeria, 1783–1992*, Trenton, NJ: Africa World Press, 2000.
Larsen, M. T. "The City and Its King: on the old Assyrian notion of kingship," in P. Garelli (ed.) *Le palais et la royauté (archéologie et civilisation)*, Rencontre assyriologique internationale, 19th, Paris, 1971, 285–300, Paris: Paul Geuthner, 1974.
——. "The Tradition of Empire in Mesopotamia," in M. T. Larsen (ed.) *Power and Propaganda: a symposium on ancient empires*, 75–103, Copenhagen: Akademisk Forlag, 1979.
Lassner, J. *The Shaping of ʿAbbāsid Rule*, Princeton, NJ: Princeton University Press, 1980.
Latham. J. D. "The Beginnings of Arabic Prose Literature: the epistolary genre," in A. F. L. Beeston, T. M. Johnstone, R. B. Serjeant and G. R. Smith (eds) *Arabic Literature to the End of the Umayyad Period*, The Cambridge History of Arabic Literature, 1, 154–79, Cambridge: Cambridge University Press, 1983.
——. "Ibn al-Muqaffaʿ and Early ʿAbbasid Prose," in J. Ashtiany, T. M. Johnstone, J. D. Latham, R. B. Serjeant, and G. R. Smith (eds) *Abbasid Belles-Lettres*, The Cambridge History of Arabic Literature, 2, 48–77, Cambridge: Cambridge University Press, 1990.
Laurès, J. *The Political Economy of Juan de Mariana*, New York: Fordham University Press, 1928.
Lawson, F. H. "Social Bases for the Hamah Revolt," *MERIP Reports* no. 110, November–December 1982: 24–28.
Layish, A. "Saudi Arabian Legal Reform as a Mechanism to Moderate Wahhabi Doctrine," *JAOS* 107, 1987: 279–92.
Layne, L. L. *Home and Homeland: the dialogics of tribal and national identities in Jordan*, Princeton, NJ: Princeton University Press, 1994.
Lecomte, G. "L'Introduction du *Kitāb adab al-kātib* d'Ibn Qutayba," in *Mélanges Louis Massignon*, 3 vols, 3: 45–64, Damascus: Institut français de Damas, 1956–7.
——. *Ibn Qutayba (mort en 276/889): l'homme, son oeuvre, ses idées*, Damascus: Institut français de Damas, 1965.
Leemans, W. F. "King Ḫammurapi as Judge," in J. A. Ankum, R. Feenstra and W. F. Leemans (eds) *Symbolae Iuridicae et Historicae Martino David Dedicatae*, 2 vols, 2: 107–29, Leiden: Brill, 1968.
Lentz, T. W. and Lowry, G. D. *Timur and the Princely Vision: Persian art and culture in the fifteenth century*, Washington, DC: Smithsonian Institution Press, Arthur M. Sackler Gallery, and Los Angeles County Museum of Art, 1989.

Lerner, J. "Sasanian and Achaemenid Revivals in Qajar Art," in V. S. Curtis, R. Hilllenbrand, and J. M. Rogers (eds) *The Art and Archaeology of Ancient Persia: new light on the Parthian and Sasanian empires*, 162–7, London: IB Tauris with the British Institute of Persian Studies, 1998.

Lesch, A. M. "The Muslim Brotherhood in Egypt: reform or revolution?" in M. C. Moen and L. S. Gustafson (eds) *The Religious Challenge to the State*, 182–208, Philadelphia, PA: Temple University Press, 1992.

Lev, Y. "The Suppression of Crime, the Supervision of Markets, and Urban Society in the Egyptian Capital during the Tenth and Eleventh Centuries," *MHR* 3, 1988: 71–95.

Levanoni, A. *A Turning Point in Mamluk History: the third reign of al-Nāṣir Muḥammad Ibn Qalāwūn (1310–1341)*, Leiden: Brill, 1995.

Leveau, R. "Stabilité du pouvoir monarchique et financement de la dette," *Maghreb-Machrek* 118, Oct.–Dec. 1987: 5–19.

Levend, A. S. "Aḥmed Rızvān'ın İskender-nāmesi," *Türk Dili* 1, 1951: 143–51.

LeVine, M. *Why They Don't Hate Us: lifting the veil on the axis of evil*, Oxford: Oneworld, 2005.

Levy, R. *The Social Structure of Islam*, Cambridge: Cambridge University Press, 1957.

Lewis, B. "Some Reflections on the Decline of the Ottoman Empire," *SI* 9, 1958: 111–27.

——. *The Emergence of Modern Turkey*, Oxford: Oxford University Press, 1961.

——. "Ottoman Observers of Ottoman Decline," *IS* 1, 1962: 71–87.

——. "Some English Travellers in the East," *MES* 4, 1968: 296–315.

——. "On the Revolutions in Early Islam," *SI* 32, 1970: 215–31.

——. "Egypt and Syria," in P. M. Holt, A. K. S. Lambton and B. Lewis (eds) *The Cambridge History of Islam*, vol. 1A: *The Central Islamic Lands from pre-Islamic times to the First World War,* 175–230, Cambridge: Cambridge University Press, 1970.

——. "Ibn Khaldun in Turkey," in M. Sharon (ed.) *Studies in Islamic History and Civilization in Honour of Professor David Ayalon*, 527–30, Jerusalem, Cana, and Leiden: Brill, 1986, repr. in *Islam in History: Ideas, People, and Events in the Middle East*, 233–6, new ed., Chicago and La Salle, Open Court, 1993.

——. *A Middle East Mosaic: fragments of life, letters and history*, New York: Random House, 2000.

——. "Monarchy in the Middle East," in J. Kostiner (ed.) *Middle East Monarchies: the challenge of modernity*, 15–22, Boulder, CO: Lynne Reinner, 2000.

——. *What Went Wrong? Western impact and Middle Eastern response*, Oxford: Oxford University Press, 2002.

Lewis, W. H. "Rural Administration in Morocco," *MEJ* 14, 1960: 45–59.

Lewy, G. *Religion and Revolution*, New York: Oxford University Press, 1974.

Lingwood, C. "Jami's 'Salaman va Absal' as an esoteric mirror for princes in its Aq-Qoyunlu Context," PhD diss., University of Toronto, 2009.

Little, D. P. "A New Look at *al-Aḥkām al-Sulṭāniyya*," *MW* 64, 1974: 1–15.

Lobmeyer, H. G. "*Al-dimuqratiyya hiyya al-hall?* The Syrian opposition at the end of the Asad era," in E. Kienle (ed.) *Contemporary Syria: liberalization between cold war and cold peace*, 81–96, London: British Academic Press, 1994.

Lockman, Z. "Imagining the Working Class: culture, nationalism, and class formation in Egypt, 1899–1914," *Poetics Today* 15, 1994: 157–90.

Loeffler, R. "Tribal Order and the State: the political oranization of Boir Ahmad," *IranS* 11, 1978: 145–71.

——. "Economic Changes in a Rural Area since 1979," in N. R. Keddie and E. Hooglund (eds) *The Iranian Revolution and the Islamic Republic*, rev. ed., 93–109, Syracuse: Syracuse University Press, 1986.

——. *Islam in Practice: religious beliefs in a Persian village*, Albany: State University of New York, 1988.

London, J. A. "'Speaking through the Voice of Another': forms of political thought and action in medieval Islamic contexts," PhD diss., University of Chicago, 2009.

Long, D. E. "The Board of Grievances in Saudi Arabia," *MEJ* 27, 1973: 71–5.

L'Orange, H. P. "Expressions of Cosmic Kingship in the Ancient World," in *The Sacral Kingship*, Studies in the History of Religions (Supplements to *Numen*), 4: 481–92, Leiden: Brill, 1959.

Losensky, P. E. "*Fanā* and Taxes: a brief literary history of a Persian proverb," *Edebiyat* 7, 1996: 1–20.

Lowry, H. W. *The Nature of the Early Ottoman State*, Albany: State University of New York Press, 2003.

Lukens-Swietochowski, M. "The School of Herat from 1450 to 1506," in B. Gray (ed.) *The Arts of the Book in Central Asia: 14th–16th centuries*, 179–214, Boulder, CO: Shambhala-UNESCO, 1979.

Lybyer, A. H. *The Government of the Ottoman Empire in the Time of Suleiman the Magnificent*, Cambridge, MA: Harvard University Press, 1913.

Mabro, R. *The Egyptian Economy, 1952–1972*, Oxford: Clarendon, 1974.

——. and O'Brien, P. "Structural Changes in the Egyptian Economy, 1937–1965," in M. A. Cook (ed.) *Studies in the Economic History of the Middle East: from the rise of Islam to the present day*, 412–27, London: Oxford University Press, 1970.

McChesney, R. D. "Four Sources on Shah 'Abbas's Building of Isfahan," 5, 1988: 103–34.

Macdonald, D. B. *The Development of Muslim Theology, Jurisprudence and Constitutional Theory*, London: 1903; repr. Lahore: Premier Book House, 1972.

McGowan, B. "Ottoman Political Communication," in H. D. Lasswell, D. Lerner, and H. Speier (eds) *Propaganda and Communication in World History*, 3 vols, 1: 444–92, Honolulu: East-West Center and University Press of Hawaii, 1979.

——. *Economic Life in Ottoman Europe: taxation, trade and the struggle for land, 1600–1800*, Cambridge: Cambridge University Press, and Paris: Maison des Sciences de l'Homme, 1981.

——. "The Study of Land and Agriculture in the Ottoman Provinces within the context of an expanding world economy in the 17th and 18th centuries," *IJTS* 2.1, 1981: 57–63.

——. "The Age of the Ayans, 1699–1812," in H. İnalcık with D. Quataert (eds) *An Economic and Social History of the Ottoman Empire*, 2: 637–758, Cambridge: Cambridge University Press, 1994.

Machinist, P. "Assyrians on Assyria in the First Millennium B.C.," in K. Raaflaub and E. Müller-Luckner (eds) *Anfänge politischen Denkens in der Antike: Die nahöstlichen Kulturen und die Griechen*, 77–104, Munich: R. Oldenbourg, 1993.

Mackey, S. *Saudis: inside the Desert Kingdom*, New York: Penguin/Signet, 1990.

——. *The Iranians: Persia, Islam and the soul of a nation*, New York: Penguin/Dutton, 1996.

McLachlan, K. *The Neglected Garden: the politics and ecology of agriculture in Iran*, London: IB Tauris, 1988.

Madelung, W. "The Assumption of the Title Shāhānshāh by the Būyids and 'The Reign of the Daylam *(Dawlat al-Daylam)*'," *JNES* 28, 1969: 84–108, 168–83.

——. "Naṣīr ad-Dīn Ṭūsī's Ethics between Philosophy, Shi'ism, and Sufism," in R. G. Hovannisian (ed.) *Ethics in Islam*, 85–101, Malibu, CA: Undena, 1985.

——. *Religious Trends in Early Islamic Iran*, Albany, NY: Persian Heritage Foundation, 1988.

——. "A Treatise of the Sharīf al-Murtaḍā on the Legality of Working for the Government *(Mas'ala fi 'l-'amal ma'a'l-sulṭān)*," *BSOAS* 43, 1980: 18–31.

Mahdavy, H. "Patterns and Problems of Economic Development in Rentier States: the case of Iran," in M. A. Cook (ed.) *Studies in the Economic History of the Middle East: from the rise of Islam to the present day*, 428–67, London: Oxford University Press, 1970.

Mahdi, M. *Ibn Khaldūn's Philosophy of History: a study in the philosophic foundation of the science of culture*, Chicago, IL: University of Chicago Press, 1964.

Majd, M. G. *Resistance to the Shah: landowners and ulama in Iran*, Gainesville: University Press of Florida, 2000.

——. "Small Landowners and Land Distribution in Iran, 1962–71," *IJMES* 32, 2000: 123–53.

Makdisi, G. "Les rapports entre calife et sulṭân à l'époque saljûqide," *IJMES* 6, 1975: 228–36; repr. in G. Makdisi, *History and Politics in Eleventh-Century Baghdad*, Aldershot, UK: Variorum, 1990, VII.

——. *The Rise of Humanism in Classical Islam and the Christian West: with special reference to scholasticism*, Edinburgh: Edinburgh University Press, 1990.

Makdisi, U. "Corrupting the Sublime Sultanate: the revolt of Tanyus Shahin in nineteenth-century Ottoman Lebanon," *CSSH* 42, 2000: 180–208.

——. "Ottoman Orientalism," *AHR* 107, 2002: 768–96.

Makiya, K. (al-Khalil, S.) *Republic of Fear: the inside story of Saddam's Iraq*, Berkeley: University of California Press; New York: Pantheon Books, 1989.

Manz, B. F. "Administration and the Delegation of Authority in Temür's Dominions," *CAJ* 20, 1976: 191–207.

——. "Tamerlane and the Symbolism of Sovereignty," *IranS* 21.1/2, 1988: 105–22.

——. *The Rise and Rule of Tamerlane*, Cambridge: Cambridge University Press, 1989.

——. "Mongol History Rewritten and Relived," *RMMM* 89–90, 2000: 129–49.

Manzalaoui, M. A. "The Pseudo-Aristotelian *Kitāb sirr al-asrār*: facts and problems," *Oriens* 23/24, 1974: 147–257.

Ma'oz, M. "The Impact of Modernization on Syrian Politics and Society during the Early *Tanzimat* Period," in W. R. Polk and R. L. Chambers (eds) *Beginnings of Modernization in the Middle East: the nineteenth century*, 333–49, Chicago, IL: University of Chicago Press, 1968.

——. *Ottoman Reform in Syrian and Palestine, 1840–1861: the impact of the Tanzimat on politics and society*, Oxford: Clarendon, 1968.

——. "Society and State in Modern Syria," in M. Milson (ed.) *Society and Political Structure in the Arab World*, 29–92, New York: Humanities Press, 1973.

Marashi, A. *Nationalizing Iran: culture, power, and the state, 1870–1940*, Seattle: University of Washington Press, 2008.

Marcotte, R. D. "Anūshirvān and Buzurgmihr–the Just Ruler and the Wise Counselor: two figures of Persian traditional moral literature," *RO* 51.2, 1998: 69–90.

Mardin, Ş. "The Mind of the Turkish Reformer, 1700–1900," *Western Humanities Review* 14, 1960: 413–36.

——. *The Genesis of Young Ottoman Thought: a study in the modernization of Turkish political ideas*, Princeton, NJ: Princeton University Press, 1962; repr. Syracuse: Syracuse University Press, 2000.

——. "Power, Civil Society and Culture in the Ottoman Empire," *CSSH* 11, 1969: 258–81.

——. "Center-Periphery Relations: a key to Turkish politics?" *Daedalus* 102.1, 1973: 169–90.

——. "Freedom in an Ottoman Perspective," in M. Heper and A. Evin (eds) *State, Democracy and the Military: Turkey in the 1980s*, 23–35, Berlin: Walter de Gruyter, 1988.

——. "The Just and the Unjust," *Daedalus* 120.3, 1991: 113–29.

——. "The Nakşibendi Order in Turkish History," in R. Tapper (ed.) *Islam in Modern Turkey: religion, politics and literature in a secular state*, 121–42, London: IB Tauris, 1991.

——. "Some Notes on Normative Conflicts in Turkey," in P. L. Berger (ed.) *The Limits of Social Cohesion: conflict and mediation in pluralist societies*, 207–32, Boulder, CO: Westview, 1998.

Marino, B. "L'approvisionnement en céréales des villes de la Syrie Ottomane (XVIe–XVIIIe siècles)," in B. Marino and C. Virlouvet (eds) *Nourrir les cités de Méditerranée: antiquite-temps modernes*, 491–517, Paris: Maisonneuve et Larose, 2003.

Marlow, L. *Hierarchy and Egalitarianism in Islamic Thought*, Cambridge: Cambridge University Press, 1997.

——. "Kings, Prophets and the 'Ulamā' in Mediaeval Islamic Advice Literature," *SI* 81, 1995: 101–20.

Marr, P. "Iraq: Its Revolutionary Experience under the Ba'th," in P. J. Chelkowski and R. J. Pranger (eds) *Ideology and Power in the Middle East: studies in honor of George Lenczowski*, 185–209, Durham: Duke University Press, 1988.

al-Marṣafī, Ḥusayn, *Risālat al-kalim al-thamān*, Cairo: al-Maṭba'a al-Sharafiyya, 1881.

Marsans-Sakly, S. "The Networks of Tunisia's 1864 Revolt," paper presented at American Historical Association Conference, 4 January 2003.

——. "The Revolt of 1864 in Tunisia: History, Power, and Memory," PhD diss., New York University, 2010.

Marshak, B. I. "The Decoration of Some Late Sasanian Silver Vessels and Its Subject-Matter," in V. S. Curtis, R. Hillenbrand, and J. M. Rogers (eds) *The Art and Archaeology of Ancient Persia: new light on the Parthian and Sasanian empires*, 84–92, London: IB Tauris, 1998.

Marshall, S. E. "Islamic Revival in the Maghreb: the utility of tradition for modernizing elites," *Studies in Comparative International Development* 14.2, 1979: 95–108.

Marsot, A. L. "Muhammmad Ali's Internal Policies," in *L'Égypte au XIXe siècle* 153–73, Paris: CNRS, 1982.

——. *Egypt in the Reign of Muhammad Ali*, Cambridge: Cambridge University Press, 1984.
——. "Religion or Opposition? urban protest movements in Egypt," *IJMES* 16, 1984: 541–52.
Martin, V. *Islam and Modernism: the Iranian Revolution of 1906*, Syracuse: Syracuse University Press, 1989.
——. *The Qajar Pact: bargaining, protest and the state in nineteenth-century Persia*, London: IB Tauris, 2005.
——. "Women and Popular Protest: women's demonstrations in nineteenth-century Iran," in S. Cronin (ed.) *Subalterns and Social Protest: history from below in the Middle East and North Africa*, 50–66, London: Routledge, 2008.
Martinez, A. P. "Bullionistic Imperialism: The Īl-Xānid Mint's Exploitation of the Rūm-Saljūqid Currency, 654–695H./1256–1296 A. D.," *AOtt* 13, 1993–94: 169–276.
——. "Changes in Chancellery Languages and Language Changes in General in the Middle East, with particular reference to Iran in the Arab and Mongol periods," *AEuras* 7, 1987–91: 103–52.
——. "Regional Mint Outflows and the Dynamics of Bullion Flows through the Īl-Xānate," *JTS* 8, 1984: 121–73.
——. "Some Notes on the Īl-Xānid Army," *AEuras* 6, 1986: 129–242.
Masters, B. "The View from the Province: Syrian chroncles of the eighteenth century," *JAOS* 114, 1994: 353–62.
Matar, F. *Saddam Hussein: the man, the cause and the future*, London: Third World Centre, 1981.
Matkovski, A. "L'insurrection de Patrona Halil à Istanbul (28 septembre 1730) et sa répercussion en Macédoine," *Balcanica* 13–14, 1982–3: 105–15.
——. "La résistance des paysans macédoniens contre l'attachement à la glèbe pendant la domination ottomane," in *Actes du Ier Congrès International des Études Balkaniques et Sud-Est Européennes*, Vol. 3: *Histoire*, 703–8, Sofia: Academie Bulgare des Sciences, 1969.
Matthee, R. "The Egyptian Opposition on the Iranian Revolution," in J. R. I. Cole and N. R. Keddie (eds) *Shi'ism and Social Protest*, 247–74, New Haven, CT: Yale University Press, 1986.
Matuz, J. "Über die Epistolographie und Inšā'-Literatur des Osmanen," *Deutscher Orientalistentag 17, 1968*, *ZDMG* Supplementa, I, pt. 2, 1970: 574–94.
Mayfield, J. B. *Rural Politics in Nasser's Egypt: a quest for legitimacy*, Austin: University of Texas Press, 1971.
Meeker, M. E. *A Nation of Empire: the Ottoman legacy of Turkish modernity*, Berkeley: University of California Press, 2002.
Mehmet, M. A. "La crise ottomane dans la vision de Hasan Kiafi Akhisari (1544–1616)," *Revue des Études Sud-Est Européenes* 13, 1975: 385–402.
Mehrchid, "Ali Shariati: une théologie de la liberation?" *Soual* no. 5, April 1985: 97–111.
Meisami, J. S. "Kings and Lovers: ethical dimensions of medieval Persian romance," *Edebiyat* 1, 1987: 1–27.
——. *Medieval Persian Court Poetry*, Princeton, NJ: Princeton University Press, 1987.
——. "Ghaznavid Panegyrics: some political implications," *Iran* 28, 1990: 31–44.
——. "Rāvandī's *Rāḥat al-ṣudūr*: history or hybrid?" *Edebiyat* 5, 1994: 183–215.
——. "Places in the Past: the poetics/politics of nostalgia," *Edebiyat* 8, 1998: 63–106.
——. *Persian Historiography: to the end of the twelfth century*, Edinburgh: Edinburgh University Press, 1999.
——. "Why Write History in Persian? historical writing in the Samanid period," in C. Hillenbrand (ed.) *Studies in Honour of Clifford Edmund Bosworth*, vol. 2: *The Sultan's Turret: studies in Persian and Turkish culture*, 348–74, Leiden: Brill, 2000.
——. "Rulers and the Writing of History," in B. Gruendler and L. Marlow (eds) *Writers and Rulers: perspectives on their relationship from Abbasid to Safavid times*, 73–95, Wiesbaden: Reichert, 2004.
Melikian-Chirvani, A. S. "Le *Shāh-nāme*, la gnose soufie et le pouvoir mongol," *JA* 272, 1984: 249–337.
——. "Le Livre des Rois, miroir du destin," *StIr* 17, 1988: 7–46.
——. "Le Livre des Rois, miroir du destan. II: Takht-e Soleymān et la symbolique du *Shāh-nāme*," *StIr* 20, 1991: 33–148.
——. "The Light of the World," in R. Hillenbrand (ed.) *The Art of the Saljūqs in Iran and Anatolia*, 146–55, Costa Mesa, CA: Mazda, 1994.

——. "Conscience du passé et résistance culturelle dans l'Iran mongol," in D. Aigle (ed.) *L'Iran face à la domination mongole*, 135–77, Tehran: Institut Français de Recherche en Iran, 1997.

Mélikoff, I. "Un document akhi du XIIIe siècle," *Res Orientales* 6, 1994: 263–70.

——. "Qui était Sarı Saltuk? Quelques remarques sur les manuscrits du Saltukname," in C. Heywood and C. Imber (eds) *Studies in Ottoman History in Honour of Professor V. L. Ménage*, 231–8, Istanbul: İsis 1994.

——. "The Worship of Shah Isma'il in Turkey in Past and Present Time," *Journal of Azerbaijani Studies* 1, 1998: 62–70.

Melville, C. *The Fall of Amir Chupan and the Decline of the Ilkhanate, 1327–37: a decade of discord in Mongol Iran*, Bloomington, IN: Indiana University Research Institute for Inner Asian Studies, 1999.

Menashri, D. "The Persian Monarchy and the Islamic Republic," in J. Kostiner (ed.) *Middle East Monarchies: the challenge of modernity*, 213–34, Boulder, CO: Lynne Reinner, 2000.

——. *Post-Revolutionary Politics in Iran: religion, society and power*, London: Frank Cass, 2001.

Meriwether, M. L. "Urban Notables and Rural Resources in Aleppo, 1770–1830," *IJTS* 4.1, 1987: 55–73.

Mernissi, F. *The Forgotten Queens of Islam*, trans. M. J. Lakeland, Minneapolis: University of Minnesota Press, 1993.

Messick, B. *The Calligraphic State: textual domination and history in a Muslim society*, Berkeley: University of California Press, 1993.

Metral, F. "State and Peasants in Syria: a local view of a government irrigation project," *Peasant Studies* 11.2, Winter 1984: 69–90.

Mez, A. *The Renaissance of Islam*, trans. S. Khuda Bakhsh and D. S. Margoliouth, London: Luzac, 1937, repr. New York: AMS Press, 1975.

Mezhoud, S. "*Glasnost* the Algerian Way: the role of Berber nationalists in political reform," in E. G. H. Joffé (ed.) *North Africa: nation, state, and region*, 142–69, London: Routledge, 1993.

Michalowski, P. "Charisma and Control: on continuity and change in early Mesopotamian bureaucratic systems," in M. Gibson and R. D. Biggs (eds) *The Organization of Power: aspects of bureaucracy in the ancient Near East*, 55–68, Chicago, IL: Oriental Institute, 1987.

——. and Walker, C. B. F. "A New Sumerian 'Law Code'," in H. Behrens, D. Loding, and M. T. Roth (eds) *Dumm-e$_2$-dub-ba-a: studies in honor of Ake W. Sjöberg*, 383–96, Philadelphia, PA: Samuel Noah Kramer Fund, 1989.

Midhat, A. H., *The Life of Midhat Pasha*, London: John Murray, 1903; repr. New York: Arno Press, 1973.

Mikhail, H. *Politics and Revelation: Mawardi and after*, Edinburgh: Edinburgh University Press, 1995.

Miller, J. (ed.) *Absolutism in Seventeenth-Century Europe*, Basingstoke: Macmillan Education, 1990.

Miller, J. and Mylroie, L. *Saddam Hussein and the Crisis in the Gulf*, New York: Times Books, Random House, 1990.

Miller, R. A. *Legislating Authority: sin and crime in the Ottoman Empire and Turkey*, New York: Routledge, 2005.

Milstein, R., Rürdanz, K. and Schmitz, B. *Stories of the Prophets: illustrated manuscripts of* Qisas al-Anbiya', Costa Mesa, CA: Mazda, 1999.

Minorsky, V. "A *Soyūrghāl* of Qāsim b. Jahāngīr Aq-qoyunlu (903/1498)," *BSOAS* 9, 1937–9: 927–60.

——. "The Poetry of Shāh Ismā'īl I," *BSOAS* 19, 1940–2: 1006a–53a.

——. "Jihān-Shāh Qara-Qoyunlu and His Poetry," *BSOAS* 16, 1954: 271–97.

——. "The Aq-qoyunlu and Land Reforms," *BSOAS* 17, 1955: 449–62.

——. "La Domination des Dailamites," in *Iranica: twenty articles*, Publications of the University of Tehran, 775, Hertford, UK: Steven Austin, 1964, 12–30.

——. "Pūr-i Bahā and His Poems," in *Iranica: twenty articles*, Publications of the University of Tehran, 775, Hertford, UK: Steven Austin, 1964, 292–303.

Mitchell, E. B. "Institution and Destitution: patronage tales of Old Stamboul," PhD diss., University of California, Los Angeles, 1993.

Mitchell, R. P. *The Society of the Muslim Brothers*, New York: Oxford University Press, 1969.

Mitchell, T. "The Object of Development: America's Egypt," in J. Crush (ed.) *Power of Development*, 129–57, London: Routledge, 1995.

Miura, T. "The Structure of the Quarter and the Role of the Outlaws–the Ṣāliḥīya quarter and the Zuʿr in the Mamlūk period," in *Urbanism in Islam: the proceedings of the International Conference on Urbanism in Islam*, 4 vols, 3: 401–37, Tokyo: Research Project "Urbanism in Islam" and Middle East Culture Center in Japan, 1989.

Moaddel, M. "Shiʿi Political Discourse and Class Mobilization in the Tobacco Movement of 1890–92," in J. Foran (ed.) *A Century of Revolution: social movements in Iran*, 1–20, Minneapolis: University of Minnesota Press, 1994.

Moghadam, V. "Islamic Populism, Class, and Gender in Postrevolutionary Iran," in J. Foran (ed.) *A Century of Revolution: social movements in Iran*, 189–222, Minneapolis: University of Minnesota Press, 1994.

Monroe, W. S. "*Via Iustitiae*: the Biblical sources of justice in Gregory of Tours," in K. Mitchell and I. N. Wood (eds) *The World of Gregory of Tours*, 99–112, Leiden: Brill, 2002.

Morgan, D. O. "The Mongol Armies in Persia," *Der Islam* 56, 1979: 81–96.

——. "The 'Great *Yāsā* of Chingiz Khān' and Mongol Law in the Īlkhānate," *BSOAS* 49, 1986: 163–76.

——. "Mongol or Persian?: the government of Ilkhānid Iran," *HMEIR* 3, 1996: 62–76.

——. "The 'Great *Yasa* of Chinggis Khan' Revisited," in R. Amitai and M. Biran (eds) *Mongols, Turks, and Others: Eurasian nomads and the sedentary world*, 291–308, Leiden: Brill, 2005.

Morimoto, K. "What Ibn Khaldūn Saw: the judiciary of Mamlūk Egypt," *MSR* 6.1, 2002: 109–31.

Morony, M. G. "Conquerors and Conquered: Iran," in G. H. A. Juynboll (ed.) *Studies on the First Century of Islamic Society*, 73–87, Carbondale: Southern Illinois University Press, 1982.

——. *Iraq after the Muslim Conquest*, Princeton, NJ: Princeton University Press, 1984.

Morsy, M. "Arbitration as a Political Institution: an interpretation of the status of monarchy in Morocco," in A. S. Ahmed and D. M. Hart (eds) *Islam in Tribal Societies: from the Atlas to the Indus*, 39–65, London: Routledge & Kegan Paul, 1984.

Morton, A. H. "The Letters of Rashīd al-Dīn: Ilkhānid fact or Timurid fiction?" in R. Amitai-Preiss and D. O. Morgan (eds) *The Mongol Empire and Its Legacy*, 155–99, Leiden: Brill, 1999.

Mottahedeh, R. P. *Loyalty and Leadership in an Early Islamic Society*, Princeton, NJ: Princeton University Press, 1980.

——. "Bureaucracy and the Patrimonial State in Early Islamic Iran and Iraq," *al-Abḥāth* 29, 1981: 25–36.

——. "Some Attitudes towards Monarchy and Absolutism in the Eastern Islamic World of the Eleventh and Twelfth Centuries A.D.," in J. L. Kraemer and I. Alon (eds) *Religion and Government in the World of Islam*, *IOS* 10, 1983: 86–91.

——. *The Mantle of the Prophet: religion and politics in Iran*, New York: Pantheon Books, 1985.

Moynihan, E. B. *Paradise as a Garden: in Persia and Mughal India*, New York: George Braziller, 1979.

Mujaheri, M. *Islamic Revolution: future path of the nations*, Tehran: The External Liaison Section of the Central Office of Jihad-e Sazandegi, 1982.

Müller, C. *Gerichtspraxis im Stadtstaat Córdoba: Zum Recht der Gesellschaft in einer mālikitisch-islamischen Rechtstradition des 5./11. Jahrhunderts*, Leiden: Brill, 1999.

Mumcu, A. *Osmanlı devletinde rüşvet (özellikle adlî rüşvet)* Istanbul: İnkilâp, 1985.

——. *Osmanlı hukukunda zulüm kavramı: deneme*, 2nd ed. Ankara: Birey ve Toplum, 1985.

Munson, H., Jr. *Religion and Power in Morocco*, New Haven, CT: Yale University Press, 1993.

Murphey, R. "Provisioning Istanbul: the state and subsistence in the early modern Middle East," *Food and Foodways* 2, 1988: 217–63.

——. "Mustafa Ali and the Politics of Cultural Despair," *IJMES* 21, 1989: 243–55.

——. "Ottoman Census Methods in the Mid-Sixteenth Century: Three Case Histories," *SI* 71, 1990: 115–26.

——. "Süleymân's Eastern Policy," in H. İnalcık and C. Kafadar (eds) *Süleymân the Second and His Time*, 229–48, Istanbul: İsis Press, 1993.

——. "Ottoman Historical Writing in the Seventeenth Century: a survey of the general development of the genre after the reign of Sultan Ahmed I (1603–1617)," *AOtt* 13, 1993–94: 277–311.
——. "The Conceptual and Pragmatic Uses of the 'Summary' (Idjmal) Register in Sixteenth-Century Ottoman Administrative Practice," *AOtt* 14, 1995–96: 111–32.
——. "Süleyman I and the Conquest of Hungary: Ottoman manifest destiny or a delayed reaction to Charles V's universalist vision?" *JEMH* 5, 2001: 197–221.
Musallam, A. A. "Sayyid Quṭb and Social Justice, 1945–1948," *JIS* 4, 1993: 52–70.
Naff, A. *A Social History of Zahle, the principal market town in nineteenth-century Lebanon*, PhD diss., University of California, Los Angeles, 1972.
Najjar, F. M. "*Siyasa* in Islamic Political Philosophy," in M. E. Marmura (ed.) *Islamic Theology and Philosophy: Studies in Honor of George F. Hourani*, 92–110, Albany: State University of New York Press, 1984.
Najmabadi, A. *Land Reform and Social Change in Iran*, Salt Lake City: University of Utah Press, 1987.
al-Naqeeb, K. H. "Social Origins of the Authoritarian State in the Arab East," 36–70, in E. Davis and N. Gavrielides (eds) *Statecraft in the Middle East: oil, historical memory, and popular culture*, Miami: Florida International University Press, 1991.
Nardoni, E. *Rise Up, O Judge: a study of justice in the Biblical world*, Peabody, MA: Hendrickson, 2004.
Nasr, S. H. and Leaman, O. (eds) *History of Islamic Philosophy*, 2 vols, London: Routledge, 1996.
Navaro-Yashin, Y. "Uses and Abuses of 'State and Civil Society' in Contemporary Turkey," *New Perspectives on Turkey* 18, Spring 1998: 1–22.
——. *Faces of the State: secularism and public life in Turkey*, Princeton, NJ: Princeton University Press, 2002.
Nawid, S. "The State, the Clergy, and British Imperial Policy in Afghanistan during the Nineteenth and Early Twentieth Centuries," *IJMES* 29, 1997: 581–605.
Nazim, M. *The Life and Times of Sultān Mahmūd of Ghazna*, Lahore: Khalil, 1931, repr. 1973.
Necipoğlu, G. "From International Timurid to Ottoman: a change of taste in sixteenth-century ceramic tiles," *Muqarnas* 7, 1990: 136–70.
——. *Architecture, Ceremonial and Power: the Topkapı Palace in the fifteenth and sixteenth centuries*, Cambridge: MIT Press, 1991.
——. "A Kânûn for the State, a Canon for the Arts: Conceptualizing the Classical Synthesis of Ottoman Art and Architecture," in G. Veinstein (ed.) *Soliman le magnifique et son temps*, 195–216, Paris: La Documentation Française, 1992.
——. "Framing the Gaze in Ottoman, Safavid, and Mughal Palaces," *ArsOr* 23, 1993: 303–42.
Netton, I. R. *Muslim Neoplatonists: an introduction to the thought of the Brethren of Purity*, Edinburgh: Edinburgh University Press, 1991.
Newman, A. J. *Safavid Iran: rebirth of a Persian empire*, London: IB Tauris, 2006.
——. (ed.) *Society and Culture in the Early Modern Middle East: studies on Iran in the Safavid period*, 237–47, Leiden: Brill, 2003.
Nezam-Mafi, M. E. "The Council for the Investigation of Grievances: a case study of nineteenth century Iranian social history," *IranS* 22.1, 1989: 51–61.
Nielsen, J. S. "*Maẓālim* and *Dār al-'Adl* under the Early Mamluks," *MW* 66 1976: 114–32.
——. *Secular Justice in an Islamic State: maẓālim under the Baḥrī Mamlūks, 662/1264–789/1387*, Istanbul: Nederlands Historisch-Archaeologisch Instituut, 1985.
Nobari, A.-R. "An Exile's Dream for Iran: an interview with the Shi'ite leader Ayatollah-Khomaini," in A.-R. Nobari (ed.) *Iran Erupts: Independence: news and analysis of the Iranian national movement*, 9–17, Stanford: Iran–America Documentation Group, 1978.
Norton, A. R. "Shi'ism and Social Protest in Lebanon," in J. R. I. Cole and N. R. Keddie (eds) *Shi'ism and Social Protest*, 156–78, New Haven, CT: Yale University Press, 1986.
Northrup, L. S. *From Slave to Sultan: the career of al-Manṣūr Qalāwūn and the consolidation of Mamluk rule in Egypt and Syria (678–689A.H./1279–1290A.D.)* Stuttgart: F. Steiner, 1998.
Noth, A. and Conrad, L. I. *The Early Arabic Historical Tradition: a source-critical study*, trans. M. Bonner, Princeton, NJ: Darwin, 1994.

Novak, M. "The Artificial Paradise: programme and ideology of royal gardens," in S. Parpola and R. M. Whiting (eds) *Sex and Gender in the Ancient Near East*, 2 vols, 2: 443–60, Helsinki: Neo-Assyrian Text Corpus Project, 2002.

Nsouli, S. M., Eken, S., Enders, K., Thai, V.-C., Decressin, J. and Cartiglia, F., with Bungay, J. *Resilience and Growth through Sustained Adjustment: the Moroccan experience*, Occasional Paper 117, Washington, DC: International Monetary Fund, 1995.

O'Brien, P. *The Revolution in Egypt's Economic System: from private enterprise to socialism, 1952–1965*, London: Oxford University Press, 1966.

Ocak, A. Y. *La révolte de Baba Resul ou la formation de l'hétérodoxie musulmane en Anatolie au XIIIe siècle*, Ankara: Türk Tarih Kurumu, 1989.

——. *Sarı Saltık: popüler İslâm'ın Balkanlar'daki destanî öncüsü (XIII. yüzyıl)*, Ankara: Türk Tarih Kurumu, 2002

Oğuzoğlu, Y. *Osmanlı Devlet Anlayışı*, Istanbul: Eren, 2000.

O'Kane, B. *Timurid Architecture in Khurasan*, Costa Mesa, CA: Mazdâ/Undena, 1987.

Okazaki, S. "The Great Persian Famine of 1870–71," *BSOAS* 49, 1986: 183–92.

Oktay, A. S. *Kınalızâde Ali Efendi ve Ahlâk-ı Alâî*, Istanbul: İz Yayıncılık, 2005.

O'Leary, D. E. *How Greek Science Passed to the Arabs*, London: Routledge and Kegan Paul, 1948.

Olivier, J. P. J. "Restitution as Economic Redress: the fine print of the Old Babylonian *mēšarum*-edict of Ammiṣaduqa," *Zeitschrift für Altbabylonische und Biblische Rechtsgeschichte* 3, 1997: 12–25.

Olson, R. W. "The Esnaf and the Patrona Halil Rebellion of 1730: a realignment in Ottoman politics'" *JESHO* 17, 1974: 329–44.

——. "Some Comments on Eighteenth Century Ottoman Historiography," in R. Olson and S. A. Ani (eds) *Islamic and Middle Eastern Societies: a festschrift in honor of Professor Wadie Jwaideh*, 137–51, Brattleboro, VT: Amana Books, 1987.

Omid, H. *Islam and the Post-Revolutionary State in Iran*, New York: St. Martin's, 1994.

Oppenheim, A. L. "A Note on the Scribes in Mesopotamia," in *Studies in Honor of Benno Landsberger on His Seventh-Fifth Birthday*, Oriental Institute Assyriological Studies, 16, 253–6, Chicago, IL: University of Chicago Press, 1965.

——. *Letters from Mesopotamia: official, business, and private letters on clay tablets from two millennia*, Chicago, IL: University of Chicago Press, 1967.

Ortaylı, İ. "On the Role of the Ottoman Kadı in Provincial Administration," *Turkish Public Administration Annual* 3, 1976: 1–21.

Ostapchuk, V. "The Ottoman Black Sea Frontier and the Relations of the Porte with the Polish-Lithuanian Commonwealth and Muscovy, 1622–1628," PhD diss., Harvard University, 1989.

Owen, R. "Large Landowners, Agricultural Progress and the State in Egypt, 1800–1970: an overview with many questions," in A. Richards (ed.) *Food, States, and Peasants: analyses of the agrarian question in the Middle East*, 69–95, Boulder, CO: Westview, 1986.

Özcan, A. "Fatih'in teşkilât kanunnâmesi ve nizam-ı alem için kardeş katli meselesi," *TD* 33, 1980–1: 7–56.

Özdemir, B. *Ottoman Reforms and Social Life: reflections from Salonica, 1830–1850*, Istanbul: İsis, 2003.

——. "Being a Part of the Cinderella Service: Consul Charles Blunt at Salonica in the 1840s," in C. Imber, K. Kiyotaki, and R. Murphey (eds) *Frontiers of Ottoman Studies: state, province and the West*, 2 vols, 2: 241–52, London: IB Tauris, 2005.

Özel, M. (ed.) *Mustafa Kemal Atatürk*, Ankara: T. C. Kültür Bakanlığı, 1996, 1998, 2001.

Özel, O. "Limits of the Almighty: Mehmed II's 'land reform' revisited," *JESHO* 42, 1999: 226–46.

——. "Population Changes in Ottoman Anatolia during the 16th and 17th Centuries: the 'demographic crisis' reconsidered," *IJMES* 36, 2004: 183–205.

——. "The Transformation of Provincial Administration in Anatolia: observations on Amasya from 15th to 17th centuries," in E. Kermeli and O. Özel (eds) *The Ottoman Empire: myths, realities and 'black holes': contributions in honour of Colin Imber*, 51–74, Istanbul: İsis, 2006.

Özveren, E. "Black Sea and the Grain Provisioning of Istanbul in the *Longue Durée*," in B. Marino and C. Virlouvet (eds) *Nourrir les cités de Méditerranée: antiquité-temps modernes*, 223–49, Paris: Maisonneuve et Larose, 2003.

Paidar, P. *Women and the Political Process in Twentieth-Century Iran*, Cambridge: Cambridge University Press, 1995.

Palairet, M. "Farm Productivity under Ottoman Rule and Self-government in Bulgaria c. 1860–1890," in S. J. Kirschbaum (ed.) *East European History*, 89–124, Columbus, OH: Slavica, 1988.

Pamuk, Ş. *A Monetary History of the Ottoman Empire*, Cambridge: Cambridge University Press, 2000.

——. "The Price Revolution in the Ottoman Empire Reconsidered," *IJMES* 33, 2001: 69–89.

——. "Prices in the Ottoman Empire, 1469–1914," *IJMES* 36, 2004: 451–68.

Paul, J. "*Inshā'* Collections as a Source on Iranian History," in B. G. Fragner, C. Fragner, G. Gnoli, R. Haag-Higuchi, M. Maggi, and P. Orsatti (eds) *Proceedings of the Second European Conference of Iranian Studies*, 535–50, Rome: Istituto Italiano per il Medio ed Estremo Oriente, 1995.

——. "The Seljuq Conquest(s) of Nishapur: a reappraisal," *IranS* 38, 2005: 75–85.

Peacock, A. C. S. *Mediaeval Islamic Historiography and Political Legitimacy: Bal'amī's Tārīkhnāma*, London: Routledge, 2007.

——. *Early Seljūq History: a new interpretation*, London: Routledge, 2010.

Peirce, L. P. *The Imperial Harem: women and sovereignty in the Ottoman Empire*, New York: Oxford University Press, 1993.

Pennell, C. R. *Tyranny, Just Rule & Moroccan Political Thought*, Nairobi: University of Nairobi Department of History, Staff Seminar Paper no. 8: 1986/87, May 1987.

Penrose, E. and Penrose, E. F. *Iraq: international relations and national development*, London: Ernest Benn; Boulder, CO: Westview, 1978.

Perho, I. "The Sultan and the Common People," *Studia Orientalia* 82, 1997: 145–57.

Perry, J. R. "Justice for the Underprivileged: the ombudsman tradition of Iran," *JNES* 37, 1978: 203–15.

——. *Karim Khan Zand: a history of Iran, 1747–1779*, Chicago, IL: University of Chicago Press, 1979.

Perthes, V. *The Political Economy of Syria under Asad*, London: IB Tauris, 1995.

Peters, E. *Lord of the Silent*, New York: HarperCollins, 2001.

Peters, F. E. *Aristoteles Arabus: the Oriental translations and commentaries on the Aristotelian corpus*, Leiden: Brill, 1968.

Peters, R. "Islamic and Secular Criminal Law in Nineteenth Century Egypt: the role and function of the qadi," *ILS* 4, 1997: 70–90.

——. "Administrators and Magistrates: the development of a secular judiciary in Egypt, 1853–1871," *WI* 39, 1999: 378–97.

——. "'For His Correction and as a Deterrent Example for Others': Meḥmed 'Ali 's first criminal legislation (1829–1830)," *ILS* 6, 1999: 164–92.

Petran, T. *Syria*, London: Ernest Benn, 1972.

Petit, O. and Voisin, W. *La poésie arabe classique: études textuelles*, Paris: Publisud, avec le Centre Nationale des Lettres, 1989.

Petrushevsky, I. P. "Rashīd al-Dīn's Conception of the State," *CAJ* 14, 1970: 148–62.

Petry, C. F. *Twilight of Majesty: the reigns of the Mamlūk Sultans al-Ashraf Qāytbāy and Qānṣūh al-Ghawrī in Egypt*, Seattle: University of Washington Press, 1993.

——. *Protectors or Praetorians 'the last Mamlūk sultans and Egypt's waning as a great power*, Albany: State University of New York Press, 1994.

——. "Royal Justice in Mamlūk Cairo: contrasting motives of two sulṭāns," in *Saber religioso y poder político en el Islam* 197–211, Madrid: Agencia Española de Cooperación Internacional, 1994.

——. "'Quis Custodiet Custodes?' Revisited: the prosecution of crime in the late Mamluk sultanate," *MSR* 3, 1999: 13–30.

——. and Daly, M. W. (eds) *The Cambridge History of Egypt*, 2 vols, Cambridge: Cambridge University Press, 1998.

Pfeifer, K. "Algeria's Implicit Stabilization Program," in H. J. Barkey (ed.) *The Politics of Reform in the Middle East*, 153–81, New York: St. Martin's Press, 1992.

Poliak, A. N. "The Influence of Chingiz-Khan's Yāsa upon the General Organization of the Mamlūk State," *BSOAS* 10, 1942: 862–76.

Poliakova, E. A. "The Development of a Literary Canon in Medieval Persian Chronicles: the triumph of etiquette," *IranS* 17, 1984: 237–56.

Polk, W. R. *The Opening of South Lebanon, 1788–1840: a study of the impact of the West on the Middle East*, Cambridge, MA: Harvard University Press, 1963.

Porter, B. N. *Images, Power, and Politics: figurative aspects of Esarhaddon's Babylonian policy*, Philadelphia, PA: American Philosophical Society, 1993.

Postgate, J. N. "Royal Exercise of Justice under the Assyrian Empire," in P. Garelli (ed.) *Le palais et la royauté (archéologie et civilisation)*, Rencontre assyriologique internationale, 19th, Paris, 1971, 417–26, Paris: Paul Geuthner, 1974.

——. "'Princeps Iudex' in Assyria," *RA* 74, 1980: 180–2.

——. "The Land of Assur and the Yoke of Assur," *World Archaeology* 23, 1992: 247–63.

Potts, D. T. *The Archaeology of Elam: formation and transformation of an ancient Iranian site*, Cambridge: Cambridge University Press, 1999.

Pourshariati, P. *Decline and Fall of the Sasanian Empire: the Sasanian-Parthian confederacy and the Arab conquest of Iran*, London: IB Tauris, 2008.

Powers, D. S. *Law, Society, and Culture in the Maghrib, 1300–1500*, Cambridge: Cambridge University Press, 2002.

Pritsak, O. "The Khazar Kingdom's Conversion to Judaism," *Harvard Ukrainian Studies* 2, 1978: 261–81.

al-Qāḍī, W. "The Term 'Khalifa' in Early Exegetical Literature," *WI* 28, 1988: 392–411.

——. "The Religious Foundation of Late Umayyad Ideology and Practice," in *Saber Religioso y Poder Político en el Islam*, 231–73, Madrid: Agencia Española de Cooperación Internacional, 1994.

Quataert, D. "The Commercialization of Agriculture in Ottoman Turkey, 1800–1914," *IJTS* 1.2, 1980: 38–55.

——. "Machine Breaking and the Changing Carpet Industry of Western Anatolia, 1860–1908," *JSH* 19, 1985–6: 473–89.

——. "Rural Unrest in the Ottoman Empire, 1830–1914," in F. Kazemi and J. Waterbury (eds) *Peasants and Politics in the Modern Middle East*, 38–49, Miami: Florida International University Press, 1991.

——. "The Age of Reforms, 1812–1914," in H. İnalcık with D. Quataert (eds) *An Economic and Social History of the Ottoman Empire*, 761–943, Cambridge: Cambridge University Press, 1994.

Qubain, F. I. *The Reconstruction of Iraq: 1950–1957*, New York: Frederick A. Praeger, 1958.

Rabbat, N. O. "The Ideological Significance of the *Dār al-'adl* in the Medieval Islamic Orient," *IJMES* 27, 1995: 3–28.

Rabi, U. "The Kuwaiti Royal Family in the Postliberation Period: reinstitutionalizing the 'first among equals' system in Kuwait," in J. Kostiner (ed.) *Middle East Monarchies: the challenge of modernity*, 151–65, Boulder, CO: Lynne Reinner, 2000.

Rabie, H. *The Financial System of Egypt, A.H. 564–741/A.D. 1169–1341*, London: Oxford University Press, 1972.

Rabinovich, I. *Syria under the Ba'th, 1963–66: the army-party symbiosis*, Jerusalem: Israel Universities Press, New York: Halsted Press/John Wiley & Sons, 1972.

Rabo, A. "Nation-State Building in Syria: Ba'th and Islam–conflict or accommodation?" in K. Ferdinand and M. Mozaffari (eds) *Islam: state and society*, 117–26, London and Riverdale: Curzon Press/Riverdale, 1988.

Radwan, S. *Agrarian Reform and Rural Poverty, Egypt, 1952–1975*, Geneva: International Labour Office, 1977.

Rafeq, A.-K. "The Local Forces in Syria in the Seventeenth and Eighteenth Centuries," in V. J. Parry and M. E. Yapp (eds) *War, Technology and Society in the Middle East*, 277–307, London: Oxford University Press, 1975.

Rahme, J. G. "'Abd al-Raḥmān al-Kawākibī's Reformist Ideology, Arab Pan-Islamism, and the Internal Other," *Journal of Islamic Studies* 10, 1999: 159–77.

Rahnema, A. and Nomani, F. *The Secular Miracle: religion, politics and economic policy in Iran*, London: Zed Books, 1990.

al-Rasheed, M. "God, the King and the Nation: political rhetoric in Saudi Arabia in the 1990s," *MEJ* 50, 1996: 359–71.

Ratchnevsky, P. *Genghis Khan: His Life and Legacy*, trans. T. N. Haining, Oxford: Blackwell, 1991.

Raymond, A. "Quartiers et mouvements populaires au Caire au XVIIIème siècle," in P. M. Holt (ed.) *Political and Social Change in Modern Egypt: historical studies from the Ottoman conquest to the United Arab Republic*, 104–16, London: Oxford University Press, 1968.

Rebstock, U. "Observations on the Diwan al-Kharaj and the Assessment of Taxes in Umayyad Syria," in M. A. Bakhit and R. Schick (eds) *The History of Bilad al-Sham During the Umayyad Period (Fourth International Conference, 1987)*, 229–46, Amman: Bilad al-Sham History Committee, 1989.

Redford, S. "The Seljuks of Rum and the Antique," *Muqarnas* 10, 1993: 148–56.

——. "Just Landscape in Medieval Anatolia," *Studies in the History of Gardens and Designed Landscapes* 20, 2000: 313–24.

——. *Landscape and the State in Medieval Anatolia: Seljuk gardens and pavilions of Alanya, Turkey*, Oxford: Archaeopress, 2000.

Regourd, F. "Le rôle de l'élite perse dans la formation de l'armée et de l'état achéménides," *Commémoration Cyrus, Hommage universel: actes du congrès de Shiraz 1971*, AcIr 1–3, ser. 1, vols 1–3, 2: 101–8, Leiden: Brill, 1974.

Reid, D. M. *The Odyssey of Farah Antun: a Syrian Christian's quest for secularism*, Minneapolis and Chicago, IL: Bibliotheca Islamica, 1975.

——. "The Postage Stamp: a window on Saddam Hussein's Iraq," *MEJ* 47, 1993: 77–89.

Reinkowski, M. "The State's Security and the Subjects' Prosperity: notions of order in Ottoman bureaucratic correspondence (19th century)," in H. T. Karateke and M. Reinkowski (eds) *Legitimizing the Order: the Ottoman rhetoric of state power*, 195–212, Leiden: Brill, 2005.

Rejwan, N. *Nasserist Ideology: its exponents and critics*, New York: John Wiley and Sons, 1974.

Remler, P. "New Light on Economic History from Ilkhanid Accounting Manuals," *StIr* 14, 1985: 157–77.

Richards, A. "Primitive Accumulation in Egypt, 1798–1882," *Review: Fernand Braudel Center* 1.2, Fall 1977: 3–49.

——. "Economic Imperatives and Political Systems," *MEJ* 47, 1993: 217–27.

Richards, D. S. "A Fatimid Petition and 'Small Decree' from Sinai," *IOS* 3, 1973: 140–58.

——. "A Mamlūk Petition and a Report from the *Dīwān al-Jaysh*," *BSOAS* 40, 1977: 1–14.

Richter, G. *Studien zur Geschichte der älteren arabischen Fürstenspiegel*, Leipzig: J. C. Hinrichs, 1932.

Richter-Bernburg, L. "*Amīr-Malik-Shāhānshāh*: 'Aḍud ad-Daula's titulature re-examined," *Iran* 18, 1980: 83–102.

Ringgren, H. "Some Religious Aspects of the Caliphate," in *The Sacral Kingship*, Studies in the History of Religions, 4 (Supplements to *Numen*), 737–48, Leiden: Brill, 1959.

Rizvi, S. R. A. *Nizam al-Mulk Tusi: his contribution to statecraft, political theory and the art of government*, Lahore, Sh. Muhammad Ashraf, 1978.

——. "Political and Administrative Measures of Nizām al-Mulk Tūsī," *IS* 19, 1980: 111–19.

Roaf, M. "Persepolitan Echoes in Sasanian Architecture: did the Sasanians attempt to re-create the Achaemenid empire?" in V. S. Curtis, R. Hillenbrand, and J. M. Rogers (eds) *The Art and Archaeology of Ancient Persia: new light on the Parthian and Sasanian Empires*, 1–7, London: IB Tauris, 1998.

Roberts, H. "The FLN: French Conceptions, Algerian Realities," in G. Joffé (ed.) *North Africa: nation, state, and region*, 111–41, London: Routledge, 1993.

——. *The Battlefield Algeria, 1988–2002: studies in a broken polity*, London: Verso, 2003.

Robinson, B. W. *Fifteenth-Century Persian Painting: problems and issues*, New York: New York University Press, 1991.

Robinson, C. F. *Empire and Elites after the Muslim Conquest: the transformation of northern Mesopotamia*, Cambridge: Cambridge University Press, 2000.

Rogers, J. M. "Evidence for Mamlūk-Mongol Relations, 1260–1360," in A. Raymond, M. Rogers, and M. Wahba (eds) *Colloque international sur l'histoire du Caire*, 385–403, Gräfenhainichen: Ministry of Culture of the Arab Republic of Egypt, 1969.

——. "The Chester Beatty Süleymânnâme Again," in R. Hillenbrand (ed.) *Persian Painting from the Mongols to the Qajars: studies in honour of Basil W. Robinson*, 187–200, London: IB Tauris, 2000.

Rood, J. M. "Mehmed Ali as Mutinous Khedive: the roots of rebellion," *IJTS* 8, 2002: 116–28.

Root, M. C. *The King and Kingship in Achaemenid Art: essays on the creation of an iconography of empire*, AcIr 19, ser. 3, vol. 9, Leiden: Brill, 1979.

Rosen, L. "Islamic Concepts of Justice," in M. King (ed.) *God's Law versus State Law: the construction of an Islamic identity in Western Europe*, 62–72, London: Grey Seal, 1995.

——. *The Justice of Islam: comparative perspectives on Islamic law and society*, Oxford: Oxford University Press, 2000.

Rosenthal, E. I. J. *Political Thought in Medieval Islam: an introductory outline*, Cambridge: Cambridge University Press, 1962, repr. Westport, CT: Greenwood Press, 1985.

——. *Averroes' Commentary on Plato's Republic*, Cambridge: Cambridge University Press, 1969.

——. "The Role of the State in Islam: theory and medieval practice," *Der Islam* 50, 1973: 1–28.

Rosenthal, F. "State and Religion According to Abū l-Ḥasan al-'Āmirī," *IQ* 3, 1956: 42–52; repr. in *Muslim Intellectual and Social History: a collection of essays*, London: Variorum, 1990, VII.

——. *A History of Muslim Historiography*, 2nd rev. ed. Leiden: Brill, 1968.

——. "Political Justice and the Just Ruler," in J. L. Kraemer and I. Alon (eds) *Religion and Government in the World of Islam*, *IOS* 10, 1983: 92–101.

——. "Abū Zayd al-Balkhī on Politics," in C. E. Bosworth, C. Issawi, R. Savory, and A. L. Udovitch (eds) *The Islamic World from Classical to Modern Times: essays in honor of Bernard Lewis*, 287–302, Princeton, NJ: Darwin, 1989.

Roth, M. T. with a contribution by Hoffner, H. A., Jr. *Law Collections from Mesopotamia and Asia Minor*, ed. P. Michalowski, 2nd. ed. Atlanta, GA: Scholars Press, 1997.

Rubin, A. "Legal Borrowing and Its Impact on Ottoman Legal Culture in the Late Nineteenth Century," *Continuity and Change* 22, 2007: 279–303.

Rubin, Z. "The Reforms of Khusro Anūshirwān," in A. Cameron (ed.) *The Byzantine and Early Islamic Near East, III: states, resources and armies*, Princeton, NJ: Darwin, 1995.

Rührdanz, K. "About a Group of Truncated *Shāhnāmas*: a case study in the commercial production of illustrated manuscripts in the second part of the sixteenth century," *Muqarnas* 14, 1997: 118–34.

Russell, J. M. *Sennacherib's Palace without Rival at Nineveh*. Chicago, IL: University of Chicago Press, 1991.

Rustow, D. A. "Ataturk's Political Leadership," in R. B. Winder (ed.) *Near Eastern Round Table, 1967–68*, 143–55, New York: Near East Center and the Center for International Studies, New York University, 1969.

Ryan, C. R. *Jordan in Transition: from Hussein to Abdullah*, Boulder, CO: Lynne Rienner, 2002.

Rypka, J. *History of Iranian Literature*, Dordrecht, Neth.: D. Reidel, 1968.

Saab, G. S. *The Egyptian Agrarian Reform, 1952–1962*, London: Oxford University Press, 1967.

Saad, R. *Social History of an Agrarian Reform Community in Egypt*, Cairo Papers in Social Science, 11, Cairo: American University in Cairo Press, 1998.

Sabari, S. *Mouvements populaires à Bagdad à l'époque 'abbasside, IXe–XIe siècles*, Paris: Adrien Maisonneuve, 1981.

Sabra, A. *Poverty and Charity in Medieval Islam: Mamluk Egypt, 1250–1517*, Cambridge: Cambridge University Press, 2000.

Sachedina, A. A. *Islamic Messianism: the idea of Mahdi in Twelver Shi'ism*, Albany: State University of New York Press, 1981.

——. *The Just Ruler (al-sultān al-'ādil) in Shī'ite Islam: the comprehensive authority of the jurist in Imamite jurisprudence*, Oxford: Oxford University Press, 1988.

Sadan, J. "A New Source of the Buyid Period," *IOS* 9, 1979: 355–76.

——. "A 'Closed-Circuit' Saying on Practical Justice," *JSAI* 10, 1987: 325–41.

——. "'Community' and 'Extra-Community' as a Legal and Literary Problem," in J. L. Kraemer and I. Alon (eds) *Religion and Government in the World of Islam*, *IOS* 10, 1983: 102–15.

Sadiki, L. "Popular Uprisings and Arab Democratization," *IJMES* 32, 2000: 71–95.

Sadowski, Y. M. "Political Power and Economic Organization in Syria: the course of state intervention, 1946–1958," PhD diss., University of California, Los Angeles, 1984.

——. *Political Vegetables? businessman and bureaucrat in the development of Egyptian agriculture*, Washington, DC: The Brookings Institution, 1991.

Safi, O. *The Politics of Knowledge in Premodern Islam: negotiating ideology and religious inquiry*, Chapel Hill: University of North Carolina Press, 2006.

Safran, N. *Egypt in Search of Political Community: an analysis of the intellectual and political evolution of Egypt, 1804–1952*, Cambridge, MA: Harvard University Press, 1961.

Sagaster, K. "Herrschaftsideologie und Friedensgedanke bei den Mongolen," *CAJ* 17, 1973: 223–42.

Saggs, H. W. F. "Historical Texts and Fragments of Sargon II of Assyria," *Iraq* 37, 1975: 11–20.

Sainte-Marie, A. "La commune d'Azeffoun à la fin du XIXème siècle," *Revue algérienne des sciences juridiques, economiques, et politiques* 9, 1974: 435–59.

Sajdi, D. "Decline, Its Discontents and Ottoman Cultural History: by way of introduction," in D. Sajdi (ed.) *Ottoman Tulips, Ottoman Coffee: leisure and lifestyle in the eighteenth century*, 1–40, London: Tauris Academic Studies, 2007.

Salibi, K. S. *The Modern History of Lebanon*, New York: Praeger, 1965.

Salles, J.-F. "The Arab-Persian Gulf under the Seleucids," in A. Kuhrt and S. Sherwin-White (eds) *Hellenism in the East: the interaction of Greek and non-Greek civilizations from Syria to Central Asia after Alexander*, 75–109, London: Duckworth, 1987.

Salzmann, A. "Citizens in Search of a State: the limits of political participation in the late Ottoman Empire," in M. Hanagan and C. Tilly (ed.) *Extending Citizenship, Reconfiguring States*, 37–66, Lanham: Rowman and Littlefield, 1999.

——. "The Age of Tulips: confluence and conflict in early modern consumer culture (1550–1730)," in D. Quataert (ed.) *Consumption Studies and the History of the Ottoman Empire, 1550–1922: an introduction*, 83–106, Albany: State University of New York Press, 2000.

Samadi, S. B. "Some Aspects of the Theory of the State and Administration under the Abbasids," *IC* 29, 1955: 120–50.

Samuel, A. E. "The Ptolemies and the Ideology of Kingship," in P. Green (ed.) *Hellenistic History and Culture*, 168–210, Berkeley: University of California Press, 1993.

Sancisi-Weerdenburg, H. "Political Concepts in Old-Persian Royal Inscriptions," in K. Raaflaub and E. Müller-Luckner (eds) *Anfänge politischen Denkens in der Antike: Die nahöstlichen Kulturen und die Griechen*, 145–63, Munich: R. Oldenbourg, 1993.

Sanders, P. "From Court Ceremony to Urban Language: ceremonial in Fatimid Cairo and Fusṭāt," in C. E. Bosworth, C. Issawi, R. Savory, and A. L. Udovitch (eds) *The Islamic World from Classical to Modern Times: essays in honor of Bernard Lewis*, 311–22, Princeton, NJ: Darwin, 1989.

——. *Ritual, Politics, and the City in Fatimid Cairo*, Albany: State University of New York Press, 1994.

Şaşmazer, L. M. "Policing Bread Price and Production in Ottoman Istanbul, 1793–1807," *TSAB* 24.1, Spring 2000: 21–40.

Sato, N. "'We Are No More in Bondage, We Are Peasants': memory and the construction of identity in the Syrian Jazirah," *Journal of Mediterranean Studies* 7, 1997: 195–217.

Sato, T. *State and Rural Society in Medieval Islam: sultans, muqta's and fallahun*, Leiden: Brill, 1997.

Savory, R. M. "The Struggle for Supremacy in Persia after the Death of Tīmūr," *Der Islam* 40, 1965: 35–65.

——. "Notes on the Safavid State," *IranS* 1, 1968: 96–103.

——. "The *Qizilbāsh*, Education and the Arts," *Turcica* 6, 1975: 168–76.

——. "Social Development in Iran during the Pahlavi Era," in G. Lenczowski (ed.) *Iran under the Pahlavis*, 86–128, Stanford, CA: Hoover Institution Press, 1978.

Sawyer, C. "Sword of Conquest, Dove of the Soul: Political and Spiritual Values in Aḥmadī's *Iskandarnāma*," in M. Bridges and J. C. Bürgel (eds) *The Problematics of Power: Eastern and Western representations of Alexander the Great*, 135–48, Bern: Peter Lang, 1996.

Sayer, D. "Everyday Forms of State Formation: some dissident remarks on 'hegemony'," in G. M. Joseph and D. Nugent (eds) *Everyday Forms of State Formation: revolution and the negotiation of rule in modern Mexico*, 367–77, Durham: Duke University Press, 1994.

Sayılı, A. *The Observatory in Islam and Its Place in the General History of the Observatory*, Ankara: Türk Tarih Kurumu, 1960.

Schacht, J. *An Introduction to Islamic Law*, Oxford: Clarendon Press, 1964; repr. 1982.

Schaendlinger, A. C. "Ämter und Funktionen im Reiche der Rūmseltschuken nach der 'Seltschukengeschichte des Ibn Bībī'," *WZKM* 62, 1969: 172–92.

Schilcher, L. S. "The Great Depression (1873–1896) and the Rise of Syrian Arab Nationalism," *NPT* 5–6, 1991: 167–89.

——. "Violence in Rural Syria in the 1880s and 1890s: state centralization, rural integration, and the world market," in F. Kazemi and J. Waterbury (ed.) *Peasants and Politics in the Modern Middle East*, 50–84, Miami: Florida International University Press, 1991.

Schirazi, A. *Islamic Development Policy: The Agrarian Question in Iran*, trans. P. J. Ziess-Lawrence, Boulder, CO: Lynne Reinner, 1993.

Schlumberger, O. "Transition to Development?" in G. Joffé (ed.) *Jordan in Transition*, 225–53, London: Hurst & Company, 2002.

Schmidt, J. *Pure Water for Thirsty Muslims: a study of Muṣṭafa 'Ālī of Gallipoli's* Künhü'l-ahbār, Leiden: Het Oosters Instituut, 1991.

Schneider, I. *The Petitioning System in Iran: state, society and power relations in the late 19th century*, Wiesbaden: Harrassowitz, 2006.

Schölch, A. *Egypt for the Egyptians! the socio-political crisis in Egypt 1878–1882*, London: Ithaca Press for the Middle East Centre, St. Antony's College, Oxford, 1981.

Schulze, R. C. "Colonization and Resistance: the Egyptian peasant rebellion, 1919," in F. Kazemi and J. Waterbury (eds) *Peasants and Politics in the Modern Middle East*, 171–202, Miami: Florida International University Press, 1991.

Schurmann, H. F. "Mongolian Tributary Practices of the Thirteenth Century," *HJAS* 19, 1956: 304–89.

Scott, J. C. *The Moral Economy of the Peasant: rebellion and subsistance in Southeast Asia*, New Haven, CT: Yale University Press, 1976.

——. *Weapons of the Weak: everyday forms of peasant resistance*, New Haven, CT: Yale University Press, 1985.

——. "Everyday Forms of Peasant Resistance," *Journal of Peasant Studies* 13, no. 2, 1985/86: 5–35.

Scurlock, J.-A. "'Freedom' and 'Justice': the Neo-Assyrian response to socio-economic crises (934–612 B.C.)," paper presented to the Association of Ancient Historians, Madison, WI, 5 May 1983.

——. "Assyrian 'Colonization'," paper presented to the Association of Ancient Historians, Lubbock, TX, 1 May 1986.

Seddon, D. "Politics and the Price of Bread in Tunisia," in A. Richards (ed.) *Food, States, and Peasants: analyses of the agrarian question in the Middle East*, 201–23, Boulder, CO: Westview Press, 1986.

——. "Riot and Rebellion in North Africa: political responses to economic crisis in Tunisia, Morocco and Sudan," in B. Berberoglu (ed.) *Power and Stability in the Middle East*, 114–35, London: Zed Books, 1989.

Semah, D. *Four Egyptian Literary Critics*, Leiden: Brill, 1974.

Seyf, A. "Despotism and the Disintegration of the Iranian Economy, 1500–1800," in E. Kedourie and S. G. Haim (eds) *Essays on the Economic History of the Middle East*, 1–19, London: Frank Cass, 1988.

Shafi, I. M. "Fresh Light on the Ghaznavids," *IC* 12, 1938: 189–234.

Shahbazi, A. S. *Ferdowsī: a critical biography*, Costa Mesa, CA: Harvard University and Mazda, 1991.

Shaked, S. "Some Legal and Administrative Terms of the Sasanian Period," *Monumentum H. S. Nyberg*, AcIr 4–7, ser. 2, vols 1–4, 2: 213–25, Leiden: Brill, 1975.

——. "Administrative Functions of Priests in the Sasanian Period," in G. Gnoli and A. Panaino (ed.) *Proceedings of the First European Conference of Iranian Studies*, pt. 1, *Old and Middle Iranian Studies*, 261–73, Rome: Istituto Italiano per il Medio ed Estremo Oriente, 1990.

——. "From Iran to Islam: notes on some themes in transmission," *JSAI* 4, 1984: 31–67; repr. in S. Shaked, *From Zoroastrian Iran to Islam: studies in religious history and intercultural contacts* Aldershot, UK: Variorum, 1995, VI.

——. "From Iran to Islam: on some symbols of royalty," *JSAI* 7, 1986: 75–91; repr. in S. Shaked, *From Zoroastrian Iran to Islam: studies in religious history and intercultural contacts*, Aldershot, UK: Variorum, 1995, VII.

Shamir, S. "The Modernization of Syria: problems and solutions in the early period of Abdülhamid," in W. R. Polk and R. L. Chambers (eds) *Beginnings of Modernization in the Middle East: the nineteenth century*, 351–81, Chicago, IL: University of Chicago Press, 1968.

——. "Midhat Pasha and the Anti-Turkish Agitation in Syria," *MES* 10, 1974: 115–41.

Shankland, D. "Old Ideas in New Forms: millennial movements in the Republic of Turkey," in F. Bowie with C. Deacy (eds) *The Coming Deliverer: millennial themes in world religions*, 224–37, Cardiff: University of Wales Press, 1997.

——. *Islam and Society in Turkey*, Hemingford Grey, UK: Eothen Press, 1999.

Shaw, S. J. *The Financial and Administrative Organization and Development of Ottoman Egypt, 1517–1798*, Princeton, NJ: Princeton University Press, 1962.

——. "Some Aspects of the Aims and Achievements of the Nineteenth-Century Ottoman Reformers," in W. R. Polk and R. L. Chambers (eds) *Beginnings of Modernization in the Middle East: the nineteenth century*, 29–40, Chicago, IL: University of Chicago Press, 1968.

——. "The Nineteenth-Century Ottoman Reforms and Revenue System," *IJMES* 6, 1975: 421–59.

——. and Shaw, E. K. *The History of the Ottoman Empire and Modern Turkey*, 2 vols, Cambridge: Cambridge University Press, 1976.

Shay, M. L. *The Ottoman Empire from 1720 to 1734 as revealed in despatches of the Venetian Baili*, Westport, CT: Greenwood, 1978.

el-Shayyal, G. "Some Aspects of Intellectual and Social Life in Eighteenth-century Egypt," in P. M. Holt (ed.) *Political and Social Change in Modern Egypt: historical studies from the Ottoman conquest to the United Arab Republic*, 117–32, London: Oxford University Press, 1968.

Shboul, A. M. H. *al-Mas'ūdī and His World: a Muslim humanist and his interest in non-Muslims*, London: Ithaca Press, 1979.

Sheikholeslami, A. R. "The Patrimonial Structure of Iranian Bureaucracy in the Late Nineteenth Century," *IranS* 11, 1978: 199–257.

——. *The Structure of Central Authority in Qajar Iran, 1871–1896*, Atlanta, GA: Scholars Press, 1997.

Sherwin-White, S. "Seleucid Babylonia: a case study for the installation and development of Greek rule," in A. Kuhrt and S. Sherwin-White (eds) *Hellenism in the East: the interaction of Greek and non-- Greek civilizations from Syria to Central Asia after Alexander*, 1–31, London: Duckworth, 1987.

——. and Kuhrt, A. *From Samarkhand to Sardis: a new approach to the Seleucid Empire* Berkeley: University of California Press, 1993.

Shoshan, B. "Grain Riots and the 'Moral Economy:' Cairo, 1350–1517," *Journal of Interdisciplinary History* 10, 1980: 459–78.

——. "Fāṭimid Grain Policy and the Post of the Muḥtasib," *IJMES* 13, 1981: 181–9.

——. *Popular Culture in Medieval Cairo*, Cambridge: Cambridge University Press, 1993.

Shukri, S. J. A. *Social Changes and Women in the Middle East: state policy, education, economics and development*, Aldershot, UK: Ashgate, 1999.

Siddiqi, A. H. "Caliphate and Kingship in Medieval Persia," *IC* 9, 1935: 560–79; 10, 1936: 97–126, 260–79, 390–408; 11, 1937: 37–59; repr. as *Caliphate and Kingship in Medieval Persia*, Philadelphia, PA: Porcupine Press, 1977.

Siddiqi, B. H. "Ibn Miskawaih's Theory of History," *Iqbal* 12, 1963/64: 71–80.

Silverman, S. "Patronage as Myth," in E. Gellner and J. Waterbury (eds) *Patrons and Clients in Mediterranean Societies*, 7–19, London: Duckworth, 1977.

Silverstein A. J. *Postal Systems in the Pre-Modern Islamic World*, Cambridge: Cambridge University Press, 2007.

Simidchieva, M. "*Siyāsat-nāme* Revisited: the question of authenticity," in B. G. Fragner, C. Fragner, G. Gnoli, R. Haag-Higuchi, M. Maggi, and P. Orsatti (eds) *Proceedings of the Second European Conference of Iranian Studies*, 657–74, Rome: Istituto Italiano per il Medio ed Estremo Oriente, 1995.

Simpson, M. S. *Sultan Ibrahim Mirza's Haft Awrang: a princely manuscript from sixteenth-century Iran*, New Haven, CT: Yale University Press, 1979.

Sims, E. G. "The Turks and Illustrated Historical Texts," in G. Fehér (ed.) *Fifth International Congress of Turkish Art*, 747–72 Budapest: Akadémiai Kiadó, 1978.

——. "Two Turkish Paintings in a Mid-Fifteenth Century Persian Nizami in the Topkapı Sarayı Library," in H. G. Majer (ed.) *VI. Internationaler Kongress für Turkische Kunst*, 93, Munich: Institut für Geschichte und Kultur des Nahen Orients so wie Turkologie, 1979.
——. "Ibrahim-Sultan's Illustrated *Zafarnama* of 1436 and Its Impact in the Muslim East," in L. Golombek and M. Subtelny (eds) *Timurid Art and Culture: Iran and Central Asia in the fifteenth century*, 132–43, Leiden: Brill, 1992.
——. "The Illustrated Manuscripts of Firdausī's *Shāhnāma* Commissioned by Princes of the House of Tī mūr," *ArsOr* 22, 1992: 43–68.
Singer, A. "Peasant Migration: law and practice in early Ottoman Palestine," *NPT*, no. 8, Fall 1992: 49–66.
——. *Palestinian Peasant and Ottoman Officials: rural administration around sixteenth-century Jerusalem*, Cambridge: Cambridge University Press, 1994.
Sinor, D. (ed.) *The Cambridge History of Early Inner Asia*, Cambridge: Cambridge University Press, 1990.
Sivan, E. *Radical Islam: medieval theology and modern politics*, New Haven, CT: Yale University Press, 1985.
Slama, B. *L'insurrection de 1864 en Tunisie*, Tunis: Maison Tunisienne de l'Édition, 1967.
Smith, J. M., Jr. "Mongol and Nomadic Taxation," *HJAS* 30, 1970: 46–85.
——. "Turanian Nomadism and Iranian Politics," *IranS* 11, 1978: 57–81.
——. "The Mongols and World Conquest," *Mongolica* 5, 1994: 206–14.
Smith, R. R. R. *Hellenistic Royal Portraits*, Oxford: Clarendon Press, 1988.
Smith, S. "The Practice of Kingship in Early Semitic Kingdoms," in S. H. Hooke (ed.) *Myth, Ritual, and Kingship: essays on the theory and practice of kingship in the ancient Near East and in Israel*, 22–73, Oxford: Clarendon, 1958.
Snider, L. W. "The Lebanese Forces: their origins and role in Lebanon's politics," *MEJ* 38, 1984: 1–33.
Sohrabi, N. "Revolution and State Culture: the Circle of Justice and constitutionalism in 1906 Iran," in G. Steinmetz (ed.) *State/Culture: state-formation after the cultural turn*, 253–88, Ithaca: Cornell University Press, 1999.
Sohrweide, H. "Dichter und Gelehrte aus dem Osten im osmanischen Reich (1453–1600): Ein Beitrag zur türkisch-persischen Kulturgeschichte," *Der Islam* 46, 1970: 263–302.
Sonbol, A. E. "Egypt," in S. T. Hunter (ed.) *The Politics of Islamic Revivalism: diversity and unity*, 23–38, Bloomington: Indiana University Press, 1988.
——. *The New Mamluks: Egyptian society and modern feudalism*, Syracuse: Syracuse University Press, 2000.
Sonn, T. "Bandali al-Jawzi's *Min tārīkh al-ḥarakāt al-fikriyyāt fi'l-Islām*: the first Marxist interpretation of Islam," *IJMES* 17, 1985: 89–107.
Soucek, P. "The Manuscripts of Iskandar Sultan: structure and content," in L. Golombek and M. Subtelny (eds) *Timurid Art and Culture: Iran and Central Asia in the fifteenth century*, 116–31, Leiden: Brill, 1992.
Soucek, S. *A History of Inner Asia*, Cambridge: Cambridge University Press, 2000.
Soudavar, A. "The Saga of Abu-Sa'id Bahador Khan," in J. Raby and T. Fitzherbert (eds) *The Court of the Il-khans, 1290–1340*, 95–218, Oxford: Oxford University Press, 1996.
——. *The Aura of Kings: legitimacy and divine sanction in Iranian kingship*, Costa Mesa, CA: Mazda, 2003.
Sourdel, D. *Le vizirat abbaside de 749 à 936 (132 à 324 de l'Hégire)*, 2 vols, Damascus: Institut français de Damas, 1959–60.
——. "Questions de cérémonial abbaside," *REI* 28, 1960: 121–48.
Sperl, S. "Islamic Kingship and Arabic Panegyric Poetry in the Early 9th Century," *Journal of Arabic Literature* 8, 1977: 20–35.
Springborg, P. *Western Republicanism and the Oriental Prince*, Austin: University of Texas Press, 1992.
Springborg, R. "Patrimonialism and Policy Making in Egypt: Nasser and Sadat and the tenure policy for reclaimed lands," *MES* 15, 1979: 49–69.
——. "Baathism in Practice: agriculture, politics, and political culture in Syria and Iraq," *MES* 17, 1981: 191–209.
——. "Infitah, Agrarian Transformation, and Elite Consolidation in Contemporary Iraq," *MEJ* 40, 1986: 33–52.

Spuler, B. "Iran: the persistent heritage," in G. E. von Grunebaum (ed.) *Unity and Variety in Muslim Civilization*, 167–82, Chicago, IL: University of Chicago Press, 1955.

——. "The Evolution of Persian Historiography," in B. Lewis and P. M. Holt (eds) *Historians of the Middle East*, Historical Writing on the Peoples of Asia, 4, 126–32, Oxford, New York: Oxford University Press, 1962.

——. *Die Mongolen in Iran: Politik, Verwaltung und Kulture der Ilchanzeit 1220–1350*, Berlin: Akademie-Verlag, 1968.

——. "The Disintegration of the Caliphate in the East," in P. M. Holt, A. K. S. Lambton, and B. Lewis (eds) *The Cambridge History of Islam*, vol. 1A: *The Central Islamic Lands from pre-Islamic times to the First World War*, 143–74, Cambridge: Cambridge University Press, 1970.

Sprengling, M. "From Persian to Arabic," *American Journal of Semitic Languages and Literatures* 56, 1939: 175–224, 325–336; 57, 1940: 302–05.

Staffa, S. J. *Conquest and Fusion: the social evolution of Cairo, AD 642–1850*, Leiden: Brill, 1977.

Stchoukine, I. *Les peintures des manuscrits de la "Khamseh" de Nieqāmī au Topkapı Sarayı Müzesi d'Istanbul*, Paris: Paul Geuthner, 1977.

Steinkeller, P. "The Administrative and Economic Organization of the Ur III State: the core and the periphery," in M. Gibson and R. D. Biggs (eds) *The Organization of Power: aspects of bureaucracy in the ancient Near East*, Studies in Ancient Oriental Civilization, 46, 19–41, Chicago, IL: Oriental Institute, 1987.

Stern, S. M. "Al-Mas'udi and the Philosopher al-Farabi," in S. M. Ahmad and A. Rahman (eds) *al-Mas'udi Millenary Commemoration Volume*, 28–41, Calcutta: The Indian Society for the History of Science and The Institute of Islamic Studies, Aligarh Muslim University, 1960.

——. "Petitions from the Mamlūk Period (notes on the Mamlūk documents from Sinai)," *BSOAS* 29, 1966: 233–76.

——. *Aristotle on the World State*, Columbia: University of South Carolina Press, 1968.

——. "Ismā'īlīs and Qarmatians," in *Studies in Early Ismā'īlism*, 289–98, Jerusalem: Magnes Press, 1983.

Stetkevych, J. *The Zephyrs of Najd: the poetics of nostalgia in the classical Arabic nasib*, Chicago, IL: University of Chicago Press, 1993.

Stetkevych, S. P. *Abū Tammām and the Poetics of the 'Abbāsid Age*, Leiden: Brill, 1991.

Stone, M. *The Agony of Algeria*, New York: Columbia University Press, 1997.

Strauss, J. "*'Kütüp ve resail-i mevkute'*: printing and publishing in a multi-ethnic society," in E. Özdalga (ed.) *Late Ottoman Society: the intellectual legacy*, 225–53, London: RoutledgeCurzon, 2005.

Subtelny, M.E. "Centralizing Reform and Its Opponents in the Late Timurid Period," *IranS* 21.1/2, 1988: 123–51.

——. "A Medieval Persian Agricultural Manual in Context: the *Irshād al-Zirā'a* in Late Timurid and Early Safavid Khorasan," *StIr* 22, 1993: 167–217.

——. "A Late Medieval Persian *Summa* on Ethics: Kashifi's *Akhlāq-i Muḥsinī*," *IranS* 36, 2003: 601–14.

——. *Timurids in Transition: Turko-Persian Politics and Acculturation in Medieval Iran*, Leiden: Brill, 2007.

Sullivan, D. J. *Private Voluntary Organizations in Egypt: Islamic development, private initiative, and state control*, Gainesville: University Press of Florida, 1994.

Susser, A. "The Jordanian Monarchy: the Hashemite success story," in J. Kostiner (ed.) *Middle East Monarchies: the challenge of modernity*, 87–115, Boulder, CO: Lynne Reinner, 2000.

Swearingen, W. D. "Agricultural Policies and the Growing Food Security Crisis," in J. P. Entelis and P. C. Naylor (eds) *State and Society in Algeria*, 117–49, Boulder, CO: Westview, 1992.

Tabak, F. "Agrarian Fluctuations and Modes of Labor Control in the Western Arc of the Fertile Crescent, c. 1700–1850," in Ç. Keyder and F. Tabak (eds) *Landholding and Commercial Agriculture in the Middle East*, 148–54, Albany: State University of New York Press, 1991.

——. *The Waning of the Mediterranean, 1550–1870: a geohistorical approach*, Baltimore: Johns Hopkins University Press, 2008.

Tabbaa, Y. "Circles of Power: palace, citadel, and city in Ayyubid Aleppo," *ArsOr* 23, 1993: 181–200.

——. *Constructions of Power and Piety in Medieval Aleppo*, University Park: Pennsylvania State University Press, 1997.

Tadmor, H. "The Campaigns of Sargon II of Assur: a chronological-historical study," *Journal of Cuneiform Studies* 12, 1958: 22–40.

——. "Monarchy and the Elite in Assyria and Babylonia: the question of royal accountability," in S. N. Eisenstadt (ed.) *The Origins and Diversity of Axial Age Civilizations*, 203–24, Albany: State University of New York Press, 1986.

——. "Propaganda, Literature, Historiography: cracking the code of the Assyrian royal inscriptions," in S. Parpola and R. M. Whiting (ed.) *Assyria 1995: proceedings of the 10th anniversary symposium of the Neo-Assyrian text corpus project*, 325–38, Helsinki: The Neo-Assyrian Text Corpus Project, 1997.

——. "Sennacherib, King of Justice," in C. Cohen, A. Hurvitz, and S. M. Paul (eds) *Sefer Moshe: the Moshe Weinfeld jubilee volume*, 385–90, Winona Lake, IN: Eisenbrauns, 2004.

Tamimi, A. S. *Rachid Ghannouchi: a democrat within Islamism*, Oxford: Oxford University Press, 2001.

Tapper, R. "Shāhsevan in Ṣafavid Persia," *BSOAS* 37, 1974: 321–54.

Teitelbaum, J. "Saudi Arabia," in *Middle East Contemporary Survey*, vol. 16, 1992, ed. A. Ayalon, 668–701, Boulder, CO: Westview, 1995.

——. *Holier than Thou: Saudi Arabia's Islamic opposition*, Washington, DC: Washington Institute for Near East Policy, 2000.

Tessler, M. "Tunisia at the Crossroads," *Current History* 84.502, May 1985: 217–20, 229–30.

——. "The Origins of Popular Support for Islamist Movements: a political economy analysis," in J. P. Entelis (ed.) *Islam, Democracy, and the State in North Africa*, 93–126, Bloomington: Indiana University Press, 1997.

Tezcan, B. "The Definition of Sultanic Legitimacy in the Sixteenth Century Ottoman Empire: the *Ahlâk-ı alâ'î* of Kınalızâde Alî Çelebi (1510–1572)," MA Thesis, Princeton University, 1996.

——. "The 'Kânûnnâme of Mehmed II:' a different perspective," in K. Çiçek (ed.) *The Great Ottoman-Turkish Civilisation*, 4 vols, 3: 657–65, Ankara: Yeni Türkiye, 2000.

——. "Ethics as a Domain to Discuss the Political: Kınalızade Ali Efendi's *Ahlâk-ı alâî*," in A. Çaksu (ed.) *Learning and Education in the Ottoman World*, 109–20, Istanbul: IRCICA, 2001.

——. "Searching for Osman: a reassessment of the deposition of the Ottoman sultan Osman II (1618–1622)," PhD diss., Princeton University, 2001.

Thapar, R. "The State as Empire," in H. J. M. Claessen and P. Skalník (eds) *The Study of the State*, 409–26, The Hague: Mouton, 1981.

Thieck, J.-P. "Décentralisation ottomane et affirmaiton urbaine à Alep à la fin du XVIIIème siècle," in Mona Zakaria (ed) *Mouvements communautaires et espaces urbaines au Machreq*, 117–68, Beirut: Centre d'études et de recherches sur le Moyen-Orient contemporain (Cermoc), 1985.

Thomas, L. V. *A Study of Naima*, ed. N. Itzkowitz, New York: New York University Press, 1972.

Thompson, E. "Ottoman Political Reform in the Provinces: the Damascus Advisory Council in 1844–45," *IJMES* 25, 1993: 457–75.

——. "The Climax and Crisis of the Colonial Welfare State in Syria and Lebanon during World War II," in S. Heydemann (ed.) *War, Institutions, and Social Change in the Middle East*, 59–99, Berkeley: University of California Press, 2000.

——. *Colonial Citizens: republican rights, paternal privilege, and gender in French Syria and Lebanon*, New York: Columbia University Press, 2000.

Thompson, E. P. *The Making of the English Working Class*, New York: Vintage Books, 1966.

——. *Customs in Common: studies in traditional popular culture*, New York: The New Press, 1993.

Thompson, J. H. and Reischauer, R. D. (eds) *Modernization of the Arab World*, Princeton, NJ: Van Nostrand, 1966.

Thomson, W. "The Character of Early Semitic Sects," in S. Löwinger and J. Somogyi (eds) *Ignace Goldziher Memorial Volume*, 2 vols, 1: 89–116, Budapest: Globus, 1948; Jerusalem: Rubin Mass, 1958.

al-Tikriti, N. "Şehzade Korkud (ca. 1468–1513)," in K. Çiçek (ed.) *Pax Ottomana: studies in memoriam Prof. Dr. Nejat Göyünç*, 659–74, Haarlem, Ankara: SOTA-Yeni Türkiye, 2001.

Tilly, C. *Coercion, Capital, and European States, AD 990–1990*, Cambridge: Basil Blackwell, 1990.

Titley, N. M. *Persian Miniature Painting and Its Influence on the Art of Turkey and India: the British Library collections*, London: The British Library, 1983.

Tlili, B. "Éléments pour une approche de la pensée socio-économique de Kheredine (1810–1889)," *RMMM* 9, 1971: 119–52.

Todorova, M. "Midhat Paşa's Governorship of the Danube Province," in *Decision Making and Change in the Ottoman Empire*, ed. C. H. Farah, 115–28, Kirksville, MO: Thomas Jefferson University Press, 1993.

Togan, A. Z. V. "The Composition of the History of the Mongols by Rashīd al-Dīn," *CAJ* 7, 1962: 60–72.

——. "Mogollar Devrinde Anadolu'nun İktisadî Vaziyeti," *THİTM* 1, 1931: 1–42; trans. G. Leiser, "Economic Conditions in Anatolia in the Mongol Period," *AI* 25, 1991: 203–40.

Togan, İ. *Flexibility and Limitation in Steppe Formations: the Kerait Khanate and Chinggis Khan*, Leiden: Brill, 1998.

——. "Patterns of Legitimization of Rule in the History of the Turks," in K. A. Ertürk (ed.) *Rethinking Central Asia: non-Eurocentric studies in history, social structure and identity*, 39–53, Reading, UK: Ithaca Press, 1999.

Toledano, E. R. "The Legislative Process in the Ottoman Empire in the Early *Tanzimat* Period: a footnote," *IJTS* 1.2, 1980: 99–106.

Touchan, R., Akkemik, Ü., Hughes, M. K. and Erkan, N. "May-June Precipitation Reconstruction of Southwestern Anatolia, Turkey, during the Last 900 Years from Tree Rings," *Quaternary Research* 68, 2007: 196–202.

Treadwell, L. "*Shāhānshāh* and *al-malik al-mu'ayyad*: the legitimation of power in Sāmānid and Būyid Iran," in *Culture and Memory in Medieval Islam: essays in honour of Wilferd Madelung*, 318–37, London: IB Tauris, 2003.

Tripp, C. *Islam and the Moral Economy: the challenge of capitalism*, Cambridge: Cambridge University Press, 2006.

Tucker, W. "Environmental Hazards, Natural Disasters, Economic Loss, and Mortality in Mamluk Syria," *MSR* 3, 1999: 109–28.

Turan, O. "Selçuk Türkiyesi Din Tarihine dair bir Kaynak: *Fusṭāṭ ul-'adāle fī kavā'id us-salṭana*," in *Fuad Köprülü Armağanı, 60. doğum yılı münasebetiyle: mélanges Fuad Köprülü*, 531–65, Istanbul: Ankara Üniversitesi Dil ve Tarih-Coğrafya Fakültesi, 1953.

——. "The Ideal of World Domination among the Medieval Turks," *SI* 4, 1955: 77–90.

Türköne, M. "The Tanzimat Charter and Mehmed Sadık Rıfat Pasha," in K. Çiçek (ed.) *The Great Ottoman-Turkish Civilisation*, 4 vols, 3: 99–110, Ankara: Yeni Türkiye, 2000.

Tushingham, A. D. "The *Takht-i Marmar* (Marble Throne) in Teheran," in C. J. Adams (ed.) *Iranian Civilization and Culture: essays in honour of the 2,500th anniversary of the founding of the Persian Empire*, 121–7 and plates, Montreal: McGill University Institute of Islamic Studies, 1972.

Tyan, É. *Histoire de l'organisation judiciaire en pays d'Islam*, 2 vols, Paris: Recueil Sirey, 1938–43.

——. *Institutions du droit public musulman*, 2 vols, Paris: Recueil Sirey, 1954.

Üçel-Aybet, G. "An Analytical Study of the Administrative and Social Policy of the Ottoman State (16th and 17th centuries)," in J.-L. Bacqué-Grammont and E. van Donzel (eds) *Comité international d'études pré-ottomanes et ottomanes: VIth symposium*, 159–70, Istanbul: Divit, 1987.

Ülken, H. Z. "Tanzimattan Sonra Fikir Hareketleri," in H.-A. Yücel (ed.) *Tanzimat I: yüzüncü yildönümü münasebetile*, 757–75, Istanbul: Maarif, 1940.

Uzunçarşılı, İ. H. *Anadolu beylikleri ve Akkoyunlu, Karakoyunlu devletleri*, Ankara: Türk Tarih Kurumu, 1937.

——. *Osmanlı devleti teşkilâtından kapukulu ocakları, II*, Ankara: Türk Tarih Kurumu, 1944.

——. *Osmanlı devletinin merkez ve bahriye teşkilâtı*, Ankara: Türk Tarih Kurumu, 1948.

——. "Onaltıncı asır ortalarında yaşamış olan iki büyük şahsiyet: Tosyalı Celâl Zâde Mustafa ve Salih Çelebiler," *Belleten* 22, no. 87, 1958: 391–441.

——. and Karal, E. Z. *Osmanlı tarihi*, 8 vols in 10, Ankara: Türk Tarih Kurumu, 1947–62.

Valensi, L. *Tunisian Peasants in the Eighteenth and Nineteenth Centuries*, Cambridge: Cambridge University Press, and Paris: Edition de la Maison des Sciences de l'Homme, 1985.

——. *The Birth of the Despot: Venice and the Sublime Porte*, Ithaca: Cornell University Press, 1993.

van der Spek, R. J. "The Babylonian City," in A. Kuhrt and S. Sherwin-White (eds) *Hellenism in the East: the interaction of Greek and non-Greek civilizations from Syria to Central Asia after Alexander*, 57–74, London: Duckworth, 1987.

Vanderwalle, D. "Ben Ali's New Era: pluralism and economic privation in Tunisia," in H. J. Barkey (ed.) *The Politics of Reform in the Middle East*, 105–26, New York: St. Martin's Press, 1992.
van Koppen, F. "The Geography of the Slave Trade and Northern Mesopotamia in the Late Old Babylonian Period," in H. Hunger and R. Pruzsinszky (ed.) *Mesopotamian Dark Age Revisited*, 9–33, Vienna: Österreischischen Akademie der Wissenschaften, 2004.
Vatikiotis, P. J. "A Reconstruction of the Fatimid Theory of State," *IC* 28, 1954: 399–409.
——. "al-Hakim bi-Amrillah: the god-king idea realised," *IC* 29, 1955: 1–8.
——. *The Fatimid Theory of State*, Lahore: Institute of Islamic Culture, 1957; 2nd ed. 1981.
Veinstein, G. "İnalcık's Views on the Ottoman Eighteenth Century and the Fiscal Problem," *Oriente Moderno*, n.s. 18.1 (79.1), 1999: 1–10.
——. "La voix du maître à travers les firmans de Soliman le Magnifique," in G. Veinstein (ed.) *Soliman le magnifique et son temps*, 127–44, Paris: La Documentation Française, 1992.
Vernadsky, G. "The Scope and Contents of Chingis Khan's *Yasa*," *HJAS* 3, 1938: 337–60.
Vincent, A. *Theories of the State*, Oxford: Blackwell, 1987.
Voet, G. and van Lerberghe, K. "A Long Lasting Life," in H. Behrens, D. Loding, and M. T. Roth (eds) *Dumm-e$_2$-dub-ba-a: studies in honor of Ake W. Sjöberg*, 525–38, Philadelphia, PA: Samuel Noah Kramer Fund, 1989.
Voegelin, E. "The Mongol Orders of Submission to European Powers, 1245–1255," *Byzantion* 15, 1940–1: 378–413.
von Grunebaum, G. E. *Medieval Islam: a study in cultural orientation*, Chicago, IL: University of Chicago Press, 1946.
——. "Firdausi's Concept of History," in *Fuad Köprülü Armağanı, 60. doğum yılı münasebetiyle: mélanges Fuad Köprülü*, 177–93, Ankara: Ankara Üniversitesi Dil ve Tarih-Coğrafya Fakültesi, 1953.
——. "Firdausī's Concept of History," *The American Anthropologist* 57.2 (no. 81), 1955: 168–89.
von Sivers, P. "The Realm of Justice: apocalyptic revolts in Algeria (1849–1879)," *Humaniora Islamica* 1, 1973: 47–60.
Vrolijk, A. "No Conscripts for the *Nizâm*: the 1850 events in Aleppo as reflected in documents from Syrian and Dutch archives," *JTS* 26, 2002: 311–38.
Vryonis, S., Jr. "Seljuk Gulams and Ottoman Devshirmes," *Der Islam* 41, 1965: 224–52.
——. "Byzantium and Islam: seven-seventeenth century," *East European Quarterly* 2, 1968/9: 205–40; repr. in *Byzantium: its internal history and relations with the Muslim World,* London: Variorum, 1971, IX.
Waines, D. "The Pre-Buyid Amirate: two views from the past," *IJMES* 8, 1977: 339–48.
Walbank, F. W. "Monarchies and Monarchic Ideas," in *The Cambridge Ancient History*, 2nd ed., vol 7, pt. 1, *The Hellenistic World*, 62–100, Cambridge: Cambridge University Press, 1984.
Walbridge, J. "The Political Thought of Quṭb al-Dīn al-Shīrāzī," in C. E. Butterworth (ed.) *The Political Aspects of Islamic Philosophy: essays in honor of Muhsin S. Mahdi*, 345–78, Cambridge, MA: Harvard University Press, 1992.
Warriner, D. *Land Reform and Development in the Middle East: a study of Egypt, Syria, and Iraq*, 2nd ed., London: Oxford University Press, 1962.
Waterbury, J. *The Commander of the Faithful: the Moroccan political elite – a study in segmented politics*, New York: Columbia University Press, 1970.
——. "An Attempt to Put Patrons and Clients in Their Place," in E. Gellner and J. Waterbury (eds) *Patrons and Clients in Mediterranean Societies*, 329–42, London: Duckworth, 1977.
Watkins, C. *How to Kill a Dragon: aspects of Indo-European poetics*, New York: Oxford University Press, 1995.
Watson, A. M. *Agricultural Innovation in the Early Islamic World: the diffusion of crops and farming techniques, 700–1100*, Cambridge: Cambridge University Press, 1983.
——. "Botanical Gardens in the Early Islamic World," in E. Robbins and S. Sandahl (ed.) *Corolla Torontonensis: studies in honour of Ronald Morton Smith*, 105–11, Toronto: TSAR and The Centre for Korean Studies, 1994.
Watt, J. W. "Syriac and Syrians as Mediators of Greek Political Thought to Islam," *Mélanges de l'Université Saint-Joseph* 57, 2004: 121–49.

——. *Muslim Intellectual: a study of al-Ghazali*, Edinburgh: Edinburgh University Press, 1963.

——. *Islamic Political Thought: the basic concepts*, Edinburgh: Edinburgh University Press, 1968.

——. "The Significance of the Early Stages of Imami Shi'ism," in N. Keddie (ed.) *Religion and Politics in Iran: Shi'ism from quietism to revolution*, 21–32, New Haven, CT: Yale University Press, 1983.

Wedeen, L. *Ambiguities of Domination: politics, rhetoric, and symbols in contemporary Syria*, Chicago, IL: University of Chicago Press, 1999.

Weintritt, O. "Concepts of History as Reflected in Arabic Historiographical Writing in Ottoman Syria and Egypt (1517–1700)," in T. Philipp and U. Haarmann (eds) *The Mamluks in Egyptian Politics and Society*, 188–204, Cambridge: Cambridge University Press, 1998.

Weiss, D. "Ibn Khaldun on Economic Transformation," *IJMES* 27, 1995: 29–37.

Welch, A. "Worldly and Otherworldly Love in Safavi Painting," in R. Hillenbrand (ed.) *Persian Painting from the Mongols to the Qajars: studies in honour of Basil W. Robinson*, 301–17, London: IB Tauris, 2000.

Welch, S. C. *A King's Book of Kings: the Shah-nameh of Shah Tahmasp*, New York: Metropolitan Museum of Art, 1972.

——. "The *Shāhnāmeh* (Book of Kings) of Shah Tahmasp," in T. Falk (ed.) *Treasures of Islam*, 68–93, London: Sotheby's/Philip Wilson, 1985.

Wenke, R. J. "Imperial Investments and Agricultural Developments in Parthian and Sassanian Khuzestan: 150 B.C. to A.D. 640," PhD diss., University of Michigan, 1975.

Werkmeister, W. *Quellenuntersuchungen zum Kitāb al-'Iqd al-farīd des Andalusiers Ibn 'Abdrabbih (246/860–328/940): Ein Beitrag zur arabischen Literturgeschichte*, Berlin: Klaus Schwarz, 1983.

Westenholz, A. "How Do We Understand Ancient History, And Why Study It At All?" *Kaskal: rivista di storia, ambiente e culture del Vicino Oriente Antico* 1, 2004: 179–86.

White, J. B. *Islamist Mobilization in Turkey: a study in vernacular politics*, Seattle: University of Washington Press, 2000.

——. "The Islamist Paradox," in D. Kandiyoti and A. Saktanber (eds) *Fragments of Culture: the everyday of Modern Turkey*, 191–217, London: IB Tauris, 2002.

Widengren, G. "The Sacral Kingship of Iran," in *The Sacral Kingship*, Studies in the History of Religions, 4 (Supplements to *Numen*), 242–57, Leiden: Brill, 1959.

Wiesehöfer, J. *Ancient Persia: from 550 BC to 650 AD*, trans. A. Azodi, London: IB Tauris, 1996.

Wilber, D. N. *Persepolis: the archaeology of Parsa, seat of the Persian kings*, rev. ed. Princeton, NJ: Darwin, 1989.

Williams, S. J. *The Secret of Secrets: the scholarly career of a pseudo-Aristotelian text in the Latin Middle Ages*, Ann Arbor: University of Michigan Press, 2003.

Winter, I. J. "The King and the Cup: iconography of the royal presentation scene on Ur III seals," in M. Kelly-Buccellati (ed.) *Insight through Images: studies in honor of Edith Porada*, Bibliotheca Mesopotamica, 21, 253–68, Malibu, CA: Undena, 1986.

——. "Legitimation of Authority through Image and Legend: seals belonging to officials in the administrative bureaucracy of the Ur III state," in M. Gibson and R. D. Biggs (eds) *The Organization of Power: aspects of bureaucracy in the ancient Near East*, Studies in Ancient Oriental Civilization, 46, 69–93, Chicago, IL: Oriental Institute, 1987.

——. "'Seat of Kingship'/'A Wonder to Behold': The Palace as Construct in the Ancient Near East," *ArsOr* 23, 1993: 27–56.

Winter, M. "The Islamic Profile and the Religious Policy of the Ruling Class in Ottoman Egypt," in J. L. Kraemer and I. Alon (eds) *Religion and Government in the World of Islam*, *IOS* 10, 1983: 132–45.

——. "Attitudes toward the Ottomans in Egyptian Historiography during Ottoman Rule," in H. Kennedy (ed.) *The Historiography of Islamic Egypt (c. 950–1800)*, 195–210, Leiden: Brill, 2001.

Winter, S. H. "Shiite Emirs and Ottoman Authorities: the campaign against the Hamadas of Mt. Lebanon, 1693–1694," *AOtt* 18, 2000: 209–45.

Wittek, P. "Notes sur la tughra ottomane," *Byzantion* 20, 1950: 267–93.

Wittfogel, K. A. *Oriental Despotism: a comparative study of total power*, New Haven, CT: Yale University Press, 1957

Wojtilla, G. "The Royal Diary in Ancient India and Its Criticis," in I. Tar and G. Wojtilla (eds) *Speculum Regis*, Acta Antiqua et Archaeologica, 26, 7–12, Szeged, Hungary: Universitas de Atilla Jószef, 1994.

Wolski, J. *L'Empire des Arsacides*, AcIr 32, ser. 3, vol. 18, Louvain, Peeters, 1993.

Woodhead, C. "An Experiment in Official Historiography: the post of şehnāmeci in the Ottoman Empire, c. 1555–1605," *WZKM* 75, 1983: 157–82.

——. "After Celalzade: The Ottoman *Nişancı* c. 1560–1700," in A. Christmann and R. Gleave (eds) *Studies in Islamic Law: a festschrift for Colin Imber*, 295–311, Oxford: Oxford University Press for the University of Manchester, 2007.

Woods, J. E. "Timur's Genealogy," in M. M. Mazzaoui and V. B. Moreen (eds) *Intellectual Studies on Islam: essays written in honor of Martin B. Dickson*, 85–125, Salt Lake City: University of Utah Press, 1990.

——. *The Aqquyunlu: Clan, Confederation, Empire: a study in 15th/9th century Turko-Iranian politics*, Minneapolis: Bibliotheca Islamica, 1976; rev. ed. Salt Lake City: University of Utah Press, 1999.

Yalçınkaya, M. A. "The Provincial Reforms of the Early Tanzimat Period as Implemented in the Kaza of Avrethisarı," *OTAM* 6, 1995: 343–85.

Yalman, N. "On Land Disputes in Eastern Turkey," in G. L. Tikku (ed.) *Islam and Its Cultural Divergence: studies in honor of Gustave E. von Grunebaum*, 180–218, Urbana: University of Illinois Press, 1971.

Yanagihashi, H. "The Judicial Functions of the *Sulṭān* in Civil Cases According to the Mālikīs up to the Sixth/Twelfth Century," *Islamic Law and Society* 3, 1996: 41–74.

Yang, Z. "King of Justice," *Aula Orientalia* 9, 1991: 243–49.

Yarshater, E. "Observations on Nâsir al-Dîn Shah," in C. E. Bosworth and C. Hillenbrand (eds) *Qajar Iran: political, social and cultural change, 1800–1925*, 3–13, Costa Mesa, CA: Mazda, 1983.

——. "Were the Sasanians Heirs to the Achaemenids?" in *La Persia nel Medioevo*, Accademia Nazionale dei Lincei, Quaderno No. 160, 517–31, Rome: Accademia Nazionale dei Lincei, 1971.

al-Yassini, A. *Religion and State in the Kingdom of Saudi Arabia*, Boulder, CO: Westview, 1985.

Yi, E. *Guild Dynamics in Seventeenth-Century Istanbul: fluidity and leverage*, Leiden: Brill, 2004.

Yıldırım, O. "Bread and Empire: the workings of grain provisioning in Istanbul during the eighteenth century," in B. Marino and C. Virlouvet (eds) *Nourrir les cités de Méditerranée: antiquité-temps modernes*, 251–72, Paris: Maisonneuve et Larose, 2003.

Yıldız, F. "A Tablet of Codex Ur-Nammu from Sippar," *Orientalia* 50, 1981: 87–97.

Yılmaz, H. "Osmanlı tarihçiliğinde Tanzimat öncesi siyaset düşüncesine yaklaşımlar," *TALID* 1.2, 2003: 231–98.

——. "The Sultan and the Sultanate: envisioning rulership in the age of Süleymān the Lawgiver (1520–1566)," PhD diss., Harvard University, 2005.

Yoltar-Yıldırım, A. "A 1498–99 *Khusraw va Shīrīn*: turning the pages of an Ottoman illustrated manuscript," *Muqarnas* 22, 2005: 95–109.

Zaehner, R. C. *The Dawn and Twilight of Zoroastrianism*, New York: G. P. Putnam's Sons, 1961.

Zakeri, M. "'Alī ibn 'Ubaida ar-Raihānī: a forgotten belletrist *(Adīb)* and Pahlavi translator," *Oriens* 34, 1994: 76–102.

Zaman, M. Q. *Religion and Politics under the Early 'Abbāsids: the emergence of the proto-Sunnī elite*, Leiden: Brill, 1997.

Zarinebaf, F. "Tabriz under Ottoman Rule (1725–1730)," PhD diss., University of Chicago, 1991.

——. "Women, Law and Imperial Justice in Ottoman Istanbul in the Late Seventeenth Century," in *Women, the Family, and Divorce Laws in Islamic History*, ed. A. El Azhary Sonbol, 81–95, Syracuse, NY: Syracuse University Press, 1996.

——. "Ottoman Women and the Tradition of Seeking Justice in the Eighteenth Century," in M. C. Zilfi (ed.) *Women in the Ottoman Empire: Middle Eastern Women in the Early Modern Era*, 253–63, Leiden: Brill, 1997.

——. *Crime and Punishment in Istanbul*, Berkeley: University of California Press, 2010.

——. Bennet, J. and Davis, J. L. *A Historical and Economic Geography of Ottoman Greece: the southwestern Morea in the 18th century*, [Princeton, NJ]: The American School of Classical Studies at Athens, 2005.

Zartman, I. W. *Destiny of a Dynasty: the search for institutions in Morocco's developing society*, Columbia, SC: University of South Carolina Press, 1964.

——. "King Hassan's New Morocco," in *The Political Economy of Morocco*, ed. I. W. Zartman, 1–33, New York: Praeger, 1987.

——. "The Challenge of Democratic Alternatives in the Maghrib," in J. Ruedy (ed.) *Islamism and Secularism in North Africa*, 201–18, New York: St. Martin's Press, 1994.

Zens, R. "Pasvanoğlu Osman Paşa and the Paşalık of Belgrade, 1791–1807," *IJTS* 8, 2002: 89–104.

Ziadeh, F. J. "Integrity *('Adālah)* in Classical Islamic Law," in N. Heer (ed.) *Islamic Law and Jurisprudence*, 73–93, Seattle: University of Washington Press, 1990.

Zick-Nissen, J. "The Turquoise 'Jām' of King 'Jamshīd'," in R. Hillenbrand (ed.) *The Art of the Saljūqs in Iran and Anatolia*, 181–91, Costa Mesa, CA: Mazda, 1994.

Zisser, E. *Asad's Legacy: Syria in transition*, London: Hurst, 2001.

Zürcher, E. *Turkey: a modern history*, London: IB Tauris, 2004.

Index